SOURCES OF VIJAYANAGAR HISTORY

SOURCES OF VIJAYANAGAR HISTORY

Selected and Edited by

S. KRISHNASWAMI AYYANGAR

GYAN

Sources of Vijayanagar History

ISBN : 978-81-212-0038-7

Rs. 900

Reprinted in 2010 in India by
Gyan Publishing House
23, Main Ansari Road, Daryaganj,
New Delhi - 110002
Phone : 23282060, 23261060
Fax : (011) 23285914
e-mail : books@gyanbooks.com
gyanbook@vsnl.com
website : gyanbooks.com

Printed at : G. Print Process, Delhi

PREFACE

THE collection that follows is primarily the work of Mr. A. Rangaswami Sarasvati, B.A., University Research Student, working under me. As he had done some work in this line before obtaining the University studentship, he was set to make a systematic collection of all passages in both Telugu and Sanskrit literature, bearing upon the history of the Empire of Vijayanagar. His collection was found to be of considerable value and the Syndicate of the University of Madras sanctioned publication, by the University, of selected passages under my editorship. Of the historical value of references in literature generally Sir George Grierson says in a letter to me: "I cordially agree with you in the importance you attach to casual references in non-historical Indian literature. These have too often been neglected by students, and they not uncommonly afford historical data which cannot be found elsewhere." Several passages in the following collection offer very good illustration of this position. The extracts are taken from unpublished manuscripts in several cases, and in case of published work the works laid under contribution have so far been but very imperfectly exploited for the purpose. The introduction will give an idea of the salient features of this collection. The work of the student deserves commendation.

The course of his work was much facilitated by the ready assistance that he always received from the Librarian and the staff of the Government Oriental Manuscripts Library. In the present stage of manuscripts cataloguing in this part of the country much has to be left for chance. A few of the most important among the works laid under contribution in the following selection are found to be in the libraries but not catalogued. While, therefore, the collection presented here may, from our present knowledge of manuscripts, be considered fairly exhaustive, it will not be surprising at all if many more come to light through the active work of the various search parties that are out at work from the Government Manuscripts Library now. When practically the whole work was in type, the student lighted upon the work Śivatattvaratnākara from which three excerpts, throwing new light upon the later history of Vijayanagar, are made. If other works like this should be forthcoming, it need not cause any surprise at all.

In the work of selecting and editing, I had throughout the willing assistance of the student himself which rendered the work much less onerous to me than it would otherwise have been. It only remains to acknowledge the assistance rendered in proof-reading by the other Research student of mine, Mr. R. Satyanatha, B.A. (Hons.), and the excellent work of the Government Press in putting the matter through the press. Those interested in historical research will surely feel grateful to the Madras University Syndicate for their enlightened policy in promoting the publication of this work, which, let me hope, is but the beginning of a long series to come.

S. KRISHNASWAMI AYYANGAR.

MADRAS,
6th February 1919.

ADDENDA ET CORRIGENDA.

Page 26, *line* 8.—*Rājagambhiram*: There was a Rājagambhīra Sambuvarāyan with a date Śaka 1180 (A. D. 1258). There is an inscription of his at Paḍaivīḍu (*S.I.Ins.* I. 78). It was probably from him that Paḍaivīḍu got this name either because he fortified the hill, or made it the citadel of his kingdom. There seems little doubt that this Paḍaivīḍu in the Arni taluk is what the poetess had in mind.

Page 27, *line* 28.—*The Sultan of Madura killed by Kampa* seems to be the fifth Sultan of Madura, Nasir-ud-din Dāmaghan Shah, on whose accession Ibn. Batura left Madura finally. There is only one coin of his available of A.H. 745, and that of his successor Adil Shah bears date A.H. 757. This seems to indicate an interregnum of about twelve years, and it is probable that Nasir-ud-din killed Beḻḻāla IV and put an end to the dynasty. For a full discussion see my forthcoming work "Muhammadan Invasions of South India," Lecture VI.

Pages 35 *and* 38, *line* 38.—*Jyotishkuḍi*: This is the place to which fugitives under Piḻḻai Lokāchārya took the Ranganātha image from Srīrangam for safety, and where the Achārya died. The identification of this place depends upon the actual route taken by the party, as there are places of the name in the vicinity of Aḻagar Tirumalai (Sundarāchallam of the poet). Kāḷaiyārkoil seems to answer best as there was a Vishnu temple also in it, though at present it is only a Śaiva centre. It had the reputation of having been an impregnable forest of Jyoti trees (*Cardiospermum halicacabum*) and had a fortress known to classical Tamil literature as Kānappēr, which name figures among those of the strongholds taken by the Ceylon general in the war of succession for the Panḍya throne in the sixties of the twelfth century. There is a Sodugudi about two miles from Iḷayānkudi formerly a Dharmāsanam (charity-gift), but now a Muhammadan village in the Śivaganga zamindari, about seven miles north of Paramagudi railway station. There is an obscure Brahman village of the name about ten miles from Aḻagar koil (Tirumālirum̃jolai), but there is nothing to recommend the place to these fugitives. For a fuller discussion, as the result of my own investigations of the locality, please refer to my forthcomming work quoted above.

Page 88.—*Manḍuva*: This place is identified with *Manve* in certain places in the course of the book. This can be either of two places: Manḍu, the Mahammadan capital of Malva, at this period; or Manvē between Raichur and Mudgal, near the north bank of the Tungabhadra in the Nizam's Dominions. It was probably at this latter that the battle between Ramarāja Tirumala and the Adil Shah of the time took place in the reign of Vīra-Narasimha Rāya (p. 205). It is very likely that this place is referred to as Mānava-durga in the campaigns of Narasa (pp. 106 and 108 R). The actual place referred to in any case will have to be settled by the context.

Page 138.—*Kembāvi*: This word means 'red well,' and Krishna Dēva Rāya says in the colophon to the fifth canto of his work *Amuktamālyadā* (p. 158) that it had walls 'reaching up to the skies' and he made the name real by filling the whole place with the blood of the Yavanas (Muhammadans) thereby indicating that he fought a great battle against the Muhammadans. This achievement of his comes after his invasion of Orissa, where one would expect a reference to the battle of Raichur. Kembāvi is not very far from Raichur according the late Dr. Fleet's note in the *Epigraphia Indica*, volume XII, 291-2. It seems likely that Krishna refers by Kembāvi to the battle generally spoken of as the battle of Raichur.

Page 269, *Extract* 89.—Raghunātha claims in this passage credit for having invented a permanent arrangement of the steps for the vīna by means of which any tune can be played upon the instrument without a special adjustment on each occasion. The credit of this invention is popularly given to one Venkaṭēśa Makhi, one of the sons of Govinda Dīkshita, the family minister of this dynasty of Tanjore nāyaks, on the authority apparently of *Chaturdanḍiprakāsika* of Venkatēsa. That the vīna had not this arrangement is clear from the following verse in the *Manucharitram* of Peddana, the Poet Laureate of Krishna Dēva Rāya. Peddana says in effect that the instrument left adjusted for the Rāga *nāṭai* by the sleepy musician began automatically to play the tune, out of time, moved by the morning breeze, when the proper tune should have been *Dēsātchi*.

Aśvasa III.

శా॥ వాలారుంగొన గోళ్ల నీవలసతిన్ వాయించిచో నాటకున్-
మేళంబైన విపంచి నిన్న మొదలున్ నీవంటమింజేసియున్ ।
యాలాపంబెయ వేళంబల్కెడుఁ బ్రభాతాయాంతవాతాహతా
లోల తంత్రుల మేళవింపఁ గద వేలో లాక్షి దేశాక్షికిన్ ॥ 57 ॥

Possibly the Raja made the suggestion and the Pandit worked it up.

Pages 334 *and* 335.—Vijayarāghava Nāyaka of Tanjore is said to have constructed four forts apparently to guard his frontier, namely Paṭṭukkoṭṭa, Atanḍagi, Rēḷātali and Tiruppattūr. Of these the first is undoubtedly the modern Paṭṭukkoṭṭa; the second is what is now called Araṁtāngi and the last is Tiruppattūr in the Rāmnād district on the road to Madura from Trichinopoly. The third name seems to be miswritten for Kīḷānilai. I was able to trace an old road from Araṁtāngi to Tiruppattūr for a little over a mile on either side of Kīḷānilai. Its old fort had seen much active war around it in the British campaigns against Chinnamarudu and Ūmayan. The error seems to have crept in owing to a copyist's blunder, which is quite possible in regard to this name, written in Telugu.

[*N.B.*—The following do not include what are errors in the originals themselves, several passages having been extracted from single MSS.]

Page 26, *line* 22.—*For* 'अंथ वश्चितखङ्ग' *read* 'अथ वश्चि । — खङ्ग'

Page 52, *line* 11.—*For* 'पदाम्बुरुहच्छया' *read* 'पदाम्बुरुहच्छाया'

Page 59, *line* 6.—*For* 'జల ˜గ' *read* 'జలశ్రీగ'

Page 75, *line* 12.—*For* 'साहस्स' *read* 'साहस्र'

Page 81, *line* 16.—*For* 'బెటుసరు' *read* 'బెట్టుసరు'

Page 86, *line* 23.—*For* 'మల్లుంశరెడ్డి' *read* 'మల్లుఁడరెడ్డి'

Page 91, *line* 6.—*For* 'come' *read* 'comes.'

Page 105, *line* 9.—*For* 'దుర్గధ' *read* 'దుర్గస'

Page 106, *last line*.—*For* '—జి' *read* 'రాజి'

Page 109, *line* 4.—*For* 'शार्यं' *read* 'शौर्यं'

Page 111, *line* 12.—*Read* 'Leave out' after 'both the works.'

Page 131, *line* 33.—*For* 'Āraviṭṭivāru' *read* 'Āravīṭivāru.'

Page 137, *line* 22.—*For* 'బదురు' *read* 'బ్ధురు'

Page 148, *line* 10.—*For* 'గోపనమంతి' *read* 'గోపనమంత్రి'

Page 152, *line* 5.—*For* 'गापसचिवः' *read* 'गोपसचिवः'

Page 155, *line* 11.—*For* 'अनुगृहीतवाम्' *read* 'अनुगृहीतवान्'

Page 158, *line* 2.—*For* 'Rāianātha' *read* 'Rājanātha.'

Page 188, *line* 20.—*For* 'దైహిత్రు' *read* 'దౌహిత్రు'

Page 193, *line* 22.—*For* 'सङ्गाति' *read* 'सङ्गीत'

Page 197, *line* 11.—*For* ‘ क्रमादेनंमुदन्तं ’ *read* ‘ क्रमादेनमुदन्तं ’

Page 200, *line* 17.—*For* ‘ तद्दूर्ग ’ *read* ‘ तद्दुर्ग ’

Page 205, *line* 21.—*For* ‘ brothers ’ *read* ‘ the brothers ’

Page 207, *line* 12.—*For* ‘ అరమభాణ ’ *read* ‘ అసమబాణ ’

Pages 225 *and* 226—Title *For* ‘ Narasabūpālīyamu ’ *read* ‘ Narasabhūpālīyamu.’

Page 228, *line* 15.—*For* ‘ महिनत्यागमो ’ *read* ‘ महिपानत्यागमो ’

Page 236, *line* 32.—*For* ‘ నేనుల ’ *read* ‘ నేస్గుల ’

Page 241, *line* 1.—*For* ‘ కుపాండుషా ’ *read* ‘ కుల్లీపాముషా ’

Page 258, *line* 21.—*For* ‘ పటైన ’ *read* ‘ పట్టైనా ’

Page 265, *line* 34.—*For* ‘ భావచితంబు ’ *read* ‘ భావచిత్రంబు ’

Page 281, *line* 19.—*For* ‘ श क्ष्मापतीन् ’ *read* ‘ शत्रुक्ष्मापतीन् ’

NOTE—On the genealogical table on page 254 please draw a line to indicate Raghunatha's queen Kalāvati was the daughter of Vemparāja and Lakshmāmba.

GENEALOGICAL TABLES.

I.—The Sangama or First Vijayanagar Dynasty.

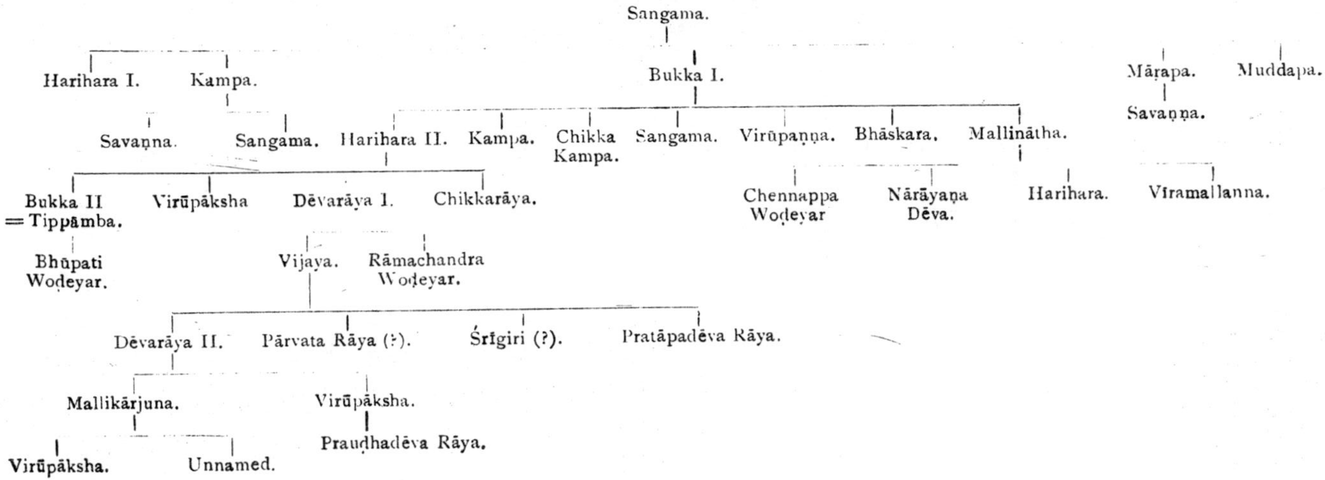

II.—The Sāluva or Second Vijayanagar Dynasty.

The Moon.
Budha.
Purūravas.
Vankidēva.
Gunda I = Kamalā Dēvi.

- Gunda II Bomma.
- Mādirāja.
- Gauta
- Vīrāhobala.
- Sāluva Mangi.
  - Gauta II (one of six sons).
    - Gunda = Mallāmba.
      - Narasimha = Śrirangāmba (Ś. 1378--1408).
        - Not named; killed by an agent called Tymarasa as stated by Nuniz.
        - Immadi Nrsimha or Dharmarāya or Tammaya Dēva (Śaka 1414—1427).
      - Timma.
    - Sāluva.
      - Parvatarāja (Śaka 1378).
    - Tippa = Harima, sister of Dēvarāya II (Ś. 1352—64).
      - Gopa (Śaka 1352).
        - Tippa, author of the commentary on the Kāvyālankāra Sūtra and Tāladīpika.
        - Timma, patron of the Tamil poets Irattaiyar and Kālamēghappulavar.
- Sāvitri Mangi.

III.—The Tuluva or Third Vijayanagar Dynasty.

Moon.
Budha.
Turvasu.
Timma = Devakī.
Īśvara = Bukkama.

- Narasa.
  - By Tippāmpa.
    - Vīranarasimha.
  - By Nāgamāmba.
    - Krishna Dēva Rāya.
      - Tirumala.
      - Tirumalāmba married Aliya Rāma Rāya.
        - Krishna.
        - Pedda Timma.
  - By Obamāmba.
    - Achyuta.
      - China Venkatādri.
    - Ranga.
      - Sadāśiva.
- Timma.

IV.—The Āraviḍu or Fourth Vijayanagar Dynasty (Collateral Branches).

- The Moon.
  - Tātapinnama.
    - Sōmadēva.
      - Rāghavadēva Rāja.
        - Pinnama.
          - Āravīṭi Bukka, General of Sāḷuva Narasimha.
            - = Abbala Dēvi.
              - Singarāja.
                - Nandyāla Narasinga.
                  - Aubhaḷarāja.
                    - Obalarāja.
                      - Chinna Aubala, ruler of Udaiyagiri.
                  - Nāra parāja.
                    - Narasingarāja.
                      - Timma, ruler of Gaṇḍikota.
                      - Krishna of Nandyāla, patron of Kaḷāpūrṇodayam.
            - = Ballāmbika.
              - Rāmarāja = Lakkāmbika.
                - Timmarāja by Gopama.
                  - Tirumala.
                  - Viṭṭhala.
                  - Chinna
                  - Pāpatimma.
                  - Chinakoṇḍa = Konamma.
                    - Chinna Timma.
                    - Apparāja.
                    - Rangarāja.
                    - Konēti Timma.
                      - Konētirāma.
                - Pedda Koṇḍarāja = Koṇḍāmbika.
                  - Konētirāja = Tirumalāmbika.
                    - Aubhala.
                    - Koṇḍarāja.
                    - Timmarāja of Udaiyagiri.
                    - Rangarāja.
                - Srīranga = Tirumalāmba (*continued in the next table*).

V.—Āraviḍu or Fourth Vijayanagar Dynasty (Imperial Branch).

- Srīranga Rāya, M. Tirumalāmba.
  - Kona.
  - Timma.
    - Krishna.
    - Peda Timma.
    - Konḍa.
      - Rāmarāja.
  - Aḷiyarāma Rāya.
    - China Timma.
    - Srīranga.
      - (6) Pedda Venkaṭa II.
      - Chinna Venkaṭa.
        - Tirumala.
        - Venkaṭa.
          - (8) Kodandarāma.
            - Pedda Venkata.
            - Chinna Venkaṭa.
            - Kodandarāma.
            - Venkaṭa.
          - Timma.
            - Srīranga.
          - Venkata.
            - Chinna Venkata.
        - (7) Śrīranga III (adopted by Gopāla).
          - Two sons to whom Sivāji made a grant.
  - (1) Tirumala I.
    - Raghunātha.
    - (2) Srīranga I.
    - Rāma.
      - Tirumala
      - (4) Śrīranga Chikka Rāya II.
        - (5) Rāmadēva Rāya.
    - (3) Venkata I.
  - Venkaṭādri.
    - Rama.
    - Śrīranga.
      - Venkaṭa.
      - Gopāla adopts (7) Śrīranga III.
        - Two sons to whom Śivāji made a grant.
  - Lakkāmba M. Obularaja of the Solar race.
    - Narasarāja, patron of Narasabhūpātiyam.
  - Obāmba M. Timmarāja of the Solar race.
    - Gobbūri Narasa.
  - Konāmba M. Obularāja.
    - Śrīranga Rāya.
    - marāja, Governor of Kondavidu and author of Paramayogivilāsam.
  - Daughter name not known.
    - Mādirāju Nagappadeva Mahārājā.

(*N.B.*—The Arabic numerals indicate the order of succession in the empire, Rāma not having ruled *de jure*.)

VI.—The Keḷaḍi Dynasty.

- Basava = Basavamma.
  - Chauḍa.
    - Sadāśiva.
      - Doḍḍa Sankaṇṇa Nāyaka = Vīrāmbā.
        - Venkaṭappa Nāyaka = Abhinava Vīrāmba.
          - Bhadrappa Nāyaka
            - Vīrabhadra Nāyaka.
        - Rāmarāja Nāyaka.
      - Chikka Sankaṇṇa Nāyaka.
        - Siddhappa Nāyaka.
          - Śivappa Nāyaka.
            - Bhadrappa Nāyaka.
            - Somasēkhara Nāyaka = Chennamāmba.
              - Basavappa Nāyaka.
          - Venkaṭappa Nāyaka.
    - Bhadra.
  - Bhadra.

CONTENTS.

SOURCES OF VIJAYANAGAR HISTORY.

INTRODUCTION.

A HISTORY OF THE EMPIRE OF VIJAYANAGAR FROM ORIGINAL SOURCES.

THE history of the empire of Vijayanagar, which till recently was as good as lost to us, was recovered through the efforts of Mr. R. Sewell, whose work in South Indian Archæology and Epigraphy naturally gave him the qualifications to take up the work. He brought out his work 'A Forgotten Empire' of Vijayanagar early in 1900 based upon his previous knowledge of the antiquities of the Madras Presidency, and of the information he derived from two Portuguese chronicles which were unearthed in the archives of Lisbon, and which he translated and appended to his work. Excellent as the work was for the time, and for the sources and historical material at his disposal, it suffered from the neglect of the evidence available in various forms in literature which go a long way towards filling up the many gaps that Epigraphy leaves in respect of that history. These sources are collected together in the following pages and they will speak for themselves. A constructive study of these goes a long way in correcting the chronicles in many places, and conveys information which would make a fuller history of the Empire of Vijayanagar possible. It is these untapped sources only that are brought together in the following extracts from various works, Sanskrit and Telugu principally, which bear on the particular period. Many of these are taken from manuscripts and published works now out of print. Some of the passages extracted are taken from works which may be available, but not in a form that would be useful to students not acquainted with Telugu. There is besides the advantage of these being brought together in a collection which otherwise it would be possible for one to get at only by voluminous reading. Each one of these extracts is provided with an English introduction which without pretending to be a literal translation of the passages, contains a faithful summary of the historical facts traceable in the extracts.

I. KUMĀRA KAMPAṆA'S CONQUESTS.

It would be useful in this introduction to draw attention to those salient features of the history of Vijayanagar which these extracts either bring to light for the first time or clear up from the mist that surrounded them in various ways. None of these throws any light upon the actual circumstances under which the empire was founded. But the first problem that suggested itself to the reader of the history of Vijayanagar, as we had hitherto known it, is what exactly was the political condition of the south, and how the southern states were gathered together under Vijayanagar. The extracts from the work 'Kamparāyacharitam' or 'Madhurā Vijayam' (since published in Trivandrum), by Gangādēvi, wife of Kampaṇa, throws the much needed light upon this dark spot. Various other works confirm what this single poem has to say regarding this matter. Of these latter, mention must be made of the Telugu Jaimini Bhāratam, the Sanskrit works Sāḷuva-abhyudayam and Rāma-abhyudayam and the Vaishṇava works on hagiology, the Prapannāmṛtam and Āchārya Sūktimuktāvali. All these join in saying that Kumāra Kampaṇa, son of Bukka Rāya, one of the five brothers who founded Vijayanagar, proceeded from his viceregal headquarters at Mulbāgal into the Toṇḍa-maṇḍalam country, then under the rule of a dynasty of Śambuva Rāyans who sprang into importance in the dismembered Chōḷa Empire. In this good work he was assisted by the Brahman general Gōpaṇa, and Sāḷuva Mangu, the ancestor of the usurper Sāḷuva Narasimha, the most distinguished of a body of distinguished generals. These together swept the country clear of the Mussalman garrisons throughout the localities, killed the Muhammadan governor at Madura, and restored the temple of Śrīrangam to its former condition by repairing the damages that it had suffered in the series of Muhammadan raids that took place for well-nigh half a century. The idol of Ranganātha which has had a long journey to various localities for safety was ultimately restored to its own home.

II. MĀDHAVA VIDYĀRANYA.

The next group of extracts following bear upon the now somewhat debated question of religious reconstruction at the time of the foundation of this empire. A body of learned men with the two famous brothers, Mādhavāchārya and Śāyana at their head, were at the instance of Bukka himself, set to work upon committing to writing various works and commentaries bearing upon the religion of the Vēdas. The fact that Bukka asked Mādhavāchārya to set about this indicates the exalted position which the latter held at court. The date of death of Mādhavāchārya is now ascertained to be A.D. 1387 on epigraphical evidence, and he himself says that he lived 85 years. So the period of his life is clearly A.D. 1302 to 1387. He must have been a ripe scholar of great reputation at the beginning of the empire of Vijayanagar, and that Bukka entrusted him with this extraordinary commission is only confirmatory of his great reputation for learning. Apart from all other considerations, it seems very likely that this was the man who is known to tradition as Vidyāraṇya, notwithstanding the fact that this Mādhavāchārya is nowhere actually equated with the name 'Vidyāraṇya.' The confusion has arisen apparently from another minister and general of Bukka, who lived about the same time and is sometimes described as 'the establisher of the path of the Upanishads.' The two Mādhavas were of different gōtras and sūtras as is clear from the extracts. The actual difficulty is that the one seems to have been a Śaiva, and the other an Advaitin. The designation 'establisher of the path of the Upanishads', as applied to the second Mādhava, seems deliberately intended to distinguish him from the other, who is described as the 'establisher of the path of the Vēdas.' The former designation seems to be the result of an effort to make rigid Śaivism conform to the path of the Upanishads. This Mādhava was the son of Chauṇḍappa, who has again been confounded with the author of a Vaidic Work, Prayōgaratnamālā, a commentary on the Śrauta Sūtras. At the commencement of this work, which was written by him in the court of Bukka II, he says that he wrote the work at the request of Vidyāraṇya, and acknowledges that in the commentary he follows the instruction he derived from Vidyāraṇya. The following six lines give a character to Vidyāraṇya which agrees point by point with the description of Mādhavāchārya, the brother of Śāyana, we get from other extracts :—

पदवाक्यप्रमाणानां पारदृश्वा महामतिः ।
साङ्ख्ययोगरहस्यज्ञो ब्रह्मविद्यापरायणः ॥

वेदार्थविशदीकर्ता वेदवेदाङ्गपारवित् ।
विद्यारण्ययतिर्ज्ञात्वा श्रौतस्मार्तक्रियापरैः ॥
श्रीचौण्डपार्यप्रमुखैः विद्वद्भिर्ब्राह्मणोत्तमैः ।
व्याचक्ष्वाध्वरतन्त्रं त्वं समन्त्रार्थमिति स्फुटम् ॥

Thus it is clear that this Chaundappa, the minister of Bukka II, could not be the father of Mādhavamantrin, a general of Bukka I, who died in A.D. 1384. This Mādhavamantrin cannot be the Vidyāraṇya described in the terms quoted above. The very terms in which Chaunḍappa refers to Vidyāraṇya unmistakably indicate Mādhavāchārya, the brother of Śāyana, to be the Vidyāraṇya of tradition.

III. OVERSEA TRADE OF VIJAYANAGAR.

The end of the first dynasty of Vijayanagar was almost coeval with the coming of the Portuguese on the West Coast. While we have so much information about the internal organization of Vijayanagar, we have had absolutely no information about any organization which the empire had for its foreign trade. The Haravilāsam of Śrīnātha, who enjoyed the patronage of Dēva Rāya II and Sarvagña Śingama, has an interesting statement regarding another patron of his, Avachi Tippayya Śeṭṭi of Nellore (Vikrama Simhapura). This Śeṭṭi, to whom Śrīnātha dedicates his work, had his own ships and traded overseas on his own account. He imported horses from Ormuz, elephants from Ceylon, camphor from the Punjab, fine silks from China, various other articles from places which are not yet capable of identification. He enjoyed the monopoly for the supply of the articles in demand at the courts of Harihara II, Firōz-shah Bhāmani and Kumāragiri Reḍḍi of Konḍavīḍu. The arrangement for provision and protection of private trade like this, detailed in Marco Polo and in the Mōṭupalli inscription of the Kākatīya king Gaṇapati, seems to have continued intact.

IV. VIJAYANAGAR EXPANSION TOWARDS THE TELINGANA COAST.

The next item of information calling for remark in this collection is the existence of a Vijayanagar governorship at Vinikoṇḍa, a railway station south-west of Gunṭūr in latitude little beyond 16° and longitude 79° 30″. The translation of a kind of Sanskrit drama called 'Prēmābhirāmam' into Telugu under the name of

'Krīḍābhirāmam' was made by one Vallabha Rāya who calls himself the Governor of Vinikoṇḍa. He gives a number of details about his ancestors who were all officers of distinction under the predecessors of Dēva Rāya II. He himself was the Governor of Vinikoṇḍa and enjoyed the revenues of certain villages as salary of the office.

This seems the first instance of a governorship in this particular frontier under Vijayanagar. It was under Sultan Firōz of the Bhāmani kingdom that the effective conquest of the territories of Warrangal was undertaken by the Bahmani Sultans. This vigorous policy was continued by his two successors, Sultans Ahmad and Allau-d-din. The transfer of capital from Gulburga to Bidar, otherwise called Ahamadabad-Bidar, seems to have been done with the same object. Allau-d-din's wars against his Muhammadan neighbours of Khandesh and Malwa and sometimes even of Gujarat, almost undid the work of his predecessors in the east. When he felt himself free to adopt a vigorous policy in the east, he found the work too much for him single-handed, and he had to call in the assistance of Orissa, now coming into prominence under Kapilēśvara Gajapati. This alliance it was that gave possession of the Telingana coast to the monarch of Orissa while the Bahmani Sultans themselves had to remain content with that part of Warrangal which was within the eastern frontier of the present Nizam's dominions. This advance of Orissa accounts for the loss of the influence of the Reḍḍi chiefs who regarded themselves politically independent of all suzerain authority.

V. THE SUCCESSORS OF DĒVA RĀYA II AND THE ADVANCE OF ORISSA TOWARDS THE SOUTH.

With the death of Dēva Rāya II a dark half-century sets in and all the information we had hitherto of this period was based on a few inscriptions and the confused accounts in the Portuguese chronicles, which only contributed to make the confusion worse confounded. An interesting extract from a contemporary Sanskrit drama called the 'Gangādāsapratāpavilāsam', of which we have so far only the rather full abstract of Professor Eggeling in part 7 (No. 1610) of Sanskrit Manuscripts in the India Office Library, throws the much needed light upon this dark point. So far as is known at present this is the only work which gives a specific reference to a joint invasion of Vijayanagar by the Bahmani Sultan and the Gajapati king of Orissa. The death of the great monarch was taken advantage of by these two rulers to carry their expansion southwards, Orissa along the Telingana coast and the Bahmani Sultan over the rest of the frontier of Vijayanagar. The invasion was obviously beaten off as the extract says, and Mallikārjuna, the son of Dēva Rāya, succeeded to the throne. But the danger from Orissa continued to be real and it had very important consequences. The aggressiveness of Orissa is seen in the claim made in behalf of the Gajapatis of a successful advance by them as far as Kanchi, in a dramatic romance called 'Kanji-Kāvēri-Pothi.' It is this successful aggression on the part of Orissa that gave the occasion for Sāḷuva Narasimha to build up his power and ultimately to occupy the imperial throne.

VI. VIRŪPĀKSHA'S SUCCESSION—A USURPATION.

Who succeeded Mallikārjuna after his comparatively short rule, and what exactly was the nature of the succession, have been problems for which an answer seemed till lately impossible to attempt. One of the extracts given from the 'Prapannāmṛtam' read in the light of the Śrīśailam plates inscription (published as an appendix to my article on Virūpāksha II of Vijayanagar in the Bhandārkar Commemoration Volume) from which an extract is also given, makes it quite clear now that Virūpāksha usurped the throne. He succeeded his elder brother by setting aside his two nephews of whom we have had a few inscriptions all along. There is the further information in the extract that either on the occasion of the usurpation, or more probably a little later, he perpetrated a massacre of all those near enough to him to set up a counter-claim, a very faint glimmering of which we find in the Portuguese chronicles themselves. It is this usurpation that must have compelled Sāḷuva Narasimha to decide upon usurping the empire, and given him the necessary moral support of the other chieftains of the empire. There is a statement in the extract which is worth noting here: Virūpāksha, in gratitude for the *raising of the ghosts* that afflicted him, as the result of the devotional reading of the Rāmāyaṇa in his behalf by Eṭṭūr Narasimhāchārya, changed his sign-manual from Śrī Virūpāksha of this dynasty to 'Śrīrāma' which may partially explain the appearance of this sign-manual in some of the later inscriptions.

VII. SŌMADĒVA RĀJA—'THE CAPTURER OF THE SEVEN FORTS'.

There is one interesting extract from a professedly historical work known as 'Rāmarājīyamu' of which an edition was issued by Dr. Oppert though the book has been for some time out of print. A number of historical passages are extracted in the course of this collection as the historical matter in it has not been properly exploited till now. The extract under reference here relates to the period of the first dynasty, and refers to the ancestor of the famous brothers who lost the battle of Tālikoṭa. He is called Sōmadēva Rāja and was the fifth ancestor of Āravīṭi Bukka who was one of the officers of Sāḷuva Narasimha and the great-grandfather of Rāma Rāya who fell in the battle of Tālikoṭa. This Sōmadēva among his many achievements is said to have fought against the Muhammadan ruler Muhammad and taken him prisoner. It is he that is credited with the capture of seven forts rhetorically described as having been taken in a day. The importance of this consists in the explanation that this provides for certain expressions occurring in epigraphical records the meaning of which has been much misunderstood. The capture of the seven forts is a fact, and perhaps the capture was made in one campaign. The campaign was in all probability against Muhammad Shah I, Bahmani.

VIII. SĀḶUVA NARASIMHA.

The next following group of extracts all relate to Sāḷuva Narasimha and throw considerable light upon the course of Sāḷuva Narasimha's rise in the Empire of Vijayanagar. The chief place is to be given to the yet unpublished work 'Sāḷuva-abhyudayam' of which so far only one manuscript is available, which is itself in a condition hardly suitable for publication. This throws much needed light upon this dark period of Vijayanagar history, and gives a clear idea of the circumstances that led to Sāḷuva Narasimha's usurpation. We already referred to a joint invasion of Vijayanagar by the Bahmani Sultan and Kapilēśvara Gajapati of Orissa, immediately after the death of Dēva Rāya II. That seems to have been the beginning of the southward march of the Gajapati ruler who had won the mastery over the Telingana coast. Though beaten off from the walls of Vijayanagar by Mallikārjuna, the successor of Dēva Rāya II, the Gajapatis extended their conquests southwards. When Sāḷuva Narasimha appears on the scene, we find the Gajapati already in effective possession of the Nellore district, giving his boasted advance upon Kanchi, a historical foundation. The whole of the region between Kanchi and Rajahmundri was in the possession of the Orissa monarch and Sāḷuva Narasimha's first service to the empire was the beating back of this enemy right up to Rajahmundri where the Bahmani Sultan, Muhammad, found him strongly entrenched in one of his campaigns. As the 'Burhan-i-Ma'sir' puts it, when the army arrived in the neighbourhood of the fortress of Rajahmundri, "they saw an immense city, and on the farther side of the river the infidel Narasimha Rāya with 700,000 cursed infantry, 8,500 elephants like mountains of iron, had taken his stand. On this side of the river he had dug a deep ditch, on the edge of which he had built a wall like the rampart of Alexander, and filled it with cannon and guns, and all the apparatus of war." The date of this is 1474-5. This position of Sāḷuva Narasimha makes it clear that his operations against the Gajapati were crowned with success. It is not likely that he made any further advance into the Gajapati's territory proper. During the same period of time he also brought under his influence several of the provinces of the empire in the middle and in the west, without his action being called in question from headquarters, or meeting with serious opposition from the governors themselves. Such a state of things is a sure indication of the unpopularity of the imperial headquarters as the extract from the Prapannāmṛtam, regarding Virūpāksha, shows. He began with his ancestral Chandragiri, took possession of Udayagiri, which was the headquarters of an early viceroyalty, and a number of other possessions up to the frontier of the Godavari. He is then said in these extracts to have mastered possession of Penukoṇḍa, Kongu, Dhārāpuram, Gingi. His inscriptions are found scattered across the region extending from Chandragiri to Nāgamangala, not far from Seringapatam. The usurpation merely completes this gradual acquisition of power and position. For further information relating to this dark period reference may be made to my 'A Little Known Chapter of Vijayanagar History.'

IX. NARASA NĀYAKA.

Among the distinguished generals who were the companions of Sāḷuva Narasimha in all his early campaigns that ultimately led him to the empire, there figured four men most prominently; they are Āravīṭi Bukka and his son Rāma, and Īśvara Nāyaka and his son Narasa. All these four distinguished themselves in the campaigns of Narasimha against the last great Bahmani Sultan Muhammad of Bidar. The youngest of all the four probably was Narasa, and he is certainly the most distinguished among those that served Sāḷuva Narasimha. Narasa had his baptism of fire in a battle against the Sultan of Bidar referred to in Telugu works, as Beḍanda-Koṭa where the brunt of the fighting on the side of Vijayanagar appears to have fallen on his father Īśvara. In various works, both Sanskrit and Telugu, which describe the campaigns in which he played any part, the general order observed seems to be that adopted in the Sanskrit work called Varadāmbikā-Pariṇayam compiled in honour of Achyuta Rāya's marriage with Varadāmbā or Varadāmbikā. The poem seems the earliest composed among the works dedicated to Achyuta Rāya, as it stops short soon after the birth of his son, whereas the Achyuta-Rāya-abhyudayam begins with his coronation, when that son was anointed in the Yauva-Rājya (heir apparentcy) at the same time. This authority may be followed as being the nearest to Narasa, among the works that describe his early career. After the affair against the Sultan of Bidar, he is said to have carried on the campaign against the Telugu country. This was very likely in the company of Sāḷuva Narasimha against the Gajapati of Kalinga and the Bahmani Sultan in the north. Then he is said to have gone to the south against the Chōḷa country. It may be that in this part of the campaign as well he accompanied his master, but there are specific achievements ascribed to him in this campaign which are not mentioned in the various accounts relating to Sāḷuva Narasimha. He is said to have marched against Madura, defeated the Chōḷa, perhaps killed a Pānḍya, who is called Mānabhūsha in one, and simply Marava in another. He is then said to have marched northwards to Seringapatam where he defeated the Heuna, governor or general, at the place, and took possession of the island, having constructed a bridge, when the river was in floods, to cross it. He is then said to have marched westwards from there through a few places which are not identifiable, to Gōkarṇa on the West Coast. His having gone to Rāmēśvaram might have been in the company of Sāḷuva Narasimha or by himself alone. According to the order of campaigns set forth in this account he must have been on the banks of the Godavari in 1475 with his master. It may be then that he marched southwards in the company of his master. The circumstances necessitating a campaign against Madura must then have arisen, and he must have been deputed on that commission.

Since the campaign of Kumāra Kampaṇa, Madura seems to have been at least nominally under the empire. The two famous brothers Lakkanna and Mādanna were respectively governors of Madura and the Chōḷa country under Dēva Rāya II. The former had for his sphere of office 'the Lordship of the Southern Ocean' along with the governorship of Madura when he was promoted from the middle division, Dēva Rāya's brother-in-law Sāḷuva Tippa taking his place there. What happened in the Pāṇḍya country after Lakkanna left Madura to go to headquarters is not quite clear. There are inscriptions of a few chieftains whose titles were Vāṇādi Rāyar and their inscriptions range from A.D. 1453 to 1476 or thereabouts. In all likelihood the province of Madura was organized by Lakkanna, and these Bāṇa chieftains whose original homes should have been in the North Arcot district were put in charge of various localities as sub-governors under him. They perhaps attempted to make themselves independent when the troubles in the empire assumed great dimensions under Virūpāksha. It may be something like this that called for the active intervention of the imperial general Narasa Nāyaka. There is another alternative possible; it may be that the Pāṇḍyas, who had practically retired into the Tinnevelly district by now, attempted to regain their former position in the Madura district. This would account for the defeat of the Pāṇḍya king Mānabhūsha as some of the inscriptions state. We have a Mānābharana among the Pāṇḍyans whose descendants were associated with Tenkāsi, a city founded by one of them. What provision he made for carrying on the administration of Madura after he left, we have no means of knowing. But obviously there was no trouble in that frontier till we come to late in the reign of Krishṇadēva Rāya. After the progress through Seringapatam to Gōkarṇam, is described in some detail, the campaign against Suratrāṇa (Sultan) at a place called in Sanskrit Mānavadurga (Mānvi in the territory of Bijapur). This seems to be a campaign against the Adil Shah of Bijapur. This is the last warlike achievement of Narasa after which he is said to have entered Vijayanagar. This is in all probability the campaign undertaken by Narasa as Regent against Yusuf Adil Shah immediately after the death of Sāḷuva Narasimha in A.D. 1493. Even inscriptions do not seem to mention any campaign in which he took part after this year. Narasa's warlike life seems to begin in the fifties of the 15th century and takes him through all the campaigns of his master Sāḷuva Narasimha, and one great campaign which included Madura, Seringapatam and the West Coast by himself alone, before we come to his last war as Regent of Vijayanagar. While the details are abundant, we have as yet no means of arranging them in any chronological order with absolute certainty, so far as this particular portion is concerned.

X. KRISHNADĒVA RĀYA.

The next group of extracts bear upon the reign of the greatest ruler of Vijayanagar, Krishṇadēva Rāya. His rule made such an impression upon the people that his name is handed down in tradition as 'the king.' There is no need to discuss the extracts in detail in this introduction as the matter is fully treated in my published paper on this subject. It would be enough to point out here that these together correct in many essential particulars the Portuguese chronicles on which Mr. Sewell mainly relied for his account of this great monarch. One extract from the 'Pārijātāpaharaṇam' makes the relation clear between the rebellion of Ganga Rāja of Ummattūr and the capture of Sivasamudram. The hitherto not well exploited 'Krishṇa Rāya Vijayam' and the 'Rayāvā chakamu' throw much light upon the actual cause of Krishṇa Rāya's campaign against Orissa. What is more, the statement in the Prabōdha Chandrōdaya Vyākhya of Nādiṇḍla Gōpa, a nephew of Krishṇa's chief minister Sāḷuva Timma, makes it absolutely certain that Krishṇa Dēva did marry the Gajapati Pratāpa Rudra's daughter, a marriage on which some doubts were cast, not altogether without reason. The fact that the other two queens figure prominently in some of the records of the reign, while the Orissa princess figures nowhere, lends colour to the tradition that she was neglected. We cannot at this distance of time say why. The five stanzas ascribed to her are included in this collection for whatever historical value they may have. All that is said in the Portuguese chronicles of the last ten years of the reign of Krishṇa Dēva Rāya, it is to be regretted, we have no means of checking from literary sources, though the large number of inscriptions of this monarch makes it clear that the chroniclers had not access to unimpeachable sources of information. Krishṇa Rāya was a great patron of letters and himself somewhat of a voluminous writer. There are only two works of his, however, that have come down to us, the Telugu Āmuktamālyadā and the Sanskrit drama 'Jāmbavatī Kalyāṇam', from both of which short extracts are given.

XI. ACHYUTA.

With the death of Krishṇa Rāya we come upon a period which is anything but clear to the historian. Krishṇa died in 1530 and was succeeded by his surviving brother Achyuta. According to the Achyuta-Rāya-abhyudayam he succeeded without any trouble and had himself anointed at Tirupati, quite close to Chandragiri, where he was at the time. His uterine brother Ranga seems to have died by this time, leaving a son who later on ascended the throne as Sadāśiva. Achyuta himself had been a married man for some time, and had a son old enough to be installed as Yuva Rāja on the occasion of his coronation. His name is given in the manuscript part of the work referred to above, as Venkaṭa. Though Nuniz was a contemporary of Achyuta and was actually in Vijayanagar in Achyuta's reign, what he has to say of this reign is so utterly confused that it is difficult to say whether any reliance can be placed on his account at all. According to the Achyuta-Rāya-abhyudayam, Achyuta was anything but a coward. The first affair to draw his attention was a rebellion in the middle of the empire. A certain governor who seems to have attained to rank and influence in the reign of Krishṇa Dēva Rāya rose in rebellion. This person seems to have enjoyed the title of Sāḷuva Nāyaka and is described by the name Vīra Narasimha Rāya. He is described in one of his records as the son of a Taḷuva Kuḷaindān Bhaṭṭar, and seems to have gone by the familiar name of Śellappa (the pet one or the dear one) Sanskritised in the above work as Chēllappa. Achyuta marched against him soon after his coronation. Why Vīra Narasimha revolted and why he fled for protection to the Travancore country, and when actually the rebellion took place, are matters which it would be of the utmost importance to definitely settle in the history of this transaction. All that the poem says is that this Chēllappa, the Governor of the Chōḷa country, created trouble, and when he was defeated in the field, fled for protection to the Travancore country (Tiruvaḍi Rājyam). A Pāṇḍya seems to have carried the complaint to Achyuta who himself marched at the head of his army on this mission to Śrīrangam. While in camp there his brother-in-law volunteered to go forward and carry the enterprise to a successful conclusion if Achyuta would only consent to give him the commission. This brother-in-law Salaka Rāju Timma Rāju marched to the Tiruvaḍi country, defeated the king who gave asylum to the rebel and returned to Śrīrangam, bringing as prisoners Vīra Narasimha and the Tiruvaḍi Rāja himself. This is the transaction as it is described in the Sanskrit epic under reference.

The epigraphical records of Vīra Narasimha range between 1510 and 1528, and he seems to have been one of the trusted officers of Krishṇa-dēva-Rāya occupying a very high and responsible position in the heart of the empire. Why he should have taken a sudden fancy to revolt, and flee for protection to Travancore after being defeated in the field, does not appear anywhere. Tradition, as embodied in the Mackenzie records, says that during the last years of Krishṇa's reign, one of the foremost of his generals was governing in the Pāṇḍya country, having gradually dispossessed the titular Pāṇḍyan of his territory. The dispossessed Pāṇḍyan is said to have carried a complaint to Krishṇa-dēva-Rāya himself that Nāgama Nāyaka, who was sent to help him against his Chōḷa rival Vīra Śēkhara, had by slow steps superseded him in authority, making the Pāṇḍya kingdom his own. Krishṇa then called for volunteers to go on this expedition, from among the most valiant of his generals, and Nāgama's young son Viśvanātha volunteered his services to go and defeat his father, and bring the head of the rebel to the king. Having obtained the commission, the story goes on to say, Viśvanātha defeated his father and returned to the capital bringing Nāgama as prisoner with him. If this embodies correct tradition, and if Achyuta Rāya's invasion at the request of a Pāṇḍya king took place immediately after his coronation, it is likely that Vīra Narasimha's revolt has some connexion with Nāgama's disobedience. The truth seems to be, both Nāgama and Vīra Narasimha were masterful men who carried on their administration in a thorough-going fashion, making encroachments upon the sovereigns of the localities still left with petty possessions of proud kingdoms, showing by their acts a tendency to set up kingdoms if the headquarters showed weakness. If Krishṇa sent a punitive expedition against Nāgama in Madura near the close of his reign, he might have sent a similar one against the rebel Vīra Narasimha Rāya as well. It was probably an expedition like that which defeated the powerful governor who fled for safety to the Travancore country. He could not, however, be allowed to remain there to work further mischief, and Achyuta's expedition might have been in continuation of what Krishṇa Rāya began.

While it seems very probable that the last years of king Krishṇa were troubled with these rebellions which the great monarch manfully struggled to bring under control with considerable success, the invasion of Achyuta after Krishṇa's death and the restoration of the Pāṇḍyan monarch which the poem records, seem apparently to go against the foundation of the Nāyakship of Madura by Viśvanātha. Viśvanātha is generally recognized as the founder of the Nāyak kingdom of Madura, and Nelson, when he wrote the Manual of the Madura country, found the most convenient time for this achievement of Viśvanātha in A.D. 1559. Whatever excuse Nelson might have had for doing so, those that have followed him blindly had some material before them to consider whether this dating of Nelson could be reconciled with the facts which have since become accessible. Without going into a full discussion of the matter, we might state it here that Nāgama was an officer of reputation in Vijayanagar already in the days of Sāḷuva Narasimha. There are inscriptions (No. 318 of 1909, Madras Epig. Col.) that make him the foremost general of the time. He must have been a very old man under Krishṇa, and the description which tradition gives of him as embodied in the various records agrees with this position of his, as we make out from his inscriptions. Viśvanātha was appointed governor in succession to his father according to the same tradition. If this were true what is his position in relation to Achyuta and what actually did happen to him as a result of Achyuta's invasion of the Pāndya and Travancore country? What again was his position in the period intervening Achyuta's invasion and the end of the period of Rāma Rāja Viṭṭala's activity in that part of the country? We shall consider these questions later. Returning to Achyuta, he set forward to his capital from Śrīrangam, and went to Seringapatam on the way. Starting from there again, he marched across his territory to Raichur. Raichur seems by now to have passed into the hands of the Adil Shah and Achyuta had to lay siege to it. The poem, Achyuta-Rāya-abhyudayam, gives him credit for a victory, and ascribes to the Adil Shah an abject submission. This statement of the poem finds support in an inscription (No. 47 of 1900), dated A.D. 1534, according to which Achyuta Rāya made a grant for the merit of his mother, while encamped on the banks of the Krishna river. So far then Achyuta shows himself quite a worthy successor of king Krishṇa-dēva-Rāya. Some change obviously comes over him now, and the rest of his reign is one of internal trouble and confusion, if we are to take the account of Nuniz and Ferishta which alone are the sources of information available to us.

About this time it is quite likely that the two brothers-in-law both of them called Tirumala, distinguished Pedda (elder) and Pinna (younger) sons of Salaka Rāju, and brothers of the Queen Vāradāmba, seem to have become prominent in the administration of the empire. It is the advent of these officers to high position at court that seems to have carried with it the seed of all the trouble. All that we are able to see from the traditions that have come down to us is that these brothers concentrated all power in their hands and created for themselves a powerful opposition which centred round the family of the late monarch Krishṇa. The two queens of the late monarch appear to have been yet alive, and wielded some influence at court. Achyuta's nephew Sadāśiva seems to have had their support. These queens had each one a daughter according to these accounts, who were married respectively to Rāma Rāja and Tirumala, two among the three famous brothers who fought the battle of Tālikoṭa. These last belong to an influential family themselves, were sons-in-law of the late great king and had a counter-claimant to the throne under their influence. Thus there were all the necessary elements for internecine quarrels ready to hand. If Achyuta continued personally to exercise his authority vigorously as he did in the first years of his reign, he might have kept these disturbing elements under control. Whether he actually did so is very doubtful from the glimpses that we are able to get of the latter half of his reign. Both Nuniz and Ferishta record an invasion of Vijayanagar itself by the Adil Shah. If that could be taken for a fact, that is certain evidence of disaffection on the part of the three brothers, the cause of which could only be the abdication of all direct authority by Achyuta Rāya himself and the unpopularity of his brothers-in-law in the exercise of that authority. More than that it would be difficult to say from the material at our disposal. In all probability these brothers had to bide their time till Achyuta should die. Achyuta's son naturally succeeded, his uncles continuing to exercise all real authority. Among them the elder who appears to have been the one more directly implicated, got rid of his nephew by assassination. That was the signal for the brothers to throw off the mask, put their own candidate Sadāśiva on the throne and carry on the administration in their turn for Sadāśiva. Finding himself unequal to the three brothers, the elder Tirumala who is described as a mad man, invited his Muhammadan neighbours to his assistance. According to the annals of Haṇḍē Anantāpura, the three brothers overpowered the mad man first, and killed him, and marched forward to meet the allied Sultans of Ahmadnagar, Bidar and Golkoṇḍa. Having defeated them in the field the brothers returned to headquarters and installed Sadāśiva duly as the Emperor.

XII. SADĀŚIVA AND RĀMA.

The whole group of extracts relating to these two fall into three divisions, not in the arrangement of order or chronology, but in respect of their subject matter. One group of them refers to Rāma Rāya's wars against Salakam Timma Rāju, the brother-in-law of Achyuta, and the installing of Sadāśiva on the throne. Our authorities only mention, as usual without date, that Rāma Rāya and his brothers retired to Gutti (Gooty) out of dissatisfaction with the management of affairs at headquarters by Salakam Timma. Adoni, Gooty, Penukoṇḍa, Gaṇḍikōṭa, Kandanol (Kurnool) were the districts where they found the most support. Having gathered such forces as they were able to raise in these districts which seem to have been all along their special charge, they marched upon Vijayanagar, defeated Timma Rāju outside the capital, and entering the city installed Sadāśiva on the throne of Vijayanagar.

That done, they had to march forward to meet the allied armies of Ahmadnagar, Bidar and Golkoṇḍa, and beat them back from the territories of Vijayanagar to which they had marched, as was stated in the previous section, on the invitation of Timma the Mad. This is the beginning of a series of wars with the Muhammadans, a number of which are described in some detail, both in the 'Rāma rājīyamu' and the other works from which extracts are made. The three brothers Rāma, Tirumala and Venkaṭa, the four sons of the first, two sons of the next and at least two nephews of these brothers, all of these figure in the various engagements against one or other or all of these Sultans in combination. The localities mentioned are all of them either on the northern frontier of Vijayanagar or within the territories of these Sultans. Though by themselves their historical value may not be very much, they are of very great value read in combination with Ferishta for this period. It is hardly necessary to go into a detailed investigation in this introduction.

The only other matter of importance calling for notice here is the expedition sent out under Rāma Rāju Viṭṭala and Tirumala (usually known Chinna Timma) to the south. The two leaders were first cousins of Rāma Rāja and are said in the contemporary sources to have marched successfully across the Chōḷa and the Pāṇḍya countries into Travancore. They are given credit for having set up a pillar of victory on the Tāmraparṇi and even to have sent out an invasion to Ceylon. These documents do not enlighten us as to what exactly was the important cause that called for this imposing expedition within a decade of the more or less similar expedition undertaken at the beginning of the reign of Achyuta Rāya. It is possible to suggest two causes of vital importance to the Empire. The accession of Sadāśiva to the throne coincided almost with the extraordinarily successful effort of the sovereign of Travancore, Udaya Mārtāṇḍa Varman to extend his dominion across the peninsula. He had established himself so far successfully in the south that he held Kāyal on the fishery coast in his possession and appointed a viceroy. This hemmed in the Pāṇḍya feudatories of the Empire, who, since the advent of the Vijayanagar authority in the south, had retired to the western parts of the Tinnevelly district and had broken up into five comparatively petty chieftaincies. Imperial intervention might have been called for in their behalf. The next cause is the politically disintegrating activity of the Portuguese government and the missionaries on the pearl fishery coast, the industrious inhabitants of which were being converted to Christianity in large numbers under pressure of circumstances, which conversion appears to have been held to imply a transfer of political allegiance to the Portuguese. The expedition must have been somewhat thorough-going in its operations. The conquest and the organization of the territory under a vigorous and more satisfactory administration required the presence of these princes of the Empire for more than ten years in the far south.

During the interval between the death of Krishṇa Dēva Rāya, just before which we already stated the foundation was laid of the Nayakship of Madura under Viśvanātha, and the termination of office of Pinna Timma, what exactly was the position of Viśvanātha and his successor does not appear to be specifically defined anywhere in the available sources. The course of this dark period of history seems to have run somewhat as follows in respect of the foundation of the dynasty of the Nāyakas of Madura. Inscriptions up to A.D. 1528 (Śaka 1450) show that Vīra Narasimha Rāya held the position of governor of the south. He must have revolted soon after, being defeated and turned out of the country in consequence. As he found asylum in Travancore Achyuta Rāya had to undertake a war against that country. We have already pointed out that in all probability Nāgama Nāyaka had been sent to Madura before this, and had made an attempt to secure himself there, with a view ultimately to attain to independence. He was defeated by his son Viśvanātha who in turn was appointed Governor of Madura. This dignity of the Governorship of Madura for Visvanātha Nāyaka could not have carried with it the freedom of action that the greater governors or viceroys enjoyed. If Viśvanātha was a governor he must have played a very subordinate part in Salaka Rāju Timma's campaign in Travancore. He must have played the same part in the still greater campaign carried on by Rāma Rāju Viṭṭala and his brother in the same region. What is more, during the period of little more than a decade when Chinna Timma was actively organizing the province of Madura, Viśvanātha must have played the same subordinate rôle. His son Kumāra Krishnappa it is likely bore his own share in these campaigns as his name is mentioned in inscriptions (417 of 1905, *Mad. Epi. Rep.*). Thus while on the one side the comparatively subordinate position of Viśvanātha is made clear, the great probability of Viśvanātha having been governor of Madura during this period is also established. This position of his, finds confirmation in a few inscriptions which mention his name specifically as Viśvanātha Nāyaka, son of Nāgama Nāyaka, of dates A.D. 1535 and 1560 (113 of 1908, *Mad. Epi. Rep.*; Sewell's *Lists of Antiquities*, I, 209, Aṇṇiyūr). The conclusion seems therefore warranted that the foundation of the Nāyakship of Madura under Viśvanātha has to go back to a date at least a quarter of a century earlier, may be about thirty years. The date A.D. 1559 given by Nelson may have now to be definitely abandoned.

The extracts under this head give a number of details in regard to the campaigns of Rāma Rāya against the Muhammadans which ultimately brought about the epoch-making battle of Tālikōta. It would be far too elaborate to deal with this matter in this introduction. It would be enough for our purpose to say here that in the battle of Tālikōta, all the three brothers Rāma, Tirumala and Venkaṭādri fought. Rāma was undoubtedly killed, and Tirumala lost one of his eyes which Cæsar Frederick has noted. This detail is referred to very cleverly in a verse-extract in Telugu which addresses the king saying "You are God Śiva himself when you sit along with your wife and you are Śukrāchārya seated alone, being in either case the 'all knowing' (Sarvagña)". The point of the joke consists in this. The comparison is to two people who are all-wise, which is the compliment the author obviously intended to pay. Śiva and his wife constitute one body with the ordinary two eyes and the third eye in the forehead peculiar to Śiva, Tirumala having only one eye and his wife two. Śukra was blinded of one eye when he attempted to prevent Mahābali from gifting away the three feet of earth prayed for by the dwarf Vishṇu.

XIII. TIRUMALA AND THE EMPIRE.

It was the next brother of Rāma that succeeded him in the administration, Sadāsiva continuing to be the ruler in name.

Tirumala was as much of a scholar as a general. He seems to have removed the capital definitely from Vijayanagar to Penukoṇḍa, where he had to withstand an attack by the Muhammadans whom, according to these authorities, he succeeded in ultimately beating off. He was able to hand down the empire intact, though in so doing he appears unwittingly to have sowed the seed of its dismemberment. Of his four sons, three were alive, the eldest of whom Śrīranga succeeded him in the Empire, Sadāsiva being no more. The next son Rāma was appointed to the Viceroyalty of Seringapatam and the last Venkaṭapati was given charge of Madura and the other viceroyalties with headquarters at Chandragiri. Śrīranga had like his father to stand a siege in Penukoṇḍa by the Sultan of Golconḍa, possibly with the assistance of one or more of his brother Sultans. In the course of the wars connected with this, he was defeated, and he fell a prisoner into the hands of the Muhammadans. In consequence of this misfortune, the Muhammadans were able to gain effective possession of the territory north of Penukoṇḍa. This happened about the year 1579–80. One of the consequences of this misfortune was the second change of capital from Penukoṇḍa, this time to Chandragiri. The general course of history following this war is that Śrīranga died in 1586 leaving no children. Rāma seems to have died in Seringapatam a little before Śrīranga, leaving two sons, the elder of whom was still too young to take his place. So the empire became united under Venkaṭapati who ruled from 1586 to 1614 from Chandragiri as his capital. Tirumala, his young nephew of Seringapatam was sent to put down a rebellion in Madura, who rewarded his uncle's confidence by practical defection to the enemy with whom he came to an understanding and retired to his viceroyalty of Seringapatam, where he tried to set up independently. This defection met its reward about the year 1610, when he fell ill of a serious disease. One of the smaller chieftains under the viceroyalty, Rāja Woḍeyar of Mysore, laid siege to Seringapatam and captured it. He got himself confirmed in the possession of the viceroyalty by a grant that he obtained from Venkaṭapati Rāya, the Emperor, in A.D. 1612. This was the first province effectively lost to the empire through defection. Venkaṭapati seems energetically to have asserted his authority over the southern provinces till his death in 1614 when he was succeeded by an adopted son of his, Śrīranga, generally known as Chikka Rāya.

XIV. ŚRĪRANGA II.

This was the second son of Rāma, and the younger brother of the Viceroy of Seringapatam. He seems to have been adopted for succession by Venkaṭapati and thus became heir to the empire with consequences tragic in the extreme. One of the queens of Venkaṭapati pretended to have a son who was a lad probably old enough to succeed, but perhaps Venkaṭapati was aware of the truth and adopted the course that he did. The Rāmarājīyamu which is circumstantial in regard to the other queens of Venkaṭapati, does not give the parentage of one of them who goes by the name Venkaṭamma. It is just possible that she was the queen designated Bāyamma by Barrados, as any lady could be called Bāyamma in Telugu. The accession of this ill-fated Śrīranga II at once threw the empire into two hostile sections, one loyalist and the other traitor to the empire. It is hardly necessary to repeat the story of the massacre of the royal family at the instance of one Jagga Rāya, either the brother-in-law or the father-in-law of the late king Venkaṭapati. One child out of the royal family, by name Rāma, was smuggled out before the massacre at the instance of the loyalist Yāchama Nāyaka, the founder of the Venkaṭagiri family. Practically all the other chieftains of the empire ranged themselves on the side of the traitor with the exception of the Nāyaka of Tanjore. Yāchama had to fight single handed against Jagga Rāya and his confederates, and was able to beat a successful retreat with the prince in his possession to the Court of Tanjore, where after his arrival and having regard to the forthcoming war, the old Nāyaka Achyuta abdicated in favour of his son Raghunātha. Raghunātha assumed power, and having disposed of his other enemies such as the cruel Śōḷaga, who had his stronghold on an island at the mouth of the Coleroon, and the Feringhis of Ceylon (Portuguese) who took possession of Jaffna, was ready to meet his enemies marching rapidly to Śrīrangam to effect a junction with the Nāyak of Madura before advancing upon Tanjore. Information came to Raghunātha that they had cut open the Grand Anicut and were awaiting perhaps to cross the river to effect the junction. Raghunātha marched at once, met the enemy at Tōpūr (now Tōhūr) not far from the Grand Anicut, and defeated them completely. The traitor Jagga Rāya fell in battle and the imperial fugitive was raised to the throne as Rāma II.

XV. LAST DAYS OF THE EMPIRE.

We have already stated, in the section immediately preceding, that with the exception of Yāchama Nāyaka and his cousins, and

Raghunātha Nāyaka of Tanjore, all the more important chieftains of the empire had banded themselves together on the side of the traitor Jagga Rāya. Though the battle actually went against Jagga who fell in the course of the engagement, the empire did not return to its normal condition. A series of campaigns were required to defeat the several enemies, and a number of actions took place between the loyalist chieftains and one or other of the confederates. The Muhammadans on the northern frontier did not fail to take advantage of the bad plight of the empire, and kept constantly harassing the northern frontiers of it. Even Venkaṭapati Rāya himself in his last days found his position in Chandragiri dangerous. This might have been the cause that led to Chenna, the brother-in-law of Yāchama Nāyaka, going to war with Linga of Vēlūr. Chenna took possession of the fort in behalf of his master. Vēlūr seems thenceforward to have become the actual capital of the Vijayanagar Empire. Some of Chenna's sons attained to considerable distinction; one of them Venkaṭa distinguished himself in the wars against the Nāyakas of Gingi and constructed a tank in the North Arcot district, which he named Chenna Sāgaram after his father. Another of his brothers Anka was a literary man, in addition to being perhaps a warrior also. One of his works has come down to us, 'Ushāpariṇayam' by name. This gives us the interesting piece of information that the town of Madras was built by a half-brother of his, Ayyappa, who interposed this town between the Portuguese at Mylapore and the Dutch at Pulikat (Praḷaya Kāveri) to prevent their constant quarrels on this boundary. He called the town Chennapaṭna in the name of his father. This Ayyappa lived on to make another exhibition of his loyalty in behalf of Rāma's successor Śrīranga in a battle at Erode where a confederacy of Chokkanātha of Madura, the general of the Tanjore Nāyak, this Ayyappa and one of the officers even of Bijapur supported the claim of Śrīranga against Mysore. Ayyappa fell in this battle. Śrīranga had therefore to betake himself to the only other chieftain of the empire who was willing to help him, and that was the usurper Śivappa Nāyaka of Ikkēri. Śivappa Nāyaka had already rendered valuable service by compelling the enemies of Śrīranga to raise the siege of Vellore which was the imperial capital at the time, and led an invasion in the name of Śrīranga against Chikka Dēva Rāya of Mysore. He was defeated at Hassan, and Sakkarepaṭna, and the result of this war was the extension of the Mysore boundary up to these places. Śrīranga passes out of the scene unknown after this particular incident. The only other incident which might be said to belong to the history of Vijayanagar Empire is an invasion of the Mysore territories by Kōdanda Rāma, a nephew of this Śrīranga, the last scion of the imperial family of Vijayanagar so far known. He defeated in battle the army of the Rāja of Mysore, at a place called Āsana (Hassan) in Mysore. It was to him that the work Rāma-rājīyamu or Narapativijayamu was dedicated.

By this time, after a series of invasions both by Bijapur and by Golkonda, a considerable portion of what was Vijayanagar had passed into the hands of the Muhammadans. The southern invasions of these Bijapur Sultans were entrusted to Shaji, Sivaji's father, and Venkāji or Ekoji, Śivaji's brother. It is well known that both Gingi and Tanjore fell into the hands of the Mahrattas. The Mysore general who is said to have been defeated by Kodandarāma at Hassan was one by name Daḷavāy Kumārayya. He laid siege to Trichinopoly according to the Mackenzie MSS. and was defeated and driven into Mysore by the Mahratta armies of Sivaji and Ekoji of Gingi. By the time that Mysore had established itself firmly as an independent kingdom, the Vijayanagar Empire had passed out of existence. With the purchase of Bangalore from Ekoji by Chikka Dēva Rāya in 1687-8, the modern Mysore State comes into existence, the only part of the Empire of Vijayanagar which might lay claim to continue the traditions of Hindu rule.

XVI. CONCLUSION.

Besides the obvious value of these extracts to the historian of Vijayanagar, they throw considerable light upon the position of various subordinate families of the empire. It will be clear from them even to a casual reader that the imperial family and the subordinate chieftains alike, were patrons of literature both Sanskrit and Telugu. It is their extraordinarily liberal patronage of letters that gave a special stimulus to the development of later Sanskrit culture. It is hardly necessary to go into more detail in this introduction. The publication of this collection would, it is to be hoped, exhibit the Vijayanagar Empire in its proper setting in respect of its character and significance in the history of Hindu India.

1

KAMPARĀYACHARITAM OF GANGĀ DĒVI.

This very important historical poem was written by Gangā Dēvi, one of the wives of Kamparāya, the son of the Emperor Bukka. It describes the achievements of her husband Kamparāya and narrates the history of his expedition to the south. Canto I of the book contains, after the usual invocation, a short description of the capital city of Vijayanagar on the banks of the Tungabhadra with its suburb containing the temple of Virūpāksha. Bukka was its ruler and he had several wives of whom Dēpāyi was the favourite. Canto II. Bukka had by his wife Dēpāyi three sons, Kampana, Sangama and Kampana, the younger. Canto III. When the prince Kampana grew up to manhood his father Bukka advised him on the duties of royal princes and pointed out to him the work that lay before him. He asked Kampana to march against the Tuṇḍīra country (Toṇḍamaṇḍalam) and after defeating its ruler Champarāya to reduce Kanchi. After subduing the several "forest chiefs" (Vanyarajas, Tam. Kāḍavar) he was directed to proceed against the king of the Turushkas who had his headquarters at Madura. Kampana after this exhortation returned home having resolved on leading the expedition to the south. Canto IV. Kampa started upon his expedition to the south. He crossed the country of Karṇāṭa in five or six days and reached the town of Kanṭakānana (Ver. Muḷvāy or Mulbāgal). Thence he started against Champa, crossed the Kshīratarangiṇi (Pālār) and made his camp at Virinchipuram. There the forces of the Dramiḍa (Tamil) King (Champa Rāya) opposed him. The forces of Champa Rāya were defeated and fled for safety to their citadel, Rājagambhīram (? Paḍaivīḍu). Kamparāya proceeded against that place also and laid siege to the fort. When pressed hard Champa sallied out of the fort sword in hand and there was a duel between him and Kampana. In the duel Champa was killed and Kamparāya proceeded to the town of Kānchi and stationed his forces there. Canto V. Kampana stayed in the town of Marakata (Virinchipuram), and spent the rainy and winter seasons there. Canto VI describes the life of Kampana in camp. Canto VII describes some conversation between the prince and his consort Gangā, the authoress of the book, but the narrative is there broken as the portion of the manuscript at this point is lost. Canto VIII. A goddess appears before the prince Kampana and after describing to him the disastrous consequences of the Mussalman invasions of the south and the sad plight of the southern country and its temples, exhorts him to extirpate the invaders and restore the country to its ancient glory, presenting him at the same time with a divine sword. Kamparāya then proceeded against Madura and, in a battle, killed the Sultan ruling in the place. He then made grants to several temples.

Here the manuscript breaks off.

Canto I.

आसीत्समस्तसामन्त मस्तकन्यस्त शासनः ।
बुक्कराज इति ख्यातो राजा हरिहरानुजः ॥
तस्यासी द्विजयानाम विजयार्जित सम्पदः ।
राजधानी बुधैः श्लाघ्या शक्रस्येवामरावती ॥
सुरलोकान्त सङ्क्रान्त स्वर्णदीमत्सरादिव ।
परिघाकारतां यान्त्या परीता तुङ्गभद्रया ॥
यच्छाखा नगरीं रम्यां अनेक धनदाश्रितां ।
अधितिष्टन्विरूपाक्षो नस्मरत्यलकापुरीं ॥
देपायीनाम तस्यासीत् देवी वसुमतीपतेः ।
पद्मापद्मेक्षणस्येव शङ्करस्येव पार्वती ॥
सत्स्वन्येष्वपि दारेषु तामेव मनुजाधिपः ।
बहुमंस्त निशानाथो नक्षत्रेष्विवरोहिणीं ॥

Canto II.

सुखायमानां सुतजन्मवार्तां सहर्षमावेदयतेजनाय ।
अवाञ्छदात्मान मपिप्रदातुं कुतूहली कुन्तल भूमिपालः ॥
अकम्पयिष्यत्ययमेकवीरः सङ्ग्रामरङ्गे सकलानरातीन् ।
इत्येवनिश्चित्य स दीर्घदर्शी नाम्नासुतं कम्पन इत्यकार्षीत् ॥
अथक्रमात्पार्थिवधर्मपत्नी सुतावुभौकम्पन सङ्गमाख्यौ ।
असूत चिन्तामणि पारिजातौ पयःपयोधेरिव वीचिरेखा ॥
सराजपुत्रस्सहसोदराभ्यां . . . . ।
. . . . ॥

पशुपतिरिवनेत्रैः सोमसूर्याग्निरूपैः
नय इव निरपायैः प्राभवोत्साहमन्त्रैः ।
भव इव पुरुषार्थैः धर्मकामार्थसंज्ञैः
त्रिभिरपि नरपालस्तैस्तनूजै रभासीत् ॥

Canto III.

तदेवमुज्जृम्भित भूरिपौरुषः पराक्रमंवैरिषु कर्तुमर्हसि ।
उपप्लुताशेष जगत्सुशोषणे वृषेव शातां शतकोटिमद्रिषु ॥
उपेत्यतुण्डीर मखण्डितोद्यमः प्रमथ्यचम्पप्रमुखात्रणोन्मुखान् ।
प्रशाधिकाञ्ची मनुवर्तितप्रजः पतिर्निधीना मलकापुरीमिव ॥
अथाभिभूताखिल वन्यभूभृतः तुलुष्कभङ्गस्तवनैव दुष्करः ।
निगीर्णशाखा शतसंवृतः कथं तरुप्रकाण्डं नदहेद्दवानलः ॥
अनेनदेशानधिकृत्य दक्षिणान् वितन्यतेराक्षस राजदुर्नयः ।
त्वयापिलोकत्रयतापहारिणा विधीयतां राघवकर्म निर्मलम् ॥
इतीरयित्वाविरते नरेश्वरे प्रवृष्टपाथोधर साम्यधारिणि ।
कृतप्रणामश्शिरसा प्रतीष्टवान् गुरूपदेशं गुणिनां पुरस्सरः ॥
ततोमहार्हैर्गुरुणा विभूषणैः प्रसाधितस्वावयवावतारितैः ।
परेद्युनिर्धारित जैत्रनिर्गमो निजाधिवासं प्रमनाः समासदत् ॥

Canto IV.

अथकम्प महीपालः कम्पयन्द्विषतां मनः ।
प्रतिष्ठितादिशंभेजे मलयाचल मुद्रिताम् ॥
अथ लङ्घितकर्णाटः पञ्चषैरेव वासरैः ।
प्रापत्कम्प महीपालः कण्टकानन पट्टणम् ॥
सतत्रदिवसान् कांश्चिदतिवाह्य महाबलः ।
अभिषेणयितुं चम्पमुपाक्रमत कालवित् ॥
प्रसृतैस्तच्चमूधूलिस्तोमैः क्षीरतरङ्गिणी ।
कीर्त्याचम्पक्षितीन्द्रस्य साकंकलुषतामगात् ॥
सदुग्धवाहिनीवीचिमारुताधूतशाखिनि ।
विरिञ्चनगराभ्यर्णेन्यवेशय दनीकिनीम् ॥

अथ सन्नद्धसैन्यस्त मरुन्धद्द्रामिडाधिपम् ।
घनीकृतहिमानीको हेमन्त इव भास्करम् ॥
सावर्तमारुताक्षिप्त समुद्रद्वय सन्निभौ ।
व्यूहौद्रविडकर्नाट नाथयोस्सन्निपेततुः ॥
ततः कम्प नरेन्द्रस्य भटैर्भुजबलोत्कटैः ।
पलायत पराभूता द्रविडेन्द्रवरूथिनी ॥
अथ तस्यपुरीमेव नीत्वा शिबिरतां नृपः ।
अचलं राजगम्भीर मरुन्धद्विषदाश्रितम् ॥
प्रवाताभिमुखाघूर्णैः पताकापाणि पल्लवैः ।
आरोहणाय राजेन्द्र माजुहावेव भूधरः ॥
अलब्धनिर्गमंदुर्ग मासी देवमुपद्रुतम् ।
निर्जगाम निजागारा च्चम्पक्ष्मापोपि कोपनः ॥
कृपाणपाणिर्वल्मीकात् जिह्माल इवजिह्मगः ।
अहंपूर्विकया वीरे प्वभितो युद्धकाङ्क्षिषु ।
प्रत्यग्रहीन्महीपालः चम्पंसिंह इवाद्विपन् ॥
तौनिकुञ्चितपूर्वाङ्गौ निश्चलाक्षौकृपाणिनौ ।
उचितस्थानकावास्तां चित्रन्यस्ताविवक्षणम् ॥
कक्ष्याविभक्त वपुषो श्चारिभिश्चरतोस्तयोः ।
पश्यद्भिस्सौष्टवं देवैः अनिमेषत्वमादृतम् ॥
अन्तर्बिम्बितचम्पेन्द्रा कम्पेन्द्रस्यासिपुत्रिका ।
अप्सरीभ्यः पतिंदातुं अन्तर्वत्नीकिलाभवत् ॥
अथ वञ्चित खड्ग प्रहारः कम्पभूपतिः ।
अकरोदसिनाचम्प ममरेन्द्रपुरातिथिम् ॥
इत्थं सङ्गरमूर्ध्नि चम्पनृपतिं नीत्वाकथा शेषतां
श्रीमान्कम्प नरेश्वरोजनयितुस्सम्प्राप्तवान्शासनम् ।

*

काञ्चीन्यस्त जयप्रशस्तिरमितः सङ्कीर्णवर्णाश्रमम्
नीत्वा नित्यनिरत्ययर्द्धि रशिषच्चुण्डीर भूमण्डलम् ॥

---

* This inscription does not appear so far to have been noticed.

Canto V.

अथ सतत्रमहीतल मण्डने मरतकाह्वय भाजिमहापुरे ।
विरचितस्थितिरप्रतिशासनम् जगदशेषमरक्षदनाकुलम् ॥

Canto VII.

अथ कम्पनृपोपि कृत्यवित् कृतसन्ध्या समयोचितक्रियः ।
अवदत्स(-)धिस्थितां प्रियां भुविगङ्गेत्यभिनन्दिताह्वयाम् ॥
कमलाक्षि कटाक्ष्यतामयं समयोवर्णनया रसार्द्रया ।
जनएष वचस्तवामृतम् श्रवसीपाठयितुं कुतूहली ॥
इति सादयितेनभाषिते दरनम्रं दधतीमुखाम्बुजम् ।
वदतिस्मशनैश्शुचिस्मिता सरसोदारपदां सरस्वतीम् ॥

Canto VIII.

. . . . व्याघ्रपुरीति सायथार्थम् ॥
अथिरङ्गमवाप्त योगनिद्रम् हरिमुद्वेजयतीतिजातभीतिः ।
पतितंमुहुरिष्टकानिकायम् फणचक्रेण निवारयत्यहीन्द्रः ॥
. . . नुघूर्णद्घूर्णनाभम् नववेतण्ड विमर्दिनीमवस्थाम् ।
विरतान्यपरिच्छदप्रपञ्चो भजतेहन्त गजप्रमाथि नाथः ॥
घुणजग्धकवाट सम्पुटानि स्फुटद्र्वाङ्कुर सन्धिमण्डपानि ।
श्लथगर्भगृहाणि वीक्ष्यदूये भृशमन्यान्यपि देवताकुलानि ॥
मुखराणि पुरामृदङ्गघोषैः अभितो देवकुलानियान्यभूवन् ।
तुमुलानिभवन्ति फेरवाणां तुमुलैस्तानि भयङ्करैरिदानीं ॥
अतिलङ्घ्य चिरन्तनींस्वसीमा मपदेष्वर्पित जीवनप्रवृत्तिः ।
मुहुरुत्पथगामिनी तुलुष्कान् अधुनाहानु करोतिसह्यकन्या ॥
सतताध्वरधूमसौरभैः प्राङ् नियमोद्घोषणवद्भिरग्रहारैः ।
अधुनाजनि विस्रमांसगन्धैः अधिकक्षीबतुलुष्क सिंहनादैः ॥
मधुरोपवनं निरीक्ष्यदूये बहुशःखण्डित नालिकेर खण्डम् ।
परितोनृकरोटि कोटिहार प्रचलच्छूल परम्परापरीतम् ॥
रमणीयतरोबभूव यस्मिन् रमणीनां मणिनूपुर प्रणादः ।
द्विजशृङ्खलकार बलाक्रियाभिः कुरुते राजपथः स्वकर्णशूलम् ॥

परितस्तत तन्तुवायतन्तु व्यतिषङ्गाज्जनितानि जालकानि ।
पुरगोपुरसालभञ्जिकानाम् दधते चीनपटावकुण्ठनत्वम् ॥
हिमचन्दन वारिसेक शीतान्यभवन्यानि गृहाङ्गणानि राज्ञाम् ।
हृदयं मम वेदयन्तितानि द्विजबन्दी नयनाम्बुदूषितानि ॥

* * * *

सुवतेन यथा पुरंवसूनि क्षितयोवर्षति पूर्ववन्नशक्रः ।
शमनोऽपिजनं नयत्यकाण्डे विषयेऽस्मिन्यवनैर्हता वशिष्टम् ॥
श्वसितानिलशोषिताधराणि श्लथशीर्णायित चूर्णकुन्तलानि ।
बहुबाष्प परिप्लुतेक्षणानि द्रविडानां वदनानि वीक्ष्यदूये ॥
श्रुतिरस्तमिता नयः प्रलीनो विरता धर्मकथा च्युतं चरित्रम् ।
सुकृतं कृतमाभिजात्यमस्तं किमिवान्यत्कलिरेकएवधन्यः ॥

* * * *

इति सा निखिलं निवेद्यराज्ञे यवनानां जनगर्हितं चरित्रम् ।
अतिभीषण मात्मनः प्रभावात् कमपिप्रादुर भावयत्कृपाणम् ॥

* * *

अधुनाशुविशस्य दक्षिणस्यां मधुरायांपुरि कंसवन्नृशंसम् ।
यवनाधिपतिं बलोत्तरस्त्वम् विदधाथाः स्पुटमच्युतावतारम् ॥
अनिदं प्रथमोहिधार्यतेऽसौ भवतान्यैर्मनसाप्यधारणीयः ।
भुवनत्रय रक्षणैकदीक्षा विधिशंसी कटकः पदाम्बुजेन ॥
. . . . |
कम्पक्षितीन्द्रं यवनाधिराजः प्रत्यग्रहीद्वृत्र इवामरेन्द्रम् ॥

* * * *

पराक्रमान्न्यकृतचोलपाण्ड्यं बल्लालसम्पल्लतिका कुठारम् ।
रणोन्मुखं कम्पनृपोऽभ्यनन्दीत् वीरस्सुरत्राणमुदग्रशौर्यः ॥
प्रशान्तदावेन वनान्तलक्ष्मीः गतोपरागा गगनस्थलीव ।
कलिन्दजामर्दितकाळियेव दिग्दक्षिणासीत्क्षतपारसीका ॥
अथावशिष्टानथवैरियोधान् संरक्ष्यपादप्रणता . . . ।
. . . . ॥ *

* These passages were extracted from the copy in the Madras Government Oriental Manuscripts Library. The work has since been published in Trivandrum by Pundit V. Srinivasa Sastri of the Travancore Archæological Department.

2

JAIMINI BHĀRATAMU, AŚVAMĒDHAPARVAMU.

[*By Pillalamaṟṟi Pinavirabhadra.*]

This work is dedicated to Sāḷuva Narasimha, the first king of the Second Vijayanagar or Sāḷuva dynasty. In the introduction it gives some information about the ancestors of Sāḷuva Narasimha of whom the chief was Sāḷuva Mangu. During the reign of the Emperor Bukka he was one of the generals that took part in the expedition to the South under Kampana Uḍayar, the son of Bukka and his Minister Gopaṇārya. The expedition was directed against the chief, Śambuva-rāya and the Muhammadans who were then masters of the Madura and Trichinopoly districts. In this extract he is said to have defeated the Sultan of the south and given his territory to Śambuva-rāya, to have established Śambuva-rāya on his throne, to have established the God of Śrīrangam in his temple and made a present to it of 60,000 Maḍas (of gold) and to have killed the Sultan of Madura in battle.

Canto I 30. మ. జననంబందిరిగుండభూవిభునకున్ సంధాకబంధారిగా
తనయున్ శ్రీనిధివీరయాంబళుఁడునుద్యత్కీర్తిమాదయ్యయున్
ఘనతేజోనిధి గుండబమ్మఁడును సంగ్రామస్థలీపార్థ స
జ్జనమందారులు సాళ్వమంగనృపుఁడున్ సావిత్రి మంగాంకుఁడున్.

31. క. వీరలలో నుతికెక్కెను
వీరాగ్రేసరుఁడులోక విశ్రుతవిభవ
స్వారాజుసాళ్వమఁగ
క్ష్మారమణుఁడుసుగుణరత్నకలశాంబుధియై.

32. సీ. దురములో దక్షిణ సురతాను నెదిరించి
కొనివచ్చిసంపరాయనికినిచ్చె
సామ్రాజ్యముఁనిల్పి సాంపరాయస్థాప
నాచార్య బిరుదవిఖ్యాతిఁగాంచె
శ్రీరంగవిభుప్రతిష్ఠించియఱ్వదివేల
మాడలద్దేవునుమ్మడికినొసఁగ
మధురాసురత్రాణు మడియించిపరపక్షి
సాళువబిరుదంబు జగతినెఱపె

గీ. గబ్బితనమునఁ దేజిమొగంబుఁగట్టి
తఱిమినగరంపుగవఁకులు విఱుగఁద్రోలి
తానువ్రేసినగౌరునుద్దవిడిఁదెచ్చె
సాహసంబుననుప్పొంగుసాళ్వమంగు.

33. గీ. అట్టిసాళ్వమంగయకుసింగవిభుగుండ
శౌరిగౌతరాజుసావడిత్తి
తీశహన్మమానవేశ్వరుంగ్నామల్లి
నాథుఁడనఁగసుతులునమదహితులు.

3

SĀḶUVĀBHYUDAYAM.

[*By Rājanātha Diṇḍima.*]

This historical poem describing the achievements of Sāḷuva Narasimha who became Vijayanagar Emperor, and his ancestors, was written by his court poet Rājanātha Dinḍima. It gives important information about Sāḷuva Mangu. His expeditions against the chief Śambuva-rāya and the Sultan of Madura are described, and the several titles which he took as a result of his achievements and which his descendents assumed after him, are explained. His munificence to the temple of Śrīrangam, as the gift of 1,000 Sāḷagramas and the presenting of eight villages to represent the eight syllables of the Ashṭākshara, is described at length. All this took place during Kampana Uḍayar's invasion of the Chola and Pandya countries in the reign of Bukka, in which Sāḷuva Mangu took a leading part as a general.

Canto I.

श्रीगुण्डयस्साळुवमाङ्गि देवस्सावित्रिपूर्वोऽपिच मङ्गिदेवः ॥ ४२ ॥
वीरोबळोगौतयमादिराजौ षट् तेनतस्यांजानिताः कुमाराः ।
शम्भोःषडङ्गैरिवतैः प्रसूतैः तस्मात्स्वतेजःपरिपूरिताशैः ॥ ४३ ॥
जगद्यथासीघ्रि कृतङ्कुलंतत् षोढाविभिन्नं भुविशोभतेस्म ।
तेषामनुज्ञामवगम्यवीरः शौर्योदाधिस्सालुवमाङ्गिदेवः ॥ ४४ ॥

आशाविजित्यापिचदाक्षिणात्य मसौसुरत्राणमगाज्जिगीषुः ।
यस्मिन्खरादीनहितान्विजित्य रामस्सुरत्राणवशंवदोऽभूत् ॥ ४५ ॥
अहन्सुरत्राणमसह्यवीर्यः . . . न्नहोसालुवमाङ्गिदेवः ।
कृतीततःकेरळराजचोळ पाण्ड्यादिभूपेषु भयद्रुतेषु ॥ ४६ ॥
शौर्येणजित्वायुधिचम्भुरायम् तमप्यसौ स्थापयतिस्म(?राज्ये) (?)
तत्स्थापनाचार्यतयातदादि तथास्ववंश्याननयत्प्रतीतिम् ॥ ४७ ॥
निर्न्येयथागुर्जरनिर्जयेन सगुर्जरीयट्टविपाटसंज्ञां ।
प्रत्यार्थिनस्तेनप . . . तयत् पतत्त्रिणस्साळुवपत्त्रिणेव ॥ ४८ ॥
तदादिसर्वोपिचसाळुवेन्द्र संज्ञांभजन्तिस्मतदीयवंश्याः ।
कटारिकास्त्रेणकमप्यजैषीत् यदायमुद्यद्वि . . . . दादि ॥ ४९॥
तेसाळुवायान्तिजगत्युदग्राम् कटारिकासाळुवइत्यभिख्याम् ।
आलङ्कमामेरुरिपूनशेषान् अशोषयत्साळुवमङ्गिदेवः ॥ ५० ॥
षडङ्गवाणीमयतुङ्गशृङ्ग श्रीरङ्गमोङ्कारमयागतोभूत् (?)
आलोकयन्यत्रनिमीलिताक्षम् अन्तस्थिताशेषसुखासुखानि ॥ ५१ ॥
दीनावनेजाग्रदुपैतितीव्रम् नानाजगन्नर्तनसूत्रधारः ।
सह्यात्मजाद्वीपतटेयदीय सुवर्णगेहं स्वपदम्बुजाक्षम् ॥ ५२ ॥
अन्तर्निलीनाद्भुतचञ्चरीक हेमारविन्दभ्रममातनोति ।
ममात्मजासावितिक्लृप्तवादा गङ्गादिभिःकिंजलधेःपुरन्ध्री ॥ ५३ ॥
नीत्वायदन्तर्नियतंसकान्तां लक्ष्मींपरीत्यावनिसह्यकन्या ।
महीपतेर्मान्यसहस्रसाल ग्रामान्प्रदातुंकृपणावनस्य ॥ ५४ ॥
अष्टाक्षरी . . ध्यवधिव्रतार्थ मष्टाग्रहारार्पणमद्भुतर्द्धिम् ।
जेतुर्दिशामष्टदिगीशमूर्तेः अष्टाङ्गयोगादधिरूढभूम्नः ॥ ५५ ॥
अष्टाग्रहारार्पणमस्ययुक्त माराधनायाभवदष्टमूर्तेः ।
श्रीरङ्गसंस्थापनजातकीर्ति मारभ्यतंचन्द्रकुलावतंसाः ॥ ५६ ॥
सर्वेप्यगच्छन्विरुदंधरण्याम् तत्स्थापनाचार्यइतिप्रतीतिं ॥
आशानिग्रहतोविगृह्यसकलानन्तस्थितानप्यरीन्
स्वाधीनः प्रकृतौस्थितस्सकरुणं पश्यज्जगत्स्वात्मवत् ।
सोदर्यैस्सहपञ्चभिस्समरसै र्भूतैरिवात्मापरान्
स्वीकुर्वन्विषयान्गुरोःपदमगाच्छ्रीमङ्गिदेवस्ततः ॥

4

RĀMĀBHYUDAYA.

[*By Sāḷuva Narasimha.*]

This poem narrating the story of the Rāmāyaṇa is said to have been written by the Vijayanagar king Sāḷuva Narasimha of the second dynasty. As is usual, in the beginning of the first canto the author gives some information about his family and ancestors. The descent of the family is traced from the moon, and after a few mythological names the name of a chief Gunḍa is given. His capital was at Kalyāṇa. He proceeded from his capital against a fort called Ramadurga ruled by a Śabara (forest) King and captured it. Gunḍa had six sons, Gunḍa, Mādirāja, Vīrāhobala, Gautama, Sāḷuva Mangi and Sāvitri Mangi; of these Sāḷuva Mangi was a friend of Kampa-rāya (the prince Kampana, the son of the emperor Bukka) and in order to help him, accompanied him on his expedition to the south. After defeating Champurāya he proceeded against the Southern Sultan who had his headquarters at Madura. There was fought a hard battle between Sāḷuva Mangi and the Southern Sultan in which the latter lost his life. The victor after erecting a pillar of victory on the banks of the Tāmraparṇi proceeded north to the temple of Śrīrangam. There he is said to have made extensive grants to the god the most important being the gift of a thousand *sāḷagramas* and eight villages.

* तदन्वयेसमभवंश्चत्वारोधरणीभुजः ।
गुण्डदेवोमाल्लिदेवःमङ्गिदेवश्चमङ्गधः ॥
गुण्डदेवोनृपस्तेषुगुणपौरुषभूषणः ।
अशेषामाशिषच्छेषनिर्विशेषभुजो भुवम् ॥
आसत्किल्याणनगरमावासस्तस्यभूपतेः ।
ध्रुवंयद्विजितामेरु शृङ्गंप्राप्तामरावती ॥
यत्कान्तामुखसौन्दर्य दर्शनात्तसत्रपश्शशी ।
प्रवत्स्यतीवपातालं परिघाम्भासिबिम्बितः ॥

* For this extract I am obliged to M.R.Ry. Rao Bahadur K. V. Rangaswami Ayyangar Avargal of Trivandrum for having obtained the extract for me from the library of the Maharaja of Travancore.

प्रासादगोपुरागारै र्यत्ररुद्धरथैरवौ ।
दीर्घिकाचक्रनामानो दैर्घ्यादह्नामहंयवः ॥
संघृष्टं निशिसौधेषु यत्रस्त्रीणांमुखेन्दुभिः ।
विवेक्तुमिन्दुं शक्नोतिमुहूर्तंनविधुंतुदः ॥
नगराद्गुण्डदेवोऽपिनिरगाद्दिग्जिगीषया ।
रामदुर्गंगतस्तत्रनिरर्गळमदग्रहम् ॥
निगृह्यशबराग्रण्यमग्रहीष्टतदास्पदम् ।
गुण्डदेवोमादिराजोवीराहोबलगौतमौ ॥
. . सालुवसावित्रीमङ्गि देवौतदात्मजौ ।
तेषांमध्येसालुवादिमङ्गिदेवोमहाभुजः ॥
अभौक्षीद्वसुधांसर्वामसपत्नामसौकृती ।
सौहार्दात्कम्पराजस्यचम्पुरायाभयार्पकः ॥
अगाज्जिगीषुस्तदरीनगरस्य युवतींदिशाम् ।
महनीयापदानस्यमधुरापुरवासिनः ॥
तस्यासीद्दाक्षिणसुरत्राणेनसमरोमहान् ।
धनुर्ज्या संश्रयोदश्वदच्छमल्लच्छटान्विते ॥
अफल्गुवल्गुनोदग्रखड्गिवर्गनिरर्गळे ।
गन्धवाहोल्लसत्पत्रबृन्दस्यन्दनदन्तुरे ॥
अखर्वगर्वदुर्वारगतिगन्धर्वबन्धुरे ।
अवर्ण्यतद्रणारण्येपततांभूभृतामसौ ॥
पक्षांक्षिपन् क्षणात्साक्षात् साळुवाध्यक्षतांव्यधात् ।
स्वयंततोमङ्गिदेवःसुचिरंरचिताहवः ॥
ताद्विषोऽपातयच्छित्वा साकंभुवनपीडया ॥
सनिखायजयस्तम्भं ताम्रपर्णीतटेततः ।
शृङ्गंनिराकरगिरां श्रीरङ्गमगमन्नृपः ॥
प्रदक्षिणंवितन्वानाप्रायोवीचिकराहृतैः ।
अर्चयन्तीवकमलैरच्युतंयत्रसह्यजा ॥

सह्यजायांततःस्नातः सालग्रामसहस्रदः ।
साकंषोडशदानानि तत्राकार्षीत्ससाल्वः ॥
सुवृत्तान् शुचिभावाढ्यान्सुदृग्यःसुगुणोत्तरान् ।
अष्टाग्रहारानदिशत् अष्टदिग्विजयीनृपः ।
अनेकसालग्रामादिदानाद्द्विजवरानपरम् ।
नातर्पयद्द्विजवरारूढंचपुरुषंपरम् ॥

5

PRAPANNĀMṚTAM.*

[*By Anantārya.*]

This work deals with the history of Śrīvaishṇavaism in South India and the lives of successive Achāryas (pontiffs) of the religion. In the lives of Piḷḷai Lōkāchārya and Vēdānta Dēśika it gives some account of contemporary political events. Once when the God of Śrīrangam was taken out for a festival to the river Coleroon, and while his worship was going on there, a messenger arrived before Lōkāchārya and informed him that a fierce yavana (Muhammadan) was marching with troops towards Śrīrangam, and that he was destroying all the temples and Brahman villages on his way.

The people of the place did not know what to do since they could not leave the place with the idol in the middle of the festival. So they all consulted together and drew lots before the God whether to stay or fly. According to the result of the drawing they resolved to stay and proceeded with the festival. Some time later another messenger arrived with the news that the invader had reached Khanḍanapura (Kaṇṇanūr) and was thence marching on Śrīrangam itself.

This time Lōkāchārya consulted Vēdānta Dēśika as to what should be done in the circumstances. According to the direction of Vēdānta Dēśika, Lōkāchārya and others took the idols of Ranganātha and his Queens with them, and escaped by way of Gōshṭīpura (Tirukkōṭṭiyūr). After their departure Vēdānta Dēśika walled up the innermost shrine of the temple (Garbhasadana) and prepared to fly along with the others.

---

* This work of 125 cantos is not yet available to the scholarly public as there has so far been only a Telugu edition which is out of print. Entire manuscripts seem so far difficult of getting. The historical matter contained in this work is valuable.

The Muhammadan invader then marched upon Śrīrangam and breaking open the gates massacred a large number of the inhabitants. Just before the occurrence Sudarśana Bhaṭṭa of the Kūram family called Vēdānta Dēśika before him and, fearing that he might not survive the onslaught of the invaders, entrusted to him the only manuscript of his commentary on the Śrī Bhāshya called Śrutaprakāśikā, as also his two young sons. Vēdānta Dēśika escaped with the two boys and the book to Yādavādri (Melkote in the Mysore territory). Lōkāchārya and his followers proceeded to the Pāṇḍya country with the idols. On their way all the valuable jewels of the God as well as the property of Lōkāchārya were plundered by robbers in the forest. Not caring to live after this and learning of the sad plight of those that remained behind at Śrīrangam, Lōkāchārya breathed his last at a place called Jyotishkuḍi, and from there the God was taken to Sundarāchalam (Aḷagar Tirumalai near Madura). The God was taken from place to place in the Kērala (Málayāḷam) country and thence to the temple at Yādavādri (Tirunārāyaṇapuram or Melkote) in Mysore. After a time he was removed to the temple of Śrīnivāsa at Tirupati and was worshipped at the place for some years.

Some time after the occupation of Śrīrangam by the Muhammadans a Tamil (Drāviḍa) Brahman called Narisimhadēva managed to get the favour of the conqueror. He persuaded the conqueror to remove to Śamayavaram from Śrīrangam and had himself appointed manager of the place. He protected the shrine and the survivors from massacre, and some of the fugitives returned once more to their homes.

At that time there was a chief called Gōpaṇa ruling at Nārāyaṇapuram. Once God Ranganātha is said to have appeared before him and exhorted him to lead an invasion against the Muhammadans; and after defeating them, to establish him once more in his temple. This Gōpaṇa was a Brahman general in the army of the prince Kampana, son of the Vijayanagar emperor Bukka, during his invasion of the Pāṇḍya country. He went to Tirupati and taking the idols along with him marched with his army towards the south. He then went to the town of Chenji (Ginji), where for a time, he kept the idols in a rock-cut temple at Śingavaram. Staying at Gingi, Gōpaṇa obtained information as to the strength of the Muhammadans and on a favourable opportunity proceeded to Śrīrangam with his army. He then destroyed all the Muhammadans at Śamayavaram and consecrated the idols once more in their temple. When Vēdānta Dēśika heard of this he hastened to Śrīrangam. After worshipping the God he composed a verse in praise of Gōpaṇa and his conquest, and had it inscribed on the wall of the temple.

Adhyāya 120.

ततः कदाचिच्छ्रीरङ्गे पूर्ववत्सुमहोत्सवः ।
आसीत्तत्रगतास्सर्वेजनास्तेपूर्ववत्तदा ॥
नदीमहोत्सवेतत्रनद्यां श्रीरङ्गशायिनम् ।
वेदिकायांप्रतिष्ठाप्य लक्ष्मीक्ष्मासहितंहरिम् ॥
अभिषेकादिकार्याणियदाचक्रुर्द्विजर्षभाः ।
तत्रचारस्समागत्यचाराणांकश्चिदग्रणीः ॥
लोकाचार्यंसमालोकच व्याजहारवचस्तदा ।
चतुरङ्गबलोपेतोयवनोबलवत्तरः ।
अलक्ष्यतमहान्कश्चित्सकालयवनोयथा ॥
देवब्राह्मणसंम्बन्धान् यवनोब्रह्मघातुकः ।
देशान्विध्वंसयामाससर्वान्कंसोयथापुरा ॥
ततोययौचोळदेशंलोकाचार्यंमहाबलः ।
देवब्राह्मणसम्पन्नंयवनोयवनैस्सह ।।
एतद्वृत्तान्तमाकर्ण्यलोकाचार्यादयस्तदा ।
महान्तोऽपितदातत्रसुतरांसाध्वसंययुः ॥
तद्वाकचश्रवणेनैवसर्वेषांचमहात्मनाम् ।
तत्रत्यानांसुमहतीचिन्ताकाचिदजायत ॥
अयमुत्सवकालोऽस्यसमाप्तिश्चनदृश्यते ।
रङ्गंप्रत्यधुनाशीघ्रंवदन्तियवनागमम् ॥
ततस्सम्मन्त्रसहसालोकाचार्यादयस्तदा ।
रङ्गेशमेवतत्प्रष्टुंमहायत्नप्रचाक्रिरे ॥
ततःश्रीवैष्णवैस्सर्वैः श्रीरङ्गेश्वरसन्निधौ ।
गम्यतांस्थीयतांवेतिनिक्षिप्तंपत्रिकाद्वयं ॥
भाविकार्यानुगुण्येनरङ्गेशः स्थितिपत्रिकाम् ।
ददौदेवस्तदातेषां सर्वज्ञस्तत्रवासिनाम् ॥

प्रतिगृह्यप्रहृष्टास्तेपात्रिकांतामनिन्दिताम् ।
रङ्गेशमेवसंसेव्यसंतस्थुर्गतसाध्वसाः ॥
यानिमङ्गळकार्याणिकर्तव्याणितदाहरेः ।
सर्वाणितानिकुर्वन्तः तन्मयत्वेनतेस्थिताः ॥
लोकाचार्यस्यनिकटं कश्चिच्चारस्समागत ।
अवोचत्सहसाकर्णेयवनागमनंतदा ॥
इदानींयवनःप्राप्तः सबलःखण्डनंपुरम् ।
आगमिष्यत्ययं क्षुद्रोह्यत्रैवाद्याशुनिश्चयः ॥
प्रतिगृह्यवचस्तस्य सहसानिपुणस्तदा ।
वेदान्तदेशिकायैवतन्निवेद्यजगद्गुरुः ॥
तच्चासनात्सरङ्गेशं समादायसदारकम् ।
तंगोष्टीपुरपन्थानं अनुसृत्यययौतदा ॥
तद्वृत्तंशनकैस्सम्यक् अभूत्क्लिष्टतरततः ।
तेनोद्विग्नाःप्रजास्सर्वे तस्थुस्तत्रभयार्दिताः ॥
ततस्तत्राञ्जसाधीमान् महान्वेदान्तदेशिकः ।
अखण्डदीपंप्रज्वाल्यसन्निधौ रङ्गशायिनः ॥
तद्गर्भसदनद्वारंइष्टकाभिः पिधायच ।
पलायनपरस्तस्थौसर्वै श्श्रीवैष्णवैस्सह ॥

इति श्रीप्रपन्नामृते रामानुजचरित्रे श्रीरङ्गवासिनांयवनबाधाप्राप्तिर्नाम विंशत्युत्तरशततमोऽध्यायः ।

Adhyāya 121.

यवनःखण्डनपुरात्स तदा देवकण्टकः ।
निर्ययौसैनिकैस्सार्थं श्रीरङ्गंप्रतिसत्वरम् ॥
यवनोयवनैस्सार्थं अगाच्छ्रीरङ्गमञ्जसा ।
मधुरांकालयवनः कोटिभिस्तिसृभिर्यथा ॥
श्रीरङ्गवासिनस्सर्वे भयार्तास्तेन ते जनाः ।
यथैवभयमापन्नाः मधुरापुरवासिनः ॥

मधुरावासिनांतेषांद्वारकाप्रापणेमनः ।
यथाचकारभगवान् श्रीकृष्णोयोगमायया ॥
तथैवरङ्गराजोऽपि श्रीरङ्गपुरवासिनाम् ।
चकारतेनव्याजेन वैकुण्ठप्रापणेमनः ॥
तद्दासुदर्शनोनाम भट्टार्यः कूरवंशजः ।
वृद्धस्समेत्यमतिमान् वेदान्तार्यं महौजसम् ॥
पुत्रद्वयंररक्षेतितस्यहस्तेऽञ्जसाददौ ।
वेदान्तार्यस्ससर्वज्ञःतत्पुत्रद्वयमञ्जसा ॥
श्रुतप्रकाशिकांचैव तत्कृतांलोकरक्षणे ।
अङ्गीकृत्यररक्षाथ रङ्गेशकृपयातदा ॥
ततोनिर्भिद्यसहसा कवाटानि दृढान्यपि ।
विविशुस्तहसारङ्गम् यवना बलवत्तराः ॥
ब्रह्मवैर्निहतास्सर्वे वैष्णवावीतकल्मषाः ।
तत्रास्थितास्तैर्यवनैः निश्शेषमभवंस्तदा ॥
श्रीभाष्यंवेङ्कटेशश्च सुदर्शनसुतद्वयम् ।
समादायञ्जसाधीमान् यादवाद्रिंतदाययौ ॥
लोकाचार्यसहायेन रङ्गेशःपाण्ड्यमण्डलम् ।
प्रतस्थेसहसारण्य वर्त्मनादुर्गमेनच ॥
सर्वंच रङ्गिणस्तत्र चोरैरपहृतंधनम् ।
अग्रयायीसलोकार्यः तत्श्रुत्वापि नविव्यथे ॥
तत्रगत्वाञ्जसाधीमान् स्वकीयंधनमादरात् ।
तस्मैचोरजनाश्चैव प्रददौ स्वयमेव सः ॥
ज्योतिष्मतीपुरं प्रापलोकार्येणसरङ्गराट् ।
रङ्गक्षेत्रस्यवृत्तान्तं तं सर्वंराङ्गिणस्तदा ॥
श्रुत्वासाहिष्णुर्लोकार्यः प्रपेदेपरमंपदं ।
लोकाचार्यवियोगेन रङ्गेशोभृशदुःखितः ॥
ज्योतिष्मतीपुरंहित्वा प्रपेदेसुन्दराचलम् ।
कूपंस्वनाम्नातत्रैकं विधायच स रङ्गराट् ॥

विहायपाण्ड्यकटकं केरळंदेशमभ्यगात् ।
चतुर्दशविलोकयाशु विष्णुस्थानानिकेरळे ॥
सदारोरङ्गराट्शीघ्रम् प्रपेदेयादवाचलम् ।
यादवाचलनाथेन सम्पत्पुत्रेणसादरम् ॥
स्थित्वाथ तत्ररङ्गेशः काश्चित्कालंजगत्पतिः ।
आजगामाञ्जसारङ्गी भगवान्वेङ्कटाचलम् ॥
पूजितःश्रीनिवासेनरङ्गेशो वेङ्कटाचले ।
निवृत्ताध्वश्रमस्तस्थौ कश्चित्कालंयथासुखम् ॥
श्रीरङ्गं यवनाक्रान्तं बभूव सुमहद्यदा ।
तदा नृसिंहदेवाख्यः कश्चिद्द्राविडभूसुरः ॥
अक्रूर इव कंसस्य यवनस्य बभूव सः ।
सबलं यवनं नीत्वा समयाख्यपुरं प्रति ॥
रङ्गाधिकारं संप्राप्य सद्विजो यवनाधिपात् ।
ररक्ष रङ्गं सुमहत् हतशेषांश्च वैष्णवान् ॥
हतशेषास्तदा तत्रकेचिद्वैष्णवपुङ्गवाः ।
नृसिंहदेवकृपया श्रीरङ्गं विविशुर्जनाः ॥

* * * *

इति श्रीप्रपन्नामृते श्रीरङ्गेशस्य वेङ्कटाचलागमनं नाम एकविंशत्युत्तरशततमः अध्यायः ।

Adhyāya 122.

गोपणो नाम धर्मात्मा कश्चिद्भागवतोत्तमः ।
शशास राज्यं धर्मेण नारायणपुरे तदा ॥
तस्य प्रसन्नो भगवान् स्वप्ने श्रीरङ्गनायकः ।
व्याजहार शुभं वाक्यं गोपणाख्यं महौजसम् ॥
हत्वा म्लेच्छबलं सर्वं स्वबलेन मदाज्ञया ।
रङ्गस्थलं प्रापयाद्य रङ्गेशं मां महाबल ॥
ततः स्वप्नात्समुत्थाय गोपणाख्यस्सविस्मयः ।
वेङ्कटाचलमारुह्य श्रीरङ्गेशं प्रणम्य च ॥

तदर्चकमुखात्सर्वं ज्ञात्वा वृत्तान्तमादरात् ।
रङ्गेशं पुरतः स्थाप्य लक्ष्मीक्ष्मासहितं हरिम् ॥
प्रतस्थे रङ्गनगरं सुमुहूर्तेमहाबलः ।
स चञ्जीनगरं प्राप्य चतुरो गोपभूमिपः ॥
यवनस्याशु निपुणैःचारैः र्ज्ञात्वा बलाबले ।
रङ्गेशसहितस्तस्मात् निर्गत्य निशि निश्चलः ॥
सर्वं म्लेच्छबलं हत्वा निश्शेषं समये पुरे ।
रङ्गेशं रङ्गनगरे तं प्रतिष्ठाप्य पूर्ववत् ॥
तुतोष सुमहातेजाः गोपणाख्यो महाबलः ।
वेदान्तदेशिकः श्रीमान् श्रीरङ्गंप्राप्य सादरम् ॥
मङ्गळाशासनं कृत्वा रङ्गेशाय महौजसे ।
श्रीगोपणाख्यविषयं श्लोकमेकमकल्पयत् ॥
अद्यापि रङ्गप्राकारे स श्लोकः परिदृश्यते ।
आनीयानीलशृङ्गद्युतिरचितजगद्रञ्जनादञ्जनाद्रेः
चञ्च्यामाराध्य कंचित्समयमथ निहत्योद्धनुष्कांस्तुलुष्कान् ।
लक्ष्मीक्ष्माभ्यामुभाभ्यां सह निजनगरे स्थापयन्रङ्गनाथं
सम्यक्चर्यां सपर्यां पुनरकृत यशःप्रापणो गोपणार्यः ॥

6

ĀCHĀRYASŪKTIMUKTĀVALI.

[*By Nambūri Kēśavāchārya.*]

This work deals with the history of Śrīvaishṇavism in Telugu. It recounts the events of the sack of Srīrangam and the vicissitudes of the idol of Śrīranganātha till it was taken back to the temple of Śrīrangam. It gives in addition a tragic incident of how a dancing girl of the temple of Śrīrangam prevented the utter destruction of the temple by beguiling the Muhammadan chief who was enamoured of her, and treacherously murdering him by throwing him down from one of the gopurams of the temple. She is said to have committed suicide immediately by throwing herself from the same tower. The descendants of this courtesan are entitled to certain privileges in the temple of Śrīrangam even today in commemoration of this act of their ancestress.

ఉల్లాసము 3.

సీ. మధురాపురముఁ దొల్లి మందాత్ముఁడా కాల
యవనుఁ డగణ్యసైన్యములతోఁడ
నాక్రమించినగతి నతితామసతురుష్క
పతియొకండశ్వాది బలముగొలువ
వచ్చి రంగాధిపప్రాకారములుకొన్ని
యాక్రమించినఁ జూచి యచటివారు
రంగశాయికి మాటు రచియించి తద్బహి
ర్వేదియందొక విష్ణువిగ్రహంబు
నుంచి కస్తూరిరంగనియుక్తగాత్రు
లందు గైకొని కానల కరుగుచున్నఁ
గాంచి శ్రీలోకగురుఁడును గదలెననుచు
వాదిభీకరగురుఁడనె మోదమలర.

సీ. చక్రవర్తిసుతుండు జనకాత్మజను గూడి
దండకావనములం దుండఁ గోరి
చనుచున్నఁ జూచి యా జాయాపతులకప్పు
డఖిలకైంకర్యము లాచరింప
సౌమిత్రి చనినట్లు జగదార్యుఁ డారంగ
నాథుని వెంటఁ గానలకుఁ జనియె
నంతరంగేశ్వరుం డభ్రమండలమునఁ
దరుగఁడు చనుమాడ్కి నమ్మహాగ్ర.

గీ. కాననముఁ జొచ్చి జరుగుచుఁ గన్న వ్రోల
భవ్యవృత్తినిఁ గైతవభక్తిసల్పు
దాసులకుఁ జేసె సర్వస్వదానమనుచు
వాదిభీకరగురుఁడనె మోదమలర.

సీ. స్వామికిముందఱజనుచున్న లోకార్యుఁ
డావార్తవిని వేగ నరుగుదెంచి
తానును సర్వస్వదానమా దాసచే
తనులకొనర్చి శ్రీధరుని వెనుక

పల్లనఁ జనుచుండఁ గల్లవాండ్రొకకొంద
ఱతనికికపటోపచారములిడ
నవిగొనమెల్లక యార్యుఁడువారిభా
వమెఱింగి వేవేగవచ్చి వచ్చి
గీ. జ్యోతిషకుఁడియనుచు విఖ్యాతమైన
గ్రామమునను న్న శ్రీరంగరాజహరిని
గాంచితత్సన్నిధినివసియించెననుచు
వాదిభీకరగురుఁడనె మోదమలర.

వ. ఇట్లు లోకగురుండు శ్రీరంగరాజస్వామిసన్నిధిం గొన్నిదినము లుచితకైంకర్యంబులు సల్పుచుండి తిరుమేనియందుం దిరునోవుధరియింపఁ జూచి నిజాశ్రితులు . . . .
యర్చిరాదిమార్గంబున జని పరమపదవ్యోమధామం బలంకరించె నంత.

సీ. జ్యోతిషకుఁడియందు జొత్తిల్లుచును గొన్ని
దివసములుండియద్దేవదేవు
డచటినుండి మనోహరారణ్యములయందు
విహరింపఁదనమది వేడ్కఁబొడమ
నర్చకపరిచారకాదిధన్యులుగొల్వ
నిరుగెలంకులసిరి ధరయుమెఱయ
స్వస్తివాచనశుభ వాద్యనర్తనగీత
ఘనరవంబులు జగత్కలుషమడఁప
గీ. బ్రహ్మరుద్రాదులును మింటఁబ్రస్తుతింప
బూలవానలుగురియంగ మునులుపొగడ
గదలిచనిచని వనగిరిగనియెననుచు
వాదిభీకరగురుఁడనె మోదమలర

* * *

గీ. యట్టియళహరితిరుమలకరిగిరంగ
రాజు మంగళదేవతామణితోడ
వనవిహారములొనరించె వాంఛననుచు
వాదిభీకరగురుఁడనె మోదమలర.
సీ. బోలుపారుమళయాళభూములకేతెంచి
దేవియుగంబుతోఁ దేఱరిల్ల

తెలిసిదక్షిణదివ్య దేశాధిపతులెల్ల
వచ్చి శ్రీరంగాధిపతినిఁ జూచి
యతనిచే బహుమతి గాంచియఱుగుచుండ . . .

సీ. అంతరంగేశుఁడు యాదవాద్రికిఁ జని
యందుఁ గొన్నిదినంబు లధివసించి
యచటినుండే తెంచి యంజనాచలమున
వేంకటేశునియింట విభవమలర
ద్వాదశాబ్దములు సన్మానింపనంతటఁ
జెంజినుండి వృషాద్రిఁ జెందిగోప
నాయఁడు వేఁకట నాథుని సేవించి
యందు రంగేశుని యంఘ్రికమల

గీ. యుగముఁ గనుగొని మ్రొక్కిఁ డియుక్తవేళ
రంగధాముని జెంజి పురంబుకడకు
దోడుకొనివచ్చె మిగులసంతుష్టి ననుచు
వాదిభీకరగురుఁడనె మోదమలర

సీ. శింజీపురము చెంత సింగరాయపురాఖ్య
మగ్రహారముఁ జేసి యందుఁ బసిడి
కోవెలఁ గట్టించి గోపనాయఁడు రంగ
పతినిఁ బ్రతిష్ఠించె భక్తినచట
నట శ్రీరంగమునందు శింగప్పిరా
న నెసు విప్రుఁడు గణకాన్వయుండు
యావనవిద్యయందతినిపుణుఁడు గాన
నాతురువఱప్రభునాశ్రయించి.

గీ. మంత్రియైవానితోఁ దొడ్డ మైత్రిఁ జేసి
రంగమందిర గోపురారామనగర
సాలములతోంటిగతిఁ బాగుసలిపెననుచు
వాదిభీకరగురుఁడనె మోదమలర

వ. అయ్యవసరంబున.

సీ. సర్వాంగసౌందర్య చాతుర్యలావణ్య
యావనసౌకుమార్యాభిరామ

న్యాయవర్తి నిరంగనాథమాణిక్యాభి
ధానయునగు దేవదాసియొకతె
నద్దివ్యదేశస్థులచటఁ గన్గొనియాతు
రుష్కబలాబ్ధిలో రంగపదము
చండవాతక్షుబ్ధ జలధిమధ్యమునఁ దుఁ
గడుఁగాసివడుచున్న కలముకరణి

గీ. నుండెగావున నీస్థలముద్ధరింపు
మమ్మ యెట్లయిన నొకయుపాయంబుఁ జేసి
వసుధయశమగు నీకని పలికిరనుచు
వాదిభీకరగురుఁడనె మోదమలర

* * * *

సీ. ముప్పిరిగొన్నట్టి మోహముచేవాఁడు
తన్మృదూక్తులనమ్మి దానితోడ
వెల్లగోపురమెక్కి వింతలఁజూచుచు
ద్వారముకడను కందర్పదర్ప
పారవశ్యముఁ జెంద వంచించియడివాని
దూర్పువీధినిఁ బడఁద్రోబ్బి తాను
పడమటితట్టునఁ బడి ప్రాణములమాని
మణిమయదివ్యవిమానమెక్కి

గీ. యర్చిరాదికమార్గమునాశ్రయించి
సురలుకొనియాడఁ జనిచని పరమపదము
జెందియందులభించె నానందమనుచు
వాదిభీకరగురుఁడనె మోదమలర

సీ. అంతసింగప్పిరాన నెదురిపుడు చెంజి
గోపనాయనితోడఁ గూడి ఘోర
చతురంగబలముల సమకూర్చుకొని వచ్చి
యాతురుష్కుల సైన్యమంతమాపి
సింగరాట్పురినుండి శ్రీభూసమేతుని
రంగనాథునిఁ దెచ్చి రంగమునను
శకము శతోత్తర సాహస్రసంఖ్యచే
వెలయు పరీధావి వృషభమాస

గీ. మునుఁబదేడవతిథియందు మాఘభూత
రంగపతికడఁ గస్తూరిరంగవిభుని
నిలిపి సంప్రోక్షణాదుల సలిపెననుచు
వాదిభీకరగురుడనె మోదమలర.

వ. ఇట్లు రంగనాథుండు నిజస్థానంబునం గ్రమ్మరం బ్రతిష్ఠితుండైన నాటనుండి నేటికైనను దనవే.సుమాని యద్దివ్యదేశంబుద్ధరించిన శ్రీరంగనాథమాణిక్యాభిధానదేవదాసీరత్నంబునం దనుగ్రహంబుచే సహస్రంబు నిజారాధనోత్సవాదికాలంబులందు శ్రీ రంగనాథమాణిక్యతాళుకుఱరుళిప్పాడనితన్నామంబుచ్చరించి తదీయాన్వయులకుం గుంభనీరాజనాదికైంకర్యంబులసేయ నియోగించి మఱియును దద్వంశోత్పన్నులైన వారెవ్వరైన మృతిఁజెందిరేని వారి చరమసంస్కారంబులకు శ్రీమహానసాగ్నియు నిజధాన్యకోశాగారంబునందు వస్త్రప్రేక్షణీయతండులంబులియ్య నియమించి లోకసంరక్షణతత్పరుండైయుండె నంత.

7

THE ANNALS OF HANDĒ ANANTAPURAM.

Chapter I.

This extract is taken from the beginning of the work called 'The Wars of the Rajahs' or 'the Annals of Haṇḍē Anantāpuram' which appears to have formed one of the Mackenzie collection of manuscripts. It gives a continuous account of the history of the villages Bukkasamudram and Anantasāgaram, also called Haṇḍē Anantāpuram.

While Bukka was ruling from the city of Vidyānagar, his pradhāni or minister Chikkappa Oḍeyar constructed an enbankment across the river Pānḍu which rises in the Kambugirisvāmi hills and formed a big tank filled with its waters in the year Krōdhi corresponding to Ś. 1286. This was near Dēvarakonḍa in the province of Nandēla (Nandyal) south of Vidyānagar. On each side of the embankment he constructed a village; that on the eastern side was called Bukkarāyasamudram after the king, while the one on the western side was called Anantasāgaram after his queen.

Chikka Oḍeyar also constructed a dam across the river Chitrāvati rising in the hill sacred to the God Venkaṭēsvara of Varagiri

(Varagonḍa) in the Elamanchi district, sixteen miles south of Bukkarāyasamudram and constructed a big tank. On the eastern side of the tank he constructed the village Bukkapaṭnam and on the west Anantasāgaram.

Chikkappa Oḍeyar, the minister, who constructed the tanks and the villages departed his life at Anantasāgaram.

Another Kaifiyat (written statement) of the same place in the collection says that Chikka Oḍeyar also constructed a temple on a hill near Anantasāgaram and gives the date of its construction as Thursday, the fifth of the dark fortnight of the month of Kārtika in the cyclic year Krodhi, corresponding to Ś. 1286.

పంపాతీరమందు, విద్యానగరమును బుక్కరాయలవారు యేలుచుండగా, ఆతని ప్రధానియైన చిక్కప్ప వొడయరు శాలివాహనశకం 1289 అగు నేటి క్రోధి సంవత్సరమందు ఆ విద్యానగరమునకు దక్షిణ ప్రాంతమందు, నందేల తాలూకాలో దేవరకొండ దగ్గిర కంబుగిరిస్వామి కొండలో పుట్టి వస్తూవుండిన పాండునదిని చూచి, దాన్ని దేవర కొండకు అడ్డముకట్టి, వొక తటాక నిర్మాణము చేసి, ఆ తటాకపు రెండు మరవల రెండు గ్రామములు కట్టించి, తూర్పు మరవను వున్న గ్రామమునకు బుక్కరాయసముద్రమని తన దొరవారి పేరున్ను, పడమటి మరవను వున్న గ్రామమునకు అనంతసాగరమని తమ దొరసాని పేరున్ను పెట్టెను. ఆ బుక్కరాయ సముద్రమునకు దక్షిణం 16 కోసులమీద యేలమంచినాడు తాలూకాలో నరగిరి వెంకటేశ్వరుని కొండలో పుట్టి ప్రవహిస్తూవున్న చిత్రావతి నదిని చూచి, అచ్చుటనున్నా మునుపటివలెనే వొక తటాకమును నిర్మాణము చేయించి దానికి వుభయ పార్శ్వముల రెండు గ్రామములు కట్టించి తూర్పు మరవను వున్న గ్రామమునకు బుక్కపట్నమనిన్ని పడమటి మరవను వున్న గ్రామమునకు అనంత సాగరమనిన్ని పేర్లు బెట్టి ఆ స్థలమందే అదృశ్యమై పోయెను.

8

MĀDHAVĪYA DHĀTUVṚTTI.

[*By Śāyanāchārya.*]

This book dealing with the roots of verbs in Sanskrit grammar is written by the famous Śāyanāchārya, the author of the commentary on the Vedas and is called after his brother Mādhavāchārya

(Vidyāraṇya), Mādhavīya Dhātuvṛtti. The book is dedicated to the prince Sangama, the son of Kampa, the second of the five brothers who founded the empire of Vijayanagar. He was viceroy of Udayagiri Mahārājya in which high office his son Sangama succeeded him. The passage is in praise both of the patron, prince Sangama, and of Śāyana.

अस्ति श्रीसङ्गमक्ष्मापः पृथ्वीतलपुरन्दरः ।
यत्कीर्तिमौक्तिकादर्शे त्रिलोक्या प्रतिबिम्ब्यते ॥
यशःक्षीराहुतीकृत्य यत्प्रतापहुताशने ।
परे यान्ति पदं दिव्यं राजानो रणदीक्षिताः ॥
तूर्णं कर्णान्तिकं प्राप्ते यत्प्रतापधनञ्जये ।
पुरो निधाय गाङ्गेयमात्मा संरक्ष्यते परैः ॥
कुर्वन्शत्रुयशांसि धूमपटलीं कूलंकषाज्यारवदः
काष्ठासङ्गविवर्जितः प्रकटयन्भूतिं नवां भूयसीं ।
आतन्वन्नितरप्रतापदहनं स्फूर्जत्स्फुलिङ्गाकृतिं
प्रायो यच्छति यत्प्रतापदहनः कस्मै न विस्मेरताम ॥
तस्य मन्त्रिशिरोरत्न मस्ति मायणसायणः ।
यः ख्यातिं रत्नगर्भेति यथार्थयति पार्थिवीम् ॥
नित्योन्मीलितदानवारिरधिकं निर्धूतपङ्कोदयो
दूरापास्तहराशिलङ्घनविधिः भङ्गप्रसङ्गोज्झितः ।
क्ष्माभृत्क्षोभकृतिक्षमः क्षणिकयन्दोषाकरोद्घोषगान्
आनन्दायचकास्ति यस्त्रिजगतामाश्चर्यरत्नाकरः ॥
यत्कीर्तौ जाह्नवीस्फूर्तौ कीर्त्या विद्विषनामपि ।
कलिन्दनन्दिनी कान्ति स्पर्धयेव प्रपद्यते ॥
येन निर्मीयते नित्यं धनैरायोधनैरपि ।
श्रेयसे यशसे दानं विदुषां विद्विषामपि ॥
न ध्यानं न व्रतं नार्चा न समाधिर्नवा जपः ।
मन्त्रसिद्धा बलं यस्य मतिरेव महीयसी ॥
तेन मायणपुत्रेण सायणेन मनीषिणा ।
आख्यया माधवीयेयं धातुवृत्तिर्विरच्यते ॥

Colophon.

इति श्रीपूर्वदक्षिणपश्चिमसमुद्राधीश्वरकम्पराजसुतसङ्गमराज महामन्त्रिणा मायणपुत्रेण सायणाचार्येण विरचितायां माधवीयायां धातुवृत्तौ . . . . ॥

9

VĒDA BHĀSHYA.

[*By Sāyaṇāchārya.*]

This is the introduction to the commentary of the Vedas by the famous Mādhavāchārya (Vidyāraṇya). It is said to have been written at the direction of Bukka whose Minister the author was.

यस्य निश्वसितं वेदाः यो वेदेभ्योऽखिलं जगत् ।
निर्ममे तमहं वन्दे विद्यातीर्थमहेश्वरम् ॥
यत्कटाक्षेण तद्रूपं दधद्बुक्कमहीपतिः ।
आदिशन्माधवाचार्यं वेदार्थस्य प्रकाशने ॥
ये पूर्वोत्तरमीमांसे तेव्याख्यायातिसङ्ग्रहात ।
कृपालुर्माधवाचार्यो वेदार्थं वक्तुमुद्यतः ॥

Colophon.

इति सायणाचार्यविरचिते माधवीये वेदार्थप्रकाशे . . . ॥

10

UDĀHARAṆAMĀLĀ OF BHŌGANĀTHA AS QUOTED IN SĀYAṆA'S ALANKĀRA SUDHĀNIDHI.*

From the following stanza we learn that Sāyana had three sons, named Kampaṇa, Māyaṇa and Śingaṇa, and that the first son was a musician, the second a poet and the third a student of the Veda.

* The following extracts from this work are taken from an article contributed to the *Indian Antiquary* for January and February 1917, by Rao Bahadur R. Narasimha Acharya of Mysore.

तत्संव्यज्ञय कम्पण व्यसानिनस्सङ्गीतशास्त्रे तव
प्रौढिं मायण गद्यपद्यरचनापाण्डित्यमुन्मुद्रय ।
शिक्षां दर्शय शिंगण क्रमजटाचर्चासु वेदेष्विति
स्वान्पुत्रानुपलालयन् गृहगतः सम्मोदते सायणः ॥

From the following extract we infer that Kampaṇa died either before Sangama II was born, or when he was a mere child, and that Sāyaṇa administered the kingdom as regent during the minority of Sangama II.

सङ्गमेन्द्र नरेन्द्र त्वय्यकृतास्यपरिग्रहे ।
विधायोर्वीधुरमगात् स्वाराज्यं कम्पणः कथम् ॥
सत्यं महीं भवति शासति सायणार्ये
सम्प्राप्तभोगसुखिनः सकलाश्च लोकाः ॥
शौर्योच्छ्रुंखलसङ्गमेश्वर महासाम्राज्यसम्पादन-
प्रोद्यत्सायणमन्त्रिवर्यरभसक्षुण्णक्षमासंपदाम् ।
गूढं काननगह्वरेषु चरतामस्माकमत्युन्नतै-
रेभिः किं घनगर्जितैर्मदनतैः किंवासहैतैर्हयैः ॥
सायणसचिवायत्तं सङ्गमराजस्य पश्य राज्यमिदम् ॥

The following shows that Sāyaṇa himself taught Sangama II from his childhood and gave him a liberal education befitting his position.

बाल्येऽपि प्रतिबोधयस्यवाहितं श्रीसङ्गमक्ष्मापतिं
बोधैकास्पदसायणार्यभगवद्व्यासावतार . . ॥
आन्वीक्षक्यामधिकविहृतौ हर्षशोकव्युदासे
मार्गोल्लेखं विदधति नृणां माध(न?)वे धर्मशास्त्रे ।
सम्यक्शिक्षां सचिवगमितः शैशवे सायणार्य
प्रौढिं गाढां प्रकटयति ते सङ्गमेन्द्रः प्रयोगे ॥

The next passage refers to the martial valour and conquests of Sāyaṇāchārya. The last verse refers to a victory gained by Sāyaṇa over a king named Champa. This king is evidently the same as the chief Śambuvarāya against whom Kumāra Kampaṇa, the son of Bukka I, Gopanārya and Saḷuva Mangu are said to have fought. His capital was at Virinchipuram and he ruled the country round Kanchi. Information about him is found in the Telugu Jaimini Bhāratam and the Sanskrit poems Madhurāvijayam of Gangādēvi, Sāḷuvābhyudayam of Rājanātha Ḍinḍima and Rāmābhyudayam of Sāḷuva Narasimha. There is a reference in Bhoganātha's Udāharaṇamāla to an attack on a place called Garuḍanagara by Sangama II and Sāyaṇa, and the defeat of the chief of that place.

अमुं शमितशात्रवस्थिरभुजावलेपोदयं
समीक्ष्य युधि सायणं समधिको भवेद्विस्मयः ।
नखाग्रहतवैरिणो नरहरेर्हरस्याथवा
नवाम्बुजदळोल्लसन्नयनमात्रदग्धद्विषः ॥
जगद्वीरस्य जागर्ति कृपाणः सायणप्रभोः ।
किमित्येते वृथाटोपा गर्जन्ति परिपन्थिनः ॥
आकर्ण्य यात्रापटहप्रणादान् अपोढनिद्रैस्तव सायणार्य ।
आरण्यसिंहैररिभूपतीनां आहन्यते चित्रगतोऽपि हस्ती ॥
समरे सपत्नसैन्यं सायण तव बिम्बिनं वहन्खड्गः ।
क्रीडति कैटभरिपुरिव बिभ्रत् क्रोडे जगत्त्रयं जलधौ ॥
दिष्ट्या दैष्टिकभावसम्भृतमहासम्पद्विशेषोदयं
जित्वा चम्पनरेन्द्रमूर्जितयशाः प्रत्यागतः सायणः ।

11

DĒVYAPARĀDHASTOTRA OF VIDYĀRAṆYA.

The following verse from the Dēvyaparādhastotra of Vidyāraṇya shows that he should have lived more than eighty-five years.

परित्यक्ता देवा विविधपरिसेवाकुलतया
मया पंचाशीतेरधिकमपनीते तु वयसि ।
इदानीं चेन्मातस्तव यदि कृपा नापि भविता
निरालम्बो लम्बोदरजननिके यामि शरणम् ॥

12

COLOPHON OF TARKABHĀSHA VYĀKHYĀ OF CHENNUBAṬṬA.

We learn from this that the author was patronized by Harihara II.

इति श्रीहरिहररायपालितेन सहजसर्वज्ञविष्णुदेवाराध्यतनूजेन सर्वज्ञानुजेन चेन्नुभट्टेन विरचितायां तर्कभाषाव्याख्यायां ॥

13

TĀTPARYA DĪPIKA, COMMENTARY ON SŪTASAMHITA.

[*By Mādhavāchārya.*]

This passage is the introduction to the commentary on Sūtasamhita by Mādhavāchārya,* disciple of Kriyāśakti Dēśika, who was a general under the first Vijayanagar emperors, and was ruling Goa and the territory near it on the west coast. He was a great scholar and is called the 'establisher of the path of the Upanishads'. He should not be confounded with his namesake, the author of the commentaries on the Vedas who lived during the same period.

प्रणमामि परं ब्रह्म यतोऽव्यावृत्त वृत्तयः ।
अविचारसहं वस्तु विषयीकुर्वते धियः ॥
श्रीमत्काशीविलासाख्यक्रियाशक्तीशसे विना ।
श्रीमत्र्यम्बकपादाब्जसेवानिष्णातचेतसा ॥
वेदशास्त्रप्रतिष्ठात्रा श्रीमन्माधव मन्त्रिणा ।
तात्पर्यदीपिका सूतसंहिताया विधीयते ॥
क्रियते तत्तत्प्रकरणतात्पर्यप्रथनपूर्वकं विशदम् ।
विषमपदवाक्यविवरणम् धियामनुग्रहाय भक्त्या च ॥

* This Mādhava belonged to the Gōtra of Angiras while the commentator of the Vedas belonged to the Bhāradvaja Gōtra. Again Chaunḍapa, the father of this scholar, has been confounded with his namesake Chaunḍapāchārya, the author of Prayōgaratnamālā (vide No. 16). Mādhavāchārya and his father Chaunḍapa belonged to the Āngirasa Gōtra, while the author of Prayōgaratnamālā belonged to the Vasishta Gōtra. Again the second Chaunḍapāchārya lived in the time of the king Bhūpati Uḍayar, who was the great-grandson of Bukka I in whose reign Mādhava, the son of the other Chaunḍapa, died. This makes it absolutely impossible for the two Chaunḍappas to be the same.

Colophon.

इति श्रीमत्काशीविलासाख्यक्रियाशक्तिपरमभक्तत्र्यम्बकपादाम्भोजसे-वापरायणेन उपनिषण्मार्गप्रवर्तकेन श्रीमाधवाचार्येण विरचितायां सूतसंहितातात्पर्यदीपिकायां . . . . . ॥

14

NĀNĀRTHA RATNAMĀLĀ.

[*By Irugapa Danḍanātha.*]

This passage is the introduction to the Sanskrit book of synonyms Nānārtha Ratnamālā. It was composed by the Jain general Irugapa Danḍanātha, born in the family of Chaicha Danḍēśa. Harihara II 'was delighted to let the burden of Emire rest on Irugapa'.

यत्पदाम्बुरुहच्छया देव चूडामणीयते ।
यस्य ज्ञानादयोऽनन्ताः स देवः श्रेयसेऽस्तु नः ॥
अस्ति श्रीमन्निरुगपदण्डनाथः प्रचण्डधीः ।
सद्वृत्तैश्चैचदण्डेशवंशमुक्तामणिर्गुणैः ॥
द्वितीयमन्तःकरणं राज्ञो हरिहरस्य यः ।
राजकार्यं प्रजारक्षां द्वयं धत्ते कुलव्रतम् ॥
भारं हरिहराधीशो भुवः कूर्मादिदुर्वहम् ।
बुद्धौ कुशाग्रसूक्ष्मायां यस्य विन्यस्य मोदते ॥
तिस्रो दधानश्चतुरः पञ्चप . . यथोचितम् ।
प्रयुञ्जानो नयन्वृद्धिं सप्ताष्टौ यो जिगीषति ॥
विविधग्रन्थसन्दर्भविमर्दविमलीकृतम् ।
यस्य चेतस्सरस्वत्या विलासमुकुरायते ॥
सोयं ग्रथ्नाति नानार्थरत्नमालां गुणोज्ज्वलां ।
श्रीमानिरुगपदण्डेशो नात्यल्पं नातिविस्तरम् ॥

Colophon.

इति जगदुपकारिण्या मिरुगपदण्डाधिनाथरचितायाम् ।
एकाक्षरकाण्डोऽयं पूर्णो नानार्थरत्नमालायाम् ॥

15

NĀRĀYAṆĪVILĀSAM.

[*By Virūpāksha.*]

This is a Sanskrit drama composed by Prince Virūpāksha, otherwise known as Udayagiri Virūpanna Uḍayār I. grandson of Bukka I, and son of Harihara II.

In this drama the author calls himself the governor of the Karṇāṭa, Tunḍīra, Chola and Pāndya Manḍalas, and claims to have had a pillar of victory in the island of Simhaḷa (Ceylon). He is also said to have performed the various *mahādānas* (great gifts), and to have been a master of all arts. The first extract is from the beginning of the drama, and, the next the colophon.

सूत्रधारः—

पौत्रो बुक्कनरेन्द्रस्य दौहित्रो रामभूपतेः ।
विद्यते हि विरूपाक्षो राजा हरिहरात्मजः ॥

नटी—प्रसिद्धः खलु सः भरतविद्यायाम् ।

सू—तस्य राज्ञः कर्णाटतुण्डीरचोळपाण्ड्यमण्डलाधिपतेः सिंहलद्वीपजयस्तम्भस्य महादानदीक्षितस्य सकलकलाविलासिनीस्वयंवरपतेः कृतिषु नारायणीविलासं नाम नाटकं प्रयोक्ष्ये ।

नटी—सुकवीविरूपनरेन्द्रः चरितं नारायणस्य रमणीयम् ।
रसिकबहुळा परिषन्निपुणा अस्माकमपि शोभनं सर्वम् ॥

भरतवाक्यम् ।

एष वीरो विरूपाक्षः शेषसारेण बाहुना ।
एकच्छत्रीकरोत्वेनां भूतधात्रीं नयोन्नतः ॥

16

PRAYŌGARATNAMĀLA (ĀPASTAMBA ADHVARA-TANTRA VYĀKHYĀ.)

[*By Chaunḍapāchārya.*]

This is a commentary on the sacrificial ritual according to the Sūtras of Āpastamba. The Sage Vidyāraṇya was asked by

Chaunḍapāchārya and other scholars to explain the sacrificial ritual as followed in the school of Āpastamba. Vidyāraṇya did so. There was a king, who levied tribute on all the world, called Harihara who performed all the sixteen dānas (gifts) as laid down in the Purāṇas. He had a son called Yuva Bukka, Bukka the younger, whose wife Tippāmba excelled other women in merit. To them was born a king whose name was Bhūpati. He was once asked by scholars to get the sacrificial ritual commented. He consulted many scholars, and entrusted the work to Chaunḍapārya. Chaunḍapāchārya was born in the gōtra of Vaśishṭa and was the son of the Chinnayārya and Kāmāmba, and had two brothers Āditya Dēva and Manchapārya.

नमो विरिञ्चिविष्ण्वीशभेदेन परमात्मनः ।
सर्गस्थितिविनाशानां व्यक्तयेऽव्यक्तमूर्तये ॥

* * * *

पदवाक्यप्रमाणानां पारदृश्वा महामतिः ।
साङ्ख्ययोगरहस्यज्ञो ब्रह्मविद्यापरायणः ॥
वेदार्थविशदीकर्ता वेदवेदाङ्गपारवित् ।
विद्यारण्ययतिर्ज्ञात्वा श्रौतस्मार्तक्रियापरैः ॥
श्रीचौण्डपार्यप्रमुखैः विद्वद्भिर्ब्राह्मणोत्तमैः ।
व्याचक्ष्वाध्वरतन्त्रं त्वं समन्त्रार्थमिति स्फुटम् ॥
प्रार्थितो बहुशः श्रौतं विशदीकर्तुमुद्यतः ।
कल्पसूत्रेष्वनेकेषु सर्वत्र तु समन्वयात् ॥
आपस्तम्बाचार्यसूत्रं प्रधानं प्रचुरं त्विति ।
तत्सूत्रमेव व्याचष्टे हौत्रौद्गात्रप्रसङ्गतः ॥
करपूरितसर्वाशः श्रीमान्हरिहरेश्वरः ।
शश्वदाकामितानाब्धि भुवं नानानृपाश्रयाम् ॥
व्यधादपि पुराणानि महादानानि षोडश ।
तस्मादभूद्भूरिधामा युवबुक्कमहीपतिः ॥

* * * *

तिप्पाम्बा नाम तस्याभूद्राज्ञी गुणगरीयसी ।

* * * *

तस्मादस्यां समुद्भूद्भूपतिः श्रीभुवो पतिः ।
कर्मब्रह्माध्वनीनेन कविर्येन कृतीकृतः ॥
स कदाचिद्भूपतीन्द्रः पालयन्धर्मतः प्रजाः ।
संप्रार्थितो द्विजैः श्रौतं विशदीकर्तुमुद्यतः ॥
विचार्य विदुषां मध्ये चौण्डपार्यमदीदिशत् ।
व्याचक्ष्वाध्वरतन्त्रं त्वं समन्त्रार्थमिति स्फुटम् ॥
किं स्तुमश्चौण्डपाचार्यं जातं तत्र महाकुले ।
वसिष्ठारुन्धतीमुख्या यत्कुले गृहमेधिनः ॥
विशिष्टवासिष्ठकुले चिन्नयार्यः सतां मतः ।
कामाम्बा गृहिणी तस्य भारद्वाजकुलेऽजनि ॥
आर्यादिवातो मिथुनात् उद्भवन्निहितास्सुताः ।
चौण्डपार्यादित्यदेवमश्वपार्याभिधास्त्रयः ॥

* * * *

Colophon.

इति श्रीमद्राजाधिराजपरमेश्वरश्रीवीरहरिहरमहाराजसाम्राज्यधुरन्धरप्रतापवीरयुवबुक्कभूपालक्षीरार्णवपूर्णचन्द्रस्य राजव्यासवाल्मीकेः कर्मब्रह्माध्वनीनस्य श्रीवीरभूपतिभूमिपालस्य मन्त्रिणा चिन्नार्यनन्दनेन आदित्यदेवमश्वपार्याग्रजन्मना चौण्डपाचार्येण विरचितायां आपस्तम्बीयाध्वरतन्त्रस्वतन्त्रव्याख्यायां प्रयोगरत्नमालायां परिभाषापरिच्छेदः—

कर्मब्रह्माध्वनीनस्य मन्त्री भूपतिभूपतेः ।
व्याचष्टे चौण्डपाचार्यः प्रकृते(दर्शपूर्णिमे) ॥

17

KRĪḌĀBHIRĀMAM OF VINUKONḌA VALLABHARĀYA.

This is a translation into Telugu of the Sanskrit Prēmābhirāmam, a drama belonging to the class called Vīdhi in Sanskrit dramaturgy of the poet Rāvipāṭi Tripurāntaka of the court of Pratāpa Rudra II of Warrangal. It has been translated into Telugu by Vinukonḍa Vallabharāya, a Governor of the fort of Vinukonḍa in the Krishna district during the reign of the Vijayanagar

Emperor Dēva Rāya II or Prauḍha Dēva Rāya. In verse 7 of the work the author Vallabharāya says that his great-grandfather Chandra was very famous, and served as a minister of the Karnāṭa Emperor Bukka I, who is here called Pedda Bukka or Bukka the elder.

Verse 16 says that the author Vallabha's uncle Linga was celebrated for his courage, and was a general under the Emperor Harihara whose prosperity he increased by his valour.

In verse 19 it is said that Linga's brother Tippa or Tripurāri served under Harihara as the controller of the Ratna-Bhanḍāra or the storehouse of precious gems. Verse 23 says that Tripurāntaka's son Vallabharāya was Governor of Vinukonḍa, that he enjoyed the revenues of the village Mopūru in Mulki Nāḍu with three other villages, was a learned man and was the *Head Comptroller of the Storehouse of precious stones* in the court of Dēva Rāya.

7. సీ. కర్ణాటక్షితినాథుఁడైన పెదబుక్కక్ష్మాప దేవేంద్రున
భవ్యామాత్యుని నఖేచరునిఁ జంద్రాధీశు బంధుప్రియుఁ
వర్ణించుంగవికోటిశంకర జటావాటీతటాంతర్నదీ
స్వర్ణద్యంబు తరంగరింఖణలసత్సాహిత్యసౌహిత్యయై

16. మ. కనకాద్రిప్రతిమానధైర్యనిధి లింగక్ష్మాపమంత్రీంద్రుఁడో
ననతారాతి నృపాలమంత్రి జనతాహంకారతారాహిమా
రుచునితో రూపగతీంద్రుతో హరిహరక్షోణీంద్రసామ్రాజ్యవ
ర్ధనుతోసాటి సమానమీడుగలరా రాజన్య సైన్యాధిపుల్.
గీ. . . . .
భద్రుతోడను రామ భద్రుతోడ.

19. గీ. సాటియనఁదగు ధారుణీపాలసభల
వీరహరిహరరాయపృథ్వీ కళత్ర
రత్నభాండారసాధికార ప్రగల్భు
మల్లికార్జున త్రిపురారి మంత్రివరుని.

23. సీ. మూడుగ్రామ గ్రాసములతోడఁ గూడఁగ
మోపూరు పాలించె ముల్కినాట
నాశ్వలాయన శాఖయందు ఋగ్వేదంబు
కరతలామలకంబుగాఁ బఠించె

బ్రత్యక్ష మొనరించి భైరవస్వామిచే
సిద్ధసాగస్వత శ్రీవరించె
గామకాయనస విశ్వామిత్రగోత్రంబు
వంశగోత్రంబుగా వార్తకెక్కె

గీ. నెవ్వఁడా త్రిపురాంతకాధీశ్వరునకు
రాయనవరత్నభాండాగ రక్షకునకు
బ్రియతనూజుండు చంద్రమాంబిక సుతుండు
మనుజమాత్రుండె వల్లభామాత్యవరుఁడు.

18

HARAVILĀSAM OF ŚRĪNĀTHA.

This book was written by the famous Telugu poet Śrīnātha and dedicated to a very wealthy merchant of Simhavikrama Paṭṭaṇa (Nellore), Avachi Tippaya Śeṭṭi by name. The merchant used to import valuable articles from very distant countries, both by sea and land, for supplying them to the sovereigns of his country. He is said to have imported camphor plants from the Punjab, gold from Jalanogi (?), elephants from Ceylon, good horses from Hurumanji (Ormuz), musk from Goa, pearls from Āpaga (?), musk from Chotangi (Chautang ?) and fine silks from China. The merchant and his brothers were very enterprising and used to supply articles to the Courts of Harihara Rāya, Emperor of Vijayanagar, Feroz Shah, the Bahmani Sultan and the Gajapati ruler of Orissa. They had the monopoly of supplying all the articles necessary for the grand Spring Festival (Vasantotsava) celebrated by the Reḍḍi king, Kumāragiri of Koṇḍavīḍu.

త్రిపురాంతకదేవదివ్య శ్రీపాదపద్మారాధకుండును పరమసాధకుఁడు నుఁగమలభవోరు సంభవవిమలవంశావతారుండును ధర్మద్రావిడబిరుద ధారుండును సుజన విధేయుండునుఁ గర్పూర వసంతరాయుండును గీర్తిల తావల్లభుండును ప్రతిదిన సమారాధిత పరమేశ్వరుండును మాణిక్యసింహా సనాధీశ్వరుండును నంగీకృత భూసురాశీర్వాదుండును దానధర్మ పరా యణుండును నిమ్మడిగరుడ నారాయణుండును నిజకీర్తి శాసనస్తంభాయ మానదిగంత దంతావళ దంతుండును సభయద్రావిళుండును గిషిరంధా

చల క్రీడావినోదుండును వశీకృత నిఖిల భూభుజుండును సతతత్యాగధ్వజుండును వినిర్మల కులశీలుండును పాండ్యరాయకందుక క్రీడావిలోలుండును గవిజనస్తోత్ర పాత్రుండును గౌండిన్యగోత్ర పవిత్రుండును జతుష్షష్టి విద్యా జన్మభూమియు నయోధ్యానగరస్వామియొయనంబరఁగి జంబూద్వీపభూభువనమండలీమకుట మండనాయమానంబగు కొండవీడు పురంబు రాజధానిగాఁ గీర్తిలతాధిష్ఠితాష్టాదశద్వీపాంతరాళుండునగు కొమరగిరివసంత నృపాలువలన నాందోళికా ఛత్రచామరతురంగాది రాజ్యచిహ్నములు వడసియమ్మహారాజునకుం బ్రతిసంవత్సరోత్సవంబున కుందగిన కస్తూరీ కుంకుమ ఘనసార సంకుమద హిమాంబుకాలాగరు గంధసారప్రభృతి సుగంధ ద్రవ్యంబులొండఁ గూర్చియుఁ జీనిసింహళతవాయి హురుమంజి జలనోగి ప్రభృతి నానాద్వీప నగరాకరంబులగు ధనకనకవస్తు వాహన మాణిక్య గాణిక్యంబులు తెప్పించియుఁ గవినైగమిక వాడి వాంశిక వైతాళికాదులగు నర్థిజనంబులకు నర్థంబుల నొప్పించియు ధీరుండును నుదారుండును గంభీరుండును సదాచారుండును ఘనవిఖ్యాతి గాంచిన యవచిదేవయతిప్ప ప్రభుండొకనాఁడా స్థానమంటపంబున సుఖోపవిష్టుండై.

* * * *

తే. సింహవిక్రమ పట్టణ శ్రేష్ఠుఁడైన
సెట్టి జగజెట్టి పావాణి సెట్టి విభుఁడు
ఘనుడునగరీశ చంద్రశేఖర పదాబ్జ
వందనానందితాత్ముండు వంశకరుఁడు.

క. శ్రీపర్వతసోపాన
స్థాపకు డగు రెడ్డి వేమజగతీపతికిన్
బ్రాపైనయవచిదేవయ
యాపావాణికిజనించె నభ్యుదయముతోన్.

మ. ఖుసిమీరన్ సురధాణిచేఁ దుకొలువైకూర్చున్నచోనీకరా
భ్యసనంబున్నుతియించు రాయవచితిప్పా చంద్రసారంగనా
భిసముత్పాదిత తాళవృంత పవనప్రేంఖోల్లసత్ప్రక్రియా
వసరోదంచితసార సౌరభరసవ్యాలోల రోలంబముల్.

* * * *

చ. హరిహరరాయ ఫేరోజసహాసురధాణ గజాధిపాది భూ
వరులు నిజప్రభావమభివర్ణన సేయఁ గుమారగిర్యధీ
శ్వరుని వసంతవైభవము సర్వమునాకడ నిర్వహించు మా
తిరుమలనాథసెట్టికిని దీగుణభట్టికి నెవ్వరీడగున్.

*   *   *   *

సీ. పంజాబుకర్పూర పాదపంబులు తెచ్చి
జలనోగ బంగారు మొలక తెచ్చి
సింహళంబున గంధసింధురంబులు తెచ్చి
హురుమంజిబలు తేజిహరులు తెచ్చి
గోవసంశుద్ధసంకు మదద్రవము తెచ్చి
యాపగ నాణిముత్యములు తెచ్చి
చోటంగిఁ గస్తూరి కాటఁకములు తెచ్చి
చీని చీనాంబర శ్రేణి తెచ్చి
గీ. జగదగోపాలరాయ వేశ్యాభుజంగ
పల్లవాదిత్య భూదానపరశురామ
కొమరగిరిరాజ దేవేంద్రు కూర్మిహితుఁడు
జాణ జగజెట్టి దేవయ చామిసెట్టి
గీ. తమ్ములిద్దఱుఁ దనయాజ్ఞ తలధరించి
యన్నిదీవుల దెచ్చు లాభార్థకోటి
యర్థులకునిచ్చి కీర్తిబేహారమాడు
నవచిత్రిపురాంతకుండు వంశాబ్ధివిధుఁడు.

మ. తరుణాచీనితవాయి గోవరమణాస్థానంబులం జందనా
గరు కర్పూరహిమాంబు కుంకుమరజఃకస్తూరికా ద్రవ్యముల్
శరధిం గప్పలి జోగులన్ విరివిగా సామాన్లఁ దెప్పించు నే
ర్పరిఁగా వైశ్యకులోత్తముండ వచితిప్పండల్పుడే యిమ్మహిన్.
గీ. పండువాఢిల్లిరాఘాది పట్టణముల
యధిపతులుమౌళి చాల్చురత్నాంకురంబు
లవచిత్రిపురాంతకానీత యానపాత్ర
సింహళద్వీప మండలక్షేత్రజములు.

19

MAHĀNĀṬAKA SUDHĀNIDHI.

[*By Immaḍi Dēva Rāya.*]

This is a Champu Kāvya in Sanskrit dealing with the story of the Rāmāyana. It is said to have been written by Immaḍi Dēva Rāya or Dēva Rāya II.

श्रीमानिम्मडिदेवरायनृपतिस्स्वर्लोककल्लोलिनी-
कल्लोलप्रतिमल्लसूक्तिविभवो विद्वज्जनश्लाघितः ।
धीमानादिमकाण्डवस्तुविषयान्व्यस्तान्महानाटक-
श्लोकान्वर्णपदक्रमोज्ज्वलतरान् रम्यानकार्षीद्विभुः ॥

20

CHĀṬU VERSES ABOUT ŚRĪNATHA'S VISIT TO VIJAYANAGAR.

Śrīnātha, the famous Telugu poet of the Reḍḍi courts is said to have visited the capital Vijayanagar. When he was there he was asked about his native kingdom, i.e., the eastern seaboard then ruled by the Reḍḍi Kings. In this his reply, he praises the Reḍḍi territory whose capital was Konḍavīḍu.

సీ. పరరాజ్యపరదుర్గ పరవైభవశ్రీల
గొనకొనివిడనాడు కొండవీడు
పరిపంథిరాజన్య బలములఖండించు
కొమరుమించిన జోడు కొండవీడు
ముగురురాజులకును మోహంబుపుట్టించు
గుఱుతైన యుఱిత్రాడు కొండవీడు
చటులవిక్రమ కళాసాహసంబొనరించు
కుటిలాత్ములకు గాడు కొండవీడు

గీ. జవనఘోటక సామంతసరసవీర
భటనటానేకహాటక ప్రకటగంధ
సింధురారవ మోహన శ్రీలదనరు
కూర్మినమరావతికి జోడుకొండవీడు.

The following is another piece said to have been composed by Śrīnātha during his visit to the capital Vijayanagar. There was some delay in his being introduced to the emperor. Śrīnātha did not like the habits and fashions of the capital which were very different from those of his province, and did not relish the food served to him in a hotel. He addresses in this verse the goddess of the Kannaḍa Kingdom, and, describing his plight, prays that he may return to his country soon.

శా. కుల్లాయుంచితిఁ గోకసుట్టితిమహా కూర్పాసముం దొడ్గితిఁ
వెల్లుల్లిన్దిలపిష్టముఁ మెసవితిఁ విశ్వస్థ వడ్డింపగాఁ
సల్లానంబలి ద్రావితిఁ రుచులు దోసంబంచు బోనాడితిఁ
తల్లీ! కన్నడ రాజ్యలక్ష్మి! దయలేదా నేను శ్రీనాథుఁడఁ.

These verses are said to have been composed when he visited the court of the Velama ruler Sarvagña Singa Bhūpāla addressing the goddess of learning, Sarasvati, wherein he recounts his own achievements. He says that in the Pearl Hall of the Southern Ruler (the Emperor of Vijayanagar) he was bathed in gold coins (Dinaras and Ṭankas). Goddess Sarasvati helped him to compose the Mahākāvya Naishadham in Telugu and to have the bell-metal drum (Kanchu Ḍhakka) of the Gauḍa Ḍinḍima Bhaṭṭa broken after a stiff contest with him. She got for him the title of Kavi Sārvabhauma before Chandrabhūsha Kriyāśakti Rāya.* He prays to her that she may help him to come out successful in the discussions of the Court of Sarvagña Singa also.

సీ. దీనారటంకాలఁ దీర్థమాడించితి
దక్షిణాధీశు ముత్యాలశాల
పలుకుఁదోడై తాంధ్రభాషా మహాకావ్య
నైషధగ్రంథ సందర్భమునకు
పగులఁగొట్టించి తుద్భటవివాదప్రౌఢి
గౌడడిండిమభట్టు కంచుఢక్క
చంద్రభూషక్రియాశక్తి రాయలయొద్ద
పాదుకొల్పితి సార్వభౌమబిరుద

---

* This is a distinct person from Kāsīvilāsa Kriyāsakti, the preceptor of Mādhava Mantrin and Gangā Dēvi, the first member of the full title being the personal designation of the occupant and the second that of the office.

గీ మెటుల మెప్పించెదో నన్ను నింక మీద
గావుసింగమహీపాలు ధీవిశాలు
నిండుకొలువున నెలకొనియుండి నీవు
సకలసద్గుణ నికురుంబ శారదాంబ.

This verse from the Kāśikhanḍam of Śrīnātha refers to his achievements. He says that the Reḍḍi King Vīrabhadra was praised by the poet Śrīnātha who was declared the king of poets (Kavirāṭ) by the bathing in gold which took place in the Pearl Hall of the Emperor of Karnāṭa (Vijayanagar).

సీ. కర్ణాటక్షితిపాలమౌక్తికసభాగారాంతరాకల్పిత
స్వర్ణస్నానజగత్ప్రసిద్ధకవిరాట్సంస్తుత్య చారిత్రధు
గ్ధార్ణోరాశిగభీర ప్రాహ్ణముఖమధ్యాహ్నపరాహ్ణార్చితా
పర్ణావల్లభరాజశేఖరమణీ పంటాన్వయగ్రామణీ.

21

COMMENTARY ON THE KĀVYĀLANKĀRA SŪTRA OF VĀMANA.

[*By Sāḷuva Gopa Tippa Bhūpala.*]

Sāḷuva Gopa Tippa was the grandson of Sāḷuva Tippa who ıarried Harima, elder sister of Dēva Rāya II, and son of Sāḷuva ɪopa. He was the governor under Dēva Rāya II and later, in the iceroyalty of Muḷbāgal. He was a great Sanskrit scholar and has eft several works of his in the language. The following are xtracts from his commentary on Vāmana's Kāvyālankāra Sūtra :alled Kāmadhēnu.

कल्याणानि तनोतु नस्स भगवान्क्रीडावराहाकृति-
र्दंष्ट्राग्रेण नवप्ररोहपुलकां देवीं धरामुद्वहन् ।
यस्याङ्गेषु वहन्ति लोमविवरालग्ना महाम्भोधयः
कान्तास्पर्शसुखादिव प्रकटितां स्वेदोदबिन्दुश्रियम् ॥

* * * *

प्रबन्धं तालानां भवनुतिमिषेणातनुत यः
शिवाङ्कूताकारा नटनकरणानामपि भिदाः ।
स वृत्तेर्व्याख्यानं सरलरचनं वामनकृतेः
विधत्ते गोपेन्द्रस्त्रिपुरहरभूपालतिलकः ॥

पावनपदविन्यासा समग्ररसदोहशालिनी भजताम् ।
घटयति कामितमर्थं काव्यालङ्कारकामधेनुरियम् ॥

इति कृतरचनायामिन्दुवंशोद्वहेन त्रिपुरहरधरित्रीमण्डलाखण्डलेन ।
ललितवचसि काव्यालङ्कियाकामधेनावधिकरणमयासीत्पञ्चमं पूर्तिमेतत् ॥

इति श्रीगोपेन्द्रतिप्पभूपालविरचितायां वामनालङ्कारसूत्रवृत्तिव्याख्यायां काव्यालङ्कारकामधेनौ प्रायोगिकं नाम पञ्चममधिकरणम्.

22

COLOPHON ON TĀḶA DIPĪKA.

[*By Sāluva Gopa Tippa Bhūpala.*]

In the introduction to the Kāmadhēnu the prince Gopa Tippa says that he also wrote a book on music determining the different ways of keeping time, and another on dancing. The following is the colophon of the Tāḷadīpika, the book on music:—

इति साळुववंशार्णवपूर्णिमाचन्द्रस्य भरतमतपारावारपारीणस्य श्रीगोपतिप्पभूपाळस्य तालदीपिकायां ताळप्रस्तारादिप्रत्ययनिरूपणप्रकरणम्.

23

VIKRAMĀRKA CHARITRAMU.

[*By Jakkana.*]

This is a Telugu poem written by the poet Jakkana and dedicated to Vennelaganṭi Siddamantri. He and his son Jannamantri were greatly patronised in the court of Dēva Rāya II. Siddhamantri is said to have been rewarded with Chāmaras, Chhatra (umbrella) and the Palanquin by the Minister Chāmanāmātya of Dēva Rāya II.

సీ. విమలవర్తనమున వేదశాస్త్రపురాణ
వాక్యార్థసరణికి వన్నె వెట్టఁ
పరమహృద్యంబైన పద్యశతంబున
దేవకీతనయువిధేయుఁ జేసె
రసికత్వమున దేవరాయమహారాయ
కరుణాకటాక్షవీక్షణముగాంచె

కర్ణాటకటకముల్గలయంతయును మెచ్చ
గణకవిద్యాప్రౌఢి ఘనత కెక్కె

గీ. గురుఁ బోషించె సత్కవివరుల మంచెఁ
బ్రజలఁ బాలించె భాగ్యసంపద వహించె
హరితమునిముఖ్యవంశరత్నాకరేంద్ర
చంద్రుఁడై యొప్పు సిద్ధయ జన్నమంత్రి.

మ. అగసెన్ బంధుల వైభవోన్నతులఁగా నాదిప్రధానావళిన్
దొరసెన్ నీతివివేకవిస్ఫురణచేఁ దోరంపుసత్కీర్తులన్
ఒరసెన్ పూర్వవదాన్యవర్గములనో హో యెందు నే మంత్రులున్
సరియే సిద్ధయజన్నమంత్రికి మనీషాదేవతామంత్రికిన్.

సీ. చిత్రగుప్తునకైనఁ జింతింపనరుదైన
గణితవిద్యాప్రౌఢి ఘనత కెక్కె
నవరసంబులయందు నవ్యకావ్యంబులు
కవిజనంబులు మెచ్చ గా నొనర్చె
నాణిముత్యముల సోయగము మించిన వ్రాలు
వరుసతో సిరుగేల వ్రాయ నేర్చె
నాత్మీయలిపి యట్ల లన్యదేశంబుల
లిపులను జదువంగ నిపుణుఁడయ్యె.

గీ. దేవరాయ మహారాయ ధీవిధేయ
మంత్రివల్లభ చామనామాత్యదత్త
చామరచ్ఛత్రశిబికాదిసకలభాగ్య
చిహ్నములనొప్పె జన్నయసిద్ధమంత్రి.

* * * *

క. శ్రీమద్వల్లయవరసుత
చామనదండాధినాథసామ్రాజ్యరమా
సామగ్రీసంపాదక
సాహాదిక చతురుపాయసంపన్నకరా.

Canto III

స. శ్రీకర్ణాటమహామహేశ్వర సదా సేవాప్రధానోత్తమా
నీకస్తుత్యలిపిక్రియానిపుణపాణిద్వంద్వపంకేరుహా
యాకల్పాంతః నిత్యకీర్తి జలజాస్యాకేళిగేహీభవ
ల్లోకాలోకధరాధరావృతధరా లోకైక రత్నామణీ.

24

ŚĒSHADHARMAMULU.

[*By Paiḍigantam Śaraṇamantri.*]

In this poem the author says that one of his ancestors Ambamantri lived in the court of Prauḍha Dēva Rāya who being pleased with his writing presented him with a gold style.

సీ. బహుపురాణగ్రంథపరనార్ధకరణాఢి
శూరుండుమీయన్న సూరమంత్రి
మహితసభాభిరామముఖకావ్యంబులు
ధరనిల్పె మీతాత శరణమంత్రి
తగవరియైయన్న దానంబుసేయుచు
వెలసె మీపెదతండ్రి విస్సమంత్రి
వేదపర్వతమనవినుతులఁగాంచెను
సరసుండుమీతాత చండమంత్రి.

గీ. ప్రౌఢనాయలమెప్పించిరాయసమున
పైడిగంటంబుగొని వ్రాసిభద్రలీలఁ
బైడిగంటంబువారని పద్దుదెచ్చి
యలరె మీతాతముత్తాతయంబమంత్రి.

25

GANGĀDASAPRATĀPAVILĀSAM.

[*By Gangādhara.*]

This is a Sanskrit drama celebrating the triumphs won by Gangādāsa, Raja of Pāvāchala, against the Sultan of Guzerat. In the beginning of the drama there is a short account given of how it came to be written and acted. As soon as the Emperor of Vijayanagar, Pratāpadēva Rāya (Dēva Rāya II) died and was succeeded by his son Mallikārjuna his enemies, the Sultan of the South (the Bahmani Sultan) and the Gajapati, taking advantage of the youth of the monarch, marched upon the city of Vijayanagar with a large army and closely invested it. But Mallikārjuna sallied forth from his capital, like a lion from his den, and routed the armies of the besiegers after completely defeating them.

Soon after this Mallikārjuna made enquiries in his court about the whereabouts of a poet of his father's court. He had been presented by Pratāpa Dēva Rāya with very valuable jewels and titles, and had gone on travel into other kingdoms in order to hold disputations with their court poets. Then a vaitāḷika (*court bard*) who had just returned to his court after a triumphal journey in the north gave an account of his tour.

After leaving the court of Dēva Rāya with presents and honours he made a pilgrimage to Dvāraka and went to the court of the Sultan of Guzerat. He there silenced all the scholars of the place and receiving presents from the sovereign stayed for six months.

He then went to the court of Prince Gangādāsa, the ruler of the state Pāvāchala, with its capital at Champakapura. He pleased Gangādāsa greatly by his achievements and scholarship. Then Gangādāsa requested him to compose a drama in Sanskrit celebrating his achievements. The poet accordingly composed a high class drama, for which the prince honoured him with a Kanakābhishēka (bathing in gold). The *vaitālika* then said that, having got the drama composed, Gangādāsa and his court were looking for the proper person to stage it.

Mallikārjuna was very glad to learn about his achievements. Immediately an actor of his court rose and proposed to go to the court of Gangādāsa and stage the newly-written play.

नाट्यकारः ॥ नाट्यरसिको नाम नाट्यकारोऽहम् ।

राजा ॥ कुतो देशादागम्यते ।

नाट्यकारः ॥ कर्णाटात् ।

राजा ॥ तत्र किमपूर्वमत्रागमने किं कारणम् ।

नाट्यकारः॥ आकर्ण्यताम् । पूर्वपश्चिमदक्षिणसमुद्राधीश्वरे, हयपतिगजपतिनरपतिरायसुवर्णपुत्तलाङ्कितवामचरणबिरुदतोडराडम्बरे, महाराजाधिराजराजपरमेश्वरे, राजगजबेटकारे, राजकठारित्रिणेत्रे, रिपुराजगजगण्डभेरुण्डावतारे, विजयनगरीपुरन्दरे, श्रीमत्प्रतापदेवराजे महेन्द्रसभालङ्कारे सति तत्कुमारेण श्रीमल्लिकार्जुनराजेन साम्राज्यसिंहासनमधिष्ठितम् । तदाकर्ण्य दक्षिणसुरत्राणेन गजपतिनाच पूर्वपराभूताभ्यां उभाभ्यां अमितहयगजपदातिभ्यां सम्भूयाभिषेणनमकारि । विजयनगरमावृत्य स्थितं तावदसहमानो गजबलं मृगेन्द्रशाब इव गिरिकन्दराद्विजयनगरतः श्रीमल्लिकार्जुनराजो बहिर्निर्गत्य निशिततरकरवालधाराजलप्रवाहवाहिनीपूरं हयपतिगजपतिसैन्यमशेषममज्जयत् । गजपतिः स्व

देहमात्रावशेषः पलाय्य निरगाद्यवनाधिपतिश्च । तदनन्तरं श्रीमल्लिकार्जुनराजेन रणद्यूतविजितान् हयगजान् सकलमहीमण्डलकलावत्करकमलसात्कृतवता तस्यामेव वेलायां निजजनकेनश्रीप्रतापदेवराजेन दिव्यरत्नरचितकटककुण्डलहारकनकदण्डचामरयुगलमौक्तिकच्छत्ररिपुराजगजगण्डभेरुण्डनिजाबिरुदपदकहयगजनरपतिराजकविपुत्तलाङ्कितं बिरुदतोडरं दत्वा निजकीर्तिजगङ्गाया भगीरथीकृत्य सम्मानितरुचिराङ्गधरोऽनवद्यविद्याबलेन दिग्विजयाय यातः सम्प्रति क्वास्त इति पृष्टम् । तदा तदानीमेव उत्तरदिगन्तराळात् समागतेन केनचिद्वैताळिकेन "महाराज महाराजस्य कीर्तिमाहिमाचलं कृत्वा द्वारकायात्रां विधाय अह्मदाबादनगरे गूर्जरसुरत्राणस्य महाद्वारे वामचरणे बिरुदतोडरं निधाय सभाकोविदान्मूकीकृत्य षण्मासानुषित्वा ततो निर्गम्य पावाचलाधीश्वरं चम्पकपुरपुरन्दरं श्रीगङ्गादासभूवल्लभं द्रष्टुं समागतः । तत्र श्रीगङ्गादासभूवल्लभेन लोकोत्तरविद्योर्जितां कवितां विलोक्य सन्तुष्टेन बहुमानदानैः परितोष्य मच्चरित्राभिनयनाटकं भवता विधेयमित्युक्तं करोमीति स्वीकृत्य लोकोत्तरं नाटकमकार्षीत् । तदद्भुतमाकर्ण्य गङ्गादासभूवल्लभो बहुकनकरत्नैः आपादतलमस्तकं तमापूरयत् । अस्य नाटकस्य अभिनयं कर्तुं कांश्चिन्नाट्यकारः समागच्छेदिति राजा चिन्तां करोती" त्युक्ते श्रीमल्लिकार्जुनराजेन साधु कथितं अस्मच्चिन्ता दूरीकृतेति बहुमानपुरस्सरं स वैताळिकः संमानितः । तदानीं तदास्थानस्थितेन रिपुनाट्यकारवारणमदनिवारणपञ्चाननेन मया तदाकर्ण्य तन्नाटकमहं नाट्यरसिकोऽभिनेष्यामीति अत्रसोत्कण्ठमागतोऽस्मि । तावन्मम भाग्यगुणेन महाराजोऽपि महाकालीमहामहोत्सवे कलाकुतूहलानि विलोकयन्नेव मन्नयनगोचरः समजनि । तदहं महाराजस्य युवराजत्वमारभ्य रूपकाभिनयाय गच्छामि । पश्यतु महाराजः । इति निष्क्रान्तः ॥

26

ŚRĪŚAILAM PLATES* OF VIRŪPĀKSHA.

These copper plates contain engraved upon them the grant by the last Emperor of the first Vijayanagar dynasty of the village Sirumala Ātukūru to the Śaiva teacher by name Siddha Bikshāvṛitti. They begin with the usual verses giving the pedigree of

* These were obtained from Mr. Kōka Rangaswami Nayudu, Tahsildar of the Podili division of the Venkatagiri Zamindari, who has possession of them.

the family from the moon to Yadu, and say that in his family was born the king Sangama. He had a son called Bukka who by his valour destroyed all his enemies and caused great prosperity to the world. The genealogy is then continued down to Vijaya. Through Nārāyaṇīdēvī, Vijaya had a son called Pratāpadēva Rāya. Possessed of many virtues and famous for his good acts he got the kingdom of Penukoṇḍa (Ghanādri) from his elder brother and was the best (Pārijāta) among men. He had a wife called Siddhala Dēvi. From her Śiva was born as the lord of kings, Virūpāksha who was the personification of generosity and an ocean of kindness. He got the kingdom 'by his own valour', and, endowed with all fortunes and having conquered all his enemies 'at the point of the sword', he rules the world a veritable storehouse of valour. Then follow two verses praising the sovereign. On the banks of the Tungabhadra, in the temple of Virūpāksha, surrounded by Brahmans and the virtuous people of his court, on the date of his coronation, i.e., in the year of Śaka counted by the Vasus, eight, the gunas and the earth or 1388,* in the month Kārtika in the dark fortnight he granted the village called Sirmaṇa Ātukūru situated in the Rajya of Pratāpagiri to the sage living in Śrī Parvata, worshipping Mallikārjuna called Siddha Bhikshāvṛtti along with 400 pagodas. Then follow two verses in praise of the donee. The boundaries of the village granted are then given and it is renamed Virūpākshapuram. The last verse says that the sage was immensely pleased with the gift and blessed the king with long life.

This inscription is important for more reasons than one. First, it gives the proper reading of the name of the Queen of Dēva Rāya which had been hitherto read as Simhala Dēvi. Again instead of saying *nijāgrājāprāptam anādirājyam* in the verse referring to Prauḍha Dēva Rāya which was interpreted as 'who got his ancient kingdom from his elder sister' the plate reads *nijāgrajāt-prapta-Ghanādrirājyam* which would mean who got the kingdom of Ghanādri or Penukoṇḍa from his elder brother. This would suggest that Dēva Rāya II had an elder brother, whose name we do not know, who conquered the kingdom of Penukoṇḍa, from whom, we do not know.

Then after Dēva Rāya II, it omits completely all reference to the king Mallikārjuna who ruled between Dēva Rāya II and Virūpāksha;

* I am obliged to the Hon'ble Diwan Bahadur L. D. Swamikannu Pillai for the equivalent Christian date which is Friday, 8th November A.D. 1465. The day may be Thursday, the 7th.

and says that Virūpāksha got the throne of his ancestors (pitṛyam simhāsanam) by his own valour (nijapratāpadadhigatya), after conquering all his enemies at the point of the sword (khaḍgā-gratassarvaripūn vijitya). This suggests that he came to the throne not by natural succession after his elder brother's death, but as a result of a successful usurpation. Hence it might have been that he omitted altogether any reference to his elder brother Mallikārjuna.

* * * *

अभूदस्मिन्महावंशे प्रभूतभुजविक्रमः ।
सञ्जात लक्ष्मीसम्पन्नस्सङ्गमो नामभूपतिः ॥
विजित्यशत्रूनखिलाञ्जगत्प्रभुः संमोदते वीरविलाससंश्रयः ।
समस्तविद्यानिपुणः प्रतापी धर्मैकभूस्सर्वकलासु कोविदः ॥
अभूदस्मान्महाभूपाद्बुक्करायमहीपतिः ।
प्रचण्डतरदोर्दण्ड खण्डितारातिविक्रमः ॥
कर्णाटलक्ष्मीस्सविलासमास यस्मिन्महीपे महनीयकीर्तौ ।
भूमिस्त्रियैवाप वसुन्धरात्वं स्थिरेतिनाम प्रथमं गुणौघैः ॥
क्षोणीपालनमेव कर्तुमनिशं जातौ त्रिलोकाधिपौ ।
एकीभूय च बुक्करायनृपतौ पीताम्बरेशावुभौ ।
नाम्नाचापितयोः प्रसिद्धिमगमद्भूवल्लभः श्रीयुतः
सर्वां सागरमेखलां भुवमिमां संपालयन्दीव्यति ॥
राजा हरिहराख्योऽसौ महादानानि षोडश ।
विधायलक्ष्मीसम्पन्नो भाति सर्वगुणाश्रयः ॥
तस्य मेलाम्बिकाजानेः प्रादुरासीद्यशोधनः ।
प्रतापदेवरायाख्यः तनयोविनयान्वितः ॥
प्रतापवह्नौ परिजृम्भमाणे शुष्कास्तुरुष्का अपि यस्यराज्ञः ।
रिपुक्षितीन्द्राः स्वनिरस्तधैर्याः कान्तारवल्मीककृतात्मरक्षाः ॥
तस्य देमाम्बिकाभर्तुः पुत्रश्शत्रु निषूदनः ।
विद्याविनयसम्पन्नो वीरो विजयभूपतिः ॥
तस्य नारायणीदेव्यामुत्पन्नश्शुभलक्षणः ।
प्रतापराय इत्याख्यामगमत्पार्थिवोत्तमः ॥

गुणैरनेकैरवनीतलेऽस्मिन् विराजमानः सुकृताप्तकीर्तिः ।
निजाग्रजात्प्राप्त धनाद्रिराज्यः साधीकृतार्थो जनपारिजातः ॥
तस्य सिद्धलदेवीति भार्या लक्षणसंयुता ।
लक्ष्मीर्नारायणस्येव जाता त्रिजगदम्बिका ॥
तस्यां शिवः प्रादुरभूद्गुणाढ्यो नाम्ना विरूपाक्ष इति प्रसिद्धः ।
राजाधिराजः क्षितिपालमौलिः वदान्यमूर्तिः करुणैकसिन्धुः ॥
निजप्रतापादधिगत्य राज्यं समस्तभाग्यैः परिसेव्यमानः ।
खड्गाग्रतस्सर्वरिपून्विजित्य संमोदते वीरविलासभूमिः ॥
खिलीकृतसुरत्राणो द्रावितान्ध्रमहीपतिः ।
हिन्दुरायसुरत्राणस्त्रिराज्यभुजगोन्नतः ॥
वैरिराजगजेन्द्राणां पञ्चास्यः परभीतिकृत् ।
सुहृत्पद्मसुधाभानुरित्यादिबिरुदोन्नतः ॥
तुङ्गभद्रानदीतीरे विरूपाक्षस्य सन्निधौ ।
पित्र्यं सिंहासनं प्राप्य पालयन्धरणीमिमाम् ॥
पुण्यश्लोकाग्रगण्योऽसौ विरूपाक्षक्षितीश्वरः ।
धर्मास्थानगतैस्सद्भिः संयुतो धरणीसुरैः ॥
शालिवाहननिर्णीतशकवर्षक्रमागते ।
वस्वष्टगुणभूयुक्ते पार्थिवाख्ये च वत्सरे ॥
कार्तिकाख्ये च मासेऽस्मिन्नसिते पञ्चमीतिथौ ।
राजाधिराजस्सर्वज्ञो यो राज्ञां परमेश्वरः ॥
विरूपाक्षक्षितीपालो विरूपाक्षस्य सन्निधौ ।
निजपट्टाभिषेकस्य पुण्यकाले नृपोत्तमः ॥
प्रतापाह्वयविख्यातगिरेराज्ये तथैव च ।
कांनाडौ शिर्मणाख्यात आतुकूरेतिविश्रुतम् ॥
कैलासस्थितएव शम्भुरधुना श्रीपर्वते सर्वदा
पार्वत्या सह संवसन्नतिमुदा लोकत्रयं पालयन् ।
यस्तिष्ठत्यथ तस्य सेवकविधौ श्रीलिङ्गचक्रेश्वरः
श्रीमान्पर्वतमल्लिकार्जुनमहादेवस्य पादार्चकः ॥

कैलासोपरि ये स्थितामरगणा तेवा पृथिव्यां च-
मुख्यासिद्धगणाम . प्रभृतयः तैस्सार्थमत्रापि यः ।
वाराणस्यधिवासतामधिगतः श्रीपर्वतेयंमुदा
श्रीसिद्धप्रतिपन्नवैभवतया बिक्षां प्रवर्तेत च ॥
अङ्गरङ्गादिभोगाय पर्वमासोत्सवाय च ।
तपस्वि . न्नदानाय विरूपाक्षक्षितीश्वरः ॥
ददौ स्वाभिमतावाप्त्यै श्रीगिरौ सन्निवासिने ।
प्रतापाख्यगिरे राज्ये वराहाणां चतुश्शतम् ॥
अष्टरापरिविख्यातं आतुकूरेति निश्चितम् ।
विरूपाक्षपुरं चेति प्रतिनाम विधाय च ॥
सहिरण्योदकदानधारापूर्वं यथाविधि ॥

* * * *

ददौ पर्वतसंस्थस्य मल्लिकार्जुननामतः ।
दीप्यमानस्य(दे?)वस्य विरूपाक्षक्षितीश्वरः ॥
तपस्वी स च सन्तुष्टो संयुतः परया मुदा ।
राजानमाशिषं चक्रे चिरञ्जीवी भवत्विति ॥

27

PRAPANNĀMṚTAM.

[*By Anantāchārya.*]

In giving the life of Ēṭṭūr Singarāchārya or Nṛsimha Guru, it narrates the following story. Eṭṭūr Nṛsimhāchārya with his younger brother, Śrīrangāchārya, being very poor started from their village Ēṭṭūr for Vijayanagara, the capital of the empire, 'to earn money.' At that time the kingdom was ruled by a sovereign called Virūpāksha. His cousin-claimants being jealous of his power wanted to injure him, and he was forced to leave his capital and take refuge elsewhere. From there he secretly collected an army, marched one night upon the capital and, putting to death all his enemies, began to rule his kingdom as before. But all his relatives who were secretly murdered in the palace became ghosts, haunted his palace, and caused him very great annoyance day and night. To escape this Virūpāksha was compelled to abandon the old palace and construct a new one. But the old palace continued to be haunted, and the ghosts gave great trouble to the neighbourhood by their noise and wailings. The king performed many austerities and gave large gifts for getting rid of the trouble, but in vain.

Nṛsimhāchārya and his younger brother as they entered the city during night, mistook this haunted palace for the king's residence and entered it, Rāmāyaṇa in hand. At their approach the ghosts (piśāchas) remained quiet; and they were admitted into the palace. Entering the palace they found the ghosts holding court with king, council and attendants. On their approach all the ghosts bowed to them and showed them the respect due to scholarship, and the ghost-minister enquired who they were and for what purpose they had come there. They narrated their whole story on which the king directed them to come secretly every night and read to them the Rāmāyaṇa for which he promised to pay them at the rate of one *nishka* every day. This they did for sometime. When they came to the end of the Rāmāyaṇa, Nṛsimhāchārya and the brother directed them to make due preparation for the celebration of the coronation (paṭṭābhishēka) of Rama as is usually the practice even now. On the day of reading the paṭṭabhishēka portion of the Rāmāyaṇa the brothers were presented with many thousands of gold coins and precious stones. After the reading was over the ghosts narrated to the brothers their story as follows: "We are all related to Virūpāksha, the present sovereign of the country, and have been foully murdered by him in our sleep. This horrible death has forced us to haunt the palace. It was on our account that Virūpāksha left this palace and built another seeking to get rid of us by vows and charities. But all that was of no avail. You two holy people by coming here every night and reading to us the Rāmāyaṇa have rid us of our sins, and we now go to the heaven of *Sāntānika*." They took leave of the two brothers thus, and went to heaven. The palace became rid of the ghosts and the whole neighbourhood, to its great relief, were rid of the nightly disturbance. They reported the matter to Virūpāksha, and Virūpāksha on learning after inquiry what had taken place, summoned the two brothers before him.

He enquired who they were and why they went to the haunted palace. They told him that they belonged to the village Ēṭṭūr, and were the descendants of the famous Śrīśailapūrṇa whom the God Venkaṭēśvara called 'grandfather,' and who explained the Rāmāyaṇa in twenty-four different ways to Rāmānuja. They then gave a full account of their going to the haunted palace and of what transpired there.

On hearing the whole story king Virūpāksha felt great reverence for the Rāmāyaṇa, the God Rama and the preceptor Nrsimha. The king was soon admitted into the Vaishṇava faith by him as before that time he was a Vīra Śaiva. After Virūpāksha became a Vaishṇava he directed his new preceptor Nṛsimhāchārya to expound to him the Rāmāyaṇa which he did. On the day of the reading the Paṭṭābhishēka sarga the king had him 'bathed in gold,' and Nṛsimhāchārya continued from that time to live in the capital itself. When Virūpāksha became a Vaishṇava, all his subjects also became followers of Vaishṇavism. The king from that time gave up the use of the old seal with the sign manual Virūpāksha on it, and adopted a new one on which was inscribed the name 'Śrī Rama.'

Sarga 123.

तस्य रामानुजार्यस्य नृसिंहार्योऽभवत्सुतः ॥
नृसिंहार्यो महातेजास्सर्वशास्त्रविशारदः ।
एटूरुनामनगरं स प्राप सुमहायशाः ॥
तस्मिन्नेटूरुनगरे कंचित्कालं समास्थितः ।
तस्मिन्काले महातेजाः विरूपाक्षो महाबलः ।
शशास राज्यं धर्मेण विजये नगरे नृपः ॥
दृष्ट्वासहिष्णवस्सर्वे विरूपाक्षस्य वैभवम् ।
ज्ञातयोऽहिंसितुं यत्नंचक्रिरे बलदर्पिताः ॥
विरूपाक्षो विदित्वाथ तेषां तत्कर्मकृत्स्नशः ।
देशान्तरमवस्थाय निर्गत्य नगराद्बहिः ॥
गूढोरहसिकस्मिंश्चित्कंचित्कालं निनाय सः ।
ततस्सम्पाद्य महतीं सेनां स चतुरङ्गिणीं ॥
केनाप्यज्ञातवृत्तान्तो निशीथेसबलो महान् ।
विजयं नगरं प्राप्य विरूपाक्षो नृपोत्तमः ॥
निश्शेषं सर्वशत्रूणां वधं चक्रे महाबलः ।
विजयाख्ये ततस्तस्मिन्नगरे पूर्ववत्तदा ॥

राज्यं प्रशासयंस्तस्थौ सर्वलोकमहीपतिः ।
निशीथेबान्धवास्सर्वे तेन ये निहतानृपाः ॥
पिशाचभूतास्तेसर्वे पुत्रपौत्रादिका जनाः ।
तं नृपं पीडयामासुर्विरूपाक्षं दिवानिशम् ॥
विसृज्य राज्यभवनं विरूपाक्षो महामतिः ।
पुनरन्यद्विधायाशु राजवेश्ममहाबलः ॥
राज्यं प्रशासयंस्तस्थौ तत्र सर्वजनैस्सह ।
प्रतिरात्रं पिशाचानां तेषां कोलाहलोरवः ।
प्रलापश्च महांस्तत्रश्रूयते राजवेश्मनि ॥
पैशाच्यमोचनार्थाय तेषां राज्ञा महात्मना ।
कन्यागोभूमिदानानि गृहदानान्यनेकशः ॥
पुण्यव्रतान्यनेकानि कृतान्यन्यानि यानि च ।
सातैर्नमोचिता दानैर्घोरापैशाच्यवेदना ॥
नृसिंहार्यस्तदातस्मा देटूरुनगरान्महान् ।
निर्गत्यनिखिलान्देशांश्चरित्वा धनकाङ्क्षया ॥
असंप्राप्तधनः प्राप विजयं नगरं प्रति ।
स राजदर्शनाकाङ्क्षी सानुजश्शास्त्रवित्तमः ॥
रामायणं समादाय पूर्वराजगृहं प्रति ।
मया (अनभि ?) वज्ञातवृत्तान्तो निशायां वैष्णवोत्तमः ॥
सानुजस्स नृसिंहार्यो रामायणसमन्वितः ।
विवेश राजभवनं पिशाचशतसङ्कुलम् ॥
पिशाचास्सौम्यरूपेण संहृष्टास्तेऽखिलास्तदा ।
दर्शनात्क्षीणकर्माणः तयोर्वैष्णवमुख्ययोः ॥
दृष्ट्वा तौ द्वारपालास्ते हस्तपुस्तकधारिणौ ।
प्रणम्य मार्गं दत्वा ते विनयेन समास्थिताः ॥
तेन सन्तुष्टहृदयौ राजान्तिकमुपागतौ ।
प्रणम्य स नृपश्शीघ्रं तयोः श्रेष्ठासनंमहत् ॥
कल्पयित्वा यथान्यायं अर्चयित्वा विशेषतः ।
दृष्ट्वाचानामयं सम्यक्सन्तोषं परमं ययौ ॥

कृत्वाशिषो नृसिंहार्यः सानुजस्सनृपाय च ।
तस्मै प्रहृष्टस्सुतरां निषषादासने तदा ॥
राज्ञा संचोदितस्तेनमन्त्री तावब्रवीत्तदा ।

* * * *

Adhyāya 124.

ते सर्वे वैष्णवं दृष्ट्वा पिशाचास्तं मुदान्विताः ।
पूजां चक्रुर्यथापूर्वं प्रत्युत्थानाभिवादनैः ॥
भद्रपीठे सुखासीनो वैष्णवो वीतकल्मषः ।
पट्टाभिषेकसर्गं च कथयामास शास्त्रवित् ॥
मुखावलोकने सक्ताः वाचकस्य मुदान्विताः ।
रामाभिषेकं श्रृण्वन्तोभक्त्या सर्वेसमास्थिताः ॥
रामाभिषेकं श्रुत्वा ते हर्षनिर्भरमानसाः ।
पूजां पौराणिकायाथ चक्रुस्सर्वे महात्मने ॥
अनेकशतसाहस्र दीनारान्भूषणैस्सह ।
अमूल्यानि च रत्नानि राजभोग्यानि यानि च ॥
तानि सर्वाणि दत्वाशु संप्रणम्य पुनःपुनः ।
नृसिंहाचार्यवर्याय सानुजाय महात्मने ॥
बद्धाञ्जलिपुटास्सर्वे वचनं तमथाब्रुवन् ।
अस्माकं सर्ववृत्तान्तं वक्ष्याम श्रूयतामिदम् ॥
अस्मद्वृत्तान्तकथने माभयं कुरुतं युवाम् ।
विरूपाक्षस्य नृपतेस्ते सर्वे ज्ञातयो वयम् ॥
व्याजेन केन चिद्राज्ञा निशीथे राज्यकाङ्क्षया ।
विरूपाक्षेण निहतास्सुषुप्तिसमये वयम् ॥
तेन प्राप्तास्स्म पैशाच्यं सर्वे सपरिवारकाः ।
अस्मद्भयाद्विरूपाक्षः तदिदं भवनं जवात् ॥
विहायचान्यभवनं विवेश समहीपतिः ।
अस्मदर्थमनेकानि धर्माणि विविधानि च ॥
विरूपाक्षेण भूपेन भक्त्या तेन महात्मक ।
कृतानि तेन पैशाच्यं निवृत्तं नाभवत्तदा ॥

युवाभ्यां रामभक्ताभ्यां पैशाच्यमतिदुस्सहम् ।
विनिवृत्तं तदस्माकं सांप्रतं घोरकर्मणाम् ॥
युष्मन्मुखाब्जनिष्यन्ददिव्यरामकथामृतैः ।
परितृप्ता वयं सर्वे भवामोऽद्य न संशयः ॥
सान्तानिकं लोकमद्य गन्तुकामा वयं स्थिताः ।
अनुज्ञां देहि नो ब्रह्मन् सर्वेषामाशु साम्प्रतम् ॥
विमानबृन्दमाकाशे दृश्यते सूर्यसन्निभम् ।
इतो विदूरे सन्तानलोकादद्यागतं शुभम् ॥
पिशाचेष्वित्युक्तवत्सु स गुरुस्सानुजस्तदा ।
तेभ्यो मन्त्राक्षतान्दत्वा स्वान्तःकरणपूर्वकम् ॥
अनुज्ञां प्रददौ शीघ्रं तेषां मुक्तौ कृपानिधिः ॥

* * * *

Adhyāya 125.

ततः पौरजनास्तस्य समीपगृहवासिनः ।
केचिद्राजगृहं प्राप्य तं विरूपाक्षमब्रुवन् ॥
सञ्जातं किञ्चिदाश्चर्यं पट्टनेऽस्मिन्नृपाद्य नः ।
पूर्वराजगृहे राजन् पिशाचानामहर्निशम् ॥
श्रूयते खलु घोराणां नित्यं कोलाहलारवः ।
स महान् श्रूयते नाद्यकिमाश्चर्यं विचार्यताम् ॥

* * * *

विरूपाक्षनृपो भक्त्या दृष्ट्वा तौ सद्द्विजोत्तमौ ।
प्रणिपत्य प्रसन्नात्मा वचनं चेदमब्रवीत् ॥
कौ युवां देवसङ्काशौ वेदज्ञौ वैष्णवोत्तमौ ।
पूर्वराजगृहं कस्मात्प्रविष्टौ प्रेतसङ्कुलम् ॥
यत्कार्यं तत्र सञ्जातं भवदागमनान्महत् ।
तत्सर्वं वदतं सत्यं माभयं भवतो ध्रुवम् ॥
इत्युक्तस्तेन भूपेन नृसिंहगुरुपुङ्गवः ।
संप्रहृष्टोऽब्रवीद्वाक्यं गतभीस्तं महीपतिम् ॥

श्रूयतामभिधास्यामि विरूपाक्ष महीपते ।
वृत्तान्तमेतं सकलं पवित्रं पापनाशनम् ॥
पुरा यमाह ताततेति भगवान्वेङ्कटेश्वरः ।
श्रीमद्रामायणस्यार्थं चतुर्विंशतिवर्त्मना ।
महते भाष्यकाराय यतिराजाय योऽदिशत् ॥
भूरिश्रीशैलपूर्णस्य तस्य वंशे महात्मनः ।
सञ्जातोऽहं महाभाग सर्वलोकैकविश्रुते ॥
नृसिंहार्य इति ख्यातः सर्वशास्त्रविशारदः ।
रामभक्तो विशेषेण नित्यं रामकथाप्रियः ॥
ममानुजोऽयं मतिमान् श्रीरङ्गाचार्यनामवान् ।
सर्वशास्त्रविदां श्रेष्ठः सर्वज्ञस्साधुसत्तमः ॥
अवेहि तदिदं राजन् श्रीरामायणपुस्तकम् ।
एटूरु नगरस्थोऽहं दरिद्रो वेदपारगः ॥
सोऽहं यवीयसानेन सहितो धनकाङ्क्षया ।
तदिदं नगरश्रेष्ठं विजयाख्यं समागतः ॥
कदाचिद्रात्रिवेलायामज्ञानेन महोच्छ्रयम् ।
तद्राजभवनं दिव्यं संप्राप्तोऽभव मादरात् ॥
तत्रत्यास्ते मया दृष्टाः पिशाचा राजसत्तम ।
राजमन्त्रिप्रधानादिरूपेण नरमूर्तयः ॥
ते सर्वे प्रीतिसंयुक्ताः पूजां चक्रुर्यथाविधि ॥
मह्यं तत्र प्रविष्टाय सानुजाय महीपते ॥
ममैतं सर्ववृत्तान्तं श्रुत्वा ते मन्मुखात्तदा ।
मामवोचन्महीपाल भक्त्याशुभतरं वचः ॥
यूयमत्र निशाकाले समागत्य दिनेदिने ।
ब्रूत रामायणं निष्कं दास्यामो भवतां ध्रुवम् ॥
एतद्वृत्तान्तलेशोऽपि न प्रकाश्यं कदाचन ।
द्रव्यलोभान्नृपास्माभिः यथोक्तं तत्तथाकृतम् ॥
एवं नीतास्त्रयो मासाः श्रीरामकथयानृप ।
पट्टाभिषेकसमये तैर्दत्तो द्रव्यसञ्चयः ॥

आवयोः पश्यतो स्सर्वे पिशाचास्ते नृपोत्तम ।
ततस्सन्त्यज्य पैशाचशरीराणि जवात्तदा ॥
अनुज्ञाता मया सर्वे दिव्यरूपधरास्तदा ।
दिव्यं विमानमारूढा विचित्रं मयि पश्यति ॥
सन्तानलोकमुद्दिश्य ते गता राजसत्तम ।
इदं सत्यमिदं सत्यं ममैवोक्तं नृपोत्तम ॥
तैर्दत्तं द्रव्यसङ्घातं पश्येदं नृपभूषणम् ।
इत्युक्त्वा देशिकश्रेष्ठो नृसिंहार्यो महामतिः ॥
विरूपाक्षाय भूपाय दर्शयामास तद्धनम् ।
विलोक्य तद्धनं सर्वं अनर्घं राजभूषणम् ॥
विस्मयं परमं गत्वा विरूपाक्षो मुमोदह ।
रामायणे रामभद्रे नृसिंहगुरुपुङ्गवे ॥
आचार्यदैवप्रामाण्यभावं चक्रे महामतिः ।
मन्त्रे तद्देवतायां च तथा मन्त्रप्रदे गुरौ ॥
त्रिषु भक्तिस्सदा कार्या सा हि प्रथमसाधनम् ।
एवं भक्तिस्सुसञ्जाता विरूपाक्षमहीपतेः ।
तत्रत्यानां च सर्वेषां जनानां तद्विचित्रितम् ॥
विरूपाक्षस्ततो धीमान् वीरशैवमतोपि सः ।
श्रीशैलवंशसम्भूतौ ज्ञात्वा तौ रामलक्ष्मणौ ॥
पुत्रमित्रकलत्रादिसहितश्च सनागरः ।
श्रीशैलवंशतिलकात् नृसिंहार्याज्जगद्गुरोः ।
पञ्चसंस्कारसम्पन्नो बभूव सुमहायशाः ॥
श्रुत्वा रामायणं सर्वं नृसिंहार्याद्गुरूत्तमात् ।
रामभक्तो विरूपाक्षः कृतकृत्यो मुमोदह ॥
पट्टाभिषेकसमये नृसिंहगुरवे मुदा ।
स्वर्णाभिषेकमकरोद्भक्त्या पार्थिवसत्तमः ॥
नृसिंहार्यस्ततस्तेन सन्तुष्टस्सानुजस्तदा ।
तत्रैव राजनिकटे सदारस्सुखमास्थितः ॥

श्रीवैष्णवे विरूपाक्षे प्रशासति महीमिमाम् ।
आसंच्छ्रीवैष्णवास्सर्वे यथा राजा तथा प्रजाः ॥
विरूपाक्षाभिधां मुद्रां विरूपाक्षो विहाय च ।
राजाङ्गुळीये श्रीराममुद्रां दृढतरां व्यधात् ॥
श्रीराममुद्रा सर्वत्र तदाप्रभृति विश्रुता ॥
विरूपाक्षनृपात्पूर्वं शैवास्सर्वेऽभवन्नृपाः ।
तत्पश्चाच्चाभवंत्सर्वे विख्याता वैष्णवा नृपाः ॥

एवं नृसिंहगुरुराडिह सर्वलोकान् रामानुजार्यपदपङ्कजभृङ्गराजान् ।
कुर्वन्निरन्तरमतन्द्रितलोकरक्षः तस्थौ सुखेन विजये नगरे जितारिः ॥

28

RĀMARĀJĪYAMU OF VENKAYYA.

[*Somadēva Rāja.*]

This extract from the Narapativijayam gives some account of Somadēva Rāja, with whom the genealogical list of the last Vijayanagar dynasty seems to pass from legend to history. He was the son of Tātapinnama Rāja. In the *birudagadyam* list of titles, which the work attributes to Tātapinnama, he is called *Cheruku Rācha Nāyaka Saptānga haraṇa* (who defeated the army and captured the 'seven constituents of royalty' of Cheruku Rācha Nāyaka). This seems to refer to a historical event, but we do not know who the Cheruku Rācha Nāyaka was whom Tātapinnama defeated. Referring to his son Somadēva Rāja the work gives a number of historical events. He defeated the chiefs Naḍabāla Nāyaka, Gujjula Vīri Nēḍu, Rudrapa, Gaurā Reḍḍi and Gangi Nāyaka). Opposite to the eastern gate of the fort of Ganginēnikoṇḍa, the capital of Gangināyaka, he erected a *toraṇa* or triumphal arch in token of his conquests.

Somadēva also fought against the Muhammadan ruler Muhammad and, completely defeating his army, took him prisoner. But Somadēva let him go after making obeisance. The Sultan presented him with 6,000 horse, promising that he would name his own son after his captor.

Somadēva is said to have conquered the following seven forts* (1) Ganginēnikonḍa, (2) Kandanavolu (Karnul), (3) Kaluvakolu, (4) Kōṭa Rāchūru (Raichur), (5) Mosalimaḍugu, (6) Yatagiri (Yadgir) and (7) Sātānikoṭa. Of these it is not possible to identify Nos. (1), (3) and (7). All the rest are situated in the border land between the Vijayanagar empire and the Bahmani kingdom where there was continuous fighting throughout the period of Vijayanagar history. The other three places are also likely to be found in the same region.

The work also gives a long *(birudagadya)* list of titles of this prince, some of which seem to refer to the conquests in which he took part. In addition to the titles referring to his conquest of the seven previously mentioned forts, he is said to have achieved victory at the following places and got the title Vīrakshētrabhāratī-malla with reference to them. The places are Ākulapāḍu, Mudugal (Mudgal), Anegondi (the northern suburb of the capital Vijaya-nagar) and Kuntisara (?). There are also a number of titles in the list which are merely of general interest and do not refer to any historical events.

Somadēva Rāja was succeeded by his son Rāghavēndra. Rāghava was a pious king and performed many acts of charity. His son was Pinnama who is called the lord of the town of Āravīḍu. His son was Āravīṭi Bukka, general of the Emperor Sāḷuva Narasimha.

చ. అతనికిసోమదేవమనుజాధిపుఁడుద్భవమంది నిర్జితా
హితుఁడయితాల్చె భూభరమహీనపరాక్రమ రేఖనెన్నఁగా
క్షితిధర జామదగ్న్యహరునకుంబ్రతియౌచును నీతిచేబృహ
స్పతిసరిఁ బోలిధర్మమునఁబాండుసుతాగ్రజుఁజోడుకోడెమై.

---

* The statement in the copperplate grants of the last Vijayanagar dynasty that Somadēva, the ancestor of those kings, captured seven forts in a single day, has hitherto been considered an empty boast. But this account in the Narapativijayam tells us where the seven forts were and from whom he captured them. It does not say that he captured them all in a single day, which statement is an addition made by the latter day courtiers of the empire. We know the approximate date of these events. Āravīti Bukka, who was a general under Sāluva Narasimha, was the great-grandson of Somadēva, and Sāluva Narasimha lived in the latter part of the fifteenth century. Allotting twenty-five years for each generation we would have to fix the latter portion of the fourteenth century for Somadēva. He must have been one of the generals under the early Vijayanagar Emperors Harihara, Bukka and Harihara II. Muhammad whom he defeated seems to be the son of the founder of the Bahmani kingdom.

సీ. బలవంతుఁడగునడబాలనాయకునిని
ఘూరుఁడౌగుజ్జులవీరినేని
రౌద్రరసోన్నిద్రురుద్రపాథిపుమహా
శౌర్యగౌగారెడ్డిసాహసాంకు
గంగినాయకుని సంగ్రామరంగంబున
సింగంబు మత్తమతంగజములఁ
బట్టుకైవడిఁ బట్టిచట్టలెత్తించికి
నఱునసహుండునై గంగినేని

గీ. కొండప్రాగ్ద్వార సీమనుద్దండవృత్తిఁ
గంబములఁ బాఁతితోరణగాఁగఁగట్టి
వినుతికెక్కెను సకలభూజనులచేత
సోమదేవనృపాల సుత్రాముఁడెలమి.

సీ. కదనరంగంబునఁ గరితురంగమవీర
వితతితోఁ బలుమారువిఱుగఁదోలి
యమితోగ్ర శౌర్యమహమ్మదుఁబట్టినీ
పేరుబెట్టెదను గుమారునకది
గాకభవత్పాద కమలంబునుదురంట
దండంబుఁబెట్టెదఁ దన్నుఁగాచి
విడువుమన్నను గాచివిడిచియర్థులకును
షష్టిశతంబునశ్వములవాని

గీ. చేతనిప్పించి శరణన్నఁ బ్రీతిఁగాచు
బిరుదుతగునీతని కెయనిధరణిపతులు
సన్నుతింపగనాది రాజన్యచర్యఁ
దేజరిలె సోమదేవధాత్రీవరుండు.

సీ. దండెత్తి చనిమ ఘూద్దండ వృత్తినిగంగి
నేనికొండవలీలగానుగట్టి
కందనవోలును గలువకోలునుగోట
రాచూరునెటువంటి రాజుకైన
సాధింపరాని మొసలిమడుగుమరియా
తగిరినగరము సాతానికోట

వరుసతోసాధించి పరమహర్షంబునఁ
దత్తన్మహాజనతతులఁ బ్రోచి

గీ. ధరకుఁదోడవని వినుతింపఁదగినయట్టి
యారవీటి పురాధ్యక్షుఁడగుచుఁదాత
పిన్నన్నృపసోమ దేవుండెయెన్నఁదగియె
నఖిలసత్కవి సురభూజమనుచు నెపుడు.

బిరుదగద్యము.—జయజయ, నిఖిలమహాభాగవత ముఖ్యవిఖ్యాతకీర్తి ఏకదివసఘటికైక ఘాటీహఠాహృతకోటరాచూరు సాతానికోట కందనవోలు యాతగిరికలువకొల్లు మొసలిమడుగు గంగినేని కొండాభిధాన సప్తదుర్గ ప్రవర్తి స్థలదుర్గజలదుర్గగిరిదుర్గవనదుర్గ చౌరాశీ దుర్గవిఫాళ, సముద్ఘుష్య మానబిరుదాపదాన హాళహాళికా కర్ణకపుల కితకపోల, నాకులపాటి ముదుగంట్యానెగొంది కుంతిసరవిజయలక్ష్మీ సమటీకరణలక్షిత, నాకులపాటి వీరక్షేత్ర భారతీమల్ల, ముదుగంటివీరక్షేత్ర భారతీమల్ల, ఆనెగొందివీరక్షేత్ర భారతీమల్ల, కుంతివీరక్షేత్ర భారతీమల్ల, వీరక్షేత్ర భారతీమల్ల బిరుదభరితానుభావ, స్వభావగంభీరాంభోనిధి, సత్వగుణవాసుదేవ, సకలనరదేవ చూడామణి, అసిభరణపటిమ సహదేవ, ఆదిదేవ, సుపర్వరమణీ మణిస్తుత, వరద, భయద, హాసబిరుదరగండ, వీరప్రతాప బిరుద, బిరుదుమన్నెరగండ, పురిగోలసురత్రాణ, శరణాగతత్రాణ బిరుద, రాయరణరంగ భీభత్స, రాయరాహుత్తరగండ, వైవరగండ, గండరగండ, తాతపిన్నమరాజతనూజ, సోమదేవరాజ, విజయీభవ, దిగ్విజయీభవ.

తే. సోమకులదీపకుండగు సోమదేవ
రాజవరునకునుదయించి రాఘవేంద్రుఁ
డఖిలనృపతులు ముకుళితహస్తులగుచుఁ
గొలువధరయేలె నతఁడు దోర్బలము మెఱసి.

చ. పరబలవేది రాఘవనృపాలుఁడు పంకజనాభుగూర్చియ
ధ్వరములు నగ్రహారములు దాత్తమతిన్ దగఁజేసిధారుణీ
సురులకొసంగెఁ బర్వముల శుద్ధసువర్ణగవాది దానముల్
గరిమనుబిన్నశౌరిని జగద్వినుతున్ ఘనుఁగాంచెవేడుకన్.

29

RĀMĀBHYUDAYA

[*By Sāḷuva Narasimha.*]

In the introduction the author, after recounting the achievements of Sāḷuva Mangi,* says that he had a son called Gāutama, whose son Gunḍaya Bhūpati is praised in very high terms. Gunḍa had a wife called Mallāmbika. As they had no issue for a considerable time they had recourse to a number of vows and retired to Ahobilam for performing penance to the God Narasimha of that place. Pleased with their devotion the God appeared before the king in a dream, and, expressing his satisfaction at their devotion, promised them a son possessed of all virtues and ordained to rule the whole world. The king awoke from his dream and communicated it to his wife. After a short time a son was born to them whom they called Narasimha after the God. The military genius and excellent qualities of Narasimha are then described at length. He is said to have ruled over the territory comprising the Kalyāṇa, Kanchi, Kaṭak, Kuntala, Chōḷa and Pundraka. The poets and scholars of his court one day, after extolling his great qualities, requested him to display his scholarship by the composition of a poem (Kāvya) on the life of Rāma.

पुत्रेषु तस्य बहुषु (मङ्गिदेवस्य) भुवनश्रुतकीर्तिषु ।
क्षमामपालयत्कृत्स्नां ख्यातो गौतमभूपतिः ॥
साहित्यसारसादित्यः सङ्गीतामृतचन्द्रमाः ।
यश्चतुर्दशविद्यानां निषद्येति (?) निगद्यते ॥
पद्मानुत्कण्टकान् वक्ष्यः शौरेश्च मणिशार्करम् ।
अपहायेन्दिरावात्सीदंसेतस्यातिमांसले ॥
अखण्डमहसस्तस्माद्भूद्गुण्डयभूपतिः ।
अकुण्ठशक्तिः श्रीकण्ठा न्नीलकण्ठरथो यथा ॥
मल्लाम्बिका महाभागा तस्यासीत्सहचारिणी ।
देवी दशरथस्येव कौसल्या कुलभूषणम् ॥
ततः कदाचिदेकान्ते स गुण्डयमहीपतिः ।
चिन्तामनन्तामतनोत्सन्तानाप्तिविलम्बनात् ॥

---

* V:de extract No. 4 for Sāḷuva Mangu.

अतर्पिताग्निसवनमलाक्षितपथं नभः ।
अनुद्गतेन्दुमम्बोधिमपुत्रं मां प्रचक्षते ॥
अन्यादृणाद्विमुक्तोयं (हं) यदि राज्यसुखाय मे ।
सुखोदर्कमिदं कर्तुं सुप्रसन्नो हरिः प्रभुः ॥
इति चिन्तापरो ध्यात्वा नृहरिं कुलदैवतम् ।
स तया सहचारिण्या तपः कुरुत दुश्चरम् ॥
तपसा तेन सन्तुष्टस्तस्य स्वप्ने पुरोऽभवत् ।
अहोबलनृसिंहस्तमब्रवीदद्भुतं वचः ॥
शौर्यगाम्भीर्यसौन्दर्यधैर्यौदार्यादिभूषणः ।
तवास्तु तनयो वत्स ! सर्वोर्वी चक्रनायकः ॥
इत्युदीर्य वचोभक्त्या हर्षितस्यास्य भूपतेः ।
अहोबलनृसिंहोयमधितान्तर्दयानिधिः ॥
अथ स्वप्नावसानेसावानन्दामृततुन्दिलः ।
हरिप्रसादमाचष्ट देव्यादर्शितकौतुकः ॥
तथा गुण्डयभूभर्तुः तनयोऽभूत्ततः फलात् ।
नानागुणगणस्तस्यां नरसिंह इति श्रुतः ॥
धन्विनो दानशौण्डस्य शास्त्राणां पारदृश्वनः ।
भूम्ना यस्य चिरादासीत् भुवि धर्मः प्रतिष्ठितः ॥
तरङ्गसदृशोत्तुङ्गतुरङ्गमखुराङ्किताः ।
यस्य दिग्विजयक्रीडांशंसन्ति कुलभूभृतः ॥
प्रतापाग्निपरिप्लुष्टप्रत्यर्थिपुरभस्मना ।
सुत्रामसम्पदो यस्य शोधितः कीर्तिदर्पणः ॥
कल्याणकाञ्चीकटकशालिनीं करदायिनीम् ।
सकुन्तलां सचोलां गां यो भुङ्क्ष्वक्ष्मां सपुण्ड्रकाम् ॥
न हैमा गिरयस्सर्वे न द्विपास्सकला मृगाः ।
नार्थिनो निखिला यस्य स्थूललक्षस्य दत्तये ॥
न वाञ्छिताधरं दानं न न्यूनं कोटितोऽपि यत् ।
नापत्रगामितद्यस्य बभूव ब्रह्मविन्न तत् ॥

न चोरः कोप्यभूत्तस्मिन्नक्षतां रक्षति क्षितिम् ।
यद्येको नवनीतस्य सोऽपि द्वापर एवहि ॥
दिशस्त्वया जितास्सर्वाः सीमायां स्थापितं जगत् ।
काव्ये दर्शय सामर्थ्यमित्यसौ कथितो बुधैः ॥
तदिदं रामचन्द्रस्य चरितं तत्प्रसादतः ।
उच्यते तेन विदुषा नरसिंहमहीभुजा ॥

Colophon.

इत्युद्दामवरप्रसादकवितासिंहासनाध्यासिनः
क्षोणीमंसरगण्डगुण्डयपतेः क्ष्माकण्टकोत्खण्डिनः ।
विष्णोः श्रीनरसिंहविग्रहभृतो भावोर्मिसेतौ कृतौ
श्रीरामाभ्युदयेऽत्र पूर्तिमगमत्सर्गश्चतुर्विंशकः ॥

30

COLOPHON OF CANTO V, RĀMABHYUDAYA.

In the colophon of canto V of the above work it is said that the author was Śoṇādrinātha, otherwise styled Ḍinḍima Sārvabhauma, son of Abhirāmā and Rājanāṭha, and the work is called Mahānāṭakasyāgrajātakāvya. (महानाटकस्याग्रजातकाव्य.)

शोणाद्रीन्द्रं कवीन्द्रं श्रवणकटुरटड्डिण्डिमं सार्वभौमं
प्रासूताम्बाभिरामा नवनवकविताभाजनं राजनाथात् ।
तस्यैतस्मिन्नयातिक्रमविषयमहानाटकस्याग्रजाते
काव्ये सर्गो निसर्गोज्ज्वलरसविलसत्पञ्चमोऽयं जगाम ॥
इति डिण्डिमसार्वभौमकृतौ रामाभ्युदये पञ्चमस्सर्गः ।

31

JAIMINI BHĀRATAMU

[*By Pillalamṛri Pinavirabhadra.*]

This is a poem dedicated to the Vijayanagar Emperor Sāḷuva Narasimha, the founder of the second Vijayanagar dynasty. In the introduction the poet gives a long account of the achievements of the king's ancestors from Sāḷuva Mangu. He explains the meanings of the various titles that Narasimha assumed, and says that he conquered the Tiguḷa Bhūmi, meaning by that term the Tamil country, deprived the Oḍḍiya (the sovereign of Orissa) who invaded his kingdom, of his strength; captured the fort of Bāladurgam * and having gone to Penukoṇḍa destroyed the Pikkiḷḷu and other enemies of his. Week after week the king Sāḷuva Narasimha made extensive gifts to Brahmans. He is said to have conquered many forts the chief among which being Bonagiri (Bhuvanagiri), Gingi, Kongudhārāpuri † and Penukoṇḍa.

ఉ. భారతవంశమండనుఁడు పాండవగాండివముక్తబాణసం
భారతతప్రభావనుతిపారగుఁడంచిత గోమహీతులా
భారతదంగదాన పరిపాకసమగ్రయశోవిలాసశో
భారతశాలిగుండ నరపాలనృసింహుఁడుగహ్వారీస్థలిన్.

సీ. తనభుజాపరిఘచేత ధరావరారోహ
భరియించి బర్బర బాహుఁడయ్యె
తనప్రతాపంబుచేత దిగంతరంబుల
దీపించి యంబరాదిత్యుఁడయ్యె
తనదానగరిమచేతసురాగముల పెంపు
దండించి యైవరగండడయ్యె
తనమహత్త్వంబు చేతఁ బురాణపురుషుని
మఱపించిచౌహత్త మల్లుండయ్యె

గీ. రాజమాత్రుండె ధరణీవరాహబిరుద
వర్ణఫలకాయ మానదుర్వారగర్వ
తాహితోర్వీశవిపుల దోరంతరుండు
సాళ్వగుండయ నరసింగ జనవిభుండు.

సీ. తిగుళభూముఖ తెంకులుగఁ జరించినదొడ్డ
చెవులపోతుల నెల్లఁ జెండివైచి
ఘనమైన కండక్రొవ్వునఁ బాఱుతెంచిన
యొడ్డీని పెనులావులూడఁదన్ని

* Seems to represent Udayagiri.

† The printed editions give the word as Kommadhārāpura, an apparently wrong reading. The place seems to stand for Dhārāpuram in the Coimbatore district.

పఱతెంచి చక్కఁగఁ బాలదుర్గము మెట్టి
సుడివడ్డచామలఁ జుట్టిముట్టి
పెనుకొండ కడప్రాలిపికిఁళ్లు మొదలైన
ప్రతిపక్షులను హతాహతము చేసి.

*　　　*　　　*　　　*

గీ. సతఁవుల త్రుప్పుడుల్పు వసంతవేళ
రాయమీసరగండ ధరావరాహ
విజయ విఖ్యాతగుండ భూవిభునృసింహ
సార్వభౌముని బిరుదైన సాళువంబు.

క. శ్రీవెంకటాద్రినాథద
యావర్ధిత రాజ్య సన్నుతార్థి జనమహీ
దేవాగ వైరినృపరా
జీవనికరచంద్ర నారసింహనరేంద్రా.

మ. కనకాద్రి ప్రతిమానధైర్య జగదేకస్తుత్య సౌభాగ్యమో
హనలీలానవపంచబాణనిజబాహాశౌర్య వీరావిరా
జినయోపాయవిహార బోనగిరి చెంజీకొంగుధారాపురీ
పెనుకొండాద్య ఖిలైక దుర్గహరణ ప్రేంఖత్ప్రతాపోదయా.

శా. పాంచాల ద్రవిళాంగ మాళవశక ప్రాగ్జ్యోతి షక్షోణిభృ
త్పంచాస్య ప్రతివర్ష దత్తవివిధోప గ్రాహ్యరత్నాంశుమ
త్కాంచీ వేంకట కాళహస్తినగరీ కల్యాణ సౌధాంచల
ప్రాంచచ్ఛాసన సాళ్వశంకితశశ ప్రాలేయరుఙ్మండలా.

32

VARĀHAPURANAM

[*By Nandi Mallayya and Ghanṭa Singayya.*]

Varāhapurāṇam, a Telugu poem written by the two poets Nandi Mallayya and Ghanṭa Singayya, is dedicated to Narasa Nāyaka, the general of Sāḷuva Narasimha. In the beginning the authors give a genealogy of their patron and the achievements of the several members of his family, as well as the achievements of their patron's sovereign Sāḷuva Narasimha. Of Īśvara, the general of Sāḷuva Narasimha, the poem says that he was in very great favour with Sāḷuva Narasimha. He was the generalissimo of all his forces. With this army he conquered and reduced the following places:—Udayādri (Udayagiri), Huttari (?), Gaṇḍikoṭa, Penukoṇḍa, Bangalore, Kovela Nellūru (?), Kundāṇi, Goduguchinta, Bagūr, Naragoṇḍa, Āmūr and Śrīrangapaṭṭaṇa. The poem further states that Īśvara Nāyaka, at the direction of Narasimha, marched with a large army against the Muhammadans (Yavanas) of Bidar (Beḍandakoṭa) and destroyed their cavalry completely near the town of Kandukūr.

The poem goes on to say that Narasa Nāyaka, the son of Īśvara, was a patron of letters, and had the works Varalakshmīkalyāṇam and Narasimhapurāṇam dedicated to himself. The work also mentions Narasa as praised for his greatness by the sovereigns of Manḍuva (Manve), Beḍandakoṭa (Bidar) and Māhura (Māhūr).

వ. . . . కృతిపతికిం బతియైన సాళువ నరసింగ రాజరాజ మౌళి పావనాన్వయంబు మొదల వర్ణింతుము. చింతారత్న కామగవి కల్ప వృక్ష లక్ష్మీపక్ష్మలాత్రులతోడంబుట్టి మిన్నుముట్టిన పాలమున్నీటి పట్టి సాయంతనసమయ సంఫుల్ల మల్లీమతల్లికా గుళుచ్ఛ స్వచ్ఛకాంతి నిస్తంద్రుండు చంద్రుండు వంశకర్తగా సకల కవికలుషాపహర్త వంకిదేవమహీభర్త కీర్తికార్తిక చంద్రికాప్రభావంబులు విసర్మించి దశదిశాంచలంబులు ముంచెఁ దత్తనూజుండు చతుష్షష్టి విద్యావినూతనభోజుండు గుండ్రాజుదుండగపురాజతండంబులఁ జెండాడి మండలగ్రావంబు కెలంకుల గెలుపు గంబంబులు నిలిపెఁ దత్సూనుండు గాండివధన్వసమానుండు సాళువరాజు ఘోరాహవపట్టంబునం బారసిక తురగఘట్టంబులఁ గనుపుగొట్టె ధరావరాహబాహుపీఠంబునం గుదురుపఱిచెఁ దత్పుత్రుండు నిరాతంకప్రతాప కమలమిత్రుండు గౌతరాజు రాజసంబున గుణలతావితానంబులు సేతుశీతాచల మధ్య పృథ్వీమండలంబున మెండుగొలిపెఁ దత్సుతుండు వీరలక్ష్మీసమన్వితుండు గుండరాజు విరోధిరథినీ విఖండన ప్రచండదోర్దండమండలాగ్రుండును సముద్దండ సాహసక్రియాసమగ్రుండునునై నిరవధికప్రభావ దుందుమారులం దిమ్మనాథ నరసింగ పార్థివులంగాంచె వారిలోన.

* * * *

వ. అట్టి నరసింగరాజరత్నంబుచేత మన్ననవడసి సైన్యనాయక పట్టభద్రత్వంబున నిర్నిద్ర విజయలక్ష్మీమహత్వంబున మదవదఖిలయాతి భయదసత్త్వంబున దీర్ఘాయురైశ్వర్యధుర్యుండైన యీశ్వరనాయకుని

కుం బ్రియతనూభవుండు నరసవసుధాధ్యక్షుండు నిర్వంచితానుగ్రహం
బునం బరిగ్రహించి యిమ్మహాప్రబంధంబునకు శృంగారవిభూషణంబుగాఁ
దదీయవంశావతారంబు రచియింతుమది యెట్టిదనిన :—

* * * *

సీ. ఉదయాద్రి భేదించె వుత్తరి నిర్జించె
గండికోటపురంబుఁ గదలఁద్రవ్వె
పెనుకొండ సాధించె బెంగుళూరు హరించెఁ
గోవెల నెల్లూరు గుంటఁ బఱచె
కుందాణి విదళించె గొడుగుచింత జయించె
బాగూరు పంచము పాడుచేసె
నరుగొండ వెకలించె నామూరు మర్దించె
సీరంగపట్నంబు బారిసమరె

గీ. రాయచౌహత్తమల్లధరావరాహ
మోహనమురారిబర్బర బాహుసాళ్వ
నారసింహప్రతాపసన్నాహుఁడగుచు
విశ్వహితకారి తిమ్మయ యీశ్వరుండు.

మ. నరసింగక్షితిపాలుపంపునుడుగౌనాఁ జేసి దండెత్తి యీ
శ్వరభూభర్త బెడందకోటయవనాశ్వవ్రాతముఁ బీమసం
గరరంగంబునఁ గొల్లవట్టుకొనిపీఁ కంగందుకూరీపురాం
తరసీమంబునఁ జక్కఁగా నఱకె దుర్దాంతారి సంతానమున్.

* * * *

క. వాణీకగవీణాని
క్వాణరతికి వినయమతికి వరలక్ష్మీక
ల్యాణ నరసింహవిజయపు
రాణకథారమణితానురాగస్థితికిన్.

క. పరిచితబోధునకు నిరం
తరకాంత ఘృణాసనాథునకు సాళ్వశ్రీ
నరసింగవిభుచమూపే
శ్వర నృపతికుమారనరసజననాథునకున్.

ఉత్సాహ. మండువా బెడందకోట మాహురాది మేదినీ
మండలేశ్వరస్తుతాసమాన మానుషోదయా
భండనాంజిత ప్రచండపటహనిస్స్వనార్భటీ
హిండితాష్టదికుడుంగ యీశ్వరాత్మసంభవా

క. శ్రీవేంకటాద్రిపతిసం
సేవాహేవాకనిపుణ శేషాహిఫణా
ళీవినమనకరకరిసే
నావిభ్రమ యీశ్వరేంద్రు నరసింహనృపా.

33

SĀḶUVĀBHYUDAYAM *

[*By Rājanātha Diṇḍima.*]

(Continued from extract No. 3.)

Canto I.—Among the sons of the famous Sāḷuva Mangu who destroyed the Muhammadans in the south and restored the temple of Śrīrangam was Gauta, to whom was born, like Abhimanyu to Arjuna, Gunḍa, the third of that name in the family. Gauta leaving the responsibility of ruling the kingdom to his children, retired to the forests to spend the evening of his life in preparation for the next.

Canto II describes the penances of Gunḍa III and his consort Mallāmbikā at Ahōbilam, the appearance of God Naraśimha in his dream and his promise to enter human life as Gunḍa's son. Mallāmba becomes pregnant and gives birth to Narasimha. His youth and early education are then described. Gunḍa then instals his son as his successor on the throne and retires to the forests as a Vānaprastha.

Canto III.—The ministers advise Nṛsimha not to give himself up to sorrow at the departure of his parents, lest it should afford a favourable opportunity to his enemies. They urge him to start on an expedition of conquest against his enemies and exhort him that if Udayagiri is captured there would be nothing to obstruct him on that side. In the last verse of the canto god Vishṇu worshipped

* The two extracts are taken from a single Manuscript, with many lacunae, in the Madras Government Oriental Manuscripts Library, No. 11819 of volume XX of Descriptive Catalogue (1918). The passages are extracted as they are in the manuscript.

at Venkaṭādri (Tirupati) is contrasted with Narasimha, his avatar who was at Chandragiri. Narasimha resolves to set out on an expedition of conquest and orders a public announcement of this resolve.

Canto IV.--Narasimha's army marches against Kalinga. The Ruler of Kalinga come out to meet him at the head of his army. Then a battle takes place between the two armies which is described at great length. The Kalinga Ruler is defeated, and retires to his city which is laid siege to. A breach is at last effected in the fort and the Kalinga Raja surrenders.

Canto V.--Narasimha then turned his attention to the south. After worshipping the god Śiva (probably at Chidambaram) he proceeded against the Chōḷa king who fled away on hearing of the march. On his way Narasimha sighted the Gōpura of Tiruvaṇṇāmalai at a distance and made his obeisance. He then went to Madhyārjunam (Tiruviḍaimarudūr) and thence to Kumbakōnam. Then by the northern bank of the Kaveri he proceeded to Śrīrangam. He spent a few days here to satisfy himself that the benefactions of his ancestors were being properly applied, and to pay his homage to God Śiva at Jumbukēśvaram. Thence he went to Madura and Rāmēśvaram. He thence went across as far west as Trivandrum (Anantaśayanam). After worshipping god at all these places he turns back. He receives tribute from the kings all along the way, and there is no record of war at all except on the Travancore frontier. Even the Ceylon king shows ready inclination to enter into a treaty with him.

Canto VI.—At the instance of a chief who is called Kuṭavāchalēndrataṭavāsin, Nṛsimha invaded Nāgamanḍala (perhaps the same as Nāgarakhanḍa). He left a garrison there and returned with a desire to conquer Pṛthugiri (big hill, Penukonḍa). At that place he was attacked by a Muhammadan army. He won a complete victory over the Muhammadans and justified his titles Dharaṇīvarāha and Sāḷuvēndra. After this the poem goes on to describe the conventional invasion by Narasimha of the territory of the king of Daśārṇa who was defeated. He is said to have continued his march northwards as far as the Himalayas and to have set his boar (Varāha) signet on the face of the Himalayas. After that Narasimha conquers some more northern countries and goes finally to Benares (Kāśi) where he is anointed as Chakravarti by the various kings in attendance upon him in front of the god Viśvēśvara. On the occasion of the anointing of Narasimha there was a shower of flowers and sound of music from heaven in token of the approval of the gods.

Canto VII.—Description of Narasimha in court.

Canto VIII describes Narasimha's hunting expeditions to the Vindhyan forest which is of course an epic invention.

Canto IX.—Narasimha returns from the banks of the Narbada to Venkaṭādri (Tirupati). He made Chandragiri his residence for the purpose of worshipping Vishṇu at Tirupati. He is then said to have descended from the hill Venkaṭa (Tirupati) and ascended the hill called Airāvata (?).

Canto X describes the seasons of winter, summer and spring, and how Narasimha spent them.

Canto XI.—Sāḷuva Narasimha resides in a fort on the banks of the Suvarṇamukhi where he performed the gift of Suvarṇamēru during Śivarātri. He then receives a very large amount of money heaped up before him by the kings of the several countries, and after receiving their respects distributes among scholars all the presents the kings brought to him.

Canto XII describes the return of Narasimha to his capital and the joy of his people in consequence. All the vassal kings show their respect to him by accepting various subordinate functions. The last portion praises the greatness of Narasimha, and declares that the kingdom was very happy, from which various vices and sins disappeared in his reign.

Canto XIII praises the great qualities of Narasimha, his great gifts performed year after year, his patronage of poets and the protection of the Dharma; and closes with a benediction that he may rule the world for all time.

Canto I.

तेष्वेकोऽजनि गौतयः त्रिभुवनख्यात स्ततो वीर्यतः
कर्णाद्येषु पृथासुतेष्वनुपमं पार्थोऽभिमन्युं यथा ।
प्रासूत प्रथितं कुमारमतुलं श्रीगुण्डदेवाह्वयं
यं वैकुण्ठमखण्डभूमिभरणोत्कण्ठावतीर्णं विदुः ॥
निष्कण्ठकीकृत्यधरामसो . . निवेश्य राज्ये च नृपात्मजाभिः ।
कृती ततो गौतमभूमिपालः शमोन्मुखः पुण्यमगादरण्यम ॥

Canto II.

रत्नाकरोरुरशनां ललितार्थभोगहृद्यां प्रजोदयकृते करदां रसेन ।
मल्लाम्बिकां समहिषीपदमाननीयां क्षोणीमिवा . गुण्डयभूमिपालः ॥

* * * *

आशीर्भिरासुमनसामखिलाश्रमाणां भाग्यैस्त्रिलोकतपसा च पचेलिमेन ।
पञ्चग्रहोच्चगतिशालिनि सन्मुहूर्ते मल्लाम्बिका सुतमसूत मनोजरूपम् ॥

* * * *

वर्णैश्चतुर्भिरिह वर्णचतुष्टयस्य भर्तेतिवा नृवरइत्यपदानतो वा ।
· ▪ ख्यया नरहरेर्न परं व्यतानीत् नामार्भकस्य नरसिंह इति क्षितीशः ॥

* * * *

विद्यापारमवापितद्गुरुजनैर्नीतं पुरो वीक्ष्य तं
साष्टाङ्गप्रणतं सुतं स विनयं सस्नेहमुत्थापयन् ।
आलिङ्ग्यो त्पु(लकं?) पुनःपुनरसावाघ्राय मूर्ध्न्यादरात्
अन्तर्लीन इवात्मनात्मनि सुखादामीलिताक्षोऽभवत् ॥
सकलामुपदिश्य धर्मनीतिं निजसाम्राज्यधुरं निधाय तस्मिन् ।
अगमद्वनमात्मवंशरीत्या सह मल्लाम्बिकया स गुण्डयेन्द्रः ॥

Canto III.

निजगुरुविरहान्नितान्तखिन्नो यदि भवसीह रमासखावतारः ।
अनिशविवरवीक्षणोन्मुखानाम् अवसर एष न संभवेदरीणाम् ॥

* * * *

अयमवसर एव जैत्रयात्रामनुपमपौरुषवारिधे विधेहि ।
समुचितसमयोप्तबीजरीत्या प्रकृतमिमंफलवद्भवेत्प्रकामम् ॥
शिशुरयमचिरागतप्रतिष्ठः श्रयति न मूलबलं स्थिरावलम्बम् ।
इति किल भवतो निरस्तशङ्कं नृपतिकुलं निखिलं निरुद्यमं यत् ॥

* * * *

तदिह सकुलरक्षसावधानो विहरति शार्ङ्गधरोऽहि वेङ्कटाद्रौ ।
सविधभुवि तदाहितावनायां नृपवरचन्द्रगिरौ नि . . . ॥
शिरसि मुनिभयाद्दधत्किलाब्धिः यदुदयदुर्गगिरिस्तटाकलक्ष्यात् ।
स्फटिकमयदर्शमुखप्रकाशैः हसति किमाद्रिमगस्त्यशीर्णशृङ्गम् ॥
(उ)दर(य)गिरिदुर्गराजधान्यां हरिणदृशाममरावतीसमायाम् ।
अधिगतशिखरास्वभेदभाजाम् अमरवधूष्वनिमेषतो विशेषः ॥

* * * *

असममिह गिरीन्द्रदुर्गमादौ स्ववशयतो भवतः सुमेरुपूर्वाः ।
अपि कुलगिरयो भवेयुरात्मध्वजकिरिलेख्यजयाङ्कसूत्रधाराः ॥

*   *   *   *

इति सचिवगिरा स राजसिंहः तदचलदुर्गवरे निवेश्य सर्वम् ।
अचकमत दिगीश्वरांशजोऽसावखिलदिशां विजयाय दण्डयात्राम् ॥

*   *   *   *

विभुरथ स विमृश्य मन्त्रिवर्गं विरचितसान्ध्यविधिर्विशेषवेदी ।
सह कवितिलकैस्सभामकार्षीत् सरस . . . भोगरागी ॥

*   *   *   *

आनन्दामृततुन्दिनः कुलगुरोरालोकहर्षादिव
श्वः प्रातर्हरितां जयोद्य महतिस्वोद्योगमुद्घोषयन् ।
सर्वान्पार्श्वगतान्विसृज्य च कवीन् सन्नाहिना चेतसा
निर्णिद्रो नृपतिर्जयश्च हरितां वाञ्छन्ननैषीन्निशाम् ॥

Canto IV.

नृसिंहधात्रीशनिदेशतस्ततो निशात्यये सैनिकबोधहेतवे ।
जयानको द्वेषिहृदां भयानको विमुच्य निद्राभरणं च (ते भ)टाः ॥
यथोचिताहार्यभृतो रसोत्तरा रणे द्विषो नर्तयितुं किलोद्यता ।
विधाय सान्ध्यं विधिमुज्झितस्ततो द्विजोदिताशीः कवचः शुभग्रहैः ॥
सहा . . . शङ्करमग्रतः स्मरन् जनाधिपः प्रस्थितदिग्जिगीषया ॥

*   *   *   *

जिगीषुरागादि . . . कलिङ्गभङ्गाय कढारिसाळुवः ।
अशङ्कमाकर्ण्य जयानकारवम् कलिङ्गराजः करिभिर्विशृङ्खलैः ॥
भुजङ्गराजं खगपुङ्गवो यथा नृपं क्रुधाङ्कूरदहङ्कियोभ्ययात् ॥

*   *   *   *

हतावशिष्टैश्च गजैरगात्पुरं कलिङ्गराजो युधि खण्डितादरः ।
सशैलदुर्गं तपनाध्वरोधकृत् विशालसालं बहुयन्त्रसाधनम् ॥

*   *   *   *

समन्ततः साळुवभूपतिस्ततः कलिङ्गभङ्गाय विशृङ्खलो . . ।
विलङ्घ्य सालं विशति स्म सत्वरं निरन्तरं तत्पुरनीडकोटरम ॥

*   *   *   *

अथ शरणं गता हतावशिष्टैः सह सुभटैस्सहसार्पितोपहारम् ।
अहितमधिकदीनमन्वगृह्णात् कलितदयस्सकठारिसालुवेन्द्रः ॥

* * * *

Canto V.

अथ पटहनिनादैरात्तबोधैरशेषैः नियमकृदवनीन्द्रो निर्गतः सैन्यवर्गैः ।
बहुवसतिरगात् भीषयन् . . . . दक्षिणाशां जिगीषुः ॥
पुरमनुपममग्रे पुण्डरीकाक्षमैशं क्षितिपतिरथ दृष्ट्वाकेवलोभ्येत्य भक्त्या ।
अनमदवनहेतोराहितानन्दनृत्तं शिशिरकरवतंसं . . . कुंसम्

* * * *

तदनुपटहनादात्तं विभाव्याभियान्तं प्रसृमरभयभारः प्राद्रवच्चोलभूपः ।
प्रलयपवनवाते वातुमुच्चैः प्रवृत्ते तुलितकुलगिरीन्द्रे तूलवार्ता कुतः स्यात् ॥
अनमदवनिपालो गोपुरं वीक्ष्यदूरे सुरसरणिमतीतं शोणवन्येशशम्भोः ।
हतमपिसहभोक्तुं भैरवस्याज्ञयाम्बा तनयमनलपक्कं तच्च यात्राजुहाव ॥
असितसरसिजालिं स्वाश्रयामात्तगन्धान् रचयितुमुपयातान्वारयद्भिर्द्विरेफान् ।
मलयपवनलोलैः शालिभिः पाकनम्रैः अवनिपतिरनर्घाश्चोलदेशानपश्यत् ॥

* * * *

तुलितसुकृतघण्टामर्जुनीं द्वारि दृष्ट्वा रथहतमपि वत्सं स्वं च पुत्रं रथस्थम् ।
व्यदलयदपि बालं यत्र चोलस्तथासीत् स्वयमपि . . मेकश्शूलपाणेः पुरस्तात् ॥
निरगमदथ नत्वा कुम्भघोणेशमीशं नृपतिरुपरिविष्टस्तत्र नीत्वा च रात्रिं ।
गणितसमयवीक्षाक्लृप्तरागे जने यत् सरसि दुरितशान्त्ये . . . सन्निधत्ते ॥
अवि तकृतदेवागारसौधप्रकाशैरनुगतहरशैलानात्मभक्तावनार्थम् ।
हरविहितविहारान्तानसौ वीक्ष्य देशान् सलिलनिधिपुरन्ध्रीमासदत्सह्यकन्याम् ॥

* * * *

स्नपनविधिकृदस्यां पात्रदत्तार्थसार्थो नृपतिरुपगत श्रीरङ्गमोङ्कारशृङ्गम् ॥
फणिककुदिशयानं तं प्रणम्याम्बुजाक्षं फलमभजत दृष्टोस्तत्प्रसादेनसाकम् ॥

निजकुलजनुषाशानिर्जयादार्जितार्थै-
र्महिपतिरथ दृष्ट्वा मंगिदेवेन क्लृप्तम् ।
सदन(म ?) युतसालग्रामदात्राभिरामं
तदधिकमदितास्मै साभ्यसूयः किलासौ ॥

तमसिगजवनेशं प्राप्य नत्वा गिरीशं
न्यवसदथ तदग्रे श्रीनृसिंहास्त्रिरात्रम् ।
जगति यमधिजम्बूमूलमाराध्य लोको
भजति सकलजम्बूद्वीपमेकातपत्रम् ॥
सुशकुनकथितैष्यत्स्वेष्टसिद्धेस्ततोऽस्मा
न्निखिलबलनिकायैर्निर्गतश्चाग्रतोऽस्य ।
तुरगखुरजधूलीक्लृप्त . . . .
. . . . . पार्श्वैः पाण्ड्यभूपोऽक्षिलक्ष्यः ॥
स्वबलमथ सशङ्कं वीक्ष्य सोत्प्रासहास-
स्तदभिमुखमशेषं वारयत्येष यावत् ।
शरणमुपगतोऽग्रे तावदश्वस्य वेगा-
दनमदवनिपाल . . . . पाण्ड्यभूपः ॥
मलयशिखरवासी यस्य वंशोद्भवानाम्
अभिमतकृदगस्त्योऽप्यागता ताम्रपर्णी ।
निगलितजलदानान्निर्जराधीशमौलि-
र्वलयकषणचिह्नाद्भक्ति बाहापदानम् ॥
. . . . प्रीणयन्हस्तपद्मा-
दभयकृदुपकारालोकमात्रेण पाण्ड्यम् ।
दशभिरथ दिनैस्तद्दर्शिताध्वानगर्या-
मभजत मधुरायामात्तवासं महेशम् ॥

* * * *

दृढकुतुकमयासीत् दर्भशय्यापवित्रं दशवदननिहन्तुर्दक्षिणाम्भोधितीरम् ॥
अपि रघुकुलकेतुप्रेयसींयातुनेतुः स्वविषयमपि नेतुं . सनोत्पातकेतुः ।
जलनिधिपरिमातुर्मानदण्डो विधातुर्दिविषदुभयहेतुस्तेन दृष्टोऽथ सेतुः ॥

* * * *

अथ नृपतिरनंसीद्रामनाथाख्यमीशं स्फुरितमहिमकाशीपुण्यसाफल्यहेतुम् ।
द्रुहिणकुलजहत्यादोषशान्त्यै प्रणीतो रघुकुलजनुषा यः सैकतं यत्र लिङ्गम् ॥
तमभिलषितसिद्धिं प्रार्थयंस्तत्र दृष्टः सुशकुनमुखतो स्यादेष निर्याति यावत् ।
तदभिगमनभीतास्तं शरण्यं प्रयाताः धृतबहुविधदिव्योपायना द्वीपपालाः ॥

शरणमयति दत्तोपायनः सिंहलोसाविह विनमति जैनो लक्ष्यते पादनम्रः ।
इति निजसचिवोक्त्या मानयन्नेष राज्ञामभयमदित तेषामम्बुजाक्षावतारः ॥
जलधिसलिलमग्नोन्मग्नमुद्वीक्ष्य सेतुं दशरथसुत . . . ते स्म क्षितीशः ।
निजपटहनिनादान्निर्जितद्वीपपालं तदधिकममुमन्ये त्वद्भुतं मन्यते स्म ।
कतिपयदिवसैस्तत्काङ्क्षयासावनन्ते पवद(?)शयनमेत्य प्राणमत्प्राण . . ॥

* * * *

. . . . तत्र बन्दीकृतानाम्
विहतिरिह भटानां शारिकाणामिहासीत् ।
अपि रिपुबलबद्धो मन्त्रिणाऽमोचि भूपो
हयपदनिहितोऽग्रे रक्ष्यभावात्पदाती ॥

मदगजगति . . . तोरच्छदाङ्गस्तदजनि चतुरङ्गक्रीडितं सार्थमासीत् ॥
अतिबलमतिरङ्गः संहितं वीक्ष्य सिंहध्वनिपटुभटासिंहैः संहताशं हताशम् ।
रणभुवि नरसिंहो रंहसारुह्य वाहं गजकुलमिव सिंहः संहरन्बृंहति स्म ॥

* * * *

स चतुरमथ हुत्वा तत्र संशप्तकानां
नियुतमपि च भीष्मान् सुप्रतीकान्द्विषांश्च ।
शकलितगुरुकर्णो दुर्नयानां प्रतूर्णं
तदकलयदपार्थं पार्थिवः पार्थकीर्तिम् ॥
अयमथ शबरेन्द्रौ भिन्दुरायस्य बाहू
धनुषि च कृतशिक्षौ दक्षिणादक्षिणौ तौ ।
विजयसदृशवीर्यावुद्धतौ द्वावपि द्रा-
गचलयदपराब्धेरध्वरोधात्तयुद्धौ ॥

* * * *

दृष्ट्वा विद्रवतो दिशो दश भयादृत्तापयो द्वेषिणः
सोत्प्रायो नरसिंहभूपतिरसौ स्वानीकिनीं चाभवत् ।
श्रान्तां तत्र निवेश्य तत्क्षण . ते तीरेम्बुधेर्मन्दिरे
विश्रान्तो रचिताह्निकादिरनयत् वीराग्रणीस्तां निशाम् ॥

* * * *

Canto VI.

कुटवाचलेन्द्रतटवासिकलितोपदेशतः ।
सह्यभुवमपि विलङ्घ्य नरसिंहभूभृदथ नागमण्डलम् ॥ ८ ॥
अपवाह्य सैन्यानिवहेन कतिपयदिनान्यपश्रमः ।
तत्र कतिचन निधाय भटान् अगमच्छनैः पृथुगिरिं जिगीषया ॥ ९ ॥

* * * *

धवळितपत्रनवचन्द्ररुचि . . . भटविधूतचामरम् ।
तत्र नृपतिरवलोकितवान् छत्रं तृणीकृतजगत्त्रयं बलात् ॥ ११ ॥
करविधृतखड्गखेटकं निखिलैर्बलैः सह नृसिंहभूपतिः ।
चरमाङ्गसङ्गतनिषङ्गततिभिरथ शार्ङ्गपाणिभिः ।
साकमधिगततुरङ्गशतैः स्वबलैस्तमेनमरुधत् तुरुष्कराट् ॥ १३ ॥

* * * *

स विधाय तज्जनपदं च निगमनिरतं निजाज्ञया ।
तत्र गमितरजनिः सबलो निरगात्ततोऽपि च नृसिंहपार्थिवः ॥३८॥

* * * *

असुरांशसम्भवदशार्णव नृपतिबलमोहनादसौ ।
सार्थमकृत नरसिंहनृपो भुवनेऽत्र मोहनमुरारिकीर्तनम् ॥ ४९ ॥
विविधेषु तेषु विषयेषु विहितवसतिर्बलैस्समम् ।
हैमवतसविधभूमिमगमत् नरसिंहभूपतिरसह्यविक्रमः ॥ ४६ ॥

* * * *

अवगम्य तत्पदमगम्यामिति किल निवृत्तधीस्ततः ।
हैमवतकटकमेष जयी तदमुद्रयन्निव वराहमुद्रया ॥ ४८ ॥

* * * *

अपि तच्छिरस्सु निजपादमभयकरमर्पयन् स तैः ।
वेतिपुरमिति(?)पुरोगमितैः अयते स्म काशिनगरं नृपाग्रणीः ॥ ९१ ॥

* * * *

तदनु प्रसादमुदितः प्रमाणिभिः प्रवयोभिरभ्रसरितः पयोहरैः ।
क्षितिचक्रवर्तिपदसिद्धये नृपैः अभिषिक्त एष पुरहर्तुरग्रतः ॥ ५९ ॥

* * * *

Canto VII.

कामं ततः शात्रवकाकलोकमामन्त्रयन्नात्मजयानकेन ।
सीमन्तयन् प्रस्थितविन्ध्यशैलं सामन्तबृन्दैस्सह साळुवेन्द्रः ॥ ९ ॥

उग्रास्ति पञ्चाननविन्ध्यवासदुर्गाश्रयादिष्टगुहाः किलेति ।
वर्गाविमुक्तं द्विषतां नृपेण व्यग्राभयेनाप्यसतां विनाशे ॥ १० ॥

किम्मीरबङ्गाळकळिङ्गगौडहम्मीरसौराष्ट्रशकोष्ट्रपूर्वान् ।
उन्मूलयन्नुत्कलमप्युदग्रमुन्मूलितौजा जयति स्म राजा ॥ ११ ॥

आनर्तितानर्तकबन्धबृन्दः पिष्ट्वा महाराष्ट्रमपि प्रहृष्टः ।
काम्भोजजिन्निर्जितभोजराजः प्राग्ज्योतिषेशं जयति स्म सज्जम् ॥ १२ ॥

शार्ङ्गायुधान्वेगसरत्तुरङ्गसङ्घातिरूढान् दृढकङ्कटाङ्गान् ।
उदग्रकीडक्वधरांस्तुरुष्कान् उग्रान् सुरत्राणमुखानजैषीत् ॥ १३ ॥

आकर्णमाकृष्टधनुः सुपर्णो गोकर्णयूथं किल चूर्णयित्वा ।
गोकर्णराजं व्यरुचत्सुवर्णं विनिर्णयज्ञः शतपर्णनेत्रः ॥ १४ ॥

आलङ्कमामेरुनयप्रशस्त्यै कोलं निजाङ्कं कुलपर्वतेषु ।
कृत्वा निवृत्तः किल पादभाजां दत्ताभयोऽप्येष न तृप्तिमागात् ॥ १५ ॥

भद्राधिकोऽसावथ तीर्णतुङ्गभद्रापगो दुर्मदतुङ्गभद्रः ।
विद्रावयन् व्याधबलौघमात्म . . . पुनर्व्यतानीत् ॥ १६ ॥

* * * *

क्लृप्ताहारपरिग्रहो . . . रसां कृत्वा कवीन्द्रैस्सभां
सान्ध्यं कर्म विधाय मन्त्रितिलकैः सम्मन्त्र्य कार्यं समम् ।
उद्रोमाश्चमतीतयुद्धकथनावेशाच्च नम्रानगैः(नो?)
निर्णिद्रो नरसिंह एष नृहरेरंशोऽनय(त्तां नि)शाम् ॥ ४३ ॥

Canto VIII.

तं तादृगाशाजयिनं समेत्य विन्ध्याचलप्रान्तविहारभाजाम् ।
बृन्दाऽयाचन्त ततो मृगाणां सन्त्रासशान्तिं मुनयो वनस्थाः ॥ १ ॥

* * * *

आत्मांशुजालान्यभितो वितत्य निरस्य ऋक्षप्रकरं निमेषात् ।
भास्वानगात्पश्चिमसिन्धुतीरं रेवातटं श्रान्तहयश्च राजा ॥ १६ ॥

* * * *

कैश्चिन्नृपोऽथ कविभिस्सह कायमाने
काव्यानि दिग्जयकथाद्भुतमांसलानि ।
कर्णामृतानि रसयन् कविताधिराज्य-
. . . रसादनुभवन् रजनीमनैषीत् ॥ ६३ ॥

Canto IX.

अथ क्षितीशैर्विजितैरशेषैरासेव्यमानो धरणीवराहः ।
विलङ्घ्य मार्गं बहुभिः प्रयाणैः विष्णोः प्रियं वेङ्कटशैलमागात् ॥ १ ॥

* * * *

महीमहेन्द्रो दिशति स्म तस्मै महार्घरत्नं मकुटं नवीनम् ।
वक्षोमणिर्यन्महसा हतश्रीर्जातेन नूनं दिवसप्रदीपः ॥ ७ ॥

* * * *

निशम्य तस्येति वचोनुरूपं नृपालसिंहोऽतितरां प्रहृष्टः ।
आराधनायैव हरेर्निवासमैच्छन् नृपश्चन्द्रशिरोनगर्याम् ॥ २१ ॥

* * * *

विष्णुःप्रसन्नोऽयमिति क्षितीशो विभाव्य तस्मादवरुह्य शैलात् ।
शैलोपमंदानहरीसमेतम् ऐरावताख्यं गिरिमध्यरुक्षत् ॥ २३ ॥

* * * *

आरूढवाहतिलकानथ राजपुत्रा-
नाह्लादयन्नमृतवर्षिभिरक्षिपातैः ।
श्रान्तां सुवर्णमुखरीतटसीम्नि भूमि-
न्यावीविशदथ श्रमशान्तिहेतोः ॥ ३४ ॥

* * * *

Canto X.

तत्तत्कालविलोकनात्प्रमुदितः कृत्वाथ सान्ध्यं विधिं
कर्णायुष्यकरोक्तिभिः कविवरैः साकं रसान् सल्लपन् ।
अङ्गैः काव्यरसप्ररूढपुलकैरावेदयन्नात्मनः
साहित्यानुभवं नृसिंहनृपतिस्तत्रानयत्तां निशाम् ॥ ३४ ॥

Canto XI.

अथ वायुलिङ्गधरसात्कृताखिलद्रविणोऽपिशम्भुनिशिधीरधीरसौ ।
विदुषां चिकीर्षुरवनं विशाम्पतिः द्रविणैरभूजितनृपोपहारितैः ॥ १ ॥

सचिवस्तादिङ्गित . . . तनोत्ततस्सहसा सुवर्णमुखरीतटान्तरे ।
नगरीं वसन्तदिनदानहेतवे नवरत्नसालगृहभासुरां नवाम् ॥ २ ॥

* * * *

. . . . . . करहाटलाटपविरण्डकीकटैः ॥
अपलज्जितं तद . गूर्जरादिभिः धनमूर्जितं . . जगत्पतेः ।
लसति स्म यद्द्रविणराशिरुन्नतो निहितः पुरोऽस्य नृवरस्य राजभिः ॥ २८॥
शिवरात्रिदत्तधनतृप्तमृत्युजित्
प्रतिपादिताप्रतिमहेतिचापवत् ।
धनसंहतिं कनकशैलसन्निभाम्
अवलोक्य दानविधयेऽग्रतः कृताम् ॥ २९ ॥

* * * *

वस्त्राद्यश्च वसन्तदानविषये दत्तं महार्घं नृपैः
सर्वं तद्विदुषाश्चिकीर्षुरुचितत्यागं नृपः सत्वरः ।
सम्मर्दोद्यत . . . कृतिजरद्वेतिप्रहारत्रुटन्
क्ष्माभृद्रत्नकिरीटमांसलरवणात्कारं व्यभाङ्क्षीत्सभाम् ॥ ३९ ॥

Canto XII.

वाहाधिरूढोऽथ समं महीपैर्वसन्तदानत्वरया मनोज्ञाम् ।
प्राविक्षदिन्द्रप्रतिमप्रभावो नवां पुरीं तां नरसिंहराजः ॥ १ ॥

* * * *

इति विजिताष्टदिक्क्षितिपदत्तबहुद्रविणैः
मधुसमये चिकीर्षुरधिकं वरदानविधिम् ।
वितरणघोषणापटहमष्टदिशावसते-
रुपगमतार्थमेष समघोषयदर्थिततेः ॥ ६ ॥

Canto XIII.

आदाय वर्षवरवेषमशेषभूपैः अग्रेसरद्भिरवलोकनमात्रधन्यैः ।
आसेवितस्ततइतो निरगात्कवीनामातर्पणाय कुतुकी नरसिंहराजः ॥ १ ॥

* * * *

अम्भोधरं धिगविशेषविदं प्रदेशे यस्योत्तरे सद्दशावर्षणमूषरेऽपि ।
सर्वस्वदस्य शिवरात्रितिथौ तवेशो . मचलं विरचय्य हैमम् ॥ २७ ॥

* * * *

आकर्ण्य वाचमिति सादरमश्चितार्थामभ्यर्हणां विरचयन्नुचितामपुष्यै ।
अव्याजबन्धुरवति स्म महीमशेषाम् आश्चर्यहेतुचरितो नरसिंहराजः ॥ ३८॥

34

RĀMARĀJĪYAMU—ĀRAVĪṬI BUKKA AND HIS CHILDREN.

This extract from the Rāmarājīyamu deals with the descendants of Sōmadēva Rāja who lived during the reigns of Sāluva Narasimha and his immediate successors. Among these, Bukka is called the firm establisher of the kingdom of Sāḷuva Narasimha (Sāḷuva Narasimha-rājyapratiṣṭhāpanāchārya). He is also given other titles in praise of his bravery and munificence. His rule is said to have prospered on account of the service he rendered always to the God Venkaṭāchalapati. He married two wives Abbala Dēvi and Baḷḷā Dēvi. By Abbala Dēvi he had several sons of whom Singa was the eldest and he gave them the district of Nandēla (Nandyal) to rule. By his other wife Baḷḷā Dēvi he had a son called Rāma Rāja.

Rāma Rāja is said to have marched against the fort of Kandanavōl (Karnūl) which was in the occupation of a chief called Savāi and laid siege to it. Each unit of his army during this siege is said to have consisted of one elephant, 20 horses, 60 archers, 60 swordsmen and 60 spearsmen. Of such units there were 3,500 in his army. We do not know whether these numbers are accurate. He defeated Bibbi and capturing Kandanavōl made it his own capital. His relatives becoming jealous of him are said to have, at one time, commissioned a young boy to offer him poisoned water to drink. But when the boy hesitated he himself took it from him and drank it all. He overcame its effects, however, by the power of his devotion to God.

There is also a Birudagadyam (string of titles) attributed to this prince. From some of these we are able to get some historical information about him. He defeated the chief Kāsappa Oḍeya who had his headquarters at Ādavāni (Adōni) and drove him from the place. The name of this chief appears as Kācha in the work

Bālabhāgavatam. He is also said to have captured the army of the redoubtable Savāi and to have conquered the seven elements of royalty (Rājasaptānga) of Savāi Bibbi. We do not know whether the two names Savāi and Savāi Bibbi refer to the same individual. In the copperplate inscriptions of the descendants of this Rāma Rāja we find the word Savāi Sanskritised into Sapāda, Savāi in Hindustani and Sapāda in Sanskrit both mean one and one-fourth. Savāi is usually given as a title to Indian heroes when they show themselves of more than ordinary quality, e.g., Savāi Mādhava Rao, Savāi Jai Singh. It seems to be classed along with such titles as Immaḍi and Mummaḍi attached to names meaning respectively twice and thrice. But Ferishta in his work says that Savoyi was the name by which Yūsuf Adil Shah was known and was so called because he was born in a village of the name in Persia.

It is just possible that in one of the two places where the word occurs in the extract it refers to Yūsuf Adil Shah, and Kandanavōl might have been captured from him. We do not know whether Ferishta's derivation of the word is correct. Persons who can have had nothing to do with Persia at any time are given the title Savāi. For instance, the Moghul Emperor Akbar conferred the title upon a celebrated Jain Guru, Hīra Vijaya Sūri *, who visited his court and whom he honoured. Another title from the Gadyam says that Rāma Rāja captured seven hundred horse from a chief called Hallisusena (Ali Hussain ?).

Rāma Rāja married Lakkamāmba and by her had three sons Timma, Koṇḍa and Śrīranga. Of these Timma became governor of Avuku (Owk), Koṇḍa governor of Ādavani (Adōni); their respective descendants referred themselves to these places in describing themselves.

క. ఆరాజేంద్రుఁడు బుక్కధ
రారమణునిఁ గాంచెనతఁడు రాజకులసుధా
పారావార నిశాకరుఁ
డైరాజిలె నరసనక్ష్మారూఢి మెయిన్.

బిరుదగద్యము. జయజయ, స్వస్తిశ్రీ సంతత వేంకటాచలపతి చరణారవింద సేవాకందళిత సామ్రాజ్య సుఖోపభోగ, సాళువ నరసింహరాయ రాజ్యప్రతిష్ఠాపనాచార్య, శౌర్యగరిష్ఠ సకలకళావిశారద,

* Vincent A. Smith's Akbar, pp. 166-68.

దైనందిన వితరణ నానాదిగంతరాగతవనీపకజాల పరిపాలన గుణవిశేష, అసహాయశౌర్య, సుమేరుధైర్య, అష్టాదశవిద్యాప్రజ్ఞాప్రవీణ, రాజకులాభరణ, రాజరాజేశ్వర, పిన్నశౌరిరాజతనూజ, బుక్కరాజ, విజయాభవ, దిగ్విజయాభవ

సీ. ఆబుక్కరాజేంద్రుఁ డబ్బలదేవిబ
ల్లాదేవియను సతులనువరించి
యబ్బళదేవియం దాత్మజులను సింగ
విభుఁ డాదిగాఁగను వేడ్కఁ గాంచి
నందేలయొసగ నానందనులాపురిఁ
దమకును నిజరాజధానిగాఁగ
నేలుచుఁ గాలము నందేలపేరధరిత్రిఁ
దనరఁగఁ బుత్రపౌత్రాభివృద్ధి

గీ. నతిశయిల్లిగి మఱియును నానృపాలుఁ
డనఘతనుఁడు బల్లాదేవియందు రామ
భద్రవరలబ్ధ జనితు నక్షుద్రశౌర్య
భానునృపతేజు రామభూపాలుఁ గనియె.

సీ. మదకరి కొంకటికిర్వదిగజ్జములు గుజ్జి
మునకును విలుకాండ్రు మూఁ గురువిచ్చు
కత్తులవారికై కొఁడ్రట్లు వర్తిల్ల
నిట్టియేనుఁగులను జుట్టుమూఁడు
వేలయేనూఱును హృత్తితోనడపంగఁ
గందనోల్పాధిఁపఁగా దలఁచి
మొనఁద్రుంచిగట్టిగా ముట్టడిదిగెనవా
బిబ్బని మిక్కిలి యుబ్బణంచి

గీ. ప్రకటసప్తాంగములఁగొని రామవిభుఁడు
కందనోల్రాజధానియుఁగాఁగవసుమ
తియును నేలి మహాహవ దీక్షఁబూని
బలిమికలిమినాశావనీపకులఁ బెనుప.

చ. మగఁటిమికోర్వలేక దయమాలటుజ్ఞాతినియుక్తబుద్ధి చే
సగరతఁగన్నతీర్థమిషఁజాలక యర్భకుఁడున్నఁజూపిశ్రీ

నగధరనీవేదికరనిజనంబులు గస్థానసంతతిఁగ్రోలియా
సగరునిఁబోలి రామనృపచంద్రుఁడు చెందఁడు తద్వికాగముల్.

బిరుదగద్యము. జయజయ, స్వస్తిసమస్త సమరసమయ బలరజోమిళిత సప్తసాగర ఘుంఘుమిత కల్లోలజాల, శరణాగతపాల, హాల్లిసుసేనోల్లాసిత సప్తశత సైంధవగ్రహణపరాక్రమధుర్య, రత్నసానుస్థైర్య, దుర్వారతర సవ్వాయి సైనికహరణ, సవాబిబ్బిరాజ సప్తాంగహరణ మార్గచరణ, రణభయానక జయానకారవ ముఖరీకృత కులగిరిదరీనికర, పోషితావని సుకరప్రకర, నిరావాపాదః నీదుర్గనివాసికాసవుడయ దుర్మదఖలనిర్మథన, ధర్మధౌరేయ, దానరాధేయ, వీరరమాసమారోహణారంభసోపానదోస్స్తంభ, వాకరంభీనస సార్వభౌమారంభ, పరిపంథినృప పుండరీకాధిపరాజమండలకబళనవ్యగ్రిమోపగ్రమండలాగ్ర, సింహీకాతనూజ రామరాజ, విజయీభవ.

చ. సరసిజసద్మతోమిగులసాటగుఁతుణంతీతాంగియై
పరఁగినలకరమాంబను వివాహము బుకరన్నృపాలురామభూ
వరుఁడయి యాపులోమజయువాసవుఁబోలిమహోనురక్తిసు
స్థిరతరభోగభాగ్యములఁ దెప్పలఁదేలెను లకరమాంబతోన్.

క. ఆరామనృపతికిమహో
దారుఁడగు తిమ్మరాజు ధన్యుఁడుకొండ
క్ష్మారమణుఁడు బుధనుతస
చ్చారిత్రుఁడు రంగవిభుఁడు జనియించిరొగిన్.

క. ఆతిమ్మనృపతిభూకాం
తాతిలకంబై నయవుకుఁ దా నేలుచుఖ్
ఖ్యాతిగనప్పురిపేరన్
ప్రీతిని దనకులమువెలయఁ బెంపొందెమహిన్.

క. దీనావనుఁడౌ కొండమ
హీనాథుండాదవేల నేలుచు బరఁగెన్
దానను సుతులును దత్సం
తానంబాయాదవేనిథామముపేరన్.

క. ఆరాజన్యుల తమ్ముఁడు
శ్రీరంగాధీశ్వరుండు శ్రితసంరక్షా
ధౌరంధర్యముచేనా
శ్రీరంగాధీశుఁడనఁగ క్షితినుతిఁగాంచెఁ.

35

PĀRIJĀTĀPAHARANAMU.

[*By Nandi Timmana.*]

In the beginning of this Telugu pœm dedicated to the Emperor Krishna Rāya, the poet Nandi Timmana gives a short account of the family of his patron. In the family of Turvasu of the Lunar race was born a king by name Īśvara who excelled by his virtues even god Śiva, who is also called Īśvara. In the battle at Kandukūr which he fought with the cavalry of the Muhammadan ruler of Bēdar (Beḍandakoṭa) he caused their blood to flow in many streams. Īśvara married Lakkāmba and got a son Narasa, by her. This Narasa became a very great warrior. He was famous for his conquests and munificent gifts. He ascended the throne of Vijayanagara which was a mirror to the whole world. When the lord of the Kuntala (Vijayanagar) country was in trouble he exhibited his valour and captured the city of Vidyāpura (Vijayanagar). He killed the Persian (Muhammadan) ruler in the battle of Mānavadurga (Manvī). He captured the town of Madura after killing the Chola ruler, and exhibited his swordsmanship to the Heuṇa ruler of Seringapatam. He performed the sixteen sacred gifts at Rāmasētu.

Narasa had two wives Tippāmba and Nāgāmba through whom he got the sons Vīra Narasimha and Krishna Rāya.

క. ఉర్వీశమౌళియగునా
తుర్వసువంశంబునందు దుష్టారిభుజా
దుర్వారగర్వరేఖా
నిర్వాపకుఁడీశ్వరాఖ్యనృపతి జనించెఁ.

ఉ. రాజులనెత్తుటం బరశురాముఁడు వంతలుసేసె రెండుమూఁ
డేజగతిన్, గణింపనది యెంతటివిస్మయ! మబ్జినీసుహృ
త్తేజుఁడు కందుకూరికడఁ దిమ్మయయీశ్వరుచే జనించె ఘో
జిబెడందకోట యవనాశ్వికరక్తనదీసహస్రముల్.

క. శాశ్వతవిజయుఁడు తిమ్మయ
యీశ్వరనృపతికిని గౌరి కెనయగుతత్ప్రా
ణేశ్వరిలక్కాంబికకున్
విశ్వాతిగయశుఁడు నరసవిభుఁడుదయించెన్.

సీ. ఎవ్వాని విజయంబు లెఱిఁగించు శాసన
స్తంభంబులాశాంత శైలవితతు
లెవ్వానియరిగాఁపులే పారుకాళింగ
యవనాదివివిధ దేశాధినాథు
లెవ్వాని నిత్యదానైక విలాసంబు
లాగూఢతరతులాపూరుషంబు
లెవ్వాని చిరకీర్తి యింద్రలోకాంగనా
భోగినీగీతికా భోగపదము

తే. వాఁడు వొగడొందు సర్వసర్వంసహాధి
దేవతాముఖదర్పణద్విజయనగర
భద్రసింహాసనస్థుఁడున్నింద్రతేజుఁ
డీశ్వరాధిపునరసభూమీశ్వరుండు.

సీ. కుంతలేశ్వరుఁడు సికురుపడంగ విద్యాపు
రంబు సైకొని నిజప్రౌఢి నెరపెఁ
పారసీకునకు దుర్భరమానవత్వంబు
దొలఁగించె మానవదుర్గసీమ
చోళవల్లభునకు సురవధూమధురాధ
రములిచ్చి మధురాపురంబు గొనియె
శ్రీరంగపట్టణసీమ ఖడ్గనటీవి
నోదంబు హేయసేంద్రునకుఁ జూపె

తే. సతతసుతికెక్కె రామసేత్వంతరాళ
కలిత షోడశదాన విఖ్యాతయశుఁడు
మండలీకరమేఘమార్తాండబిరుదుఁ
డీశ్వరాధిపు నరసపృథ్వీశ్వరుండు.

క. ఆనరసమహీమహిళా
జానికిఁ గులసతులు పుణ్యచరితలు తిప్పాం

బానాగాంబిక లిరువురు
దానవదమనునకు రమయు ధరయునుబోలెన్.

క. వాకలలోఁ దిప్పాంబకు
మారుఁడు పరిపంథికంధి మంథాచలమై
వీరనరసింహరాయఁడు
వారాశిపరీతభూమి వలయంబేలెన్.

36

ACHYUTARĀYĀBHYUDAYAM

[*By Rājanātha Kavi.*]

In the beginning of this historical poem dealing with the life and victories of Achyutarāya there is a short account of his predecessors. In the Lunar race was a king by name Timma who had a son called Īśvara who was a great warrior and who 'had set his foot upon the heads of his enemy kings'. By his wife Bukkama Īśvara had two sons Narasimha and Timma. Of these Narasimha was famous for his heroic deeds even from his youth. He captured the fort of Mānava (Manuva ?) Durga from its Muhammadan ruler and gave it back to him. He laid a bridge across the Kaveri and captured the town of Seringapatam. He then marched against Madura and, defeating and killing its Marava ruler in a battle, captured the place. He then defeated in battle a chief called Konēṭirāja who opposed him with his elephant hordes. He made the city of Vidyāpura his capital. He had three queens who were called Tippāmba, Nāgamāmba and Obamāmba. Of these by his wife Tippāmba he got a son called Vīra-Narasimha, by Nāgamāmba Krishna Rāya and by Obamāmba, Achyuta Rāya.

नालीकिनीनायकवद्धहेषु नीहारभूमी धरवन्नगेषु ।
वलासुहृद्धारणवद्गजेषु तेषु प्रतीतोऽजनि तिम्मभूपः ॥ २३ ॥
प्रतिक्षमापावलिपर्यटन्त्या वीरश्रियो विस्मयहेतुबाहुः ।
श्रीतिम्मभूपाज्जितभूस्ततोऽभूद्यशोधनादीश्वरभूमिपालः ॥ २९ ॥
क्रमादभूतामथ बुक्कमायां नृसिंहतिम्मक्षितिपालसिंहौ ।
प्रतीकवन्तावित दोःप्रतापयशोगुणावीश्वरभूवलारेः ॥ २७ ॥

आरभ्य बाल्यादजनि प्रजानामानन्दहेतुर्नरसावनीन्द्रः ।
प्रौढोऽर्भको वा पतिरुत्पलिन्याः प्रमोदनत्वे परिहीयते किम् ॥ २८ ॥
महीपतिर्मानिवनामदुर्गं शकाधिनाथेन समं गृहीत्वा ।
स्फुटीचकारास्य पुनर्वितीर्य शार्यं तथौदार्यमवार्यचर्यम् ॥ २९ ॥
प्रायोऽर्णवे सेतुकृतोऽवतारः प्राग्जन्मसंस्कारवशादिवैषः ।
सेतुं विधायाम्भसि सह्यजायाः श्रीरङ्गपूर्वां नगरीं जहार ॥ ३० ॥
कंसं यथा कैटभजिद्बलेन समन्वितः सैनिकमल्लहन्ता ।
मदप्रवृत्तं मरवं मथित्वा महीमहेन्द्रो मधुरामहार्षीत् ॥ ३१ ॥
महेन्द्रलोकं मरवाय दत्वा मध्येसमीकं मधुरां स जह्रे ।
महीयसामेष महीपतीनां नयो विपक्षेष्वपि नान्यथा स्यात् ॥ ३२ ॥
क्रुधापतन्तं सह कुञ्जरौघैः कोनेटिराजं क्षुभितान्यसैन्यः ।
जग्राह पाणौ जगदेकवीरो जयाब्धिकन्यामपि जन्यभूमौ ॥ ३३ ॥
प्रयाणमाशाविजयाय तस्य प्रायो गृहप्राङ्गणभूविहारः ।
दानान्यहो षोडश विश्रुतानि जातानि दैनंदिनमेव कृत्यम् ॥ ३४ ॥
वस्वोकसारेव विभोर्वसूनां वलाभियातेरमरावतीव ।
विद्यापुरीविस्मयभूरमुष्य विशिष्य राज्ञोऽजनि राजधानी ॥ ३९ ॥
तिस्रो नृपस्येत्यभवन्माहिष्याः तिप्पाम्बिका तासु च नागमाम्बा ।
पट्टाभिषिक्ता पतिदेवतानाम् उत्तंसभूषामणिरोबमाम्बा ॥ ९२ ॥
तिप्पाम्बिकायां द्विजसंसदेऽभूत् विख्यातिमान्वीरनृसिंहरायः ।
नागाम्बिकायां नरसावनीन्दोः कीर्त्याकरोऽजायत कृष्णरायः ॥ ५३ ॥
अनन्यसामान्यतया धरायां दानेन तौ ख्याततरावभूताम् ।
आद्यस्तयोर्दैन्यमुषा द्विजानामन्योऽपि वैगुण्यमुषा परेषाम् ॥

37

ĀMUKTAMĀLYADĀ

[*By Krishṇa Dēva Rāya.*]

After giving the genealogy of his family down to Narasa Krishna Rāya in this work says that he had two wives Tippāmba and Nāgamāmba by whom he had two sons Vīra-Narasimha an

Krishna Rāya respectively. Narasa conquered all the countries and defeated their rulers, and was a patron of poets. His son Vīra-Narasimha is also said to have destroyed his enemies and brought the whole kingdom under his umbrella.

సీ. అంబోధివసన విశ్వంభరావలయంబు
తనబాహుపురిమారతకముఁ జేసెఁ
గకుబంతనిఖిలరాణ్ణికరంబుఁ జరణమం
జీరంబు సాలభంజికలఁ జేసె
మహనీయనిజవినిర్మలయశస్సరసికిఁ
గగనంబుఁ గలహంసకంబుఁ జేసె
నశ్రాంతవిశ్రాణనాసారలక్ష్మికిఁ
గవికదంబముఁ జాతకములఁ జేసె

గీ. నతిశితకృపాణకృత్తమత్తారివీర
మండలేశసకుండల మకుటనూత్న
మస్తమాల్యపరంపరా మండనార్చి
తాశ్వరుండగు నారసింహేశ్వరుండు.

తే. ఆనృసింహప్రభుండు దిప్పాంబవలన
నాగమాంబికవలన నందనులఁ గాంచె
వీరనరసింహరాయభూవిభునినచ్యు
తాయతాంశజు శ్రీకృష్ణరాయనిన్.

క. వీరనృసింహుఁడు నిజభుజ
దారుణకరవాలపరుష ధారాహతవీ
రారియగుచు నేకాతప
వారణముగ నేలెఁ ధరనవారణ మహిమన్

38

RĀYAVĀCHAKAMU—ACCOUNT OF KRISHNA RAYA'S CAMPAIGNS.

This is an account of the reign of the Emperor Krishna Dēva Rāya of Vijayanagar. It is written in colloquial Telugu prose. It purports to be written to the governor of a province under

Krishna Dēva Rāya, by name Viśvanātha Nāyanayya by an agent (sthānāpati) of his at the imperial headquarters. The chief referred to in this connexion seems to be Viśvanātha Nāyaka, son of the general Nāgama Nāyaka, who fought successfully against his own father when he rebelled, and was eventually appointed as viceroy of the Pāndya country. The account of Krishna Rāya, as it is given in this work, agrees in the main with that of the poem Krishna Rāya Vijayam of Kumāra Dhūrjaṭi dedicated to the later Vijayanagar prince Chinna Venkaṭa Rāya. As in the latter work, the father of Krishna Dēva Rāya is called Vīra-Narasimha instead of Narasa and he is immediately succeeded by his son Krishna Dēva Rāya. Thus both the works Vīra-Narasimha, the elder brother of Krishna Rāya, who preceded him on the throne for some years. Both these works may have borrowed their story from the same source, or one may have been modified from the other, but we cannot at present say anything decisive about this.

After examining his treasury and army, and making all the necessary preparations for the expedition against his enemy with the assistance of the able minister Appāji (Sāḷuva Timma), Krishna Dēva Rāya entertained all the Boya nobles (Doras) and the men of the eighteen Kappanas (provinces ?) at a grand feast. He then ordered them to proceed to a distance of about three āmaḍas (30 miles) into the enemy territories and gather from there men, cattle, sheep and goats that they may not be available to the enemy. Leaving a company of horse to guard the city along with the minister Sāḷuva Timma and ordering all the subordinate chiefs (Doramannelu), horsemen, elephants, mahouts and the people of the Viniyogams (divisional officers ?), he directed the war-drum to be sounded and with them set out from the city.

He then proceeded against the fort of Śivasamudram which belonged to the chieftainship of Ummattūr and fought with Ganga Rāja, the chief of the place. The place was reduced after a single day's fighting. Leaving there his own servants he proceeded towards Śrīrangapaṭṭanam. He examined the fortifications of the place and worshipping the God Ādi-Ranganāyaka proceeded towards Ikkēri Ārangam ? There he inspected the troops of Sukkula Nāyaka. After that he directed his army to proceed towards the frontiers of Vijayāpura (Bijapur). On hearing of Krishna Dēva Rāya's march the garrisons of the several frontier forts were much afraid and began gradually to desert their stations. Therefore he easily introduced his own garrisons into such forts as

Rāchūru (Raichur), Mudikallu (Mudkal), Addanki * and Ādavani, and, by forced marches, capturing at the rate of one fortress a day, approached the frontiers of Golkonda.

There the three Muhammadan Sultans (Adil Shah of Bijapur, Kuṭb Shah of Golkonda and Barid Shah of Bidar) had collected their troops, and crossing the river (Krishna) had fixed their camp on its southern bank with 100,000 horse and a thousand elephants. The emperor also learnt from his spies their respective strength, and heard of the atrocities they had committed in his territory. Krishna Rāya was very angry on hearing of the atrocities of the Muhammadans in his own territory to the south of the Krishna. He summoned from among his Amaranāyakam generals, the chief Pemmasāni Ramalinga † and telling him about the Muhammadan advance to the south of the Krishna consulted him how best to act under the circumstances. The general Pemmasāni Ramalinga said that it was no serious matter, and promised that, if he were entrusted with the attack, he would march on their camp and cut the ropes of their tents. If, at a given signal, the emperor's troops attacked the enemy their camp could be broken and the enemy routed. Moreover he impressed upon the emperor the fact that the Muhammadan soldiers coming from cooler climates could not stand and fight with the emperor's soldiers during the hot summer.

Pleased with the general's reply, the emperor presented him with betel and nut in token of his approval of his leading the attack. Rāmalinga returned to his troops and told them the Emperor's Commission. He impressed upon them that the opportunity had arrived for showing their gratitude to the emperor for having maintained them, to fight that they may win high favour here and everlasting glory hereafter. So saying he exhorted all brave men in his camp to follow him, and, asking the rest to stay away, he marched towards the enemy's camp. He was followed by eighty thousand redoubtable swordsmen 'who march to the battle as to a marriage.' To oppose these heroes the enemy concentrated sixty thousand

* This Addanki cannot be the well known place of the name. It is situated in the south of the modern district of Guntūr to the north of the Nellore border. It must be placed not on the Bijapur but on the Golkonda frontier.

† He seems to have been an ancestor of the general Pemmasāni Timma who was the Viceroy of Koṇḍavīḍu under Aḷiya Rāma Rāya, and was the chief in whose jurisdiction the village Garikipāḍu which was granted to the famous philosopher and logician Annambhaṭṭa lay. For the text of this inscription *vide* Mackenzie Manuscripts, the inscriptions from Garikipāḍu.

broadswordsmen assisted by 10,000 well caparisoned horses and one thousand elephants. They first attacked the elephants and the cavalry of the enemy with their broadswords and their javelins. After a short fight 4,000 horses of the enemy were killed. He then proceeded against the rest and managed to kill 4,000 out of the 60,000 horsemen. Rāmalingama Nāyuḍu then managed to approach the tents and give the signal to Krishna Dēva Rāya's main army by cutting the ropes. Upon this the triumphal band of the emperor struck up, and the emperor Krishna himself started on his state elephant with all the royal insignia, closely followed by 120 *ghaṭṭams* of elephants, 60,000 horse and 500,000 infantry in a body. Simultaneously with this pressing attack of Krishna on this side, the river Krishna rose in floods on the other, and flowed full to the brim. When the attack was directed against the elephant corps, the elephants not being able to stand the pressure of the attack and suffering very much on account of the summer heat, were attracted by the cool breeze from over the flooded Krishna, ran to the river and fell into the water. The remaining troops also could not stand the pressure and began to escape across the river by swimming. Most of the people that thus tried to escape lost their lives in the flood.

Only a third of the troops remained on the southern bank of the river. The elephants could not be pursuaded to leave the cool waters and so the mahouts over them thought it unwise to stay longer and themselves escaped. The Muhammadan soldiers of the three kingdoms crossed the river on elephants and barges, and retreated respectively to their capitals Bijapur, Golkonda and Ahmadnagar.

Krishna then came to the edge of the river and ordered the capture of all the ownerless elephants and horses, and of the tent equipage and bands of the enemy's camp. He then held court along with his minister Appāji and the generals Ayyamarusu, Koṇḍamarusu and Bācharusu; and poets like Mukku Timmanna, Allasāni Peddanna and Mādayagāri Mallanna. When the emperor asked them to describe to him the day's victory Mukku Timmanna composed a verse the substance of which is "O! Krishna Rāya, your Muhammadan enemies broke and fled at the mention of your name, and their elephants turned and fled seeing in you the God Vishṇu, the rescuer of the lord of elephants".

The ministers advised Krishna to cross to the other side of the Krishna only after the rainy season was over and the floods had subsided. Meanwhile they advised him to reduce the fortresses of

Udayagiri, Kandūr? (Kandukur), Koṇḍavīḍu, Bellamkoṇḍa, Nāgārjunakoṇḍa belonging to the enemy from any one of which he could attack him on the flank after getting into the interior of the enemies' territory. The emperor accepted the advice and started on the campaign. Then the manuscript gives two triumphal verses which his court poets composed at his starting.

He marched by way of Gutti and Gaṇḍikoṭa to Udayagiri and reduced a fortress called Hurmatti * at the place. On occupying it the emperor was surprised that the enemy should have surrendered the fort when they had it so well provisioned. He then placed his own garrison in the fort under the general Kampanna and proceeded to Kandūr (Kandukur). The garrison at this place left the fort when they heard of the approach of the emperor's army. The emperor was about to proceed to Koṇḍavīḍu when his agents reported to him that the garrisons in the several fortresses were afraid when they heard that Krishna was proceeding against them, and began to desert in bodies. It was also reported that Boya (the hunter caste) chieftains and the chiefs of the eighteen Kappaṇas were scouring the whole country and giving the people great trouble.

Krishna Dēva Rāya marched to Koṇḍavīḍu and laid siege to the fortress. The garrison in the place could not defend themselves and after one and half days surrendered the fort. The general Koṇḍayya (Rāyasam Koṇḍamarusu?) was placed in garrison there. Then the army was directed to Vinukoṇḍa which place also soon surrendered. The general Bhāskarayya (Rāmaya Mantri Bhāskara) was posted to govern the fort with a garrison. The emperor then reduced the forts of Bellamkoṇḍa and Nāgārjunikoṇḍa and placed there garrisons under the generals Vīrabhadrayya and Ayyalayya. Krishna then marched into the enemies' territory and approached the town of Ahmadnagar (Ahmadabad-Bidar). He easily captured the outskirts of the place and fought a pitched battle with the enemy's horse outside the city. In a very short time 2,800 of the enemy's cavalry were destroyed and the emperor gained a complete victory. The garrison within the fort thought

* According to this manuscript Hurmattu appears to be the name of a fortress near Udayagiri. But in the Krishna Rāya Vijayam the word occurs in the phrase ఒకహుర్మత్తున meaning in one hurmattu and refers to the conquest of Śivamsamudram. It there appears to be an adverb. The proper meaning of hurmatti is not known and there is no fort of that name near Udayagiri so far known.

they could not stand a siege by Krishna, and in order to avoid the storming of the fort, evacuated it and retreated to the interior. Krishna Rāya thus got possession of the fort very easily and directed the fortifications to be destroyed. He then ordered that castor-seeds should be sown where the fortifications stood and proceeded towards the frontier of the kingdom of the Gajapati.

The minister Appāji and other courtiers advised the emperor that he had already defeated all his enemies and annexed portions of their territories. It was not desirable that he should enter further into the interior of the Gajapati's country as he might be attacked on the flank by the Muhammadans who might succeed in cutting off his supplies. But Krishna Rāya disregarded this counsel and continued his march. When his army was marching through the ghats (kanumas) it was attacked by a chief (Chitāpra) Chitāph Khān * at the head of 60,000 archers. There was a severe battle between the two armies, but Chitāph Khān's archers were easily hemmed in by the army of the emperor, a company of which went over the ghats and attacked Chitāph Khān in the rear. The army of Chitāph Khān was defeated after a loss of 23,000 archers and 4,000 horse and retreated from the place. Krishna Rāya left 30,000 of his own troops to guard the passes, marched on capturing the districts of the Gajapati's kingdom and encamped at Poṭlūri Simhādri (Simhādri Poṭṭunūr).

After having advanced so far, Krishna Rāya learnt of the great preparations made by the Gajapati and his sixteen Mahāpātras to repel his army. Fearing that their opposition might be much stronger than anything which he had met with so far, he was doubtful of success and consulted with the minister Appāji privately. In the consultation the minister advised the emperor that he could defeat the enemy only by a stratagem. With the consent of the emperor the minister despatched some chests full of gold and valuables to the sixteen Pātras along with secret letters. The letters said that the boxes were despatched to them according to the agreement between the Pātras and Krishna Rāya, and exhorted them to act up to it by deserting the Gajapati during the

* A chief of this name is known to us in Warrangal about the year A.D. 1503. A record of his in the fort (No. 110 of 1902, Madras) states that he belonged to the Bhogikula (Nāgavamsi?), and that he conquered Warrangal from the Muhammadans reinstating there Pānchālarāya. It is probably this chief of Warrangal that is referred to above. It is difficult in the face of this to accept Col. Haig's statement that he was a Muhammadan. Vide Land marks of Dekhan History, pp. 60 and 85.

battle. Some of these boxes of presents were captured by Gajapati's messengers and taken to him. When he read the contents of the letters and saw the treasure that accompanied them he began to fear for his own safety. He escaped from his camp without being noticed by anybody, and went a long distance to the north.

When the sixteen Pātras went to court the next day and learnt about the flight of their master they retired to their respective fortresses. Getting to know of this Krishna Rāya appointed his own followers to guard the Gajapati's palace and the city. He planted a pillar of victory at Poṭṭunūri Simhādri. Then he summoned before him the minister of the Gajapati and said that he had invaded the country for victory rather than permanent conquest and was prepared to give back his kingdom to the Gajapati and return to his own capital. The minister informed his master about this and the Gajapati returned to his capital and apologised to Krishna Rāya for having fought with him. The sixteen Pātras were also sent for and they also begged pardon of him.

Highly pleased with their action Krishna Dēva Rāya mad them presents of gold and jewels. The Gajapati gave his daughter Jaganmohini * to Krishna Rāya in marriage and made him presents of valuable gems, ornaments, elephants, horses, scents, etc. He also returned the boxes containing the treasure which Appāji sent to the Pātras in order to deceive him. He ceded all the country to the south of the river Krishna to Krishna Dēva Rāya as the dowry of his daughter.

After the marriage festivities were over Krishna Dēva Rāya started back to his own territory escorted by the Gajapati's minister and officers. When the rulers of Golkonda, Bijapur and Ahmadnagar learnt of this they thought that they could never more defeat Krishna Rāya and meeting him on his way concluded peace with him after apologising for past misconduct. When he went as far as Tirupati in his own empire he learnt that the Muhammadans of Kalyan and Gulbarga showed signs of hostility. He marched to Gulbarga and reduced the fort after capturing 6,000 horse at the place. He then appointed Gujjari Kalyāṇa Rao as the governor of the place and returned to Tirupati.

* This marriage is also referred to in the Krishna Rājavijayam and the preface to the commentary on Prabodha Chandrodaya by Krishna Rāya's general Nādinḍla Gopa. The five verses called Tukkā Panchakam are said to have been composed by the daughter of the Gajapati when she found that the emperor's love to her had waned. In this her name is given as Tukkā.

Āt Tirupati he performed all the sixteen *dānas* as laid down in the *śastras*, and presented to the god valuable jewels and gold. He also had copper statues of himself and his two queens Tirumala Dēvi and Chinnā Dēvi, cast and set them before the god of the place that they may signify his constant worship. He thence moved to Kāḷahasti where he also made large grants to the god on the twelfth day of the bright fortnight of Aśvayuja in the year Śrīmukha.* He also constructed at Kāḷahasti several choultries. He then marched to the south visiting on his way all the chief temples. He is said to have visited the god Vandīśvara (?) who was worshipped by the Tripuras (Rakshasas). Among the places that he visited were Aḷagar Guḍi (Aḷagar Koil or Tirumālirunjolai near Madura), Madura, Srīvilliputtūr, Karuvanailūr, Śankaranārāyanarkoil, Dakshiṇa Kāśi (Tenkasi), Trikūṭāchalam (Kuṟṟālam), Agastyaparvatam (Podiyil hill), Gajēndramoksham (?) Śālivaṭam (Tinnevelly), Tōtādri (Vānamāmalai), Tirukkurunguḍi, Kanyākumari (Cape Comorin), Śrīkandūr (Tiruchendur), Nava Tirupati (near Aḷvār Tirunagari). His grants to the god Sundarēśvara and Mīnākshi at Madura, to the goddess Āndāḷ of Śrīvilliputtūr were specially valuable. He constructed the big tank at Śrīvilliputtūr and endowed a lakh of Māḍas towards the cost of the Manṭapa in its centre and the stone work. At Agastyaparvata he constructed a new Gopura (tower), and at Tinnevelly the Tāmrasabha, a big stone hall covered over with sheets of copper. He founded a village called Krishnarāyasamudram near Tinnevelly.

Krishna Rāya then went to Sētu (Rāmēśvaram) and worshipped the god there. Thence he crossed over in barges (Kāḷams) to Dhanushkoṭi. There he washed the blood *stains* off his sword and performed three Tulābhāras (weighing against gold). He stayed there for three days and thence went to Gokarṇam. After worshipping at the place he returned to his capital Vijayanagar by way of Seringapatam after a long absence. There he made very costly presents to the gods Viṭṭhala and Virūpāksha, and held his darbar on an auspicious day with all his relations and ministers. There he made Appāji sit upon a costly carpet (ratnakambaḷi), and had his Svarṇābhishēkam and Ratnābhishēkam performed. He made him presents of costly jewels and perfumery. The other generals also he rewarded each according to his merit.

---

* This is incorrect. Śrīmukha corresponds to the year A.D. 1512—3 and is much too early to be correct.

కనుక అదేరీతిని అప్పాజిరాయలవారితోను తురకాణ్యాంమీద దళమెత్తేటప్పుడు బోయదొరలందరినిన్ని రప్పించి పదునెనిమిది కప్పణాలవారినిన్ని నగరఖిందు బెట్టించి హరిబాణం కొమాళ్లతోను కార్యముఖానకు తురకాణ్యం సీమలోను ముణకలుగా బోయి దిగి మూడేశి ఆమడదూరం సారిసరాళంపోయి మనుష్యుల, పసలం, ప్రాయలు, గొర్రెలు, మేకల, గుర్రాల వుండ్డకుండ్డా కొళ్లబెట్టమనిన్ని యెదిరితోడట్టు, సకల సన్నాహములతోడట్టు, బయలుమెరశి వెలిగుడారమునకు వచ్చి నిలిచి దొరమన్నీలనున్ను, రవుతుల, మావత్తులనున్ను, వినియోగం పైకంవార్లనున్ను, మునుపటివారు వెనకటివారు, యెడవంకఱవారలనున్ను అందరినిన్ని రప్పించుక వారివార్లతో మాటపలుకులు ఆడి మీమీ స్తోమములతో ఆయత్తపాటుతో రమ్మని బలవంకఱం అమరనాయకంవార్లతోనున్ను నగరికై జీతంవారితోనున్న . . . . కొంత్త గుర్రం రాణువనున్ను విజయనగరపట్టణమునకు రక్షణియ్యముగ్గా సాళువ తిమ్మరసయ్యగారినింన్ని పట్ణమంద్దు వుంచ్చి దండుయాత్రకు జయధ్వనిగా దిక్కుల పిక్కటిల్లెటంద్దుకు భేరితాడనము శేశి డమామిటోకించమని ఉత్తరువు శేశి రౌతులకు మావుత్తులకు అమరనాయకంవార్లను, అల్లుండ్లు, కొమాళ్లకు, రాజులకు, జట్లకు, కంమ్మనాయకులకు అందరినిన్ని పయనంజెప్పి రమ్మని కటకాలవారికి వుత్తరువు యిచ్చి తామున్ను భోజనం జేసుకొని మూడోనగారాటోకించ్చమని ఆనతిచ్చి గుర్రంయెక్కికొని పయనంగతుల కదలి వుమ్మత్తూరు శివసముద్రానకు వచ్చి గంగారావు వూడెమమీంద కార్యము శేశి వుదరదోలి ఆ స్థలాలు వకఱ్ణాటనే సాధించ్చి అకఱడ వూడిగాలవార్లను వుంచ్చి అంద్దునుండ్డి శ్రీరంగపట్ణం కోటకై చని కోటకొత్తళములు జూచి మీద ఆదిరంగనాయకుల శేవించ్చి యికెర్రి ఆరంగానకు (?) వచ్చి సుకుఱలనాయడినినాయడిమూకలను జూచి విజయాపురం సరదుల నడువమనంగ్గా సరుదు స్థలాలవుండ్డి గురిమనుష్యులనుంన్ను దుర్గాలవుండే రాణువనున్ను నిర్వహించలేక విడిచి పారిపోసాగిరి. కనక అందుండి రాచూరు, ముదికల్లు, అద్దంకి, ఆదవని ఇవి మొదలైన స్థలాదులకు తాణ్యములు వుంచి దినమొకఱటిగాసారి నడవగా స్థలములవుండ్డేవారు మునకలుగానె వచ్చె దళాన్ని జూచి పారిపోయిరి గనక సాధించిన స్థలములకు తాణ్యామువుంచ్చి గోలకొండ్డవారి సరదు స్థలాలకై నడవంగా అకఱడ

మూడు తెగల రౌతులున్ను యెదురించి యేరుదాటివచ్చి మోర్చా వేసి పాళ్యముదిగినారు గనక ఆ వర్తమానం తెలిసిన వేగర్లు వచ్చి రాయలదేవునితోను తురకలు లక్షగుర్రాలుతోడట్టున్ను వేయియేనుగులతోడట్టున్ను కృష్ణదాటివచ్చి పాళ్యందిగినారని వారికలిమి బలములున్ను వారి పృథుతెలున్ను పలుకరించ్చి వారి శీమలో మనతెగల వార్లులోజొచ్చి మూడామడకు మూడామడవుండే గ్రామాదులు కొళ్లబెట్టేదిన్ని పాతరలు శోధించి ధాన్య దవసములు యెత్తేదిన్ని గృహస్థుల యిండ్లలోజొచ్చిపోయి ముందువెనక దాంచియుంచిన చందాన నిక్షేపములు యెత్తేదింని వూళ్లుపల్లెలు కాల్చేదిన్ని పసలం, ప్రాయలు, మేకలు, గొర్రెలు, గుర్రాలున్ను పట్టుకవచ్చి కాసుకు వకటిగా అమ్మేదిన్ని యీ గీతిగా నిర్నామం చేసేదిన్ని దుర్గములలో వుండే వార్లెల్లా జతనమై వున్నారనిన్ని విన్నపం శేయంగా రాయలవారు విని తురకలు కృష్ణవేణిదాంటి వచ్చి డేరిజా వేసిదిగేట్టా అని ఆగ్రహించుకొని అమరనాయకం వారలలో పెమ్మసాని రామలింగమనాయణ్ణి బిలిచి తురకలు కృష్ణవేణిదాంటివచ్చి డేరిజా వేశి పాళ్యందిగినాగట యిందులకు యేరీతున నడవవలెనో అని అడిగినందులకు తురకల కార్యమనంగా యెంతమాత్రం దేవరవారి ప్రతాపమువల్ల డేరిజాతాళ్లు తెగకోశేను. అప్పుడు భేరితాడనం శేశి నడిస్తేను తురకలు మూడుతెగలవారున్ను పటాపంచలై విరిగి యధాయథలై తమతమ స్థలాదులకు పొయ్యేటట్టు శేశేను. యిదిగాక యీ గ్రీష్మకాలాన దగదప్పలకుతాళి వాండ్లు నిలువలేరు. అని విన్నవంశాయుగా తనకు శెలవులకు యిమ్మనగా రాయలవారు చాలా సంతోషబడి రామలింగమనాయనికి వట్టీలుయిచ్చి అంపుగా రామలింగమనాయడు వెలువడినివచ్చి తనతెగ కమ్మదొరతనాల వారినందరినిన్ని రప్పించుక వారలకున్ను చెయ్యెత్తి మొక్కి యిన్నాళ్లును రాయలవారి సంబళములు బ్రసాదించి బ్రతికితిమి. యేలినవారికి యిప్పుడు కార్యాసరవి కలిగి అనిమొనకు వచ్చి యెదటి వారిమీదికి నడువమని బహుమానం వక్కలాకులు యిచ్చి వంపగాం వస్తిమి. యీ బహుమానంమీది గనక మిమ్మునను అండి మానువములున్ను ముందరిక కమ్మకులం వారికి బ్రతుకులున్ను ప్రతిష్టలున్ను కీర్తి మాటవాసులు కలుగజేసేటందులకున్ను స్వర్గాదిభోగములు అనుభవించేటందులకున్ను తనతోకూడా నడశేవారెల్లా నడువండ్డా తకిరినవారెల్లా వారులో నిలువుడా అని తొక్కినడునగా ఆయన సంతరించిన యెనబైవేల చివ్వలవారున్ను రణపెండ్లి కొడుకులై యిక్కడి ఆశపాశలు

విడిచి కయ్యమందేదే వియ్యమందేదిగా యెంచ్చి అనిమీది దృష్టిచేత రామలింగమనాయని వెంబడిని నడువంగా తురకలు యీ వార్తలువిని డెరిజావద్ద జీరా సంజ్జోగంత్తో విత్సుకత్తుల రౌతులు అరవైవేలున్ను వారినిచుట్టుక నింఢ్డు సంజ్జోకం గుఱ్ఱాలు పదినేలకున్ను వార్లను అనుభవించుకయుండె మదహత్తులు వెయ్యింటికిన్ని యీ రీతిని డెరిజావద్దవుంచ్చి మూడుతేగల తురకలున్ను తమతమ పాళ్యములో ఆ యత్తపాటుతో జాగ్రతకలిగియుండగా రామలింగమనాయుడు తురకల పాళ్యంవారి సమీపానకుపోగానే గుఱ్ఱాన్ని కత్తికేడం తీసుకొని యేనుగల బారుమీద శైల తటమునకు లంఘించు సింహ్వాపుపిల్లల చందానతొక్కిఱ నడిచి మదహత్తీల తొండముల ఖండములుగా నరికి మావటీలను యీటెలమీద కుమ్మితోయగా యేనుగల వారిమీందికి నడవగలవారు గుఱ్ఱాల పక్కెఱలెత్తి కురచ యీటెలతోనున్ను పిడి యీటెలతోనున్నూ పంది బల్లములతోనున్ను గుచ్చి తోశేదిన్ని దోసకాయల చంద్దానవేటారు తునకలుగా నరికేదిన్ని యీరీతు నొప్పించగా గుఱ్ఱాలవారు వెనుకముంద్దై పారసాగెను. అప్పుడు నాలుగువేల గుఱ్ఱాలు చాపకట్టుగా బడగా అటు వెనుక విచ్చుకత్తుల రవుతులమీద నడిచి జగడమియ్యాగా సరిచావులుగా ఆరువేలకు నాలుగువేల రవుతులుగాపడిరి. అంతట రామలింగమనాయుడు జిరీజు (?) త్రాళ్లు తెగకోయించ్చగా డిరిజా నేలకూలిన క్షణాన్నె కృష్ణరాయలవారు భేరితాడనం శేయించి మదహత్తినెక్కుఱకొని ఉభయ ఛ్ఛత్రములతోనున్ను మకరటెక్కెఱములతో నూటయిరువై ఘట్టముల యేనుగలున్ను అగవైవేల గుఱ్ఱాలున్ను అయిదులక్షల పాయదళమున్ను పొట్లముగా నడచిరి. గనక ఆ క్షణాంన్నె కృష్ణవేణి వుభయతీరాలున్ను ప్రవాహాంనిండి రాసాగెను. జగడముఖానకు తురకయేనుగల మొన చేస్తే గ్రీష్మకాలం యెండ్డచేతను డస్సిన యేనుగలు గనక దగదప్పిపుట్టి చల్లగాలిచేత కాలుజారి కృష్ణవేణిలో బోయిపడెను. గుఱ్ఱాల రౌతులు యేరు నీళ్లువచ్చెను యివతలనుండి కార్యంకాదని గుఱ్ఱాలవారు యేనుగులవెంబడినె తిరిగి మొదటిదొరలు ముగ్గురున్ను దైపీకంగా పెడతల పోటుగా ప్రవాహంవచ్చె గనక యికఱడను పాళ్యందిగి జగడమిచ్చేమంశే రస్తుసామగ్రీలున్ను అమరదు. అని దొరలు ముగ్గురున్ను నియ్యోగులతో ఆలోచనగా వారి అన్నిటికిన్ని యేరుదాంటి ఆవలనిల్చి సరిపోయినట్లు నడిపించుకొందాము శీమకు తిరుగగానే యేరునిండారుగా వచ్చెను గాయలవారున్ను వెంబడించి నడిచి జగడంశేయగా అందరున్ను విరిగి

పారిపోయిరి. కొందరు యేట్లో బడిరి గనక సగం రెండుపాళ్లు యేటి వర దపోయిరి. వఖపాలు దక్షిణపుగట్టున నిలిచెను. ఏనుగలన్నిన్ని నీళ్లు విడిచి గట్టుకురాకపాయను. గనక మావటీలు యిఖను నిలువగూడదని దిగి ప్రాణాలతోడట్టు తప్పిపారిపోయిరి. మూడుతెగల తురకలున్న అంత్తట యేనుగులమీదనుంచి వోడలమీదికి దిగి వుత్తరపు గెట్టుయెక్కి ఆలోచనపరులై యీ సమయాన నిలిచేది కార్యంకాదని తమతమ స్థలా దులకు హతశేషులైన వారి గూర్చుక గట్టెక్కిన గుర్రాలతోడట్టు విజ యాపురం, గోలకొండ, అహమ్మదానగరం చేరబోయినారు. గనక కృష్ణరాయలవారు కృష్ణవేణి వొడ్డుకువచ్చి మూడుతెగల తురకల యేను గ గుర్రాలున్న నగరకట్టి పెట్టుమనిన్ని గుడారాలు నిశానులు నగా రా మొదలైనది మెందటజగడాన దొరికింద్ది గనక అదంత్తా నగరకట్టమని అప్పాజిమొదలైన నియ్యోగులతోనున్న ముక్కు తిమ్మన్న మొదలైన కవీశ్వరుల దిక్కుజూచి నేటిజయం యే రీతు అని అడిగినందులకు ము క్కు తిమ్మన్న చెప్పినపద్యం.

క. నరసింహ కృష్ణరాయా
దురమున నీపేరు వీరందురకలంద్రుంచెర
గరిరాజ వరదుడవనీ
కరిఘటలును నిన్నుంజూచి గ్రక్కునదిరిగెర.

అని ముక్కుతిమ్మయ అలసాని పెద్దన్న మాదనగారి మల్లయ్య మొ దలైనవారు విన్నపం శేశినందులకు అప్పాజి, అయ్యమరసు, కొండమర సు, బాచరుసుగారున్ను అనేకస్తుత్యములుగా విన్నపంజేసి కృష్ణవేణి యీ సమయాన నిండేరు వచ్చినందువల్ల మ్లేచ్ఛులకు అపజయమై నిలువ లేక తమతమ స్థలాలకు పోయినట్లాయెను. యేరు నీళ్లు విడిసి కాలినక్క అయినతోడుతోనే ముందర కార్యముఖానకు నడవవలెను. యీ ఆషాఢ శ్రావణాలు రెండు నెలలున్న యేటికి దక్షిణముగానున్నే తురకల దు ర్గాలున్న కోటస్థలాలున్న గజపతి దుర్గములున్న స్థలములున్న చేకూ ర్చుక ఆతర్వాత అహమ్మదానగరం పర్యంతమున్న పోయిరావలెను. అని విన్నపంజేసినందులకు కృష్ణరాయలవారు మీరు చెప్పినది కార్య సరవి అవును. మునుకలుగాయేరుదాంటి మ్లేచ్ఛుల రాజ్యానకు కదలి పొయ్యి నట్టాయనా గజపతివారి శీమలోనున్న ఉదయగిరి, కంద్దూరు, కొండవీడు, బెల్లంకొండ, నాగార్జునంకొండ, వినుకొండ, మొదలైన దుర్గా

లలోవున్నవారు మనదండుకు రస్తు సామగ్రీలు రానీకుండా అరికట్టుదురు. ఆరీతిగాకుండా మునుకలుగా ఆయాస్థలాలు సాధించి ఆయా దుర్గాలను మనతెగ తాంణ్యములు వుంచ్తేరస్తు సామగ్రీలు నడుచును. అని ఆనతిచ్చినారు గనకవద్దనున్న పిన్నపెద్దలు కార్యముగాయెంచి ముందర తరలే యత్నంగనవలెనన్నారు. కాబట్టి రాయలవారు రవుతు రాణువ దొరమన్నీలకు అందరికిన్ని పయనంచెప్పించ్చి భేరీ ఢమామి కాహళాలవారిని రప్పించి నగారా కూచిశేయించమని వారలా భేరి పూజసేయించ్చి టోకించ్చిన జయధ్వనిపద్యం.

కం. ధాత్రీశుఁడంతఁదిగ్జయ
యాత్రాసంరంభ జృంభితాటోపగతిన్
శత్రువులగుండెలవియఁగ
జైత్రప్రస్థానభేరి సేయించుటయున్.

ఉ. భూకంపంబు జనింపరొప్పఁగ మహాంభోగాసులుప్పొంగఁగా
లోకాలోకములెల్లఁ బెల్లగిలముల్లోకంబుఘూర్ణిల్లన
స్తోకవ్యాప్తినజాండగోళ దళనోద్భూతధ్వనింబోలెవ
స్తాకాలాంబుద గర్జితధ్వని సమారంభంబులైమీఱఁగన్.

వారలున్న పయనమని డెలిశి ఆయత్తపాటున కాచివుండగా రాయలవారు బయలుమెరశి గుర్రంయెకిరి సకల సన్నాహములతోడట్టు సకల దళసమేతుడై గుత్తి గండికోట మార్గముగా ఉదయగిరికివచ్చి సహుర్మత్తు అ(న?)నే దుర్గముపై లగ్గయెకరిగా దుర్గములలోని వారు తమ చేతనైనట్టు సమరంజేసి మందుగుండు శల్లవై నిర్వహించలేక కొలిచినారు గనక కాలునదించి శత్రుజనాలు వెళ్లిపోయిన తర్వాత రాయలవారు దుర్గంపైనెకిరి జూచి యింతరస్తువుండగా యేమని కొలిచి వెళ్లిపోయిరి అని ఆశ్చర్యపడి కంపన్నను, దుర్గమందు తాణ్యాంవుంచి కందూరికిపోగా ఢమామి ధ్వనివిన్నక్షణాన్నె ఆస్థలంవారు వెళ్లిపోయిరి. గనక ఆస్థలంతొక్కిరి చూచి అచ్చట తాణ్యాంవుంచి కొండవీటికి కదలిపోగా దుర్గములలోనున్న వూడెములవారు సముద్రంపొంగి వచ్చేరీతిని సేనాసముద్రం కదలివచ్చేది గని కాలిధూళిమిన్నుముట్టి సూర్యరశ్మి గప్పినగని స్థలములువిడిచి పొయ్యేవారున్ను కాహళ ధ్వని విని పారేవారున్ను యీరీతున కొండ్డవీడు శీమకోటలు దుర్గాలలో నున్నవారలు సరాళభ్రష్టులై తమతమ దొరలున్నతావుకు పోసాగిరి. బోయదొరలు పదునెనిమిది

కప్పగాలవారున్ను మూడులక్షల పాయదళమున్ను కొండవీడు, కొండ
పల్లె, బెల్లంకొండ, వినికొండ, నాగార్జునంకొండ మొదలైన దుర్గాలకు యే
లబడియైన శీమలాద్యంత్తం నిపాతం శేస్తావున్నారు గనక ఆయా శీమలో
గల ప్రజలందరున్ను సకల మున్ను కొల్లయిచ్చి మిక్కిలి అంద్దుపడి అయిన
దుర్గాలు జేరినారు. అని వేగర్లు అక్కడక్కడ నడుచు యోగక్షేమ
ములు క్షణక్షణేవచ్చి విన్నపం శాయంగా విన్నవారై తిరుగా వార్లను
ఆయా తావులకు అంప్పించి కొండవీటికిపోయి జగడమియ్యాగా కొనమూకల
వారు విరిగినమాత్రానే కొండవీడు కోటలోని వారు తీసిబోయినారు
గనక ఆదుర్గంమీద సమరం శేయంగా దుర్గంలోవున్నవారు తమ చేత అయి
నమట్టు పక్షటిన్నరదినం పోరాడి రాత్రి దుర్గం విడిచిపోగా మరుచునాడు
దుర్గమెక్కిజూచి ఆదుర్గమందు కొండయ్యను తాళ్యంవుంచి వినికొండకై
నడువంగా వారు యీవార్తలు విని స్థలంనిర్వహింప నేరమనియెంచి
మునకలుగా వెళ్లిపోయిరి. అక్కడ భాస్కరయ్యనువుంచి బెల్లంకొండ
కైనడవగా వారు పిరంగ్గినాదంవిని బెల్లంకొండవారు పారిపోయిరి.
యిచ్చట వీరభద్రయ్యను తాణ్యముంచి నాగార్జునుకొండకై నడవగా
వారు నానాప్రయత్నముల నాటమర్నాట పోరాడి చేతగాక తమనాటికి
పోయిరి. గనుక అచ్చట అయ్యలయ్యగారినివుంచి అహమదానగరా
నకు నడవగా కొనమూకలువారు వెలిపాళ్యాలు చొరబడి చెరజోరాబట్టి
చాలా కంపోలం శేయంగా కోటలోని గుఱ్ఱాలువారు వెళ్లివచ్చి యెదుట
నిలిచి జగడమియ్యాగా మూడుంముకాలు ఘడియలలోగా రెండువేలుం
నైనమంన్నారు గుఱ్ఱాలున్ను అంన్నియు రౌతులున్ను చాపకట్టుగా
మృతంబొందిరి. గనక యీ సమాచారం కోటలోవున్న మొదటి దొ
రలయినవారు విని ఇఖను మనంకోటలో నిలిచివున్నట్టయితే చేపట్టుగా
పట్టుకపోదురు. అందునుంచి చాలా అవమర్యాద అనియెంచి యేమి
బోయినాబోని అని కోటవిడిచి పారిపోయిరి. గనక రాయలవారు కోట
యిడియకొట్టించి ఆపట్ణంయెంత మేరో అంత్త మేరానున్ను వెలిపాళ్యా
లున్ను దున్నించి ఆముదాలు, జిల్లేళ్లు విత్తించి అందుండి గజపతి రా
జ్యానకై నడవగా అప్పాజి రాయలవారితో మూడుతెగల తురకల రాజ్య
మంత్తా కపోలం శేశి వారి దుర్గాలున్ను స్థలాలున్ను కట్టుకొని అహము
దానగరం ఆమిద్యాలు విత్తించి గజపతివారి గిరిదుర్గం జలదుర్గం స్థల
దుర్గం యివి అన్నియు ఆక్రమించినట్లాయను. ముంద్దర కదలిపా

య్యేది కార్యంకాదు. కనమలు దాటిపోవలెను, కనమలలోనున్న గజపతివారి తెగవారు సామగ్రీలు రానియ్యరు అని మంత్రాలోచనగా విన్నపం శేశినందులకు ఆవిశదం రాయలవారు చిత్తాన వుంచకముందర కదలిపోవలెననే దృష్టిని తమకు యెదురు లేదని యెంచి అప్పాజిగారు విన్నపం శేశినందులకు అవుగాములు ఉత్తరమియ్యక కదలిపోగా గజపతివారి కనమలనడమ పొయ్యేటప్పుడు చితాప్రఖానుడనేవాడు అరసైవేల శింగాణిరౌతులతోడట్టు కనుమమార్గమును పొయ్యే రౌతు రాణువమీద చిత్తవానగురిశిన రీతి అమ్ములగురియించగా అమ్ములనుండి తప్పించుకొనువారున్ను అమ్ములకు యెదురై నిలిచినవారున్ను ముందువెనక తెలియక నిలిచినవారున్ను ఆడాడ దిగ్భ్రమపడి వున్నవారున్ను యీ రీతినివుండగా చితాప్రఖానునికి యెదురులేదు గనక జగడంశేయగా ఆసమయాన కర్ణాటకంపైజీతం రౌతులు చితాప్రఖానునికి పెడతలపోటుగా యిరుపార్శ్వాల కనమల పొడువునెక్కి చితాప్రఖానుని వెనకదిక్కులకై వచ్చి శింగాణులచేతనున్ను ఖడ్గములచేతనున్ను బరిజీలచేతనున్ను వేటారు తునకలుగా నరకగా చితాప్రఖానుని తెగలకు కనుమలో నిలువగూడక విరిగిపారగా వెంబ్బడించి తరుముకబోయి వారిని దుర్గం చొరదోలి తిరుగావచ్చిరి. గనక అప్పుడు చితాప్రఖానుని తెగలలో యిరువైమూడువేల స్తోమమున్ను నాల్గువేల గుఱ్ఱమున్ను వఖతావున్నె మడిసి అటు తర్వాత సమదళం ఆద్యంత్తమన్న ముందర కదలిపోయిరి. గనక ఆకనుమల్లో ముప్పైవేల స్తోమాన్ని తాణ్యాంవుంచి అవతల గజపతిగారి శీమాద్యంత్తం నిపాతం శేసుకపోయి పోట్లూరి సింహాద్రివద్ద పాళ్యం దిగిరి. . . . .

. . . .

గనక కర్ణాటకం పాళ్యానునుండి మనపాళ్యానకు వచ్చేమార్గాన అప్తులైనవార్ల నుంచి నియ్యోగులున్ను పెట్టియున్ను సముఖానకు తెప్పించుక జూడగా నిదర్శనమైతేను అందుకు తగిన ఆలోచన కనేదని వ్రాసి అంప్పగా ఆ కాకితం గజపతివారు చదువుకొని ఆతీరుననే యికఱ డివారికి వెళవియ్యాగా షోడశపాత్రులకు అనర్ఘ్యమైన భూషణములు పెట్ట్యెల కట్టించి నియ్యోగులనున్ను పదారు పెట్యెలున్ను శేపట్టుగా పట్టుకపోయి గజపతివారి ముందరవిడిచినారు. గనక గజపతివారు పెట్టల విడిపించి వారివారి పేరటవ్రాసిన నిరూపములున్ను చదివించుకొని వకఱణము విని ఆదియందు తాము అగ్రహపడిన కార్యములున్ను వుటం

గ్గించి అందుకు ప్రత్యుత్తరమున్ను అనర్ఘ్యమైన భూషణములున్ను నిదర్శనంగా చూచి షోడశపాత్రులను నమ్మి జగడాలకు పోతావుంటిమి వార్లు ఇంత ద్రోహానకులోనైరి మనపాలింటి జగన్నాథుల కృపవల్ల మునుకలుగా హెచ్చరికపడితి. ఇఖను యెవ్వరిని నమ్మరాదు అని వచ్చినపదారు నియోగ్యాగులనున్ను పట్ణంవిడిచి యేకదేశాన అవ్వల పీడతోలి గజపతివారు యేడెనిమిది ఆమడ పాడవు ఉత్తరంగా పారిపోయిరి. గనక మరుచునాడు ఉదయాన షోడశపాత్రులు ఆయిత్తపడివచ్చి నగరి వాకిట నిలిచి గజపతివారిని బయలు మెరశి రమ్మని ఘణిహారులతో చెప్పి అంపగా గజపతివారు నగరివాకిట పిన్నపెద్దలతో చెప్పిపోయినారు గనక వారు వాకిలిం వెళ్లివచ్చి గజపతివారి నడిపించిన కార్యమున్ను ప్రచ్ఛన్న వేషముగా పోయిన మార్గాలున్ను తెలువంగా షోడశపాత్రులు విని ఉత్సాహమగ్నులై ఆలోచనకులోనై గజపతివారు వున్న తావుకు పోయినాను అపవాదం కార్యముఖానకు పోయినప్పటికిన్ని వారు నడపించిన కార్య మంత్రభిన్నం ఆయన గనక తెంపుగానడిపించ్చి రింత్తెగా నగరికి హితవాచరించినవారుకారు అని అందుకు తామె తెలుసుకోనేరు అని వారువార్లు తమ తమ దుర్గాలకు సాగిపోయినారు. కాబట్టి కృష్ణరాయలవారు యీ వర్తమానములు విని జయభేరిశాయంగా మోకటిస్థలానకు వచ్చి నిలిచి యెవ్వరున్ను చేగకుండ సుబుద్ధిగారి మనుష్యుల కోట వాకిళ్లనున్ను పట్టణములోనున్ను నగరి మహాలులోనున్ను జతనంగా మనుష్యుల వుండమని నియమించి పోట్నూరి సింహాద్రివద్ద జయస్తంభము వేయించి సుబుద్ధిని బిలువనంపి ఆయనతోను మేము ప్రతాపముకొరకు వచ్చినవారము ఇంత్తె కాని రాజ్యాపేక్షకొరకు వచ్చినవారమునుగాము, గజపతివారి రాజ్యం గజపతికే నడిపించేము. మేమున్ను మాశీమకు సాగిపొయ్యేము అని ఆనతియ్యాగా సుబుద్ధి ఆవివరములకు గజపతివారికి అనుపూర్వకముగా కాకితం వ్రాసిసంపినారు. గనక బుద్ధిశాలియై నటువంటి గజపతివారు ఆ కాకితము చదువుక చాలా సంతోషపరులై తిరుగా పట్నానకువచ్చి షోడశపాత్రులవల్ల తప్పితం లేదని విచారించ్చుక చారులచేత బిలువనంప్పించగా వారలున్ను వచ్చి కనికొలిచిరి. గనక మీవల్ల కపటమున్ను లేదు. ద్రోహచింతనాను లేదు అని పలుకరించి వారలకు బహుమానములు శేశి వారల కూర్చుక రాయలవారిని సందేహించక మాటపలుకు లాడేటప్పుడు గజపతివారు రాయలదేవునితోను సమయోచితములుగా పలుకరించినందులకు.

श्लो ॥ नष्टंकुलं भिन्न तटाककूपान् विभ्रष्टराज्यं शरणागतं च ।
गोब्राह्मणान्देवगणालयांश्च यदुद्धरेत्पूर्व चतुर्गुणं तत् ॥

అని శ్లోకం చదివి మరిన్ని ఉచితమైనట్టు మాట పలుకులాడంగా రాయలవారు గజపతివారితోను మీరనిన్ని మేమనిన్ని భేదము ఉన్నదా అని ఉపచారములుగా మాటలాడి గజపతివారికి చాలా బహుమాన సన్మానములు శేశి నాలుగునగల కోకతాకలున్ను యిచ్చినారు. గనక గజపతివారు తమ కొమార్తె అయిన జగన్మోహినీ అనే కన్యకను ధారవోశి యిచ్చే సమయాన చెప్పినపద్యం.

క. హాటక పేటీ శాటీ, ఘోటీశకటీమదేభకోటీపీటీ
పేటీభృచ్ఛేటీ . . . మయూరికలు . . . వేడ్కన్.

అని నీతిచదివి ఆవలమరిన్ని అల్లునికిన్ని ఆడబిడ్డకున్ను యియ్యతగిన బహుమానోచితక్రమభూషణాలనిన్ని అంపించి, మరిన్ని తమ కొమార్తెకు పట్టు పరిమెళ వసుపులకని కృష్ణవేణికి దక్షిణపుదిక్కున నడిచే రాజ్యాలున్ను కోటకొత్తళములున్ను దుర్గాలున్ను ఇచ్చి యేనుగ గుఱ్ఱములు బంటు పరివారం దాసానుదాసులు ఆందోలిక హయలు బండి పసలం ప్రాయలు పాత్రసామగ్రిలు పగడపుకాళ్ల మంచము హంసతూలికా యివి మొదలైనవిగా ఆడబిడ్డెకు యియ్యతగ్గ వరుసలన్ని యిచ్చి అల్లునికిన్ని శాయతగ్గవరిశలు అన్నిన్ని తప్పకుండా వఖసారిగానె సకల పదార్థములున్ను యిప్పించ్చి తమ నగరగలభూషణములలో అపూర్వమైన హెచ్చుబడిన నవరత్న భూషణాదులు అపరిమితముగా యిచ్చి అప్పాజి షోడశపాత్రులకు అంప్పించ్చిన పదారు నగల నవరత్నపొడి సొమ్ములు యిచ్చి చీని చీనాంబరమైన పట్టుపతావళ్లు పీతాంబరాదిగాగల సకలమైన కోకతాకలున్ను యిచ్చి యేనుగ గుఱ్ఱం కత్తికెడం మొదలుగాగల రాజోపచారమైన బహుమానములున్ను యిచ్చి, విందు పీడుకళ్లు ప్రసాపడశేయించ్చి సుబుద్ధినిన్ని వెంబడిపూర్చి అప్పగా రాయలవారు అత్యంత సంతోషయుక్తులై నగారా శేయమని అప్పాజి సుబుద్ధినికూడా చోడోలున వుంచుకొని బయలుదేరిరాగా, యీపర్యాయములన్నిఁన్ని గోలకొండ విజయాపురం అహముదానగరం యేలే ముగ్గురు దునేదార్లున్ను విని యిఖను మనం రాయలదేవునితో యెదిరించి కత్తికట్టేది కార్యంకాదు అని యోచనచేసి భేటిశేసుకోవలెనని నిశ్చయించ్చి అందుకు అయిన సం

విధానపురస్సరముగా వచ్చి నిలిచి సవినయంబులుగా కుర్నీసులు శేశి రాయలవారి భేటి శేశుకొని కానుక నదురుదెచ్చి అపరిమితముగా పాదముల సమర్పించి భయబుద్ధికలిగి రాయలవారియొక్క దానపాత్రములు తెలుసుకొని పలుకరింప్ప శేశిన నీతిపద్యం :—

చ. మలకలుమాప్రచారములు మాముఖముల్విషవహ్నిఘోరముల్
ఖలులమురోమజాతులముగర్వులమే మొకమంచివారమే
నలినదళాక్ష ప్రాణులకునైజగుణంబులు మాన్పవచ్చునే
పెలయఁగమావికారములువేయును నెంచఁగ నేలభూవరా.

అనినీతి పద్యంచదివి, అన్యోన్యమైన మాటపలుకులు నడిపించ్చి తమ తమదేశాలకు సరుదులు యేర్పాటు శేశుకొని కనమని కొలిచేవారై రాయలవారిచేత అంప్పించుక వారివారి స్థలాదులకు పోయినారు. గనక కృష్ణరాయలవారు ఉత్తరా తురకల కార్యంజయంచేసుకొని శీమకై తిరిగి తిరుపతికిరాగా కల్యాణకలుబరిగె కోటలవారు గర్వితులై కోటమీదనుండి కూతలీంగ్గా ఆ వార్తలు రాయలవారు విని యెదిరితెగవారిని అడుగఁగామ్లేచ్ఛుల తెగవారు వున్నారు గనుక కోటమీదికై అంద్దుల మగిడించమని కలుబరిరేగ కోటలగ్గబెట్టించి మూడుముక్కాలు ఘడియలలో కోట సాధించి ఆ కోటలోవున్న యజమానుంణ్ని చేపట్టుగా పట్టుకొని ఆరు వేల గుఱ్రాలవారినింన్ని గుఱ్రాలనున్ను ఏకవాగెగా బట్టుకొని ఆ కోటకు తాణ్యాంగుజ్జరి కల్యాణరావును వుంచి తిరుపతికివచ్చి అలమేలుమంగా సమేతులయిన కల్యాణవెంకటేశ్వరుల దర్శనంబు శేశి రొఖ్ఖ రూపాయలు కానుకవేశి సకలభూషణములున్న స్వామికె సమర్పించ్చి అస్థలాన షోడశమహాదానాలున్ను శేసి సన్నిధిని నిత్యశేవగా అంజలిపుటులై పూర్వద్వారమందలి వుభయ పార్శ్వములా తిరుమలదేవి చిన్నాదేవి సహితంగావుండేటట్టుగా తాంబ్రాన ప్రతిబింబమున శేయించ్చి స్వామిని యెదురుగానిలిపి అంద్దుండ్డి కాళహస్తికివచ్చి స్వామినిదర్శించి కానుకలున్న నవరత్నాభరణములున్న సమర్పించి శ్రీముఖ సంవత్సరం ఆశ్వీజశు. 12 దినములు(? రాదిగాగల) వస్త్రములున్న గ్రామాదులున్న సమర్పించిస్వామి సన్నిధిని షోడశమహాదానాలున్న శేశి అవ్వారిగా సత్రములున్న కలుగశేశి అందుండి త్రిపురులచేత పూజకొన్న మూడుస్థలాలకున్నపోయిన స్వామి దర్శనం శేశి వంద్దీశ్వర దర్శనం శేశి అళగరుగుడికి వచ్చి శేవించి కానుకలున్న ముత్యాలకిరీటం పచ్చలపతకం సమర్పించి

మధురకువచ్చి మీనాక్షిదేవినిన్ని చొక్కనాథస్వామినిన్ని త్రిసంధ్యలయందున్ను శేవించ్చి కానుకలువేశి అనేక భూషణములు సమర్పించి అమ్మవారికి వజ్రాల కమ్మలున్ను వైడూర్యపతకములున్ను పచ్చలకమ్మలున్ను ముత్యపు ముక్కరానున్ను సమర్పించి త్రిరాత్రుల్లు వాసముజేశి శ్రీవల్లిపుత్తూరికివచ్చి చూడుకొడుత్తు నాచ్యారు సమేతముగా సంపెంగ్గిమన్నారు స్వామిని శేవించి తిరుముక్కు కెంపుల వడ్యాణం, బంగారు నూపురములున్ను నవరత్నకీతమైన సింహాముఖం ప్రభలున్ను సమర్పించి గుంటతొవ్వించి రాతికట్లానకున్ను నడిమి మంటపానకున్ను లక్షమాళ్లు యిప్పించ్చి కరువనల్లూరికివచ్చి క్షీరవర్ణస్వామిని దర్శించుక శంకరనారాయణదేవళానకువచ్చి నాగతీర్థమున స్నానం శేశి గోమేతీ సమేతముగా శంకర నారాయణస్వామిని దర్శించి దక్షిణకాశికిపోయి త్రికూటాచలమందు ఆకాశ గంగయందలి స్నానం శేశి చిత్రసభ శేవించుక అగస్త్యపర్వతానకువచ్చి కల్యాణతీర్థమందలి స్నానము శేశి అగస్తేశ్వరుని గోపురం గట్టించ్చి గజేంద్రమోక్షానకువచ్చి స్వామిని శేవించుక శాలివటపురానకువచ్చి కాంత్తమతీ సమేతముగా వేణువనేశ్వరస్వామిని దర్శనం శేశి తామ్రసభకట్టించేటందుకు కొంతరూకలుయిచ్చి కృష్ణరాయసముద్రమని తనపేర అగ్రహారముగావించి తోతాద్రిస్వామిని శేవించుక కురుంగుడికిపోయి పంచనంబ్బులనున్ను శేవించ్చి కన్యాకుమారికి జని అమ్మవారిని శేవించుక శ్రీకంకూరికివచ్చి వల్లి దేవయానసమేతముగా సుబ్రమ్హణ్యస్వామిని శేవించి నవతిరుపతులకువచ్చి ఆయా స్థలాదులకు తగిన నవరత్నపొడి భూషణాదులుయిచ్చి ఆదిసేతువుకుపోయి రఘునాయకుల సేవించ్చి కాళములమీద సముద్ర తరణమై ధనుష్కోటిలో ఖడ్గంగడిగి సేతుస్నానం తులాపురుషదానం మొదలైన దానాలాచరించి కాశీవిశ్వేశ్వరులనుంన్ను రామలింగస్వామినిన్ని సేతుమాధవస్వామినిన్ని పర్వతవర్ధన అమ్మవారినిన్ని సేవించుకొని చతుర్వింశతి తీర్థములయందు స్నానం శేశి కోటిదానం కోటి బ్రాహ్మణులకు అన్నదానము శేశి స్వామిసన్నిధిని మూండు తులలుతూంగి అమ్మవారికి సకలాభరణములున్ను నవరత్నపొడిగాయిచ్చి త్రిరాత్రి వసియించి కోటి తీర్థస్నానం శేశి స్వామిచేత అంప్పించ్చుకొని మరలినవారై గోకర్ణ స్థలమునకువచ్చి బృహదంబా సమేతముగా గోకర్ణేశ్వరుని సేవించి వకుళవన ప్రదక్షిణము శేశి గోకర్ణ తీర్థముందున్ను స్నానం శేశి అంమ్మవారికి సకలాభరణములుంన్ను సమర్పించ్చి

శ్రీరంగపట్నానికివచ్చి ఆదిరంగనాయకుల సేవించ్చి సుముహూర్తమందలి విద్యానగర ప్రవేశమై విఠల విరుపాక్షుల సేవించ్చి కానుకలున్ను అనర్ఘ్యమైనటువంటి భూషణాదులున్ను సమర్పించి నగరుప్రవేశమై పెద్దలకు మ్రొక్కి సుముహూర్తమున హజారమునకు విజయంశేశి అప్పాజిమొదలైన సకలసామాజికులనున్ను అల్లుడి కొమాళ్లనున్ను రప్పించుక నిండు కొలువిచ్చి అప్పాజీని రత్నకంబళియందు కూర్చుండబెట్టి రత్నాభిషేకం స్వర్ణాభిషేకం శేశి నాలుగునగల కోకతాకలున్ను ఇచ్చిచెసరాలున్ను పచ్చలకడియాలు, తాళిబొకట్లు, పచ్చలవొంట్లు, ముత్యాలతురాయి, వజ్రాలకంఠసరం, కెంపుల వుంగరములు ఇవిమొదలైన భూషణములున్ను యిచ్చి గంధకస్తూరి, తట్టుపునుగు, జవ్వాజిమొదలైన పరిమెశములచాత లెస్సాయిగా బహుమానములు శేశి తక్కిన వార్లకెల్ల తగుపాటి బహుమానములు శేశి సకల వాద్యఘోషములతోడట్టుగజాధిరోహులశేశి యిండ్లకు అంపించి.

39

KRISHNA RĀYA VIJAYAM.

[*By Kumāra Dhūrjaṭi.*]

This is a poem written by Venkaṭa Rāya, a poet who lived in the Court of the Prince Chinna Venkaṭa of the fourth Vijayanagar dynasty and who was the fifth in descent from the famous Kavi Dhūrjaṭi who lived in Krishna Rāya's Court. He is popularly called Kumāra Dhūrjaṭi or Dhurjati, the younger. At the request of his patron Chinna Venkaṭa he wrote this poem celebrating the victories of the famous Emperor Krishna Rāya of Vijayanagar. The poem makes a Vīra-Narasimha the father and predecessor of Krishna Rāya, but does not mention Vīra-Narasimha, his elder brother who ruled for nearly six years before Krishna Rāya succeeded. For the sake of Kāvyauchityam (literary propriety) perhaps, it says that Vīra-Narasimha Rāya (for the work calls the father of Krishna Rāya by this name), finding that he had grown old, installed his son Krishna Rāya on the throne and himself retired. The coronation ceremony was attended by all the prominent feudatory chiefs of whom the following are important : Āravīṭi Bukkarāju, the chiefs of Owk, the chiefs of Nandēla, the Velgoḍu chiefs, the Khurāsānivāru, the chiefs of Būdahaḷi.

Then Krishna Rāya enquired from the minister Sāḷuva Timma, addressing him Appa (father), what was the amount of his imperial revenue and the strength of his army. Sāḷuva Timma gave a detailed account of the number of elephants, horses and infantry that were maintained, and the expenses from the annual revenue on their account, as also the gross revenue that was collected every year and the deductions that were made from it on account of Dēvadāya, Brahmadēya (grants to Brahmans and temples) as well as the money saved from the revenues by previous rulers. He then compelled such of the governors as did not maintain the necessary forces to do so and to pay a heavy fine to the State.

Then the spies that had been sent from Vijayanagar to the neighbouring kingdoms returned bringing with them the news that the Muhammadan rulers of Golkonda and Ahmadnagar (Nizam Shah) had sent their representatives to Bijapur to consider what steps should be taken against Krishna Rāya, the young Emperor of Vijayanagar who had just succeeded; and their representatives Venkoji and Dadoji were day and night consulting each other and were corresponding with the Gajapati of Orissa. The three Muhammadan rulers had reinforced the garrisons of all the frontier fortresses and stored large quantities of provisions and ammunition there. Moreover they had made strict regulations with regard to the entry of strangers into their territories and fortresses, and established a system of sealed passports.

News was also received from the Vijayanagar spies in the territory of the Gajapati of Orissa that the envoy of the Nizam Shah had informed the Gajapati that Krishna Rāya was making preparations for war against the chiefs of Ahmadnagar, Bijapur and Golkonda, and was intending to cross the Krishna into their territories. As he might then advance even as far as Ahmadāpuram (Ahmadabad-Bidar) they cautioned the Gajapati to be on the alert and garrison his fortresses. The Gajapati agreed to do so. After the necessary preparation Krishna Rāya summoned all the important chiefs to his Court and making them the usual presents, entertained them at a banquet. Giving the necessary instructions to the officers at the capital he started with his army.

He defeated several refractory chiefs who opposed him. After capturing their fortresses and garrisoning them with his own troops he proceeded against Śivanasamudram, the capital of the Ummattūr chief Gangarāja. Having defeated him in battle, he captured the place, and after taking possession of the money in the place visited Śrīrangapaṭṭaṇam. He left the place and in a short time effected a junction with the troops of Sankula Nāyaka (of Ikkēri) and marched against the frontier fortresses of Bijapur. The garrisons in many of these fortresses surrendered after defeat, and Krishna Rāya spared the lives of their Governors. He then put fresh garrisons in the fortresses of Ādavani (Adoni), Mudugallu (Mudgal) and Rāchūru (Raichur) and directed his march towards Golkonda.

On hearing this, the three Muhammadan rulers of Bijapur, Ahmadnagar and Golkonda collected their armies on the southern banks of the Krishna to prevent Krishna Rāya's crossing the river. When Krishna Rāya heard this he held a council of war and Pemmasāni Ramalinga, one of the chief generals, came forward and requested that the attack against the enemy may be entrusted to him and promised to drive out all the enemy and capture their tents.

The troops engaged on the Muhammadan side in the war amounted according to the work to 1,000 elephants, 100,000 Bondēlas, 100,000 Pendars and 100,000 Muhammadans, whereas the Vijayanagar troops amounted to 600,000 infantry, 6,600 horse and 2,000 elephants. Krishna Rāya won a complete victory in the battle that ensued. The court poets that followed him on the campaign as Mādayagari Mallana, Allasāni Peddana and Mukku Timmana composed verses in his praise.

Krishna Rāya then consulted Appāji (Sāḷuva Timma) about proceeding further into the Mussalman territories; but Appāji replied that it was not at all desirable to enter into the interior of the enemies' territory leaving the Gajapati free to attack him on the flank in the east. The Emperor accepted the salutary advice and directed his march towards the east against the Gajapati.

The chief officers that accompanied Krishna Dēva Rāya against the Kalinga territories are then said to have belonged to the following families: the Āravīṭṭivāru, Toragaṇṭivāru, Gobbūrivāru, the Tuḷuva lords, the chiefs of Owk, Velugoṭivāru and the Rāvelavāru. They attacked the fort of Udayagiri and soon reduced it. Thence he proceeded north and in his onward march besieged and captured one after another the fortresses of Kandukūr, Koṇḍavīḍu, Koṇḍapalli and Vinukoṇḍa, and dispersed the garrisons in all of them.

After that Krishna Rāya proceeded against Ahmadnagar. This Ahmadnagar is Ahmadabad-Bidar and not Ahmadnagar, the capital of the Nizam Shahs. After reducing the place and hoisting his own standard there, he turned once more towards the interior of the territories of the Gajapati in spite of Sāḷuva Timma's remonstrances. While Krishna Rāya's troops were crossing the ghats into the Gajapati's territories he was attacked in the passes by a chief called Chitaph Khan with a large number of archers. He defeated Chitaph Khan and after driving away his troops marched into the territories of Kalinga as far as Poṭnūri-Simhādri and fixed his camp at the place.

Then as a result of a stratagem played upon him by Sāḷuva Timma, the Gajapati suspected treason among his chief generals, and thinking that everything was lost, left his capital one night and fled towards the forests. When his generals came to hear of their chief's defection they also retired to their several places and Krishna Rāya captured his city very easily. He had the great magnanimity, however, to prevent his soldiers from doing any harm to the Gajapati's palaces or family.

Krishna Rāya sent word then to the Gajapati through the latter's minister saying that he was prepared to come to terms with him and promised to give him back his territory. The Gajapati was very glad at this and, in his joy, gave to Krishna Rāya his daughter in marriage and presented to her as dowry all his territories to the south of the Krishna.

Thereupon Krishna Rāya proceeded against Kulbarga, and, reducing the fortress, returned to his capital after a long absence. Krishna Rāya then proceeded to the south on a progress through his empire and visited Śrīśailam, Kāḷahasti, Chidambaram and other Saiva shrines, Śrīrangam, Kanchi (Conjivaram), Tirupati and other shrines of Vishnu, and bathed in the sacred rivers such as the Kaveri and the Tāmraparṇi. He also had many literary works dedicated to him of which the most important was the Manucharitram.

N.B.—The original is not given here for considerations of space. The work has been published and is available to the public.

40

ĀMUKTAMĀLYADĀ.

[*By Krishnadēva Rāya.*]

In the introduction to this poem of Krishna Rāya, he says that while on his expedition against Kalinga he stayed for a few days at Vijayavāṭi (Bezwada), and went to Śrīkākulam to worship the

God Āndhramadhusūdana (Āndhra Vishṇu) of the place and spent the Ekādaśi (eleventh day after the full-moon and the new-moon) fast, at that place. On that night in the fourth watch (yāma) the God appeared to him, and, recounting the several works which he wrote in Sanskrit, Madālasa Charitra, Satyāvadūprīṇanam, Sakalakathāsārasangraham, Sūktinaipuṇīgñana Chintāmaṇi and Rasamanjari, directed him to compose the story of Godā (Āṇḍāḷ, the daughter of Vishṇuchitta, Periyāḷvar, one of the twelve Śri Vaishṇava saints) in Telugu. Telugu was according to the God the best of the Dēśabhāshās and could alone be understood by all those assembled in his court. He exhorted the king to dedicate it to God Venkaṭēśvara.

Krishna Rāya then gives a genealogy of his family from the moon. Of his own achievements which he gives us in the words of his court poets, he has a long account. The fire of his valour which was kindled by his sword coming in contact with the rocks of Udayagiri advanced to Koṇḍaviḍu, and after defeating Kasavāpātra, crossed the Jammiloya and reduced successively the district of Vegī ((Vengi), Kona (the Gōdāvari delta) and Koṭṭāmu, Kanakagiri, Poṭnūru, Māḍēmalu, Oḍḍādi and even threatened Cuttack so that the Gajapati fled from there. In another verse the Uriya-speaking Pātras of the Gajapati's army are said to have gone from Koṇḍavīḍu to heaven in large numbers having been defeated by Krishna Rāya. Later on Krishna Rāya is represented as having planted a tall pillar with inscriptions on it at Poṭnūru to commemorate his victory over the Gajapati. In the next verse (41), the Muhammadan soldiers of the cities of Kulbarga and Sagar killed in battle by Krishna Rāya are said to be in heaven giving great trouble to the gods. In verse (42), he is said to have fought with the troops of Adil Khan, and, having killed him in battle, to have exhibited his head as a sign of his glory. The next verse (43) describes his munificent benefactions. The five colophons give the important particulars of the capture of the Gajapati's uncle in Udayagiri, of his son Vīrabhadra in Koṇḍavīḍu, of Praharēśvara and his treasure at Koṇḍapalli, of his worshipping god at Simhāchallam and of the erection of the pillar of victory at Poṭnūru bearing an inscription. The final verse refers to a bloody engagement against the Muhammadans at a place called *Kembāvi* * and the destruction of its fortifications.

---

* This place is in the Nizam's Dominions in the Raichore Doab. (*Epigraphia Indica*, XII, pp. 291–92.)

వ. . . . . మున్నే కళింగదేశ విజిగీషామనీషం దండెత్తి పోయి విజయవాటిం గొన్ని వాసరంబు లుండి శ్రీకాకుళ నికేతనుఁడగు నాంధ్రమధుమథను సేవింపఁబోయి హరివాసరోపవాసం బచ్చటం గావింప నప్పుణ్యరాత్ర చతుర్థయామంబున :—

సీ. నీలమేఘముడాలు డీలు సేయఁగఁజాలు
మెఱుఁగుజామనచాయ మేనితోడ
నరవిందములకచ్చు లడఁగించుజిగిపచ్చ
నాయతంబగుకన్నుదోయితోడఁ
బులుఁగురాయనిచట్టుపలవన్నెనొఱఁబట్టు
హొంబట్టుజిలుఁగురెంటెంబుతోడ
నుదయార్కబింబంబునొఱపువిడంబంబు
దొరలంగనాడుకౌస్తుభముతోడ

గీ. దమ్మికేలుఁడఁబెఱకేలదండయిచ్చు
లేములుడిపెడు లేఁజూపు లేమితోడ
దొలుకరిదయఁదెల్పుచిఱునవ్వుతోఁడగలఁద
దంధ్రజలజాక్షుఁడిట్లనియానతిచ్చె.

సీ. పలికితుత్ప్రేక్షోపమలజాతిపెంపెక్క
రసికులౌననమదాలసచరిత్ర
భావధ్వనివ్యంగ్యసేవధిగాఁగఁజె
ప్పితివిసత్యావధూప్రీణనంబు
శ్రుతిపురాణోపసంహితలేర్చికూర్చితి
సకలకథాసారసంగ్రహంబు
శ్రోత్రఘచ్ఛటలువిచ్చుగరచించితిసూక్తి
నైపుణీజ్ఞానచింతామణికృతి.

గీ. మఱియురసమంజరీముఖ్యమధురకావ్య
రచనమెప్పించికొంటిగీర్వాణభాష
నాంధ్రభాషయసాధ్యంబెయందునొకక
కృతివినిర్మింపుమిఁకమాకుఁబ్రియముగాఁగ.

ఉ. ఎన్నినుఁగూర్తునన్నవినుమేమునుదాల్చినమాల్యమిచ్చిన
ప్పిన్నదిరంగమందయినపెండిలిసెప్పుముమున్నగొంటిమే
వన్ననదండయొక్కరుమగవాఁడిడనేనుదెలుఁగురాఁయడ
న్నన్నడరాయ యకొ్కరుదువఁగప్పుప్రియాపరిభుక్తభాకరుధర.

ఆ. తెలుఁగిదేలనన్న దేశంబు దెలుఁగేను
దెలుఁగువల్లభుండఁ దెలుఁగొకండ
యెల్లనృపులుగొలువ నెఱుఁగవే బాసాడి
దేశభాషలందుఁ దెలుఁగు లెస్స.

గీ. పొత్తమిటు సేయ నీకుత్తరోత్తరాభి
వృద్ధియని పోవ మేల్కాంచి వెఱగుతోడి
భక్తిఁ దద్గృహాగోపురప్రణతిఁ జేసి
వేఁగుటయుఁ గల్యకరణీయవిధులు దీర్చి.

క. అంకిత మోయన నీకల
వేంకటపతి యిష్టమైన వేల్పగుటఁ దదీ
యాంకితము చేయు మొక్కొక
సంకేతమ కాక యతఁడరసజ్ఞుఁ గానే.

*　*　*　*

క. ఆవిభునవంతరంబధ
రావలయము పూనితీవు రహిమై తిరుమ
ల్దేవియును నన్నపూర్ణా
దేవియుఁ గమలాబ్జముఖులు దేవేరులుగాన్.

*　*　*　*

సీ. తొలుదొల్త నుదయాద్రిశిలఁ దాఁకి తీండ్రించు
నసిలోహమున వెచ్చనై జనించె
మఱికొండవీఁ డెక్కి మాఱొకొని నలిరైన
యలకసవాపాత్రు నంటిఁ జాజె
నటసాఁగి జమ్మిలోయఁ బడి నేఁగి దహించె
గోనబిట్టేర్చెఁ గొట్టానఁ దవిలెఁ
గనకగిరిస్ఫూర్తిఁ గఱచెఁ గౌతమిఁ గ్రాచె
నవల నాపొట్నూర గవులుకొనియె.

గీ. మాడెములు వ్రేల్చె నోడ్డాదిమసియొనర్చె
గటకపురిఁ గాల్చెఁ గజరాజు గలఁగి వఱవ
దోఁకచిచ్చన నౌర నీదుర్వగాహ
ఖేలదుగ్రప్రతాపజాగ్రన్మహాగ్ని.

ఉ. చిత్రముకృష్ణరాయనృపశేఖరనీదగుధాటికోడిస
ర్వత్రనిలింపకామినులవాడకుఁగాఁపుఁబోదురుత్కల
క్షత్రియపాత్రులెల్లఁగనుఁగందనిమేనులఁదోంటిపెద్దలే
నూత్నముఁబన్నినారొబలసూదనువీఁటికిఁగొండవీటికిన్.

ఉ. కూరిమిఁగృష్ణరాయనృపకుంజరచేరెఁగళింగరాజ్యల
క్ష్మీగమనీలలామనినుమిన్నులుముట్టినమోహనాలతోఁ
గారణమట్లలక్ష్మిగనుఁగందనివేఁడుకఁగృష్ణరాయనిం
జేరునకాకవంచి పెడఁజెందు నెసోదరుఁడైనరుద్రునిన్.

* * * *

గీ. నిద్రమేలాంచి పెలయేటనీడఁగాంచి
గోపవేషంబుపైడితోంటిభూపవేష
ముగుటయవ్వనమహిమ, గానలికియచటు
విడుచుగజరాజునీధాటివింధ్యవాటి.

చ. అభిరతిఁగృష్ణరాయవిజయాంకములీవులిఖించితాళస
న్నిభముగఁబొట్టునూరికడనిల్పినకంబముసింహభూధర
ప్రభుతిరుణాళ్లకుండిగుసురప్రకరంబుగళింగమేదినీ
విభునపకీర్తికజ్జలమువేముఱుఁబెట్టిపఠించునిచ్చలున్.

గీ. తిరుగుహరిపురిసురతరుసురలమరిగి
బహుళహాళవాళిభరితకల్బరిగనగర
నగరపురవరపరివృఢజవనయవన
పృతనభవదసిననిఁదెగికృష్ణరాయ 41.

మ. అలుకస్ఖోటకఘట్టికాఖురపుటీహల్యస్థగాసానిపు
చ్ఛలువోఁదున్నిచలచ్చమూగజమదాసారప్లుతిస్ఫూర్తిపు
షల లసస్యంబిడియేకదాటిభళిరాకట్టించితౌదృష్టికే
దులఖానోగ్రక పాలమర్ధపహారిదూర్భాజాంగలశ్రేణికిన్.

చ. సుమతిప్రనఃపునారచితషోడశదానపరంపరావసం
తములననంతవిత్తముననంతనంతమహాగ్రహారబృం
దమునురొసంగునిన్నెఱసితారెనరాకకదానిలింపభూ
జములువహించుదుర్వశముషట్పదకోకిలకైతవంబునన్.

తే. ప్రబలరాజాధిరాజవీరప్రతాప
రాజపరమేశ్వరార్థదుర్గానటీశ
సాహితీసమరాంగణసార్వభౌమ
కృష్ణరాయేంద్రకృతివిసర్తింపుమసిరి.

Colophon of Canto I.

మ. ఇదికర్ణాటధరాధృతిస్థిరభుజాహేలాకళాభేదగా
డుదమోర్వీధరతత్పితృవ్యకృతనవ్యోపాయనోద్దీపర (1)
త్నదృగంచత్పదకృష్ణరాయవసుధాధ్యక్షోదితాముక్తమా
ల్యదనాశ్వాసముహృద్యపద్యములనాద్యంబైమహింబొల్పగున్

Colophon of Canto II.

మ. ఇదిభూమండనకొండవీటిధరణీభృద్దుర్గపూర్వాద్రిబా
స్వదిభేశాత్మజవీరభద్రజనజీవగ్రాహరాహుత్యమా (2)
ణదృఢాంచద్భుజకృష్ణరాయమహిరాణ్ణామాప్తదాముక్తమా
ల్యదనాశ్వాసముహృద్యపద్యముద్వితీయంబైమహింబొల్పగున్

Colophon of Canto III.

మ. ఇదిపాత్రప్రహారేశ్వర (3) ప్రభృతిబాహిస్థోత్కళానీకగు
ప్తదివిస్పృక్పటుయంత్రకొండపలిహృద్వాకాసికద్రూజజీ
వ్యదుదారోద్యమకృష్ణరాయనృపసంజ్ఞాస్తదాముక్తమా
ల్యదనాశ్వాసముహృద్యపద్యముతృతీయంబైమహింబొల్పగున్.

Colophon of Canto IV.

మ. ఇదిసింహాచలదంభకేసరిపదాభీష్టార్పనాపుణ్యాల
బమరుట్టంకణపొట్టునూరివిజయస్తంభోపలోట్టంకితాం

(1) The name of this uncle of Pratāparudra is given as Tirumala Rāghavarāya or Tirumala Kāntarāya in inscriptions (vide Nos. 37, 38, 40 and 41), Butterworth Nellore Inscriptions.

(2) At Koṇḍavīḍu Krishna Rāya is said to have captured alive not only Vīrabhadra, the son of Pratāparudra Gajapati, but several others like Naraharipātra, the son of Kumāra Hammīra Mahāpātra, Mallūkhān and Uddaṇḍakhan of Rāchūru (Raichur), Rāchirāju of Pūsapāḍu, Śrīnātharāju and Lakshmīpatīrāju, Kasavāpātra of Janyāla, Balachandra-Mahāpātra and others (vide Nos. 574 of 1902, 196 of 1903, 272 of 1897, *Madras Epig. Rep.*).

(3) Inscriptions give in addition to Praharēśvara the names of Bōḍajanna Mahāpātra and Bijilikhan as having been captured at Koṇḍapalli. The name of Praharēśvara appears in inscriptions variously as Bhūpati Pritalāḍana Śiraschandra (No. 511 of 1905), Bhūpati Pradhānarāja Śiraśchandra (No. 74 of 1903) or Bhūpati Ahlādana Śiraśchandra (No. 125 of 1904).

కద్భుతశేషాతురకృష్ణరాయనృపసంజ్ఞాప్తత్ప్రణీతాముక్తమా
ల్యదనాశ్వాసవరంబునాలవదిహృద్యంబైమహింబొల్పగున్

Colophon of Canto V.

మ. ఇదియాంధ్రక్షితియుధార్థనామయశనాస్ఫూర్జత్కెంబావివా
రిదపద్ధత్యవరోధివప్రవలయశ్రేణీవిఘాతక్రియా
స్పదసేనాగ్రదకృష్ణరాయమహిభృత్సంజ్ఞాప్తదాముక్తమా
ల్యదనాశ్వాసముపంచమంబమరుహృద్యంబైనపద్యంబులన్.

41

PĀRIJĀTĀPAHARAṆAMU.

[*By Nandi Timmayya.*]

In the reference to Krishnadēva Rāya's family at the beginning of this book Krishna Rāya is described as God Krishna himself born again into the world. In a battle which Krishna Rāya fought on the banks of the Kaveri near the Western Ghats the water of the Kaveri was made quite red with the blood of the large number of enemies whom he killed. Near Koṇḍavīḍu Krishna Rāya defeated the son of Pratāpa Rudra and having captured him, gave him back his life'. In his triumphant march in the territories of the Gajapati he captured Udayagiri, Vinukoṇḍa, Koṇḍavīḍu, Bellamkoṇḍa, Vēlupukoṇḍa, Jallipalli, Anantagiri and Kambammet; and the Gajapati was in hourly apprehension of his march upon his capital Cuttack. In a verse at the end of the first canto he is represented as hearing, along with his queens, the works composed by the poets assembled at his court for the spring festival every year. In the beginning of the second canto he is described as staying in a palace called Malayakūṭa, and in a verse at the end of the canto he is praised as having pulled down the walls of Ummattūr and Śivasamudram, the citadel of the Rāja of Ummattūr. At the end of the fifth canto the poet gives some information about his own family. He was the son of Nandi Śingāmātya and Timmāmba, nephew of the clever Malayamāruta Kavi *, and pupil of Aghōra Śivachārya. He was presented by Krishna Rāya with an agrahāra (Brahman village) for his skill at dice. In the next verse Krishna Rāya is said to have performed

* Ghanta Singayya, the joint author of Varāhapurāṇam (vide Extract 32 above).

the gift of Mauktika Tulāpurusha, i.e., weighing himself against pearls, which he distributed among the learned.

Canto I.

శా. వీరశ్రీనరసింహశౌరిపదవీవిశ్వక్షమామండలీ
ధౌరంధర్యమునన్ జగంబు ముదమందన్ నాగమాంబాసుతుం
డారూఢోన్నతిఁ గృష్ణరాయఁడు విభుండై రాజ్యసింహాసనం
బారోహించె విరోధులున్ గహనశైలారోహముల్ సేయఁగన్.

సీ. యాదవత్వమున సింహాసనస్థుఁడు గామి
సింహాసనస్థుఁడై చెన్ను మెఱయు
గొల్లయిల్లాండ్రతోఁ గోడగించుటఁ జేసి
పరకామినీసహోదరతఁ జూప
మఱి జరాసుతునకై మధుర డించుటఁ జేసి
పరవర్గదుర్గముల్ బలిమిఁ గొనఁగఁ
బారిజాతము నాసపడి పట్టి తెచ్చుట
నౌదార్యమునఁ దాని నడుగువఱుపఁ

గీ. గోరి తొలిమేనఁ గన్నకైన కొదువలెల్ల
మాన్పుకొనవచ్చి భువనైకమాన్యలీల
నవతరించిన కృష్ణుఁడౌ ననఁగ మించె
నరసవిభు కృష్ణరాయభూనాయకుండు

శా. శ్రీరంగేశ్వరనాభిపంకజరజశ్శ్రీకంటెఁ జోళేంద్రత
న్వీరాజత్కుచపాళి వంజరులకంటెన్ సహ్యభూభృత్తటీ
నీరంధ్రోజ్జ్వలగైరికద్రవముకంటెన్ స్వర్ణగావించెఁగా
వేరీతోయము గృష్ణరాయఁడహితోర్వీనాథరక్తప్రభన్.

సీ. చక్రవర్తిమహాప్రశస్తి నాఁడును నేఁడు
జెలఁగి ధర్మక్రమస్థితి ఘటించె
భూభృదుద్ధరణవిస్ఫూర్తి నాఁడును నేఁడు
గోరక్షణఖ్యాతిఁ గుదురపఱిచె
సాధుబృందావనసరణి నాఁడును నేఁడు
ఎ శౌనురాగంబు వదలఁడయ్యె
సత్యభామాభోగసక్తి నాఁడును నేఁడు
నాకల్పమవని నింపారనిలిపె.

గీ. నాఁడు నేఁడు సుయాదవాన్వయమునందు
జననమందెను వసుదేవ మనుజవిభుని
కృష్ణుఁడను పేర నరసేంద్రు కృష్ణదేవ
రాయఁడను పేర నాదినారాయణుండు.

చ. మునుకొని కొండవీటి కడ మూఢత రుద్రుఁడు కృష్ణనందను
న్మనసిజుని జయించె నది మానుష మే నరసేంద్ర కృష్ణరా
యనృపతి కొండవీటి కడ నాహవభూమిఁ బ్రతాపరుద్రనం
దనుఁడగు వీరభద్రుఁ గరుణామతిఁ గాచె జగత్ప్రసిద్ధిగన్.

చ. నెలకొని కృష్ణరాయధరణీవిభుఁ డుత్కలభూమిపాలుతో
గలన నెదిర్చి హస్తికర కాండ తతుల్ మసకంపుఁ బాములై
మలసినచోటఁ గూడిన సమగ్రయశోవసనంబుఁ గప్పి తా
వలవఁగఁ జేసె భూసతిని వశ్యవిధిజ్ఞుఁడు గాన నేర్పునన్.

సీ. ఉదయాద్రి వేగ నత్యుద్ధతి సాధించె
వినుకొండ మాటమాత్రన హరించెఁ
గూటముల్ సెదరంగఁ గొండవీడ గలించె
బెల్లముకొండ యచ్చెల్లఁ జేటిచె
వేలుపుఁగొండ యుద్వృత్తి భంగము సేసె
జల్లిపల్లె సమగ్రశక్తిఁ గూల్చె
గినుక మీఱి యనంతగిరిఁ గ్రిందుపడఁ జేసె
గంబఁబుమెట్టుఁ గ్రక్కన గదల్చె

గీ. బలనికాయము కాలుమట్టులన డంచుఁ
గటకమును లింక సనుచు నుత్కలమహీశుఁ
డనుదినమ్మును వెఱచు నెవ్వనికి నతఁడు
రాజమాత్రుండె శ్రీకృష్ణరాయవిభుఁడు.

*   *   *   *

క. ప్రతివర్షవసంతోత్సవ
కుతుకాగత సుకవినికర గుంభిత కావ్య
స్మృతి రోమాంచ విశంకిత
చతు[illegible]ంతఃపురవధూప్ర[illegible]దనరసికా.

Canto II.

క. శ్రీసదనలోచనాబ్జద
యాసారమరందపోషితార్థిభ్రమరో
ల్లాసగుణమలయకూట
ప్రాసాదనివేశకృష్ణరాయమహీశా.

శా. సమ్మర్దక్షమధీనిబంధనవిధాసంక్రందనాచార్యశూ
రమ్మన్యాచలవజ్రబాహు జగతీరక్షాంబుజాక్షాశర
ధ్యన్మార్గస్థదశాస్యరాజ్యసమసహ్యాప్రోద్భవాతీరభా
గుమ్మత్తూగిశివంసముద్రపుర వప్రోన్మూలనాడంబరా.

Canto III.

క. విదళితకాళింగమదా
స్పదసింధురకుంభరత్నశర్కరిలాగా
దుదయగిరికొండవీటీ
పదవీస్థలమండలీకభాసర్కగబిరుదా.

పంచ. మరుద్వృధాతటస్థ శత్రుమండలీగళాంతక
క్షురన్నవాస్యగా పగాభి సారికాదృతాంబుధీ
మరుత్పతిస్వరుక్షితి క్రమత్రుటత్తుర్కభృద్వర
స్ఫురద్ధ్వనిప్రవృద్ధ యుద్ధపుంఖితానకార్భటీ.

Canto IV.

క. చండతరమూరురాయర
గండమహోబిగుద ధాటికారయవిచల
తోర్దండపలికొండవీటీ
మండలకటకేశసింధుమంధరకుధరా.

Canto V.

సీ. కౌశికగోత్ర విఖ్యాతుఁడాపస్తంబ
సూత్రుఁడార్వేలపవిత్రకులుఁడు
నందిసింగామాత్యునకును దిమ్మాంబకు
దనయుండుసకలవిద్యావివేక
చతురుఁడుమలయమారుత కవీంద్రునకు మే
నల్లుండుకృష్ణరాయక్షితీశ
కరుణాసమాలబ్ధఘనచతురంతయా
నమహాగ్రహారసన్మానయుతుఁడు

గీ. తిమ్మయార్యుండు శివపరాధీనమతియ
ఘోరశివగురుశిష్యుండు పారిజాత
హరణమను కావ్యమొనరించె నాంధ్రభాష
నాదివాకరతారాసుధాకరముగ.

శా. ఏకచ్ఛత్త్రితసర్వభూతల నృసింహేంద్రక్ష్మాభృత్తపః
పాకద్యోతితరూప మౌక్తికతులాభారప్రదానోన్నతా
నేక స్తన్యసమాస్త్ర సన్నిభ హరిత్తూలంకషోద్యద్యశః
శ్రీకర్ణాటమహీశ వైరికరిఘటాసింహప్రతాపోదయా.

క. భుజనవిజయాఖ్యసంస
న్నవరత్నవిభాప్రభాతనలినాస్త్రరమా
ధవచరణకమలసేవా
ప్రవణమతీవీరరుద్రవర్యతవజ్రీ.

42

JĀMBAVATĪKALYĀṆAM.

[*By Krishna Rāya of Vijayanagar.*]

This is a Sanskrit drama written by the Emperor Krishna Rāya. In the prologue, the drama is said to have been enacted before the people assembled to witness the Chaitra (Spring) festival of Virūpāksha, the tutelary god of the Karṇāṭa Empire residing on the top of the mountain Hēmakūṭa in the city of Vijayanagar.

नान्द्यन्ते सूत्रधारः—(सानन्दं परिक्रम्य सपुष्पाञ्जलिक्षेपम्)

अद्य खलु चराचरगुरोः अपारकरुणापारावारस्य नमदमरशिरोमन्दार-मन्दारविन्दस्य विजयनगरनिवासवासनावधीरितधनदनगरविहारदोहलस्य हेमकूटगिरिकटकवास्तव्यकुटुम्बिनः कर्णाटराज्यरक्षामणेः श्रीविरूपाक्षदेवस्य चैत्रोत्सवावलोकनाय सङ्गता परिषत्.

. . . . . . श्रीकृष्णरायः कविः

सूक्तिः कर्णरसायनं सुमनसां श्लाघ्यस्वभावा सभा ।
चारित्रं यदुवंशशेखरमणेः देवस्य सर्वोत्तरः
पारम्पर्यकृतश्रमाः पुनरमी नाट्येनपारा वयम् ॥

* * * *

End.

धर्मं पादचतुष्टयेन कृतवत् स्थैर्यं समालम्बतां
चातुर्वर्ण्यमुपैतु कर्म सततं स्वस्वाधिकारोचितम् ।
शेषक्ष्माधरनायकस्य कृपया सप्तार्णवीमध्यगां
रक्षन्गामिह कृष्णरायनृपतिर्जीयात्सहस्रं समाः ॥

Colophon.

समाप्तमिदं राजाधिराज राजपरमेश्वर सकलकलाभोजराजविभव मूरुरायरगण्ड श्रीमत्कृष्णरायमहारायविरचितं जाम्बवतीकल्याणं नाम नाटकम् ॥

43

COLOPHON OF THE COMMENTARY ON AGASTYA'S CHAMPU BHĀRATA.

[*By Sāḷuva Timma.*]

Sāḷuva Timma, the famous Minister of the Emperor Krishna Dēva Rāya, has written a commentary on the Champu Bhārata of Agastya.

इति श्रीमद्राजाधिराज राजपरमेश्वर कर्णाटेश्वर श्रीकृष्णरायशिरःप्रधान सकलागमपारावारपारीण साळ्वतिम्मयदण्डनाथविरचितायां बालभारतव्याख्यायां मनोहराख्यायां पञ्चमः सर्गः ॥

44

TUKKĀ PANCHAKAM.

The following five verses are ascribed by tradition to Tukkā, the daughter of Pratāpa Rudra Gajapati, the ruler of Orissa, who was given in marriage to Krishna Rāya. She is said to have been neglected by her husband and to have led a life of seclusion at Kambam in the Cuddapah district. The big irrigation tank at Kambam is said to have been constructed at her instance. In the verses she bemoans her husband's neglect of her.

तुक्का नाम गजपतिपुत्री कृष्णदेवरायपत्नी.

चरन्वनान्ते नवमञ्जरीषु न षट्पदो गन्धफलीमजिघ्रत् ।
सा किं न रम्या स च किं न रन्ता बलीयसी केवलमीश्वराज्ञा ॥ १ ॥

मा किंशुक प्रकटयात्मनिमेषमात्रं मन्मस्तके विहरतीति मधुव्रतोऽयम् ।
किं मालतीविरहवेदनया त्वदीयं दृष्ट्वा प्रसूनमचिरादनलभ्रमेण ॥ २ ॥
भ्रमर भ्रमता दिगन्तराले क्वचिदास्वादितमीक्षितं श्रुतं वा ।
वद सत्यमपास्य पक्षपातं यदि जातीकुसुमानुकारि पुष्पम् ॥ ३ ॥
कुसुमानि लिखन्तु नाम चित्रे कतिचित्कारुविशेषरूढशिक्षाः ।
सुरभित्वममूनि किं लभन्ते किमु चैतेषु रसं पिबन्ति भृङ्गाः ॥ ४ ॥
किं मालति म्लायसि मां विहाय चुचुम्ब तुम्बीकुसुमं षडाङ्घ्रिः ।
लोके चतुर्भिश्चरणैः पशुस्स्यात् स षड्भिरत्यर्थपशुर्न किं स्यात् ॥ ५ ॥

45

PRABODHA CHANDRODAYA VYĀKHYA.

[*By Nādinḍla Gopa Mantri*].

Nādinḍla Gopa, the author of this commentary on Krishṇamiśra's Prabodha Chandrodaya, was a nephew of Krishna Rāya's well-known minister Sāḷuva Timma. In the introduction the author gives in addition to his own genealogy some account of Krishna Rāya and his great minister. Referring to Krishna Rāya the account says that Krishna Rāya married the daughter of Pratāparudra, the Gajapati King of Orissa. His minister Sāḷuva Timma is said to have governed the whole country extending from sea to sea and from the Sētu to Simhāchalam. Sāḷuva Timma's nephews, by his sister Krishṇāmbikā and Timma Mantri, were Nādinḍla Appa and Nādinḍla Gopa Mantri. Of these the elder Appa was also the son-in-law of Sāḷuva Timma. Gopa is said to have excelled, by his ability as a minister, the famous Chāṇakya, Bhaṭṭi, Śivadēva and Yugandhara. He was presented by Sāluva Timma with a palanquin, anklets (Kaṭaka), chauris, ear-rings, bracelets and other insignia of royalty. Gopa governed the district of Konḍavīḍu with Vinukonḍa and other forts, and gave to Brahmans several agrahāras like Rāmachandrapuram.

अस्ति प्रशस्तमहिमा नरसिंहसूनुः श्रीकृष्णरायनृपतिर्नृपसार्वभौमः ।
यस्योद्धता समरसीम्नि कृपाणवल्ली दूतीभवत्यमरलोकविलासिनीनाम् ॥
नास्तं याति सदोदयाद्रिशिखरे तिष्ठत्यरिक्ष्माभृतां
हस्ताब्जानि निमीलयत्यगणयन्लोकान्समाक्रामति ।

तापं छत्रभृतामहर्निशमतीवापादयत्यद्भुतं
*कर्णाटेश्वरकृष्णरायनृपतेस्तीव्रप्रतापांशुमान् ॥
प्रतापरुद्रस्य गजेश्वरस्य पुत्रीं पवित्रीकृतभूतधात्रीम् ।
प्रत्यग्रहीद्यः प्रकटप्रतापो भद्रां सुभद्रामिव पाण्डवेयः ॥
तस्य श्रीकृष्णरायस्य प्राज्यराज्यधुरन्धरः ।
कुलक्रमागतो मन्त्री साल्वतिम्मचमूपतिः ॥
आपूर्वपश्चिमसमुद्रमधत्त राज्यम् आसेतुसिंहगिरि चाप्रतिमप्रतापः ।
यः कृष्णरायनृपपालकदण्डनाथः कौण्डिन्यगोत्रतिलकः कविपारिजातः ॥
तद्भागिनेयौ तरणिप्रतापौ नादिण्डुयप्पप्रभुगोपवर्यौ ।
विराजतस्तिम्मयमन्त्रिपुत्रौ कृष्णाम्बिकागर्भपयोधिचन्द्रौ ॥
अथ मन्त्रीश्वरो ज्यायान कौशिकान्वययोस्तयोः ।
अभवत्साल्वतिम्मस्य जामाताब्धेरिवाच्युतः ॥
काशा वीतप्रकाशा रणभुवि पतिताः कुन्तलाः कुन्तलूनाः
चोला भ्रश्यन्निचोलाः निशिततरशरैः छिन्नदेहा विदेहाः ।
लाटास्तन्त्यक्तघोटाः सपदि भयवशाज्जातभङ्गाः कलिङ्गाः
यस्मिन्नादिण्डुयप्पप्रभुवरतिलके विक्रमादात्तखड्गे ॥
त्यागेन तिम्मसचिवाप्पयवत्प्रतीतो
यः कोऽपि नास्ति यदि देवमणिस्ततः किम् ।
तन्मन्दुरान्तरजुषां तुरगोत्तमानां
कण्ठेषु देवमणयः कति वा न सन्ति ॥
तस्यानुजस्तरुणभास्करदिव्यतेजाः
नादिण्डुगोपसचिवो नवमार्गवेत्ता ।
चाणक्यभट्टिशिवधर्म(देव)†युगन्धरादीन्
यः पूर्वमन्त्रितिलकानापि धिक्करोति ॥
पल्यङ्किकाकटकचामरकर्णभूषाहाराङ्गदादिवसुधाधिपलाञ्छनानि ।
श्रीकृष्णरायसचिवेश्वरसाल्वतिम्मदत्तानि तानि विविधानि समग्रहीद्यः ॥

---

* Srikanṭēśvara in the printed Nirnayasagara edition ; the manuscript reading adopted above is apparently the correct reading.

† There seems to be a reference here to Śivadēva, the famous minister of the Kākatīya King Gaṇapati and his successor Rudrāmba.

यः कोण्डवीडुनगरीं विनिकोण्डमुख्यैः दुर्गैस्समं समधिगम्य महामहिम्ना ।
प्रादान्मुदा सकलभूसुरपुङ्गवेभ्यः श्रीरामचन्द्रपुरमुख्यमहाग्रहारान् ॥
सोऽयं प्रधानोत्तममौलिरत्नं नादिण्ड्लगोपप्रभुरात्मवेत्ता ।
प्रबोधचन्द्रोदयनाटकस्य टीकां हितार्थं व्यतनोद्बुधानाम् ॥

इति श्रीमद्राजाधिराजपरमेश्वर श्रीमत्प्रतापश्रीकृष्णराय महासाम्राज्य-धुरन्धर श्रीसाल्वतिम्मदण्डनायकभागिनेय नादिण्ड्लगोपमन्त्रिशेखरविरचितायां प्रबोधचन्द्रोदयव्याख्यायां चन्द्रिकाख्यायां षष्ठोऽङ्कस्समाप्तः ॥

46

RĀJAŚĒKHARA CHARITRAM.

[*By Mādayagāri Mallana*].

This poem is dedicated by the author to Nādinḍla Appa Mantri, the nephew of Sāḷuva Timma Mantri, Krishna Rāya's Minister and the Governor over the district of Gutti. In the beginning of the work Appa's genealogy is given at length. In the Kauśika Gotra was born Nāmana Mantri who married Singamāmba, and got the three sons Mādaya, Gangana and Chiṭṭi Gangana. Of these Chiṭṭi Gangana became famous as a minister of the emperor Sāḷuva Narasimha. His elder brother Mādamantri married Amalāmba, and to them were born the five sons Nannapārya, Lingāmātya, Varada the commander of troops, Mādhava Mantri and Rāma-bhadra. Of these Varada married Gopamāmba and got three sons: Timma, China Timma and Konḍā. Of these the eldest Timma became famous as a minister and destroyed all his enemies in the battlefield. He married Krishnamāmba, the sister of Sāḷuva Timma, and got three sons by her: Kona, Appa and Gopa. Of these Gopa was the Governor of the fort of Gutti and his elder brother also became very famous. Nādinḍla Appa married Tirumalāmba, the daughter of Sāḷuva Timma, Minister of Krishna Dēva Rāya, and Lakshmama.

క. ఆకౌశికవంశాంబుధి
రాకాహిమరోచిసచివరత్నము పుణ్య
శ్లోకుఁడు వితరణరేఖా
నాకానోకహము మంత్రినామన వెలసెఁ.

చ. అతనికిసింగమాంబకుమహామహులాశ్రితవజ్రపంజరుల్
సుతులుజనించిరంచితవచోరచనాఫణిభర్తలోకస
మ్మతనుతిమార్గవర్తనుఁడుమాదయమంత్రియుగంగనార్యుఁడున్
గతకలికల్మషుండుచిటిగంగనయున్నిగమత్రయాకృతిన్.

ఉ. సాళువనారసింహమనుజప్రభుకార్యకళాధురంధరుం
డైలవణాబ్ధివేష్టితధరాధిపదుర్గతమంత్రమంత్రిశుం
డాలవితానకేసరియనంగననంగసమానరూపరే
ఖాలలితాంగుఁడట్టిచిటిగంగనయొప్పుగుణానుషంగుఁడై.

శా. అంగాధీశకళింగరాజమగధాధ్యక్షాదిభూభృత్సభా
రంగాభంగవిహారముల్ ఘనశిలాగ్రావస్థలీసంసర
ద్గంగోత్తుంగతరంగనిర్గళితనిధ్వానోద్భటప్రక్రియా
సాంగత్యంబులుచిట్టిగంగవిభువాచాసంభ్రమారంభముల్.

క. అంతగ్రజునకుధృతిజిత
మందరకుధరునకుమాదమంత్రికిసౌంద
ర్యేందిరయగునమలాంబకు
నందనులు జనించిరార్యనందితులగుచున్.

శా. ఆరూఢోన్నతినన్నపార్యుఁడును సింగామాత్యుఁడున్ సద్వి
ద్యారాజీసభవాక్కృతిన్ వరదదండాధీశుఁడున్ మంత్రిచూ
డారత్నంబగుమాధవుండునరిరాడ్గర్వచ్ఛిదాపాదన
శ్రీరామాపగమూర్తియాతఁడనఁగాశ్రీరామభద్రాఖ్యుఁడున్.

గీ. అందువరదయమంత్రిసంక్రందనునకు
గోపమాంబకునుదయించిరాపగేంద్ర
సన్నిభులుతిమ్మనార్యుండుఁజిన్నతిమ్మ
ఘనుఁడుఁగొండయమంత్రిపుంగవుఁడుననగ.

ఉ. వారలలోననగ్రజుఁడవారితశౌర్యుఁడుతిమ్మమంత్రిమం
దారముదగ్రదోరసివిదారిత దారుణవైరివీరకం
ఠీరవకంఠశోణితధునీఘనఫేనవిభాసితత్పత
స్ఫురిసితాతపత్రరణభూమియతండొకమంత్రిమాత్రుఁడే.

శా. నాదింగ్లాన్వయవార్ధిశీతరుచిదానక్షాత్రసంపన్నుఁడా
శాదంతావళదంతకుంతపటలస్ఫూర్జాలుసత్కీర్తినా
నాదేశక్షితిపాలమంత్రికులరత్నంబాశ్రితవ్రాతపీ
ఊదాక్షిణ్యనివాసభూమియనలోకఖ్యాతిమించెన్మహిన్.

గీ. సత్యగుణశీలియమ్మహాసచివమణికి
కృష్ణమాంబకుఁగోనమంత్రీశ్వరుండు
భాగ్యసంపన్నుఁడప్పనప్రభుఁడుగోప
దండనాథుండుఁబుట్టిరుద్దండలీల.

ఉ. స్థాపితరాజ్యవైభవనిరాకృతపాకవిరోధిసై నయా
గోపనమంతిధర్మధనగోపనసమ్మతికుత్తిదుర్గల
క్ష్మీపరిపాలనక్రమసమిద్ధభుజాబలశాలిరూపరే
ఖాపరమర్త్యలాంఛనుడయావహకార్యధురంధరుండిలన్.

* * * *

క. ఆయనుఁగుందమ్ముఁడువిన
యాయతమతిఁగొల్వనప్పనార్యుఁడునతఁడున్
బాయకయన్యోన్యప్రియు
లైయలరిరిరామలక్ష్మణాకృతులగుచున్.

క. ఆయప్పమంత్రిగుణములు
వేయితెఱంగులఁజెలంగివినుతియొనర్పన్
డాయఁగఁగాకోదరకుల
నాయకునకుఁగాకకవిజనంబులతరమే.

* * * *

సీ. ఏమంత్రిమణినిజస్వామికార్యక్రియా
తత్పరమానసోత్సాహశాలి
యేమంత్రిమణిమిత్రహితబాంధవాశ్రిత
ప్రకరగతక్షణకళాప్రౌఢబుద్ధి
యేమంత్రిమణివచోహేలాతినైర్మల్య
శీతలతాధూతశీతరోచి
యేమంత్రిమణిసుధాధామశాంభవధామ
ధాళధళ్యసుతుల్యధవళకీర్తి

గీ. అమ్మహామంత్రికతనియ యర్థాంగలక్ష్మి
సకలపుణ్యాంగనాజనశ్లాఘనీయ
లక్ష్మమాంబకునుదయించి లలిని మెఱయు
తిరుమలాంబిక బెండ్లియై తేజరిల్లె.

Colophon.

ఇది శ్రీమదఘోరశివాచార్యగురు కరుణా విశేషలబ్ధ సారస్వత మాదయామాత్యపుత్ర మల్లయనామధేయప్రణీతంబైన రాజశేఖరచరిత్రం బను మహాప్రబంధంబునందు సర్వంబును దృతీయాశ్వాసము.

47

KRISHṆĀRJUNASAMVĀDAM.

[*By Nādindla Gopa Mantri*].

In the introduction to this work written in Telugu Dvipada metre by Nādindla Gopa Mantri, the nephew of Sāḷuva Timma, the famous minister of Krishna Rāya, the author gives an account of his family. In the Kauśika gotra was born Timma Danḍanātha who married Krishnamāmba, the sister of Sāḷuva Timma. They both got three sons : Kona, Appa and Gopa. Of these Appa became very famous for his benefactions to the poor, was a Kirīṭi (Arjuna) in battle, and had dedicated to him the Telugu poem Rājaśēkharacharitram. He married Tirumalāmba, the daughter of his maternal uncle Sāḷuva Timma, who is called the Sāmrājya Dhurandhara (bearer of the burden of the empire of Krishnadēva Rāya), and his wife Lakshmamma. His younger brother Nādinḍla Gopa is called Nādinḍla Śāsana (ruler of his native village Nādinḍla). Through the favour of Sāḷuva Timma he was appointed governor of the fort of Konḍavīḍu. He constructed the prākāras (compound walls) and the gopura (tower) and palaces for the God Rāghavēśvara worshipped at Konḍavīḍu. Covering the temple with paintings he presented the village Maidavolu to the God.

ద్విపద. శ్రీకాంతతో సాటిసెప్పఁగా జాలి
శ్రీకరాకృతియైనకృష్ణమాంబకును
కోమరొప్పఁ బుట్టిరి కోనధీమణియు
నమరాద్రిసమధీరుఁడప్పమంత్రియును
అందునప్పయమంత్రి యాచక . . . .

మందారలోకసమానవైభవుఁడు
రాజశేఖరచరిత్రకునధినాథుఁ
డాజికిరీటిమహాభాగ్యయుతుఁడు
చింతామనోహారకాంతివి . . .
కంతుజయంతసంకాశుఁడైతనరి
శ్రీయశోనిత్యుండుశ్రీకృష్ణదేవ
రాయసామ్రాజ్యభారధురంధరుండు
బలవదరాతిభూపతినుతపాద
తలుఁడుసాళువతిమ్మదండనాయకుఁడు
లక్ష్మీమహాదేవిలాగుననొప్పు
లక్ష్మమ్మకుజనించిలాలితలీల
బెఱిగినతిరుమలాంబికఁబెండ్లియాడి
నిరుపమప్రాభవనిత్యుఁడైవెలసె
నతనికిననుజుండుననఘవర్తనుఁడు
చతురనానావిధజాలకోవిదుఁడు
భద్రలక్షణరామభద్రప్రసాద
సద్రాజ్యబహుళరక్షావిచక్షణుఁడు
సమదశాత్రవరాజసచివదుర్మంత్ర
తిమిరసూర్యుండునాదిండ్లశాసనుఁడు
వరగుణాకరుఁడువిశ్వంభరాచక్ర
పరిపూర్ణయశుఁడుగోపప్రధానుండు
దండితాహితమహీధవసాళ్వతిమ్మ
దండనాయకునిసంతతకృపామహిమను
వినుతికెక్కినకొండవీటిదుర్గంబు
ఘనతనేలుచుసొంపుగానొకనాఁడు
నవరసజ్ఞులుహితుల్ నటులుమాగధులు
కవులునురాజపుంగవులునుఁగొలువ
వన్నెగాబాంధవవర్గంబుతోడ
నున్నతశ్రీలఁబేరోలగంబుండి
మద్వంశకర్తయైమహినుతిఁగన్న
సద్వర్తనుండువిశ్వామిత్రమౌని

యజ్ఞవాటము నబాయని వేల్పుగాన
విజ్ఞానమునఁ జాల వివరించి కొండ
వీటికాభ్యంతర విలసిత యజ్ఞ
వాటికా రాఘవేశ్వరునకు వరుస
బ్రాకార గోపుర ప్రాసాద తతులు
ప్రాకట శ్రీలు జూపట్టఁ గట్టించి
నలవుతోఁ జిత్రవర్ణములు గావించి
బలితంపు హేమకుంభంబు లెత్తించి
యలఘుతర శ్రీలకాస్పదంబగుచు
యలరిన మైదవోలను పురోత్తమము
వినుతమహాత్మవిగ్రహంబులను
పెనుపొందు వేడ్కనర్పించి చిత్తమునఁ.

* * * *

48

COMMENTARY ON MAHINASTAVA, PANCHIKA.

[*By Dēśayāmātya*].

This commentary was written by Dēśayāmātya, an assistant of Nādinḍla Gopa who felt happy in having entrusted the burden of ruling the province to him. He made large additions and gifts to the God Śiva worshipped at Konḍavīḍu. Dēśaya Mantri was the son of Annayāmātya, and was a warrior as well as a scholar. He says that he comments upon the Mahimnastava through the grace of Lolla Lakshmīdhara, his guru (preceptor), whom he compares with the God Gaṇapati in wisdom. Lolla Lakshmīdhara whom he praises as his guru was a very celebrated scholar of his time. We find him as the author of the Konḍavīḍu and Kāza inscriptions* of Krishna Rāya. He has written works on Astronomy, Astrology and the Mantraśāstra, as well as on all the six Darśanas (religious schools), and Law. He was the author of the work Sarasvatīvilāsa, upon law, attributed to Pratāparudra. This Pratāparudra was the ruler of Orissa, contemporary with Krishna Rāya, who became his father-in-law. Lolla Lakshmīdhara enumerates Sarasvatīvilāsa among his works in the colophon

* Edited by Dr. Lüders in the *Epigraphia Indica*, Vol. VI, pp. 117 et seq. and 233 et seq.

to his commentary on Saundaryalaharī. He was author of a portion of the encyclopædic work on Astronomy, Astrology and allied subjects called Jyotisha Darpaṇa.

नादिण्ड्लगापसचिवः सचिवाग्रगण्यः श्रीसाल्वतिम्मसचिवेश्वरभागिनेयः ।
. . . . देचार्यमन्त्रिणि निधाय सुखं समास्ते ॥
श्रीकोण्डवीडुनगरे नगरेभहर्म्यभर्माणि भूषणवराणि वितानजालम् ।
छत्रध्वजांश्च मखवैरिमहेश्वराय प्रादत्त देचय . . . . . ॥
. . . . . सप्तभुवनव्याप्तं यशो यत्कुले
सप्तर्षिप्रभवो हि यत्कुलगुरुः कौण्डिन्यनामा मुनिः ।
यूरेग्रामनिवासवासनवशाद्यूराख्यया विश्रुतः
सोऽयं देचयमन्त्रि . . . . ॥

. . . .
शूरश्शौर्यप्रथितमहसां पुण्यवान् पुण्यवत्सु ।
प्राज्ञः प्राज्ञेष्वतुलमहिमा नीतिमान्नीतिमत्सु
श्रीमान्देचप्रभुमणिरसावन्नयामात्यसूनुः ॥
स चायं देचयामात्यो महिम्नस्तुतिपञ्चिकाम् ।
लक्ष्मीधरकटाक्षेण कुरुते गुरुतेजसा ॥
विश्वेशपार्वतीपुत्रं लोल्ललक्ष्मीधराह्वयम् ।
विद्वद्गणपतिं वन्दे द्विजराजशिरोमणिम् ॥

End.

लक्ष्मीधरकटाक्षेण देशयामात्यशेखरः ।
अकरोदाकरो वाचां महिम्नस्तुतिपञ्चिकाम् ॥

49

CHĀṬU VERSES OF PEDDANA ON KRISHNA RAYA.

1. In this verse the famous poet Allasāni Peddana of Krishna Rāya's court, who dedicated the work Manucharitram to him, bemoans Krishna Rāya's death. He blames himself for surviving such a patron, and recounts the various marks of honour which his late sovereign bestowed on him. Whenever Krishna Dēva Rāya met him outside, he made it a point to stop his elephant and to

give him a seat by his side. When the poet was taken round in procession on the occasion of dedicating his work Manucharitram to him, the emperor lifted the poet's palanquin with his own hands. When the anklet, Kavigaṇḍapeṇḍēra, was presented to Peddana signifying that he excelled all the other poets of his court, he himself put it round the poet's ankle saying "you alone of all deserve it." Krishna Rāya granted him the village Kōkaṭamu, and whatever other village or villages he chose to ask in any part of the empire. He used to address the poet Āndhrakavitā-pitāmaha (the grandfather of Telugu poetry).

2. The verse following is said to have been composed by Peddana addressing the Gajapati (of Orissa) who invaded the Karnāṭaka territories after Krishna Rāya's death. In the verse Peddana recounts the victories which Krishna Rāya won over him, drawing pointed attention to the following four incidents: (1) that Krishna Rāya devastated the Āraṭlakona with his elephants; (2) that he put up his triumphant inscription at Simhādri; (3) that he set his siege elephants to charge against the bell-metal door of the Gajapati's fort; and (4) that he gave his daughter in marriage to Krishna Rāya after putting upon his ankle the Gaṇḍapeṇḍēram (anklet) as a sign of submission. He then goes on to rebuke the impudence of the Gajapati's invading the Kanarese country after Krishna Rāya's death. Tradition has it that the Gajapati returned to his territory after the incident.

సీ. ఎదురైన చోఁదన మదకరీంద్రము డిగ్గి
కేలూత యొసఁగ యెక్కించుకొనియె
మనుచరిత్రం బందుకొను వేళఁ బురమేఁగఁ
బల్లకిఁ దనకేల బట్టియెత్తె
బిరుదైన కవిగండ పెండేరమునకీవె
తగుదని తానె పాదమునఁ దొడిగె
కోకటగ్రామాద్య నేకాగ్రహారము
లడిగిన సీమలయందు నిచ్చె

గీ. నాంధ్ర కవితాపితామహ యల్లసాని
పెద్దన కవీంద్రయని నన్నుఁ బిలుచునట్టి
కృష్ణరాయలతోఁ దివి కేఁగ లేక
బ్రతికియున్నాఁడ జీవచ్ఛవంబ నగుచు.

సీ. రాయరావుతు గండఁ రాచయేనుఁగు వచ్చి
యారట్లకోన గోరాడునాఁడు
సంపెటనరపాల సార్వభౌముఁడు వచ్చి
సింహాద్రిఁ జయశిలఁ జేర్చునాఁడు
సెలగోలుసింహంబు చేరిధిక్కృతి గంచు
వల్లుల గరుల డీకొల్పునాఁడు
ఘనతర నిర్ఝరగండ పెండెరమిచ్చి
కూఁతురాయలకును గూర్చునాఁడు.

గీ. ఒడలెఱుంగవొ చచ్చితో యుర్వి లేవొ
చేరఁజాలక తలచెడి జీర్ణమైతొ
కన్నడం బెల్లు చొచ్చెదు గజపతీంద్ర
తెలిచినిలుకుకర చొచ్చిన తెలుఁగుతోవ.

50

ŚRIVALLABHĀCHĀRYACHARITAM.

[*By Muraḷidhara Dāsa*].

In this biography of Vallabhāchārya, the great Vaishṇava teacher of Gujarat, by Muraḷīdhara Dāsa, it is said that once in his youth he went to the court of the Raja of Viśākhanagara (Vizagapatam ?), called Krishna Rāya. He was very much honoured at the court. Even his envious uncle, though personally inimical, stood up along with the other members of the court and showed him respect. Vallabhāchārya was made to take his seat on a Ratnāsana (jewelled chair). While there he learnt of a religious controversy between the Vaishṇavas and their opponents in which the latter succeeded. Not able to endure the defeat, he entered the controversy and defeated all the opponents of Vaishṇavaism. Rejoicing at this Krishna Rāya honoured him by a Kanakābhishēka. But he did not accept the wealth as he thought it was not necessary for the establishment of his religion. But he accepted ONLY four or five coins out of the money, just for the satisfaction of the king.

अन्यदिवसे प्रातर्नित्यकर्मानुष्ठानानन्तरं शिष्येण सह विशाखनगर-राजसभां प्रविवेश। सनत्कुमारशुकादिवत् स्वतेजसा राजसभां भासयामास।

असूयादग्धमातुलोऽपि सभासीनजनैस्सर्वैः भूपालेन चाप्यवशो भूत्वा प्रत्युत्थाय सम्मानयामास । राज्ञा भृशं मानितो भूत्वा रत्नासने उपविवेश । तत्पूर्वं तत्र विद्वज्जनैः कृतचर्चायां अवैष्णवजयमश्रृणोत् । स्वयं तदसहमानः राज्ञा च प्रार्थितः साक्षाद्बलदेव इव भागवतशास्त्रार्थचर्चया रिपुसमूहं जित्वा कृष्णरायनामकेन तेन भूपालेन कनकाभिषेकं प्राप्यापि स्वमतस्थापनमात्रैकप्रयोजनत्वात् भगवदितरनिस्पृहत्वं विशदयन् तीर्थयात्रार्थं प्रस्थितः राज्ञो मुदे चतुःपञ्चनिष्कमात्रं स्वीकृतवान् । कृष्णसेवामार्गवर्धकं वेदव्यासमेव स्वशिष्यकोटिषु प्रख्यापयन् मायावादिप्रभृतिनानापाषण्डमतशुष्कतृणेषु अग्निरिव चरन् नित्यदा नियमेन निकटवर्तिना परमाप्ततमेन दामोदरदासेन च अनुगतः गर्भ एव गोवर्धननाथेन स्वीयत्वेन अनुगृहीतवान् ।

51

TAMIL NĀVALAR CHARITAI.

The following verses taken from the Tamil Nāvalar Charitam refer to Krishna Dēva Rāya of Vijayanagar.

The first verse by an author called Kumāra Sarasvati refers to the conquest of Orissa by Krishna Dēva Rāya and of his marriage with the daughter of the Orissa king. The next three, ascribed to an author Tatvaprakāśar, have reference to irregularities of management in respect of daily worship in the Tiruvālūr temple. On hearing the complaint, Krishna Rāya ordered the dismissal of the culpable servants of the temple against whom is aimed these stanzas wherein the author contrasts, in bitter satire, the previous position of the priests with that to which they had reduced themselves by their own action. The last stanza draws the attention of Krishna Rāya to the destruction of the metallic images of two of the 63 Nāyanmars by the temple priest Nāgaraśa Nambi; the interesting part of the story is that the people who complained had recourse to a parrot which had been taught to recite the poem in the hearing of Krishna.

குமாரசரசுவதி, ஒட்டியனை (கிருஷ்ணராயர்) செயித்தபோது பாடியது.—

கலிங்க மிழந்துநுதிக் கைச்சங்கந் தோற்று
மெலிந்துகட கங்கழுவ விட்டாள்—மலிந்தமலர்ப்

பொன்னிட்ட மானகிருட்ண பூபாலா வுன்றனுக்குப்
பின்னிட்ட வொட்டியன்பொற் பெண் (210)

தத்துவப்பிரகாசர் திருவாரூர்க் கொடியிறக்காமற் றகைந்தது—

மருவுபுகழ்க் கிர்ஷண மகராச ராணை
அரிய வடமலையா ராணை—திருவாரூர்ப்
பாகற் கொடியறுப்பார் பாதத் திருவாணை
த்யாகக் கொடியிறக்காதே. (212)

ஊழித் துலுக்கல்ல வொட்டியான் றுலுமல்ல
வீழித் துலுக்குவந்து மேலிட்டே—யாழி
சிறந்ததே ராரூர்த் தியாகருடைப் பூசை
யிறந்ததே கிட்டிணரா யா. (213)

இது கேட்டு ராயர் சில பட்டரை மாற்றியபோது தத்துவப் பிரகா
சர் பாடியது.—

உண்ட வயிற்றி லுமிக்காந்த லிட்டதே
தொண்டரே வீழித் துலுக்கரே—பண்டெல்லா
மப்ப மவலென் றதிரசமுந் தோசைகளுங்
கப்புவது போச்சே கவிழ்ந்து. (214)

திருவாரூர் நாகரசநம்பி செய்த குற்றங்கிள்ளைக்குச் சொல்லிவித்துத் தலத்தார் ராயனுக்குச்சொல்லி யறிவித்தது.—

முன்னாளருவத்து மூவரிருந்தாரதனி
லின்னாளிரண்டு பேரேகினார்—கன்னா
னருக்கின்றான் வந்துவிட்ட நாகரசநம்பி
யிருக்கின்றான் கிட்டினராயா. (177)

52

LĪLĀVATĪ.

[*By Vallabhāchārya*, otherwise *Kavi Dēvēndra*]

This is a translation into Telugu of the Sanskrit mathematical work of Bhāskarāchārya, Līlāvatī, by Vallabhāchārya who is otherwise known by his title Kavi Dēvēndra, the Indra among poets. The author says that he wrote the work at the request of Bommalāṭa Kāḷa, son of Bommalāṭa Virūpāksha, who was the confidential servant of the emperor Krishna Rāya, and after him, his brother Achyuta Rāya. The position held by the patron of the poet at court can be gleaned from the following statement which is found in a sum given as an exercise in the work. Achyuta Rāya presented a large amount of money to his subordinate

Bommalāṭa Kāḷa of which he presented half to his religious preceptor Kumāra-Tātāchārya ; of the remainder he gave two-thirds to Brahmans ; of what remained still, he gave a fourth to poets, and, giving five-ninths of what remained yet to his friends, gave the author Kavimahēndra himself the rest which amounted 1,116 (Varāhas ?).

గీ. . . . తుఁడ
సుజన హితుఁడ నాపస్తంబ సూత్రకలిత
హారిత గోత్రపయోధినీహారకరుఁడ
నలఘుచరితుఁడవల్లభాహ్వయుఁడ నేను.

ఉ. శ్రీ నరసింహనందను నరిందమవిక్రము కృష్ణరాయ భూ
జానిని వెండియుం దనుజన్ముని నచ్యుత దేవరాయనిన్
దానధికాప్తుఁడై కొలిచి తద్దయుమన్ననగాంచి మించువి
ద్యానిధిఁ బొమ్మలాట విరుపాధిపు కాళని ప్రార్థనంబునన్.

* * * *

క. అనిపొగడఁ గణకులౌనా
ననసంస్కృతభాష భాస్కరాచార్యులు చె
ప్పిన పాటిగ లీలావతి
యొనర్తుఁ దెనుగున. . . .

సీ. నరసనరేంద్రు నందనుఁడైన యచ్యుత
దేవరాయల కృపాదృష్టిఁ జేసి
ఆందోళికారూఢుఁడగు . . బొమ్మ
లాటకాళుఁడు వేడ్కనర్థరాశి
లోనంత్మ గురునాథుఁడైన కుమారతా
తాచార్యవర్యున కర్థమిచ్చ
ద్విజులకు శేషతృతీయము రెండిడి
శేషపాదము కవిశ్రేణికొసఁగె.

గీ. స్నేహమునఁ దనచెలులకు శేషనవమ
భాగపంచక మంతయుఁ బంచిపెట్టెఁ
కవిమహేంద్రున కర్పించె మిగిలినట్టి
వేయునూట పదాఱెంత విత్తరాశి.

53

ACHYUTARĀYĀBHYUDAYAM.

[*By Rāianātha Dindima*]*

This historical poem after recounting the victories of Narasa says that Narasa's wife Obāmba gave birth to a son who was called Achyuta.

Canto II describes the youth of the prince and his studies.

Canto III.—The king Narasa got the young Achyuta married to several maidens born of various families of ruling chiefs belonging to the race of the sun as well as the moon. Of all these Obāmbika was his favourite. Narasa wished that his three sons, Vīra-Narasimha, Krishna and Achyuta should rule the empire one after the other. Of these Vīra-Narasimha ruled the kingdom in peace and released many prisoners from imprisonment. After Vīra-Narasimha, Krishna Rāya ascended the throne and was a terror to his enemies. He captured many fortresses like Koṇḍavīḍu from his enemy the Gajapati of Orissa, and planted a pillar of victory at Paṭupeṭṭanūrpura. This last name seems to have been miswritten for *Poṭṭunūrapura* near Simhādrī, in the Vizagapatam district where according to the Āmuktamālyadā, Manucharitra and other contemporary works he is said to have planted his pillar of victory. After Krishna Rāya's reign grand preparations were made by Narasa to celebrate the coronation of Achyuta. Achyuta's coronation was first celebrated at Tirupati where he was bathed in the water poured out of the conch in the hand of the God Venkaṭēśa. Afterwards Achyuta went to his capital *Vidyānagara* where his coronation was once more celebrated. There his queen Varadāmbika, the daughter of Salaka Rāju, and his son Pinna Venkaṭādri were also anointed as Queen Regnant and Crown-prince respectively. At the time of his coronation Achyuta performed the gift called Suvarṇa-Mēru and gave it to Brahmans.

Canto IV.—One day after his coronation Achyuta's minister waited upon him in the palace called Venkaṭavilāsa and reported to him on the affairs of his empire. He said that *Chellappa* (Tam. Śellappa), one of his subordinate governors, had revolted, and after being defeated in battle, escaped from his province and had taken refuge with the Travancore (Chera) king in his territory. Chellappa and the Chera king together had made war on the Pāṇḍya ruler and driven him from his ancestral territories. The minister

* Vide extract 36 above.

exhorted Achyuta to protect the Pāṇḍya who was an exile from his ancestral kingdom and place him once more firmly upon his throne, and punish Chellappa and the Chera king for their revolt. Achyuta resolved in consequence upon making war with Chellappa, and ordered his general to march with his army to the south.

Canto V.—Achyuta started on his expedition and went to Chandragiri in a few days. There he stationed his troops and went to Tirupati to worship the god at the place. He presented to the God a pair of ear-rings (kuṇḍala), a padaka (a jewelled medallion hung on the necklace and worn on the breast), and a jewelled crown, and stayed there for a few days. He then went to Kāḷahasti, worshipped the God at the place and made to him large grants. From there Achyuta proceeded with his army to Kanchi. There the king weighed himself against pearls which were distributed for charity. While at Kanchi several forest kings (Kirātās) waited upon him with tribute and presents. Accompanied by them he proceeded further south and went to Aruṇaśaila (Tiruvaṇṇāmalai). After worshipping the God of the place he entered the Chola country and after a few days' march reached Śrīrangam. Having stayed there for some time he intended proceeding further on his expedition when one of his officers, the son of Salaka, told him that it was not necessary for the king to go against a small chief like Chellappa and requested that he might be entrusted with the expedition.

Canto VI.—On the assent of the sovereign the general marched to the south past the city of Madura, and encamped on the banks of the Tāmraparṇi. Thence he despatched a subordinate officer of his to march against Tiruvaḍi, the Chera ruler. The Tiruvaḍi came with his army against him near the mountains where a great battle was fought between the two opposing forces. Having been defeated in the battle, the Tiruvaḍi with the remnant of his troops and with the Chola king (probably the ruler of the province of the Vijayanagar Empire corresponding to the Chola kingdom) approached the general and prostrating before him acknowledged his own defeat. He also handed over to him the fugitive Chola king and made presents to him of elephants and horses. The general accepted these for his sovereign, and reinstating the Pāṇḍya on his ancestral throne proceeded to Anantaśayanam (Trivandrum), to worship the god of the place.

Canto VII.—From Anantaśayanam the general went to the Sētu and bathed in the sea at the place. Thence he returned to Śrīrangam in a few days where the emperor stayed spending all the time in the company of poets and scholars. The general presented before Achyuta the Chera king and the other prisoners, and submitted to him a report of his expedition. Achyuta ordered the Chera king who had invaded the Pāṇḍya territories to be punished and the Pāṇḍya to rule over his ancestral territories.

Canto VIII describes life in Achyuta's camp and the pleasures of the king.

Canto IX continues to describe the pleasures of the king.

Canto X.—Achyuta proceeded with his army along the banks of the Kaveri to Śrīrangapaṭṭaṇam (Seringapatam). There he was met by the governors of the place who made him large presents of money. He then turned north and crossing his own territories proceeded towards the territories of the Hayapati (the Sultan of Bijapur).

Canto XI.—Achyuta marched against the territory of the Hayapati (Bijapur Sultan), and laid siege to the fort of Raichur which was garrisoned by the latter's troops. The siege is then described at length. The Sultan sent fresh troops to assist the garrison at Raichur and raise the siege. Then a battle was fought, between these troops and those besieging Raichur, which is described. The lord of the Yavanas (Muhammadans) was defeated in the battle, and he fled from the field. Achyuta after capturing the horses and elephants of the enemy's army proceeded to the Krishna on the banks of which the Sultan had collected all his troops. The armies of the Sultan and the king were ranged on the two banks of the Krishna and they were preparing for a battle when the Sultan left his army, and riding across the river, prostrated himself before Achyuta signifying submission. Achyuta then accepted the allegience of the Sultan and returned to his capital Vijayanagar after a long absence.

Canto XII describes Achyuta's triumphal entry into his capital and the grand reception he was accorded by his subjects. The manuscript is incomplete and breaks off at the thirty-seventh verse of this canto.

Canto II.

नयतो न कदाचन च्युतस्स्यादवतीर्णस्स्वयमच्युतोऽयमुर्व्याम् ।
इति शोभनलक्षणैस्स जानन् अकरोदात्मजमच्युताभिधानम् ॥ ३२ ॥

अधिरोपयति स्म हास्तिकण्ठे जनतां तोषमिषेण जातमात्रः ।
अधुना पटुतामनेकपेन्द्रे व्यवृणोदित्यपि किं नु विस्मयाय ॥ ५२ ॥

विद्यास्समेत्य विविधा नृपतेस्तदासी-
दानन्दहेतुरतिवाहितशैशवोऽयम् ।
यातः क्रमाद्विलसितानि यथा कलानां
पाथोनिधेः किमपि पार्वणशर्वरीशः ॥ ९३ ॥

Canto III.

करम्बितं यौवनकान्तिसम्पदा कुमारमालोक्य कुतूहलान्नृपः ।
अथानिनायास्य विवाहकर्मणे महीभुजां मन्त्रिमुखेन कन्यकाः ॥ १३ ॥
करेण सूनोः क्षितिपालकन्यकाकरानयं ग्राहयति स्म भूपतिः ।
प्रकाशितारुण्यरुचेः पयोजिनीप्रसूनपालीर्दिवसो यथा रवेः ॥ १४ ॥
कुलोद्वहास्वर्ककुमुद्वतीशयोर्वधूषु देवी वरदाम्बिकाभिधा ।
अमुष्य सन्तोषमपुष्यदान्तरं विशिष्य तारास्विव रोहिणी विधोः ॥ १५ ॥
तनूभुवस्त्रीनपि तादृशश्रियः समीक्ष्य साम्राज्यपदार्हलक्षणान् ।
अमन्यतैवान्तरुदन्वदम्बरां परम्पराभोज्यतया पतिः क्षितेः ॥ १६ ॥
समेत्य साम्राज्यरमां मनोरमां विनीतिमान्वीरनृसिंहभूपतिः ।
बहिर्व्यधाद्बन्धनमन्दिरादरीन्धरासुरान्किच दरिद्रताभिधात् ॥ १७ ॥
अनन्तरं कीर्तिधुरन्धरोऽदधात्स कृष्णरायः सकलां वसुन्धराम् ।
अमुष्य शीर्णैरभिषेकवारिभिः शशाम विद्वेषणशौर्यपावकः ॥ १८ ॥
स कोण्डवीटिप्रमुखानि सङ्गरे महान्ति दुर्गाणि मतङ्गजेशितुः ।
पुरा गृहीत्वा पटुपोट्टनूर्पुरे न्यधादथ स्तम्भमसौ महाबलः ॥ १९ ॥
पयोधिकाञ्चीपरिणेतृतास्पदे पदेऽभिषेक्तुं तमथाच्युतप्रभुम् ।
कुलाद्रिकूर्मोरगकुञ्जराग्रणीश्रमापहत्यै समनाहि मन्त्रिभिः ॥ २० ॥
प्रचोदितास्तैः परिचारकास्ततस्तपात्ययेन स्तनयित्नवो यथा ।
अशेषतीर्थार्णववाहिनीजलान्यनैषुराज्ञासमकालमग्रतः ॥ २१ ॥
युवानमाजानुभुजायतिं ततो निशाम्य सर्वैर्निरचायि मन्त्रिभिः ।
भुजङ्गराजन्यधृतां भुवं कृती भुजाङ्गदीकर्तुमसौ भवेदिति ॥ २२ ॥
प्रणामशीलः फणिशैलशासितुः कदाचिदग्रे करशङ्खवारिणा ।
पयोधिकाञ्चीपरिणेतृतास्पदे पदेऽभिषिक्तस्स परम्परागते ॥ २३ ॥

प्रणीय विद्यानगरीं पतिं क्षितेरहीन्द्रशैलाधिभुवास्य कल्पिताम् ।
उदारवृत्तेरुदयुञ्जतोत्सवं विधित्सवस्ते सचिवा विशेषतः ॥ २४ ॥
महत्तरे मानवलोकशासितुः मनोऽनुकूला महिषीपदे तदा ।
कृताभिषेका सळगक्षितीशितुर्वरात्मजासीद्वरदाम्बिका वधूः ॥ ४८ ॥
चकार यन्मेरुमनादिमः पुमान् सुवर्णरूपं सुरसंसदां वशे ।
सुवर्णमेरुं स्वयमस्य सेवको महीसुरेभ्योऽदित मानवेश्वरः ॥ ९० ॥
फलं यदस्याः पतिसेवया प्रभोः फणीशपर्यङ्कपदार्चया च यत् ।
चिरात्तदासीच्चिनवेङ्कटाद्रिरित्यभिख्ययाक्ष्णोरपि दीर्घमायुषि ॥ ९१ ॥
अनेन राज्ञा चिनवेङ्कटाद्रिरप्ययोजि लक्ष्मीं युवराजपूर्विकाम् ।
क्षमापतौ राज्यरमा सयौवनक्रमा च कौमारमसावसूचयत् ॥ ९२ ॥

Canto IV.

एकदा तु सचिवो यथाक्रमं प्रेषितप्रणतराजराजिकम् ।
प्राप्य वेङ्कटविलासमण्टपे प्रश्रयेण निजगाद पार्थिवम् ॥ ४६ ॥
वेत्सि कार्यमखिलं विशेषतो वेदनीयमिह ते न विद्यते ।
श्रोतुमर्हसि यदुच्यते मया मन्त्रिधर्म इति मानवेश्वर ॥ ४७ ॥
छन्नविग्रहतया पलायितश्चेल्लपो वसति चेरसीमनि ।
तच्छरण्यधरणीभुजा समं शिष्य एव स चिरायुषा त्वया ॥ ५६ ॥
प्राकृतान्निजपदात्परिच्युतः पालनीय इह पाण्ड्यभूपतिः ।
शिक्षणं मदवतां पुनः सतां रक्षणं च ननु राजलक्षणम् ॥ ९७ ॥
इत्युक्तस्सचिवेन रागकणिकामीषद्दृशोरञ्चले
बिभ्राणो दलदम्बुजोदरदरप्राप्तातपश्रीमुषम् ।
संरम्भेण चमूविनिर्गमकृते सन्दिश्य सेनापतिं
प्रस्थातुं कृतनिश्चयः समजनि प्राग्रेसरो भूभुजाम् ॥ ९८ ॥

Canto V.

स समाप्य काल्यनियमं सकलं जगदण्डलङ्घिजयशङ्खरवः ।
अधिरुह्य वाहनमहन्युचिते नृपकुञ्जरोऽपि निरगान्नगरात् ॥ १ ॥
अथ वेदिकाममरमौलिमणेरवधूतमन्दरमहेन्द्रगिरिम् ।
शनकैरगाहत स चन्द्रगिरिं नगरीश्रिया हसितनाकपुरीम् ॥ २२ ॥

अखिलानि तत्र विनिवेश्य बलान्यविलम्बितं समवरुह्य हयात् ।
हरिपादभक्तिमवलम्ब्य नृणाम् अधिपोऽध्यरुक्षदहिराजगिरिम् ॥ २३ ॥
श्रवणेकथास्यमननं च मनश्चरणे शिरः स्वयमलङ्कुरुतः ।
इति कुण्डलं पदकमेष हरेः किमिहार्पयन्मणिकिरीटमपि ॥ ४२ ॥
अनुलेपमाल्यवसनाभरणैर्हरिमन्तरन्धतमसेभहरिम् ।
न्यवसद्गिरौ परिचरन्नियमात्कतिचिद्दिनानि कमिता धरणेः ॥ ४३ ॥
अवरुह्य वेङ्कटगिरेः शिखरादधिरुह्य वाहमतिगन्धवहम् ।
स गरीयसीं सकलमुक्तिकरीमपि कालहस्तिनगरीमगमत् ॥ ४४ ॥
निकषा सुवर्णमुखरीं लहरीमुखरीभवद्वितततीरदरीम् ।
कृतधामधामनिजनामपदाङ्कनसीमभूम नमति स्म नृपः ॥ ४५ ॥
द्रविणाधिपेन दृढसख्यवता न च बिक्षुतास्यसमतक्ष्यतया ।
अपवारितेयमुपहारितया नरसात्मजेन नवसीमभुवा ॥ ४६ ॥
स विनम्य चन्द्रशकलाभरणं शिवमञ्जनेभगिरिसंचरणम् ।
अभिवाञ्छितामपि विरिञ्चिमुखैर्हरिकाञ्चिनामनगरीमगमत् ॥ ४७ ॥
अभिजातवैधहयमेधमखान्तरजातमाधिहरमानमताम् ।
कुमुदारविन्दकुलबन्धुदृशं समुदायमम्बुधिसुताक्षिमुदाम् ॥ ४८ ॥
परिचर्यया प्रणवशीर्षमणिं परितोष्य शार्ङ्गिणममुष्य पुरः ।
अधिरूढमौक्तिकतुलापुरुषोऽप्यतुलोऽजनिष्ट सदभीष्टकरः ॥ ४९ ॥
पटहोरुभाङ्करणमन्त्रवशागलितस्वगर्वगरलोष्मभराः ।
निभृताः किरातनिकरा नृपतेर्निहितोपदाश्चरणयोर्न्यपतन् ॥ ५० ॥
शिखिपिञ्छलाञ्छितशिखण्डभरैः श्रितधन्वभिः सितवराटगुणैः ।
विशति स्म तैरनुगतो विनयादधिपो नृणामरुणशैलपुरीम् ॥ ५१ ॥
कदलेक्षुकेरकलमैः स्वदृशोर्जनितोपदान् जनपदाभ्युदयान् ।
अवलोकयन्नतिशयादवनेः कमिता समाश्रुत कवेरसुताम् ॥ ५५ ॥
घननालिकेरकदलीवकुलक्रमुकाटवीजुषि तदीयतटे ।
पृतनां मुकुन्दनमनाभिमना निखिलां न्यवेशयदयं नृपतिः ॥ ५६ ॥
पृथुनीतिमार्गपथिकः पृतनापदवीश्रमापहाति तत्पयसि ।
कृतमज्जनादिनियमः क्षितिपैः सह कैश्चिदाश्रुत स रङ्गगृहम् ॥ ५७ ॥

अजमव्ययामजरं जगतामवनैकतानमनिदानदयम् ।
अभिवन्द्य कामफलदं धरणेरधिभूः समारभत गन्तुमितः ॥ ६२ ॥

नलिनेक्षणांशनरपालमणे क्षितिमण्डले तव किमस्ति समः ।
अभिगम्य एष हि मयैव विभो रणकर्म राजति न चासमयोः ॥ ६३ ॥

प्रेम्णः पात्रीकुरुष्व प्रियरमणभुवः प्रेषणादेष दोर्भ्यां
नेष्ये प्रेष्यं हि गर्वग्रहिलमिह जवाच्चेल्लपं चेरसीम्नः ।
प्रस्थाप्येत्युक्तवन्तं सलगनृपसुतं पद्मनाभान्तरङ्गे
रङ्गे भक्त्युत्तरङ्गः कतिचन दिवसान्स्थातुमैच्छन्महेच्छः ॥ ६४ ॥

Canto VI.

प्रहितः पयोधिरशनापतिना सलगेन्द्रसिन्धुरमणेन्दुरयम् ।
अगमाद्विलङ्घ्य मधुरां महतीमथ ताम्रपर्ण्यभिहितां सरितम् ॥ १ ॥

अदसीयरोधसि निवेशमसाववकल्प्य दर्पभरितस्य रिपोः ।
व्यसृजद्विमाथकरणाभिमनाः पृतनापतिं स पुरतो नृपतिः ॥ १३ ॥

अथ निर्ययौ मतिविपर्ययतो गिरिदर्यमेयजयतूर्यरवः ।
स च सङ्गराय चतुरङ्गबलैस्तिरयन्दिशस्तिरुवटिक्षितिपः ॥ १४ ॥

अविचारितस्वपरयोधमनाद्दृतजीवमस्थिरजयापजयम् ।
अजनिष्ट जन्यमनयोर्बलयोरपि नारदेन यददृष्टचरम् ॥ २० ॥

निहतावशिष्टसुभटानुगतो विजयिष्णुसैन्यमधिजन्यममुम् ।
अधिगम्य चोलपतिनानतवानपरावतारममरेन्द्रतरोः ॥ २९ ॥

अवमर्पितस्तव पदाम्बुजयोरधमः स निर्वटिरधर्मपरः ।
इति तं निगद्य समदान्द्विरदानुपदीचकार रयगांस्तुरगान् ॥ ३० ॥

अनुगृह्य नम्रमसुरक्षणतः स्थितिमान्नये तिरुवटिक्षितिपम् ।
अपि पाण्ड्यभूपमदसीयपदाभ्यधिकप्रतिष्ठमतनिष्ट नृपः ॥ ३१ ॥

शयने शयानमुदधिं समया पदसौरभोर्मिपरिणाहवति ।
अथ नन्तुमच्युतमगादवनेरधिभूरनन्तशयनाभिमुखम् ॥ ३२ ॥

मैनाकप्रमुखैर्महीधरकुलैर्माहेन्द्रभीत्याकुलैः
मत्वा शोषमपामपाङ्कितचमूराजीरजोमण्डलैः ।

अभ्युत्थानमिवाचरन्तमसकृत्प्रेङ्खत्तरङ्गच्छला·
दद्राक्षीन्निधिमम्भसां स नयनायामं मिमानं किल ॥ ३९ ॥

Canto VII.

मङ्क्त्वा मायादंष्ट्रिणोदस्यमानां मध्येपाथः क्ष्मामिवाविर्भवन्तीम् ।
नेतुं भूजामातुरिष्टानि दातुं सेतुं सीताश्वासहेतुं य एति ॥ १२ ॥
पारेसिन्धु प्राप्तसंवेशवेशं पद्मावन्धुं पार्थिवेन्दुः प्रणन्तुम् ।
मोक्षाधारं प्राविशन्मोहदूरं देवागारं दत्तनेत्रापहारम् ॥ १३ ॥
भूयो व्यावृत्तापि भूम्ना चमूनां पश्चात्कुर्वन्पाथसामेष राशिम् ।
रङ्गस्थानं राजसंसेवयाग्रे वल्गच्चेता वासरैः कैश्चिदाप ॥ १४ ॥
आसाद्योर्वीनायकस्योपकार्यामग्रद्वारे सोऽवरुह्योपवाह्यात् ।
औत्सुक्येनानीतकक्ष्याविशेषस्तं प्राणंसीत्तस्थिवांसं सभायाम् ॥ १५ ॥
केचित्स्वामिन्केरळेशप्रयुक्ता वर्तन्ते प्राग्द्वारि ते मन्त्रिवृद्धाः ।
इत्युक्त्वासावेतदीयानुमत्या तस्याभ्याशं ताननैषीत्सभायाम् ॥ १६ ॥
कर्णायुष्यस्यन्दिभिः काव्यबन्धैः कालक्षेपं कल्पयन्तं कवीन्द्रैः ।
पाण्यग्रेण प्रक्वणत्पारिहार्यं वाटीं पश्चाद्व्याहृतामाददानम् ॥ १७ ॥
देया दृष्टिः पूर्वमत्रेति पात्रे तद्भृत्यौघैर्दर्शितानर्घरत्नम् ।
व्याचक्षाणं विश्रुतैर्नीतिमार्गैः कूटस्थानां क्ष्मापतीनामिवैक्यम् ॥ १९ ॥
साक्षात्कारं शारदाया दयायाः सञ्जीवः स्याज्जन्मसाफल्यमक्ष्णोः ।
आरादालोक्यैनमौत्सुक्यभाजः सर्वे चेरोर्वीशसाचिव्यकाराः ॥ २३ ॥
शिष्टैः कैश्चित्सेव्यमानं सविद्यामानंसस्थेमानमानंसिषुस्ते ।
मर्त्याधीशो माननापूर्वमेतान् संप्रेक्ष्याग्रे वीक्ष्य सक्रोधरूक्षः ॥ २४ ॥
नीत्वा दण्डं नीयतां कंचनावित्युक्त्वा दुष्टं मन्त्रिहस्तेऽतनिष्ट ।
आक्रम्यत्वाद्राज्यमाजानसिद्धं सीमालङ्घी शिक्षितश्चेरभूपः ॥ २५ ॥
पाहि क्षोणीं प्राक्तनीमित्यभाणीत्पाण्ड्योर्वीशं पालको नीतिभाजाम् ।
राजीवाक्षस्यांशराज्योपलम्भात्सेवा श्लाघ्या श्रीमदङ्घ्रेस्तथापि ॥ २६ ॥
आराद्यातेतावदाज्ञेति चोक्त्वा भक्त्या नत्वा प्रस्थितः पाण्ड्यभूपः ।
प्रस्थानाय श्रीपतेरभ्यनुज्ञां प्राप्तुं पाण्ड्यस्थापनाचार्य एव ॥ २७ ॥
मोक्षोदारं प्राविशन्मोहदूरं देवागारं देवनेत्रोपहारम् ।
लास्योदग्रे रङ्गमेत्यान्तरङ्गे नेत्रद्वन्द्वं निर्निमेषं नृपेन्दोः ॥ २८ ॥

देवं दूरादेव देदीप्यमानं दृष्ट्वा भक्त्या क्लृप्तदण्डप्रणामः।
आसाद्यासावाद्यमभ्यर्च्य पुष्पैः . . रित्वर्चयद्वासुदेवम् ॥ ३३ ॥
क्षिप्तो भारः शिक्षणाद्दुर्मदानां इत्येवोर्व्याः श्लिष्टमीडे भवन्तम्।
स्तावंस्तावं देवमेवंविधानं वाचां गुम्भैर्वावदूकेन्द्रकल्पम् ॥ ९६ ॥
आनन्दाब्धौ क्रीडति स्माङ्गलग्नां रोमाञ्चैः किं व्यञ्जयश्चैव लीलाम् ॥ ९७॥
हरिपदनुतिचर्यानन्तरं मानवानाम्
अधिपतिरुपकर्यामासदन्नीतिधुर्यः।
अधिपदमपि विष्णोश्चारयन्गोप्रपश्चा-
नपरगिरिमकाङ्क्षीदाप्तुमह्नामधीशः ॥ ९८ ॥

. . . .

. . . .

Canto X.

आकर्ण्य कर्णमधुरामिति मागधोक्तिं
कान्तो भुवः परिसमापितकाल्यकर्मा।
प्रातिष्ठतास्तपवमानजवाभिमानम्
आरुह्य वाहमपरोक्षितताक्ष्र्यवाहः ॥ १० ॥
नासीरसीम्नि चलिता नरपालमौलेः
आशामपूरयत पाशधराधिनाथाम्।
कल्लोलजालशिखरेण कवेरजायाः
कूलाध्वनैव परिलङ्घ्य स कोङ्कदेशान् ॥ ४९ ॥
श्रीरङ्गपत्तनमगाज्जयसिन्धुकन्या-
नाव्यक्रियासमुचितं तरसावनीन्दुः।
तन्निर्गतस्तदनु ताविव (?) भूमिपालैः
आदाय दत्तमनियत्ततया स वित्तम् ॥ ४६ ॥
आशां कुबेरभरितामवगाहमानः
प्रायात् सपादमभिपालयिता धरायाः ॥ ४७ ॥
निखिलफणाधरेन्द्रनयनान्ध्यनिबन्धनकृत्
प्रतिभटतूर्यभाङ्क्रांतिविदीर्यदहार्यतटः।

पतिरवनेः क्रमेण परिलङ्घ्य निजान्विषयान्
हयपतिरक्षितां क्षितिमगादरिशिक्षयिता ॥ ४८ ॥

Canto XI.

उत्क्षिप्य क्षितिकुहरादुपात्तवृत्तेः निक्षिप्तः स्वयमिव निस्तुत (लं?) पदार्थम् ।
आलोकक्षितिपमणेरथायुधीयैराक्रान्तं हयपतिराज्यमन्यभोज्यम् (?)॥ १ ॥
प्राकारान्तरनिभृता क्षितीशसेना पाश्चात्यानथ परिवारयांबभूव ॥
पर्यायात्प्रतिभटदारुयन्त्रमुक्तैः पाषाणैरपि लगुडैः परश्वधैश्च ।
सक्रोधं तदुभयसैन्यमण्डलानां सङ्ग्रामस्समजनि साधुवादपूर्वम् ॥ ४ ॥
निर्याते मलुकनिबर्हणाय तस्मिन्
(?)पारीन्द्रप्रतिभयविक्रमे प्रतीच्याम् ।
साशङ्कस्समजनि शाङ्करस्सखापि
प्रादुष्यत्क्क खलु जिजीविषा परेषाम् ॥ १० ॥
आलीढाम्बरमपदिश्य धूमजालं निर्गच्छत्सगरनिवासदुष्कृतानि ।
भूजानेर्बलनिहतैरबर्हिषा(?)पूर्वद्वेषिक्षितिपपुराण्यहो विशुद्धिम् ॥ ११ ॥
किं वायं तव पतिरेष वा किमु स्यात् इत्येतैररिनगराक्रमेण योधैः ।
धृत्वाग्रे यवनशिरांसि दर्शयद्भिः कारुण्यं शककमलेक्षणास्वनाटि॥ १२॥
प्रज्वालो बलनिहितः प्रतीपपुर्याः प्रासादोपरि . . विजृम्भते स्म वह्निः ।
व्यालीनान्दिशिदिशिविपक्षानुकग्रीवो मनुजपतेरिव प्रतापः ॥ १३ ॥
साहंपूर्विकनृपसैन्ययोधवीरैरानीतं परिभवमाकलय्य सीम्नः ।
सम्भिभ्रद्धृतिवरणे विलुण्ठितात्मा वाहेन्द्रप्रति . वशंवदो दिदीपे॥१४॥
आबद्धभ्रुकुटिरयं वितानमालामामृद्नन् रुषमवगम्य दष्टपाणिः ।
हुङ्कारैरुपजनयन्जनस्य भीतिं वाहेन्द्रस्समगतवानरेरियरीत्या (?) ॥ १८ ॥

आतन्वन्नयमयथातथं यथावत्
कुर्वाणः किल कुरुविन्दपारिहार्गम् ।
सन्दष्टोष्टदलपरिकम्प्यमानमौलिः
सक्रोधारभटि सभासदो न्यगादीत् ॥ २० ॥
प्राचीनान्परिभवता कुतोऽस्य पित्रा
कालान्मे कथमपि कल्पितप्रमीलः ।

यस्सुप्तः किल हृदये भियातिवाहि-
न्यारावैस्त्वरितमजागरीत्सरोषः ॥ २१ ॥
गीर्वाणावसथगिरेर्गरीयसः स्यात्
चाश्चल्यं यदिसहकल्पना कृशानोः ।
संक्षोभः शकधरणीशितुस्तथा स्यात्
सङ्ग्रामे चतुरिमशालिना परेण ॥ २२ ॥
इत्युक्त्वा परिषदधीशिता हयानां
राचूराह्वयपुररक्षणाय योधान् ।
प्रस्थाप्याहवकृतिनः प्ररूढरागान्
संजज्ञे स्वयमपि सावधानचेताः ॥ २३ ॥
सक्ष्वेलारभटि चमूभटो नगर्याः
निर्यातः पटहनिनादनिह्नुताशः ।
दुर्वाराध (राच ?) श्चलनबलस्य धूलिरग्रे
नेत्राणां निपुणसुहारिणी चचाल ॥ २४ ॥
आयान्तीस्वयमवनीययावनीयं
मर्त्यानां पतिरभिमांसलानुरागा ।
संरंभात्सह बलतो बलैश्शकेन्दोः
आयासीदभिमुखमञ्जसा समीरः ॥ २५ ॥
वीरोऽयं युधि हतशेषमश्वयूथं
वेतण्डव्रजमपि विद्विषो गृहीत्वा ।
कृष्णायाः कृतवसतिं दिनैस्स कैश्चित्
नेतारं निधिमभजन्निधिं बुधानाम् ॥ ४९ ॥
श्रुत्वा तामथ मलुकप्रवृत्तिमुर्वी
सुत्राम्णा सह भद्रसौहृदं विधातुम् ।
अन्तर्निश्चितमतिरासीत्सपादो
नीतिज्ञो निजसचिवानिति न्यगादीत ॥ ५० ॥
सङ्ग्रामे नरसविभुस्सदा सपाद-
त्रातासीदयमपि तत्तपोविपाकः ।

आनम्रानवतितमां क्षमाभृदस्मान्
आचारो ननु पितुरात्मजैरलङ्घ्यम् ॥ ९१ ॥
आत्मीयैरभिनुतभाषितस्सदस्यैः
आरूढो हयमिति दूरलङ्घिताध्वा ।
कृष्णायां न्यधित बलं क्षितीशमौलेः
संच्छन्नापरतटसीम्नि सैन्यवर्गैः ॥ ९२ ॥
प्रासन्यस्थशिसरितः पयस्यमुष्याः
सङ्क्रान्तस्तदुभयसैनिकानुबिम्बाः ।
पातालादुपरिगताः प्रजा इवासन्
सन्द्रष्टुं नरपतिसैन्धवेशसिन्धुम् ॥ ९३ ॥
पर्यस्तस्तदुभयसैन्ययोः परागो
निस्साणध्वनिनिह्नुतान्तरिक्षः ।
वातोऽपि ध्वजवसनोदितो मिलित्वा
मर्त्येशाश्वपतिमताकिन्वरुन्ध ॥ ९४ ॥

वाहेन्द्रास्सिततरवारवाणधारी निर्मोकाञ्चित इव निर्विषं फणीन्द्रः ।
आनम्रीभवदतिनम्रपूर्वकायः प्राणंसीत्पतिमवनेः प्रमृष्टदर्पः ॥ ९५ ॥

चमूमयपयोनिधौ सगरकुञ्जरं साध्वसा-
वहारगलितं वराच्युतनृपस्य भक्तिं हरौ ।
अपातयत तक्षणादभयहस्तचक्रोदयात्
कथं नु भवितान्तरं कमलनाभतद्भक्तयोः ॥ ९६ ॥
संप्रेष्यासौ शकपरिवृढः शासिता दुर्मदानां
प्रत्यायासीद्विजयनगरीं पञ्चषैरेव वारैः ।

अध्वश्रान्तामिव निजचमूमग्रतो वीजयन्तीं
वारंवारं भवनवलभीवैजयन्तीसमीरैः ॥ ९७ ॥

Canto XII.

सतोरणालीं शनकैः प्रतोलीं विशामधीशेऽथ विगाहमाने ।
आलोकनायास्य निरस्य कार्यं पर्याकुलः पौरवधूजनोऽभूत् ॥ १ ॥
दिदृक्षयामुष्य मृगेक्षणाभिः क्षिप्रारणीबन्धलसद्गवाक्षः ।
पुरी च तद्वीक्षणपुङ्खिताशा विस्तारिताक्षी विललास नूनम् ॥ २ ॥

Canto XII has only thirty-seven verses and seems incomplete. There is only one manuscript of this work available and the extracts are made therefrom in this imperfect condition.

54

VARADĀMBIKĀ-PARIṆAYAM.

[*By Tirumalāmbā*].

This Sanskrit Champu (work written partly in prose and partly in poetry) deals with the marriage of princess Varadāmbikā with Achyuta, who afterwards became the emperor of Vijayanagar as Achyutarāya. It was written by a lady called Tirumalāmbā* who, in the long colophon at the end of the work, enumerates her accomplishments at great length. She was greatly admired in the Court of Achyuta for her achievements. The book seems to have been written during the reign of the Emperor Krishna Deva Raya because it comes to a close soon after the description of the youth of China Venkaṭādri, son of Achyuta. When Achyuta succeeded to the throne in the year 1530 this son China Venkaṭādri was already old enough to be installed as the heir-apparent according to the Achyutarāyābhyudayam of Rājanātha.

The work gives a genealogy of Achyuta's family. In the Lunar race of kings was born Timma who married Dēvakī, and got by her a son called Īśvara. Īśvara married Bukkama and had by her Nṛsimha or Narasa.

Narasa went to the capital Vidyāpuri (Vijayanagar), and from there spread his fame in all directions. First he marched to the east † and after defeating his enemies there, turned his attention to the south and marched with his army along the sea coast. He crossed the Tuṇḍīra country (Toṇḍamaṇḍalam) and approached the Chōḷa districts. The king (or the Governor ?) of the Chōḷa country had been opposing his (Narasa's) troops and harassing the country. Narasa crossed to the south of the river Kāvēri, and awaited the arrival of the enemy. The Chōḷa king too did not accept the advice of his ministers to come to terms with Narasa, and

* This Tirumalāmbā seems to be the same as Oduva Tirumalamma (or the student Tirumalamma) who appears in No 9 of 1904 as the composer of the verse in the inscription commemorating the gift of Svarṇamēru 'Mountain Meru of gold' performed by Achyutarāya.

† This campaign of Narasa in the east seems to be the same as that of his father Īśvara. Both of them were subordinates of the Emperor Sāḷuva Narasimha during his wars against the Uriya kings Kapilēśvara and Purushottama who had conquered some portions of the Vijayanagar empire in the north-east.

prepared to fight. A severe battle was fought between them both in which the Chōḷa was taken a prisoner by Narasa. After the capture of the Chōḷa he ordered his troops to desist from fighting, and saved the people from further molestation. He then entered the enemy's capital * which is not named in the work. The Chōḷa king then fled to the sea coast leaving all his wealth and relatives behind him.

Narasa then entered the town of Madura† and was presented by its sovereign with valuable articles, and proceeded to Rāmēśvaram across the sea. While at Ramēśvaram he made many gifts. He then proceeded against the town of Seringapaṭam situated on the island in the Kaveri. There he constructed a bridge across the river, while it was in flood, and reduced the town easily. Accepting defeat at his hands the ruler of the place surrendered himself with all his relatives. Narasa forgave him and restored him his kingdom. The Pārijātāpaharaṇam says that Narasa defeated a Hēuṇa chief at Seringapaṭam. We do not know who this chief was.

Narasa is then said to have captured the forts of Dumakur (? Tumkur?) and Taraśangi. He visited the sacred shrine of Gōkarṇa on the West Coast and performed there the Tulāpurusha and other gifts. Narasa now turned his attention to the north where the Suratrāna (Sultan), perhaps Yusuf Adil Shah, had garrisoned the fort Mānavadurga (Manuva or Manve) in Haiderabad (Dekhan). Narasa defeated the Sultan but gave back the town to him after his submission. After this achievement Narasa returned to his capital Vidyāpuri.

* We do not know who this Chōḷa was and where his capital was situated. Perhaps he was the chief ruling the Chōḷa districts from Tanjore. In our present work he is said to have been captured as a prisoner, and later on, to have escaped to the sea coast. But the Pārijātapaharaṇam dedicated to Krishnarāya says that Narasa killed the Choḷa. We cannot say which of the versions is correct.

† The ruler of Madura is according to this account said to have submitted to Narasa without fighting and to have made him valuable presents. But the copperplates of his successors and the Achyutarāyābhyudayam give a different version. According to the Achyutarāyābhyudayam he captured Madura after killing in battle its Marava ruler. Again inscriptions say that he captured it from a king called Mānabhusha. This Mānabhūsha has been identified with Arikēsari Parākrama Pāndya surnamed also as Mānābharana and Mānakavacha of the Tenkāsi Pāndyas. The Achyutarāyābhyudayam again says that Narasa defeated a chief called Konēṭirājā who opposed him with his elephant hordes. We do not know who this chief was. Konēṭirāja is perhaps a corruption of the title Konerinmaikonḍan which is one of the titles of Perumāl Parākrama Pāndyadēva alias Kulaśēkhara. (Travancore Archæological Series I, p. 104.) But he succeeded to power only in SS. 1464 or A D. 1542-3. Therefore the term Konēṭirāya of the Achyutarāyābhyudayam cannot refer to him. There were others that have had the same title and the present reference might be to one of them. No. 259 of 1911, in Kumbhakonam, of A.D. 1490-1, refers to a Konēṭiraja of Kānchi.

The work then describes Narasa's marriage with Ōbamāmba. His earlier marriages with Tippāmba and Nāgamāmba are not mentioned in this work. Ōbamāmba is described as the daughter of Rāchirāja, born in the Solar race and his wife Srirāmāmbikā. As a result of his marriage with Ōbamāmba, Narasa had a son who was named Achyuta. Narasa is said to have died after his son Achyuta was a grown-up man. After describing the youth and early life of Achyuta the work describes his marriage with Varadāmbā*. She was the younger sister of two of Achyuta's ministers both of whom were named Tirumalarāja. When Achyuta and his wife had lived happily for a considerable time they had a son by the favour of the God of Venkaṭādri (Tirupati). The child was consequently named Chinavenkaṭādri. Observing with satisfaction the character and achievements of the prince, Achyuta had him installed as Yuvarāja (heir-apparent). After this the authoress prays to the God Venkaṭesa to preserve her patron Achyuta, his queen Varadāmbā and the prince Venkaṭādri.

† अनन्यसामान्यगुणादिसान्द्रः तदन्ववायार्णवपूर्णचन्द्रः ।
कौक्षेयसाक्षीकृतवीरलक्ष्मीकरग्रहोऽभूद्भुवि तिम्मभूपः ।
पुरा हरिं पुत्रमसूत देवकीमुदूह्य कश्चिद्यदुरित्युदारधीः ।
स देवकीनाम्नि परिग्रहे शुभे सुतं प्रसूयेश्वरमत्यशेत्ततम्(?) ॥

*   *   *   *

आर्यां गुणौघैरथ बुक्कमाम्बां स राजमौलिर्विधिनोपयेमे ।
नृसिंहनामानमुदग्रशक्तिं निबर्हितारिं सुषुवे कुमारम् ॥

*   *   *   *

अद्वैतशास्त्राधिगमेन सम्यक् विद्यामिवासाद्य विवृद्धसत्वः ।
विद्यापुरीं वीरवरस्स्वधाम्ना व्यद्योतत व्याप्तजगत्रयींकः ॥
हरिद्वधूरात्मगुणानुरागिणीरनुग्रहिष्यन् अखिलाः करग्रहान् ।
प्रहीत्य दूतीमिव कीर्तिमग्रतो विभुः प्रतस्थे विजयादरच्छलात् ॥
आदौ जित्वा हरिद्दयदिशां आत्मसात्कृत्य शक्त्या
तत्रात्युग्रं दिनकरमिव स्थापयित्वा प्रतापम् ।

---

* Varadāmba is described in the Achyutarāyābhyudayam as the daughter of a chief called Salaka or Salaga (Salagakshitīśa). His two sons who had the same name Tirumala were distinguished by the preceding epithet Peda (elder) or Pinna or Chinna (younger).

† This work remained unnoticed, as it was catalogued Ambikāpariṇayam by Burnell. Its real character was discovered on reading through the MS.

क्षोणीपालः प्रथमजलधेः कूलमार्गेण गत्वा
पारावारान्तरघनचमूपङ्क्तिरागादवाचीम् ॥

* * * *

. . . . . सकलसस्यसम्पदाण्डीरभुवः तुण्डीरानतीत्य सुत्रामलोकप्रत्यादेशान् अत्यादरणीयरामणीयकनिवेशान् चोलदेशानयासीत् ॥

त्रैलोक्यसारसमवायसहोपमेयानालोक्य चोलविषयानवनीमहेन्द्रः ।
नाकार्पिणा शतमखो नलिनासनेन शंके विलोहित इति स्फुटमाशशंके ॥
भृत्येषु पीडयति यः परकीयबुद्ध्या देशानिमान्मम तु दण्ड्यतमस्स एव ।
सेनाधिपान(?)स महीपतिरादिदेश शौर्यावधारितसमस्तजगत्रयश्रीः ॥
ततो व्रजन्नेव धरेन्दुरग्रे कवेरकन्यां कलयांचकार ।
भ्रूभङ्गसङ्काशतरङ्गरेखास्फुटद्युगङ्गोपरिवासरोषम् ।

* * *

कवेरजायाः कलितोरुभागान् दृष्ट्वा पुरो दक्षिणकूलभागान् ।
वरूथिनी वर्त्मपरिश्रमार्तां निवेशयामास नृपालसिंहः ॥

अथ तत्र समागत्य . . . .
. . अमृताशापूरकृशांगीजनांगीकृतरमणाशापूरणनिपुणरणाभिनिवेशमवनीशममुमात्मचारमुखादाकर्ण्य निर्णीततन्त्रैः मन्त्रिभिः गौडकलिंगत्रिलिंगमुख्यपार्थिवानां अत्याहितच्छलमाहवकृत्यमुदाहृत्य प्राभृतार्पणप्रणत्युद्गमप्रणामादिकृत्याय प्रार्थ्यमानोऽपि प्राकृतनृपप्रत्याख्यायिनिजबलप्रत्ययेन तानवमत्य तदात्व एव सन्नद्धः चोलनृपालः केवलयुद्धाय बद्धादरो बभूव ॥

विज्ञाय चारवदनाद्व्यवसायमस्य प्रज्ञावतस्तदनु पार्श्वगतानमात्यान् ।
आलोक्य सस्मितमवोचत राजसिंहो योद्धुं प्रयाम वयमप्युचितं किलेति ॥

* * * *

कोपाटोपाच्चोलभूपालको दुष्प्रापानेकानेकपानीकपार्श्वः ।
आगाद्वेगादभ्यमित्रान्जिगीषुः छागैस्साकं केसरीन्द्रं करीव ॥

* * * *

. . . अपरावतारनारसिंहो नृसिंहभूपालश्चोलेन्द्रं कञ्चुकिनमिव वैनतेयः कुञ्जरमिव पञ्चमुखः जीवग्राहं जग्राह ॥

तस्मिन्क्षणे तस्य चमूसमूहः तत्रास कुत्रापि पदं न लब्ध्वा ।
प्रचण्डवाताहतपद्मपत्रपरिप्लवांभःक्षणिकाप्रकारः ॥

गृहीतमात्रे युधि चोलभूपे कृपानिधिः श्रीनरसक्षितीशः ।
स तां न्यषेधत्समरात्स्वसेनां सतां प्रसादस्सहजो न रोषः ॥

* * * *

. . . प्राविवेश तदानीमेव तदीयराजधानीम् । अथावगत्य वार्तामिमां उत्रारभरसमु(?) दाशयः तदात्व एव हित्वा समस्तापत्यभृत्यधरित्र्यादिकं वस्तुजातं कुत्राधुना परित्रातुं असून् विद्रवामि इति कर्तव्यं किमप्यविदित्वा विमुग्ध इव निरुद्ध इव विप्रलब्ध इव वर्तमानो(?)भरुवपाकचोनिपत्य समुद्रतीरमध्ये कुत्राप्यदुद्रुवत् ॥

तदनु विहस्य नरसिंहमहेश्वरः प्रविश्य मधुरापुरीम् तत्रत्यनृपोपदीकृतसमस्तवस्तुजात. रामेश्वरप्रणिनंसया सेतुमार्गेण निर्जगाम ।

* * * *

नानाग्रहारैर्नवरत्नहारैः सुवर्णपुष्पैरपि सूक्तिपुष्पैः ।
अभ्यर्च्य रामेश्वरमादरेण तत्सन्निधौ दानशतान्यतानीत् ॥

ततो . . . . क्रमेणापरान्तनदीकान्तवेलापर्यन्तदिशाचक्रसमाक्रमणेऽपि समग्रतरात्युग्रशौर्यसूर्योदयः सागरान्तरावासदुर्लंघां लंकामिव रघुपुङ्गवः कावेरीपरिवेष्टितां श्रीरङ्गपट्टणाभिधां आवरिष्ट पुरीम् ॥

स्थिरे जले सेतुरकारि पूर्वं तदद्भुतं नेति कवेरजायाः ।
सेतुं प्रवाहेषु गुणाभिरामः चित्ते सतामद्भुतमप्यबध्नात् ॥

. . . . निस्तन्द्रयन्त्रशिलाचक्रनिखातनिपात्यमानविजयपार्थिवशृङ्गसङ्काशविशंकटशृङ्गसंघाटां पुरीमिमां समाक्रम्य वित्रासभरपुरस्स्थापितसमस्तवित्तजातम् अपत्यकलत्रादिभिः मित्रादिभिस्समागत्य पदयोर्निपत्य आत्मनो गत्यन्तराभावं उद्योतयन्तं महावीरं पार्थिवं प्रत्यग्रकृपारसाभिषिक्तं तत्र पुरि स्थापयित्वा तदात्व एव तत्रदुमका(कू?)रादिमहादुर्गजालं सलीलमग्रहीत् ।

दुर्गं प्रगृह्य तरशंगयभिनं विपक्षात् स्वर्गं विरोचनसुतादिव शार्ङ्गपाणिः ।
गोकर्णनाथमनमत् सुतदाररोधक्रोधादिवापरपयोनिधिना परीतम् ॥

तेने तुलापूरुषदानपूर्वं(?) तेनेह नानाविधदानजातम् ।
संख्ये भवन्त्यद्यपि स्थूललक्ष' स स्थूललक्षो हि विहाय तेषु ॥

ततो विनिर्गत्य सत्वरमुत्तरां हरितं अभिप्रस्थितवति मण्डलीकसूर्येतदीयधामोष्माणमसहमानः शक्रमुखानेकमहीनायकानुगम्यमानः कांबोजबह्लीकमरुखा-

तुरुष्कारखंखाणतुरगारिंखासंवृतस्थपुटितधरणीतलोऽपि सुरत्राणः प्राणत्राणपरायणो दुर्गमं मानवदुर्गं तत्क्षणमध्यरुक्षत् ॥

त्रासाद्द्रुतं मानवदुर्गमध्ये धृत्वा सुरत्राणवराहपादम्(?) ।
अमुञ्चतानुग्रहधीस्स धीरो गृहीतमब्धिं किल कुम्भजन्मना ॥

तुङ्गतरतुङ्गभद्रातरङ्गपर्यङ्कप्रेङ्खोलित . . . . प्रत्युत्थानसमुद्यममिव विद्योतयन्तीं विद्यापुरीं प्रतिपद्य . . . . निरर्गलहृदयोल्लासः प्राविशदुदवसतिम् ।

* * * *

गृहीतस्स एष तस्याबान्धवमुखाद्वृत्तान्तमखिलं अवगत्य राज्ञो विज्ञाप्य तदनुमत्या साकं अमात्यगणेन दिवसकरकुलोत्तंसराचिराजरत्नाकररेखां श्रीरामांबिकागर्भशुक्तिमुक्ताभाणिं अन्यूनतरान्वयोचितशीललावण्यादिगुणगणधन्यां कन्यां ओबमाम्बाभिधानां आनीय यथाविधि धरणिभुजा पर्यणीनयत् ।

* * * *

दुग्धांबुराशिलहरीव तुषारभानुं अर्थं नवं . . . सत्कविभारतीव ।
प्रत्यङ्मुखस्य यमिनः प्रतिमेव वोधम् प्रासूत भाग्यमहितं सुतमोबमाम्बा ॥

* * * *

विनयनयविवेकविक्रमादिष्वखिलगुणेष्वमुमच्युतं विदित्वा ।
अभिजनकृतसम्मतिर्व्यतानीत् अवनिपतिस्सुतमच्युताभिधानम् ॥

* * * *

कालाद्बहोरथ महीं विरहासहिष्णुमाश्वास्य नव्यनिजशाश्वतकीर्तिमूर्त्या ।
नानागुणश्रवणकौतुकिनां गुणानाम् नाथेन सख्यमभजन्नरसाक्षितीशः ॥

. . . सततविरचितानेकदानयोः असाधारणभुजापधानयोः अखिललोककृतबहुमानयोः तिरुमलराजाभिधानयोः उभययोः प्रधानयो. अवरजा वरदाम्बिकाभिधाना वरवर्णिनी . . . . तपोवनमुपगतवती—

* * * *

प्रविश्य तस्मिन् प्रमना नृपालः तां राजकन्यां विधिनोपयम्य ।
श्रियं पयोधेरिव शेषशायी समानयत्तां सदनं स्वकीयम् ॥

* * * *

कालाद्बहोर्वसुमतीकमितुर्मृगाक्षी श्रीवेङ्कटाद्रिपतिसेवनपुण्यपाकैः ।
चन्द्रान्वयाभ्युदयहेतुमधत्त गर्भम् आनन्दकन्दलममेयमिवात्मविद्या ॥

* * * *

श्रीवेङ्कटाद्रीशवरप्रसादात् जातं कुमारं जगतीसुधांशुः ।
अमुं हरेरंशभवं विदित्वा नाम्ना व्यतानीत् चिनवेङ्कटाद्रिम् ॥

* * * *

अनन्तरमच्युतमहीमहेन्द्रो बाल्य एव समुल्लसदसाधारणानुभावं नारायणचरणारविन्दभावं अत्युदारं कुमारमालोक्य साकमागत्य गणेन सकलमहीतलसन्त्राणधुर्यं अवतार्य शुभंयुनि दिने . . . . शाश्वतं युवराजपदम् ॥

अत्यादरादच्युतदेवरायं वरेण्यशीलां वरदांबिकां च ।
श्रेयोनिधिं च चिनवेङ्कटाद्रिं श्रीवेङ्कटेशश्चिरकालमव्यात् ॥

55

BHĀGAVATA CHAMPU.

[*By Rājanātha Kavi.*]*

This is a poem written by Rājanātha Kavi of the Ḍinḍima family whose other work, the historical poem Achyutarāyābhudayam, has already been quoted. This poem deals with the story of the Bhāgavata, and is dedicated to the poet's patron Achyuta Rāya, whose family and genealogy are described in the introduction. In the Lunar race of kings was born Timma who married Dēvaki and got by her a son called Īśvara. This Īśvara married Bukkama who gave birth to Narasa whose son was Achyuta. Achyuta was a great king, made extensive conquests and performed all the sixteen gifts (dānas) prescribed by the Śāstras.

One day Achyuta called the poet Rājanātha Kavi, the son of Śoṇagirinātha, before him and directed him to compose a poem embodying the story of Vishnu upon which Rājanātha composed the Champu Bhāgavata.

* The author of the Sāḷuvābhyudam (Extract 33) is also a Rājanātha, son of Arunagārinātha or Śoṇādrinātha, and is likely naturally to be taken to be the same as this author. The former gives himself the titles *Dindima*, *Kavisārvabhauma* among others of a similar high character. There is besides the important fact that the Sāḷuvābhyudayam, which seems complete so far as the conquests of Narasimha are concerned, makes no reference to Narasimha as *Emperor of Vijayanagar*. On the contrary it associates him intimately only with Chandragiri. Hence it seems a work of the pre-imperial period of his rule.

Canto I.

तेजोविजृम्भणतृणीकृततिग्मधामा तेषु प्रतीतमहिमाजनि तिम्मभूपः ॥१५॥

पतिदैवतदेवकीतपस्यापरिपाको मनुनीतिपारदृश्वा ।
विदधेः परिणीरिवौषधीनाम् उदभूदीश्वरभूवलारिरस्मात् ॥ १६ ॥

दुर्गेशताविभवधूर्वहयोरहार्यधाम्नोरियान्नियतमीश्वरयोर्विशेषः ।
आपीडिताद्विजपतिः प्रथमो द्विजानाम् अव्याजपालनकलाभिरतो [द्वितीयः ॥ १७ ॥

अपास्तखेदानवनीधुरीणान् फणाधरेन्द्रप्रमुखान्विधातुम् ।
अजायतामुष्य च बुक्कमायां नयोपदेष्टा नरसक्षितीशः ॥ १८ ॥

तस्य खलु हृदयङ्गमगुणसम्पदः साम्परायिकप्रस्थानमेव संमुखापतद्विजयरमाभ्युत्थानं पटुतरगुणारोपणमेव परिपन्थिकुलपौरुषावरोपणं कोदण्डरभसकुण्डलीकरणमेव कुनृपतिमदकुण्डलीकरणम् ॥

यस्यासिना रिपुनृपैणविलासिनीनाम् अक्ष्यञ्चलादपहृतं नवमञ्जनं यत् ।
आद्यैश्च भूपतिभिरादरणीयकीर्तिः निक्षेपदर्शननिदानमभूत्तदेव ॥ १९ ॥

अस्मादच्युतभूवलारिरुदभूदव्याजबन्धुस्सताम्
अन्तेवासिपदे तरुन्दिविषदामौदार्यतः स्थापयन् ।
इन्धे पूर्वनृपानपत्रपयितुं यस्य प्रशस्यं यशो
यस्मिन्नेति दया वृषाचलपतेरेकातपत्रश्रियम् ॥ २० ॥

यस्य खलु सुघटितपात्रसंविधानेषु षोडशमहादानेषु घटीयन्त्रवदनियन्तृणैश्वर्यसलिलनिधावावृत्तिमधिगतेषु परिवहमानेन दानपयसा समन्ततोऽखिलभुवनकेदारान्तरैधंतयशःकलमसन्ततयः ॥

यस्याशास्यप्रवृत्तेर्भुजविजयरमाचारुवेण्या कृपाण्या
राजन्यैर्जन्यभूमौ रभसविदलितैरन्धितं चेन्न बिम्बम् ।
व्योमाकारे कटाहे विमलतरयशःपूरपूर्णे वितीर्णो
मार्ताण्डो नूनमह्नां मणिमयघटिकामानपात्रीभवेत्किम् ॥

. . . . रजनीकरकुलप्रदीपः सराजराज-
परमेश्वरः राजनाथकविमिदमवादीत् ।
साधु शौरिकथालापसुधापूरप्रणालिका
कृतिः कृतिजनग्राह्या भवता क्रियतामिति ॥ २३ ॥

सोयं कविस्तदनु शोणगिरीन्द्रसूनुः आज्ञागिरं नरपतेरवतंसयित्वा ।
चम्पूप्रबन्धमजहत्सरसोक्तिबन्धं वक्तुं समारभत वाग्विभवानुकूलम् ॥२४॥

56

THE ANNALS OF HANḌE ANANTĀPURAM.

This chronicle says that after the death of Krishna Rāya in S.S. 1487 (wrong) his queens Chinnā Dēvi and Tirumala Dēvi wanted that Rāma Rāya who had married the daughter of Tirumala Dēvi should rule as the Aḷiya (son-in-law) helped by his younger brother Tirumala Rāya who had married the daughter of Chinnā Dēvi. But Salakam Timmaya, who had been the treasurer of the court, taking advantage of his position managed to get the control of the army and tried to imprison both Rāma Rāya and Tirumala Rāya. Finding this out they both fled from the city and after wandering over the Penukoṇḍa Viceroyalty, collected an army and, capturing the fortress of Ādavani (Adoni), lived for four months in the place and, getting together additional troops from the side of Kandnavol (Karnul) and Gadwal, proceeded with all of them against Vidyānagara. On this Salakam Timmaya invited the assistance of Barid Shah, Nizam Shah, Ali Adil Shah, Kutb Shah and other princes of the Bahmani kingdom, and promised to hand over the whole kingdom to them if they helped him against Rāma Rāya.

On that the Muhammadan forces advanced upon the capital, Vijayanagar, and encamped within a kos of it. On this Rāma Rāya and Tirumala Rāya summoned Hanḍé Hanumappa Nāyuḍu of Sonnalāpuram, who was a great hero, and along with him encamped within two leagues of Vijayanagar on the banks of the Tungabhadra. As the Muhammadan chiefs were new to the place they placed the troops of Salakam Timmaya in the front and waited for the attack being delivered by him. Knowing this Rāma Rāya and Tirumala Rāya delivered the attack upon the forces of Salakam Timmaya, but his forces, thinking that he was only a Golla (shepherd), who wanted to snatch away the kingdom as he was rich, deserted in a body, and he was killed in the fight.

The queens of Krishna Rāya on hearing this ordered the ministers to hand over the city to Rāma Rāya and Tirumala Rāya, and the order was accordingly carried out.

Afterwards Rāma Rāya and Tirumala Rāya wished to make war on the Padishahs. Dividing their joint troops into three sections, they directed Haṇḍé Hanumappa Nāyuḍu of Sonnalāpuram to lead one section against the Muhammadans while they each led another. Hanumappa Nāyuḍu was to march against the Nizam Shah, Rāma Rāya against the Kutb Shah and Tirumala Rāya against the Barid Shah. There was a great battle between them and the Padshahs fled from the field to their own country. But Haṇḍé Hanumappa Nāyuḍu took the Nizam Shah prisoner and offered him as a present to Rāma Rāya and Tirumala Rāya. Thereupon they were very gracious to him and directed him to state what he wished from them for his services. Hanumappa Nāyuḍu stated that he would be satisfied with anything they chose to bestow upon him.

On that they bestowed upon him in the eastern country Nandēla, Bukkarāyasamudram, Dharmāvaram and Kanicallu, and in the west Baḷḷāri and Kurugoḍu with complimentary titles.

Then this Haṇḍé Hanumappa Nāyuḍu took leave of the Rajas and went to Nandēla where he took charge of his new office. He then proceeded to Bukkarāyasamudram where he beheld the lake, and, learning how great it was, caused a palace to be built in front of the fort in the village around which he erected bastions and governed the district till Śaka 1505,* Chitrabhānu when he died.

4. తర్వాత ఆవిద్యానగరమును బుక్కరాయల వంశస్థుండైన కృష్ణరాయలు రాజ్యము చేస్తూవుండి, శాలివాహన శకం 1487 అగు నేటి క్రోధన సంవత్సర జ్యేష్ఠ శు 6 భానువారమున చనిపోయెను. అతని భార్యలు చిన్నాదేవి తిరుమలదేవి అనేవారు యిద్దరు. వీరికి ఆడుబిడ్డలు మాత్రము కలిగివున్నందున, తిరుమలదేవి కొమార్తైను రామరాయల వారున్ను, చిన్నాదేవి కుమార్తైను అతని తమ్ముడైన తిరుమలరాయులున్ను, వివాహము చేసుకొనిరి. పిమ్మట ఆదొరసానులు యిద్దరున్ను ఆరామరాయులవారికి అళియపట్టము కట్టవలెనని సంకల్పించి వుండిరి.

5. ఇంతలో, లోగడ సంస్థానములోవున్న బొకరసం గొల్లసలకం తిమ్మయ్య అనేవాడు, రాజ్యము అరాజకమై బొకరసం తనస్వాధీనములో వున్నందున, చతురంగ బలాన్ని పదిల పరచుకొని, అల్లుండ్లయిన

* This date and the ones given before are alike wrong.

రామరాయ తిరుమలరాయులనుపట్టి, చెరవుంచవలెనని యోచించెను. ఈ వర్తమానమును వారువిని, ఆదేశమును విడిచి పారిపోయి, పెనుకొండ సంస్థానములో సంచరించుచు, కొంత సైన్యమును కూర్చుకొని, అదవాని చేరి, అక్కడ నాలుగు నెలలు నివాసము చేసి, కందనూలు గద్వాల ఆ ప్రాంతములయందు మరికొంత సైన్యమును కూర్చుకొని, సకల సేనా సమేతులై, విద్యానగరమునకు దండెత్తి వచ్చిరి. ఈ వర్తమానమును చారులవల్ల ఆసలకం తిమ్మయ్యవిని, తనకు సహాయం నిమిత్తము కుదుపుషహా -1- పరీదుషహా-1- నిజాంషహా-1- అల్లి అదల్ షహా-1- వీరు మొదలైనవారికి, మీరు చతురంగ బల సమేతులైవస్తే యీ రాజ్యము యావత్తు మీస్వాధీనము చేస్తానని, జాబులు వ్రాయించి పంపించెను.

6. వారు చూచుకొని, ఆప్రకారమే సకల సేనాసమేతులై వచ్చి, విద్యానగరమునకు వొకకోసు దూరమునదిగిరి. ఆ రామరాయ తిరుమల రాయులు యీ సమాచారము తెలుసుకొని సొన్నలాపురమందు వున్న హండేహనుమప్ప నాయుడు బహుశూరుడు అనేటట్టుగా విని, అతణ్ని సైన్యయుక్తముగా పిలిపించి కొలువుపెట్టుకొని, విద్యానగరానకు రెండు పరుగుల మీద తుంగభద్రానదీ తీరమందుపోయి దిగిరి. ఆపాదుషహాల సైన్యమునకు యీస్థలం కొత్తగనుక, వారు సలకం తిమ్మయ్యగారి సైన్యమును ముందువుంచుకొని, యుద్ధమునకు ప్రయత్న పడిరి.

7. ఈ సంగతి ఆ రామరాయ, తిరుమలరాయులవారు విని పట్టపగలు రణభేరివేయించి, యెదుటవున్న సలకం తిమ్మయ్య సేనమీదపడి యుద్ధముచేయగా, ఆ సలకం తిమ్మయ్య సేన "వీడు గొల్ల, ధనవంతుడై సంస్థానమును ఆక్రమించవలెనని, ప్రయత్నము చేసినాడు; వీనికి సహాయము చేస్తే, మనకు దైవసహాయము కానేరద" ని తలంచి, యుద్ధభూమిని తొలగిపోయినందున, సలకం తిమ్మయ ఆజగడములో చిక్కి, ప్రాణముపిడిచెను.

8. ఈ వర్తమానము దొరసానులు విని, ప్రధానులను పిలిపించి రామరాయ తిరుమలరాయులను పిలుచుకవచ్చి పట్టణము వారిస్వాధీనము చేయుమని సెలవు యిచ్చినందున, ప్రధానులు ఆ ప్రకారమే ఎదుర్కొని పోయి, వారిని తోడుకొనివచ్చి పట్నము వారిస్వాధీనము చేసిరి.

9. తర్వాత, ఆరామరాయ తిరుమలరాయులు పాదుషహాల మీదికి యుద్ధమునకు పోవలెనని యోచించి, స్థలములోవున్న సైన్యం తమ

దగ్గెరవున్న సైన్యం యీరెంటిని మూడు భాగములుచేసి, సొన్నలాపురం హండే హనుమప్పనాయుణ్ని పిలిపించి, నీవు బహుశూరుడవు ; నీకు కొంత సైన్యమును యిస్తున్నాము, నీదగ్గెరవున్న సైన్యమునున్ను సన్నాహము చేసుకొని, నిజాంసహా మీదికిపోయి, యుద్ధము జరిగించి, జయించి వస్తే నీమనసు ప్రకారము యియ్యనయ్యాని అనిచెప్పి, కొంతసైన్యమును యిచ్చి పంపించిరి. రామరాయులవారు కొంతసైన్యముతో కుతుబుషహా మీదికిన్ని, తిరుమల రాయులవారు కొంతసైన్యముతో వరీదుషహా మీదికిన్ని పోయి, అఘోరయుద్ధము చేయగా, పాదుషహాలు యుద్ధరంగమందు నిలువలేక పలాయితులై పోయిరి.

10. ఈ హండే హనుమప్పనాయుడు నిజాంవారిని పట్టుకవచ్చి, రామరాయ తిరుమలరాయులవారికి కానుక యిచ్చెను. అందుమీదట, వారికి బహుదయవచ్చి, మెచ్చి నీమనస్సులో యేమివున్నదో అడుగుమని హండే హనుమప్ప నాయడితో సెలవుయివ్వగా, అతడు తమరు దయ చేసి యేమియిచ్చినా, సకల బహుమానములు యిచ్చినట్టే అని మనవి చేసెను. అప్పుడు, తూర్పుదిక్కునవున్న నందేల -1- బుక్కరాయ సముద్రం -1- ధర్మవరం -1- కణికలు -1- పడమరవుండే బళ్లారి కారుగోడు -1- యీగ్రామములున్ను బిరుదులున్ను యివ్వగా, యీహండే హనుమప్పనాయుడు రాయులవారివద్ద సెలవుతీసుకొని, శాలివాహనశకం 1491వ అగు నేటి శుక్లనామ సంవత్సర మార్గశిరమాసమందు నందేలకువచ్చి చేరి, ఆతాలూకా విచారించుకొని, అచ్చటనుంచి బుక్కరాయ సముద్రమునకువచ్చి, అక్కడి తటాకమును చూచి దొడ్డదని తెలుసుకొని, యీగ్రామములోని కోటముందర నగరు కట్టించి, చుట్టూవెలపటికోట నిర్మాణము చేసుకొని, రాజ్యమును విచారిస్తూవుండి, శాలివాహనశకం 1505 అగు నేటి చిత్రభాను సంవత్సరములో కాలముచేసెను.

57

RĀMARĀJĪYAMU

(AḶIYA RĀMA RĀYA AND HIS CHILDREN).

This extract from the Rāmarājīyamu deals with Aḷiya Rāma Rāya and his successors. Aḷiya Rāma Rāya defeated the armies of Salakam Timmarāju and captured the forts of Gutti, Penukonda, Gaṇḍikoṭa, Kandanol (Karnul) and Ādavani (Adoni). Rāma Rāya is called the ruler of the city of Indraji. Assisted by his two younger brothers Tirumala and Venkaṭādri he marched against the Nizam who had disobeyed his orders, and, having captured his capital Ahmadnagar, razed it to the ground and sowed castor seeds there. Then the poem gives a long *birudagadyam* (string of titles), wherein the various conquests of Rāma Rāya are referred to. A list of the more important of the titles and their significance is here given :—

Titles.	Significance.
Kalyāṇa Puravarādhīśvara.	Ruler of the city of Kalyan.
Kanyākumārī Bhīmarathī Taṭānta Nikshēpa Vijaya-stamba.	Planter of pillars of victory at Cape Camorin and on the banks of the Bhima.
Gutti Durga Nirbhēdana.	Breaker into the Fort of Gutti.
Ādavani Durgāpaharaṇa.	Capturer of the Fort of Adoni.
Penukoṇḍa Durga Sādhaka.	Capturer of the Fort of Penu-koṇḍa.
Chandragiri Durga Rājyā-dhīśvara.	Ruler of the Fort of Chandra-giri.
Uddagiri Rājyapālaka ...	Protector of the Fort of Udaya-giri.
Rāyadurgāvana Dhuran-dhara.	Protector of the Fort of Raya-durgam.
Kandanavōlu Kavāṭā Bhē-daka.	The breaker-open of the gates of the Fort of Karnul.
Jūṭūru Samara Nirvāhaka ...	Conqueror in the battle of Jūṭuru.
Koṇḍavīṭi Durga Nāyaka ...	Ruler of the Fort of Koṇḍavīḍu.
Reṭṭahaḷḷi Sīma Pratishṭhita ? Dhāma Sāgara. Puṭṭapaḷḷi Sīma Pratishṭhita ? Dhāma Sāgara.	Constructor of tanks at Puṭṭa-paḷḷi and Reṭṭahaḷḷi.
Bankāpura Vīraramālingita.	Embracer of the Goddess of heroism at Bankāpur.
Chandraguptī Dharāntara ...	Ruler of Chandragutti.
Rāchūru Rājyaharaṇa Dhur-ya.	Capturer of the province of Rai-chur.
Muduganṭi Durgādhināyaka.	Ruler of the Fort of Mudgal.
Orugallu Nagara Poshana ...	Protector of the city of War-rangal.
Vijayāpura Bhaya Dāyaka...	Terrifier of the city of Bijapur.

Titles.	Significance.
Sollalāpura (Sonnalāpura) Sankshobhakāra.	Hero who made the town of Sollalāpapuram throb with fear.
Kalyāṇanagara Sādhaka ...	Capturer of the town of Kalyan.
Āmudānagara Sālabhanjana.	Destroyer of the fortifications of Ahmadnagar.
Dēvagiri Durga Samākrānti Dhīra.	Occupier of the Fort of Dēvagiri.
Gautamīsnānapāvanākāra ...	Hero who became holy by bathing in the Godavari (Gautami).
Balichāpalijanyadāyaka ...	Hero who fought the battle of Balichāpali (Balijepalli).
Bedadakoṭanagara Simha Samhanana.	Terrifier of the Fort of Bidar.
Kalubarigikoṭapāṭana Dhurya.	The breaker of the walls of the Fort of Kulbarga.
Sagarasamākramaṇa Dhīra.	Capturer of the Fort of Sagar.
Hamsa Durga Nibarhaṇa ...	Capturer of the Fort of Hamsa.
Jurnūru Bhaya Nirnāyaka ...	Terrifier of the town of Jurnūru.
Rāmagiri Durga Pratishṭhāpaka.	Establisher of the fortress of Rāmagiri.
Yādagiri Durga Bhēdaka ...	Capturer of the Fort of Yadgir.
Golakonḍapura Dūshaṇa ...	Chastiser of the city of Golkonda.
Ayilakonḍaharaṇa Kāutūhala.	Capturer of the town of Ayilakonḍa.
Pānuganṭi Durga Pāṭana Dhurya.	Reducer of the Fort of Pangal.
Bellamukonḍavallabha ...	Lord of the town of Bellamkonḍa.
Śāvaga Durga Bādhaka ...	Destroyer of the Fort of Śāvaga (Seogi).
Mavūra Durga Mādhaka ...	Capturer of the Fort of Māhura.
Makkhākoṭa Sikshānikara.	Punisher of the Fort of Makkha.
Dhillīpura halla-kallola ...	Terrifier of the city of Delhi.
Golēru Sandēru Bhaya-Sandhāyaka.	Hero who instilled fear to the towns of Golēru and Sandēru.
Kalamba Durga Kampāsura.	Hero who made the Fort of Kalamba shake.
Paigova Nagara Bhīshaṇa.	Terrifier of the city of Paigo (Pegu ?).

Titles.	Significance.
Konḍapalli Haraṇa... ...	Capturer of the Fort of Konḍapalli.
Vinukonḍapālaka	Protector of the Fort of Vinukonḍa.
Vinūtnakṛta Nāgārjunikonḍa Sālajālaka.	Constructor of the new fortifications of Nāgārjunikonḍa.
Avantīmadavidārana ...	Hero who destroyed the pride of Avanti.
Kaṭaka Rājaghaṭitakīrtana.	Hero who is praised by the king of Cuttack.
Rājamahēndra Rāja Dhanuś-śāsana.	Hero who reduced the king of Rajmundri with his bow.
Yēdulakhānu SaptāngahaHaraṇa.	Hero who captured the seven constituents of royalty of Adil Khan.
Imādana Malaka Māna Mardana.	Hero who destroyed the pride of Imad-ul-Mulk.
Kuṭupanamalka Daḷa Sindhūra.	Hero who defeated the troops of Kutb-ul-Mulk.
Barīdu Bala Haraṇa ...	Capturer of the forces of Barid.

Rāma Rāya is then said to have married Tirumalāmba, the daughter of the Emperor Krishna Rāya, and had by her two sons Krishnapa and Pedda Timma.

Rāma Rāya also married Appalāmba, the daughter of Peddanandi Rāju of the Jillēḷḷa family, Konḍamma and Lakshmamma, the daughters of Timma of the Pōchirāju family. By his wife Konḍama, Rāmạ Rāya had two sons Konḍa and Timma the later Governor of Raichur, and by his wife Lakshmāmba he had Śrīranga Rāya. Of these Peda Timma fought with the Muhammadan armies and after driving away their horse, was opposed by the Nizam with his elephants, but was able to defeat him completely. Konḍa, the other son, fought with the troops of the Nizam on the northern bank of the Krishna, and killed a very large number of elephants, horses and soldiers. Konḍa was ruling at Ānegondi, and his enemies, after defeat, used to flock to his court with presents, and wait for admission to audience.

This Konḍa married Tirumalāmba, the daughter of Sūrapa, Commander-in-Chief of the Cavalry (Vāhādhīśvara), and had by her the son Rama. This Rama married three wives Narasingama, the daughter of Ōba of the Gobbūri family, Ōbamma, the daughter of

Ōba of the Sūrapa family, and Jānakamma, the daughter of Pōchirāju Chenna.

Timma Rāju, the other son of Aḷiya Rāma and Governor of Raichur, married Pochama, the daughter of the Chief Pāṇerāju (the ruler of Panem).

The last son of Aḷiya Rama, Śrīranga, married Lakshmamma, the daughter of Raghunātha of the Pochiraju family, and had by her two sons who were named Pedda Venkaṭa and Chinna Venkaṭa.

గీ. అవని నిటువలెఁ బుత్రపౌత్రాభివృద్ధి
గహాని వర్ధిల్లు తిరుమలరాయవేంక
టాద్రి రాజానుద్వయ మధికభక్తి
గొలువ నళిరామభూపాలుఁడలరుమిగుల.

తే. సకలవిభు తిమ్మరాజు సేనలనుద్రుంచి
గుత్తిఁబెనుకొండ మఱిగండికోటఁ గంద
నోలుపురమాదవేనవలీలఁ గెలిచి
దొలుదొలుత రామనృపతిదోర్బలము మెఱసె.

శా. తారాధీశ్వర గోత్రపాలన చమత్కారుండు నైదానవి
స్తారోదగ్రతనద్భిమించి రిపులన్ దండించిధాత్రీజనా
ధారప్రక్రియనొందియింద్రజిపురాధ్యక్షేశుఁడై మించుమా
శ్రీరంగేంద్రుని రామరాజవిభుఁడా శ్రీరామచంద్రంబునన్.

సీ. హరిశౌర్యుఁడగు తిర్మలాధీశ్వరుండుద
దవరజుండగు వేంకటాద్రిరాజు
భుజయుగంబుగ బలస్ఫురణతోఁ గరిహరి
పరవీరభటులతో దొరలతోడఁ
దనయాజ్ఞమీఱిన కినుక నిజాముపై
దండెత్తి తఱిమి యుద్దండవృత్తి
నతఁడేలుచున్నట్టి యాముదానగరంబు
చాలెత్తి మఱియాముదాలు వేసి

గీ. సేతుకాశిమధ్య భూతలనుతజయ
శ్రీవరించివేడ్కఁజేఁ జెలంగ
రామమూర్తియైన రామరాజేంద్రుండు
సాంద్రవిభవజిత సురేంద్రుఁడెలమి.

<u>బిరుదగద్యము.</u> జయజయ, స్వస్తి, సమస్తసద్గుణస్తోమభద్ర, రణరంగరామభద్ర, కల్యాణమహీపాలభాస్వర, కల్యాణపురవరాధీశ్వర, కన్యాకుమారీ భీమరథీ తటాంతనిక్షేపవిజయస్తంభ, స్తోత్రార్హయశఃప్రక్రియాపావనచరిత్ర, * * *, విజయచరితసింహాసనాభాస్వర, విజయనగరసింహాసనాధీశ్వర, యుక్తవర్గసద్యోధనపుర, గుత్తిదుర్గనిర్ఛేదనపుర, వాదిపురతరాభరణ, ఆదవేనిదుర్గాపహరణ, ఘనచండవర్గబాధక, పెనుకొండదుర్గసాధక, మంద్రగిరిదుర్గభాస్వర, చంద్రగిరిదుర్గరాజ్యాధీశ్వర, శబ్దపరిశుద్ధపాలక, ఉద్దగిరిరాజ్యపాలక, కాయదుర్గతనయబంధుర, రాయదుర్గావనధురంధర, వందనశీలకిరీటపాదక, కందనవోలుకవాటభేదక, చాటూరుఫణితినిర్వాహక, జూటూరుసమరనిర్వాహక, చండనపాటిఖడ్గసాయక, కొండవీటిదుర్గనాయక, పుట్టపల్లిసీమాధిష్ఠితధామసాగర, రెట్టహళ్లి సీమాధిష్ఠితధామసాగర, వంకాదిమవీరసమాసంగిత, బంకాపురవీరరమాలింగిత, సాంద్రకీర్తినిరంతర, చంద్రగుప్తిధరాంతర, ఆచారరాజ్యావయవచర్య, రాచూరురాజ్యహరణధుర్య, మదచండవర్గాదిదాయక, ముదుగంటిదుర్గాధినాయక, పరిభల్లుచరణభూషణ, ఓరుగల్లునగరపోషణ, విజయకరాయతసాయక, విజయాపురభయదాయక, వర్ణనాదికరత్నోపకార, సొల్లలాపురసంక్షోభకార, కల్యాదినృపకబాధక, కల్యాణనగరసాధక, సామదానముఖ్యశీలరంజన, ఆముదానగరసాలభంజన, ధావకరమార్గవిక్రాంతిసార, దేవగిరిదుర్గసమాక్రాంతిధీర, గౌతమీస్నానపావనాకార, కౌతుకాఖిలభూజనాధార, ఖలిచాపలిజన్యదాయక, హాళిపురచాంచల్యకారక, ఘుడితకూటతమసింహాసంహనన, బెడదకోటనగరసింహాసంహనన, బలికిరికూటపాకలశౌర్య, కలుబరిగికోటపాటనధుర్య, నగరసమాక్రమణవిచార, సగరసమాక్రమణధీర, పరచండనిర్గతకింకర, పరచండదుర్గభయంకర, సంసదుర్గకేతుఃహారణ, హాంసదుర్గనిబర్హణ, సగ్ణాటకవర్గసద్గంథనాసిక, కర్ణాటకబుధధన్వాసిక, జుర్నారుభయనిర్ణాయక, నిర్నారుసామజసముద్రద్రునిష్టాధిదాయక, సామగిరిదాపక, రామగిరిదుర్గప్రతిష్ఠాపక, మేదినీతలసమగ్రసంపాదన, యాదగిరిదుర్గభేదన, శీలచండమృదుభాషణ, గోలకొండపురదూషణ, అయిలకొండచండవిమతహాలాహల, అయిలకొండహరణకౌతూహల, సానుభల్లుధృతిపరాక్రమ, సానుగల్లుకృతిపరాక్రమ, పానుగంటిదుర్గపాటనధుర్య, భూనుతసాహసధుర్య, వేల్లితచండదుర్లభ, బెల్లముకొండవల్లభ, నిలయాలోలగర్జితాకార, మలయకేళిమహిమాధార,

కామసమాచరణాక్రమణ, సోమపదిమానచణాక్రమణ, శావగదుర్గబాధక, మాపురదుర్గమాధక, ఖండితసమగ్రసంధాచణ, దండితసమస్తశత్రుగణ, అక్షారూఢరత్నానికర, మక్షాకోటదత్నానికర, మక్షాకోటశిత్నానికర, అకారూఢశిత్నానికర, ఉల్లీఘనిజాప్తకల్లోలజాలక, ఢిల్లీపురహల్లకల్లోలవాలిక, కేలీసుమందారుగతబృందాయక, గోలేరుసందేరూభయసంధాయక, కలంబవర్గసంభాసుర, కలంబదుర్గకంపాసుర, భూగోళరుచిరభూషణ, పెగోవనగరభీషణ, కొండపల్లిహరణ, చండకరనిభప్రతాపభరణ, వినుకొండపాలక, వినూత్నకృతనాగార్జునికొండసాలజాలక, అవంతీకలితపూరణ, అవంతీమదవిదారణ, కటకరాజ్యాధివర్తన, కటకరాజ్యఘటితకీర్తన, ఆజికలేంద్రదారుణశరాసన, రాజమహేంద్రరాజధనుశ్శాసన, బూదలఖానుతిక్తాంగహరణ, యేదులఖానుసప్తాంగహరణ, నిదానమలకగుణసహజాపగాధిచారక, నిదానమలకభుజాబలాపహారక, రమాధిపవినుతాపదానకీర్తన, ఇమాదనమలకమానమర్దన, భృతరిపుదళనబంధుర, కుతుపనమలకదళసింధుర, కరీశతరుణాకారీశ సుగుణాభరణ, బరీదుబలవారణ, భుజకృతరిపుధావనావధాన, గజపతినుతపరాక్రమావధాన, కలికరకశసమగ్రస్తంభీకృతారాతివర్గవిశాల, కలివర్గమననిర్గపరతరకవారాశివర్గకేళ, గిరిదుర్గ వనదుర్గ జలదుర్గ స్థలదుర్గ చతురశీతి దుర్గసమస్తదళవిభాళ, రిపురాజగోపికాపాల, గాయగోపాళ, శ్రీరంగరాజరామభూపాల, విజయీభవ, దిగ్విజయీభవ.

తే. అని హిమాచల సేతుపర్యంత ధరణి
పతుల సభలందు సతతంబుల్ ప్రణుతి సేయ
వెలసె నెంతయు నార్వీటికులపయోధి
చంద్రుఁడైనట్టి రామరాజ్ఞనవిభుండు.

తే. అనఘుఁడా వైరసేనిభీమాధిపేంద్రు
పట్టి దమయంతి చేపట్టినట్టిరీతి
రామభూపాలకుఁడు కృష్ణరాయతనయ
యగు తిరుమలాంబను ద్వాహమయ్యె వేడ్కన్.

చ. శతమఖునింబులోమజను శంకరునిన్గిరిపుత్రిశంబరా
హితురతిదేవిఁబోలుచునహీనసుఖానుభవాప్తి రామభూ
పతియును దిర్మలాంబయును భానుసమానునిఁ గృష్ణపాధ్యునం
చితగుణుఁ బెద్దతిమ్మ నృపశేఖరుఁ గాంచిరి హర్షమొప్పఁగన్.

సీ. మఱియును నారామ మానవాధీశుండు
జిల్లేళ్లకులసుధాసింధుచంద్రుఁ
డగు పెద్దనందిరాజాగ్రణిసుతనప్ప
లాంబను బోచిరాజాన్వయావ
తంసముఁ దిమ్మభూధవుప్రియాత్మజలఁ గోం
డమ్మ లక్ష్మమ్మయు ననఁగ బరఁగు
సరసిజవదనల వరుసతో నిరువుర
నతివైభవోన్నతు లతిశయిల్ల.

గీ. సతులనిట్టుమువ్వురను బంధు వితతి వొగడఁ
బరిణయంబయ్యె సంభ్రమభరితుఁడగుచుఁ
నబ్జగర్భగురుండు పీతాంబరుండు
శ్రీమహీనీళలను వరించినట్లు.

శా. ఆరామక్షితి భర్తగాంచెను బ్రమోదాయత్తుఁడై కొండమాం
బారామామణివల్లగొండ ధరణీపాలేంద్రు సద్వృత్తనుం
డై రామారిపురీశుఁ దిమ్మవిభులక్ష్మాంబాపయోజాస్యయం
దారూఢాత్మసిరంగరాజవసుధాధ్యక్షున్దయాబ్జాక్షునిన్.

క. వితరణరేఖను రాధా
సుతుఁడంచిత భోగగరిమ సుత్రాముఁడనన్
నుతిఁగాంచెఁ గృష్ణరాయ
క్షితివరుదౌహిత్రుఁడైన కృష్ణేంద్రుఁడిలన్.

ఉ. ధ్యేయుఁడు రామరాజ పెదతిమ్మవిభుండని వాఁజివోలిలోఁ
బాయని భీతిచేత మొనభగ్నము గాయవనుల్ద్రొలంగనా
బాయనిజాముఁడడ్డపడ సామజయూథముఁ ద్రుంచెఁ జూపరుల్
వాయుజుఁడంచు నెంచఁగనవార్యసముజ్జ్వలబాహుశౌర్యుఁడై.

ఉ. మావులు నేనుఁగుల్భటసమాజముపీనుఁగుపెంటగాఁగగం
గావలినుండి కృష్ణదనుకా నెనరించి నిజాముఁ దోలిరా
మావనినాథుఁ గొండవిభుఁ డాహవకేళిఁ జరించెఁ జూచియా
దేవతలెల్ల నీఘనుఁడు దేవవరాత్మజుఁడంచు నెంచఁగన్.

ఉ. ఏలుచు నానెగొందిపురమింద్రసమానుఁడు కొండధారుణీ
పాలుఁడుపొల్చె శాత్రవులు బంటుతనంబులమాని చావడిన్

వేళయెఱింగి కాంచి మఱి వేళమునన్మకుటాగ్రరత్నరు
గ్జాలముచేత నాత్మపదకంజయుగంబు నలంకరింపఁగన్.

క. సూరపవాహాధీశ్వరు
కూరిమిసుతఁ దిరుమలాంబఁ గులసతిగ మహో
దారత వరించె రామ
క్ష్మారమణుని కొండనృపతి కడువేడుకతోన్.

క. ఆమహితాత్ముని తనయుఁడు
రామాధిపుఁ డహితకమల రాకాశశియై
భూమిఁ బ్రజలెపుడు నధిక
శ్రీమించఁగ నేలెనీతి చెలువుదలిర్పన్.

సీ. గొబ్బూరి కులవార్ధి కుముదాప్తుఁ డౌనోబ
విశ్వంభరాధీశ విభునికూర్మి
తనయయౌ నరసింగమను సూరపాన్వయ
పావనుం డగునోబ పార్థివేంద్రు
పుత్రి నోబమ్మను బోచిరాట్పన్ననృ
పాధ్యునిసుత జానకమ్మ నిట్లు
వరుసతో ముప్పురఁ బరిణయంబై వాగ
లబిశంబునను రక్తి నాత్మధర్మ

గీ. వర్తనకును సహాయులై వర్తిలంగ
నఖిలతరభోగభాగ్యంబులా సతీత్ర
యంబుతోఁ గూడఁ దాఁ జాల ననుభవించె
రామభూవరు కొండ్రాజు రామరాజు.

క. రాకూరి తిమ్మరాజధ
రాచక్రేశ్వరుఁడు పాణెరాజు ప్రియసుతా
పోచమదేవిని మోద
ప్రాచుర్యము మదిఁ దలిర్పఁ బరిణయమయ్యెన్.

చ. కడిమిఁ గిరీటిమాడ్కి నుతిఁ గన్నసిరంగ మహీవిభుండు మే
ల్నడకలపోచిరాజ రఘునాథనృపాలుని కూర్మిపుత్రికన్
బుడమిపడంతి దాల్మినను బోలినలక్ష్మమనున్వరించె నిం
పడరఁగ రాఘవుండు జనకాత్మజఁ గయికొనుచందమేర్పడన్.

క. అతిగుణనిధి శ్రీరంగ
క్షితిపతికుదయించిరార్య కీర్తితసుగుణా
న్వితులు సుతులు పెదవేంకట
పతి చినవేంకటపతియనంబరగ నిరువురున్.

58

SVARAMĒLAKALĀNIDHI.

[*By Ramayāmātya Toḍaramalla.*]

In the introduction to this work on music the author traces the genealogy of his patron Rāma Rāya. In the Lunar race was born a king called Srī Ranga Rāja who married Timmāmba celebrated for her virtues. As a result of their joint penances was born to them a king called Rāma Rāja to whom Krishna Rāya gave his daughter in marriage and was proud of being the father of a daughter in consequence. He went out of Vidyāpura and retired to the fort of Gutti along with his two younger brothers; and, after conquering the traitors to the kingdom, placed the helpless Sadāśiva Rāya on the Karnāṭa throne. With his two younger brothers Timma Rāya and Venkaṭādri he shone like Yudhishṭhira with his brothers Bhīma and Arjuna, and with their help having conquered all Pārasīkas (Muhammadans), filled the whole world with his fame. He had a palace called Ratna Kūṭa constructed by his minister Rāmayāmātya and was struck with admiration as it excelled even Vaijayanta, the palace of the gods. The palace was surrounded by extensive gardens, adorned with statues, which contained cool tanks abounding with swans.

Seated within this palace Rāma Rāya spent his time in the midst of scholars versed in sāhitya (literature), music and other arts. From among them Rāmayāmātya got up and exhibited before them his skill in the art of music. Then Venkaṭādri suggested that Rāmayāmātya should write a book settling the several points of dispute among scholars about music. On this Rāmayāmātya remembering all that the king had done for him, for example, appointing him as the viceroy of the Konḍavīḍu Rājya bordering on the eastern sea; enabling him to grant many agrahāras to Brahmans, and giving him the Jēlūri Simhāsanapaṭṭana (?), resolved to write a book on music about the several points at dispute, and dedicate it to Rāma Rāya. The last verse in Prakaraṇa V of the book says that it was completed on the 10th (Daśami) of the Śukla Paksha of Śrāvaṇa in the cyclic year Sādhāraṇa corresponding to the Śaka year 1471.

एषां कुलालङ्कृतिरेष जज्ञे श्रीरङ्गनाथो जितराजराजः ।
तया सदाचारदृशा विविन्ते राजर्षिभावं रमितक्षमो यः ॥ ६ ॥
तिम्माम्बिका तस्य बभूव देवी साध्वीजनानामिव या समष्टिः ।
सती यशोदा विनतानसूया सुदक्षिणा सत्यवती सुभद्रा ॥ ७ ॥
तपोविशेषेण तयोरशेषराजाधिराजोऽजनि रामराजः ।
कन्याप्रदोऽस्मै स हि कृष्णरायः कन्यापितृत्वं बहुमन्यते स्म ॥ ८ ॥
भुजो यदीयो भुजगेन्द्रजेता भुवं बिभर्तीति न विस्मयाय ।
चेतोणुमात्रं जगदेकधुर्यं शेषाचलेशं वहतीति चित्रम् ॥ ९ ॥
यः खड्गैकसखः सहानुजयुगो निर्गत्य विद्यापुरात्
लब्ध्वा गुत्तिगिरौ सदाशिवमहीपालं निरालम्बनम् ।
स्वामिद्रोहकृतः प्रतीपनृपतीन्निर्जित्य भद्रासने
कर्णाटे भगवानिव ध्रुवमयं कीर्त्या सहास्थापयत् ॥ १० ॥
दधीचिराधेयशिबिक्षितीशजीमूतवाहादिमजीवनाङ्गैः ।
अवाप्तमूर्तैरिह येन कीर्तिः भाति प्रणीतं भुवि वल्लभत्वम् ॥ ११ ॥
तस्यानुजौ विश्रुततिम्मराजश्रीवेङ्कटाद्रिक्षितिपावभूताम् ।
अजातशत्रोरभिजातवृत्तेः भीमार्जुनौ भीमभुजाविवार्यौ ॥ १२ ॥
अमुक्तपार्श्वद्वितयोऽनुजाभ्यां रामावतारो भुवि रामराजः ।
दिवानिशं दीप्यति शीतभानुदिवाकराभ्यामिव रत्नसानुः ॥ १३ ॥
विजित्य सर्वानपि पारसीकान् रणेषु तत्कीर्तिपटच्चराणि ।
आधूय भूयो हरितो वधूटीः विशोभयत्येष यशोदुकूलैः ॥ १४ ॥
श्रीरामयामात्यवरेण रत्नकूटाभिदं कारित एष सौधम् ।
आलोकयन्निर्जितवैजयन्तं हर्षाङ्कुरो विस्मितमानसोऽभूत् ॥ १५ ॥
अनेकतेजोनिधिराजहंससमाकुलं नित्यमनन्तजिष्णुम् ।
नानासुधर्मावलिनर्मवासमन्यं सुमेरुं समुदाहरन्ति ॥ १६ ॥

मन्दानिलाकम्पितवैजयन्ती मन्दारशाखाव्यतिघट्टनेन ।
आराममलक्ष्यामरुतां तनोति हल्लीसलीलामिव सस्यलक्ष्मीः ॥ १७ ॥
पर्वेन्दुबिम्बोपलसीम्नि पादमारोप्य यस्मिन्नधिवासवत्यः ।
पाञ्चालिकानां मिथुनानि कन्याः पाणिग्रहं प्रापयितुं यतन्ते ॥ १८ ॥
सौधान्तरेऽस्मिन् कुरुते प्रमोदात् सरामराजस्समयापनोदम् ।
सङ्गीतसाहित्यकलाविशेषशेषावतारैर्विबुधैरुपेतः ॥ १९ ॥
सैलारागकदम्बमातृकलसद्द्वयप्रबन्धादिम-
द्वात्रिंशद्वरसूदकानधिगतः श्रीपञ्चतालेश्वरान् ।
श्रीरङ्गाद्विपदस्वराङ्कसहितान्सश्रीविलासादिकान्
त्रिंशद्वासरविप्रकीर्णकमहानर्घप्रबन्धादिमान् ॥ २० ॥
चेतोरञ्जनषोडशध्रुवमुखानेकार्थगम्भीरषट्-
चत्वारिंशदुदारसालकमहागूढप्रबन्धान्वितान् ।
अन्यान्विंशतिरागविश्रुततमश्रीपञ्चरत्नस्फुर-
द्गीतालङ्कृतसाक्षराक्षपनपर्यायैरुपेतानपि ॥ २१ ॥
स वैणिकैस्संसदि गीयमानान् समञ्जसश्रावककण्ठनादैः ।
श्रीरामयामात्यकृतप्रबन्धान् आकर्ण्य कर्णाभरणान्यनन्दत् ॥ २२ ॥
अत्रान्तरे संसदि रामराजं सङ्गीतसाहित्यविनोदभाजम् ।
वेलानुरूपं विनयादवादीत् श्रीवेङ्कटाद्रिक्षितिपालसिंहः ॥ २३ ॥
सङ्गीतशास्त्रे बहुधा विरोधाः सन्त्येव लक्ष्येषु च लक्षणेषु ।
सर्वं समीकृत्य स राममन्त्री तनोतु शास्त्रं वचसा तवेति ॥ २४ ॥
अथासनस्यान्तिकभाजमेनमधीतसङ्गीतकलारहस्यम् ।
श्रीरामयामात्यमिदं बभाषे श्रीरङ्गराजाधिपरामराजः ॥ २५ ॥
विजानते लक्षणमात्रमेके विदन्ति लक्ष्यं कतिचिज्जगत्याम् ।
सल्लक्षलक्ष्योभयसारवेदी सन्दृश्यते नैव भवानिवान्यः ॥ २६ ॥
विद्यानिधिः *कल्लपदेशिकस्ते मातामहो दत्तिलवन्महीयान् ।
गान्धर्वशास्त्रेषु ततोपि तानि तत्सम्प्रदायेन ततस्स्फुरन्ति ॥ २७ ॥

* This is obviously the commentator, on the Saṅgītaratnākara of Śārṅgadēva, who calls himself Kallinātha or Chatura Kallinātha. In the preamble to this commentary he refers himself to Court of Mallikārjuna (Immadidēva Rāya, as he calls him), the son of Prauḍha Dēvarāya, son of Vijaya, i.e., Dēvarāya II of history.

सङ्गीतशास्त्रेषु मतान्तराणि सन्त्येषु सारांशमुपाददानः ।
सङ्गृह्य सल्लक्षणलक्ष्ययुक्तं सङ्गीतशास्त्रं सरसं विधेहि ॥ २८ ॥
मतानुवृत्त्या भरतादिमानां स्वरप्रमाणं सुलभं कुरुष्व ।
पतञ्जलिः पाणिनिशास्त्रदृष्ट्या शब्दव्यवस्थां कृतवान्यथादौ ॥ २९ ॥
हृत्पूरितानन्दमिति ब्रुवाणः कर्पूरवीटीमददादमुष्मै ।
आदाय तामारचितानुमोदः विचारयामास स राममन्त्री ॥ ३० ॥
स एव पूर्वाधिककोण्डवीटिप्रधानदुर्गप्रतिपादनेन ।
पूर्वार्णवेनैव परीतमूर्तेः प्रभुत्वमुर्व्या विततार मह्यम् ॥ ३१ ॥
अस्य प्रसादादमिताग्रहारप्रतिष्ठयानेकमहीसुराणाम् ।
आलम्बनं तत्र विधाय तेषामनुग्रहादाप विशालकीर्तिम् ॥ ३२ ॥
जेलूरिसिंहासनपट्टणेन युक्तां सरत्नामिव हारवल्लीम् ।
वितीर्य मे सश्रमवातिराश्मेरधीशतामस्य तुलामतानीत् ॥ ३३ ॥
प्रयच्छति प्रत्यहमत्युदारां सम्माननां सादरमेष मह्यम् ।
सन्तं जगत्यामुपकर्तुकामः सराजभूरस्यपटुर्मुदेऽहम् ॥ ३४ ॥
अचिराद्विरचय्याहं स्वरमेलकलानिधिम् ।
तमस्मै चोपदीकृत्य गम्यासं कृतकृत्यताम् ॥ ३५ ॥
सोऽयं सङ्गीतसाहित्यलक्ष्मीदक्षिणनायकः ।
इत्थं विचिन्त्य तं राममन्त्री वक्तुं प्रचक्रमे ॥ ३६ ॥

Prakaraṇa V. Last verse.

शाकेनात्र धराधराब्धि धरणीगण्ये च साधारणे
वर्षे श्रावणमासि निर्मलतरे पक्षे दशम्यां तिथौ ।
रामामात्यविनिर्मितस्वरततेस्सङ्गतिरत्नाकरात्
सोयं मेलकलानिधिर्मतिमतामाकल्पमाकल्पताम् ॥

Colophon.

इति श्रीमदभिनवभरताचार्यवाग्गेयकारतोडरमल्लातिम्मामात्यनन्दनरामामात्यनिर्मिते स्वरमेलकलानिधौ रागप्रकरणं पञ्चमं सम्पूर्णम् ॥

59

ŚIVATATTVARATNĀKARA

[*By Keḷadi Basavabhūpāla.*]

This encyclopædic Sanskrit poem containing more than one hundred chapters or kallolas, divided into seven tarangas and dealing with a large variety of subjects was written by the Keḷadi chief Basava Rāja. The book was completed in the year Sarvadhāri corresponding with the Śaka year counted by the Moon (1) Agni (3) ritu (6) and kshmā (earth) (1) or 1631 Ś. corresponding to A.D. 1709. The author has skilfully woven into the body of the work a history of his own ancestors who were prominent subordinates of the emperors of Vijayanagar. At the end of kallola IV the author gives the legendary account of the foundation of the city of Vijayanagar by the sage Vidyāraṇya, and the succession of its sovereigns from the time of Vidyāraṇya as well as the length of each reign. Until we come to the time of Rāma Rāya who died at the battle of Talikota the account is more or less legendary and so not useful for purposes of history.

In taranga II of kallola V there is an account of the origin of the Keḷadi family. In the town of Keḷadi in the Kannaḍa country there was a person named Basava, who had married a woman of the same name and who was a devotee of Śiva. The couple had four sons. After the death of Basava and two of his sons, his wife was bringing up the two other sons who were named Chauḍa and Bhadra, and in due course had their marriages performed. Once when Chauḍa was attending to the ploughing of his land his ploughshare is said to have come across a large amount of buried treasure. With the aid of the treasure he managed to become a Grāmādhipa (headman of a village). He then collected a small company of soldiers. The king of the country, on hearing of this, sent for Chauḍappa. Much pleased with him on hearing his story, the king made him governor of Pulladésa with the title Keḷadi Chauḍappa Nāyaka. Then Chauḍa returned to Keḷadi and, constructing the temple of Rameśvara there, made to it large endowments. He had two sons who were named Sadāśiva and Bhadra. Having taught both of them the sevaral śāstras and arts, he nominated Sadāśiva Nāyaka as his successor and died soon after.

Sadāśiva governed his province righteously, and the people were very happy under him. He married two wives from the elder of whom he had a son Doḍḍa Saṇkaṇṇa Nāyaka, and from the younger Chikka Sankaṇṇa Nāyaka. He had these two sons properly educated. At that time Rāma Rāya, the ruler of Vidyānagara (Vijayanagar), wanted to fight with the rulers of Kalyāna and Kalubarigi, and summoned Sadāśiva Nāyaka to his aid. He then sent his own army also along with Sadāśiva Nāyaka. Hearing of this the lord of Vijayāpura (Bijapur) sent his own army to oppose. The two armies met and the Bijapur forces were defeated and driven away from the field by Sadāśiva Nāyaka. He then captured the valuable possessions of the enemy's army and accompanied by the emperor Rāma Rāya, who admired his achievements, proceeded to capture the town of Kalyān.

During the siege of the place the emperor once summoned before him all his generals and throwing the weapon called 'yamadamṣṭrika' into the fort asked which of them would enter the fort and fetch him back the instrument. When all the other generals kept quiet, Sadāśiva Nāyaka alone was able to storm the fort and bring back to his master the weapon. The sovereign was greatly pleased with this and bestowed upon him the title Koṭikolāhala, and the governorship of the three provinces of Gutti, Bārkūr, and Pangalūr. He also granted him the right to affix the title Rāya Nāyaka to his name and honoured him in other ways. Sometime after this the emperor sent him against the barbarian Nāyakas (Dasyunāyakas) of Chandragutti whom he completely vanquished. He was then sent against Barid Padishah (of Bidar) whom he captured along with the seven constituents of his royalty (Saptānga), and brought him as a present to his master. The emperor gave him the title of Śatrusaptāngaharaṇa (capturer of the seven constituents of royalty of his enemies), and honoured him in other ways. Some time after this a chief called Sāḷva Timma marched against his enemies according to his directions.*

Then Sadāśiva was directed by the emperor to march against the Tauḷavas (people of the Tulu country) and the Keraḷas (the people of Malayāḷam). He defeated the people of the places completely and planting a pillar of victory in the country added all the territory to his master's empire. Then the emperor wanted to march against two chiefs called Yaḍava and Murāri, in the country of Jālihāḷu. Sadāśiva dissuaded the emperor from undertaking the expedition himself and marching against them, defeated

* We do not know who this chief was. He is different from the famous minister of Krishna Rāya of the same name, and the Sāḷuva Nāyaka, the rebel governor of the time of Achyuta Rāya. The present passage merely mentions him as a subordinate of Sadāsiva Rāya Nāyaka, but no definite achievements are ascribed to him.

them both and brought them prisoners to him. The emperor then gave him the title Yaḍavamurāri-Koṭikolāhala. After this Sadāśiva retired to his own province. There he made extensive endowments to the God Rāmēśvara and founded the town of Sadāśiva Sāgara. He also founded the Agrahāra called Sadāśivapura and built therein several temples.

Later on when he found that the governor of Bankāpura, Mādarasā, by name, had grown conceited he marched against him and capturing him, led him a prisoner to the emperor. Then his brother Bhadrappa Nāyaka who had gone on a pilgrimage to Benares returned, and he spent some time with him. He later bestowed upon him the title of Immaḍi Sadāśiva Nāyaka and anointing him as the governor in his stead retired to the forests in the evening of his life.

After Bhadrappa Nāyaka ruled for some time he nominated the elder of his nephews Doḍḍasankaṇṇa Nāyaka as his successor and the younger Chikkasankaṇa Nāyaka as the heir-apparent, and taught both of them the science of politics.

Kallōla V. Taranga II.

देशेऽस्मिन्केलदीनाम्नि पुरे गार्हस्थ्यमाश्रितः ।
गुरुभक्तिपरस्तस्थौ शैवो बसवनामकः ॥
स नाम्न्या कान्तया युक्तः शिवया स यथा शिवः ।
तस्य पर्याप्तवसनाशनसौख्यस्य जज्ञिरे ॥
क्रमात्कुमाराश्चत्वारः पुमर्था इव धीमतः ।
कालक्रमेण सविधं शिवस्य समुपेयुषि ॥
तस्मिन्नथानुगतयोस्तं द्वयोस्सुतयोरपि ।
अवर्धेतां चौडभद्रनामानौ द्वौ कुमारकौ ॥
ताभ्यां माता बभौ भानुचन्द्राभ्यां द्यौरिवोन्नता ।
उद्वाहमङ्गलमपि कारयामास सा तयोः ।
अनन्तरं च सुखिनोस्तिष्ठतोरेकदा तयोः ।
स्वकारितां कृषिं द्रष्टुं चौडनामा विनिर्गतः ॥

*   *   *   *

तत्प्रसादमहिम्नाऽस्य कदाचित्स्वपतो निशि ।
स्वप्नो जातस्त्रियामान्ते निधिसम्प्राप्तिसूचकः ॥

ततः प्रातस्समुत्थाय तत्फलं च विमृश्य सः ।
निधानं लब्धवान्पश्चाद्बहुद्रविणपूरितम् ॥

Taranga IV.

*　　*　　*

तदुत्तरं प्रवृत्तस्तु वृत्तान्तश्चौडभूपतेः ।
उदीर्यते विस्मयकृत्क्रमादवहितश्शृणु ॥
ईश्वरानुग्रहादेनं निधिं संप्राप्य तद्बलात् ।
ग्रामाधिपत्यमासाद्योत्तरोत्तरसमृद्धया ॥
प्रसादयत्पूजया तं रामेशं लिङ्गरूपिणम् ।
ततः परिमितां सेनां संगृह्णाति परानपि ॥
तस्मिन्संगृह्णति श्रुत्वा सार्वभौमः प्रहर्षितः ।
आनाय्य तं क्रमादेनं मुदन्तं तन्मुखोक्तितः ॥
श्रुत्वायं सुमहान्शौर्यसम्पन्न इति नन्दितः ।
पुल्लदेशं वशं तस्य विधाय तदनन्तरम् ॥
नामादात्केलदीचौडप्पनायक इति स्वयम् ।
लब्ध्वा नाम च देशं चानुज्ञया तस्य निर्गतः ॥
केलदीस्थलमासाद्य तत्र रामेश्वरस्य सः ।
आलयं गुरुनिर्मायभुवं भूयो वितीर्य च ॥
उपचाराय पर्याप्ता सहर्षयदीश्वरम् ।
दुष्टानां निग्रहं स्वैरं शिष्टानां परिपालनम् ॥
कुर्वन्स्वबाहुशौर्येण सम्पदा चाभ्यवर्तत ।
सुतौ तस्मादजायेतां यथाब्धेरिन्दुकौस्तुभौ ॥
तौ सदाशिवभद्राख्यौ प्रख्यातिं प्रापुतां ततः ।
शस्त्रविद्याब्धिपारीणौ निपुणौ किंच नीतिषु ॥
वाहनारोहणाभिज्ञावुदूढसद्दशस्त्रियौ ।
विधाय च तयोर्मध्ये श्रीसदाशिवनामके ॥
उद्वोढुमक्षम इव सर्वां राज्यधुरं न्यधात् ।
नीतिं चोपादिशत्तस्मै भूमिपालजनोचिताम् ॥

*　　*　　*　　*

साधुनीतिमुदीर्यैवं सप्रपञ्चं सुताय सः ।
केलदीस्थितरामेशप्रसादात्प्राप्तवान्निधिम् ॥
चौडनायकनामाङ्को नृपः कैलासवासिनः ।
सान्निधिं दुर्लभं लब्धुमिव कैलासमासदत् ॥
ततस्तस्य सुतः श्रीमान् सदाशिवमहीपतिः ।
शशास सकलं राज्यं धर्मेणैव यशोनिधिः ॥

Taranga V.

ततस्सदाशिवनृपे बहुधा राज्यशासिनि ।
महीसुरास्सुराश्चापि बहुधाराज्यहर्षिताः ॥
ज्येष्ठायामस्य भार्यायां दोड्डसंकण्णनायकः ।
कनिष्ठायां तु सञ्जातश्चिक्कसंकण्णनायकः ॥
तावेधेतां सुतौ राज्ञो जनरागोदयाविव ।
उभयोरनयोर्विद्याभ्यासं स्वयमकारयत् ॥

* * * *

अशात्रवां महीं कुर्वन् गोपायति यदा तदा ।
विद्यानगरवर्ती यो रामराजः क्रमागतः ॥
कल्याणकलुबुरिगिवर्तिना विग्रहेच्छया ।
आनाययदमुं स्वीयैः पुरं साहाय्यकाय सः ।।॥
सहैतेन बलं स्वीयं चतुरङ्गं नियोजयत् ।
बलेनानेन सहितस्त्वमग्रे यानमाचर ॥
इत्याज्ञप्ते पुरोयाते श्रीसदाशिवनायके ।
श्रुत्वास्य पुरतो यानं विजयाख्यपुरेश्वरः ॥
तेषां सहायकोद्युक्तो जेतुमेनं पुरः स्थितम् ।
प्राहिणोद्बलिनो योद्धुं प्रमुखान्म्लेच्छनायकान् ॥
न्यरुन्ध न्नस्य ते मार्गं सन्नद्धा युद्धकर्मणि ।
जितेन लभ्यते लक्ष्मीर्मृतेनापि सुराङ्गना ॥
क्षणविध्वंसिनः कायाः का चिन्ता मरणे रणे ॥
इति युद्धाय सन्नद्धः परान्पर्यभवत्क्षणात् ।
अन्धकारानिव रविर्मेघानिव च मारुतः ॥

पलायितानां तेषां तु सर्वस्वं स्वैरहारयत् ।
सङ्केतेन तदारामराजेनाह्लादिचेतसा ॥
सहैव निर्ययावग्रे कल्याणवरणं प्रति ।
गच्छन्सच कियद्दूरं तं सन्निहितमैक्षत ॥
सार्वभौमस्तमालोक्य कौतुकेन करस्थितम् ।
यमदंष्ट्रायुधं स्वीयं प्राकारस्यान्तराक्षिपत् ॥
अथ राजा प्रतीतान्स्वान् अदिशच्चापि यूथपान् ।
वरणाक्रमणं कश्चिद्युष्मासु रचयत्विति ॥
सर्वेषु तूष्णींभूतेषु सदाशिवनृपः स्वयम ।
ततस्तस्याभ्यन्तरं च प्रविशन्यमदंष्ट्रिकाम् ॥
गृहीत्वा तां ततस्सार्वभौमायाकुरुतोपदाम् ।
सहायो यन्त्रकीलेन द्वारोद्घाटनकारिणा ॥
सार्वभौमोददौ तस्मै कोटिकोलाहलाभिधाम् ।
बिरुदानि महार्घाणि वसनाभरणानि च ॥
देशांस्त्रीन् गुत्तिबाकूरुपुङ्गलूरुपदाङ्कितान् ।
रायनायकनामापि निधायास्य महीपतेः ।
बहुधा मानयामास श्रीसदाशिवनायकम् ।
सोऽप्याख्यया तदा भूरिप्रख्यातिमपि लब्धवान् ॥
अनन्तरं कतिपयदिनेषु क्षपितेष्वसौ ।
चन्द्रगुत्तिस्थितैर्दस्युनायकैर्भूयूपद्रुतः ॥
सार्वभौमो निग्रहार्थं तेषामेनं समादिशत् ।
अयं च रचयामास तेषां निग्रहणं ततः ॥
पुनः कियद्दिनादूर्ध्वं दूतैरानाय्य तेन सः ।
बरीदपादुशाहस्य विजयाय प्रचोदितः ॥
विजितं तं करे कृत्वा सह सप्ताङ्गसम्पदा ।
उपहारं समकरोत्तस्मै साकं यदा तदा ॥
सन्तुष्टस्तु ददौ शत्रुसप्ताङ्गहरणाभिधाम् ।
किंचारुणध्वजपटं दुन्दुभिं वाद्यपञ्चकम् ॥

मनोज्ञानि च वासांसि बिरुदाभरणानि च ।
ततो याति कियत्काले साल्वतिम्माभिधानवान् ॥
तदनुज्ञां समासाद्य न्यगृह्णन्निजतेजसा ।
अनन्तरं सार्वभौमः सदाशिवनृपं प्रति ॥
मायोपायेषु चतुरान् स्वासाध्यान्केरळाधिपान् ।
तै(तौ)लवांश्च तथा जेतुमादिदेश महीपतिः ॥

*   *   *   *

तानीश्वरप्रसादेन पौरुषेण च भूयसा ।
सदाशिवमहीपालः केरळादीन्पराभवत् ॥

*   *   *   *

एवं केरळभूपादीन् सार्वभौमस्यनुज्ञया(?) ।
सबलान्परिभूयाथ गृहीत्वापि बलं ततः ॥
संस्थाप्य स जयस्तम्भं तद्देशाभ्यन्तरे क्वचित् ।
सकलान् सार्वभौमं स प्रापयामास तान् नृपान् ॥
अनन्तरं जालिहाळदेशाधीशौ विरोधिनौ ।
यडवश्च मुरारिश्चेत्युभौ बहुपराक्रमौ ॥
निगृहीतुः परासाध्यौ स्वयं यातुं चिकीर्षति ।
सार्वभौमे तान्निवृत्य स्वयं गत्वा समं बलैः ॥
तद्दुर्गवरणं सद्यः प्रविश्यानु च तावुभौ ।
जग्राह च यथा रामः कुम्भकर्णदशाननौ ॥
प्रसाध्य दुर्ग्रहं दुर्गं जित्वा दुर्निग्रहौ च तौ ।
आनीय दर्शयामास राज्ञे सोयं तदा ततः ॥
लब्ध्वा यडवमुरारिकोटिकोलाहलाभिधाम् ।
ततस्सदाशिवनृपः स्वदेशं समुपेयिवान् ॥
रामेश्वरस्य पूजार्थं ददौ क्षेत्राणि भूरिशः ।
नगरं कारयामास स सदाशिवसागरम् ॥

ततः कुशावतीतीरे सदाशिवपुराह्वयम् ।
अग्रहारं स्वनाम्नैव व्यतनोद्दीशतुष्टये ॥
विप्रैर्विमलसद्वृत्तैः सद्वृत्तजनितैरपि ।
अग्रहारः कृतो भूमेर्मुक्ताहार इवाबभौ ॥
सदाशिवेश्वरं तत्र प्रत्यस्थापयदादृतः ।
स्वनाम्नैव यथा रामः पुरा रामेश्वराभिधम् ॥
अथावरणदेवांस्तं परितोऽस्थापयत्ततः ।
तन्नित्यपूजापर्याप्तं क्षेत्रं तेभ्योऽपि सोऽमुचत् ॥
महादानोदितैः कीर्तिखण्डैष्षोडशाभिर्व्यधात् ।
सर्वेश्वरशिरः श्लाघ्यं स्वयशश्शशिमण्डलम् ॥
ततः कदाचित्साम्राज्यदर्पितं जेतुमिच्छति ।
स मादरसनामानं बंकापुरनिवासिनम् ॥
निगृह्य तं गृहीत्वाथ निनाय नृपसन्निधिम् ।
अथानुजे समायाते काश्या भद्रप्पनायके ॥
तेन साकमयं निन्ये कंचित्कालमवन्महीम् ।
तस्य दत्वेम्मडिसदाशिवनायकनाम च ॥
पट्टाभिषेकमकरोद्गन्तुकामस्तपोवनम् ।
स राज्येऽवस्थितान् बाह्यान् निगृह्य श्रेयसे रिपून् ॥
आन्तरानिव तान्जेतुमाश्रमं स्वयमाश्रयत् ।
ततस्सदाशिवनृपः काले कियति निर्गते ॥
मुञ्चन्नपि पुनर्नैव सदाशिवपदं जहौ ।
ततो महीं भद्रभूपः कंचित्कालं शशास सः ॥
ज्यायसस्सुतयोश्शस्त्रशास्त्रविद्याप्रवीणयोः ।
स्वराज्यभारं निदधौ दोड्डसंकण्णनायके ।
यौवराज्यं कनिष्ठस्य चिक्कसंकण्णनायके ।
ताभ्यां राज्यस्थिरीभावसाधनत्वमुपेयुषीम् ॥
उपादिशद्राजनीतिं प्रेम्णा भद्रप्पनायकः ।
अनन्तरं च संकण्णनायको राज्यमन्वशात् ॥

Colophon.

इति श्रीमदनाद्यनन्तसकलतत्त्वोत्तीर्णषडध्वोपादानाबिन्दुकारणचिदम्बरशाक्ति-समन्वितपरमेश्वरप्रसादासादितशिवाद्वैतविद्याविशारदश्रीमत्केळदीबसवराजेन्द्रविर-चितवेदागमान्तर्गताविविधविद्यातन्त्रसारभूताशिवतत्त्वरत्नाकरे पञ्चमकल्लोले सदाशिव-नृपचरित्रमायोपायवर्णनं नाम पञ्चमस्तरङ्गः ॥

60

PRAPANNĀMṚTAM.

[*By Anantāchārya.*]

At the close of this work the author gives a short account of his own preceptor and his family. In the family of the famous Śrīśailapūrṇa, the maternal uncle of Rāmānuja, was born Tātāchārya who was a great scholar. He was the son of Śrīnivāsa Guru and was learned in all Śāstras. He was the āchāryā (preceptor) of Rāma Rāya, emperor of Vijayanagar, who ruled after Krishna Rāya. On one occasion Rāma Rāya took his preceptor along with him to Chandragiri. At that time there was a scholar, born in the Vādhūla Gotra, called Mahāchārya (Doḍḍayāchārya). He lived at the sacred town of Ghaṭikāchala (Sholighur). He had defeated all the Śaiva scholars of Chitrakūṭa (Chidambaram) among whom there was the famous scholar Appaya Dīkshita. After the victory he wanted to establish the worship of Govindarāja once more in the temple of Chidambaram from where his idols had been removed by the Chōla king Krimikanṭha. This he was able to accomplish with the assistance of the emperor Rāma Rāya and his Guru Tātāchārya.* Appayya Dīkshita had also written a work on Advaita called Advaita Dīpika. In refutation of the work Mahāchārya wrote the Chanḍamārutam, and Tātāchārya, Panchamata Bhanjanam.

Chapter 126.

श्रीनिवासगुरोः पुत्रः तातार्यो लोकविश्रुतः ।
स तातदेशिकश्श्रीमान् महात्मा शास्त्रवित्तमः ॥
ग्रन्थं विधाय विख्यातं यः पञ्चमतभञ्जनम् ।
विख्यातस्सर्वलोकेषु महात्मा विबुधाग्रणीः ॥

---

* Chapter XII, Ancient India by S. K. Aiyangar about the temple of Govinda Raja and Vol. X, Purchus, His Pilgrimes, Chapter VII, Jesuit Observations of India.

महांस्तद्विषयश्लोको गीयते लोकविश्रुतः ।
शुकतातं त्रयीमार्गे तत्तातं तत्त्वनिर्णये ।
तत्तातततातमाचारे ताताचार्यमहं भजे ॥
श्रीरामदेवरायाख्यः कृष्णरायादनन्तरम् ।
शशास राज्यं धर्मेण गुरुभक्तिपरायणः ॥
स भूपतिर्महातेजाः ययौ चन्द्रागिरिं प्रति ।
गुरुं तातार्यमादाय रामरायाभिधस्तदा ॥
तस्मिन्काले महाचार्यस्सर्वशास्त्रविदां वरः ।
अवर्तताप्रातिद्वन्द्वो वाधूलो घटिकाचले ॥
खिलीकृतं चित्रकूटं क्रिमिकण्ठेन यत्पुरा ।
तत्प्रतिष्ठापितुं सम्यक् तदा मेने महागुरुः ॥
रामरायसहायेन महाचार्यो महायशाः ।
दुर्जयानपि निर्जित्य शैवान्शास्त्रविदुत्तमः ॥
स सम्यक् स्थापयामास गोविन्दं चित्रकूटके ।
गोविन्दराजो भगवान् महाचार्यप्रतिष्ठितः ॥
महोच्छ्रायश्चित्रकूटे ह्यद्यापि परिदृश्यते ।
शैवशास्त्रविदां श्रेष्ठो श्रीमानप्पयदीक्षितः ॥
चित्रकूटे जितारातिः अशोभत महायशाः ।
अद्वैतदीपिकाभिख्यं ग्रन्थमप्पयदीक्षितः ॥
चकार भगवद्द्वेषी शैवधर्मरतस्सदा ।
महाचार्यस्स तां श्रुत्वा तस्याः प्रतिभटे तदा ॥
चण्डमारुतनामानं विदधे ग्रन्थमुत्तमम् ।
अद्वैतदीपिकानाशस्ततोऽभूच्चण्डमारुतात ॥
प्रचण्डमारुते दीपप्रकाशस्स्यात्कथं भुवि ।
विधाय तातयाचार्यः तत्पश्चमतभञ्जनम् ॥
श्रीरामानुजसिद्धान्तमव्याहतमपालयत् ।
महाचार्यो महातेजाः स कृत्वा चण्डमारुतम ॥
अव्याहतं यतीन्द्रस्य तं सिद्धान्तमपालयत् ।

तत्र संवर्धितं सम्यक् श्रीरामानुजदर्शनम्।
आचन्द्रतारकं भूम्यामवर्धत सुविस्तरम्॥

This passage says that Appayya Dīkshita wrote Advaita Dīpika. But the work that now exists with that name is not written by him but by Nṛsimhāśrama. We do not know whether this refers to the same, in which case the statement is incorrect. Else Appayya Dīkshita should have written another work of the same name which has not come down to us.

61

BĀLABHĀGAVATAM.

[*By Konērunātha Kavi.*]

This Telugu poem dealing with the story of the Bhāgavata was written by Dōnūru Kōnērunātha Kavi and dedicated to his patron Chinna Timma Rāja of the Āravīṭi family. This chief was born in a collateral branch of the same family to which Rāma Rāya and the later emperors of Vijayanagar belonged. A lengthy account of the ancestors of the chief is given at the beginning of the work. In the family of the Lunar race of kings was born the famous Āravīṭi Bukka who was a staunch friend and supporter of the emperor Sāḷuva Narasimha. By his wife Ballāmbika he had a son called Rāma Rāya. This Rāma Rāya was the Governor of the fortress of Kandanavolu (Karnul), and defended the place against the chief Savāi who came against him with a force of 70,000 horse. Not only did he defend the place but sallied out of the fort and dealt severe destruction to the forces of the Savāi. This Savāi seems to refer to Yusuf Adil Shah, the famous founder of the line of the Bijapur Sultans, who was also called Savoyi. Ferista tells us that he was so called after a Persian village of the name where he was brought up. [But the title is also used in India with regard to people who have had nothing to do with Persia. The word has also got another form Sapāda in which form it occurs in copper-plate inscriptions, and means one and one-fourth. When applied to a man it signifies that he is a great dignitary although we are not in a position to state the exact significance.] Rāma Rāja also marched against the chief Kācha, and defeating him completely captured his fortress Adavani (Adoni). Rāma Rāja had a son called Timma by his wife Lakkāmba. Of this Timma the work narrates two miraculous exploits. He is said to have restored the lost eyesight of a shepherd. Once when he was marching with his army in a mountain pass during summer his soldiers were suffering very much from heat and thirst. The king by his devotion to the God, Doni Śrī Ranga Rāja, caused a spring to rise out of the mountain-side and was able to appease the sufferings of his soldiers.

He defeated Ēdula Khan (Adil Khan) at the battle of Mānuva (Manve). He also marched against the rebel governor of Ādavani (Adoni) and brought him a prisoner before his sovereign Vīra Narasimha Rāya and was presented by him with a Gaṇḍapeṇḍēra (Anklet) in appreciation of this service. He was also the patron of the Telugu poem Bālabhāgavatam. He married Gōpama Dēvi, and had by her several sons as Tirumala, Viṭṭhala, Chinna Timma and Pāpa Timma. He had also another wife called Tirumala Dēvi by whom he got the sons Kōnappa and Śrī Rangarāja.

Of these sons the eldest son Tirumala constructed manṭapas, choultries and a garden, and made arrangements for several forms of worship to the God Nṛsimha at Garuḍādri (Ahobilam). He also constructed the big tank of the temple of Bhārgava Nṛsimha at Ahobilam.

His younger brother Chinna Timma was the most famous of all brothers. He was a great conqueror and the Chola, Kēraḷa, Pāṇḍya, and Tiruvaḍi sovereigns used to wait upon him with presents of horses of various breeds, gold and precious gems. He restored to the Tiruvaḍi (the king of Travancore) his lost territory, and was called Tiruvaḍi Rājyasthāpanāchārya. He also defeated the Pāṇḍya sovereign who had fought against the Tiruvaḍi.

అనవద్యగుణుఁడైన యతనివంశమున
ఘనుఁడారవీటిబుక్కనృపాలుఁడెసఁగె
నరనాథమణిసాళ్వ నరసింగరాయ
వరసఖుండైబుక్క వసుధేశుఁడలరె
నామహీపతికి బల్లాంబికయందు
రామనృపాలుండు రాజేంద్రుఁడొదవె
నెందు నెన్నఁగఁజాలు నిద్ధశౌర్యమున
గందనవోలి దుర్గంబులోనుండి
బుక్కరాయరామభూభుజుఁడెల్ల నృపులు
నెకుఱవ యిదియని యెన్నంగఁజాలి
పీరులు డెబ్బదివేవురాశ్వికులు

చేరి గొల్వంగవచ్చిన సవా నెదిరి
కలనంది పంచబంగాళంబు సేసి
గెలిచెఁ దచ్చరితంబుఁ గీర్తింపఁదరమె
వినుతింపఁదగునాదవేని దుర్గమున
ననతుఁడైయుండుకాచాధీశు గెలిచి
యరుదుగా సప్తాంగహరణంబు సేసె
గరిమోన్నతుండు బుక్కరాయరామవిభుఁడు
మహిమవంతుఁడు చిత్తమతకృతాంతుండు
సహజధైర్యుఁడు రామజనపతి వెలసె
నారామనృపతిలక్కాంబికయందు
ధీరునందనుఁగాంచెఁ దిమ్మభూవరునిఁ
బరిపాటిమించు ముప్పదిరెండురాజ
వరలక్షణంబుల వఱలెడువాఁడు
ఉన్నతకీర్తుల నొనరు నర్జునున
కెన్నంగ నలువది యేనవవాఁడు
ధరణి హరిశ్చంద్ర దశరథాత్మజుల
సరసకెక్కిన నిత్యసంపదవాఁడు.

* * * *

రాజచంద్రుఁడు రామరాజు తిమ్మయ్య
యమృతదృష్టియగునొక్క యాభీరునకును
నిపుణుండు వేంకట నిలయుండు చక్రి
యొకకంటి చూపుతా నొసఁగి స్వప్నమున
బ్రకటుఁడై తిమ్మభూపాలు మన్నించి
ఓకృతకృత్య నీకుర్వీశు లెనయె
నీకహోబలపుణ్యనిధి మోక్షమిత్తుఁ
గరుణఁ గోపాలుని కడమచూపిమ్ము
నరనాథయనుచు నానతియిచ్చుటయును
గొలువులో నగ్గోపకునకుఁ జూపొసఁగె
బలబలభద్రుఁడా పాండువంశజుఁడు
ధన్యుండు రామభూధవు తిమ్మనృపతి
సైన్యసమేతుఁడై చైత్రమాసమున

దండువోవుచునుండి తనభటుల్ త్రోవ
నెండినవోళ్లదప్పెలఁగించుటయును
నిండుచిత్తమున ధోనిసిరంగరాజు
కొండనెత్తమున వైకుంఠుని దలచి
గోవిందువేఁడి గ్రక్కునఁ నెకరఁ బుగ్గ
భూవినుతంబుగాఁ బొడమఁగఁజేసె.
నందఱుఁజూడంగ నన్నీరమచటఁ
గ్రందుగావిలసిల్లె ఘటికాద్వయంబు
కడిమిమైమానువకడరణక్షోణి
గడుసరి నేదులఖానుజయించె
విక్రమంబున నాదవేనిదుర్గంబు
విక్రాంతులెన్నవే వేగసాధించి
సిరులతో వీరనృసింహరాయలకుఁ
బరుషాత్తుఁ దుర్గాధి పతినొప్పగించి
గరిమ స్వామిద్రోహగండపెండార
మరిభీకరముగ రాయఁగాఁసంగనాందె
లాలితకీర్తి విలాసుండుపద్య
బాలభాగవత ప్రబంధనాయకుడు

* * * *

నాపార్థివోత్తము నర్ధాంగలక్ష్మి
గోపమాంబిక సతిగుణనిధానంబు
గోపమాంబయుఁ దిమ్మకుంభినీశుండు
నేపైనభక్తిలక్ష్మీశుఁ బూజించి
మహిమతోఁ దిరుమలమనుజ నాథుండు
విహిత దిగ్విజయుండు విట్ఠలేశ్వరుఁడు
రాజిల్లి చినతిమ్మరాజచంద్రుండు
తేజంబుగల పాపతిమ్మభూపతియు
ననునట్టి వలువురనాత్మసంభవులఁ
గనిరిందువంశంబు ఘనతకునెక్కఁ
దెలివితో మఱియునాతిమ్మ భూవరుఁడు
తిలకించు తిరుమలదేవి జేఁపట్టి

గనియెఁ గోనపమహీకాంతు శ్రీరంగ
మనుజేంద్రు రామలక్ష్మణులఁ బోలంగ
ననితర సమవృత్తి నందగ్రజుండు
దినపతి తేజుఁడు తిరుమలనృపతి
యొనరించె శ్రీమదహోబలపతికి
వనము మంటపమును వరసత్రములున
కర్పూర కస్తూరకాగంధసేవ
యర్పించె నాగరుడాద్రి నాథునకుఁ
జెలఁగు భార్గవనిధి శ్రీనృసింహునకు
నెలకొన్నభక్తిఁ గోనేఱుఁగట్టించె
సంకీర్ణదానంబు సముదయయోగ
పంకిల నిజసభాభవనాంగణుండు
శూరుండు భూషితసోమవంశుండు
ధీరతాహేమాద్రి తిరుమలనృపతి
సకలతీర్థంబులఁ జరియింపఁగలుగు
సుకృతమాజననాథుఁ జూచినఁగలుగు
నిందఱిలోన లక్ష్మీశకారుణ్యా
నందితస్థితి కృతినాయకుండైన
యాచినతిమ్మరాజేంద్ర చంద్రముని
రాచఱిమేరికిఁ బ్రణుతింపఁదరమె
ధీరులు కేరళతిరువడిపాండ్య
చేరచోళాదిక క్షితినాథవరులు
కదిసికంఖాణ తుక్ఖారాదిభేద
విదితంబులగునట్టి వివిధవాహములు
నౌపవాహ్యత గల్గియష్టమదంబు
లేపుచూపఁగనుండు నిభవిశేషములు
గణికాగణముల లెక్కలువెట్టరాని
మణికాంచనాదుల మహితవస్తువుల
నవహితులై యుపాయనములఁ దెచ్చి
యవసరంబుల వారియాజ్ఞలోనిలిచి
తెలివి మీఱఁగఁ జినతిమ్మభూపాలు
కొలువువేళలు గాచికొనియుందురర్థి

శ్రీరాఘవుండు దక్షిణదిగంతమున
నారూఢియున్న శౌర్యము పెంపు నెఱపి
పౌలస్త్యులంకలోఁ బట్టంబుగట్టి
యాలీలనిల్పలేఁదయ్యె దిరువడిని
పదపడియారామ భద్రుఁడేతనదు
కొదువదీర్పుటకు నైగొబ్బునమఱల
చినతిమ్మనృపతి యైసిరిమించఁబుట్టి
ఘనతనిద్దిశయెల్లఁ గ్రమ్మఱఁగెలిచి
బలిమిమైఁదిరువడిఁ బట్టంబుగట్టె
నలవిమేయారాజ హారిణాంకుఁబొగడ
నిలదన విద్వత్కవీంద్రగేహములు
కలితేభమద జలగంధముల్గాఁగ
నాసక్తినొనరించునన నారెవీటి
శాసను వితరణోత్సవమెన్నఁదరమె
యీదృశగుణ రమాహితుఁడైనవిజయ
మోదవంతునకు సన్మూర్తివంతునకు

* * * *

కృతకృత్యునకుఁ జంద్రగిరిముఖ్యదుర్గ
వితత మహైశ్వర్య విలసితాత్మునకు
బాటిత కేరళ భామినీగర్భ
ధాటీలసద్ఘణంధణనాదునకు
తిరువడిరాజ్యప్రతిష్ఠాపకునకు
విరచిత పాండ్యభూవిభుశాసనునకు
చేరచోళాదిక క్షితినాథమకుట
హారనీరాజన హృద్యపాదునకు.

62

YĀDAVĀBHYUDAYA VYĀKHYA.

[*By Appayya Dikshita.*]

This is a commentary on the Sanskrit poem Yādavābhyudayam of the great Śrī Vaishṇava teacher Vēdānta Dēśika, by Appayya Dīkshita, the famous Śaiva scholar. In the beginning he says that he wrote it at the instance of his patron Chinna Timma Rāya, and gives the genealogy of his family. In the Lunar race of Kshatriyas was born a famous king called Rāma Rāja. By his wife Gopī Dēvi he had a son called Timma Rāja. This Timma Rāja had many sons on account of his devotion to Venkaṭēśa, the god worshipped at Tirupati. Of these Chinna Timma became famous on account of his valour and achievements. He planted a pillar of victory, in token of his conquest, near the mountains of Malaya (the Western Ghats in the Tinnevelly District and Travancore). He was also a good scholar and patron of poets. Once he heard the poem Yādavābhyudayam read out to him by scholars, and being struck with its many merits directed the scholar Appayya Dīkshita to write a commentary on the work.

The prince who is described in this extract, was a first cousin of the well-known Aḷiya Rāma Rāya, who was killed in the battle of Talikota. During the latter's reign he led an expedition to the extreme south of the Peninsula against the Pāṇḍya and Tiruvaḍi (Kēraḷa) chiefs; and, having subdued them completely, he planted a pillar of victory on the banks of the Tāmraparṇi.

वंशे महति सुधांशोः पाण्डुसुतप्रवरचरितपरिपूते ।
आसीदपारमहिमा महीश्वरो रामराज इति ॥ २ ॥
उदपादि तिम्माराजस्ततोऽम्बुधेरिव सुधामयान्मणिराजः ।
हृदयंगमं मुरारेर्यमलंचक्रे प्रभेव गोपी देवी ॥ ३ ॥
राजर्षिरेष सुचिरं धुरि स्थितस्सत्यसन्धानाम ।
आराध्य वेङ्कटेश्वरमलभत लोकोत्तरान् पुत्रान् ॥ ४ ॥
तेषु महितेषु जयति त्रिदिवाधीशेषु पद्मबन्धुरिव ।
श्रीचिन्नतिम्मराजः प्रतापनीराजितक्षमावलयः ॥ ५ ॥
प्लवमानस्य समुद्रे सेतोश्शैथिल्यशङ्कया निहिताः ।
कीला इव भासन्ते तत्रत्या यस्य पृथुजयस्तम्भाः ॥ ६ ॥
मलयाद्रिकटकनिकटे विन्ध्य इवाभाति यज्जयस्तम्भः ।
अद्यापि नागतोऽसीत्यगस्त्यमनुयोक्तुमन्तिकोन्मग्नः ॥ ७ ॥
सूक्तिमयैस्स्वप्रभवैरमृतैराप्याययन् सदा विबुधान् ।
कुलकूटस्थस्येन्दोराचारं योऽनुवर्तते धीरः ॥ ९ ॥

साहित्यगोष्ठीं सरसामातिष्ठन्नयमेकदा ।
यादवाभ्युदयं काव्यमश्रौषीद्विदुषां मुखात् ॥ १० ॥
अव्याख्याततया पूर्वैरनभिव्यक्तभावकम् ।
अघृष्टमिव शिल्पज्ञैरभिजातं हरिन्मणिम् ॥ ११ ॥
तदाकर्णनतस्सद्यः समुदञ्चत्कुतूहलः ।
विदुषां पुरतस्तस्य विवृतौ मां न्ययोजयत् ॥ १२ ॥

63

PARAMAYŌGI VILĀSAM.

[By Siddhirāju Timma Bhūpāla.]

This Telugu poem dealing with the lives of the Śrīvaishṇava Aḷvārs in Telugu, was written by Siddhirāju Timma Rāju, the nephew of Aḷiya Rāma Rāya and viceroy of Koṇḍavīḍu. These two verses are taken from the beginning of the work. From these we get this information: Timma Rāju was the great grandson of Siddhirāju, grandson of Ananta, and son of Obala and Kōnamāmba, the sister of the princes Aḷiya Rāma, Tirumala and Venkaṭādri. Timma Rāju fought with a Muhammadan army and defeated it near the river Krishna. He had also a younger brother Ranga Rāja.

While viceroy of Koṇḍavīḍu, he was, one day, in the company of Vaishṇava scholars and in conversation with them about the stories of Vishnu was impelled to write a Telugu poem on the lives of the Aḷvārs.

(Vide note under Gītagovinda Vyākhyā Śrutiranjani.)

సీ. ఏరాజు ముత్తాత భూరిసామ్రాజ్యల
క్ష్మీధురీణభుజుండు సిద్ధనృపతి
యేనరాధిపుతాతనానార్థిసంతాన
సంతానశాఖియనంతశౌరి
యేకణాధ్యుని తండ్రిభోగవైభవనూత్న
సుత్రాముఁడోబళక్ష్మోణిభర్త
యేవిభుండళిరామభూవరు తిరుమల
ప్రభువేంకటేంద్రుల భాగినేయుఁ

గీ. దట్టితిమ్మనృపుండాజి హతతురుష్క-
రక్తశోణనదీకృత ప్రబలసలిల
వితతకృష్ణానదీయశోర్జితుఁడుకోన
మాంబపుత్రుండు రంగరాజానుజుండు.

మ. సకలశ్రీయుతకొండవీటి నగరీ సామ్రాజ్యధౌరేయతా
ధికతన్మీఱుచు నాకర్-నాడ చల భక్తిస్ఫూర్తి శ్రీవైష్ణవ
ప్రకరంబున్భజియించుచున్ హరికథాప్రస్తావనన్ దివ్యయో
గికథల్వించుఁదదగ్ధ కావ్యరచనా కేళీసమాసక్తుఁడై.

64

ŚRUTIRANJANĪ, A COMMENTARY ON THE GĪTA GOVINDA.

[*By Tirumalarāya.*]

This commentary, Śrutiranjanī on the Gīta Govinda, was written according to some manuscripts by the Emperor Tirumalarāya and according to others by Cherukūri Lakshmīdhara.* In the introduction to the work he gives a short account of his family, agreeing with those already given.

अस्ति सोमान्ववायेन्दुरार्विटी बुक्कभूपतिः ।
यद्दानवारिवाहिन्या नित्यं परिणयोऽम्बुधेः ॥
रामराजस्ततो जज्ञे दानक्षात्रेजनुर्गहम् (?) ।
गृहीतान्येकदा येन दश दुर्गाणि विद्विषाम ॥
श्रीरङ्गराजाक्षितिपालमौळिः तस्यात्मजस्सर्वगुणाभिरामः ।
यद्वर्तनं भाविमहीपतीनाम आचारशिक्षागुरुकल्पमासीत् ॥
रामोर्वीशस्तिरुमलनृपो वेङ्कटाद्रिक्षितीशः
. . . . जगति जनिता विश्रुतास्तेन पुत्राः ।
ये साधर्म्यं दधाति धरणीपालिनामग्रगण्याः
वाणीप्राणेश्वरागिरिसुताभर्तृलक्ष्मीपतीनाम ॥

* Cherukūri Lakshmīdhara is also the author of the commentary called Abhīṣṭārthadāyini on Jayadēva's Prasannarāghava Nāṭaka which he dedicated to Siddhirāju Timmarāju, a nephew of Tirumala Rāya and his brothers. Cherukūri Lakshmīdhara also wrote Shaḍbhāshāchandrika, the Prakrit grammar and several other works.

जयति तिरुमलेन्द्रस्तेषु विख्यातकीर्तिः
नमदरिनृपमौलिस्तोमनीराजिताङ्घ्रिः ।
सुगुणसुतचतुष्कन्यस्तराज्यातिभारः
कृतबुधवरविद्यागोष्ठिरत्यूर्जितश्रीः ॥
लोकालवाला सौशील्यबीजादानाम्बुवर्धिनी ।
सुगुणप्रसवा यस्य दिक्षु भाति यशोलता ॥
यद्बाहुनांस मुत्क्षिप्ता खड्गवल्लीमताल्लिका ।
शत्रुराजप्रतापाग्नेः मणिर्भवति बन्धकः ॥
सोऽयं तिरुमलक्षोणिपतिर्गूढार्थसङ्ग्रहम् ।
शृण्वन्मृदुपदं गीतगोविन्दं ध्वनिमण्डितम् ॥
अस्यार्थदीपिकां टीकां करोति श्रुतिरञ्जनीम् ।
लोकोपकारकद्वारा रामस्य प्रीतये प्रभोः ॥
न बुध्यते बुधैर्गीतगोविन्दस्यार्थगौरवम् ।
व्याख्यानशतकेनापि विहाय श्रुतिरञ्जनीम् ॥
रागद्वेषविहीनैरतिसरसैः परगुणस्तवकैः ।
विद्वत्कविभिरासिकैः स्तोतव्या कृतिरसौ विमला ॥
रत्यलङ्कारसङ्गीतशब्दशास्त्रविचक्षणैः ।
विलोकनीया विद्वद्भिः व्याख्येयं श्रुतिरञ्जनी ॥

65

RĀMARĀJĪYAMU OF VENKAYYA: TIRUMALA RĀYA AND HIS SONS.

Tirumala Rāya defeated the forces of the Sapāda (Adil Khan), Kutb Shah and the Nizam Śhah. He married Vengalāmba and had the sons Raghunātha, Śrīranga, Rāma and Venkaṭa. Of these Śrīranga Rāya is said to have led expeditions into the territories of Bijapur, Ahmadnagar and Golkonda, and to have resuscitated the glory of the Karnāṭa empire which had waned. Śrīranga Rāya married Timmamāmba.

His younger brother Rāma is said to have defeated the troops of the Nizam Shah. He married Narasingama and had by her the sons Tirumala and Śrīranga. Of these the younger Śrīranga was adopted by the emperor Venkaṭapati Rāya and became the heir-apparent (Yuva Rāja).

సీ. పఘను సౌందర్య మిందిరానందను
నందనైసతుల కానంద మొసఁగు
. . . . .
గీ. నతఁడు నృపమాత్రుఁ డేయరయను సపాద
కుతపశాహినిజామాదికుతలపతులఁ
జెండెదోర్గర్వఖర్వితాఖండలుండు
రణజయవిహారి తిరుమలరాయశౌరి.

వ. సరసిజపత్రనేత్రుఁడగు శౌరి పయోనిధికన్యక న్వియ
చ్చరులు నుతింపఁ జేకొనినచందమున న్సుగుణాభిరాముఁడా
తిరుమలరాయశేఖరుఁడు ధీయుతులొప్పఁగ వెంగళాంబనుం
బరిణయమయ్యె వేడుక నపార మహావిభవంబులొప్పఁగన్.

శా. ఆరామామణియందుఁ దిర్మల నృపాధ్యక్షుండు ప్రేమన్గనెన్
నీరేజాప్తసమానులన్సుతుల నిర్ణిద్రప్రతాపారిసం
హారోగ్రప్రతిమానశౌర్య రఘునాథాఖ్యాతునా భర్తనున్
శ్రీరంగాధిపు రామరాజ విభున్ శ్రీవెంకటాధీశ్వరున్.

మ. సమరోర్వి న్రఘునాథ రాజవరుఁ డశ్వంబుద్ధతి న్దోలి శౌ
ర్యమృగేంద్రుండన నొప్పి త్రుంచెను తురుష్కాధీశుల న్రౌతుఁ బ
ల్లెము గుజ్జంబును నాటుతుంటలయి డొల్లన్వేటు వేటట్లు గా
నమరుల్గన్గొని మేల్సె బాసుబళియా నౌనంచు వర్ణింపఁగన్.

క. ఆరఘునాథమహీధా
త్రీరమణునియనుజుఁడైన శ్రీరంగవిభుం
డారాము మాడ్కి వసుమతి
నారూఢిగ నేలె నిర్జితాహితుఁడగుచున్.

సీ. గడివిజాపురవర కామినీగర్భముల్
భేదించు నెవ్వని భేరిరవము
దాముడిబోయి నిజాముపట్టణముల
ధూళిగాఁ జేయునే దొరబలంబు
గోలకొండ వజీర్లకోటుల కాయముల్

చించు నేరాజేంద్రు చేఁకత్తి
సకలభూపాలకాస్థానసన్నుతిఁగాంచి
వెలయు నేశూరుని విజయలక్ష్మి

గీ. యతఁడు కేవల నృపతియే యఘవిదూర
చర్యుఁడాశ్రిత రక్షావిచక్షణుఁడు
జీర్ణకర్ణాట భూపునర్జీవనుండు
రమ్యగుణశాలి శ్రీరంగరాయమౌళి

తే. రాజగుణహారి శ్రీరంగరాయశౌరి
ప్రీతితోఁ దిమ్మమాంబను పెండ్లియయ్యె
నావధూవరులఖిలసౌఖ్యములమిగుల
వెలసిరవని ధరాత్మజేశులనుబోలి.

క. ఆవిభుతమ్ముఁడు రామధ
రావల్లభుఁడలరు నాదిరాజులచర్యల్
ధీవరనుత రాకేందుయ
శోవిస్తారతను నధికశూరత్వమునన్.

ఉ. రామమహీశ్వరుండు రణరంగమునందు నిజాము సేనలన్
భీమపరాక్రమస్ఫురణఁ బీచమణంపఁగ సాటికెన్నుచున్
రామరణంబు చండమిదిరా యితఁడాతఁడెయౌనటంచునా
తామరసోద్భవోద్భవుఁడు తాళములొత్తను నాట్యమాడుచున్

క. కృతకృత్యుఁడగు రామ
క్షితిపతి నరసింగమాఖ్యసీమంతినినం
చితధర్మనిధినిఁ బరిణయ
మతిముదము దలిర్పనయ్యెనాసతివలనన్

క. ఆజనపతి కాంతివిభవ
రాజేంద్రుని విజయనిభపరాక్రమరేఖా
రాజితఘను శ్రీతిరుమల
రాజును గనియెఁ దదనంతరంబున మఱియున్

క. అతనికి శ్రీరంగమహీ
పతి కలిగెను నామహాను భావుఁడు శౌర్యో
న్నతి వెంకటపతిరాయన్న
పతిచే యువరాజ పట్టబంధమునొందెన్.

66

VASUCHARITRAMU.

[*By Rāmarājabhūshaṇa, usually known as Bhaṭṭu Mūrti.*]

This is an excellent Telugu poem written by the poet Bhaṭṭu Mūrti and dedicated to the Vijayanagar Emperor Tirumala Rāya. The poet is also called Rāmarājabhūshaṇa (jewel of the court of Rāma Rāja) because he was in high favour in the court of the Emperor Rāma Rāya. At the beginning of the poem he gives an account of the family of the sovereign. Rāma Rāja of the Lunar race of kings had three sons Timma, Koṇḍa and Śrīranga. Of these Śrīranga became famous, and had by his wife Timmāmba five sons Kōna, Timma, Rāma, Tirumala and Venkaṭa.

Of these Rāma Rāya was the most famous. Before his coronation he had to flee from the capital (Vijayanagar) with his two brothers to Penukoṇḍa, and conquering that place and Ādavani defeated the armies of the cruel Salaka (Salaka Rāju Timma, the brother-in-law and minister of Achyuta, who rebelled after the death of Achyuta Rāya to prevent the succession of Sadāśiva Rāyà). Rāma finally killed him and restored once more the empire of Vijayanagar to its ancient glory. The Nizam, Kutupasahi (Kutb Shah) and the Sapāda (Adil Shah) fled to forests at his march, or rendered abject submission to him. Rāma Rāya made war on the Nizam (of Ahmadnagar) and captured from him the city of Kalyan, and forced him to repudiate his friendship with Ibharām (Ibrahim Kutb Shah). Venkaṭādri, the last of the brothers, was also a famous general and dealt destruction to the armies of the Muhammadans that opposed him. After defeating Barid in battle he captured his standard and other State insignia, and brought them in triumph to the capital. He also drove the armies of the Nizam up to the Gōdāvari which was in floods. The Nizam Shah crossed the river in a small boat. With the help of his younger brothers Tirumala and Venkaṭādri, Rāma Rāya conquered the country as far as the Gōdāvari and is said to have washed the bloodstains off his sword in the waters of the river.

Rāma Rāya was succeeded by his younger brother Tirumala. Tirumala drove the Nizam and his army from the battlefield. He also defeated the armies of the Muhammadans sent against him, and gained a complete victory at Penukoṇḍa. He married Vengaḷāmba and had four sons Raghunātha, Śrīranga Rāya, Rāma and Venkaṭa. Of these Raghunātha defeated the armies of the Nizam Shah near the river Krishna, and drove them to the north of the river. The next brother Śrīranga was nominated Yuvarāja (heir-apparent) by Tirumalarāya and was looking after the affairs of the whole empire. The next brother Rāma was governing in peace the whole country from the Kaveri to the sea with his capital at the island town of Seringapatam. The last of the four brothers Venkaṭapati was governing as viceroy the kingdom of Chandragiri, having under his authority many feudatory princes.

శా. ఆరామక్షితిభర్తకుం బ్రథిత సత్యాలాపధర్మోద్భవ
శ్రీరమ్యుండగు తిమ్మరాజు బలలక్ష్మీధామభీమప్రధా
పారీణుండగు కొండశౌరి విజయప్రఖ్యాత చారిత్రుఁ డా
శ్రీరంగేంద్రుఁడు గల్గి రైందవకులక్షేమంకరాకారులై.

శా. ఆరాజత్రితయంబులోన సమభాణారాతివిజ్ఞాతదో
స్సారుం డాత్త సుభద్రుఁ డర్జునగుణశ్లాఘ్యుండునై పొల్చు నా
శ్రీరంగేంద్రుఁ డశేషరాజ్యపదవీ సింహాసనాక్షీణల
క్ష్మీరాజన్నిజసంతతి ప్రథితుఁడై మించెన్ ధరామండలిన్.

క. ఆమనుజేంద్రునకుం బురం
ధ్రీమణియగు తిమ్మమాంబ శ్రీరామునకున్
భూమిజ సుత్రామునకుం బు
లోమజయును బలె జగంబులో నుతికెక్కెన్.

శా. చేతోజాత సమానమూర్తియగు నా శ్రీరంగధాత్రీధవుం
డా తిమ్మాంబికయందుఁ గోనవిభుఁ దిమ్మాధీశు రామప్రభున్
ధాతాశేషవిపత్తు శ్రీతిరుమలేంద్రున్ వేంకటాఖ్యానవి
ఖ్యాతుం గాంచె సురద్రుపంచకము నయ్యంభోధిరాజుం బలెన్.

సీ. పట్టాభిషేక విపర్యయంబునఁ బ్రోలు
వెడలి ప్రియానుజుల్ వెంటఁ గొలువ
జిత్రకూటాభిఖ్యఁ జెలఁగు పెన్గొండసాం
ద్రహరిద్విపేంద్రనాదవనిఁ జెంది
ఖలజనస్థానవాసులఁ బల్వురవధించి
మహిమ సలక ఖరస్మయమడంచి
వాడివీరభటము హయోద్ధతి నబ్ధిగంపింప
దురమునఁ గది సితద్రోహిఁ దునిమి

తే. యనఘతర పార్థివేందిరనధిగమించి
సాధుకర్ణాటవిభవ సంస్థాపనంబు
పూనిశరణాగతుల నెల్లఁ బ్రోచె రాముఁ
డతఁడు నిజచరితంబు రామాయణముగ.

మ. హరిశౌర్యుండగు రామ భూవిభుని తీవ్రాటోప వద్వాహినీ
శరవేగంబున నాత్మమూల బలముల్జారం దళాడంబరం
బరుగంగొమ్మలువోవలావరినిజామాదుల్వజీరుల్ఖళిం
తురుస్రమత్త్వముఁ గానలో ముసలి మానుల్గా వితర్కింపఁగన్.

గీ. అనుచు శిరములఁ దాల్తు రెవ్వని సమగ్ర
సైన్యధుత ధూళిచకితులై చనుసపాద
కుతుపశాహి నిజామాదికుతలపతుల
తండు నృపమాత్రుఁడే రామ ధరణివిభుఁడు.

శా. విశ్వామిత్రునిఁ గొల్చి రాముఁడతఁడుర్విం జెందెఁ గల్యాణము
న్విశ్వామిత్రులు గొల్వ రాముఁడితఁడుర్విం జెందెఁ గల్యాణముల్
శశ్వత్కీర్తులు రాములయ్యిరువురున్ సాధించు కల్యాణలా
భైశ్వర్యంబులు ధర్మనిర్మథనధర్మాలంబనవ్యగ్రముల్.

సీ. ప్రబలగావలేప విగ్రహజాయమానాగ్ర
హాముడించి బహుధావ నాప్తిఁ గాంచుఁ
బురి మెల్లఁ బ్రత్యగ్రభూతి పాలుగఁ జేసి
యచలాస నాభ్యాసి యైక్యశించు
రతినిభరామానుగత మైత్రి పైరోసి
కలనైనఁ గల్యాణకాంక్షయిడఁడు
సరవిఁ బ్రాణాయామ సంసిద్ధికై సారె
సారెకుఁ గుండలి స్థానమంటు

గీ. మానక నిజాముఁ డపవర్గమార్గవృత్తిఁ
బెరయుపరబుద్ధి నెవ్వాని పేరుదలచి
యతఁడు శ్రీరాముఁడఖిల సన్నుతికిఁ దగడె
సేతుకాశీతలాంతరఖ్యాతయశుఁడు.

వ. అరిజయకీర్తిసాంద్రుఁడగు నయ్యభిరామనరేంద్రసోదరుం
దిరుమలదేవరాయలనుతింపఁ దగం బెతదీయ హేతిశాం

కరియతిలోహితావయవగాఁ దనునాత్మహృదంతరంబులం
దరలక దాల్చువారలకుఁ దార్చు సురీవరణీయవైఖరుల్.

సీ. నిరతంబు దుర్మార్గనిరతులౌ తురకల
నతులసన్మార్గసంగతులఁ జేసె
ననియత మోహాంధులౌ పారసీకుల
స్వస్త్రీసుఖైకనిశ్చలులఁ జేసె
నతినిర్దయాత్ములౌ యవనులభూతసం
తానతృప్తిప్రదాత్మకులఁ జేసె
ద్విజపక్షపాతంబు దెగడు పాశ్చాత్యుల
ద్విజపక్షపాతభావితులఁ జేసె

గీ. ననుచుఁ గడు మెచ్చి జయలక్ష్మి యాజిరంగ
కాతరబరీద కేతనఘటితభద్ర
కలశ మెదురుగఁ బూనియే ఘనునిఁ జెందె
నతఁడు సామాన్యుఁడే వేంకటాద్రివిభుఁడు.

మ. కడిమిన్ వేంకటరాయశౌరి నెదురంగా లేక నత్యాహితం
బడరం గౌతమి దాటువేళ నిజకాంతాశ్రుప్రవాహాప్తిం గా
ల్నడ దప్పన్ జడుఁడైన నిజాముఁడు డుపాలంబంబున దాటి మె
కఱ డగన్నన్ భజియించు నయ్యుడుపరేఖన్నామ మోహంబునన్

ఉ. ఏకసపాదలక్షమితమింద్రజుదోశ్చరితప్రబంధమ
స్తోకమెయంచుఁ జాపజిత ధూర్జటి వేంకటశౌరి శౌర్యదీ
ప్త్యాకృతి కర్ణభీష్మజయశక్తి ననేకసపాదలక్షసం
ఖ్యాకమనీయభూరివిభవాప్తి వహించు నుదంచితోన్నతిన్.

ఉ. ఆయనుజుల్ విశుద్ధహరిదంత మహాకరిదంతకాంతిగే
హాయతకీర్తులై కొలువ గౌతమినీటన రాతిఘాతికా
త్యేయకరక్తముల్ గడిగి శ్రీరమణీవరమూర్తి రామభూ
నాయకుఁ డుర్వి నేలె భువనస్తవనీయజయాభిరాముఁడై.

క. ఆ రామశౌరి పిమ్మట
ధీరామరశాఖి వీరతిరుమలరాయుం
డారామసేతుహిమవ
త్క్ష్మాగమణీగమణుఁడై జగంబు భరించెన్.

సీ. బహుమహీధరకూటపటలిపాఱఁగఁజేసె
గంధాంధసింధురఘటలనెల్ల
శాఖిశాఖాశిఖాచయములఁదగిలించె
నమితకోదండదండములనెల్ల
శరధికుటింబినీఝరులవెంబడిఁబంచె
రామాకుచాగ్రహారముల నెల్ల
దుర్దమకర్దమస్తోమంబులోవైచె
విజయమంగళశంఖవితతి నెల్ల

తే. తగవరిగ దానిజాముఁడుద్దండజయప
టిమ్మతిరుమలరాయధాటికిఁజలించి
పఱచు నెడశక్తిమఱచియుమఱువఁడయ్యె
దత్తదుచితప్రవేశసంధానయుక్తి.

వ. తిరుమలరాయశేఖరునిధీరచమూభటరాజియాజిభీ
కరయవనేశ్వరప్రహితఖాన బలంబులఁజకుఱ సేయని
ద్ధరఁబెనుకొండకొండలు మహద్వీపచర్మకపాలమాలికా
పరికరభూషితంబులయి బల్విడిఁగాంచెగిరీశభావమున్.

తే. అవిభుని దేవి శ్రీవెంగళాంబపుట్టి
నిల్లు మెట్టినయిల్లువర్ధిల్లఁజేసెఁ
బుట్టినింటికిమథనంబు మెట్టినింటి
కమితదోషాహతియుఁగూర్చ్నకమలఁదెగడి.

శా. రారాజద్గుణశాలితిర్మలమహారాయండు శ్రీవెంగళాం
బారామామణియందుఁగాంచెసుతులంబ్రఖ్యాతసత్కీర్తిల
క్ష్మీరాముల్ రఘునాథభూమిరమణుల్ శ్రీరంగరాయాగ్రణిన్
శ్రీరామావనినాథుఁబ్రాభవనిధిన్ శ్రీవేంకటక్ష్మావరున్.

శా. యాదోరాశిగభీరమూర్తి రఘునాథాధీశుఁడుద్దండబా
హాదర్పాంధసపాదమలిక్ కనిజామానీకముల్ ద్రుంపఁజ
న్యాదూరక్షితిఁబారుకృష్ణకును గృష్ణాంకంబునాడబ్బెబి
బ్బీదీవ్యన్నయనాబ్జకజ్జలజలాభీలప్రవాహంబునన్.

చ. హరిపదభక్తిశీలుఁడగు నారఘునాథనృపాలుకూర్మిసో
దరుఁడుసిరంగరాయ వసుధావరుఁడాత్మగుణప్రమోదవ

తిరుమలరాయ శేఖరవి తీర్ణ మహాయువరాజపట్టబం
ధురుఁడయి సర్వభూభువనధూర్వ హశక్తివహించు నెంతయున్.

మ. ఘనశౌర్యుండు సిరంగరాయ నరలోకస్వామితోఁ బుట్టురా
మనృపాలాగ్రణి సహ్యజాంబుధివయోమధ్యోర్విశ్రీరంగప
ట్టణాలంకానగరంబు పుణ్యజన పీడావార్త లేకుండఁగై
కొని యెన్మిత్రభవోపకారనిరపేక్షుండై విచిత్రంబుగన్.

క. ఆరఘునాథప్రభృతిధ
రారమణేంద్రులకు మువ్వరకు సోదరుఁడై
సారమతి వేంకటపతి
క్ష్మారమణీప్రియుఁడు వెలయు శత్రుఘ్నుఁడనన్.

మ. హరుఁడా తారకశైలదుర్గమున నధ్యాసీనుఁడై రాజశే
ఖరవిఖ్యాతివహించుఁ జంద్రగిరిదుర్గంబందు శ్రీవేంకటే
శ్వరుఁడొప్పెన్ బహురాజశేఖర సహాసం సేవ్యుఁడై యారయి
ద్ధరబం కేలికవాసితద్గిరులకుం దద్వలభ్ల శ్రీలకున్.

67

CHĀṬU VERSE ABOUT TIRUMALA RĀYA.

This verse referring to the emperor Tirumala Rāya who succeeded to the throne after the battle of Talikoṭa is taken from an anthology of the verses of various Telugu poets called Kavichamatkāraoradarśini. Bhaṭṭu Mūrti or as he is otherwise called Rāmarājabhūshaṇa (the adorner of the court of Rāma Rāya) is said to have been its author. Once Tirumala Rāya asked the poets that were assembled at his court to compose verses in description of him charging them at the same time to be true to nature and not to exaggerate. In this verse Tirumala and his wife when they are sitting together are compared to the God Siva ; and Tirumala alone to Śukrāchārya, the preceptor of the Asuras. Śiva is described in one of his forms as half man and half woman (Ardhanārīś-vara) and to have three eyes, the ordinary two with "the eye of wisdom." When Tirumala and his wife sit side by side they had only three eyes between them. Śukrāchārya, the preceptor of the demons, is said to have only one eye, the other having been blinded by God Vishnu when he took the form of the Dwarf (Vāmana)

Both Śiva and Śukrāchārya are considered to be omniscient by Sanskrit writers and are termed Sarvagña (all-knowing). The fact that Tirumala Rāya had only one eye is also recorded by Caesar Frederick (Purchas, His Pilgrimes, Vol. X, page 93). He is there said to have lost it during the battle of Talikota, A.D. 1565.

క. అన్నాతిఁగూడహరుఁడవు
అన్నాతింగూడకున్ననసురగురుండౌ।
అన్నాతిరుమలరాయా
కన్నొక్కటిలేదుగాని కాంతుఁడుగావే॥

68

RĀMARĀJĪYAMU OF VENKAYYA : VENKAṬĀDRI AND HIS CHILDREN.

Venkaṭādri defeated in battle the armies of the Barid and captured his insignia of royalty and military band. In a pitched battle he dealt destruction to the combined troops of the Nizam Adil Khan and Kutb Shah, and drove away all the three chiefs from the field. Venkaṭādri ruled with his capital at the town of Kandanol (Karnul), and his defeated enemies used to send him presents of elephants, horses, gold and precious stones to that place. Venkaṭādri performed many dānas (gifts) as ordained in the Śāstras. He married two wives Rangamma and Krishnamma and had two sons Rangappa and Rāma Rāja.

Of these Rangappa married three wives—Konēṭamma, Timmamma and Chevvamma. By Konēṭamma he had a son Venkaṭādri. By Timmamma he got the son Gopāla. Gopāla ruled a province from his capital Kandanol (Karnul). Gopāla married Vengamma, the daughter of Gobbūri Giriyappa, and Timmamma, the daughter of Jillēḷla Ranga.

ఆ. అసదృశోరుశౌర్యుఁడాహవగాండీవి
వేంకటాద్రిరాజవిబుధరాజు
అనిబరీదు గెలిచియాతనిబిరుదు మే
ళమ్ముఁగొనియెభూజనమ్ము వొగడ.

సీ. కందుకక్రీడఁగాఁగదనరంగస్థలిఁ
గడువజీరులమస్తకములఁదునిమి

హరులనుబోరిగొని కటులను దుర్మిత
దారోహకులఁద్రుంచి పీరభటవి
ఘటనంబు సేసిదుర్భరపతాకలఁగూల్చఁ
గనుఁగొని కాందిశీకత వహించి
పీఁడుబట్టను నాసవిడిచి నిజాముయే
దులఖానుకుతపశాహులకళంబు

గీ. విప్రవెన్నిచ్చి కనుకనియిచ్చఁబఱచి
మెచ్చఁజొచ్చిననభయంబునిచ్చి విజయ
కాహళులుమ్రోయనియమించె క్ష్మాజనంబు
లభినుతులొనర్పఁగా వేంకటాద్రిరాజు.

ఉ. ఏలెను గందనోలుపురమింద్ర సమానుఁడు వేంకటాద్రిభూ
పాలుఁడు ధర్మరీతి నరివర్గము బీరము దక్కి మత్తశుం
డాలతురంగహేమఘన నవ్యమణీచయమిచ్చి రేపగల్
ఫాలతలాగ్రసీమఁ గరపంకజ యుగ్మము జేర్చికొల్వఁగన్.

చ. అనిశముగోహిరణ్యవసుధాశ్వతులాదిసమస్తదానముల్
వనరుహనేత్రుఁగూర్చి ద్విజవర్గము రాగిలనిచ్చి రంగమాం
బను మఱికృష్ణమఁదగ వివాహమునైక్రమ మొప్పచారివ
ల్లనుగనె వేంకటాద్రినృపలక్ష్ముఁడు రంగపరామరాజులన్.

శా. నెమ్మిన్ రంగపరాజశేఖరుఁడు కోనేటమ్మఁ దిమ్మమ్మ చె
వ్వమ్మమ్ముప్పురఁ బెండ్లియయ్యెను ప్రమోదాయత్తుఁడై బంధులో
కమ్ముల్మెచ్చ మహావిభూతి నిటులా కాంతామణుల్దాను సౌ
ఖ్యమ్మొంగాంచెను ధర్మతత్పరత నత్యంతంబు వర్తిల్లుచున్.

క. అతనికిఁ గోనేటమ్మకు
గతకలికల్మషుఁడు విమతఖండనుఁడు గుణా
న్వితుఁడైన వేంకటాద్రి
క్షితిపతి జనియించె నార్యకీర్తన లెసఁగన్.

క. ఆరంగపరాజధరి
త్రీరమణునకుదయమయ్యె దిమ్మాంబాయో
షారత్నమువలన మహో
దారుఁడు గోపాలరాజధన్యుం డెలమిన్.

సీ. . . . .

బాహుబలోగ్రసపాదమహాబల
భంజనుండాశ్రితరంజనుండు.

గీ. సతతసేవకనరవరాంచితకిరీట
ఘటితమణిఘృణిలలితాంఘ్రికమలుఁడార
వీటిగోపాలరాజభూవిభుఁడుకంద
నోలునిజరాజధానిగా నేలెధరణి.

ఉ. శ్రీలెలమిన్నెలంగఁగవరించెముదంబున రంగపేంద్రుగో
పాలనృపాలచంద్రుఁడతిపావనిగొబ్బురిగిర్యధారుణీ
పాలునిపుత్త్రివెంగమనుపంకజనేత్రజిలేళ్లరంగగో
త్రాలలనామనోహరసుతామణిఁ దిమ్మమనుస్మహోన్నతిన్.

69

NARASABŪPĀLĪYAMU.

[*Of Bhaṭṭu Mūrti.*]

This is a work on poetics in Telugu written by Bhaṭṭu Murti, the author of Vasucharitram, who is also called Rāmarājabūshaṇa. The work is dedicated to Pōchirāju Nārasarāju, and therefore called Narasabhūpālīyam. As usual, the author gives an account of his patron's family and achievements at the beginning of the work. In the Lunar race of Kshatriyas were born the five brothers Kona, Timma, Rāma, Yeṛatimma and Venkaṭa. Of these Rāma was the most famous. He saved the Karnāṭa (Vijayanagar) empire from destruction by making war on and destroying the traitor Salakaya Timma. He protected the Kutb Mulk when he submitted to him, and helped him to get back his lost kingdom. He preserved the Sapāda (Adil Shah) in his kingdom on his agreeing to pay him tribute and hand over Raichur and Mudgal. When the Nizam (of Ahmadnagar) sought refuge with him he lent him his help and established him firmly in his kingdom. Having done all these he ruled the empire in prosperity as Rāma of old.

Venkaṭādri fought a battle with the Barid and captured his Saptānga (the seven constituents of royalty). He also fought with the Sapāda (Adil Shah) near the banks of the Bhīmarathi (Bhima) and, driving him from the battlefield, compelled him to sue for terms of peace by prostrating himself before him and touching his feet with his head. These five brothers had a sister Lakkamāmba who married Oba Rāja of the Pōchirāju family. The couple had a son called Nṛsimha who is the patron of the present work. This Narasa married Tirumalāmba, the daughter of Tirumala,* son of Rāma Rāju Timma Rāju, and had by her a son, Śrīranga Rāja.

Narasa is said to have fought with the Barid and captured all the valuable articles of his camp equipage. He is said to have established Pīnana Mulk (?) on his throne, and to have been a devotee of the God Nṛsimha. He had his capital at the fort of Toragal, and was a good bowman. He is said to have shot at the fish in the yantra like Arjuna. In one of his invasions he marched upon the towns of Makkha, Manḍuva (Manve) and Panḍuva (Panve).

క. కోనక్షితిపతితిమ్మన
సింగనాథుఁడు రామనృపతియొఅతిమ్మనగా
జాగియును వెంకటేంద్రుఁడు
భూనాయకతిలకులగుచుఁ బొల్తురు ఘనులై.

సీ. ఖలునతిద్రోహి సలర్కయతిమ్మని హరించి
సకలకర్ణాటదేశంబు నిలిపె
నతుని వర్ధితునిఁ దత్సుతునిఁ బట్టముఁ గట్టి
కుతుపనమలర్క-నష్ణోణి నిలిపెఁ
బదిలుఁడై రామూరుము దిగల్లు గప్పంబు
సేయఁగాంచ సపాదు సీమ నిలిపె
శరణన్న మలర్క నిజామునకభయంబొ
సంగి తదీయరాజ్యంబు నిలిపె

గీ. నవనియంతయు రామరాజ్యంబు సేసెఁ
దనగుణమ్ములు కవికల్పితములు గాఁగ
నలవియొరచింపసత్కావ్యములను వెలయ
భూమినొక రాజమాత్రుఁడే గామవిభుఁడు.

* * * *

* An account of this family is given in the extract from the Telugu poem Bālabhāgavatam of Kōṇerunātha Kavi, No. 6f above.

గీ. అనుచు యవనులఁ దెగడి తన్నాశ్రయించు
వారి సామ్రాజ్యలక్ష్మి నెవ్వాఁడు గొనియె
నాహవోగ్ర బరీద సప్తాంగహరణుఁ
డతఁడు విలసిల్లు శ్రీ వేంకటాద్రివిభుఁడు.

మ. బలధుర్యుండగు వేంకటేంద్రుని మహాబాహాబలాటోపవి
హ్వలుఁడై మున్న తిథావనక్రియ సపాదాభిఖ్యుఁడైనట్టి యే
దులఖానుండిదె నేఁడు గ్రమ్మఱ సపాదుండయ్యె నానర్మిలిన్
దలఁ దత్పాదముఁ దాల్చెఁ భీమరథి పొంత న్గానని తోయ్యన్నతిన్

మ. స్థిరసంగ్రామజయాభిరాముఁడగు నా శ్రీవెంకటక్ష్మావరుం
డరయన్ రాజశిఖావతంసుఁడగుఁ దథ్యంబు గాకున్న నీ
ధరణీపాలకులెల్ల మెచ్చఁగ సపాదక్షోణిభృత్ప్రాప్తిభా
సురదుర్గాధిపతిత్వవైభవభవ స్ఫూర్తిన్ విజృంభించునే.

క. ఈ రాజమణుల సోదరి
యై రాజిలు లక్కమాంబ యమృతాశనధా
త్రీరుహములకైదంటికి
నారయఁ దోఁబుట్టువగు రమాంగన వగిదిన్.

సీ. . . . . . .
నలరు నోబక్షితీంద్రు నర్ధాంగలక్ష్మి
బాంధవావనధుర్యవైభవకదంబ
లలిత సద్గుణనికురుంబ లక్కమాంబ.

క. పౌలోమికి నింద్రునకును
పోలిక తాకృపజయంతుఁ డాత్మజుఁడైన
ట్లా లక్కమాంబకోబన
పాలునకు నృసింహధరణిపతి జనియించెన్.

క. ఇతఁడిల రామయతిమ్మ
క్షితిపాలుని పుత్రుఁడగుచు చెలువొందు గుణా
న్వితుఁడగు తిరుమలధాత్రీ
పతి తనయం దిరుమలాంబఁ బరిణయమయ్యెన్

గీ. ఆమగువయందు నరసింహభూమివిభుఁడు
రసికసారంగరాజు శ్రీరంగరాజు

గనియె ననఘునిఁ దేవకీకాంతయందు
ఘనుఁడు వసుదేవుఁ డచ్యుతుఁ గన్నసగిది.

క. గర్వితబరీద సేనా
సర్వస్వహ రానివార్యశౌర్యునకుసమి
ద్ధూర్వహసపాదభయదా
ఖర్వమహావిజయభేరికాభాంకృతికిన్.

క. పీనసమలాట్స్థాపన
మానితకరుణాప్రసంగమాంగల్యునకున్
ధీనిధికిన్నృహరిచరణ
ధ్యానవిధానావధానధౌరేయునకున్.

క. తోరగంటిదుర్గరాజ్య
స్థిరసింహాసననివాసదీక్షానిధికిన్
వరయంత్రమత్స్యభేదన
బిరుదోద్దండునకుగండభేరుండునకున్.

శా. మక్షామండువపండువాభయదదోర్మాహాత్మ్యధాటీమహా
తుక్షారప్రతిరుద్ధభూభువన హిందూరాజ్యసంస్థాపనా
ప్రాక్షద్యోతకులోత్థితధ్వజ పటప్రాయప్రసర్పద్యశ
స్సాక్షీకృతశర్వకంకణ నమస్యాజాలకోలాహలా.

70

JĀMBAVATĪ KALYĀṆAM.

[*By Ēkāmranātha.*]

This Sanskrit work dealing with the story of Krishna's marriage with Jāmbavatī was written by Ēkāmranātha, a poet born in the province of Konḍavīḍu. The poet travelled all the way to Chennapatna, in the territory of the viceroyalty of Seringapatam, and dedicated it to the governor of the district Immaḍi Ankuśa. At the beginning of the work as usual the poet gives a lengthy account of the family of his patrons.

Among the members of the fourth caste (Śūdras) was a family which became famous as the Rāṇā vamśa. In that family was born Timma who married Mallamma. Their descendants are represented in the following genealogical table :—

Timma = Mallamma.
|
Singa = Gangamma.
|
Jagadēka Rāya or Pedajagadēka Rāya = Giryāmba.
|
Jagatāpa Rāya. | Jagadēka Rāya. | Jagatāpa Rāya. | Ankuśa.

Ankuśa:
= Lingamma, daughter of Vīrappa. | = Viṭṭhalamma. | = Lakshmamma, daughter of Raghuvara.

(by Lingamma) Kumārajagadēka Rāya. | Immaḍi Ankuśa. | Nṛsimha.
(by Viṭṭhalamma) Venkaṭapati.
(by Lakshmamma) Kastūri. | Siva.

Of these chiefs Jaga[illegible]ka Rāya or Pedda Jagadēka Rāya is said to have fought with the ruler of Burāṇa Nagari (the city of Burhan, Nizam Shah) and, defeating him, to have captured innumerable horses and elephants. Of his sons Jagadēka Raya was the most famous. In a battle he is said to have captured as prisoner a Muhammadan chief Chittakhan, defeated the troops of Nūru Khan and Mūrtijā Khan, and killed the chief Sujāta Khan.

Ankuśa, the last of the sons of Jagadēka Rāya, is said to have married Lingamma, the daughter of the prince Vīrappa, whom we are not able to identify.*

क्वेदं तावकचेन्नपट्टणमहो श्रीशैलमुख्याचलैः
अत्यन्तं व्यवधानवत्सुमहिता मत्कोण्डवीटी पुरी ।
मध्यस्थानखिलानतीत्य महिनत्यापागमो मामको
दूरादिम्माडिअङ्कुशाक्षितिपते सर्वज्ञताज्ञापकः ॥

* * * *

शिङ्गक्ष्माभृदजीजनद्गुणयुतं धैर्याचलं गङ्गमा-
नामाङ्कयुवतीमणेस्त्रिभुवनप्रख्यातशौर्योदयम् ।
कीर्त्याढ्यं जगदेकरायमतुलं जग्राह यस्संयुगे
सञ्जित्यागणितान् बुराणनगरीनाथं गजान्घोटकान् ॥

---

* For fuller extracts from this and the next work, see Nos. 11535 and 11816 of the Madras Manuscripts Library, Des. Cat., Vol. XX.

पश्चास्याभिख्ययाप्तः करजरुचिलसद्धेतिनिर्भिन्नवैरि-
क्ष्माभृत्कुम्भीन्द्रकुम्भव्रजाविनिपातितैर्भूरिमुक्ताफलौघैः ।
कुर्वन्व्याप्तां धरित्रीं निखिलबुधगणैश्शूरवर्याग्रगण्यो
भाति स्मायं नितान्तं भुवि पेदजगदेकावनीनाथसिंहः ॥

सूर्याभौ जगतापरायजगदेकावन्यधीशौ परं
धैर्याढ्यं जगतापरायमतुलं शौर्येङ्कुशक्ष्मापतिम् ।
गिर्यम्बाह्वययोषितीन्द्रसदृशानुत्पाद्य पुत्रानमून्
भाति स्मैष पुरा यथा दशरथो रामादिभिस्स्वात्मजैः

चित्तास्वा (नन्नू) पेन्द्रवन्धाविलसद्र (ञ्जु) स्वशौर्योदयो
नूरूमूर्तिजखानसैन्यकमहारण्यैकदावानलः ।
विष्णुर्भातिसुजातखानमक (राचेर्नमल्कं) भसं
रक्षायां जगदेकरायनृपतिर्दुष्टान्धकारारुणः ॥

71

SATYAPARINAYAM.

[*By Ēkāmranātha.*]

This is another poem written by Ēkāmranātha, and dedicated to the chief Immaḍi Ankuśa. In this work also he gives a long account of his patron's family. Referring to the achievements of Jagadēka Rāya, he says that he protected the fort of Ghanagiri or Penukonḍa by defeating the two chiefs Mūrtija Khan and Nuru Khan, captured the chief Chitta Khan and, killing the chief Sujāta Khan, gave protection to the Chief Chērna Mulk. This siege of Penukonḍa must have taken place during one of those frequent invasions of Vijayanagar territory after the battle of Talikota and the sieges of the later capital, Penukonḍa.

The chiefs that are called Jagadēva Rāya and Jagadēka Rāya in this family have nothing to do with the traitor Jagga Rāya, brother-in-law of the emperor Venkaṭapati Rāya who massacred the royal family after the death of Venkaṭapati Rāya as will be shown in the sequel. The traitor Jagga Rāya was a Kshariya and belonged to the Gobbūri family. This Jagadēva Rāya is distinctly described as a Śudra belonging to the Rāṇā family. His capital was at Chennapatna while the traitor's family was somewhere about the North Arcot district.

N.B.--Lewis Rice says (Ep. Carn., Mysore I, Introduction, page 28) that Jagadēva Rāya of Chennapaṭna defeated the Muhammadans and drove them from Penukoṇḍa in A.D. 1577. But he seems wrong in saying that he was the son-in-law of the Vijayanagar Emperor. His wife was Giriyāmba, but her parentage is not high enough for mention in the two works, Jāmbavatī Kalyāṇam and Satyāpariṇayam.

इत्थं तेन जितास्समस्तयवना युद्धेषु भीत्यान्विताः
तीक्ष्णात्युन्नतकण्टकद्रुममहारण्यानि वेगान्विताः ।
संप्राप्य स्वकमूर्धजेषु नितरामाकृष्यमाणा मुहुः
नूनं तद्गतकण्टकैस्तुनसहन्त्यद्यापि तान्मूर्धसु ॥

* * * *

योरक्षीद्दुर्गवर्यं घनगिरिमाहितौ मूर्तिजाखाननूरू-
खानौ जित्वा च शूरौ महितबलयुतं चित्तखानं च युद्धे
जीवग्राहं त्वगृह्णाद्बहुबलमपि निर्भिद्य सौजातखानं
योरक्षीच्चेर्नमल्कं स जयति जगदेकावनीनाथशौरिः ॥

72

LAKSHMĪVILĀSAM.

[*By Rāyasam Venkaṭapati.*]

This Telugu poem was written by * Rāyasam Venkaṭapati, an officer in the court of the Emperor Śrīranga Rāya. After his office the poet's family was called Rāyasam (despatch-writer). The poet says that he was the Nirvāhaka (manager) of the Sakalādhipatya (the all-secretariat functions) of the Karnāṭa empire. Śrīranga Rāya is said to have defeated the large armies of Kutb Shah and captured his royal insignia. The poet says that he was presented by Śrīranga Rāya with a village, the office Rāyasam and with gold and jewelled ornaments

* There is a Sanskrit drama called Kuvalaya Vilāsa written by a poet called Rāyasa Ahobala. This poet also says that he was a minister of Śrīranga Rāya. We do not know what, if any, connexion there was between him and Rāyasam Venkaṭapati, the author of the Telugu poem Lakshmīvilāsam.

క. సకలాధిపత్య నిర్వా
హకుఁడని జనులెన్న వెలసితో ధరఁగర్ణా
టకరాజ సభలనిహరిం
టకముగ రాయసము వేంకటపతీ సుకృతీ.

మ. అలఘుప్రాభవగర్వభాసురతురుష్కాప్రమేయ సైన్యంబున
గ్గలికంబంపులచేత గెల్చి బిరుదుల్గైకొన్న శ్రీరంగ రా
యలచిత్తం బిగురింపరాయసము వ్రాయంజాలితౌ నౌసుధీ
తిలకుండకర్ణాయమంత్రి వేంకటపతీ దీవ్యత్కళా వాక్పతీ.

* * *

ఉ. వ్రాయును రాజ్యవైభవ ధురంధరభూతి దలిర్పఁగీర్తిధౌ
రేయసిరంగరాయ మహీభృన్మణి రాయసమగ్రహార హే
మాయతరత్న భూషలు నృపాధ్యులు వర్తనలీయ నుబ్బుచున్
వేయననేమి రాయసము వేంకట మంత్రియనాయశస్వినై.

73

THE ANNALS OF HANḌĒ ANANTĀPURAM.

The son of Hanumappa Nāyuḍu, called Immaḍi Hampa Nāyuḍu, succeeded his father and governed his province from Śaka 1506, Svabhānu, to Śaka 1518, Manmatha, and died at Bukkārāya-samudram.

During the administration of his son Malakappa Nāyuḍu, Śrī-ranga Rāya (the son of Tirumala Rāya), proceeded towards Chandragiri in the course of a royal tour. The army of the Padishah again marched from the north to seize Vijayanagar, and halted at Kalyan, Kalbarga and the neighbourhood. When Śrī-ranga Rāya learnt this he rapidly returned to his capital and marched with his army against Kalyan and Kalbarga. He summoned Hanḍē Malakappa Nāyuḍu, the Governor of Bukka-samudram, and with the assistance of his troops fought with the Muhammadan invaders and routed them.

Afterwards this Malakappa Nāyuḍu took leave of the emperor, and constructing a new town at Bukkarāyasamudram ruled there till the cyclic year Vikāri. Then the Muhammadan Sultans of the north again invaded the territories of Vijayanagar, and war ensued. In the course of this war Śrīranga Rāya was defeated and taken prisoner, and the Mussalmans conquered the whole country north of Penukonḍa, and ruled it.

On hearing about this defeat of Śrīranga Rāya, Hanḍē Malakappa Nāyuḍu thinking that the Muhammadan fortunes were destined to rise and his master's to wane, transferred his allegiance to them and behaved obediently in their service. So they showed great favour to him and bestowed upon him the lands formerly granted to him by the Vijayanagar sovereigns, Bukkapatnam in the Elamanchi country, and Anantasāgaram along with the hamlets under them, with the title 'Padishah Vazir'.

11. పిమ్మట యితని కుమారుడు యిమ్మడి హంపానాయుడు రాజ్యాభిషిక్తుడై, శాలివాహనశకం 1506 అగు నేటి స్వభాను సంవత్సరం మొదలు, శాలివాహన శకం 1518 అగు నేటి మన్మథనామ సంవత్సర పర్యంతం, రాజ్యమును పాలించి, యీ బుక్కరాయ సముద్రములోనే గతించెను.

12. ఇతని కుమారుడు మలకప్పనాయుడు రాజ్యము చేయుచున్న సమయమందు, విద్యానగరమును పాలించే తిరుమలరాయుని కుమారుడు శ్రీరంగరాయలవారు, చంద్రగిరిపట్టు రాజ్యము విచారించేటందుకు పోయివుండగా, వుత్తరాననుంచి పాదుషహాలవారి సైన్యము తిరుగా విద్యానగరమును తీసుకోవలెనని వచ్చి, కల్యాణ కల్బురిగి ప్రాంత్యమందు దిగెను. ఈ వర్తమానము శ్రీరంగరాయలు విని, తాను శీఘ్రముగా విద్యానగరముచేరి అక్కడనుండి సైన్యసహితముగా కల్యాణ కల్బురిగె ప్రాంత్యమునకువచ్చి, యీ బుక్కరాయసముద్రములో వున్న మలకప్ప నాయుణ్ని సైన్యసమేతముగా పిలుపించుకొనిపోయి, యుద్ధముచేసి వారిని పరాజితులను చేసెను.

13. తర్వాత, ఆ మలకప్పనాయుడు రాయలవారివద్ద సెలవు తీసుకొనివచ్చి, బుక్కరాయ సముద్రములో నూతనముగా పేటకట్టించి, వికారి సంవత్సర పర్యంతము రాజ్యము చేస్తూవుండగా, విద్యానగరానకు తిరుగా ఆపాదుషహాలు సైన్యముతోవచ్చి యుద్ధముచేసిరి. ఆ యుద్ధములో శ్రీరంగరాయలు నిర్వాహము చేయలేక, వారిచేతికి చిక్కినందున, పాదుషహాలు పెనుకొండ మొదలుకొని సర్వరాజ్యము తమ స్వాధీన పరచుకొని, రాజ్యము చేస్తూవుండిరి. అంతట యీమలకప్ప నాయుడు శ్రీరంగరాయలవారి సమాచారమునువిని, "తురకలు ప్రబ

లులు అయినారు, యిక మీదు రాచ కార్యము చేస్తే, బాగు లేద" ని తలంచి, ఆపాదుషహాలను అనుసరించి, వారి నవుకరీలో చక్కగా నడుచుకొంటూ వచ్చెను. గనుక, యీ మలకప్పనాయుడి మీద వారికి మిక్కిలి దయవచ్చి, పూర్వము రాయులవారు యిచ్చిన రాజ్యమున్ను యలమంచి నాడుకు చెల్లే బుక్కపట్నం 1, అనంతసాగరము 1, యీ రెండు గ్రామములున్ను పాదుషహావజీరా అనేబిరుదున్ను దయచేసిరి.

74

AHOBALAM INSCRIPTION OF ŚRĪRANGA RĀYA.

The following inscription from Ahobalam is dated in the Śaka year 1506, Tārana, corresponding to A.D. 1584-5, Thursday, the fourteenth day of the bright fortnight of the month Vaiśākha. It says that while Śrīranga Rāya was ruling with his capital at Penukoṇḍa, Rāchappa Gāru, the agent of Saṭhagōpa Jiyyangāru of the Ahobalam Mutt, and the inhabitants (Sthānamvāru) of Ahobalam set up the stone inscription in favour of the Telugu Chola chief Mahāmanḍalēśvara Konḍrāju Venkaṭarāju *, the son of Timma Rāju.

It records that in the cyclic year Bahudhānya, preceding the date of the inscription, i.e., A.D. 1578-79, Vibhurāmuvāru (Ibrahim Kutb Mulk, the Sultan of Golkonda) along with Hanḍēvāru (the chiefs of the Hanḍē family)† had invaded the Vijayanagar country, and laying waste the district round Ahobalam, occupied it for five or six years. Then the religious teacher Śrī Vaṇ Śaṭhagopa Svāmi,‡ who was seventh in apostolic succession from the first Vaṇ Śaṭhagopa upon whom the God of Ahobalam himself bestowed the robes of a Sanyāsi, and the immediate disciple of the teacher, Śrī Parānkuśamahāmuni, who was highly respected by Mukunda Deva §, and who had established the idols of the Vaishṇava

* He was the chief to whom the Telugu poems Reṭṭamatam and Kāmandakam were dedicated.

† The proper name of the Hanḍē chief was Malakappa Nāyuḍu. He is said in extract No. 73 to have first fought on the side of Śrīranga Rāya, but after Śrīranga's defeat and capture by the Muhammadans, to have transferred his allegiance to them.

‡ He was the author of the Sanskrit drama Vāsantikāpariṇayam.

§ This Mukunda Dēva seems to be the same as Mukunda Harichandan who usurped the kingdom of Orissa and set up for some time as an independent sovereign. He was an ally of Aḷiya Rama Rāya of Vijayanagar. It was through his influence that the teacher Parānkuśa established the worship of the Āḻvārs at Purushottama or Jagannāth. This statement is corroborated by a passage in the Sanskrit drama, Vāsantikāpariṇayam.

Āḷvārs at Purushōtamam (Jagannāth), approached the emperor Śrīranga Rāya, and, reporting to him the sad condition of the temple of Ahobalam and the surrounding country, requested him to recover the district from the Muhammadans and restore the temples to their ancient glory.

On this the emperor Śrīranga Rāya prepared himself to lead an army to the district in person and drive out the enemy. But the 'High Priest' said that he need not lead the expedition in person, but might entrust it to his subordinates Koṇḍarāju Venkaṭarāju and Koṇḍarāju Tirumalarāju who were designated by the God of Ahobalam, in a dream, as the fittest persons to lead the attack and restore the temples. The emperor was struck with this, and presented the chiefs with jewels and titles, and ordered them to march against the enemy. Then the chiefs started with their army along with the 'Priest' and having defeated the Haṇḍē chiefs and the other allies of Ibrahim, made vast additions to the temple and bestowed on the temples more than their former prosperity. As a return for this the 'High Priest' Śaṭhagopa Svāmi granted to the chief and his descendants certain rights and privileges in the temple.

शुभमस्तु ॥

देवश्रेणी शिरोरत्नं दैत्यद्विपघटाङ्कुशम् ।
जयति श्रीनृसिह्मस्य देवदेवस्य शासनम् ॥

స్వస్తిశ్రీ విజయాభ్యుదయ శాలివాహనశకవర్షంబుల 1506 అగు నేటి తారణ సం॥ వైశాఖశుద్ధ 14 లు గు శ్రీమద్రాజాధిరాజపరమేశ్వర శ్రీవీర ప్రతాప శ్రీవీర శ్రీరంగరాయదేవ మహారాయులుగారు పెనుకొండ నగరమందు వజ్రసింహాసనారూఢులై పృథ్వీ సామ్రాజ్యము చేయుచుండగాను శ్రీమద్వేదమార్గ ప్రతిష్ఠాపనాచార్య సర్వతంత్ర స్వతంత్రోభయ వేదాంతాచార్యులయిన శ్రీ శఠగోపజియ్యంగారి కార్యకర్తలయిన రాచప్పగారున్ను శ్రీ అహోబలస్థానం వారున్ను కాశ్యపగోత్ర ఆపస్తంబ సూత్ర యజుశ్శాఖాధ్యాయులయిన సూర్యవంశోద్భవులయిన మూరురాయరబసవశంకర గుత్తిహన్నిబ్బరగండ యొరయూరి పురవరాధీశ్వరులైన శ్రీమన్మహామండలేశ్వర కొండ్రాజుతిమ్మరాజుగారి పుత్రులయిన వెంకటరాజు దేవమహారాజులుంగారికి యిచ్చిన శిలాశాసన క్రమమెట్లన్నను.

ప్రాక్ బహుధాన్యనామ సంవత్సరాన విభురామువారు హండేవారిని
కూడుకొని సీమయంతా రామూరాపట్టి అహోబాబల స్థలానకువచ్చి
అహోబాబలం అంతా పాడుసేసి అహోబాబల స్థలం అయిదు ఆరు ఏండ్లు
తమవశం చేసుక ఆక్రమించి నడుస్తూవున్న నిమిత్తం శ్రీ అహోబాబలే
శ్వరులు సన్యాసం ప్రసాదించిన ఆదిమమైన వంశఠగోప జియ్యంగారికి
పడోతరమై శ్రీ పురుషోత్తమ ఆళ్వారుల ప్రతిష్ఠసేసి ముకుందదేవుని చేత
పూజగొని రామానుజ దర్శనోద్ధారకులయిన శ్రీపరాంకుశ మహాముని
శిష్యులయినటువంటి శ్రీమచ్ఛఠకోప స్వామివారి స్థలం యీతీరున అయిన
నిమిత్తం శ్రీరంగరాయదేవ మహారాయుల సముఖాన తామువిచ్చేసి
మీరు యీతీరున రత్నసింహాసనా సీనులైవుండిన్ని మీకులస్వామియైన
అహోబళేశ్వరుని స్థళం తురుష్కాక్రాంతం అయివున్నది. వారిని
పోగొట్టి ఆప్రాంతం అంతాసాధించి అహోబళస్థళం జీర్ణోద్ధారణం
సేయవలెనని రాయలవారితోను ఆనతియ్యంగాను రాయలవారు తామె
దండెత్తివచ్చి శీమసాధించి [యి]చ్చెమని వయనం సన్నాహం కాంగాను
అందుకు అయ్యవారు ఆనతిచ్చిన విపరం వొక విభురామువారి నిమిత్యం
మీరు రావద్దు. శ్రీ అహోబాబలేశ్వరులు స్వప్నముఖాం త్రాలను తమ నిజ
దాసులైన మీబంటు అయిన [. . .] కొండ్రాజు వెంకట్రాజు తిరుమల
రాజుగారు వున్నారు వారిచేతనే సకల కయింకర్యాలు [...] యించు
కొనుము. అని రాయలవారితోను ఆనతియ్యంగాను రాయలవారు
అటువంటి నిజదాసులుగా అని సంతుష్ట చిత్తులై రాయసమును పల్ల
కిన్ని కుంచకాళాంజం కనకపదకాలయినటువంటి దివ్యాభరణాలున్ను
తమముద్ర మనుష్యులచేతను అయ్యవారివెంట అంపంగాను ఆవెంక
ట్రాజు తిరుమలరాజుగారు యెదురుగావచ్చి అవి అంతవట్టుంన్ను శిరసా
ప్రతిగ్రహించుకొని ఆక్షణమందే రథగజ తురగపదాతులు మొదలైన చతు
రంగ బలాలను గూర్చుకొని అయ్యవారిని ముందర బెట్టుక తాము అహోబా
బళానకు కదలివచ్చి ఆ విభురామువారికి సహాయం అయిన హండేవారు
మొదలైన వారిని అందరినిన్ని విరుగగొట్టి దేశమంతా కట్టించి అహోబా
బలం జీర్ణోద్ధారణం శేశి అయ్యవారిని అహోబాబళస్థళాన నిలిపి
అహోబాబళస్థళం పూర్వానికంటె యినుమడి సేసినిమిత్తం అయ్య
వార్లు అతిసంతుష్ట చిత్తులై యీ వుపకారం చేసినవారికి ప్రత్యుపకారం
మరి యేమిన్ని శేయలేమేకా . . . .

75

YAYĀTICHARITRAM.

[*By Ponnikanṭi Telaganārya.*]

This poem written in unmixed Telugu was written by the poet Ponnikanṭi Telaganārya, and dedicated to the Muhammadan Chief Amin Khan, General of Ibharam (Ibrahim Kutb Shah). Amin Khan's elder brother Gatāta Khan is said to have gone to the court of Akbar, and to have highly pleased him by his conversation. He marched against a certain Viśvanātha Dēv, and, having defeated him, captured a large number of elephants and horses. He went to the court of the Adil Khan several times and fetched the tribute he consented to pay his master. He also fought the Nizam Shah and Mādanamulk Barid and compelled them to pay tribute to his suzerain. The kings of the Karnāṭa (Vijayanagar) used to send him valuable presents, and Gatāt Khan is said to have stood high in the estimation of Ibrahim Kutb Shah. He was a very pious man and was able to understand and write several languages as Arabic, Persian, Gujarati, Telugu, Kannoji and Āremaccha (?).

Of his brother Fazl Khan, the work says that on one occasion he went with a large army to the territory of Śrīranga Rāya, and (without any fighting) by negotiation took Śrīranga Rāya to his suzerain and brought about a treaty between them, for which achievement he was greatly applauded. Fazl Khan is said to have got the following presents from various sovereigns, palanquins from the Nizam-ul-Mulk (of Ahmadnagar), Pegu ponies from the Adil Khan (of Bijapur), elephants from the chiefs of the seven Māḍems (the hilly tracts of the Orissa border), boxes of pearls from the emperor of Vijayanagar. Fazl Khan gave the valuables to his sovereign Ibrahim (Ibharām) and stood high in his estimation.

సీ. నెఱపలుకు నెఱవ్రుల నే చాల మెప్పించి
యక్బరుచే మెప్పులందుకొనియె
జని విశ్వనాథదేవునిచేత వస్తున
వెలయ నేనుఁగులఁ దెచ్చె వేనవేలు
పూనికి నేదలఖాను పీటికి నేగి
బలుమరు మించు కప్పములు గొనియె
మాదనముల్కు బరీదు నిజాంసాహుఁ
దనయేలికకుఁ బన్నుఁ బనుపనడచె.

గీ. మఱియుఁ గన్నడరాజులు మెరసిపొగడి
నెనరుదళుకొత్తఁ గ్రొత్త కానుకలు పనుప
మనియెమలిక్ఇభరాముమన్ననఁగతాత
ఖానరాయఁడు రెండవ కలువఱేఁడు.

సీ. తలిచంద్రు లేమాట తనకానతిచ్చిన
దల మోచి నడుచుగ తాతఖాను
డిభరాము పాదుషా యేలెడు పుడమిలో
దగవులగాజుగ తాతఖానుఁ
డలచిన్నిపాయంబు నందురాజులచేత
దగునిమ్మపండు గ తాతఖానుఁ
డేప్రొద్దు కూరిమి హెచ్చఁగర్తారుని
దలఁపులో నిలుపుగ తాత ఖానుఁ

గీ. డరబిపారసి గుజరాతి యారెమచ్చ
తెనుఁగు కన్నోజి మొదలుగాఁ దెలిసి వ్రాయ
దారిఁగన్నట్టివాఁడ గ తాతఖాను
డహహా యతనికి నెవ్వరీడరసి చూడ

వ. కనితను రాజులెన్నుకొనఁగాఁ బెనుపొంజులతోసిగంగరా
యనికడకేగిమాటలనె యాయనఁ దేఱిచి తెచ్చి మలక్కుఱ
మనుకువనంటుచేసి యొరిమంగడు మెచ్చులుగొన్న మేటినే
మనిపొగడంగవచ్చు నవునౌనిఁక ఫాజిలుఖానరాయనిన్.

సీ. మదిలోఁగి యుల నిజామనమలుక్ పెట్టిన
పల్లకీలొక వంకబాగు మీఱ
నుదిరియేదులఖానుఁ డొసఁగినపైగోవ
గుజ్జుముల్ బడివాఁగె గొల్చిరాఁగ
వేడుకతోనేడుమాడె-దొరలు కా
నుకలంపినట్టి యేనుఁగలు బెరయ
కన్నడరాయఁడు మన్నించియంపిన
ముత్తేల పెట్టెలహత్తి మెఱయ.

గీ. వచ్చి తెచ్చిన సొమ్ములు మచ్చికలర
నిచ్చియిభరాముశాహుచే మెచ్చుగనియె
నట్టిపాజిలుఖానరాయనికి సాటి
గలరె నేర్పరు లెల్ల జగంబులందు.

76

TAPATĪSAMVARAṆAM.

[*By Addanki Gangādhara Kavi.*]

This Telugu poem of Addanki Gangādhara Kavi is dedicated to Ibrahim Kutb Mulk, who conquered the northern province of Vijayanagar after the battle of Talikota. Kutb Mulk is said to have defeated the Savāi (Adil Khan) in the west and occupied the town of Koilkonḍa. He captured Pānugal and other forts after defeating a Muhammadan chief whose name appears corrupted here as Tamarimillā Khan. In the east he defeated the Uriya Pātras and captured from them the town of Kambhamumeṭṭu (Khammamet), and on the north he defeated the Barid and captured his fort Metuku (Metk). He also captured the fort of Konḍapalli after a signal victory over the ruler of Cuttack (Gajapati). He compelled the chief Chitaph Khan to cross the Gōdāvari. He saw the backs of (routed) the army of the Barid at a place which is not clear in the manuscript. He extended his conquests on the east as far as the mouth of the river Gōdāvari and washed the blood-stains on his sword there. When Haidar Khan, his general, laid siege to and took the big fort of Konḍapalli, he captured alive the enemy Harischandra, general of the Orissa king (possibly the same as Mukunda Harischandra, the founder of the new dynasty of Orissa).

సీ. పడమటను సవాయి బసవనిగా జేసి
యచట గోయ్యలకొండ యావరించె
(?) తమరిమల్లాఖాను దండణంబుగ గొట్టి
హరియించె బానుగల్లాది గిరులు
ప్రథమదికురాల యొడ్డె పాత్ర సామంతుల
ధట్టించెకంభముమెట్టుగొనియె
ఉత్తరంబునఁ బరీదోడి పాఁగఁదోలి
మెతుకు దుర్గంబాక్రమించిమించె

గీ. అతనిబొగడంగఁ దగదె యాచతురశీతి
రూఢిగిరి దుర్గలుంతన ప్రౌఢతేజు
వాహాసిశారిధి (?) రోహరేవంత మూర్తి
కుతపుశాహి నిజ్జాపాలుగుణ విశాలు.

సీ. కటకేశ్వరునిఁ దోలి కైవసంబుగఁ జేసె
కొండంత జయముతో కొండపల్లి
కంపమంది చితాపఖానుండు గౌతమీ
తటినిలంఘించి వోచలముపట్టె
చెటవిరావాచ (?) ప్రాంగణక్షోణిలో
వీగఁదోలి బరీదు వెన్నుచూచె
సాగరగౌతమీసంగమస్థలమున
నడిపంబుగడిగెఁ బ్రఖ్యాతిగాఁగ.

గీ. అష్టదిగ్రాజులును తనకరియు గోరు
వెట్టుకాపుల జేసి కువ్వేటుగొనియె
ఇతరధరణితలాధీశు లెవ్వరీడు
పృథివికుతుపనమలుక చక్రేశ్వరునకు.

శీ. శీవిన్ షాహి దరుఖానుఁ దుద్దవిడి వోడ్డిలన్ విభాళింపుచో
ఆవేళఁ బెదకొండపల్లి కడుజన్యక్షోణి-వీ
ఝూవైయార్తులు హాహినీపతి హరిశ్చంద్రుండు మారొరన్నచో
జీవగ్రాహముగాగ బట్టుకొనె నక్షీణప్రభావోన్నతిఁ.

77

AMINĀBAD INSCRIPTION OF AMIM MULK ON THE EASTERN GATE OF THE AMMAVĀRU (GODDESS) TEMPLE AT AMINĀBAD.

The following inscription is taken from the Mackenzie Records in the Madras Government Oriental Manuscripts Library. The inscription is dated Śaka 1514, Nandana, corresponding to A.D. 1592-93, Vaiśākha, third day of the bright fortnight, Thursday. The Persian equivalent of this date is also given. The inscription says that Hazarat Ibrahim Padishah proceeded against the Vijayanagar territory in the Śaka year 1502, Vikrama, corresponding to A.D. 1580-81, Chaitra, fourteenth day of the dark fortnight

Tuesday, captured Uddagiri (Udayagiri), and driving * Venkaṭa Rāju from the place, captured successively the fortresses of Vinukoṇḍa, Bellamkoṇḍa, Tangēḍa and Koṇḍavīḍu, and was ruling the whole of the Karnāṭa (Vijayanagar) province of Koṇḍavīḍu. Ibrahim Padishah's son Muhammad Kuli Padishah was crowned on Rabi, 21, A.H. 988; June 2. A.D. 1580.†

In the cyclic year Khara, Baḷḷē Rāya, Sābja, Alam Khan, Khaṇ Khan and other subordinates of the Padishah revolted, and captured the district of Koṇḍavīḍu. Thereupon the Hazarat Padishah sent his General Mulk Amin Mulk against the rebel chiefs from Golkonda. All the rebel chiefs fled before Amin Mulk, who crossed the Krishna, and going to Koṇḍavīḍu once more established order there by punishing the traitors and rewardiug the faithful.

స్వస్తి శ్రీ విజయాభ్యుదయ శాలివాహన శకవర్షంబులు ౧౫౧౪ అగునేటి నందన సంవత్సర వైశాఖ శుద్ధ 3 గురువారం సుస్నదిలాసుతి సైను తిస్సాలుయీాచ ౧ మాహెూహీసవ్వాలుసన అలప్ప ౧౦౦౦ సాలు అగునేటి మోడిమదౌలతు అలీయతులువియావకే అసలతనకల అయాం తుల బాహిరాములకు అమీనుమలకావొడయులుంగారు చేసిన ప్రతాప ధర్మశాసన క్రమమెట్లన్నను మొదటను శాలివాహన శకర్షషంబులు ౧౫౦౨ అగునేటి విక్రమ సంవత్సర చైత్ర బ॥ ౧౪ భౌమవారంనాడు హాజరతి ఇభురాహింపాదుషహావొడయలుంగారు తమనామజాదు పంపితేను.

ఉ. ధాటిగనేగి వుద్దగిరిదాకొని వెంకటరాజు దోలిముం
గోటలులగ్గబట్టి వినికొండయు బెల్లముకొండ తంగెడల్
పాటిపరిహరించి మరిబల్మినిగైకొనె కొండవీడుక
నాటకరాజధాని ఇభురాముడు బాహుబలంబుమీరుచున్.

ఈలాగు ప్రతాపానకొండ వీటిరాజ్యం పుచ్చుకొని రాజ్యంపాలిస్తూ వుండెను.

---

* This Venkaṭarāju seems to be no other than Srīranga's younger brother Venkaṭapati who succeeded him in the Vijayanagar empire.

† I am obliged to Mr. G. Yazdani, M.A., Superintendent, H.E.H. the Nizam's State Archæological Department, for verifying this date which, according to him, agrees with that of Ferishṭa and that on the epitāph of Ibrahim Quṭb Shah. (*Ep. Indo-Moslemica*, 1907–8, p. 24).

యిడితలయిభరాంపాదుషహాగారి పుత్రుడు మహమ్మదు కుల్లపాదు షహావొడయలుంగారు శ్రీతిమిజయసనేసాలచ ౨౧ రబ్బిలాసాని తేదిన పట్టాభిషిక్తులై రాజ్యం పాలిస్తూవుండగాను ఖరసంవత్సరములోను భల్లై రాయడు సాబ్జా ఆలముఖానుడు ఖానుఖానా మొదలయినవారున్నూ పాయకట్టు దొరలున్ను తిరగబడి హారాంఖోర్లైకొండవీటి శీమలోను వుండంగాను హజరత్ పాదుషహావొడయలుంగారు తమ పట్నానకు ప్రధాని అయిన మలిక్ అమీను మలక్కుంకు శెలవుయిచ్చి యీ తిరగబడ్డ హారాంఖోర్లను ఖండించి శీమకుదుకూ పరిచిరమ్మను శెలవు దయచేస్తేను ఆలాగేరాజుగారి ఆనతిక్రమాన మలక్ వొడయలుంగారు గోలకొండకు వెళ్లి వచ్చేనన్న ఖబరువిని యీ హారాంఖోర్లైనవాండ్లు అందరున్నూ సూర్యోదయం అయితే చీకటి విచ్చిపోయినట్టు యకడివాండ్లు అకడడనే యథాయథలై పారిపోయిరి. మలార్ వొడయలుంగారున్ను కృష్ణపాటి శీమలోకి విజయంచేసి దుష్టనిగ్రహశిష్ట ప్రతిపాలనచేశి హారాంఖోర్ల నెల్లాను ఆజ్ఞచేసిరి.

78

CHĀRUCHANDRODAYAM.

[*By Chennamarāju.*]

The author of this work Chennamarāju says that his cousin Tammaya Mantri was the right-hand man of the emperor Śrīranga Rāya, and was presented by him with elephants, horses, palanquins and white umbrellas. He was also a minister of the emperor Venkaṭapati Rāya, and compelled recalcitrant chiefs to go to him and accept his suzerainty.

His other cousin Lingamantri is said to have saved the life of the General Pemmasāni Pedda Vīra. A maddened elephant rushed on his palanquin, and, by dealing it a severe blow with his spear, Linga averted its course in the battle at Miḍigēsi. *

* The two chiefs Pemmasāni Pedda Vīra and Pemmasāni Timma were probably the descendants or relatives of the general of Krishna Dēva Rāya, Pemmasāni Rāmalinga who exhibited great valour in capturing the camp of the Bahmani Sultans in the battle of Raichur. They may also be related to Pemmasāni Timmā Nāyuḍu, the Viceroy of Konḍaviḍu, about the close of the reign of the emperor Aḷiya Rāma Rāya. The Mackenzie records contain copy of a copper-plate grant by the emperor Aḷiya Rāma Rāya of the village Garikapāḍu in the Guntūr district to the famous scholar and philosopher Annambhaṭṭa. The Viceroy of Konḍaviḍu in whose province the village was situated was Pemmasani Timma.

The author also says that his patron Pemmasāni Timma had the titles Manne Mārtāṇḍa, Gaṇḍarāditya and Gaṇḍaragaṇḍa. Once the poet carried from the emperor Venkaṭapati Rāya the several insignia of his position to his patron Pemmasāni Timma. These were the triumphal banner of Garuḍanārāyaṇa, a costly red cloth with golden flowers worked upon it, a Turāyi (Tiara), an elephant, a costly horse and a necklace called Vīra Malahari, Tāḷichaukaṭṭu (a square piece-pendant on the breast), bangles made of pearls, the anklet called Gaṇḍapenḍēram, and a sword ornamented with a tassel at the hilt. Of these the general presented the poet Chennapradhāna with the white turban, the white chanks, the palanquin and Tāḷichaukaṭṭu.

సీ. శ్రీరంగరాయ ధాత్రీతలాధ్యక్షుద
క్షిణభుజాదండమై చెలఁగినాఁడు
కర మొప్పునతనిచేగజ వాహనాంకోళి
కాసితచ్ఛత్రముల్గాంచినాఁడు
రమణ వేంకటదేవరాయేంద్రుఁడనుతింపఁ
బటుకార్యదక్షుఁడై ప్రబలినాఁడు
దనియందారులఁ దెచ్చి ఘనతనాతనికిఁ బా
దాక్రాంతుఁబుగఁ జేసి యలరినాఁడు.

గీ. బోటకర్ణాటలాటకాంభోజమగధ
గౌళనేపాళమాళవచోళసింధు
నృపవరాస్థానముల మెఱుఁగెక్కినాఁడు
మంత్రిమాత్రుండె తిమ్మయమంత్రిమౌళి.

* * * *

చ. విడువక పెమ్మసాని పెదవీరనృపాలుని యందలంబుపై
నడచునుదార ఘోరమదనాగము చేపిడియమ్ముకొద్దియె
కుఱుకువడిగ్రుద్దిపోఁదరిమె కొంచకలింగయమంత్రిసింహమిం
పడరెడు వేడ్కరాయలవురా యననామిడిగేసి చెంగటన్.

* * * *

గీ. నలరుధాత్రిని మన్నెమార్తాండుఁడట్టి
గండరాదిత్య గండరగండబిరుదు
దీపితాటోపభయద ప్రతాపతీవ్ర
ఘృణికిఁ బెమసానితిమ్మభూమీంద్రమణికి.

సీ. గరుడనారాయణ బిరుదధ్వజంబుబం
గారుపూవుల చంద్రకావిపావ
డయుతురాఘుగజంబు హయరత్నమును వీర
మలహారి ఘనకంఠమాలికయును
తాళిచౌకట్టుముత్యాల కడియములు
గండపెండేరంబు కత్తికుచ్చు
వేంకటపతిరాయ విభునిచేతను దెచ్చి
పెమసానితిమ్మ భూరమణమణికి.

గీ. నిచ్చితదనుజ్ఞకైకొంటి వెలమినీవు
రాయదత్తంబులైన కుల్లాయిమీఁది
పాగధవళశంఖంబులు పల్లకియును
తాళిచౌకట్లు చెన్నప్రధానచంద్ర,

79

RĀMARĀJĪYAMU.

VENKAṬAPATI RĀYA, HIS ADOPTED SON AND HIS CHILDREN.

The following extract from the Rāmarājīyamu says that Venkaṭapati Rāya collected his army and drove the son of Ibharām (Ibrahim Kutb Shah) who had invaded his territory, as far as Golkonda. He chased his army back and defeated it on the banks of the Pennar. The water of the river was coloured red with the blood of the Muhammadan soldiers killed in the battle. When the son of Ibrahim came as a suppliant seeking terms of peace, he settled with him that the Krishna should thenceforward form the boundary between their respective territories. He also defeated some enemies at Nandēla. This may refer to the revolt of the Nandyal chief Krishna Rāja who revolted at this time and was subdued. This revolt is referred to in the Siddhout inscription of Venkaṭapati (vide extract 81). Venkaṭapati Rāya's capital was at Vellore.

He married four wives—Venkaṭamma, Obamma, the daughter of Jillēḷḷa Ranga Rāja, Krishnamma, the daughter of Jillēḷḷa Krishna Rāju, and Koṇḍamma, the daughter of Gobbūri Oba.

Venkaṭapati Rāya adopted Śrīranga Rāya, the son of his brother Rāma, who is also called Chikka Rāya, and anointed him as the heir-apparent (Yuva Rāja). Chikka Rāya married Obamma, the daughter of Jillēḷḷa Narasimha, and got by her the son Rāma Dēva Rāya.

This Rāma Dēva Rāya was the prince rescued by the chief Yāchama Nāyaka from being massacred by Jagga Rāya along with his parents and brothers. The war that ensued after the massacre, between the young prince Rāma Dēva Rāya assisted by Yāchama Nāyaka, and Jagga Rāya, the traitor, is compared to the Mahābhārata war, and the several chiefs that took part in the war to the heroes of the Mahābhārata.

Singa Nṛpatī * is compared to Bhīma, Rāyappa to Arjuna, Ayyana and Chenna to the twins Nakula and Sahadēva, while Rāma Dēva Rāya is compared to Yudhiṣṭhira. These chiefs were assisted by Raghunātha Nāyaka (of Tanjore) who is likened to Krishna. Their enemies Chenchu, Vīrappa, Yāchana and Māka Rāju are respectively compared to Duśśāsana, Śakuni, Śalya and Karṇa, while the vile Jagga Rāya who was killed in the battle is compared to Duryodhana.

After the war Rāma Dēva Rāya ruled the empire in peace. He married two wives—Obamma, the daughter of Pochirāju Rāma Rāju, and Koṇḍamma, the daughter of the Gobbūri chief Yatirāju. Rāma Dēva Rāya is also said to have performed many dānas (gifts) as laid down in the Śastras.

క. అతనికి శ్రీరంగమహీ
పతికలిగెను నామహానుభావుఁడు శౌర్యో
న్నతి వేంకటపతిరాయ సృ
పతిచేయువరాజపట్ట బంధమునొందెన్.

తే. రాజకులభూషణుఁడు చిక్కరాయభూవ
శౌరివరియించె జిల్లేళ్లనారసింహ
రాజదేవేంద్రపుత్రియం భోజనేత్రి
యైనయోబమ్మదేవి నాయతివవలన.

* The suggestion has recently been made that Singa, Rāyappa, Ayyana and Chenna were the brothers of Rāma Rāya, since they are all compared to the five Pāṇḍavas. This interpretation is not tenable in the face of Barrado's statement and the text of the two poems Raghunāthābhudayam and Sāhitya Ratnākara that Śrīranga Chikka Rāya and all his children except Rāma were killed by Jagga Rāya.

తే. అవసుమతీశునకు రామదేవరాయ
లుదయమైననురిపురాజు లొందఁగి శైల
గుహలఁ జేరిరి రవిదోఁప ఘూకచయము
లతిభయంబున గొందులనణఁగుపగిది.

సీ. సింగనృపతి భీమసేనుఁడు రాయప్ప
శ్వేతాశ్వుఁడయ్యాన చెన్ననృపులు
మాద్రేయులితర భూమండలేశ్వరులు వి
రాటపాంచాలాది రధికవరులు
రఘునాథనాయకాగ్రణియగు కృష్ణస
హాయమ్ముగాఁ గనునాజిఁ జెంచు
వీరప్పయాచనవిభుమాకభూపదు
శ్శాసన సౌబలశల్యకర్ణ

గీ. యుక్తముగజగ్గరాజ దుర్యోధనుని వ
ధించి సంతసమున రామదేవరాయ
ధర్మతనయుండు ప్రజలు మోదంబెలర్ప
ధరణిఁబాలించె ధర్మవిస్ఫురణమెఱయ.

సీ. రాజాధిరాజవీర ప్రతాపోజ్వలుఁ
డగు రామదేవరాయ నృపతుహిన
ధాముఁడు పోచిరాడ్రామరాజాత్మజ
యోబమదేవి గొబ్బూరివంశ
పావనుఁడరిగిరి పాకారియతిరాజు
సుతకొండమయుఁగులసతులుగాఁగ
వరియించి యోషితాద్వయమతిధర్మ స
హాయమై వర్తిల్ల నధ్వరములు

గీ. భూసురోపనయనతులాపురుష కన్య
కాశ్వగజగోహిరణ్య వస్త్రాన్నభూము
ఖాదిదానంబులొనరించి యాదిరాజ
చర్యవర్తిల్లె భూజనుల్సన్నుతింప.

తే. మనుచరిత నిట్లు సుతుఁడు మన్నఁడును దనర
నలరు రామావనీభర్త కనుజుఁడైన
వీర వేంకటపతిరాయవిభుఁడు వసుధ
కెల్ల రాజయ్యె భూజను లెల్లఁ బొగడ.

సీ. బలముగూడినఁ జూచి నిలువని యిభరాము
కొడుకు భీతికి గోలకొండసాక్షి
వెన్నాడి తత్సేన వీఁగఁ దోలుటకును
బృథురక్తిమున నుబ్బ పెన్నసాక్షి
నీవాఁడ ననఁ బ్రోచి నిర్భయంబున వాని
నిమేర యిడుటకుఁ గృష్ణసాక్షి
యెదిరించు వైరుల మదమెల్ల నవలీలఁ
దూలించుటకును నందేలసాక్షి

గీ. గాఁగనసదృశబాహు విక్రమవిభూతి
దనకు వేలూరు వరరాజధాని గాఁగ
వీర వేంకటపతిరాయవిభుఁడు మిగుల
ధరణిఁ బాలించె ధర్మతత్పరతఁ జెలఁగి.

సీ. పరమపాతివ్రత్యగరిమచే మిక్కిలి
యతిశయిల్లిన వెంకటమ్మగారి
జితయశోనిధులైన జిల్లెళ్ళ రంగనృ
పాధిపుపుత్రి నోబమ్మగారి
జిల్లెళ్ళ కృష్ణరాట్ఛ్వేతమయూఖప్రి
యాత్మజయైన కృష్ణమ్మగారి
భూరిశౌర్యోగ్రగొబ్బూరి యోబళమా
ధ్యక్షుని తనూజఁ గొండమ్మగా

తే. నెమ్మి వరుసఁ బాణిగ్రహణమ్ముఁ జేసి
వీర వేంకటపతిరాయ విభుడు వేడ్క
నలరు నప్పద్మముఖులతో ననుదినంబు
నధిక సౌఖ్యాంబునిధి నోలలాడె మిగుల.

80

CHANDRABHĀNU CHARITRAM.

[*By Tarigoppula Mallana.*]

The author says that his elder brother Tarigoppula Datta Mantri was a minister (Kāryakarta) of the emperor Venkaṭapati Rāya, son of Tirumala Rāya. He was a patron of poets and excelled in diplomacy the ministers of all other kings. All the members of the emperor's court used to extol him for his patronage and helpfulness to them on various occasions.

సీ. . . . .

గీ. అనుచు బుధులెన్న వెలయు రాజాధిరాజ
రాజపరమేశ సకలకర్ణాటకాంధ్ర
రాజధౌరేయ తిరుమలరాజతనయ
చంద్రుఁడగు వేంకటపతిక్షితీంద్రమణికి.

వ. అనుపమకార్యకర్తయు మదగ్రజుఁడున్ మహనీయసత్కళా
ఖనియు నఖండకీర్తి కలికాసురభీకృత సర్వదిఙ్ముఖుం
డును నగు దత్తనార్యుఁడు ననువినయాన్వితుఁ బార్యవశక్తిఁ గ
న్గొని పలికెన్ సుధారసనిగుంభన జృంభితవాక్యవైఖరిన్.

సీ. యాదవాగ్రజుని పటాటోపమెల్ల ...

గీ. నగి తెగడి మీఱి కేరి తృణంబొనర్చి
యడచి కారించి కేరించి యడరు నేవి
వేకనిధికీర్తియందొప్పు వేంకటాద్రి
దత్తసామ్రాజ్యవిభవుండు దత్తవిభుఁడు.

మ. ఘనగోత్రోద్ధరణంబ సంఖ్యసుకవిగ్రామ ప్రధానైకసా
ధనసద్భావధురంధరత్వము మహోదర్పోద్ధతారి ప్రధా
ననిరాసోద్భటపాటవంబు నిగవొందన్ దత్తనార్యుండు శ్రీ
దనరున్ వేంకటరాజదక్షిణభుజాదండావిశేషస్థితిన్.

ఉ. నాకుపకర్తనాకు చెలినాకు సహాయుఁడు నాకుఁ బ్రాపిలన్
నాకు బహుప్రదుండనిమనంబున వేంకటరాట్ప్రభాజనా
నీకము సంస్మరింప మహనీయగుణోన్నతిఁ గన్న యుత్తమ
శ్లోకుఁడ మల్లనాహ్వయుఁ డను ప్రథమతత్కృతినాథును న్నెడన్.

81

SIDDHOUT INSCRIPTION OF MATLA ANANTA.

This inscription is found on the wall of the ruined fortifications of Siddhout. It consists of one Sanskrit verse and a long sīsa-mālika. The Sanskrit verse says that, in the Śaka year counted by the horses (7), the eyebrows (2), the arrows (5) and the earth (1), i.e., 1527 corresponding to A.D. 1605, Maṭla Ananta extended the fortifications of Siddhavaṭam (Siddhout) which had been captured by his father in the battle of Ūṭukūru.

The Telugu portion says that in the Śaka year 1527, Viśvāvasu, when Vīra Venkaṭapati Rāya was ruling from Chandragiri, Maṭla Ananta constructed the fortifications round the town of Siddhout which had been captured by his father Ella, after defeating in battle the chief Konḍrāju Tirupati Rāju.

The inscription also gives a long account of the achievements of Ananta. He was born in the solar race of Kshatriyas, and belonged to the family of Dēva Chōḍa and had the titles Aivaraganḍa, Mannehamvīra and Rāchabebbuli. He killed on the battlefield the chief Rāvela Velikonḍa Venkaṭādri. He was the conqueror in the battle of Jambulamaḍaka (Jammalamaḍugu) and reduced the fort of Cuttack. He instilled fear in the mind of Krishnamma of Nandyal and was like the right-hand of the emperor of Karnāṭa (Vijayanagar). He defeated the Chief Konḍrāju Venkaṭādri * and captured from him the town of Chennūr. He was the author of several works, as Kakutsthavijayam, which were highly praised by scholars. He constructed the large tank, Ellamarāju Cheruvu, after his father. † He protected the flying armies

* This is the chief who, according to extract 73 above, overthrew the Hanḍē chief, (Malakappa Nāyuḍu), who held Ahobalam and surrounding country in the interests of Ibrahim Kutb Shah. Konḍraju Tirupati Rāju referred to above was an elder brother of this Venkaṭa according to Reṭṭamatam, a work of Hindu Meteorology translated from the Kannaḍa original.

† Rai Sahib Mr. H. Krishna Sastrigal considers that this is in reference to the battle fought against Jagga Rāya after the massacre of the royal family by him, in which the Madura Nāyak took the side of Jagga Rāya. But the date of the present inscription A.D. 1605 is too early for that; for the massacre and revolt took place after the death of the emperor Venkaṭapati Rāya who lived for about ten years after this inscription, and died in the year A.D. 1614. The invasion here referred to may be the one mentioned in the Pudukkoṭa plates of Śrīvallabha and Varatunga Rāma Pānḍya, or that referred to in the Chikkadēva Rāya Vamśāvaḷi when the Madura Nāyak revolted and when Venkaṭapati Rāya sent his nephew from Seringapatam against him. The nephew proved a traitor to his uncle and made a treaty with the Nāyaka without any reference to Venkaṭapati Rāya who had to undertake a fresh invasion on that account. *Cf.* Ancient India, p. 274.

of the Madura chief from destruction. In the battle of Penukoṇḍa he destroyed the pride of the Muhammadan (Yavana) Padishah.

Maṭli Ananta was the son of Ellamarāju and Rangama, and his son was called Maṭli Tiruvēngaḷa.

स्वस्ति—

शाकेऽश्वाम्बकबाणभूपरिमिते वर्षेच विश्वावसा-
वौन्नत्येन चिरायुषाच गुणभाजा चन्द्रतारं भुवि ।
यस्यानन्तनृपेण तेन जनकेनैवोट्टकूरीरणे
प्राप्तास्सिद्धवटोऽयमुज्वलशिला सालो विशालः कृतः ॥

సీ. శాలివాహన నామ శకవర్షములు వేయి
నేనూట యిరువదియేడు చనిన
విశ్వావసువనంగ వెలయువత్సరమున
సకల హిందూరాజ్య సార్వభౌమ
వీరవేంకటరాయవిభుఁడు చంద్రగిరీంద్ర
సీమసామ్రాజ్యంబు సేయునపుడు
భానువంశాంభోజ భానుఁడం భోరాశి
గంభీరుఁడై వరగండమూర్తి
బిరుదసామజ సింహభీమకేతన భర్త
దేవచోడాన్వయ భూవిభుఁడు
రణభూబలీభూతరావెలవెలికొండ
వెంకటాద్రి మహీశ వీరవరుఁడు
జంబులమడక భూసంగ్రామ జయశాలి
కటకపురీ చూరకార హారి
నందేల కృష్ణమ నరనాథభయదాన
దక్షదోర్దండ విచక్షణుండు
అఖిలకర్ణాట సింహాసనాధీశ్వర
దక్షిణ బాహాభిధానధారి
విదళిత కొండ్రాజు వెంకటాద్రివిభుండు
చెన్నూరి హరణ సంపన్న గృహుఁడు
విబుధస్తుత కకుత్స్థవిజయప్రబంధాది

కావ్య నిబంధన గ్రంథకర్త
శ్రీమదెల్లమరాజు చెరువు పేర తటాక
ఘటనానుభావ సంఘటిత యశుఁడు
ద్రవిడ భూమధురాధిధాట (నాథ) చలద్రయ
బలరక్షణాక్షీణ బాహుబలుఁడు
పెనుకొండసమగయావనపాదుపాగర్వ
ఖర్వ కరణచణాఖగ్వభుజుఁడు
రంగ మాంబా[...]రవతంసరత్నంబు
పరభీమ బిరుదుల భాయబంట్టి (?)
విమతావనీశ్వర వేశ్యాభుజంగుండు
బలరంగ గండాంక భాసురుండు
మన్నెహంపీరుండు మగలరాయడు రాచ
బెబ్బులి పరరాజ భీకరుండు
మల్లితిర్వేంగళ మానవాధిపరత్న
రత్నాకరుఁడ నంతరాజశౌరి
తమతండ్రి యల్లభూరమణుండు కొండ్రాజు
తిరుపతిరాజు పైఁబెరిగకొట్టి
తనకత్తి మొనఁ దెచ్చుకొనిన సిద్ధవటంబు
చెల్లంగ తనపేరఁ చెరువుసేసె
హృదయ ముప్పొంగ సిద్ధవటేశ్వరునకు
ఔపచారికమైన సాలాంతరముగ
పురముచుట్టును వరణమై పరణమింప
ధాత్రిఁగట్టించె నాచంద్ర తారకముగ.

82

VERSES ABOUT VENKAṬAPATI RĀYA, CHINNA BOMMA NĀYAKA AND APPAYA DĪKSHITA.

The first verse says that Appaya Dīkshita wrote his work on Alankāra called Kuvalyānanda at the instance of the Emperor Venkaṭapati Rāya.

The second verse, the author of which is so far unknown, refers to the patronage which the famous scholar Appaya Dīkshita had at the court of Chinna Bomma Nāyaka, Viceroy of Vēlūr, during the reign of Venkaṭapati Rāya. It describes the ceremony of Kanakābhishēkam, or bathing in gold which Chinna Bomma Nāyaka* performed in order to honour the scholarship of Appaya Dīkshita. He is said to have with his own hands poured the gold coins out of the vessel.

अमुं कुवलयानन्द मकरोदप्पदीक्षितः ।
नियोगाद्वेङ्कटपतेर्निरुपाधि कृपानिधेः ॥

from Kuvalayānanda.

कर्णश्श्रीचिनबोम्मक्षितिपतिरभितो लम्भयन्शातकुम्भ-
स्तोमं हेमाभिषेकप्रणयन समये यस्यमूर्तिं प्रशस्याम ।
रेजे श्रीरङ्गराजाध्वरिवरकलशाम्भोधिलब्धप्रसूते-
र्विद्याकल्पद्रुमस्यस्वयमिवकलयञ्जातरूपालवालम् ॥

83

PRAPANNAMRTAM.

[*By Anantārya.*]

This extract from Prapannāmṛtam says that, after the time of Rāmarāya, there was an emperor of Vijayanagar, Venkaṭapati. He was a great and pious sovereign. He became a disciple of the Śrīvasihṇava teacher Lakshmīkumāra Tātāchārya. He entrusted the whole kingdom to his preceptor and himself led a life of retirement doing service to him like Kulaśēkhara of old. When the emperor himself became a disciple of Tātāchārya, a large number of the subjects became Vaishṇavas.

राजासीत्सर्वदेशस्य रामरायादनन्तरम ।
श्रीवेङ्कटपतिर्नाम महात्मा भगवत्परः ॥

---

* Vēlūri Linga, the donor of the Viḷāpākam Grant of Venkaṭa II (A.D. 1601) was the son of Chinna Bomma. Linga was killed and his capital taken possession of by Dāmarla Chenna after whom the town of Madras was named Chennapaṭṭaṇam.

लक्ष्मीकुमारतातार्यं महात्मानमशिश्रियत् ।
स महान्वेङ्कटपतिरायः श्रीमान्महायशाः ॥
तद्राज्यं देशिकाधीनं विधाय गुरुभक्तिमान् ।
गुरुकैङ्कर्यनिरतः कुलशेखरवत्स्थितः ॥
आक्रान्तवेङ्कटपतिरायः श्रीतातदेशिकः ।
यतीन्द्राभिमुखं सम्यक् स चकाराखिलं जगत् ॥

84

RĀGHAVĒNDRAVIJAYA.

[*By Nārāyaṇa.*]

This poem dealing with the life of the famous Madhva teacher Rāghavēndrasvāmi gives a short account of each of his predecessors in the pontifical seat of Madhva and a detailed account of the doings of Rāghavēndra and his teacher Sudhīndra.

Sarga II.—Vijayīndra succeeded Surēndra as teacher. He was well versed in several arts (vidyas) and was honoured by the Emperor Rāma Rāya with bathing in jewels (Ratnābhishēkam) for his scholarship. The emperor also presented him with several villages. He wrote works on various religious subjects. Vijayīndra was succeeded by Sudhīndra. He was also a great scholar and travelled over the country controverting the teachings of other religions. He conquered all his opponents at the court of the emperor Venkaṭapati Rāya, and was presented by the sovereign with the conch and other emblems of victory. He lived at the town of Kumbhakonam on the banks of the Kaveri, and was honoured by Raghunātha of Tanjore with Kanakabhishēkam (bathing in gold).

Sarga III.—While referring to the ancestors of Rāghavēndra on the maternal side, the author says that Krishna, the great grandfather of his mother, was a great scholar and musician who had specialised in the art of playing upon the Vīna. He taught the emperor Krishna Rāya how to play on the Vīna and got from him as gurudakshiṇa (present to the preceptor) costly pearl necklaces and jewels.

His grandson Timmaṇārya lived at the capital Vijayanagar and was a great scholar and artist.

Sarga IV.—At Tanjore the great Yagnanārāyaṇa Dīkshita* who had performed sacrifices and who had commented upon the Sulba Sūtras respected Venkaṭanātha (later on Rāghavēndra Tīrtha) very much. Seeing that Rāghavēndra came out successful in a philosophical disputation about Kākatālīya with some great scholars, the scholar Yagnanārāyaṇa himself underwent mudrānkana (the imprinting of the holy insignia of Vishnu) by him.

Sarga II.

विद्वद्वरोऽस्माद्विजयीन्द्रयोगी विद्यासु ह्यास्वतुलप्रभावः ।
रत्नाभिषेकं किल रामराजात् प्राप्याग्र्यलक्ष्मीनकृताग्रहारान् ॥ २१ ॥
वाक्ये पदे पादविलोचनोक्तौ व्यासीयशास्त्रे च कृतान्प्रबन्धान् ।
आस्तां बुधः श्रोतुमशेषमेषामाख्याः समाख्याद्यतिपण्डितोऽसौ ॥ २२ ॥
सा रामचन्द्रप्रतिमा जयीन्द्रात् सुधीन्द्रयोगीन्द्रमगात्क्रमेण ।
विस्तीर्णकीर्तिर्विबभाववन्यां विख्यातविद्वज्जनवन्द्यपादः ॥ २३ ॥
पवित्रितामेष धरां वितन्वन् संचारतो दिग्विजयापदेशात् ।
श्रीवेङ्कटक्ष्मापरिणीसमक्षे वादेन विद्वेषिबुधान्विजिग्ये ॥ २४ ॥
समेत्य शङ्खादिमजैत्रचिह्नं नृपादमुष्मादपि सह्यजायाः ।
तटस्थितां तापससेवितां तां पुरीं प्रपेदे पुनरुक्तनाकाम् ॥ २५ ॥
तस्यां नगर्यां सुकृते बदर्यां भवाब्धितर्यां बुधसिंहदर्याम् ।
विचित्रनार्यां विजितेन्द्रपुर्यां चिरं न्यवासीत्सितसौधगौर्याम् ॥ ५२ ॥
अतुलविविधविद्वन्मण्डलीलाल्यमानः
प्रभुमणिरघुनाथप्रौढभूपालकेन ।
निहितनिखिलविद्वन्मौलिपादः सुधीन्द्रः
परजनदुरवापं प्राप हेमाभिषेकम् ॥ ५३ ॥

Sarga III.

जनकोपमकन्यकेऽन्वयेऽस्मिन् निजताताधिकनन्दने गुणौघैः ।
अनुजातसमानपूर्वजातेऽभवदेको भुवि कृष्णनामधामा ॥ ५ ॥

---

* This is the author of the historical poem Sāhityaratnākara dealing with the life of Raghunātha of Tanjore. He was a son of the famous Govinda Dīkshita, Minister of the Nāyaka rulers of Tanjore, Achyuta and Raghunātha. He has written many works and is said to have co-operated with Appayya Dīkshita in writing some of his works.

उपदिश्य स कृष्णभूवलारेर्निजगान्धर्वकलां कलामगृह्णात् ।
घनमौक्तिकगुच्छहारपूर्वां बिरुदालीं गुरुदक्षिणापदेशात् ॥ ७ ॥
अधिकृत्य स बाल्य एव शास्त्राण्यधिकं वैणिकवर्णगानविद्याम् ।
नगरं विजयाख्यमध्यतिष्ठत् जननीतातसुहृज्जनाधिवासम् ॥ १० ॥

Sarga IV.

तञ्जापुर्यामन्यदा शुल्बसूत्रं व्याख्यातारं वावदूकं यजन्तम् ।
राज्ञो विद्वान्यज्ञनारायणेज्याशीलोत्तंसस्तं ननन्दातिमात्रम् ॥ १६ ॥
कालेनास्मिन्काकतालीयशब्दे जेतारं तं यायजूकान्कवीन्द्रान् ।
तस्यां पुर्यां तप्तमुद्राङ्कने च प्रौढं मेने यज्ञनारायणस्तम ॥

85

RAGHUNĀTHĀBHYUDAYAM.

[*By Vijayarāghava Nāyaka of Tanjore.*]

Vijayarāghava Nāyaka of Tanjore wrote this Telugu drama celebrating the achievements of his father, the famous Raghunātha Nāyaka. In the beginning of the drama he says that he dreamt one night that his favourite God, Mannār (Gopala) of Mannārguḍi, appeared before him and exhorted him to write the work. He thereupon consulted his spiritual preceptor Śatakratu Tātāchārya who told him that the dream showed that great prosperity was in store for him and encouraged him in the undertaking. He also gives a short account of the several members of Vijayarāghava's family and their achievements.

The several members of the family and their respective relationships may be represented by the following genealogical table:—

Krishna.
|
Timma = Bayyamba.
|
Peda Chevva. | Chinna Chevva = Mūrtimāmba. | Peda Malla. | Chinna Malla.

Chinna Chevva = Mūrtimāmba.
|
Achyuta = Mūrtimāmba.
|
Raghunātha = Kaḷāvati.
|
Vijaya Rāghava. | Rāmabhadra.

Chinna Malla.
|
Vemparāja = Lakshmāmba.

All these chiefs were born in the Śudra caste. China Chevva, the second son of Timma, was a great warrior and offered many valuable gifts to the temples of Śrīśailam and Vṛddhāchalam. He married Mūrtimāmba, who was the younger sister of the queen of Achyuta Rāya. Their son Achyuta made extensive additions and gifts to the temple of Ranganātha at Śrīrangam. His chief gifts to the place were a golden throne for the god and a costly crown, with walls to the temple compound and pleasure gardens. He fought with several chiefs and gained victories. These chiefs are not mentioned in the work.

His son Raghunātha drove from the battlefield the lord of the Tuṇḍīra (the district under the Nāyak of Gingi) and killed Jagga Rāya. He also approached the capital of the Pāṇḍya king (the Nāyak of Madura) and captured his harem. He placed Rāma Dēva Rāya firmly on the throne of Ghanagiri (Penukoṇḍa). Raghunātha made all the sixteen gifts (dānas) ordained in the Śāstras. He married Kaḷāvati, the daughter of Vempa Raja and Lakshmāmba, and had by her the son Vijayarāghava.

Vijayarāghava fought with the lord of the west and won a victory. On a day in the year of his coronation he made the sixteen gifts as laid down in the Śāstras. He fought with the chief Savaram Venkaṭapati and drove him from the field. He constructed the new fortress of Pandanallūru in a single day. When the Pāṇḍya and Tuṇḍīra chiefs (the Nāyaks of Madura and Gingi) rebelled against the emperor Śrīranga Rāya, Vijayarāghava fought on the side of the latter and compelled the enemy to sue for terms of peace at his door. He also established many choultries where a large number of people were daily fed. He presented to Rājagōpāla (the god worshipped at Mannārguḍi)* a coat made of jewels (Ratnāngi), a costly crown, costly jewelled ornaments, and the car and elephants and horses. He also constructed the prākāras (compound-walls), the towers and palaces of the temple, the Vaikunṭha Sabha, flower gardens and tanks. Vijayarāghava founded an agrahāra after his father called Raghunāthapura. He respected his father Raghunātha as a god and always worshipped him.

ద్విపద. భుజవిక్రమాధార భోజావతార
విజయరాఘవధీర వీరాదివీర

---

* In the temple of Rājagōpāla at Mannārguḍi opposite to the god there is a bronze statue of Vijayarāghava in the posture of worshipping the god.

వినవయ్య మీవంశ విస్తారమెల్ల
వినుపింతు నీకు సవిస్తర ఫణితి
వనజాక్షు పదములవరలు వాహినికి
ననుజ యైమించు నాలవజాతి జగతి
నాజాతిలో చాల నధికులైనట్టి
రాజులు గొందరు ప్రఖ్యాతిగనిరి
వారిలో కృష్ణ భూవరుఁడు లావణ్య
కారుణ్య గుణముల ఘనకీర్తిఁగాంచె
అమ్మహామహునకు నాత్మజుఁడైన
తిమ్మ భూపాలుండు ధీరత వెలసె
బయ్యాంబికవరించి ప్రౌఢివహించె
నయ్యిరువురుగాంచిరాత్మ సంభవుల
పెదచెవ్వ భూపాలుఁ చినచెవ్వవిభుని
పెదమల్ల భూజాని పినమల్ల నృపతి
వారిలోచిన చెవ్వ వసుధావలారి
మేరు ధీరుఁడ నంగమేదిని వెలసె
చిరతరంబుగ భక్తి శ్రీశైలమందు
...............వృద్ధాచలంబునను
శంకరార్పణముగా శాశ్వతానేక
కైంకర్యములఁ జేసి ఘనకీర్తిఁ గాంచె
సుగుణ సంతతికి నచ్యుతరాయ సతికి
తగిన సోదరి కృశోదరి మూర్తిమాంబ
యతనికి భార్యయై యఖిల భూపాల
సతులలో నార్యయై సన్నుతిఁగాంచె
అచ్యుతేంద్రుఁడు వారి కాత్మజుండగుచు
నచ్యుతుండితండె యని జనులెన్న
రంగధామునకు శ్రీరంగంబునందు
బంగారు సజ్జలు ప్రాకారములును
రంగుమీరు కిరీట రాజంబు మేలి
సింగారవనములు చెలువొందఁజేసి
యెదురైన మన్నీలనేపున గదిసి

కదనంబులో గెల్చె గవ్వఁడియనఁగ
సతికి భారతికి శ్రీసతి కరుంధతికి
ప్రతి వచ్చుమూర్తి మాంబను వరియించె
కౌసల్యఁ దశరథక్ష్మాభరణుండు
వాసిమీరఁగ రఘూద్వహుఁ గన్నరీతి
అలమూర్తిమాంబయు నచ్యుతేంద్రుండు
నలనిభు రఘునాథ నరనాథుఁగనిరి
రసికుఁడా యచ్యుత రఘునాథవిభుఁడు
వసుమతి రాజ్య నిర్వాహకుఁడగుచు
తుండీర వీరునిం దురములో డఱిమి
చండించి ఖండించె జగ్గభూవిభుని
ఆలంబు సేసి పాండ్యావని నాథు
పాళెంబుడాసి తద్బాలికామణుల
మొరవెట్టఁ గాతన మూకలచేత
చెరవట్టి తెప్పించి చెలఁగె నాపట్ల
మన్నారు మీయయ్య మాయవతార
మన్నమాట యథార్థ మగునైన వినుము
ఆయవతార విహారంబుకన్న
యీయవతార మందిదిగదా వింత
జలకేళి సవరించు/చరియించు జలజలోచనల
వలువలామన్నారు వంచించి తెచ్చె
రణకేళి సవరించు రాజులసతుల
మణుఁగులఁ దెచ్చె నిమ్మనుజేశ్వరుఁడు
ఇంతమాత్రము దక్క నీ యిద్దరికిని
వింతయే మున్నది వెండియునతఁడు
చెలఁగుచు ఘనగిరిసింహాసనమున
అలరామదేవరాయలఁ దెచ్చినిలిపె
ఆదరంబున పదియారుదానములు
వేదకోవిదులైన విప్రులకొసఁగి
కోదండదీక్షాదిగురుఁడైన రాముఁ
డే దైవమనియెంచు నెంచఁ డన్యులను

ఆరఘునాథ నాయక శిరోమణికి
నారీలలామమై నారాయణునకు
పట్టఁపురాణి యగు పాలమున్నీటి
పట్టికిసాటియగు పరమకల్యాణి
గుణరత్న ఖనియనికోవిదుల్బొగడ
ప్రణుతిగైకొని వెంపరాజ చంద్రునకు
పరగఁలక్ష్మాంబకుఁ బట్టియై పుట్టి
పరమ పతివ్రతా........... యించు
లావణ్యవతికి కళావతి సతికి
యావిర్భవించి నీ వభివృద్ధినొందు
విజయరాఘవనామ విఖ్యాతిఁగాంచు
నిజభుజంబున నుర్వి నిర్వహించితివి
కురులు...............కరిదొరల్బొగడ
దరములోపడమటిదొరను గెల్చితివి
పట్టాభిషేక వైభవము గైకొన్న
యట్టి సంవత్సరమం దొకనాట
నవలీలగా పదియారుదానములు
సవరించి ద్విజుల కొసంగితి వీవు
వీరుఁడౌ సవరము వేంకటపతిని
పారదోలించి నీ పంపులచేత
వచ్చిన శీమతోపందనెల్లూరు
గట్టించితివి ఘటికామాత్రముననె
శ్రీరంగరాయలఁ జేపట్టినిల్పి
యారాయకార్యంబులోఁగాదటంచు
దండగించిన పాండ్యతుండీరపతుల
ఖండించి వాకిలిగావఁ జేసితివి
కడలేని మృష్టాన్నదాన సత్త్రములు
నడపుచున్నాఁడవు నానాట హెచ్చ
రత్నాంగియుఁ గిరీట రాజంబుదివ్య
రత్న భూషణములు రథగజాశ్వములు
ప్రాకార గోపుర ప్రాసాదములును

వైకుంఠసభ పుష్పవన తటాకములు
ప్రకటించి రాజగోపాల దేవునకు
సకల కైంకర్యముల్ సంఘటించితివి
నవనవంబుగ రఘునాథపురాది
వివిధాగ్రహారము ల్వేలయఁ జేసితివి
ఏకాలమును తండ్రియే దైవమనుచు
చేకొని పూజలు చేసెదవీవు
కావున నీ నడకకు మెచ్చి యిష్ట
దైవమా దక్షిణద్వార కావిభుఁడు
నీకుఁ బ్రసన్నుఁడై నీవు గావించు
నాకావ్యమందుదు మని యానతిచ్చె
మన్ననారనుమతి మాయనుమతియుఁ
గన్నాపు గనుక నాకనకాంబరునకు
తారహారముగ మీ తండ్రి చారిత్ర
మారూఢిఁ ద్విపద కావ్యము సేయవయ్య.

86

RAGHUNĀTHĀBHYUDAYAM.

[*By Vijayarāghava Nāyaka of Tanjore.*]

The following extract from Vijayarāghava's drama gives details of the battle between Raghunātha and the fugitive emperor, and Jagga Rāya. The account is embodied in a Kammavakkaṇa (report of the doings) of a subordinate of Raghunātha, Ayyaparasu Nārappa of Guntur in the north. It is dated in the cyclic year Nala, the month of Āshāḍha, the fifth day of the bright fortnight (a date in A.D. 1617-18).

Raghunātha was in camp at the village of Paḷavānēri. After the usual morning prayers and worship, he made the usual dānas (gifts), and, receiving the blessings of Śrīvaishṇavas, took his breakfast at about 5 or 6 ghaṭikas after sunrise. He then gave his enemy notice of his march and entered the howda called Vijayagaruḍādri, on the state elephant Rāmabhadra. He was attended by his son Rāmabhadra. On one side of him rode upon another elephant the town Madālaśis, Purushottamaya and Narasappa. On the other side rode upon another elephant the two officers

Asteppa and Aḷagappa. Immediately after them upon another elephant rode the young emperor Rāma Dēva Rāya. Then followed a number of subordinate chiefs whose names are enumerated below:—

(1) Kōnēti Konḍrāju.
(2) Kaṭṭa Rangapa Rāju.
(3) Kastūri Rāju.
(4) Sampeṭa Nāga Rāju of Miṭṭapālem.
(5) Rāma Rāju.
(6) Raghunātha Rāju of Owk.
(7) Obala Rāju who is called the Māma, maternal uncle, possibly of the young emperor.
(8) Manuboli Rāju.
(9) Śrīrangapati Rāju.
(10) Śrīgiri Rāju.
(11) Vīra Rāghava Rāju.
(12) Viṭṭhala Rāju.
(13) Chiṭrāju of Nandēla.
(14) Nārapa Rāju.
(15) Kandanavol Rāju.
(16) Gaḍi Timma Rāju.
(17) The Chiefs of Kāluva.
(18) The Chiefs of Cuddapah.
(19) The Pāḷela Chiefs.
(20) The Panṭa Chiefs.
(21) Śrīpati Rāju and his merceneries.
(22) The Jūpalli people.
(23) Dēśūr Reḍḍi clans.
(24) Mūrteppa who is called Māma, the maternal uncle (of whom nothing more known).
(25) Kumāra Rangayya.
(26) Pāmināyanivāru.
(27) The Balumūri Chiefs.
(28) The Chiefs of Manḍuva (Manve).
(29) The Reḍḍis of Kambam, Konḍavīḍu and Konḍapalli.
(30) Mallappa.
(31) Mādana.
(32) Perumāḷ Mudaliar.

The battle is then described. Gobbūri Jagga Rāju, the traitor, was killed in the field. His ally Māka Rāju fled away with his followers. Daḷavāy Chenchu and Raviḷḷa Mādanna, and the Lord of Tunḍīra (the Nāyak of Gingi) also fled. Vīrapa Nāyuḍu (the Nāyak of Madura) fought till the important officers under him, Tiruvandinā Pillay, Titappa Śetti, Puram Timmā Nāyuḍu, Bhujabala Rao and Eṛṛama Śetti, the junior Captain of horse had fled. He then dismounted from his horse and fled from the field leaving behind him his harem, camp and treasury.

After that Raghunātha accepted the hand of a daughter of the Pānḍya (Nāyak of Madura) offered to him, and returned in triumph to his capital Tanjore. There he held a grand durbar in the palace Rāma Saudha containing the portrait of Rāma's Coronation in the golden pavilion over the broad blackstone.

On learning of his successes the Pādishah (of Bijapur ?) sent his ambassador Hanumoji Pantulu to his court with credentials.

అని పలుకు రఘునాథ జననాథునకు ప్రధానులు సమయ కథాను గుణ సుధామధురోక్తుల కార్యాంశంబులు విన్నవించి దినవర్గ్యలు చదివి రట యెటువలెను.

కమ్మవకరణ :—

శ్రీమన్మహాచోళ సింహాసనేంది
రామనోహరులైన రఘునాథనాయ
నయ్యవారికి యుత్తరాది గుంటూరి
యయ్యవరుసు నారప్పవిన్నపము
లంచిత నలవత్స రాషాఢ శుద్ధ
పంచమీ పుష్యార్క పరిఘుయోగమున
స్వామివారా పళవా నేరినగర
నామతీర్థము పురాణ శ్రవణంబు
రామ విగ్రహ పూజ రామ జపంబు
శ్రీ మూర్తి దానాద్యశేష దానములు
గావించి విజయంబుగలుగ నక్షతలు
శ్రీ వైష్ణవు లొసంగ శిరమునఁదాల్చి
ఆదిత్య హృదయ జపానంతరమున
నయిదారు ఘడియల యపుడారగించి
భేరుల మ్రోయించి పెండ్లికిఁబోవు
తీరునతగిన మస్తైను గావించి
యెదుటి పాళెంబున కెలుకశేయించి
కదలివచ్చి విజయగరుడాద్రి నెక్కి
రామభద్రగజాధి రాజంబు నెక్కి
రామభద్ర కుమారరత్నంబు గొలువ
మతిశాలి పురుషోత్తమయ నరసప్ప
జతగూడి నగరిమదాల శీల్ గనుక
యెదురెచ్చరించుచు నేకపార్శ్వమున
మదగజంబెక్కి సమ్మదముననడవ

అస్త్రైప్పయళగప్పయాప్తులైయొకర
మస్త్రన్గపై నెక్కిర మకుటవనఘువ
రాజులుమన్నీలురౌతులుదొరలు
తేజీలపై నెక్కిర ధీరులైకొలువ
చేరువనొకగంధసింధురం బెక్కిర
యారామ దేవరాయలుచను దేర
తరతరమ్ములకునుతగుర్రైనకతన
నెఱినమ్మఁదగినకో నేటికొండ్రాజు
కట్టరంగపరాజుకస్తూరిరాజు
మిట్టపాళెంపుసంపెటనాగరాజు
రామరాజలయాకురఘునాథరాజు
మామవోబుళరాజుమనుబోలురాజు
శ్రీరంగపతిరాజు శ్రీగిరిరాజు
వీరరాఘవరాజువిట్ఠలరాజు
నందేలచిట్రాజునారవరాజు
కందనవోల్రాజుగడితిమ్మరాజు
కాలువరాజులుకడపరాజులును
పాళెలరాజులుపంటరాజులును
శ్రీపతిగాజు కైజీతంపుదొరలు
జూపల్లివారుదేసురిరెడ్లతెగలు
మామమూర్తెప్పగుమారరంగయ్య
పామినాయనివారుబలుమూరివారు
మండువవారుకంబముకొండవీటి
కొండపల్లెడ్లునంకుశరావువారు
నొదలవచ్చిమల్లప ... టిగంటి
మాదనసేపెరుమా మొదలార
మొదలైనగురిదొరల్ ముందరనడవ
కదనరంగమునకుకదలిపోవుటకు
నేడెనిమిదివేలయెలగోలుప్రజల
కాడియపాదమునధిపతిపేసి (?)

చివగడల్ కైదువల్ సెలవు శేయించి
సవరణతో నేరుజాలకప్పించి
భ్రమసినపడమటిపాళెంబుమీఁద
దుమికిహుటాహుటిదొక్కొనినడవ
అమ్ములచేత చేయమ్ములచేత
దుమ్ములచేత దోదుమ్ములచేత
ఖల్లెలచేత తుపాకులచేత
నల్లమూకలచేత నడగొండలైన
మత్తేభములచేత మావులచేత
కత్తులచేత ఛీకాకు సేయింప
పోరిలో సమసెగొబ్బూరిజగ్గరాజు
పారెమూకలవెంటఁబడిమాకరాజు
దగదొట్టివగబుట్టిదళవాయి చెంచు
శిగవిడితెగజారశింతింపకేగె
వుడిజోయిగోటకాండూడసింబాడ (?)
విడిబడిపారెరావిళ్లమాదన్న
మధురవారినిగూర్చిమమ్మింతజేసె
విధియంచుతనపాలివిధిమూరుకొనుచు
దొరలెల్లనవ్వంగతుండీరవిభుఁడు
పరువెత్తెతనచెంజి పట్టణంబునకు
తిరువందినాపిళ్లతితెప శెట్టి
పురముతిమ్మానేండుభుజబలరావు
చినరౌతుయెఱ్ఱమ శెట్టిలోనైన
తనవద్దిదొరలెల్లతనుడించిపార
యింతులనెడబాసియిలుమూరయిచ్చి
సంతరించినబొక్కసము విడఁబుచ్చి
తురగంబుడిగ్గికైదువపారవైచి
విరిగిపారదొడంగెవీరపనేండు
జయలక్ష్మిచేపట్టిస్వామివారపుడు
దయమీరగాధర్మదారపట్టించి
బంగారుబొమ్మనుపాండ్యభూపాలుఁ

డింగితవేదిగ్గైయిచ్చినమెచ్చి
తంజాపురముచేరితనవంశవజ్ర
పంజరంబైసార్వభౌమసామ్రాజ్య
లక్షణంబులతోకళావతిసతియు
కుక్షిసంభవరాజగోపాలుఁడనగ
విజయసంధాయియైవెలయుచున్న
విజయరాఘవనామవిఖ్యాతిఁగాంచి
యాముహూర్తమునపట్టాభిరామాభి
రామమైమించుశ్రీరామసౌధమున
చలువరాజగతిపైజాళువాపసిఁడి
పలకలగొప్పచప్పరములోఁజేరి
పేరోలగంబున్నపెద్దమ్మవార
లారతులెత్తివారనివ్రాసిరాఁగ
కొలువులోచదివించుకొనిస్వామివారి
బలపౌరుషములెంచిపాచ్ఛావువారు
సమయోచితోక్తులఁజాలలాలించి
తమముద్రచేకాగితముశిక్కాచేసి
ఘనముగామీకుడుగరలుగట్టించి
హానుమోజిపంతులనంపించినారు
యిటువలెనడచినదికఱడికార్య
మటుగాననెరిగుండనవధరించేది.

87

RAGHUNĀTHĀBHYUDAYAM.

[*By Vijayarāghava Nāyaka of Tanjore.*]

The following extract from the drama of Vijayarāghava gives a description of the palace at Tanjore :—

The palace contained a big Bavanti (mansion) where the elephants belonging to the king were stabled. There was also a large building built in the Pathan style in which his horses were stabled. There was an extensive hall where the clerks (sampratis) and accountants (karaṇams) of the palace attended to their work. Opposite to one of the gates of the palace, called the Koṇe Vākili, lived the cowherds of the town. There were also a palace called Achyuta Rangakūṭam in the shade of a punnāga tree; gymnasium, and a theatre adorned with gems of all sorts. In another palace called Madanagōpāla Vilāsam the god Mannār (Gopala) was worshipped.

There was also the palace called Śrī Rāma Saudham, containing a life-like painting of the Coronation of Rāma, and the broad single stone platform of black stone, shining and transparent with the golden pavilion over it.

The palace called Vijaya Bhavana Rāja was guarded by the chamberlains (kanchukis). It was provided with golden doors and contained very costly golden and jewelled furniture. It contained portraits of Raghunātha's victory over Śōḷaga, of his raising the king of Nēpāḷa (Jaffna) to the throne, which he had lost, by defeating his enemies. There were besides representations of his successes over the Pāndya and Tundīra kings (the Madura and Gingi Nāyaks), and of his raising Rāma Dēva Rāya to his empire.

ఘనతరమదగజఘటలచే నలరు
పెనులాగడపుఁబని పెద్దబవంతి
. . హురుమంజితేజీల
నిరుపమంబగుపటానిబవంతి సెజ్జ
ప్రతిలేకనగరిసంప్రతికరణములు
జతగూడి . . విశాలశాలయును
తరతరంబులు వేణుదండముల్వాని
గురిగొల్లలున్నట్టికోణెవాకిలియు
చెంగటిపున్నాగశీతలచ్ఛాయ
రంగైనయచ్యుతరంగకూటంబు
లలితనాకపురీవిలాసగేహంబు
కులగిరిఁబోలులాగులచప్పరంబు
కవివర్ణనీయమౌగరడికూటంబు
నవరత్నమయమైననాటకశాల
మదనావతారుఁడైమన్నారుఁడున్న
మదనగోపవిలాసమందిరాంగణము
పట్టాభిరామునిభావచిత్రంబు
గట్టిబంగారుచెక్కడపుఁజప్పరము

నీలంపుజాషలునీడలు దేర
జాలవిప్రైయొప్పుచల్వరాజగతి
గలిగి రెండవపుష్పకవిమానమనఁగ
నలరు శ్రీరామసౌధాధిరాజంబు
విజయచిహ్నములచే వెలయుచునున్న
విజయభవనరాజ వేదికాస్థలిని
కంచుకివర్గంబు గాఁచియున్నట్టి
కాంచనోరుకవాటఘటితమార్గంబు
చంద్రకాంతఁపువింతసంతనపనుల
సాంద్రమై విలసిల్లుజగతిమీదటను
పగడాలజగడాలబటువుకంబములు
మగరాలనిగరాలమదనచేతులును
చిన్నారిదంతంపుజేరుల్లతుదలఁ
జెన్నారమలచినజీనిపట్టులును
పైగోవకెంపురావనులబోదియలు
బాఁగైనపచ్చరాపలకపైకప్పు
ఇంద్రనీలంబులనెస గులోవరియు
చంద్రికవెదఁజల్లుచలువగోడలును

* * * *

మేలైనపటికంపుమెటికలుగల్గి
కదనంబులోఁజోళగనిగెల్చినట్టి
పోలికల్ నేపాళభూపాలకునకు
దొరతనంబిచ్చినదోర్విలాసములు
దురములోనలపాండ్యతుండీరపతుల
జేరిగెల్చినగెల్పుసింహాసనమున
నారామదేవరాయలనిల్పుటయును
మొదలైనవిజయముల్ ముద్దులుగులుకఁ
బదరక వ్రాసినభావముల్మెఱయ
నిందిందిరాలకయిందిరామణి
కందళించినవేడుకలఁగటారింప
రమణీయమగునిందిరామందిరంబు
మొదలైనగృహరాజములుగల్గిరాజ
సదనమప్పురమునఁజాలనొప్పారు.

88

SAHITYA SUDHA.

[*By Govinda Dikshita.*]

The work, written by Govinda Dīkshita, the famous minister of Raghunātha of Tanjore, begins with a short account of the achievements of Raghunātha. The author says that when he and many other famous scholars were once sitting in the court of Chevva, Raghunātha was brought before them, a small child. Seeing the child Chevva in great delight said "This child will become great and rule the whole kingdom, and we shall become famous on his account."

Raghunātha was an expert with the sword and shield, as also in the training of elephants. He was a great scholar both in Sangīta (music) as well as Sāhitya (literary art), and a good poet in Sanskrit as well as the vernacular (bhāshā, Telugu). Raghunātha not only maintained all the charities established by his father Achyuta, but instituted new ones. At Rāmaśētu, Kumbhakonam and Śrīrangam he built temples to his favourite deity Rāmabhadra with towers, manṭapas and prākāras (compounds). He also added to the temples of Champēśa (the God of Mannarguḍi), Panchanada (Tiruvaiyār), Dhēnunātha (Paśupatikoil?) and Śrīnivāsasthala (Uppiliyappankoil near Kumbhakonam) and built the big gopuram at Kumbhakonam (of the Kumbhēśvara temple).

On several occasions he weighed himself against gold (tulābhāra) as laid down by Hēmādri. Collecting a large army he marched against his enemies and conquered them. He even reduced to subjection the inhabitants of some islands.*

He wrote the following works: Parijātāharaṇam, Vālmīkicharitram, Achyutēndrābhyudayam, Gajēndramoksham, Naḷacharitram, Rukminī-Krishnavivāhayakshagānam, and several other works besides.

---

* These achievements refer to his conquest of the turbulent chief Soḷaga who, occupying the island Dēvakoṭṭa near the mouth of the Coleroon, was giving great trouble to the neighbouring country by his atrocities. He was an ally of the Portuguese and the Nāyaka of Gingi. Raghunātha defeated the chief, reduced his island to subjection and brought him a prisoner. The other achievement of Raghunātha against an island was with reference to Jaffna which is called in the Telugu and Sanskrit works of the time, Nēpāḷa. The Portuguese (who are in these accounts called Parangis) occupied the island and the rightful sovereign fled for protection to Raghunātha. Raghunātha for his sake marched to the island with his army crossing the straits by a bridge of boats, defeated the Portuguese and drove them from the island and celebrated the coronation of the rightful king. *Danvers' Portuguese in India* II, Ch viii, and *Purchas His Pilgrimés*, Vol. X, *Jesuit Observations of India*, page 218.

तत्रेन्दिरामन्दिरनामधेये सभाविशेषे सह मन्त्रिवर्गैः ।
कविप्रकाण्डैरपि कालिदासमयूरसौमिल्लमुरारिदेश्यैः ॥
कर्णाटकान्ध्रद्रमिलप्रबन्धनिर्माणविद्यानिपुणैश्च कैश्चित ।
वाग्गेयकारप्रमुखैरनेकैः विचित्रगीतादिकलाप्रवीणैः ॥
आस्तेऽधिभद्रासनमच्युतेन्द्रतनूभवश्श्रीरघुनाथभूपः ।
आज्ञप्तिमेनां शिरसा प्रगृह्य प्रावेशयत्सोऽपि बुधान्समस्तान् ॥

* * * *

पूर्वं समेता वयमत्र युष्मत्पितामहं चेव्वमहीमहेन्द्रम् ।
आशीर्भिरानन्दयितुं तदग्रे त्वय्याददाने खुरळीषु केळीम् ॥
तदा भवन्तं स विलोक्य हर्षात् अस्मान्मुदावाचमिमामवोचत् ।
अस्माकमेतेन भवेत्प्रतिष्ठा धर्तुं समर्थश्च स एष राज्यम् ॥
आशीर्विशेषाच्चिनचेव्वनेतुः आसीरिदानीमधिकस्ततोऽपि ।
कृपाणिकाखेटकनैपुणेन गजस्य चाकर्षणचातुरीभिः ।
सङ्गीतसाहित्यकलाविलासैः भाषाप्रपन्धेषु भृशं पटिम्ना ।
चित्तानुवृत्त्या चिरमच्युतेन्दुः अमन्दमानन्दभरं बभार ॥
तदीयधर्मान्परिपालयंस्त्वं चोळावनीं पालयसि प्रकर्षात् ।
श्रीरामसेतावपि कुम्भघोणे श्रीरङ्गधामन्यपि रामभद्रम् ॥
देवं प्रतिष्ठाप्य तदोन्नतानि प्राकारसद्गोपुरमण्टपानि ।
. . . . चम्पेशितुः पञ्चनदेश्वरस्य ॥
श्रीधेनुनाथस्य महेश्वरस्य श्रीश्रीनिवासस्थलसीम्नि विष्णोः ।
श्रीरङ्गनाथस्य वरप्रदातुः महत्तरं मण्डपमादधास्त्वम् ॥
श्रीकुम्भघोणेश्वरगोपुराग्र्यं हेमाद्रिकल्पप्रतिपादितानि ।
मुहुस्तुलापूरुषपूर्वकानिदत्तैस्त्वयार्थैः परितुष्टचित्ता ॥
श्चोळेषु काश्यामखिलेचदेशे भवज्जयस्तम्भानि(?)द्विजेन्द्राः ।
कृताग्निहोत्राः कतिनो जयन्ति नित्यान्नदानं कुरुषे द्विजानाम् ॥
असङ्ख्यकानामनिवारितस्त्वं सम्पाद्य सेनां बहुधात्युदग्रान् ।
जित्वा सपत्नानपि भूमिपालान् समुद्रमध्याग्रयिणस्समस्तान् ॥

क्षिप्रान्निराकृत्य सुखं विधत्से . . . . ।
श्रीपारिजाताहरणप्रबन्धं चित्रं च वाल्मीकिचरित्रकाव्यम् ।
तथाच्युतेन्द्राभ्युदयं गजेन्द्रमोक्षं चरित्रं च नळस्य चित्रम् ॥
श्रीरुक्मिणीकृष्णविवाहयक्षगानं प्रबन्धानपि नैकभेदान् ।
निर्माय वाग्भिर्निपुणार्थभाग्भिः विद्वत्कवीनां विदधासि हर्षम् ॥

89

SANGĪTA SUDHA.

[*By Raghunātha Nāyaka.*]

At the beginning of this excellent treatise on Hindu music by Raghunātha Nāyaka one of his courtiers is made to narrate the achievements and accomplishments of Raghunātha Nāyaka and his predecessors. After referring to his conquests and his literary works both in Sanskrit and Telugu, the account says that Raghunātha was a great authority in music. He had invented new Rāgas like Jayantasēna, and new Tālās like Rāmānanda. He is also said to have taught the art of playing on the Vīna to many musicians. He had invented a new Mēḷa after his own name in which any recognized Rāga could be played.

जयन्तसेनादिमरागरामानन्दादितालान् रचयन्नवीनान् ।
सङ्गीतविद्यां समुपादिशस्त्वं विपश्चिकावादविचक्षणानाम् ॥
किंच त्वमंचद्रवदीयनाम मेळान्तरं सम्प्रति कल्पयित्वा ।
मेळान्तरे तत्र समस्तरागान् प्रकाशयोग्यान्सुलभान्करोषि ॥

90

SĀHITYARATNĀKARA.

[*By Yagñanārāyaṇa Dikshita.*]

This Sanskrit poem deals with the life and achievements of the famous Tanjore Nāyaka ruler Raghunātha. It was written by Yagñanārāyaṇa Dīkshita, son of the famous Govinda Dīkshita, minister of the Tanjore Nāyaka rulers Achyuta and Raghunātha.

Sarga I.—After the usual salutations to the Gods, the author salutes his own father Govinda Dīkshita who was a great authority in the Advaita Vēdānta and in the six Darśanas. The poet then praises his patron, Raghunātha, in very high terms. He is said to have given back his throne to the king of Nēpāḷa and to have defeated the Pāṇḍya king. He built a bridge across the ocean like Rāma of old and subdued some islands. He is also said to have been a great scholar and poet, and a patron of poets and musicians.

Sarga II is devoted to a description of the Chola country (Kaveri Delta) and its capital Tanjāpurī (Tanjore).

Sarga III.—There was a king called Chevva ruling at Tanjore. He built the big gopuram and the large tank of the temple of Sōnagirīśa (the God of Tiruvaṇṇāmalai). He married a wife called Mūrtimāmba and had by her the son Achyuta. Achyuta made presents of very valuable ornaments to Ranganātha of Śrīrangam. The canto closes with the praise of Achyuta.

At the end of this canto in the last verse in which the author praises his patron, he says that he was maintaining 1,000 Brahman families at Champakāṭavi (Mannarguḍi), and was in the habit of celebrating the Tulāpurusha (weighing against gold) every year at Bhavasthala (Śivapuram ?).

Sarga IV describes the birth of a son to Achyuta and his wife Mūrtimāmba. The son is named Raghunātha.

Sarga V describes the early education of young Raghunātha. After his training in Sāhitya (Arts) was complete he was directed by his father to compose a poem dealing with the life of Krishna, since by literary works alone could one become immortal. On that Raghunātha wrote his poem Pārijātāharaṇam within the period of two yāmas (six hours), and the scribes wrote it down with difficulty as he dictated it so rapidly. Highly pleased with the performance, the king Achyuta had him bathed in gold and precious stones (Kanakaratnābhishēkam). He later on wrote many other works like Achyutābhyudayam and the total number of his works exceeded a hundred.* Achyuta then sent his son on horseback

* We do not know whether this statement is a mere exaggeration. About a dozen of his works in Sanskrit and Telugu have come down to us. The author of the present work says that he was himself a student of Raghunātha and that Raghunātha presented him with costly jewels instead of receiving anything in the shape of Gurudakshina from him. Rāmabhadrāmba, one of the many poetesses that adorned his court and the authoress of his biography Raghunathābhyudayam, pays a very high tribute to his scholarship and acknowledges that she herself learnt many things from Raghunātha. His Telugu poem the Ramāyanam is highly praised for its merits, and it has been translated into Sanskrit by Madhuravāṇi, another poetess that adorned his court. In his treatise on music Sangīta Sudhā, Raghunātha himself says that he was a great master of music and had invented some new rāgas.

to get a personal knowledge of his father's territory. Raghunātha travelled over many districts and returned to his father's capital.

Soon after Raghunātha's return to his capital there was heard in the palace of Tanjore the voices of many royal ladies crying for help from outside. This was caused by the ladies belonging to the family of the Nēpāla* king who had been driven from his capital, with his family, by his enemies the Pārasīkas. When Achyuta heard of this he said that formerly the Pārasīkas had been defeated by himself and driven away by him from Negapatam. He took pity upon the position of the king of Nēpāḷa, and promised for his sake to make war on the Pārasīkas and drive them from his island. He allotted one of his own palaces for the Nēpāḷa king to live in, and presented him with ornaments suited to his position and dignity. Having done this he was waiting for the coming of autumn to march with his army against the usurping Pārasīkas.

Sargas VI to VIII describe the life of Achyuta and Raghunātha at court during the several seasons.

Sarga IX.—As soon as the autumn set in, the king Achyuta remembering the promise he had made to the Nēpāḷa king held council along with his minister Govinda Dīkshita and his own son Raghunātha in the palace Lakshmīvilāsam.

Sarga X.—Achyuta, Raghunātha and Govinda Dīkshita hold council in the palace of Lakshmīvilāsam. Govinda Dīkshita described the aggressions of the Pārasīkas (Portuguese) upon the Nēpāḷa king. Then he proceeded to give an account of Cholaka (Śoḻaga) their ally. This Śoḻaga having occupied an island near the coast was giving great trouble to the people of the neighbouring country. He used to inflict inhuman punishments upon the innocent people of the land. He would bind them up in empty sacks and having well beaten them with pestles would throw the sacks containing the men into the water to be devoured by crocodiles. He would also subject the kaḷamāḷ (perhaps means Kaḷḷamars or Kaḷḷars) of Achyuta's territory to unheard of atrocities by

* This Nēpāla king seems to be the ruler of the island of Jaffna. The name of Jaffna (Yāḻpāṇa) seems here to have been corrupted out of all recognition into Nēpāḷa. The Pārasīkas who drove the Nēpāḷa king from his territory are called in the Raghunāthābhyudayam of Rāmabhadrāmba Parangis which word signifies the Portuguese. The Portuguese seem to have interfered with the affairs of the island of Jaffna at this time and espousing nominally the cause of a rival to the throne drove the ruler of the island away and themselves occupied it. (*Danvers' Portuguese in India*, II, Ch. vii.)

passing sharp needles into the roots of their hair. These do not cover even a small portion of the cruelties practised by Śōḷaga. If Achyuta were to subdue him and put an end to his atrocities, then the Portuguese (Pārasīkas) could be easily subdued and the Nēpāḷa (Jaffna) king once more raised to his throne.

Govinda Dīkshita then proceeded to say that the king of Pāṇḍya (the Nāyak of Madura) had without any cause been entertaining a feeling of hostility towards him. He had also concluded alliances with Śoḷaga and the king of Tuṇḍīra (the Nāyaka of Gingī, at this time Krishnappa Nāyaka).* Considering the strength of the coalition formed against Achyuta it would not be advisable on his part to fight with them at once.

* The king of Tuṇḍīra or the Nāyaka of Gingi, with whom Soḷaga allied himself, was according to the poem Raghunāthābhyudayam of Rāmabhadrāmba, Krishnappa Nāyak. He had been imprisoned at Penukoṇḍa by the emperor Venkaṭapati Rāya for an act of revolt. After Raghunātha of Tanjore had marched to Penukoṇḍa to help the emperor and defeated his enemies, the Muhammadans, and driven them from Penukoṇḍa, he interceded on behalf of the prisoner Krishnappa Nāyaka and got him released. As a mark of his gratitude for this kind service, Krishnappa Nāyaka gave one of his daughters in marriage to Raghunātha. In spite of this past service Krishnappa Nāyaka allied himself later with the enemies of Raghunātha like the Nāyaka of Madura, Jagga Rāya, the Portuguese (Parangis) and the chief Śoḷaga.

There is an interesting account of Krishnappa Nāyaka in Purchas, His Pilgrimes, volume X, chapter VII, Jesuit Observations of India. Krishnappa Nāyaka was at the town of Chidambaram in the year 1599 A.D. superintending the improvements made in the temple of Gōvinda Rāja, within the great Śiva temple, as the construction of the Dhvajasthambha. The magnificence of his court is described in detail. The Śaiva priests of the temple of Śiva at Chidambaram protested against the Nāyak's improvements in the Vishnu temple and some of them even killed themselves by falling from the top of the tower. But Krishnappa Nāyaka accomplished his purpose in spite of their opposition.

Krishnappa Nāyaka is also said to have constructed a new port named Krishnapaṭam after himself near the mouth of the river Veḷḷār (Velarius), and allowed the Portuguese to construct two churches in it. This forms now the Hindu part of Porto Novo. Krishnappa Nāyaka is also said to have previously been imprisoned by his uncle, but escaping from his prison he managed to blind his uncle and imprison him in turn. His capital Gingī is described as a great city, the biggest that Pimenta, the Jesuit, saw in India, and bigger than any in Portugal, Lisbon excepted.

We do not know how Krishnappa Nāyaka was related to the chiefs Sūrappa Nāyaka and his father Pōta Bhūpāla who were the Nāyaks of Gingī before him if they were related at all. The famous poet Ratnakhēṭa Śrīnivāsa Dīkshita lived in the court of Sūrappa Nāyaka and dedicated to him the drama Bhāvanāpurushottama. According to this source Pōta Bhūpālā had by his wife Vengalāmba two sons Divākara Nāyaka and Bhairava Nāyaka in addition Sūrappa Nāyaka. He founded villages called after himself and his parents respectively: Sūrasamudra, Pōtasamudra and Vengalāmbāpura. One of his titles in the work is the firm establisher of the throne of Karnāṭa, (Karṇāṭasimhāsanapratisṭhāpanāchārya). This seems to refer to the help which the chief rendered to the emperor of Vijayanagar (Tirumala Rāya or Srīranga Rāya) during one of the Muhammadan invasions into the Vijayanagar empire soon after the battle of Talikota.

Soon after this, a spy sent to collect information about the Pāṇḍya returned and gave startling news. When the Pāṇḍya and his allies had come to an understanding and were about to proceed against Achyuta, they were joined by Jagga Rāya, who long a relative and servant of the Emperor of the Karṇāṭa, had treacherously assassinated the emperor and his near relations. After the emperor of the Karṇāṭa (Vijayanagar) had thus been murdered in his capital, his only surviving son, a child, had been rescued by the nobleman, Yācha, who with other chiefs was proceeding to Achyuta for help. Achyuta had to effect a junction with Yācha and the young emperor before the Pāṇḍya and his allies met the troops of Jagga Rāya at Śrīrangam as arranged between them.

After enumerating these events Govinda Dīkshita praised Achyuta for his long and beneficent rule, for his destruction of his enemies and his liberal patronage of learned men. He said that Achyuta had become old and requested him to instal his son Raghunātha on the throne that he might carry on the impending wars with greater vigour and bring them to a successful close. Achyuta accepted the advice of the minister and directed him to make arrangements for the coronation of Raghunātha. He also said that the ensuing Saumyavāsara (Wednesday) was an auspicious day and directed that the coronation take place then.

Sarga XII gives a description of the coronation of Raghunātha as it was performed by Govinda Dīkshita. After the coronation was over Achyuta retired to the sacred Śrīrangam to spend his later days in the worship of the God of the place.

Sarga XIII.—A spy in the service of Raghunātha returned with news of the enemies of Raghunātha, the Pāṇḍya and his confederates. He gave a description of the fire-arms used by the soldiers of the enemy and of the field pieces worked for them by the Pārasīkas (Portuguese). He also gave a short description of the foreign (Pārasīka or Portuguese) Captains in the enemy's army. They had long whiskers, red as copper. They had no mark on their faces, and their ears had no holes (to wear the ear-rings). They had long faces with crooked eyebrows. They wore red trousers and had red feathers on their caps. They chewed no betel and their breath smelt of toddy. Their bodies were covered with armour, and they were provided with big swords, quivers full of arrows and bows.

The messenger was then taken to Govinda Dīkshita to whom he gave the following account of the enemy. The traitor Jagga Rāya along with his friends went to the emperor as if for some act of service, and when the emperor was asleep one night murdered him along with his children and friends. Then having been joined by the Dravida, Chera and Pāṇḍya kings he is wandering with his forces near Śrīrangam. The noble Yācha, however, managed to rescue one of the late emperor's sons from the massacre by a stratagem, and is now proceeding to the south for assistance. He requests to be assisted by you in the cause of your common master the Karṇāṭa emperor.

Hearing that Yācha and his army are proceeding towards you with the emperor's son, and that they may not effect a junction with your troops, the Pāṇḍya king (the Madura Nāyak) at the instance of Jagga Rāya has cut the great anicut across the Kaveri.

On hearing this news, king Raghunātha decided to proceed to Kumbhakonam to effect a junction with the emperor's son Rāma Rāya, and celebrate his coronation at the place. The king then vowed that he would proceed against Śoḷaga in his island and destroy him along with his relations. He would then proceed against the Pāṇḍya and his allies and having captured the chiefs in the battle-field, would take away all the wealth in the camp and set their empty camp on fire. He would also destroy in battle Jagga Rāya and his other allies, and with their skulls reconstruct the anicut (Śētu across the Kaveri), and put up there an inscription in memory of his great triumph there. Speaking thus, Raghunātha entrusted the whole management of the kingdom to his minister Govinda Dīkshita, and in great anger ordered his army to get ready for the march.

Sarga XIV describes Raghunātha's army. Raghunātha vowed to his favourite god Raghutilaka (Rama) that he would build for him a temple at his enemy's capital if he blessed him with success in the war.

Sarga XVI.—Raghunātha sets out with his army ready equipped from the fort of Tanjore.

N.B.—Here the manuscripts break off and the remaining portion is not available.

Sarga I.

अद्वैतविद्याविभवावलम्बान् गोविन्दयज्वेन्द्रगुरूनुपासे ।
निर्मथ्य षड्दर्शननीरधीन्ये धियैव सारान् ददते बुधेभ्यः ॥

* * * *

नित्यावर्तितनैकदानविनमन्नेपाळसिंहासन-
प्रत्यापत्तिविधानशौण्डमदवत्पाण्ड्यक्षिपापण्डित ।

जिह्वास्पन्दनमात्रजृम्भितवचस्सन्दब्धनानाकृते
प्रह्वाशेषनृपप्रजावनविधो मूर्त्यम्बिकानन्दन ॥
जलनिधिगर्भवासवशनिर्भरदर्परिपु-
प्रतिहतिहेतुसेतुकृतिनूतनदाशरथे ।
कविबुधगायकाभिमतकल्पनकल्पतरो
जय करुणासनाथ रघुनाथ जनाधिपते ॥

Sarga II.

रङ्गाधिभूमिरमानुनीतिशृङ्गारवीक्षामृतपूरितायाः ।
सह्यात्मजायास्सलिलैस्सदैव सह्यादृतो दीव्यति चोळदेशः ॥ १ ॥

* * * *

तत्तादृशे काचन चोळदेशे रमानटीनर्तनरङ्गशाला ।
तञ्जापुरी नाम दरी हरीणां धराभुजां राजति राजधानी ॥ ४० ॥

* * * *

Sarga III.

पुरीमथासाद्य भुजेन तादृशीं भुजङ्गमेन्द्रप्रतिमेन मेदिनीम् ।
असारकेयूरसमं महायशाः बभार चेव्वक्षितिपालशेखरः ॥ १ ॥
सरोगभीरं पुरि गोपुरं च यस्समुन्नतं शोणगिरीशितुर्व्यथात् ।
अशक्तयोरङ्घ्रिशिरो विलोकितुं महापथा माधववेधसोरिव ॥ ६ ॥
सुधांशुचूडस्य यथा सुता गिरेः पयोजनाभेरिव पङ्कजालया ।
विधेस्सवित्रीव गिरां विशां विभोरमुष्य जायाजनि मूर्तिमाम्बिका ॥ १५ ॥
पुरन्ध्रिरस्मादवनीपुरन्दरात् असूत सा शूरमथाच्युताधिपम् ।
कुलाचलाधीशकुमारिकामणिर्धरेन्द्रचापादिव तारकाहितम् ॥ १७ ॥
अनर्घरत्नाङ्कितमेष भूषणं वितीर्य रङ्गाधिपतेर्विशां पतिः ।
अनुत्तमं रत्नममुष्य कौस्तुभात् परं नहीति प्रणुनोद दुष्प्रथाम् ॥ ४७ ॥
अलङ्क्रियाप्रेम यदब्धिकन्यकाविभोः प्रसिद्धं तदयं विशां पतिः ।
अमुष्य रङ्गाधिपतेस्समर्पयन् अपूरयद्भूरिविभूषणानि सः ॥ ४९ ॥
ससंभ्रमं विरचितचम्पकाटवीसहस्रभूविबुधकुटुम्बसम्भृते ।
भवस्थले प्रतिशरदप्रवार्तितस्फुरत्तुलापुरुषयशो विशोभते ॥ ८० ॥

Sarga IV.

अमुमद्भुताकृतिममुं विलोकयन्नशरीरवाक्यमपि चानुचिन्तयन् ।
उचितं तयोरथ तनूजमुर्वरारमणश्चकार रघुनाथभूपकम् ॥ ९४ ॥

Sarga V.

रामो दशस्ववतरेष्वपि राजतेऽसा-
वद्यापि कीर्तिवपुरादिकवेर्निबन्धात् ।
तस्माद्विधेहि समतामवधेहि ताव-
द्यत्नं विभोर्यदुपतेश्चरितप्रबन्धम् ॥ २७ ॥

माकन्दकन्दळदमन्दमरन्दबन्धु
त्वंपारिजातहरणं त्वरया निबन्धुम (?) ॥

यामद्वयेन यदुनेतरि पारिजात-
माजीहरत्सरसमच्युतभूपसूनुः ।
काव्यं तदत्र विबुधैस्तु कथंकथंचि-
दालोखि चित्रमवधाय फणीन्द्रकल्पैः ॥ ३० ॥

एवं वदंस्तनयमेष कृपारसौघैः
जाताभिषेकमपि तं जगतीबिडौजाः ।
तत्राभ्यषिञ्चत मणीभिरसौ सभाया-
मासीत्स एव वसुधेशपटाभिषेकः ॥ ३९ ॥

अस्याच्युताभ्युदयपूर्वशतप्रबन्ध-
कर्तुर्महीतलशतक्रतुरात्मजस्य ।
अ(श्वो)रसानि गजतां रत्नविभूषणानि
देशान् बहूंश्च दयमानमना व्यतारीत् ॥ ३७ ॥

जातु क्षमामथ विजापयितुं समस्तां
नानानरेन्द्राविधृतां निजनन्दनेन ।
सञ्चिन्तयन्स नृपतिश्रवसोरतानीत्
कोलाहलं कमपि भूपकुलाङ्गनानाम् । ६९ ॥

भो रक्ष रक्ष सहसा भुवनैकवीर विद्राविताન्निजपदाद्भ्रमतैस्त्वमस्मान् ।
नेपाळनेतुरवरोधनितम्बवत्यः पत्या वयं पदमिताश्शरणं तवेति ॥ ६६ ॥

(?) कार्पण्यगर्भमवकर्ण्य तु कर्णरन्ध्रनाराचकल्पमुदितं नतमध्यमानाम् ।
आधारमावहदपारकृपारसार्द्रं वाचां हृदैष निमिषं वसुधासुधांशुः ॥ ६७ ॥
ते नागपट्टणगतेन मया निरस्ताः
पूर्वं समेत्य पुरमस्य समुद्रवेयम् ।
नेपाळभूविभुमतो निरकासयन्किं
भङ्क्ष्यामि तत्पुनरहं युधि पारसीकान् ॥ ६८ ॥
नेपाळभूविभुमसौ निजभर्मगेह-
द्वारि स्थितं द्रुतमुपेत्य तमित्युवाच ।
प्राक्पीतशेषरुधिरान्युधि पारसीक-
प्राणान् हरेयुरधुना तु त एव बाणाः ॥ ६९ ॥
प्राणस्य मे हृदि गतं तदनेन बुद्धं
विज्ञापनोक्तरचनेन विना तदद्य ।
द्वीपं हृतं जितमपि द्विषतामनीकं
नेपाळभूमिपरिणीरिति निश्चिकाय ॥ ७० ॥
स्नेहः परं मयि विभो तव कल्पनीयः
तेनैव सिध्यति समीहितमेतदास्ताम् ।
द्वेष्या न किं तु सुहृदो मम पारसीकाः
सन्दर्शनस्य भवतो यदमी निमित्तम् ॥ ७१ ॥
एवं वदन्तममुमेष महीमहेन्द्रो
नेपाळभूपमबलासहितं निनाय ।
स्वावासगेहसदृशं सहसोपकार्य-
द्रव्याणि च स्वधृतरत्नविभूषणानि ॥ ७२ ॥
नेपाळक्षोणिपालं सपदि निजपदभ्रंशितं पारसीकैः
प्रत्यासन्नं वितन्वन्प्रबलभुजमहो नर्तयित्वा समित्याम् ।
भूमीपालश्चिरायागमयत समयं भूभृतो जैत्रयात्रां
सर्वे कुर्वन्ति यस्मिञ्जलनिधिशयनस्वापमुद्रादरिद्रे ॥ ७३ ॥
द्वीपान्सप्त द्विजेभ्यो वितरसि रघुनाथेन्द्र ते सान्द्रतेजः
कुत्राप्यत्राश्रितान्न स्वधनमिति धिया कौतुकाधानधीरान् (?) ।

अन्यत्रास्माकमस्माद्वसतिमतिसृजेत्यन्तरीपान्तरस्थैः
नेपालक्षोणिपालप्रभृतिभिरभितः प्रार्थितो द्वीपदाने ॥ ७४ ॥

Sarga IX.

स्वस्वारिक्षितिपालकप्रतिहतिस्वच्छन्दनैकावनी-
पाकारातिजयप्रयाणनिहतैः प्रौढा मुहुर्भाङ्कृतिः ।
निस्साणैस्समुद्रिराद्रिरजर्निनिणिद्रभावभ्रुवं (?)
पाथोराशिवरे चिरेण शयितः पद्मालयावल्लभः ॥ ४४ ॥

*　　　　*　　　　*

सोऽयं नेपाळनेतुः पुनराधिनगरि स्थापनार्थं तदीये
सर्वान्दुर्वारगर्वानपि धरणिभृतस्सत्वरं निर्जिगीषन् ।
जम्भारातिस्सुधर्मामिव धिषणजयन्तान्वितो मन्त्रहेतोः
भूपः प्रापद्यताथो सचिवसुतयुतो जातु लक्ष्मीविलासम् ॥ ७९ ॥

Sarga X.

ससुतो वसुधासुधाकरोऽसौ सह गोविन्दमरविन्दुना सभायाम् ।
समगादथ तत्र गोत्रभेदे सजयन्तो गुरुणा यथामराणाम् ॥ १ ॥
प्रभुरेष तथा नु भद्रपीठे सचिवेनात्मभुवं समं निवेश्य ।
अपराङ्गमुपाश्रितोपबर्हं विमताज्ञातमुपाविशाद्वितन्वन् ॥ २ ॥
प्रभुतत्सुतमन्त्रिणस्सभायां वरमेते सममस्मरन्वसन्तः ।
प्रथमं मिळितं प्रपञ्चसृष्टेः पुरुषाणां त्रितयं पुरातनानाम् ॥ ३ ॥
अचिरादनरेन्द्रमन्त्रसाध्यः प्रबलोऽयं नृपपारसीकदेहान् ।
प्रविशन्नसिपन्नगस्त्वदीयः पिबतु प्राणसमीरणं रणाग्रे ॥ १४ ॥
अधिनेतरयन्ति पारसीकान् युधि नेपाळपरम्परा भवन्तः ।
अधुना खलु चोळकं सहायं विधुनानं तव शासकं बलेन ॥ १९ ॥
नृपचन्द्रनृशंसवृत्तिरास्ते स तथा संप्रति चोळको धरायाम् ।
प्रवदन्ति जना यथा मुनीनां प्रवरं हन्त दशाननं चरित्रैः ॥ १६ ॥
अभवद्बहुकाळकूटबाधा नभवस्तोयनिधेश्चिरंतनो यः ।
अधुना स निजान्तरैकवासं सहतश्चोळकमस्यसाधनैव ॥ १७ ॥

पथिकान्मिळितःपथिष्वजस्त्रं बत गोणीकृतभस्त्रिकासु बद्ध्वा ।
मुसलैस्स विभो मुहुः प्रहार्य क्षिपति ग्राहमुखेषु निर्निमित्तम् ॥ १८ ॥
वनदंष्ट्रिभिराहता त्वदीयैः कळमाळित्यभिधायिनां जनानाम् ।
अधिरोपयतेऽधिरोमकूपं शितसूचीरिह पाययत्यजस्रमः ॥ २० ॥
इयता वचसा यदेकदेशोप्यधुनाभिहितस्तदस्य सर्वम् ।
चरितं हतकस्य शक्यते तन्न मयाकर्णयितुं नमश्शिवाय ॥ २१ ॥
भवता नरपालकेन्द्र भग्ने निहते चोळगनाम्नि नीतिमार्गात् ।
प्रभवो न भवन्ति पारसीकाः पुरि नेपाळविभुं पुनर्निरोद्धुम् ॥ २२ ॥
सचिवोक्तमिति श्रवःपुटाभ्यां परिगृह्णन् रघुनाथपार्थिवेन्द्रः ।
अगदीदिति दन्तदीधितिभ्यो जनयन्नर्म दिवापि चन्द्रिकाणाम् ॥ १३ ॥
निहते युधि चोळगे नृशंसे निहता एव भवन्ति पारसीकाः ।
नरनाथनिजाश्रयस्य बाधे नयसिद्धो न किमाश्रितस्य बाधः ॥ २४ ॥
अवनीन्द्र तवाश्रितस्य पादौ पुरि नेपाळविभोः पुनः प्रतिष्ठाम् ।
अयमाशु विधातुमभ्युपायः परमस्मिन्प्रतिभाति किञ्चिदेवम् ॥ २५ ॥
अविवेकनिधिस्स पाण्ड्यभूपो भुवि वेतण्ड इव भ्रमन्मदेन ।
नरपालमृगाधिपे स्वशक्त्या निरपाये त्वयि शात्रवं विधत्ते ॥ २६ ॥
प्रबलं बत शात्रवं स पाण्ड्यः प्रभुचन्द्र त्वयि शीलयत्यहेतुः ।
अधुना तु स चोळकस्य तस्मिन्नपि तुण्डीरविभोः प्रवर्तनेन ॥ २७ ॥
ब(हुमर्थ ?) मेकदापरैर्यत् प्रबलोऽपि क्षितिपालको न कुर्यात् ।
तदमी विषयेषु विप्रकीर्णा धरणीन्दो युगपत्त्वया न योध्याः ॥ २८ ॥
अवतंस्य वचस्तदस्य मन्त्री नयसिन्धो रघुनाथमेदिनीन्दोः ।
अवदत्स वदावदप्रवेकः परमानन्दधुरन्धरान्तरङ्गः ॥ २९ ॥
अयतेऽस्य वचोऽनवद्यमर्थं श्रयतेऽर्थो नृपचन्द्रनीलतत्वम् ।
तनुतेऽपि च नीतितत्त्वमेतत्प्रकृतेऽतिप्रवणं मतिं विधेये ॥ ३१ ॥
प्रभुरेष तथेति भाषितेन प्रसवेनेव सदाळिमोददात्रा ।
सरसेन फलैकसाधनेन व्यतनोन्मन्त्रिणमुल्लसद्वतंसम् ॥ ३२ ॥
अनयैव किल त्वयानुपूर्व्या वदता कश्चन वैरिणां नृपाणाम् ।
प्रणिधिश्चरितस्य पाण्ड्यभूपप्रभृतीनां प्रहितो विचारणाय ॥ ३३ ॥

भुजधाम यशोऽपि तादृशं ते भुवनान्यस्य तदेतदच्युतेन्दो।
अहमेव विदिक्षु दिक्षु सीमास्वपि सर्वासु चरश्चिराय जाने ॥ ३४ ॥
विजिता बहुधा पृथक्पृथक्ते विमताः पाण्ड्यमुखास्त्वया रणेषु।
मिळिताश्शपथैर्मिथस्समस्ताः पुनरप्यत्र पुराभिषेणयन्ते ॥ ५४ ॥
अनुजीव्य चिरादनन्यमित्रं पुरि कर्णाटकभूपतिं सबन्धुम्।
निजनाथमहो निहत्य कैश्चित् समगात्पाण्ड्यनृपेण स जग्गराजः ॥५५॥
पुरि तत्र हते स्वपुत्रपौत्रैः सह कर्नाटनृपे तदावशिष्टम्।
परिगृह्य तदात्मजं स याचप्रभुरन्यैश्च समायियासतीह ॥ ५६।
अधिरङ्गममी मिळन्ति यावत् युधि मत्ता रिपवस्सपाण्ड्यभूपाः।
पुर एव ततोमुना विधेयं तव कर्नाटनृपात्मजेन सख्यम् ॥ ५७ ॥
(?) समनोजवसेनकिंविधेयात् सुमनोराजनिभस्सुतो विधेयम्।
अहितास्सकला युयुत्सया ते प्रांहितास्तत्र मिळन्तु भूप मा वा ॥ ५८ ॥
नृपधूर्वहतां निजे तनूजे वसुधावास्तटिनीवराव्रता यः।
वितनुष्व रणेष्वसौ विशङ्को विमतानाशु विनाशयत्ययत्नम् ॥ ६० ॥
अनपायविभुत्वहेतुमेतत्सनिपायस्पशवाक्यमच्युतेन्द्रः
प्रतितं वचनं प्रमोदमानः प्रथितं किंचन वर्णयांचकार ॥ ६१ ॥
विजिता बहवो विशामधीशाः बहुधाभोजि वसुन्धराप्यशेषा।
विदुषामपि संभृतं व्यतारि द्रविणं किं परमस्ति किं विधेयम् ॥ ६२ ॥
परमेतादिहावशिष्यते मे परमेऽस्मिन्रघुनाथनाम्नि पुत्रे।
अवनीभरमाकलय्य शत्रूनविनीतानमुना विजापयिष्ये ॥ ६३ ॥
तदमुं धरणीतलेन्द्रतायाम् अभिषिञ्चे त्वमपि द्रुतं विकीर्णैः।
सविधं मम कैश्चन क्षितीन्द्रैः सह कर्णाटनृपात्मजं नयस्व ॥ ६४ ॥
इतितामिति सोयमुर्वरेन्दोर्वदनात्कल्पकमञ्जरीं वतंस्य।
निरतोमहति स्पशो विधेये निरगाद्भूभृदगारतोऽतिवेगात् ॥ ६५ ॥
निजपार्श्वभुवं प्रसाधयन्तं नृपचन्द्रो रघुनाथपार्थिवं तम्।
अवलोक्य समन्त्रिणाथ वाणीमवतंस्यामिति वर्णयांबभूव ॥ ६६ ॥
इत्यात्मजं निजमसाविममच्युतेन्दुः
अत्यादरेण धृतनीतिमथादधानम्।

आविप्रमोदमुचितामवलोक्य वाणीम्
गोविन्दयज्वतिलकं गुणवानवादीत् ॥ १०२ ॥
सौम्ये भाविनि वासरे शुभतरे शौण्डीर्यमुख्यैर्गुणैः
प्रख्यातं रघुनाथनायकममुं प्रौढापदानं सुतम् ।
क्षिप्रं त्वं चतुरर्णवीपरिवृतक्षोणीतलप्राभवे
कुर्याः कौतुकतोऽभिषिक्तमखिलैर्गोविन्दयज्वाग्रणीः ॥ १०३ ॥
कुर्वन्तद्वचनं वतंसमुचितं गोविन्दयज्वाततः
पौराणामभिषेकमङ्गळकृते प्रावीवृतत्सम्भ्रमम् ।
सोऽपि श्रीरघुनाथभूमिरमणः स्वावासगेहं मुदा
प्राग्भारेण समं समाविशति (च) प्रह्वैः परीतो नृपैः ॥ १०४ ॥

Sarga XII.

भद्रासनस्थितिविधिप्रथितं विभूत्या
नित्याग्निहोत्रभवया निटिलो महीन्दोः ।
आचन्द्रतारकमधीश्वरतानिदानं
गोविन्ददीक्षितगुरुः कुरुते स्म पट्टम् ॥ ४९ ॥
सर्वं धैर्यविधूतमेरुविभवे सर्वंसहाया भरं
प्रौढेऽस्मिन् रघुनाथनाम्नि निदधत्पुत्रेऽच्युतक्ष्मापतिः ।
श्रीरङ्गस्थलसङ्गतो बुधकुलं शीतांशुरुर्वीमिव
प्राप्तस्सैष पुपोष शेषशयने भक्तः परे धामनि ॥ ९४ ॥

Sarga XIII.

चारो नेत्रा चोदितस्सप्रजानां दृष्ट्वा श क्ष्मापतीन्द्रप्रवृत्तीन् ।
वक्तुं वेगादागतो वासधाम्नः कक्ष्यामग्र्यामस्य कामप्यवाप ॥ १ ॥
आपूर्यन्तिःप्रौढलोहाग्नियन्त्रेष्वाविर्ध्वानो यत्समीपे समीरः ।
सख्यास्तस्यारातिसैन्याक्षिपायाम् उद्योगित्वं नित्यमुद्घुष्यतीव ॥ ८ ॥
हस्तग्राह्यापारलोहाग्नियन्त्रक्रूरैर्हालास्वादनाघूर्णिताक्षैः ।
सन्नद्धैर्या सन्ततं पारसीकैः उत्साहैर्वा सप्रतीकैरुपेता ॥ ९ ॥
वेद्यां तस्यां भूपतेर्वेत्रहस्तैः द्वित्रैरेव स्थापितान्द्रप्रवृत्तीन् ।
कालस्येवालोकयत्कालभेदान् सोऽयं भीतो नित्यशुष्कांस्तुलुष्कान्॥ १४ ॥

सद्योमृष्पृस्वच्छताम्रोपमानैः दीर्घश्मश्रुश्रेणिदीप्तैर्महाद्भिः ।
शून्याळीकैरक्षतश्रोत्रयुग्मैः वक्त्रैः क्रूरान्वाक्रितभ्रूकुटीकैः ॥ १९ ॥
उद्भ्रान्ताक्षान्लोहितोष्णीषबन्धान् ताम्रच्छायैस्सावतंसान्गरुद्भिः ।
वज्रप्रायैर्वर्मितान्वारवाणैः निस्ताम्बूलान्मद्यानित्यावलिप्तान् ॥ १६ ॥
कव्यालम्बिप्रौढकौक्षेयसक्तं तूणीभारं बिभ्रतो दुर्विदग्धान् ।
सव्येनोच्चैः पाणिना शार्ङ्गचापं द्वित्रानन्येनापि तीक्ष्णान्पृषत्कान्॥ १७

* * * *

विज्ञाप्य नैकधरणीविभुचेष्टितानि
वक्तुं समागतममुं वसुधासुधांशुः ।
आलोक्य चारमयमाह पुरो निषण्णं
गोविन्दयज्वतिलकं गुणिनां प्रवेकम् ॥ ७० ॥
अभिधाय पटाञ्चलाञ्चिताभ्यां स विनीतो वदनं चरः कराभ्याम् ।
अगदीद्द्विषतामथापदानान्यनुयुक्तो मखिनामधीश्वरेण ॥ ७३ ॥
स्वामिद्रोही जग्गराजः स्वमित्रैः कैश्चिद्भूपैः प्राप्य कर्णाटभूपम् ।
सेवाव्याजेनाशु सेनासनाथः सुप्तं रात्रौ सोऽवधीत्बन्धुमित्रैः ॥ ७४ ॥
स मित्रसुतबान्धवैस्सह निहत्य कर्णाटक-
प्रभुं स्वकुलपोषकं प्रबलपापदुष्यन्मतिः ।
ततोनु सहितो नृपैः द्रमिडचेरपाण्ड्यादिभिः
भ्रमत्यनुचितक्रियः परवशोऽधिरङ्गस्थलम् ॥ ७९ ॥
हतेऽथ कर्नाटनृपे सहात्मजैः ततोऽवशिष्टं पृथुकं तदात्मजम् ।
कमप्युपायादवहृत्य यत्नतः कथंचिदायाति स याचभूपतिः ॥ ७६ ॥
आलम्ब्य मंक्षु धरणीन्द्रमहानुभावम्
आगन्तुकैकशरणं प्रबलं बलेन ।
याचक्षमापतिरसाविह याचति त्वां
सख्याश्रितो रिपुनृपैस्स विभुत्वहेतुम् ॥ ७७ ॥
कर्णाटप्रभुसूनुमात्मावमतं कंचिद्गृहीत्वा शिशुं
त्वामभ्यागमदेष याचमहिपस्तूर्णं भियेत्यन्वहम् ।

पाण्ड्यश्रेरसखोऽथ जग्गविभुना पापेन च प्रेरितः
कावेरीतटधर्मसेतुमचलं कैश्चित्क्रुधाभेदयत् ॥ ७८ ॥
गत्वा संप्रति कुम्भघोणमुचितं कर्णाटनेतुस्सुतं
बालं तं शरणागतं विरचये पट्टाभिषिक्तं बलात् ।
प्रौढश्रीरधिभद्रपीठि निवसन्पाथोधिभिः प्रावृतां
सर्वामप्यवनिं स राममहिपः स्वैरं चिरं रक्षतु ॥ ८० ॥
अन्तरीपगतमम्बुधेरहं चोलकं सपदि चोदितैर्नृपैः ।
कैश्चिदेव युधि खण्डये पुरा वन्धुपुत्रसहितं प्रतापतः ॥ ८१ ॥
पाण्ड्यं तुण्डीरचेरद्रमिडमगधभूपालमुख्यैस्सपत्नैः
हस्तग्राहं गृहीत्वा सपदि समिति तत्तत्समस्तार्थजातम् ।
योधैराहार्यशूरैः पटगृहमखिलं (?) याधयित्वा च वह्निं
ज्वालाभिर्भासयेऽहं दिशिदिशि सततं जैत्रवृत्तिर्महांसि ॥ ८२ ॥
छिन्नैर्जग्गनृपादिबाहुजनुषां सेतुं शिरःकूर्परैः
कावेर्यां युधि बन्धयामि सुदृढं कामं तथाहं भटैः
स्पष्टं तैः विधृताभिरेवं लिपिभिस्स्वायंभुवीभिर्यथा
कर्तव्यं जयरेखिकाविरचनं कल्प्येत कल्पावधि ॥ ८३ ॥

इतीरयन्वचनमिलावलाहितो
धराधुरां निजसचिवे निवेश्य च ।
सरोहितात् सदसि सरोषमीक्षणात्
अनीकिनीमथ समनीनहत्क्षणात् ॥ ८४ ॥

Sarga XIV.

प्रत्यर्थिप्रभुविजयप्रयाणयोग्यं
सन्नद्धं महति बले स भूषणानि ।
आहत्य प्रकृतिमनोहरैरथाङ्गैः
आकाङ्क्षीन्महिपरिणीरनुग्रहीतुम् ॥ १ ॥
द्वीपस्थं रघुतिलकं द्विषं मथित्वा
तस्याहं पुरि कलये तव प्रतिष्ठाम् ।

साहाय्यं युधि मम संविधेहि तत्रे-
त्यभ्यर्थ्य क्षितिभृदथ प्रतिष्ठते स्म ॥ ३९ ॥
आधूनखड्गलतिका मुहुराननतानि कृत्वा शिरांसि परिक्लृप्तगभीरघोषम् ।
दूरादकुर्वत तुरुष्कभटा धरित्रीपाकद्विषस्सविनयं प्रणयं हयस्थाः ॥६९

Sarga XVI.

अम्लानाभिरपास्तरञ्जनहनक्लेशाभिरम्भोरुह-
स्रग्भिस्सौधजुषामपाङ्गजनिभिस्सश्लाघमेणीदृशाम् ।
आयुष्मान्रघुनाथभूमिपरिणीरभ्यर्चितो भूयसा
सञ्जातप्रमदो बलेन निरगात्तञ्जापुरीतो बहिः ॥ ७४ ॥

91

RAGHUNĀTHĀBHYUDAYAM.

[*By Rāmabhadrāmbā.*]

This important historical poem dealing with the life and achievements of Raghunātha Nāyaka of Tanjore was recently found in November 1916 by Professor S. Krishnaswami Ayyangar of the University in the course of his search, with the assistance of Pandit Rāmaswami Sastriyar of the library, for historical manuscripts bearing-on the history of Vijayanagar. It is not noticed in Burnell's catalogue of the Tanjore library. The work was written by the talented poetess Rāmabhadrāmba of the Court of Raghunātha.

Sarga I.—She praises the great qualities of Raghunātha and says that he had written many literary pieces (Prabandhas). She invokes the assistance of her patron in her task of writing his life.

Sarga III.—Raghunātha is referred to as able to pay attention to a hundred subjects at a time (Śatāvadhānam), and issue his instructions with regard to all of them. His magnanimity even excelled that of the great ocean itself, and, as if to signify this, the king of *Nēpāḷa* (Jaffna) and the inhabitants of other islands sought refuge with him.

Sarga VI.—The king *Raghunātha* holds his court in the palace Lakshmīvilāsam, and his bards are made to sing the praises of his family. In the Śūdra caste, born from the feet of Vishnu, was born a king called *Timma* who had married Bayyāmbika. They got a son called Chevva (Śiva). He constructed the tall gopura (tower) of *Śōṇādri* (Tiruvaṇṇāmalai), the gopura and Dhvajastambha (flag-column) at Vṛiddhāchalam, and the compound walls and the steps leading to the temple of Śrīśailam. In all these places he made arrangements for the permanent worship of God. He made many offerings (gifts) and established many agrahāras (Brahman villages) on the banks of the Kaveri. He married Mūrtyamba, the sister of the Queen of Achyuta Rāya.

They had for son Achyuta. He constructed the beautiful golden Vimāna (tower over the sanctum) at Śrīrangam, and presented to the God of the place a crown (Kirīṭa) and a throne. He made many gifts to the God Śiva worshipped at Ramēśvaram and restored the many tīrthas (holy bathing ghats) of the place which were in ruins. He constructed many temples, granted agrahāras and performed gifts like muktātulāpūrusha (weighing himself against pearls and distributing the pearls in charity). Achyuta married Mūrtyamba and to her was born the son Raghunātha.

When Raghunātha grew up, his great qualities pleased his father very much. He had several princesses of the Pāṇḍya and other kingdoms married to him. Achyuta made Raghunātha Yuvarāja (heir-apparent). At that time the Karṇāṭa (Vijayanagar) emperor Venkaṭadēva Rāya was opposed by the Pārasīkas (Muhammadan rulers of Bijapur and Golkonda). In order to defend the empire against them, he requested Achyuta to send the prince Raghunātha to his assistance. At the direction of Achyuta Raghunātha started on the expedition followed by hundreds of tributary chiefs. He went to Chandragiri, and from there reached Penukoṇḍa the hereditary capital of the Karṇāṭa (Vijayanagar) kings in a few days. The emperor Venkaṭadēva Rāya on hearing of his arrival received him with great honour and made him stay in Penukoṇḍa. Many of the enemies of the emperor fled from Penukoṇḍa when they learnt of the arrival of Raghunātha with troops, while a few mounting their horses opposed him. But they were easily defeated by the valiant Raghunātha and were scattered as the Rákshasas were by Rāma. On their defeat they submitted to Raghunātha and retired. After this victory Raghunātha was opposed by the Murasas (the people of the Morasanāḍu, the district embracing the northern portion of North Arcot and the adjacent parts of the neighbouring districts) from their forts like Baḷḷāḷapura. Having defeated all these enemies he brought all the territory and the fortresses of Karṇāta once more under the emperor Venkaṭadēva

Rāya. After this victory the emperor Venkaṭadēva Rāya in the public court acknowledged the great assistance rendered by Raghunātha, and said that he was able to destroy his enemies only with the assistance of Raghunātha. He also honoured him with presents of horses and jewellery. Raghunātha then learnt from some relatives of the chief that the lord of Tunḍīra (the Nāyaka of Gingi), Krishnappa Nāyaka, was wasting away in the emperor's prison. Raghunātha took pity upon him and by his influence got Krishnappa Nāyaka released by the emperor. The lord of Tunḍīra then prostrated himself with his queen before Raghunātha, and showed his gratitude by giving Raghunātha his daughter in marriage. When Achyuta heard that his son Raghunātha was returning after accomplishing his mission with the emperor of Karṇāṭa he proceeded some distance from his capital to meet him and give him a fitting reception.

Sarga VIII.—Raghunātha was then raised to the throne.* Soon after this, news was brought to Raghunātha of the atrocities of a chief called Śoḷaga. This chief was so powerful that he had defied even powerful viceroys like Viṭṭhala Rāja.† He was a worshipper of the God Bhairava. He had occupied an island near the sea, and was giving great trouble to the surrounding country. He used to carry away women from the neighbouring country and was giving the people no peace.‡

When Raghunātha heard this he promised to relieve the suffering people by the destruction of Śoḷaga.

* This must have been when his father Achyuta was still living. In the poem Sāhityaratnākaram of Yagñanārayana Dīkshita, dealing with the life of Raghunātha, Achyuta is said to have been living after the death of the emperor Venkaṭapati Rāya, and the massacre of the royal family by Jagga Rāya. When he heard that the only surviving son of the murdered emperor and the general Yāchama were proceeding to the south for assistance to Tanjore, and that Jagga Rāya and his ally, the Nāyak of Gingi were marching south to effect a junction with the Nāyak of Madura, Govinda Dīkshita persuaded Achyuta to resign in favour of his son Raghunātha, who was young and vigorous to carry on the war. Achyuta did as he was advised and retired to Śrīrangam to spend his remaining days.

† We do not know whether the Viṭṭhala here referred to could be Rāma Rāju Viṭṭhala, a cousin of the Emperor Aḷiya Rāma Rāya who led an invasion to the extreme south of the peninsula. We do not know whether Śoḷaga against whom Raghunātha fought about 1615 could have also fought with Rāma Rāju Viṭṭhala who invaded the south more than half a century before the event.

‡ The atrocities of Śoḷaga are described in worse colours in the Sāhityaratnākaram. He used to throw his prisoners to his trained crocodiles. He used to pass sharp needles into the roots of the hairs of his prisoners. This chief Soḷaga was an ally of the Portuguese, and the Jesuit writer Pimenta gives an account of him in Purchas His Pilgrimes, Volume X, Chapter vii.

Soon after this the servants of Raghunātha's Court announced to him that the king of Nēpāḷa* had gone to him with his relatives and assistants, and was waiting to be admitted to his presence. When the king of Nēpāḷa (Jaffna) was brought before him he made due obeisance to Raghunātha and narrated how Raghunātha's grandfather China Chevva and his father Achyuta were great supporters of his kingdom. The Parangis (Portuguese) had on several occasions been defeated by his ancestors, and they had been waiting to wreak their vengeance upon the king of Nēpāḷa.† Roving the seas in their ships they now attacked his capital while he was himself away from it and captured it. He was obliged to flee in a ship across the sea and seek refuge at the court of Raghunātha. Raghunātha promised to render assistance to the king and restore him his lost kingdom.

After this there arrived at his court some envoys from the court of the emperor of the Karṇāṭa. When they were introduced into his presence they narrated how after the death of the Emperor Venkaṭadēva Rāya all the officers raised the son of the crown prince,‡ Śrīranga Rāya to the throne. After the new emperor had ruled for some time the nobleman Jagga Rāya, along with his

* The king of Nēpāḷa was the ruler of the island of Jaffna. He was driven away from his kingdom by the Portuguese who are called Parangis in this poem and Pārasikas in the Sāhityaratnākara. They nominally espoused the cause of a rival to the throne and took the opportunity of getting hold of the island by driving out the ruler in possession (vide Danvers: The Portuguese in India II, pp. 206–7).

† In 1591 under Andreu Fustado the Portuguese undertook an invasion of Jaffna, as they heard that both the king of Kandy and himself persecuted those of their subjects that professed Christianity. Fustado occupled Jaffna, killed the king and his eldest son. The younger son Pararājaśēkhara Pandara, a boy of seven, was placed on the throne by Fustado in anticipation of the Viceroy's sanction, which was ultimately accorded on terms later, with an uncle of the prince as regent, until he should come of age. This ruler died in 1617 leaving a young son and an uncle for regent. One Sangili Kumāra killed the regent and usurped the throne; but he was driven out by a rebellion of the people. He managed, however, to get the help of the Naik of Tanjore and establish himself on the throne, the Portuguese recognizing him as king. They dethroned him ultimately and occupied Jaffna. A rebellion was soon stirred up in behalf of a prince who was then at Remancor by one Arache Dom Luiz. This was put down. The prince surrendered himself after the defeat of the allies. Arache Dom Luiz fled to Tanjore and persuaded the Naik to take possession of Jaffna. The first Tanjore invasion under Khem Naik, who assisted Sangili Kumāra not long before, failed. Another and larger expedition had no better result. The Jaffna prince who found sanctuary with some Franciscan friars to escape Sangili Kumāra became Christian in 1620, making over his claim to the kingdom to the Portuguese. The text above seems apparently to refer to Sangili Kumāra's defeat by the Portuguese in 1617 (vide F. C. Danvers: The Portuguese in India, II, Ch. viii).

‡ This must refer to Rama Rāya, father of Śrīranga, and brother of Venkaṭapatirāya. He died as Viceroy at Seringapaṭam.

younger brother, surrounded the palace one night with his troops, and massacred the emperor, his wives and children. From among the children of the emperor a boy was very skilfully rescued from the palace, in the dead of night, by a washerman. Some grateful officers of the late emperor had taken up the child's cause, and not being able to fight against their enemy were going to Raghunātha for help. The envoys then requested Raghunātha to take up the cause of the fugitive emperor, and rescue the empire *once more* from destruction as he had done before in his youth, and to destroy the party of Jagga Rāya. When Raghunātha heard this he told his ministers that the three tasks of destroying Śōḷaga in the island, driving out the enemies of the Nēpāḷa (Jaffna) king, and celebrating the coronation of the new Karṇāṭa emperor would constitute his digvijaya (conquest of the four quarters).

Having ordered all his generals to get ready, and apppointed proper officers for governing the capital during his absence, Raghunātha set out with his army along the banks of the Kaveri to Kumbhakonam. He worshipped the gods of the place and marched towards the island of Śōḷaga on the seashore. Śōḷaga was afraid of the great heroism of Raghunātha, although he was himself a warrior, and requested the assistance of his ally Krishna (Krishnappa Nāyaka of Gingi). His own courtiers sought to dissuade Krishnappa Nāyaka from making war against Raghunātha who had saved him when he was captured by his powerful enemy, the emperor. But he did not listen to their counsel and marched towards the island of Śōḷaga. Seeing that Śōḷaga did not surrender and still stood defiant, Raghunātha ordered his men to construct a bridge of boats and himself crossed over to the island on an elephant. They then began to lay siege to the enemy's fort, but the garrison within it did great injury to his army by raining upon it stones and fire. The king then in great anger ordered his army to destroy the fortifications or enter the fort with scaling ladders. When the fort fell into the besiegers' hands Śōḷaga tried to escape, but he was taken prisoner and Raghunātha ordered his life to be spared. Seeing that the Śōḷaga had been captured, his ally * Krishnappa Nāyaka, the Nāyaka of Gingi, escaped to his own capital. Advised by his ministers not to show any consideration to Śōḷaga and to throw him into prison, Raghunātha ordered accordingly.

* In 'Purchas, His Pilgrimes,' Vol. X, page 218, there is an interesting account of Krishnappa Nāyaka, the ruler of Gingi and of the manner of his accession to this position. He escaped from the prison himself and had his uncle blinded and put into it.

Sarga IX.—After Raghunātha's victory over the Śōḷaga his ministers reminded him of the expedition against the usurping Portuguese (Parangis) in the island of Nēpāḷa (Jaffna). He proceeded on his elephant to the seacoast followed by his army and ordered the construction of a bridge of boats for his army to cross over to the island. When his army was crossing over to the island by the bridge it was opposed by the troops of the Portuguese who used fire-arms. The battle between the two forces is then described. Seeing that the forces of the king (Raghunātha) were irresistible the Parangis fled before them and leaving behind them their money and arms and ammunition, escaped into the sea. Raghunātha then placed his own garrison in the island and celebrated the coronation of his ally, the Nēpāḷa (Jaffna) king, as Rama performed the coronation of Vibhīshaṇa.

The envoys sent from Raghunātha's court then brought to him an account of the traitors to the empire (Jagga Rāya and his allies).* They had effected a junction with the rulers of Tunḍīra (Gingi) and Pānḍya, and with their armies were hunting for the late emperor's surviving son to put him to death. Raghunātha ordered his army to march west to Topur † which was the headquarters of the enemy. He then intimated to every captain in his army that they should deliver the attack upon the enemy the next day, and stationed sentinels at several places in the field. The troops are then described as they appeared in the night with their torches and watch fires. Seeing the extraordinary preparations of Raghunātha, his enemies, the Pānḍya and his allies also made themselves ready.

Sarga X.—When the allies were attacked by the troops of the king, the scene resembled the meeting of the eastern ocean with the western. In the beginning there was an artillery duel between the two contending armies. After that the cavalry of Raghunātha proceeded in semi-circular formation, and attacked the enemy

---

* Vide Sewell's Forgotten Empire, Chap. XVII. Barradas says that Jagga Rāya did this in order to bring about the succession of his own nephew. One of the queens of Venkaṭapati Rāya, who is called Bāyamma was very sorry that she had no issue and pretending that she was pregnant introduced into the palace a stranger child and brought him up as her own son. He was brought up in the court itself, but his origin was known to the emperor who on his death-bed nominated as his successor Śrīranga Rāya alias Chikka Rāya, son of his brother Rāma who was crown-prince. Jagga Rāya took up the cause of the boy who was brought up by Bāyamma as her own son. He was father or brother of Bāyamma. He surrounded the palace one night with his soldiers and massacred the whole of the royal family except a single child who was skilfully saved by the noleman Yāchama Nāyaka.

† Now called Tohur, about two miles from the grand anicut, on the south bank of the Kaveri.

closely followed by his infantry which was irresistable. The troops of the Pāṇḍya could not stand the attack, broke and fled from the field. Jagga Rāya then advanced and opposed Raghunātha's troops. The sight of the traitor Jagga Rāya made Raghunātha very angry. In the ensuing attack Jagga Rāya and his relatives were all killed by the spears of Raghunātha's infantry. The anicut across the Kaveri which had been breached by Jagga was apparently the one he reconstructed 'with the skulls of his troops and cemented by their blood'. Seeing that Jagga and his troops were completely destroyed in the battle, the Pāṇḍya began to feel anxious for the safety of his own territory. Leaving his elephants, horses, treasury and harem in the camp he fled a krosa (a league). The ruler of Tuṇḍīra (Gingi) also fled from the field making himself ridiculous in the eyes of his own officers. When he saw the troops of his allies flying from the field Rāviḷḷa Venka lost courage and fled along with the others, as also Māka Rāja who had come to the field in a braggart spirit. Their ally Rāyadallāpi (?) Chencha* who had never seen a battle from his birth became afraid when he saw from a distance royal corpses weltering in their blood and fled in great hurry. Raghunātha then pardoned the Pāṇḍya who was captured and brought before him. and spared his life gaining great glory by the act. Raghunātha then had a pillar of victory erected on the banks of the Kaveri.

Some envoys of Raghunātha's court who had gone to enquire about the proceedings in the territory of the Nāyak of Gingi returned to his court and reported that, after having been defeated by his army and driven away from the field, he had joined with other chiefs like himself and was projecting measures of hostility against Raghunātha. Raghunātha on hearing that, proceeded with his army along the bank of the Kaveri to Panchanada (Tiruvaiyār or Tiruvāḍi) and there waited for news of the success of the army he had despatched under his general against Krishnappa of Gingi. His victorious generals returned from the campaign and gave him an account of it. They first proceeded against Bhuvanagiri and other fortresses in the enemy territory, and captured them dispersing the garrisons stationed there by the enemy. Then they were attacked by Krishnappa Nāyaka with his allies like Yatirāja who like himself had fled from the field. Raghunātha was greatly pleased with the news of the victory and rewarded his generals

* This Chencha is referred to as Daḷavāi Chenchu in Vijayarāghava Nayaka's poem, Raghunāthābhyudayam (Extract No. 86). He seems to be the same Chenchu referred to among the allies of Jagga in the Rāmarājīyamu (Extract No. 79). Dallāpi is possibly an error for Daḷavāi.

amply. He then returned to his capital Tanjore after a long absence, being waited upon on his journey by the princes of ancient clans.

Sarga XI.—After Raghunātha returned to his capital he held court to examine the achievements of the accomplished ladies of his court. They are said to have been proficient in composing the four kinds of poetry (Chitra, Bandha, Garbha and Āśu) and in explaining the works written in various languages. They were skilful in the art of Śatalēkhini and filling up literary verse puzzles (padyapūraṇam). They were able to compose verses at the rate of one hundred in an hour (ghaṭikāśata), and to compose poetry in eight bhāshas (Sanskrit, Telugu and the six Prākrits). They knew how to interpret and explain the poems and dramas (kávyas and nāṭakas) composed by the famous poets, and to explain the secrets of the music of the two sorts (Karṇāṭa and Dēśa). They were able to sing very sweetly and to play on the vīṇa and such other musical instruments as the Rāvaṇahasta. Raghunātha examined the proficiency of all of them and presented them with Kanakābhishēka (bathing in gold).

Sarga XII.—Raghunātha heard the songs sung before him and witnessed the dances of the accomplished ladies of his court. Some of the rāgas, etc., that were sung before him were designed by Raghunātha himself who was a master of the art. The chief rāgas that they sung were Jayamangaḷa, Simhaḷalīla, Jayanissāru(?) and Kachachcharitra (?). Some of the tāḷas to which they were played were Ratilīla, Turangalīla, Rangābharaṇa and Anangaparikramaṇa, Abhinandana, Nandanandana and Abhimāla. Among the dances that were exhibited before him there was one called Raghunāthavilāsa named after himself.

In the colophon the talented authoress says that she got her learning by the favour of the god Rāmabhadra, and that she was an expert in the arts of Śatalēkhini and Samayalēkhini, that she was able to write the four sorts of poetry in all the eight languages (Sanskrit, Telugu and the six Prākrits). She also says that she was installed on the throne of Sāhitya Sāmrājya (empress among poets).

Sarga I.

रसप्रधानान् रघुनाथनेतुः प्रबन्धभेदान्मम भावयन्त्याः ।
प्राङ्निर्मितानेककविप्रबन्धप्रस्तावनाय प्रभवेन्मतिं किम् ॥ ९ ॥
शब्दार्थयोर्मर्म समप्रधानं वशंवदं यस्य वदन्ति सर्वे ।
कृती स एवात्र कृतौ सहायो नाथो मम श्रीरघुनाथनामा ॥ १० ॥

Sarga III.

चिन्तासमस्याशतमेकदैष वक्तीति वार्ता न हि वर्णनाय ।
अशेषलोकाशयवृत्तभेदप्रस्तारविद्याप्रथितस्य यस्य ॥ १९ ॥
अन्तःपुरान्तर्हरिणेक्षणासु त्रिहायणीनामपि दीप्यमानान् ।
विलोक्य विद्याविभवानजस्रं वशंवदां यस्य वदन्ति वाणीम् ॥ २० ॥
अमुष्य गाम्भीर्यमपांनिधानमपाकरोतीति तदन्तरस्थाः ।
नेपालभूपादिनृपेश्वराणां भयाकुला यं शरणं भजन्ते ॥ २६ ॥

Sarga VI.

ततस्सभां तां मगधौ समेत्य लक्ष्मीविलासाभिधया लसन्तीम् ।
वंशानुपूर्वीं वसुधासुधांशोराशंसतां वाग्भिरतिप्रगल्भाम् ॥ १ ॥
तस्यां प्रसूताः धरणीमहेन्द्राः महौजसः केचन माननीयाः ॥
तेषु प्रतीतेष्वजनि प्रकामं तिम्मक्षमाभृत्तिलकः प्रतीतः ॥ ३ ॥
सरोजगर्भस्य सरस्वतीव पद्मेव पाथोरुहलोचनस्य ।
पतिव्रतासु प्रथमाभिधेया बय्यांम्बिका तस्य बभूव भार्या ॥ ४ ॥
ततः प्रभावेन तयोरवन्यां प्रमोदहेतुस्सकलप्रजानाम् ।
. . . . इवाजनिष्ट चव्वाभिधानः क्षितिपालचन्द्रः ॥ ५ ॥
शोणाद्रिनाथं सुपदास्समेत्य पुरास्समस्तास्सुकरं भजन्ताम् ।
इत्येव यो हेममयं महेन्द्रपुरातिगं गोपुरमाततान ॥ ७ ॥
वियत्तले यो विबुधाग्रसीम्नि नित्यं नटन्त्यां निजकीर्तिनव्याम् ।
स्तम्भं यथा वृद्धगिरौ चकार स्फुरन्मणीगोपुरमिन्दुमौलेः ॥ ८ ॥
श्रीशैलनाथस्य सितांशुमौलेः प्राकारसोपानपरम्परादीन् ।
स्वनामचिह्नान् सकलोपचारान् चक्रे स्थिरं यो नृपसार्वभौमः ॥ ९ ॥
महान्ति दानानि मरुद्वृधायाः तटान्तिके दैवतमन्दिराणि ।
महाग्रहारांश्च महीमहेन्द्रश्चकार यश्शाश्वतधर्मकेतुः ॥ १० ॥
भार्याभवत्तस्य धरावलारेः मूर्त्यम्बिका मूर्तिमतीव कीर्तिः ।
आढ्या गुणैरच्युतरायदेव्याः सहोदरा श्लाघ्यतरप्रभावा ॥ ११ ॥
अपत्यभावेन तयोरवन्याम् अजायताम्भोजदलाक्ष एव ।
अनेकजन्मार्जितभाग्यराशिराकारवानच्युतभूमिपालः ॥ १२ ॥

विधाय हेम्ना रुचिरं विमानं रत्नैश्चिरत्नैरपि रङ्गधाम्नः ।
किरीटराजं च कृती चकार सिंहासनं चापि च राजसिंहः ॥
रामेश्वरे राजकलाधरस्य समर्प्य कैंकर्यशतानि सम्यक् ।
खिलानि तीर्थाण्यखिलानि सोऽयं चकार तत्रैव जगत्प्रसिद्धम् ॥ १४ ॥
मुक्तातुलापूरुषमुख्यदानान्यसंख्यदेवायतनान्यवन्ध्याम् ।
महाग्रहारान्स महामहिम्ना नित्यानि चक्रे नृपचक्रवर्ती ॥ १९ ॥
सती गुणानां वसतिस्सतीव पद्मेव वाणीव जगत्प्रतीता ।
मूर्त्यम्बिका शोभनमूर्तिरस्य भार्याभवद्भव्यतरस्वचर्या ॥ २० ॥
पुरातनैरद्यतनैश्च पुण्यैः पुत्रत्वभाजः पुरुषोत्तमस्य ।
राजा स चक्रे रघुनाथनाम शास्त्रोक्तमार्गेण सधर्मदारः ॥ ५६ ॥

Sarga VII.

एवं शुभाकारसमेतमेतं हर्षोदयादच्युतभूमहेन्द्रः ।
अग्राहयत्पाणिमथात्मजातं पाण्ड्यादिभूपालककन्यकानाम् ॥ ३४ ॥
अनन्तरं श्लाघ्यगुणातिरेकलक्ष्यं प्रजारक्षणलक्षणाढ्यम् ।
ऐच्छद्विधातुं विभुरत्युदारंयुवानमेनं युवराजसंज्ञम् ॥ ३९ ॥
ऊढं प्रयत्नाच्चिरमुर्वरायाः भरं तनूजाय भरं वितीर्य ।
अवाप तस्मादवनीसुधांशुः अमन्दमानन्दभरं स्वयं च ॥ ४२ ॥
अतिप्रगल्भैरथ पारसीकैः समं प्रवृत्ते सति साम्पराये ।
कर्णाटरक्षाकरणे नितान्तं विचारवान्वेङ्कटदेवरायः ॥ ४३ ॥
गन्धान्धभूमीधवगन्धनागकण्ठीरवं शौर्यकथानिदानम् ।
रणे सहायं रघुनाथदेवं अयाचतोर्जस्वलमच्युतेन्द्रम् ॥ ४४ ॥
गुरोर्निदेशाद्गुरुराजकन्या(कार्य)म् निर्वाहको नीतिपराध्वनीनः ।
सामन्तभूपालशतानुयातो जयप्रयाणाय समुद्यतोऽभूत् ॥ ९६ ॥
समासदच्चन्द्रगिरिप्रतीतां पुरीं नृपालः पुरुहूतकल्पः ।
कटाक्षयंस्तामथ कैश्चिदेव प्रभुः प्रयाणैः पेनुकोण्डनामा(म्नी?) ।
कर्णाटनेतुः कुलराजधानीमालोककासेचनिकामयासीत (?) ॥ ६० ॥
वीराग्रणीर्वेङ्कटदेवरायः विनिर्मितैर्नैकविधोपचारैः ।
उदूढवेषैः स नवोपकार्यामध्यास्त तस्यामवनीशसूनुः ॥ ६२ ॥

कर्णाटरक्षाकरणाय तूर्णं समागतं तं सह सैन्यसंघैः ।
आकर्ण्य चारैरभजन्सदारा वनानि केचिद्यवना निगूढाः ॥ ६३ ॥
आरक्तनेत्राञ्चलभीषणास्यैः अमुक्तगर्वोन्मिषिताट्टहासैः ।
आरूढकाम्भोजहयैर्भटौघैः अभिक्रमत्कैस्तु (?) तदा तमन्ये ॥ ६४ ॥
नाराचपातैर्नरदेवसूनोः पलायमानाश्चरणे पतन्तः ।
अत्याकुलत्वादभयार्थिनस्ते रामास्त्रतो रात्रिचरा इवासन् ॥ ६५ ॥
प्रख्यातबल्लालपुरादिसर्वदुर्गान्तरस्थाः परदुर्निरीक्ष्याः ।
मुहुर्नदन्तो मुरसामहीपं प्रत्युद्व्रजन्तिस्म रणे प्रतीतम् ॥ ६६ ॥
विजित्य युद्धे विमतानशेषान् कर्णाटभूमीकमितुस्तदानीम् ।
स्थलानि दुर्गाणि जगत्प्रसिद्धं वशंवदास्य(न्य)स्य विभुर्व्यतानीत् ॥६८।
अभ्यागमात्तस्य निजारिवर्गविसंस्थुले वेङ्कटदेवरायः ।
प्रमोदमानस्सह बन्धुवर्गैः अमन्यत स्वं स्थिरमाधिराज्यम् ॥ ६९ ॥
राज्ञां समक्षं रघुनाथभूपं प्रशस्य भूमीपतिरेवमूचे ।
अभ्यागमादेव तवाजनिष्ट निष्कण्टकं राज्यमिदं नृपाल ॥ ७० ॥
इति ब्रुवन्नादरमेव योग्यान् भूमीभुजे वाहनभूषणादीन् ।
वितीर्य तं वेङ्कटदेवरायो बलाढ्यमेनं बहुमन्यते स्म ॥ ७१ ॥
अत्रान्तरे भूपकुलावतंसः तुण्डीरनाथं परिदूयमानम् ।
काराश्रितं तत्प्रमदाकदम्बात् आकर्णयद्दीनजनावलम्बः ॥ ७२ ॥
तदात्ययोवार्तधराधिनाथः रक्षैकतानो रघुनाथभूपः ।
काराश्रितं कृष्णपनायकं तं व्यमोचयद्वेङ्कटदेवरायात् ॥ ७३ ॥
तुण्डीरनाथस्सवधूरनाथः प्रणम्य भक्त्या पदयोरमुष्य ।
करं स्वसुर्ग्राहयति स्म सद्यो रक्षाधुरीणं रघुनाथमेनम् ॥ ७४ ॥
कर्णाटसिंहासनकार्यभारं निर्वर्त्य सर्वं विनिवर्तमानम् ।
अथाच्युतक्ष्मापतिरात्मसूनुं प्रत्युज्जगाम प्रमदातिरेकात् ॥ ७६ ॥

Sarga VIII.

अथाच्युतक्षितिरमणात्मसम्भवो निषेवितः प्रबलनृपालपालिभिः ।
अधिष्ठितो मणिमयमासनं व्यधात् भुवं श्रितस्सदसि पुरन्दरो यथा ॥ १ ॥
भूमीश्वरैर्जगति विट्ठलराजपूर्वैः अन्यैरमेयबलशालिभिरप्यजेयः ।
आराध्य भैरवमवाप्य वरं दुरापं शूराग्रणिश्चरति चोलगनामधेयः ॥ ७ ॥

अथिपयोधि दशास्य इवापरः प्रबलबाहुबलः परदुस्सहः ।
जगदशेषमिदं जगतीपते क्षुभितमेव करोति स चोलगः ॥ ८ ॥
कथमिदं कथयामि कृपानिधे श्रुणु नृपाल स चोलगरावणः ।
प्रतिदिनं हरते पतिदेवताः परवधू रनिवार्यपराक्रमः ॥ ९ ॥
श्रुत्वा तदा सदसि चोलगदुष्टचेष्टा-
मापाद्य भूदिविषदामभयप्रदानम् ।
वीराग्रणीस्स रघुनाथविभुस्समस्तैः
अस्तूयत द्विजवरैरतिमोदमानैः ॥ १२ ॥
अथ वेत्रिजनोऽवदन्महीशं नृप नेपालनृपोऽतितूर्णम् ।
भवनाङ्गणमेत्य बन्धुवर्गैः समयं संप्रति वीक्षते त्वदीयम् ॥ १३ ॥
इतीरयन्तं तमवेक्ष्य सोऽयम् आनीयतामित्यवनीबिडौजाः ।
अर्हैः पुरस्कार्य तदात्मनीनैः आस्थानसीमानमनीनयत्तम् ॥ १४ ॥
स्वागतं वदतिनागमे(रमे?)नम् ! मञ्जुवाग्भिरवनीमिहिकांशौ ।
अन्तरीपपतिरानतमौलिः व्याहरद्विनयतो निजवृत्तम् ॥ १५ ॥
चिनचेव्वयभूपशेखरेण प्रथितेनाच्युतभूमिपालकेन ।
मकुटाभरणं ममैव वंश्याः रघुनाथक्षितिनाथरक्षितास्ते ॥ १६ ॥
महीपते मम कुलजैर्महाभुजैः पराजितास्समिति परङ्गिवंशजाः ।
तदादि ते मनसि दृढं विरोधितां प्रवर्धयन्त्यवमतिपङ्करूषिताः ॥ १८ ॥
तत्तादृग्भुजमहसस्तरीमेता
मत्तास्ताकरवलमानमण्डलाग्राः ।
कल्पान्तज्वलनकरालनेत्रकोणाः
निश्शङ्कं सलिलनिधौ चरन्ति नित्यम् ॥ १९ ॥
मय्यारामालोकने मग्नचित्ते वेलां सर्वे ते विचार्यैव तूर्णम् ।
वप्रैर्दीप्रां वार्धिखेयां पुरीं मे संघीभूयच्छद्मकृत्यैरगृह्णन् ॥ २० ॥
नगपते सकलं नगराद्बहिः विरचितं विमतैर्विषमं तदा ।
परमुखादवकर्ण्य सरित्पतिं परिविलङ्घ्य भवन्तमशिश्रियम् ॥ २१ ॥
इति धरणिधवेऽस्मिन्नीरयत्यात्मवृत्तं
सदसि स रघुनाथक्ष्मापतिः प्रत्यवादीत् ।

अखिलमपिच भूयोऽप्याधिपत्यं समस्तं
निजकरगतमेवावेहि नेपालभूप ॥ २२ ॥
इतिवादिनि मेदिनीश्वरेऽस्मिन् अवहत्सम्मदमन्तरीपभूपः ।
अथ कश्चिदुपागतो विनीत्या समयज्ञैस्समभाषतावनीशम् ॥ २३ ॥
कर्णाटभूपाश्रयिभिः कृतज्ञैः कैश्चिन्महीशैर्नृपराजकार्यम् ।
संजल्पितुं सम्प्रति सम्मुखे ते संप्रेषितास्सत्वरमेव चाराः ॥ २४ ॥
इतीरयित्वा स महेशमौलेः अपाङ्गसंज्ञामवगम्य चारान् ।
अनीनयत्सम्मुखमानतास्ते न्यवेदयन्नीतिविदे विधेयम् ॥ २५ ॥
विष्णोः पदं श्रयति वेङ्कटदेवराये
सर्वे तदीयसचिवा युवराजसूनुम् ।
भद्रासने तदनु भूभरणाय तूर्णं
श्रीरङ्गरायनृपशेखरमभ्यषिञ्चन् ॥ २६ ॥
तस्मिन्महीं शासति तं समस्ताः पुरातना भूपतयो भजन्तः ।
द्रोहं विधातुं द्रुतमेव तस्मै जनाधिनाथाय स जग्गराजः ॥ २७ ॥
सानुजो निशि स जग्गमहीशः पार्थिवस्य भवनं परिवेष्ट्यच
भूपतिं तदनु पुत्रकलत्रैः निर्घृणो निहतमातनुते स्म ॥ २८ ॥
तनयेषु नृपाल तस्य कश्चित् शिशुमाप्तो रजकस्समेत्य शीघ्रम् ।
अनयन्नगराद्बहिर्निशायाम् अतिचौर्याद्द्विषतामनक्षिलक्ष्यम् ॥ २९ ॥
केचिदेनमुपगम्य कृतज्ञाः पार्थिवास्तदहितान्प्रतिकारम् ।
नेतुमक्षमतया नृपतेऽस्मान् प्रापयन्परिसरं भवदीयम् ॥ ३० ॥
आपदां पदमनन्यशरण्यं राजपुत्रमवनीरमणस्त्वम् ।
सिंहपीठमधिरोपय शीघ्रं जग्गराजमपि (संहर) युद्धे ॥ ३१ ॥
बाल्येऽपि सिंहासनकार्यभागः कृतः स्वयं कीर्तिनिधे पुनश्च ।
स एष कार्यस्सकलप्रयत्नात् भुजाबलाढ्यो भुवने त्वमेव ॥ ३२ ॥
इत्थंचारैरीरितं रायवृत्तं श्रुत्वा सर्वं क्षोणिपालाग्रगण्यः ।
कर्तुं तूर्णं कार्यमेतत्तदानीं वीरोत्तंसो व्याहरन्मन्त्रिवर्यान् ॥ ३३ ॥
सिन्ध्वन्तरीपगतचोळगशिक्षणं च नेपाळदेशनृपशात्रवनिग्रहश्च ।
कर्णाटभूपतिनवीकरणं च सर्वमापाद्यमेव मम दिग्विजयापदेशात् ॥ ३४ ॥

एवं तदानीमवनीशमौळिः आज्ञाप्य सर्वानपि वाहिनीशान् ।
अर्हान्नियुज्यात्मपुरावनाय यात्राप्रयाणाय समुद्यतोऽभूत् ॥ ७१ ॥

अवलोकयन्नमितवस्तुसम्भृताः पथि कल्पिताः बहुविधोपकारिकाः ।
अधिसह्यजातटमतीवपावनीमुदकुम्भघोणनगरीमगान्नृपः ॥ ७२ ॥

अथ तत्र विन(?)तः सुदेवतौघं प्रबलेनात्मबलेन सेव्यमानः ।
शकुनैश्शुभसूचकैस्सहर्षं निरगान्निश्चितदिग्जयो नृपालः ॥ ७६ ॥

परितो बलरेणुभिः प्रगल्भैः परिघां शात्रवपट्टणस्य सिन्धुम् ।
अवनीपतिराविलङ्घ्य . . . . ॥ ७७ ॥

अवार्यशौर्यादवनीवलारेः शूरोऽपि भीतो हृदि चोळगोऽस्मात् ।
अयाचतास्मैरध कृष्णभूपं बलैस्समेतं प्रधने सहायम् ॥ ७८ ॥

तदा ब्रुवन् कृष्णधराधिनेतुः मनीषिणो मन्त्रिजना विनीत्या ।
विशांपतेऽस्मद्विदितं तवाद्य विज्ञापयामस्सविमर्श एव ॥ ७९ ॥

बलवत्परिपन्थिभिर्गृहीतो बहुधा त्वं परिमोचितोऽपि तेन ।
प्रभुणा रघुनाथपार्थिवेन प्रधनं भूमिपते न ते प्रशस्तम् ॥ ८० ॥

एवं तदानीं हितवादिनस्तान् निरस्य भूपो निजमन्त्रिवृद्धान् ।
प्रचोदितो दुर्विधिना बलौघैः उपागमत्तं नगरोपकण्ठम् ॥ ८१ ॥

मध्येसमुद्रमतिमानुषविक्रमं तम्
आलोक्य भूपतिरुपायशतैरसाध्यम् ।
प्राग्जन्मदाशरथिरेष बलानि दृष्ट्वा
बन्द्धुं न्ययुङ्क्त सहसा पतिमापगानाम् ॥ ८४ ॥

सिन्धौ प्रवृत्ते सति सेतुबन्धे तदाप्यनम्रं तमतीव गर्वात् ।
विक्ष . . मालोच्य विशामधीशो विशिष्य रोषारुणवक्षिणोऽभूत् ॥ ८६ ॥

अथावनीपतिराधिरुह्य वारणं विलङ्घ्य तं सलिलनिधिं विरोधिनः ।
पुरीं रयादाधिगतवीर(?) पुंगवां न्यरुद्ध तां निरुपमविक्रमक्रमः ॥ ८७ ॥

प्राकारचारिभटमुक्तशिलाकलापदृष्ट्या सधूमविसरो वियति व्यलोकि ।
पाषाणवर्षपरिपूरितदिग्विभागा कल्पान्तदुस्सहघना घनमण्डलीव ॥ ९२ ॥

अथादिशद्विभुरतिरोषभीषणः चमूं निजां वरणसमीपचारिणीम् ।
पुरःस्थितं विकलयितुं पुरं रयात् विरोधिनो विविधबलैराधिष्ठिते(तं) ॥ ९३ ॥

निश्श्रेणिकाभिर्नृपसैन्यसङ्घैः प्राकारमाक्रामति तद्भटौघः ।
प्रणामपूर्वं प्रणिगद्य सान्त्व मदुद्रुवत्तूर्णमवाप्तशस्त्रः ॥ ९४ ॥
अत्याहिताद्गळितधैर्यमवाप्तशस्त्रम्
आलोक्य सैन्यमभितः परिधावमानम् ।
शोकाकुलं सपदि चोळगमेक्ष्य शोच्यं
कारुण्यमाविरभवत्कमितुर्धरायाः ॥ ९५ ॥
कान्तायुक्तं क्लृप्त . . . . हन्तव्यो मा मां शरण्यं प्रपन्नः ।
एवं भृत्यानीरयन्भूमिपालो जीवग्राहं तूर्णमग्राहयत्तम् ॥ ९६ ॥
अरिवशंगतवत्यथ चोळगे गळितधियन् (?) कृष्णपनायकः ।
अधिकभीरथी . . पवनवेगे . . . मतीव पलायितः ॥ ९७ ॥
करुणा तव चोळगे न कार्या नृप कारानिलये निधेहि शीघ्रम् ।
इति विप्रवरैरुदीरितस्तं धरणीपालमणिस्तथा व्यतानीत् ॥ १०० ॥

Sarga IX.

अथाखिलाशाविजयोत्सुकाय महीभुजे चोळगमानहन्त्रे ।
नेपाळभूमौ निजकार्यभागं व्यजिज्ञपन्मन्त्रयतो विनीत्या ॥ १ ॥
वेलापथे तस्य विभोर्गजानां कर्णानिलैः केतकगर्भरेणुः ।
प्रसारितस्तत्र पयःपयोधिमाकल्पयन्तं लवणाम्बुराशिम् ॥ ३ ॥
विना प्रगल्भं विमतान्जिगीषुः महीपतिस्तत्र महाम्बुराशौ ।
तरीभिरेतत्तरणाय तूर्णम् अकल्पयत्सेतुमनन्यसाध्यम् ॥ १२ ॥
आरभ्य वेलामभितोऽम्बुराशेः मनीषिणां सत्वरमापतन्तीम् ।
आलोक्य तामाहवकौतुकोत्कैः अभावि नेपालनृपालवर्गैः ॥ १४ ॥
अयोमयाभिर्नळिकावलीभिः अपाङ्गकोणैरपि रोषशोणैः ।
अवाकिरं स्त्वग्निकणान्विपक्षा भूपालसैन्येषु पुरःस्थितेषु ॥ १८ ॥
परंगियोधप्रहितैः क्षुरप्रैः विभोधभून्नेवचमूर्तिहस्ता (?) ।
परागजातं किमु पद्मजातं प्रगल्भते शोषविधौ पयोधेः ॥ १९ ॥
उदस्तनानायुधमुत्पताकमभिद्रवन्तीमवनीशसेनाम् ।
आलोकितुं स्थातुमशक्नुवन्तो भयात्पलायन्त परंगिवंश्याः ॥ २१ ॥
धनानि धा(दा?) रैः सममार्जितानि शस्त्राणि शौर्येण समं धृतानि ।
विहाय सर्वे भयविह्वलास्ते निधौ जलानां न्यपतन्सवेगम् ॥ २२ ॥

विधाय विद्वेषिपदं स्वयोधैः विभाषणं राम इवात्मभक्तम् ।
नेपालभूपं रघुनाथनेता तदास्पदे तत्र तमभ्यषिञ्चत् ॥ २३ ॥
अथावनीवासवमभ्युपेत्य चाराः प्रक्लृप्ताखिलदिक्प्रचाराः ।
व्यजिज्ञपन्कार्यविदो विरोधिप्रवर्तितं वृत्तमिति पृथिव्याम् ॥ २४ ॥
सिंहासनद्रोहविधानशीला जिघांसवस्तं क्षितिपालबालम् ।
तुण्डीरपाण्ड्यादिमदुष्टभूपैः विचारयन्ते विपदं जगत्याम् ॥ २५ ॥
अदभ्रवीचीभ्रमदभ्रकल्पगन्धर्वरेखान्वितगन्धनागः ।
महारवस्तस्य महीसुधांशोश्चमूसमूहस्समजृम्भताग्रे ॥ २६ ॥
आत्मीयसैन्याहृतचन्दनौघं पाटीरशैलं यशसा प्रसाद्य ।
अथ प्रतीच्यामरिराजधानीं तोपूरभिख्यामगमत्ससतूर्णम् ॥ २७ ॥
परेद्यवि प्रौढरणःपरैर्नो भविष्यतीति प्रतियूधनाथन् ।
न्यवेशयन्वेत्रधरा निशायां निदेशतस्तत्र नृपालमौळिः ॥ ४८ ॥
व्यधुः पुरा सह्यसुताविभंगं योभूमिह(?) स्तानिह पाटयामः ।
एवं सजातीयतया धरेन्द्राश्चमूद्विपेन्द्रच्छलतो न्यगच्छन् ॥ ६० ॥
भटावलीरायुधयन्त्रभाजो वर्तिज्वलद्वह्निकणा(?)व्यराजन् ।
प्राणानिलग्रासपरा परेषान अहीन्द्रपाळीव विषाग्नियुक्ता ॥ ६६ ॥
अभिषेणनमद्भुतं रणोर्व्यां रघुनाथक्षितिपेन रच्यमानम् ।
अवलोक्य भयात्तदाहवोत्कैः तरिभिः पाण्ड्यनृपादिमैरभावि ॥ ६७ ॥

Sarga X.

अभ्यायान्तीमभ्यगच्छन् महीन्दोः नेपाल(?)पाण्ड्यक्ष्मापसेनाथ तूर्णम् ।
पूर्वाम्भोधिं घोषसंपूरिताशं प्रौढध्वानः पश्चिमो वा पयोधिः ॥ १ ॥
अन्योन्येषामग्नियन्त्रादुदीतैः धूमैर्यूधा दुर्निरीक्षा रणोर्व्याम् ।
अश्वान् रोषाविष्कृतात्मापदानैः अन्यान्ज्ञात्वा सैन्ययोरात्तशौर्यान् ॥ २ ।
सङ्ग्रामान्तस्सादिवर्गेण क्लृप्ताः काम्भोजानां मण्डलाकाररेखा ।
पादातानामच्युतक्ष्मापसूनोः प्राकारोऽभूद्दुर्निरीक्षं विपक्षैः ॥ १४ ॥
पाण्ड्यक्षोणीपालसैन्यैः स्वसैन्यैः प्रत्यावृत्तैः जग्गराजस्सबन्धुः ।
बद्धोत्साहः प्रत्यगात्पार्थिवेन्द्रं भास्वन्तं द्राक्पावकं वा पतङ्गः ॥ २८ ।
अग्रे योधैरच्युतक्ष्मापसूनोः (आलोक्याराद्च्युतक्ष्मापसूनुः)

क्रोधावेशाद्वृम्भितः कुन्तजातैः (कोपारक्तापाङ्गकोणोऽजनिष्ट) ।
भ्रश्यत्प्राणो बन्धुवर्गेण साकं जन्यक्षोण्यां जग्गराजः पपात ॥ २९ ॥
छिन्नं सेतुं शीर्षजालैर्नवीनं पाथः पूर्णं कण्ठरक्तैः परेषाम् ।
सन्तन्वानस्सह्यजायास्तदानीम् आभाचौर्यामच्युतक्ष्मापसूनुः ॥ ३३ ॥
जन्यैस्सैन्यैर्जग्गाराजादिमेषु व्यापन्नेषु व्याप्तिभिः पाण्ड्यवीरः ।
क्षोणीरक्षाक्षोभ्यबाहाबलाढ्यो ह्यात्मप्राणत्राणयत्नाकुलोऽभूत् ॥ ३४ ॥
स्कन्धावारे गन्धनागाश्वसंघान् योषारत्नद्रव्यभूषाविशेषान् ।
पाण्ड्यस्त्यक्त्वा प्राणभीत्या समित्यां धीमान्क्रोशं प्राद्रवद्दीनदीनः ॥ ३५
तुण्डीराणामीशिता दुर्नयेन प्रापय्यैवं पाण्ड्यमत्यन्तभङ्गम् ।
सद्योऽधावीत्तेन साकं रणोर्व्याम अग्रेस्सैन्यैर्हास्यमानोऽस्तलज्जम् ॥ ३६॥
वीरे वीराशंसने घोषपूर्वं धैर्यं त्यक्त्वा धावतां क्ष्मापतीनाम् ।
संघैस्साकं स्रस्तहस्तायुधस्सन् विघ्नोऽधावीत्तत्र राविल्लवेंकः ॥ ३७ ॥
व्यर्थान्भूयो व्याहरन्वीरवादान् युद्धक्षोणीं शूरवद्योद्धुमेत्य ।
प्रागेव द्राक्प्राद्रवत्पाण्ड्यभूपात् मध्येसैन्यं माकराजन्यदैन्यम् ॥ ३८ ॥
जन्मारभ्यादृष्टसङ्ग्रामरङ्गः चश्चद्दर्वी रायदल्लापिचश्चः ।
रक्तासिक्तान्राजराजीकबन्धान् द्वारे दृष्ट्वादुद्रुवद्धूयमानः ॥ ३९ ॥
धीरोदात्तो दीनरक्षाधुरीणः सद्यो भूपस्सह्यकन्यातटाग्रे ।
प्रौढां कीर्तिं प्रातुकामो व्यतानीत् पाण्ड्यक्षोणीपालकप्राणदानम् ॥ ६१ ॥
अथ सह्यसुतातटाग्रभूमावुदयत्कीर्तिलतातते रुपघ्नम् ।
. . . वीरविग्रह . . . विजयस्तम्भं च विशामधीशः ॥ ६३ ॥
तुण्डीरेभ्यो दृष्टराजालयेभ्यः चाराः केचित् दृष्टकार्यप्रचाराः ।
अभ्यागच्छन्नच्युतक्ष्मापसूनोः आस्थानीं तामक्षिसाफल्यधात्रीम् ॥ ६० ॥
भटैः पुरा तव समरे पराजितः त्रपां विना धरणिधवैस्स्वसन्निभैः ।
विचारयन्त्यधिपमणेर्विरोधितां स कृष्णभूपतिरतिसत्ववानिव ॥ ६९ ॥
अवनीपतिराशये विधेयं सकलं हस्तगतं विचार्य सम्यक् ।
अथ पञ्चनदं शनैरयासीत् तटमार्गेण मरुद्वृधाताटिन्याः ॥ ६७ ॥
अधिवसन्नथ तत्र सभान्तरे समुपगम्य समाचरितानतीन् ।
उपगतोत्तरदिग्विजयोत्सवान् प्रभुरलोकत यूधपतीन्निजान् ॥ ७४ ॥

अधिपतिरविदन्नथागतास्ते विमतधराधरवीररक्षितानि ।
भुवनगिरिमुखानि भूपदुर्गाण्यहृत स सत्वरमस्मदीययोधैः ॥ ७५ ॥
अथ कृष्णजनाधिपः समेतो यतिराजप्रमुखैरतीव यत्नात् ।
समराय समागतोऽस्मदीयैः भटवर्यैर्विदितः पलायितोऽभूत् ॥ ७६ ॥
एवंवादिषु यूधनाथ . . . .
. . . . . . रघुनाथभूपतिरुकस्संभाव्य तान्सादरम् ।
प्रौढक्ष्मापकुलावतंसविलसत्पार्श्वद्वयीकैर्बलैः
आनन्दातिशयादयान्निजपुरीं तञ्जाभिधानां तदा ॥ ७७ ॥

Canto XI.

ततस्स तासां धरणीपुरन्दरः चतुर्विधोद्दामकवित्वचातुरीम् ।
अशेषभाषानुगुणप्रपञ्चितप्रबन्धसन्दर्भविशेषपाटवम् ॥ २३ ॥
सम(?)प्रधानं शतलेखिनीसमं प्रक्लृप्तनानाविधपद्यपूरणम् ।
सलीलजाग्रद्घटिकाशतोचितक्रमाष्टभाषाकविताविजृम्भणम् ॥ २४ ॥
कविप्रणीताखिलकाव्यनाटकप्रबन्धतत्त्वप्रतिपादनक्रमम् ।
कर्णाटदेशादिमकल्पितश्रुतप्रगल्भगूढार्थविवादपाटवम् ॥ २५ ॥
सुधारसस्यन्दिसुगीतिचातुरीप्रवीणवीणाप्रतिमानवादनम् ।
स्वरानुकूला . . . . ॥ २६ ॥
अनेकधा रावणहस्तपूर्वकप्रसिद्धयन्त्रस्वनरक्तिपाटवम् ।
यथाक्रमप्राञ्चितमध्यरागसत्पदाद्यपद्यद्विपदप्रपञ्चनम् ॥ २७ ॥
परीक्ष्य सम्यक् प्रतिबोध्य चाधिकं विशेषमुर्वीविभुरत्युदारधीः ।

* * * *

Sarga XII.

चञ्चत्पुटाद्यैर्नृपतेः समीपे भवान्यजातैर्नटनप्रपञ्चम् ।
प्रपञ्चयत्पञ्चविधैस्सलीलं मृगेक्षणा काचन मार्गतालैः ॥ २३ ॥
जयमङ्गलसिंहललीला जयनिस्सारुणकचच्चरित्रभिन्नैः (?) ।
रतिलीलतुरंगलीलरंगाभरणानंगपरिक्रमादितालैः ॥ २४ ॥
अभिनन्दननन्दनन्दनाद्यैरभिमालादिभिरन्यकैश्च तालैः ।
रघुनाथविलासमुख्यलास्यान्यबला काचिदकल्पयत्सलीलम् ॥ २५ ॥

Colophon.

इति श्रीरामभद्रकरुणाकटाक्षलब्धसारसारस्वतप्रवर्धमानशतलेखिनीसम-
यलेखिनीद्याष्टभाषाकल्पितचतुर्विधकवितानुप्राणितसाहित्यसाम्राज्यपदपीठा-
रूढरामभद्राम्बाविरचिते रघुनाथाभ्युदये महाकाव्ये द्वादशः सर्गः समाप्तः ॥

92

CHIKKADĒVARĀYA VAMŚĀVALI.

[*By Tirumalārya.*]

This history of the Woḍeyars of Mysore was written in Kanarese by Tirumalārya, the prime minister of Chikkadēvarāja Woḍeyar. In the beginning of the work some account is given of the origin of the Woḍeyars and their relation to the empire of Vijayanagar. In the empire of Vijayanagar after the reigns of the emperors Narasa, Vīranarasimha, Krishnarāya, and Achyuta, Sadāśivarāya succeeded. During his reign all power was vested in his brother-in-law and commander-in-chief Rāma Rāya, born of a Telugu family. In one of his invasions against the Yavana (Muhammadan) kingdoms of the north he lost his life. His younger brother Yeṛa Timma Rāja then made himself the ruler setting aside the nominal sovereign Sadāśiva. After a short time he changed his capital from Vijayanagar to Penukoṇḍa (Ghanagiri) on account of the constant attacks of the Muhammadans. Of his three sons Śrīranga Rāya was the viceroy of the whole Telugu country with his capital at Penukoṇḍa. His brother Rāma Rāya ruled the whole Kanarese country from his capital Seringapatam. Venkaṭapati, the third brother, was the viceroy of the Tundīra, Chōḷa and Pāṇḍya countries with his capital at Chandragiri. Of these three Srīranga Rāya died without issue and his younger brother Venkaṭapati succeeded him at Penukoṇḍa as emperor.

Rāma Rāya, the other brother of Śrīrangarāya, died after a short time leaving his sons Tirumala Rāya and others. These brothers left the administration of the viceroyalty in the hands of their Daḷavāi Rēmaṭi Venkaṭayya.

Later on Venkaṭapati Rāya declared war against Vīrappa Nāyaka of Madura, and laid siege to the Fort of Madura with a large army. But Vīrappa Nāyaka managed to bribe the several generals of the emperor's army. Tirumala Rāya, the emperor's nephew, was also one of those that accepted the bribe and retired, without continuing the siege of Madura, to the capital of his own viceroyalty, Seringapatam. Hearing of these events the Mysore chief Rāja Woḍeyar resolved to drive the traitor Tirumala Rāya from his viceroyalty and sent his spies to test the feeling among Tirumala Rāya's feudatories.

ಅತ್ತಲುತ್ತರದೇಶದೊಳ್ ತುಂಗಭದ್ರಾ ತೀರದೊಳ್ ವಿದ್ಯಾನಗರಿಯ ನಾಳ್ದ ಹರಿಹರಬುಕ್ಕರ್ಮೊದಲಾದ ಕುಱುಂಬರಾಯರ ಅನನ್ತರದೊಳರಸುಗೆಯ್ದ ತುಳುವಕುಳದೀಕ್ಷ್ವರ ನರಸ ವೀರನರಸಿಂಗ ಕೃಷ್ಣಾಚ್ಯುತರೆಂಬ ರಾಯರ್ಗ್ಯವರ ತಱುವಾಯಿಂ ಮುಂದೆದೊಳಿಳೆಯಂ ಪೊರೆದಿ ಸದಾಶಿವರಾಯಂಗೆ ಸೇನಾನಿಯೆನಿಸಿದ ಆಂಧ್ರಕುಲದ ರಾಮರಾಜಂ, ನಿಜರಾಜಂಗೆ ದ್ರವಿಡಾನ್ಧ್ರ) ಕರ್ಣಾಟ ಸಾಮ್ರಾಜ್ಯಮಂ ಸಾರ್ಚಿ ಪತಿಕಾರ್ಯದೊಳರ್ಪಿತಪ್ರಾಣನನಿಸಿ, ಒರ್ಮೆಯುತ್ತರದಿಗ್ವಿಜಯದೊಳುದ್ವೃತ್ತಯವನ ಸೇನಾ ಚಕ್ರಮನೊಕ್ಕಲಿಕ್ಕಿ ಯಶಶ್ಶೇಷನಪ್ಪನು ಮವನನುಜಂ ಎರದಿಮ್ಮರಾಜಂ ಅಂದಿನಾಜಿಯೊಳಱಿದುಱಿದರನೊಡಗೊಂಡು ಊರ್ಗೆ ನಡೆತಂದಾಳ್ದನ ಸಿರಿಗೆಳಸಿಯವನಂ ಭಂಗಿಸಿ, ತಾನೆ ರಾಯನೆನಿಸಿದ್ದೆಳಗಜ್ಜ ದಂಡಾವಿದ್ಯಾನಗರಂ ಕಿಱಿದುಂದಿನಕ್ಕೆ ತುರುಷ್ಕರಿಂದೆಱಿಯೆಲೊಡಂ; ಅಲ್ಲಿಂ ಪೆನಗೊಂಡೆಗೆಯ್ತಂದು ಒಂದೆರೆಬ್ಬರಿಸಮಿರ್ದುಪೋಂಪಿ ಪೋಪಾಗಳ್, ತನ್ನ ಮೂವರ್ಕುವರರೊಳ್ ಮೊದಲಿಗನಾದ ಶ್ರೀರಂಗರಾಜನಂ ಪೆನಗೊಂಡೆಯೊಳಟ್ಟಾತಂಗೆ ತೆಲುಂಗನಾಡೊಡೆತನವಂ, ಎರಡನೆಯ ರಾಮ ರಾಯನಂ ಶ್ರೀರಂಗಪಟ್ಟಣದೊಳಿರಿಸಿಯವಂಗೆ ಕರ್ಣಾಟದೇಶಾಧಿಪತ್ಯಮಂ ಮೂಱನೆಯ ವೆಂಕಟಪತಿರಾಯನಂ ಚಂದ್ರಗಿರಿಯೊಳಟ್ಟು ಆತಂಗೆ ತುಂಡೀರಚೋಳಪಾಂಡ್ಯಮಂಡಲೇಶ್ವರತ್ವಮನಿತ್ತಂ. ಇವರೊಳ್ ಶ್ರೀರಂಗರಾಜಂ ಅಪುತ್ರನಾಗಿ ಬರ್ದಿಲವೆುನ್ನೆದಲೊಡಂ, ಆ ವೆಂಕಟಪತಿರಾಯಂ ಪೆನಗೊಂಡೆಯೊಳಿರ್ದೆಳೆಯಂ ಪರಿಪಾಲಿಸುತ್ತಿರೆ;

ಇತ್ತಲೀ ರಾಮರಾಜಂ ಕೆಲವುಂಕಾಲಕ್ಕೆ ಕಾಲಧರ್ಮಮನೆಯ್ದಿದಬೞಿಕ್ಕೆ ತಿರುಮಲರಾಜಂ ಮೊದಲಾದ ಅವನ ಕುವರರ್ ಶ್ರೀರಂಗಪಟ್ಟಣದಲ್ಲಿ ರೇಮಟಿ ವೆಂಕಟಯ್ಯ ನೆಂಬ ತಮ್ಮಡೆಱವಾಯನಿರಿಸಿ ತಾಮೆಳವರಯದವರಾದುದಱಿಂದೆ ಪೆನಗೊಂಡೆಯಂ ಪೊರ್ದಿ ಕಿಱಿಯಯ್ಯನ ಬೞಿಯೊಳಿರ್ದುಬಳೆದರ್,

ಬೞಿಕ್ಕಾ ವೆಂಕಟಪತಿರಾಯಂ ಮಧುರೆಯವೀರಪ್ಪನಾಯಕನೊಳ್ಮುನಿದು, ದಂಡೆತ್ತಿ ನಡೆದು, ಪಾಣ್ಡ್ಯಮಣ್ಡಲದ ಮಧುರಾಪುರಮಂ ಸುತ್ತಿಮುತ್ತಿರ್ಪಿನಂ; ಆವೀರಪ್ಪನಾಯಕಂ ಭೇದೋಪಾಯಮನವಲಂಬಿಸಿ, ರಾಯನ ಸೇನಾನಾಯಕರ್ಗೆ ದ್ರವ್ಯಭೂಷಣಂಗಳಂ ಕಳುಪಲೊಡಂ, ಈ ತಿರುಮಲರಾಯನಾಲಂಚಮಂ ಕೊಂಡದರ್ಕೆ ವಿವೇಕದೊಡನೆ ತನ್ನುಮಂ ಕೀರ್ತಿಯುಮಂ ಸುಕೃತಮುಮಂ ಮಾಱಿ ತಂದೆಯುಮಾಳ್ದನು ಮಪ್ಪ ಕಿಱಿಯಯ್ಯನೊಳ್ಗಂಟುಗೊಂಡು ತನ್ನ ಕರಿ ತುರಗ ಪದಾತಿಗಳ್ವೆರಸಿ ಅತ್ತಣಿಂ ಶ್ರೀರಂಗಪಟ್ಟಣಕ್ಕೆ ಬಂದನೆಂಬ ವಾರ್ತೆ ಬರ

ಲೊಡಂ, ಅದಂ ಕೇೞ್ದು ರಾಜನೃಪಂ ತನ್ನನುಜಸೇನಾನಿಮಹಾವಮಾತ್ಯಮಿತ್ರ ರೊಡನಾಳೋಚಿಸಿ ನಿಶ್ಚಯಂಗೆಯ್ದು ಈ ಪಿತೃಘಾತಿಯಸೇಪಟ್ಟಣದಿಂ ಪೊಱ ಮಡಿಸವೇೞ್ಕುಂ, ಅದರ್ಕಿವರ ಸಪ್ತಾಂಗದಿರವನಾರಯ್ವೆನೆಂದು ಗೂಢಚಾರರಂ ಪ್ರಣಿಧಿಗಳುಮಂ ಕಳುಪ್ರಪಿನಂ, ಅವರ್ ಅಲ್ಲಿ ಕೆಲವುಂದಿನಮಿರ್ದು ಮಗುೞ್ದಾಳ್ದ ನೆಡೆಗೇೞ್ತಂದು ಒಳ ಓಳಗದೊಳ್ಕೈಮುಗಿದು ಬಿನ್ನಪಂಗೆಯ್ದರದೆಂತೆನೆ.

93

BAHUḶĀŚVACHARITRAM.

[*By Dāmarla Vengaḷabhūpāla.*]

This Telugu poem was written by Dāmarla Vengaḷabhūpāla, a member of the Kāḷahasti family of feudatory chiefs. He lived during the reigns of the Vijayanagar emperors Rāma Rāya I and Śrīranga Rāya III. He dedicated the poem to his brother-in-law, the famous Velugōṭi Yācha.

From the introduction to the book we are able to frame the following genealogical table of the Kāḷahasti princes and their relation to the contemporary Velugoṭi chiefs :—

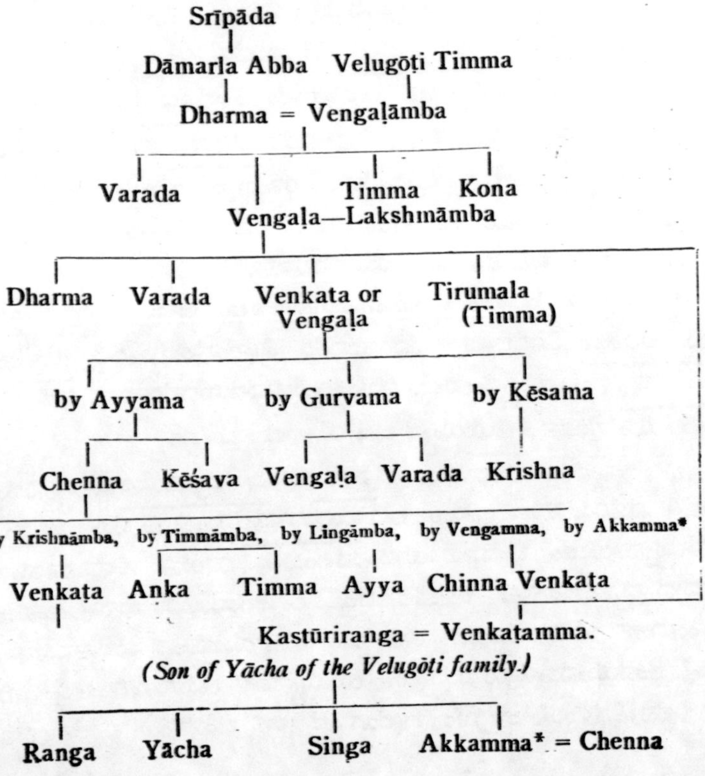

Of these Timma or Tirumala, the son of Vengaḷa and the brother-in-law of Velugoṭi Kastūriranga, was a great conqueror. On merely hearing that he was invading their territories, the Muhammadan chiefs of the north fled from their capitals in great fear; the lord of Bijāpur to Pannāla, the Mulka (Kutb Mulk of Golkonda) to Paigova (?), the Nizam of (Ahmadnagar) to Makka (?) and the ruler of Agra to Gaya.*

His younger sister Venkaṭāmba married Kastūriranga of the Yācha family and had by him three sons Ranga, Yācha and Singa, and a daughter Akkamāmba. Of these Yācha, son of Kastūriranga and brother-in-law of *Chenna*, defeated the chief Dāvalu Pāpa† at Uttaramallūru. He marched as far as Tirumala (Tirupati in the Chittoor district), defeated the mountain chiefs there, and captured Chengalpaṭ (Chengleput). Outside the fort of Pālembukoṭa (Palemkota, South Arcot) he fought with the chief Yatirāju and defeated him. He fought with Jagga Rāya and the rulers of Gingi, Madura and Trichinopoly at Topur.‡ He there killed Jagga Rāya, defeated the troops of the Nāyaks of Madura and Gingi, and drove the Nāyak of Trichinopoly from the field.

His brother-in-law Chenna defeated Linga of Vēlūr § (Vellore) in the plains of Munnali (Minnal ?). He defeated his enemies at a place called *Kūḍalāttūr*. He also fought with the Pandya ‖ (the Nāyak of Madura) and put him to flight. He got the title Gaḍikoṭamalla (the capturer of enemy fortresses). Chenna also captured the fortress of Vellore with its high fortifications and deep moat. Yāchama Nāyaka got presents of elephants and

* This seems to be merely an exaggeration. The chief might have fought with the Bāhmani rulers of Bijapur, Golkonda and Ahmadnagar in the wars between those chiefs and the later Vijayanagar emperors; but he could never have come in contact or even within a reasonable distance of the territory of the Moghul Empire of Delhi.

† The Jesuit Father Pimenta has something to say of this chief—vide Purchas, His Pilgrimes, X, Chap. vii.

‡ The present name of this place is Tohur. It is situated near the Grand Anikut across the Kaveri. Gagga Rāya and his troops effected at this place a junction with the troops of the Nāyaks of Gingi and Trichinopoly. But they were completely defeated by Yāchama Nāyak and Raghunātha Nāyaka of Tanjore who espoused the cause of the fugitive emperor Rāma Rāya.

§ Linga of Vellore was the son of Chinna Bommu Nāyaka of Vellore who was the patron of the scholar Appaya Dīkshita. He is the donor of the Viḷāpāka grant of Venkaṭa. His defeat and the capture of his capital by Chenna must have occurred after the date of the Viḷāpāka grant (Epigraphia Indica, IV, No. 39). The capture of the place was possibly the immediate cause of the change of capital from Chandragiri to Vellore by Venkaṭapati Rāya.

‖ This possibly means that he took part in the war between the fugitive emperor Rāma Rāya and Jagga Rāya. He may have fought on the side of Rāma Rāya along with his brother-in-law Yāchama Nāyaka.

horses from the Nizam Shah, Adil Shah and Kutb Shah. He was high in the estimation of the people of the cities of Cuttack, Delhi, Agra, Ahmadnagar, Māhūr, Shiraj, Kalamba, Manḍuva, Makkha, Beḍandakoṭa (Bidar), Hukumi (?) and Māhishmati.

మ. భయవిభ్రాంతి విజాపురీశుఁడరిగెం బిన్నాలకున్మల్కాయుం
బయిగోవంబడియెన్నిజాముచనియెన్మక్కాపురక్షోణికిఁ
గయకున్వెల్వడె నాగరానగరభూకాంతుండు దామర్లతి
మ్మయదంతావళ ఘోటికా భటసముద్యద్ధాటిసామన్యమే.

చ. తదనుజనైన లోకహితధర్మవిశంకట వేంకటాంబికం
గదన కిరీటియాచవిభు కస్తురిరంగనృపాలవర్యుఁడిం
పొదవవరించి కాంచెవిభవోజ్వలు రంగయయాచభూవరు
న్విదిత గుణాఢ్యుసింగపృథివీవర చంద్రునినక్కమాంబికన్.

సీ. ఉత్తరమల్లూరియొద్ద దావలుపాప
విభునిఁగొట్టిననాఁటి విజయకలన
తిరుమలఁజేరిధాత్రిని మన్నెరాజులఁ
బాఱఁద్రోలిననాఁటి బాహుబలము
చెంగలుపట్టు వీక్షించి లగ్గలువట్టి
యాక్రమించిననాటి విక్రమంబు
పాలెంబుకోటవెల్పట నాజి యతిరాజు
జరగఁజేసిననాటి శౌర్యపటిమ

గీ. మున్నెతోపూర జగ్గరాణ్ముఖులనొంచి
మధురదొరచెంజిమన్నీని మదమడంచి
తిరుచెనాపలిదొరఁదోలు తేజముగల
మేటివెలిగోటియాచని సాటిగలరె.

సీ. మునుమున్నయేరాజు మున్నలిబైళ్లను
వేలూరిలింగ భూవిభునిఁగొట్టె
పంచవన్నియడాలు వట్టించెనేరాజు
పరవీరభద్రేభ పటలిరెబ్బ
ధీరతఁ గూడలాతూరిలోనేరాజు
శాత్రవబలముల సంహరించె

శుక్రవారమునాఁడె చోరఁ బారియేరాజు
పాండీనిబలముల భంగపఱచె

గీ. నతఁడుసామాన్యుఁడే దామరాన్వవాయ
కలశవారాశి పూర్ణరాకాశశాంకు
డనఁగగడికోటమల్లశుభాంకయుతుఁడు
వేంకటేంద్రునిచెన్నభూవిభువరుండు.

మ. పరిఘాసౌధగభీరతోన్నతులచే బ్రలాయిడింజెందియుఁ
దరియంజాలరు పన్నగామరులనన్భాసిల్లునాదిప్రవ
ప్రరమన్వేలురి రాజధానిని దృణప్రాయంబుగాఁగొన్నయ
న్నరనాథాగ్రణిఁ జెన్నభూపమణినెన్నన్శక్యమేయేరికిన్.

క. ఇలవెలయునేచభూవరు
చెలియలి నలయకక్కమాంబఁజెన్నక్షోణీ
తలపతి పరిణయమయ్యెం
జలనిధిసుతఁ బెండ్లియైనశౌరియపోలెన్.

కవిరాజ విరాజితము

వితరణజృంభణ శక్రతరుక్రమ విక్రమనూతనశాతఘృణీ
తతరణబృందపురందర నందనధన్య మహీమహిళాగ్రహిళా
యతభుజగాగ్రభుజాగ్ర మహోగ్రజయాంక నిజామశహైదులశా
కుతుపనశాహసమాగత ఘోటకఘోటకరిప్రవరా.

Canto II.

సుగంధి. కటకఢిల్లిపురమతల్లికాలిజాగరాముదా
కటకమాహురీశిరాజిఘటకలంబముండువా
ఘటచకోరలోచనా కుచద్వయీలసత్తటో
త్కటపటీరశాదసదృశదళదిశావిశద్యశా.

Canto IV.

శా. తుఖ్ఖారాదిహయాధిరోహణకళాదో్యరత్న తుఖేఁచనా
మఖ్ఖాఢిల్లిబెడందకోటహుకుమీమాహిమ్మతీమాహురీ
దిఖ్ఖండేందునిటాలకాకుచఘటీదేశార్ద్రకాశ్మీరస
మ్యఖ్ఖాభ్రామ్యదతి ప్రతాపతపనీయాహార్యధైర్యోదయా.

94

CHATU VERSE ABOUT JAGGA RĀYA AND YĀCHAMA NĀYAKA.

This verse has been taken from a collection of Chāṭu (fugitive) verses called Chāṭupadyaratnākaram. It refers to the war between Jagga Rāya, Māka Rāja and Rāviḷḷa Venku on one side and Yāchama Nāyaka on the other. This refers to the war between the chiefs to secure the succession of Rāma Rāya and punish the murderer Jagga Rāya. The substance of the verse is that a crore of Jagga Rāyas, seventy crores of Māka Rāja's father and one lakh and a sixteen Rāviḷḷa Venkus put together would not be a match for Yācha, who bears the title of Ibbara Gaṇḍa, just as any number of goats joining together would not be a match for the tiger.

ఉ. గొబ్బున జగ్గరాజులొక కోటియు డెబ్బదికోట్లమాకరా
జబ్బులు లక్ష మీఁదఁ బదియార్గురు రావిల వెంకులైన మా
నిబ్బరగండ యాచ ధరణీపతి ముందట నిల్వ శక్తు లే
కబ్బులు లేక, బెబ్బులిముఖాముఖి మేఁకలు నిల్వనేర్చునే.

95

USHĀPARIṆAYAM.

[*By Dāmarla Ankabhūpāla.*]

In the introduction to this work written by the Kāḷahasti chief Ankabhūpāla and dedicated to his father Chenna, he gives a short account of his family. His elder brother Venkaṭa marched with his army against the ruler of Gingi, Krishnappa Nāyaka, and after defeating him constructed in his territory a large tank and named it Chennasāgaram after his father.*

His younger brother Ayya† saw that the people of Praḷayakāveri (the Dutch at Pulicat) were incessantly fighting with the people of Mailāpūr (the Portuguese at St. Thomé in Mylapore), and to put an end to the fighting, founded the town of Chennapaṭnam (Madras) between them.

---

* Vide Nos. 61–64 of Epigraphist's collection for the year 1906.

† This is the Dāmarla Ayyapēndra who fought on the imperial side against Chikka-dēvarāja Woḍeyār of Mysore at Erode. He fell in the battle. (Epigraphia Carnāṭaka, Mysore, part I, Sr: 14). Refer to genealogical table on page 304 above.

మ. రహిన వ్యేంకటధారుణీరమణుఁడౌరా తండ్రిపేరొప్పఁగా
మహిఁజిత్రంబగు చెన్నసాగరము ధర్మస్ఫూర్తిఁగట్టించెన
త్యహరీశోదిత తేజుఁగ్రష్ణఘన వాహాధీశజున్నావలిబ
ల్వహినేచెంజిరమాధ్యుంద్రుంచిశుభలీల న్గాంచెరామోన్నతిన్.

ఉ. అయ్యధరాధినాయకుఁడహార్పతి తేజుఁశుమీర జంద్రుతో
వియ్యముజెందజాలు ముఖబింబము దానగుణంబుజెందుచున్
దొయ్యలులెల్లజూచి పరితోషముగాంచుచు మానసంబులన్
దియ్యనివిల్లుడాచి జగతిన్జరియించు మనోజుఁడోయనన్.

గీ. ప్రళయకావేరి మైలాపురంబుగల్మి
బీరమునబోర నడిమట్టుపెట్టదండ్రి
పేరదన్మధ్యభూమిని వృథువిభూతి
నలవరిచెఁ జెన్నపట్టణమయ్యన్నృపతి.

96

CHIKKADĒVA RĀYA VAMŚĀVAḶI.

[*By Tirumalārya : Śrīranga Rāya III of Vijayanagar.*]

At the end of this work there is an interesting account of Śrīranga Rāya III, the last great ruler of the decaying Vijayanagar empire. Śivappa Nāyaka, the younger brother of Vīrabhadra Nāyaka of Ikkēri, murdered the latter and himself became the ruler of Ikkēri. After this he sent some of his officers with presents to Chikkadēva Rāya of Seringapatam requesting an alliance with him. But Chikkadēva Rāya rejected the offer seeing the nature of Śivappa Nāyaka's accession to power.

Wroth at this Śivappa Nāyaka took up the cause of Śrīranga Rāya III, the nominal emperor of Vijayanagar, against Chikkadēva Rāya. Śrīranga Rāya had by that time lost all his northern possessions like Chandragiri and Vellore on account of the invasions of the Muhammadans. He then retired to the territories of the Nāyakas of Gingi, Tanjore and Madura. When these latter failed him he was wandering over the country for want of supporters. Śivappa Nāyaka now came to his help and ceded to him the districts of Hāssan and Bēlūr. By the influence of the nominal emperor, Śivappa Nāyaka got in return the help of the chiefs of Aigur, Tāriyakere, Harpanahalli, Chintanakal, Maddagiri and

Gadag. With the aid of these chiefs he made war on Chikkadēva Rāya of Seringapatam.*

(ಚಿಕದೇವರಾಯ.)— ಇವನುಮುಪೇಂದ್ರನಂತೆ ಅರಸುಗೆಯ್ಮೆಯ ಪ್ರೋಷೆಯ
ನಿತುವಮಂ ಪೊತ್ತು ಜೈತ್ರಯಾತ್ರೋತ್ಸವಂಗಳನೊಡರ್ಚುತಿರೆ; ರಾಯನುಂ ಮಹೇಂ
ದ್ರನಂತೆ ನಿರ್ಭರನಾಗಿ ದಿವ್ಯಭೋಗಂಗಳನನುಭವಿಸುತ್ತಿರೆ; ಒರ್ಮೆ ಮಾನೋಮಿ
ಯುತ್ಸವದೊಳೆಣ್ದೆಸೆಯ ಧೊರೆಗಳನಿಬರುಂ ಕಪ್ಪಕಾಣ್ಕೆಗಳಂ ತಂದೊಪ್ಪಿಸುವೆಡೆ
ಯೊಳ್, ಇಕ್ಕೇರಿಯೊಳ್ ಶಿವಪ್ಪನಾಯಕಂ ತನ್ನಾಳ್ದನಪ್ಪ ವೀರಭದ್ರನಾಯಕ
ನೊಳ್ ದ್ರೋಹಮನೆಣಿಸಿ, ಅವನಂ ಕವಡಿನೊಳ್ ಮಡುಪಿ, ಆ ದೊರೆತನಮಂ
ಕೊಂಡು, ತಾನುಂ ಪಾವುಡಮಂ ಕಾಣ್ಕೆಗಳಂ ಕಳುಪುವಿನಂ; ಅವನ ತಪ್ಪುಗೆ
ಯ್ಮೆಗಳನೆಣಿಸಿ ನೀಟ್ಕರಿಪ ಬಂದ ಗುಜುವಾನಿಸನಂ ಬಂದಂತೆ ಕಳುಪಲೊಡಂ;
ಅದರ್ಕಾ ಧೊರೆ ಪಿರಿದುಂ ಬಿಗುರ್ತು ನೆರವನರಸೆ ಮುಂತನ್ನಂತೆ ಬಿಜ್ಜಾನಗರಿಯ
ಧೊರೆತನಮನಾಳ್ದ ತೆಲುಂಗರಾಯರ ಬಗೆಯೊಳೊರ್ವಂ ಶ್ರೀರಂಗರಾಯನೆನಿಸು
ವಂ ತನ್ನ ಬೇಲೂರ್ ಚಂದ್ರಗಿರಿ ಮುಂತಾದ ಕೋಟೆದುರ್ಗಂಗಳಂ ತುರುಕರ್ಗೆ
ಸೂರೆಗೊಟ್ಟು ತನ್ನ ಪರಿಜನಂಬೆರಸು, ಪಿರಿಯ ತಿರುಕಾಳಿಯೆನಿಸಿ ಚೆಂಜಿ, ತಂಜಾ
ವೂರ್ಮಧುರೆಯ ಮನೆಗಳೊಳೆಡೆದು ಅವರಿತ್ತುದಂ ತುತ್ತಿಯವರಂಜನ - -
- - - - ಗಣಿಂದೆಚಿತ್ತಲುಮತ್ತಲುಂ ಎತ್ತಲುಂ ನೆಲೆಗಾಣದಿರೆಯವನ
ನೆಜಸಿ ಕಂಡು ಕಾಲ್ಗೆರಗಿಯೊಡಗೊಂಡು ಬಂದು ತನ್ನ ಮುಂದಣ ಕಡೆಯಗಡಿ
ಯೆನಿಸುವ ಹಾಸನ ಬೇಲೂರ್ಗಳನಿತ್ತು ನೆಲೆಗೊಳಿಸಿ ಯವನತ್ತಣಿಂದ ಐಗೂರು
ತರಿಯಕೆರೆ ಹರಪನಹಳ್ಳಿ ಚಿಂತನಕಲ್ ಮದ್ದಗಿರಿ ಗಿಡುಗ - - - ದ ಪಲ
ವುಂ ಪಟ್ಟಕೊಟ್ಟದ ಧೊರೆಗಳ ಬಲಮುಂ ತನ್ನ ಮೂಲಬಲಮುಂ ತನ್ನ ಸೇರಿದ
ತುಳುವ ಕೊಂಕಣ ಕೊಡಗ ಮಲಯಾಳಂಗಳ ಮೂಲಬಲಮುಂ ಕೊಂಡು ಪಟ್ಟ
ಣಕ್ಕೆ ನಡೆತಂದು - - - ||

97

RĀMARĀJIYAMU.

[*By Venkayya.*]

PEDDAVENKATA, CHINNAVENKATA AND HIS CHILDREN.

Sriranga, the son of the famous Aliya Rāma Rāya who died in the battle of Talikota, had two sons Peddavenkata and Chinnavenkaṭa. Of these † Peddavenkaṭa ruled peacefully the whole empire extending from the Krishna to the Sētu. He married Bangāramma, the daughter of Gobbūri Oba, who had the title Hannibbaraganda.

* Here the work breaks off and is incomplete.

† He was the donor of the Kuniyūr plates of Venkaṭa II (*Ep. Ind.*, Vol. III, No. 34, of A.D. 1634).

His younger brother Chinnavenkaṭa* while on his return from a visit to the temple of Virūpāksha in the imperial capital had a vision that the God Kodaṇḍa Rāma appeared before him and told him that he would be born as the eldest son of his son Tirumala. Chinna Venkaṭa married Tiruvengaḷāmba, the daughter of Jillēḷḷa Nārapa, and had by her three sons Tirumala, Venkaṭapati and Śrīranga (hitherto called Śriranga VI).

Of these Śrīranga was adopted by Gopāla, the grandson of Venkaṭādri, the brother of Aḷiya Rāma Rāya, and was nominated by him to rule his kingdom after him. He ruled the kingdom in peace from his capital Vellore, and made many dānas (gifts) and maintained dharma. Once Śrīranga Rāya marched from his capital against the hill fort of Udayagiri which was occupied by the Kutb Shah and utterly defeated him. He married three wives, Pāpamma, the daughter of Gobbūri Vengaḷa, Rāghavamma, the daughter of Pochirāju Venga, and Vengamma, the daughter of Pochirāju Venkaṭa.

Śrīranga's elder brother Venkaṭapati was a beneficent ruler, and he married three wives, Appalāmba, daughter of Sūrapa Krishnapa, and the two daughters of Pochirāju Raghunātha, namely, Vengamma and Kōnēṭamma. Of these three Appalāmba was his favourite. Venkaṭapati had by his wife Appalāmba, three sons Rāma, Timma and Venkaṭādri.

Of these sons Timma or Tirumala built the tall eastern gōpura (tower) of the temple of Virūpāksha at the capital Vijayanagar (then almost ruined). He was a very pious king, did many acts of charity and maintained the worship of Virūpāksha. He composed the story of the Rāmāyana in dvipada metre and dedicated it to Virūpāksha of Pampa (Hampe). He made an extensive and cool garden by the side of the Tungabhadra in Kishkinda (Vijayanagar), and there built the temple of Śrīranganātha resembling Śrīrangam on the banks of the Kaveri.

Tirumala married Kōnēṭamma, the daughter of Konḍa of the Jillēḷḷa family, and Tiruvēngaḷāmba, the daughter of Pochirāju Rāma. Of these Kōnēṭamma was a patron of poets and wanted to emulate by her action "the famous predecessors of the family, Krishna Rāya, Rāma Rāya and Tirumala Rāya. Tirumala had by his wife Kōnēṭamma two sons Śrīranga and Chinnavenkaṭapati."

---

* It is to this Chinna Venkaṭa that the Krishnarājavijayamu was dedicated. (No. 39). Dedicated to his elder brother Pedda Venkaṭa is the Telugu work Venkatapatirāya-daṇḍakam.

The elder brother of Tirumala, Rāma or Kōdaṇḍarāma ruled his kingdom with fame assisted by his younger brother. Kōdaṇḍarāma fought a battle with his enemies outside the town of Jūṭūr, and utterly defeated them. Again he fought another battle with the troops of Mysore near the town of Āsana (Hassan) under their Daḷavāi (commander) Kumārayya.* Some of the subordinate chiefs that fought under him in the battle were Kāsarakōṭa Timmayya, Sabinīsu Krishnayya and Maṭli Venkaṭapati. Kōdaṇḍarāma routed his enemies on the field and returned in triumph to his capital.†

శా. శ్రీరంగాధిపు పెద్ద వేంకటధరిత్రీ జాని యుద్యద్భుజా
సారంబొప్పఁగ నేలె నెంతయును గృష్ణా సేతుమధ్యక్షితిన్
మారీ భూతవిపక్షమానవ వరస్తోమప్రచారంబుగా
నాకూఢిన్ధరణీజనుల్సకల సౌఖ్యావాప్తిరాణింపఁగన్.

క. గొబ్బూరివంశమణిహా
న్నిబ్బరగండఁడగు నోబ నృపవరుసుతయా
నబ్బింగారమ్మనుమది
నుబ్బుచుఁ బెద వేంకటపతి యొనరవరించెన్.

క. అతని సహోదరుఁడబ్జా
హితకుల కలశాబ్ధిపూర్ణహిమరుచిబుధస
మ్మతమతియౌచిన వేంకట
పతిగుణతతినుతి కలవియె ఫణిపతికైనన్.

సీ. ఒకనాఁడు చినవేంకటోర్వీశ్వరుఁడు విరూ
పాక్షసేవాసక్తినచ్చటికిని
నరిగెక్రమ్మఱఁద్రోవ యందొకర యెడరామ
సుత్రాముఁడును బొడచూపినట్లు

* According to the Mackenzie MSS. quoted by Nelson in his Manual of the Madura Country, a Daḷavāi Kumarayya of Mysore figures among those that laid siege to Trichinopoly along with Sivaji and Venkaji, his brother. He was defeated and compelled to retire into Mysore territory by Sivaji.

† Mr. Jayanti Ramayya Pantulu has in his possession a silver plate grant of Sivaji, the great Mahratta ruler, recording the provision he made for the widow and the two sons of Srīranga III who is said to have died a fugitive 'in the west country.' The position of the widow and the sons was brought to the notice of Sivaji by their Vakil Venkaṭakrishnayya.

తోఁచినభయము సంతోషంబుఁ బెనఁగొన
బ్రకటరోమాంచకంచుకితగాత్రుఁ
డైవచ్చి నెమ్మదివారిఁదల్చి నిద్రింప
దంబైన మణికిరీటంబుఁ దాల్చి

గీ. దివ్యభూషణములు దివ్యమాల్యంబులు
దివ్యగంధములును దివ్యవస్త్ర
ములును దాల్చి దివ్యమూర్తితోఁ గోదండ
పాణియైన రామభద్రుఁ డెదుట.

క. వచ్చుటయు నిల్చినఁ గనుఁగొని
యచ్చెరు వీరాజిచటికి నరుదెంచుట యే
మిచ్చ యుదలంచుకనోయది
యొచ్చెముపడనీక దానినొనఁగూర్పఁదగుఁ.

సీ. అనుచును దలపోయనంతనో చినవేంక
టాధిపనీవు వంశాధినాథు
డగునీశు భజియించియరుదేరఁ ద్రోవను
బోడనూపినట్టియా భూమిభుజుఁడ
నేను నా పేరు నీ కెఱిఁగింతుఁ గోదండ
పాణియౌ శ్రీరామభద్రుఁ డంద్రు
మమ్ము భూజనులన్న మాట విన్నంతన
నిటలతటాగ్రసంఘటితహస్త

గీ. కమలుఁడై దండములఁ బెట్టి కనకపీఠ
మందు నాసీనుఁ గాఁ జేసి యాగమోక్త
సరణిఁ బూజించి తత్పాదజలజములకు
భక్తిఁ బ్రణమిల్లి యిట్లని ప్రణుతిఁ జేసె.

గీ. అనుచు వినుతింప నారాముఁ డటయె చిన్న
వేంకటపతి క్షమానాథపను మునీదు
పుత్రుఁడగు పీక వేంకటభూవరునకు
నగ్రసుతుఁడు ధృఢవిల్లు మదంశమునను.

మ. పరమప్రీతి జిల్లేళ్లనారప మహీపాలేశు సత్పుత్రిఁ దా
మరసాక్షిం దిరువేంగళాంబ నరిసంహారైకశూరుండు భా

సురధైర్యుండగు చిన్న వేంకటపతిక్షోణీంద్రుఁడు ద్వాహను
య్యె రమన్బన్నగ రాజతల్పుఁడు వివాహంబైన చందంబునన్.

మ. జననంబందిరి చిన్న వేంకట మహీశస్వామికిన్నందనుల్
ఘనచారిత్రుఁడు తిర్మలాధిపుఁడు సంగ్రామార్జునుండంచుభూ
జనసంస్తుత్యతఁగాంచు వేంకటపతిక్ష్మాజానియున్ధర్మవ
ర్తనగాణించు సిరంగరాయమనుజాధ్యక్షేశుఁడన్మువ్వరున్.

సీ. గోపాలమూర్తియౌ గోపాలభూపాల
చంద్రుఁడు తనదురాజ్యంబునకును
బట్టంబుఁగట్టిన బాహాబలస్ఫూర్తి
మెఱసిధర్మంబున ధరణినేలి
వర్ణాశ్రమంబుల వరుసతోనడపుచు
నీతిబాధలులేక ప్రీతిజనులు
సంపదలనుదేల సవనోత్సవంబులు
దఱచుగానూరూర జఱుగుచుండ

గీ. సకలనరనాయకులు గనుసన్న మెలఁగ
దనకు వేలూరు నిజరాజధానిగాఁగ
బరఁగెఁగడుఁ జిన్న వేంకటపతికుమార
రత్నమైనట్టి శ్రీరంగరాయమౌళి.

సీ. ధాటీనిరాఘాట ఘోటకోద్ధుత పాంసు
పటలంబు నల్లడఁబాఱఁజల్లి
బంధురతరగంధసింధురనికరశీ
కరమునిబ్బరముగఁ జిలికిచిలికి
వితతదోర్బల విజృంభితయోధశరవర
దండాహతులఁజాల బెండువఱిచి
వీరరసావేశ ఘోరసద్భటపద
ఘట్టనలనుజాపచుట్టువెట్టి

గీ. యుదయగిరికొండ వెలుఁగొందుచుండుకుతుప
శాహుబలదర్ప దవహుతాశనునినడఁచి
వినుతిఁగాంచెను సకలభూజనులచేత
రమ్యగుణహారి శ్రీరంగరాయశౌరి.

క. శ్రీరంగరాయశశిగో
బ్బూరికులుండైన వెంగళోర్వీశతనూ
జారత్నముఁ బాపమ్మన
పారవిభవమలరఁగా వివాహంబయ్యెన్.

సీ. మతిపోచిరాజుకులమండనుఁడగు వెంగ
భూనాయకాగ్రణి పుత్రికైన
రాఘవమ్మను బోచిరాజు వేంకటరాజు
తనయ వెంగమ్మను ద్వాహమయ్యె
నా సతీత్రయమును ననురక్తితో సర్వ
ధర్మసహాయమై తగభజింప
నతిశయభోగభాగ్యాభివృద్ధినిఁ జాల
గాంచి ధర్మమార్గప్రచారి

గీ. యనుచు విద్వజ్జనంబులు వినుతిసేయ
వెలసె నెంతయు నసహాయ విక్రమార్కుఁ
డారవీటిపురాధీశుఁడైన చిన్న
వేంకటపతీంద్రుఁ శ్రీరంగవిభుఁడు మిగుల.

క. ఇట్టి గుణములఁ గలతోఁ
బుట్టువులనురక్తిఁ గొలువఁ బోరులరిపులన్
గొట్టి మనుమార్గచర్యకుఁ
బట్టగుచును వేంకటేశపార్థివుఁడలరున్.

సీ. రాజాధిరాజవీరప్రతాపాంకుఁడౌ
వేంకటపతిరాయ విభుఁడు వేడ్క
నూరప కృష్ణవతీశుసత్పుత్రి
నప్పలాంబను నమరాద్రిధైర్యు
డనఘుండు పోచిరాజాన్వయుం డగు రఘు
నాథ రాజేంద్రుని నందనలను
విమలసచ్చారిత్ర వెంగమ్మ పద్మాయ
తాక్షి నేటమ్మ యనని రువురఁ

గీ. నొగి వరించెను సతులను ముగురి యందు
నశ్వినియునాదియగు తారకాళిలోక

మణుని యనురక్తిఁ గాంచు రోహిణివిధమున
నలరుఁ బతిమన్ననల నప్పలాంబ మిగుల.

క. వారిరువురు గనిరనఘుల
వీరాగ్రణి రామరాజవిభునిన్ శౌర్యో
దారుండనఁ దగుతిమ్మధ
రారమణుని వేంకటాద్రి రాజబిడౌజున్.

సీ. కట్టించె నేరాజు గగనంబునొరయవి
రూపాక్ష ప్రాగ్ద్వారగోపురంబుఁ
బెట్టించె నేనృప భిదురపాణిహృదిష్ట
మృష్టాన్నసత్రంబు నిత్యఁగూర్చి
చేయించె నేపుణ్యశీలుండు ద్విజులకు
వడుగులు పెండ్లిండ్లు కడుముదమునఁ
గావించె నేమహీకాంతుఁడు ముప్పొద్దు
పంపాధిపతికి సపర్యభక్తి

గీ. దలచు నేధన్యుఁ డాత్మను దనకుఁ గలుగు
మాన్యైశ్వర్యమీశ్వరాధీనమనుచు
నతఁడు మనుజేంద్రమాత్రుఁడె యధిపమౌళి
రాయలాధిపు తిరుమలరాయమౌళి.

ఆ. ఆరవీటితిరుమలాధీశ్వరుఁడు రామ
భద్రకథ లఘుద్విపదనొకర్థి
పరమభక్తినాప్రబంధంబు శ్రీవిరూ
పాక్షుపేరఁ జేసె నంకితముగ.

సీ. శ్రీరంగనాథుఁ గవేరజాతటమున
మును ధర్మవర్మప్రార్థననొనఁ
నిలిపినవైఖరిఁ మహీధరశ్రేష్ఠ
మైనకిష్కింధాభిధానదివ్య
నగభేదినైరమానాయక దేహశ్ర
మాంబుస్వరూపంబు ననఘమూర్తి
యగుతుంగభద్రామహానదిమధ్యమ
శ్రీరంగమందిర క్షేత్రమునను

గీ. క్రముకముఖభూజములమల్లికాప్రభృతుల
తాళిఁగలవనమును వేసియాయుపవన
సీమయందును శ్రీరంగధామునునిచె
రాయలోర్వీశుతిరుమలరాయవిభుఁడు.

తే. పటుయశోనిధిచిన్నవేంకటపతీంద్ర
వీరవేంకటపతిరాయవిభుతిరుమల
నృపతిశ్రీల్లెళ్ల కొండమహీవరాఢ్యు
తనయయైనట్టికోనేటమనువరించె.

సీ. దుర్జయరాజన్య దోశ్శక్తులుడిగించి
సర్వసర్వంసహాచక్రభార
భరణదక్షతమహాప్రౌఢులౌ శ్రీకృష్ణ
రాయలునార్వీటి రామరాజ
తిరుమలరాయాది ధరణీనాయకులును
వారలదేవులు వసుధఁగీర్తి
గనరెయాకీర్తికిజననంబుపోషిత
కవిజనసన్నుతిగాదెయట్టి

గీ. కవిజనాధారవిఖ్యాతిఁగాంచిమిగులఁ
గవులఁబోషించి తన్నుతికబ్బములను
తింపవెలసెను నార్వీటితిరుమలక్ష
మావరేంద్రుకోనేటమ్మ మహినిమిగుల.

శా. దీనత్రాణుఁడు తిమ్మరాజమహిభృద్దేవేంద్రుఁడుద్యద్భుజా
నూనస్ఫారబలావహాతాహితమహీశోత్సాహుఁడౌ పోచిరా
డ్భూనాథోత్తమరామరాజతనయన్ బూతాత్మఁదిర్వేంగళాం
బానారీమణినగ్నిసాక్షిగను జేపట్టెం బ్రమోదాత్ముఁడై.

మ. అమరాహార్యసమానధైర్యుఁడరివర్యధ్వంసిసద్వైభవా
నిమిషేంద్రుండగుతిమ్మరాజమణికోనేటమ్మ శ్రీరంగభూ
రమణున్ శ్రీచినవేంకటక్షితిపునిన్ రాజద్గుణాంభోనిధిం
బ్రమదంబొప్పఁగఁగాంచిరెంతయు బుధవ్రాతంబుగీర్తింపఁగన్.

తే. ఇట్లు సుతయుక్తమిలనుతికెక్కె—యనుఁగుఁ
దమ్ముఁడౌ తిమ్మభూభర్తనెమ్మిఁగొలువ

రాజకులమణికోదండరామవిభుఁడు
డనరుఁగర్ణాటరాజ్యపదస్థుఁడగుచు.

విజయసీసమాలిక.

శ్రీమన్మహాసుధాధామవంశంబుర్వి
వినుతికెక్కఁగనుద్భవించినట్టి
రఘురామమూర్తియా రామరాజతిమా
పాలుండుజాబూరి బైటమున్న
భండనభూమినిఁ బన్నినపగతుర
బారికినడచియపారశౌర్య
గరిమచేఁగరులను హరులఁబదాతులఁ
బోరిగొనిజయలక్ష్మిఁ బొందెనట్టు
లాసనమను పేర నమరినపురియొద్ద
మైసూరివారటు మాఱుకొనను
గణుతికెక్కిన గంధసింధురతురం
గమవీరభటనికాయములు పెక్కు
గలదళములవాగ దళవాయిమైనకు
మారయ్యచను దెంచి బారుఁదీర్ప
గనికరిఘటఁగన్నకంఠీరవేంద్రని
కైవడిమిగులదుర్గర్వమెసఁగ
మేటైనకాసరకోటతిమ్మయసచి
నీసుకృష్ణయకార్యనిపుణుఁడైన
మట్టివేంకటపతిబ్రహ్మపాలుఁడాదిగాఁ
గలవారల్ చతురంగబలముతోడ
నిరుగడవెనుకముందఱఁద్రొక్కినడవంగ
ధరణీవరాహపతాక మెఱయ

*   *   *

జాఱగాఁగొనిజయభేరులుమ్రోయంగ
సైన్యంబులుభయపార్శ్వములఁగొలువ
నిజశిబిరంబున నిండువేడుకఁదల
పూవువాడకసుఖంబునవసించి

క్షితిసురౌఘమ్ములాశీర్వాదమొనరింపఁ
ప్రమదలు నీరాజనములొసంగ
రామరాజకులాబ్ధిరాకాసుధాకర
రాజాధిరాజ వీరప్రతాప
రాజమార్తాండసుత్రామసన్నిభ యష్ట
దిగ్రాజభయదారక తేజరాజ
పరమేశ యనుచును భటకవిగాయకుల్
వినుతింపనసదృశ విజయరమను

గీ. బొందెఁగడు శ్రీవిరూపాక్షుభూరికరుణ
స్థిరముగా నెంతయును దనుఁ జేరనార
వీటిపురవంశమణియార్యవినుతచరితుఁ
డైనకోదండరామరాయనరవరుఁడు.

98

TANJĀVŪRI ĀNDHRA RĀJULA CHARITRA.

This is an account of the Telugu Nāyakas of Tanjore who were the viceroys under the emperors of Vijayanagar, written in colloquial Telugu prose. It seems to have been one of the manuscripts of the Mackenzie collection.

When the great emperor Krishna Dēva Rāya was ruling in peace and prosperity in Vijayanagar after conquering the whole of the country extending from Cuttack to Cape Comorin, Chandraśēkhara Pāṇḍya and Vīraśēkhara Chōla were governing as his subordinates the Pāṇḍya and Chōla territories. Vīraśēkhara Chōla then made war on Chandraśēkhara, and having defeated him ruled over both the Chōla and the Pāṇḍya provinces. Then Chandraśēkhara fled to the emperor in Vijayanagar, and lodged a complaint against the Chōla for making war on him and driving him out of his kingdom. Then Krishna Rāya in great anger summoned his general Nāgama Nāyaka who is called Tōsēkhānā Adhikāri (officer of the treasury) and directed him to march against the refractory Chōla, and, after punishing him for his transgression, to reinstate the Pāṇḍya on his ancestral throne.

Nāgama Nāyaka marched against the Chōla. He defeated the Chōla and annexed his kingdom after executing him. Later he marched to Madura and drove out the garrison left at the place by Vīraśēkhara Chōla. But he did not restore the Pāṇḍya kingdom to the rightful ruler, but instead began to rule it in his own name. He also established order there and brought under subjection many refractory places which had not rendered submission to any ruler for a considerable time. Once more the Pāṇḍya went to Vijayanagar and complained about the high-handedness of Nāgama Nāyaka. Krishna Rāya sent an order to Nāgama Nāyaka reprimanding him for his conduct, and directing him to give his kingdom back to the Pāṇḍya and return with his army.

But Nāgama Nāyaka wrote back in reply that the Pāṇḍya had till then no hope of bringing back all the parts of his kingdom under his control after having been reinstated; that he waited on saying he would be content with a maintenance pension till Nāgama had brought the whole province completely under subjection; and that, seeing the success of Nāgama, he had begun to covet his old kingdom and complain against Nāgama. Nāgama further wrote that if the kingdom were once more given to the Pāṇḍya the emperor would not be able to collect even the quit-rent from the province. He then proceeded to recount all his past services to the emperor, and said that he had spent a large sum of money out of his own wealth, in addition to the money belonging to the treasury, in conquering the province, and wound up by saying that he would not return before recouping all the money that he had advanced, from the revenues of the province. He also added that Chandraśēkhara was not the rightful heir of the Pāṇḍyas, but only an illegitimate son and that that was the cause of the previous war between him and the Chōla.

The emperor in great anger called out which of his generals would immediately march on Nāgama Nāyaka and bring him the rebel's head. Then Viśvanātha Nāyaka, the son of Nāgama, rose and offered his services. Upon that Krishna Rāya said that he could hardly believe that the offer was made in good faith and suggested that it was only a blind for the son to join the father in the revolt. Viśvanātha Nāyaka made protestations of good faith and said that he would never be faithless to the ruler whose salt he had eaten. He pointed out that the duty he owed to his emperor was far superior to the duty he owed to his own father. After getting the emperor's consent Viśvanātha marched against his father with his own contingent of 2,000 horse and 6,000 infantry without any addition from the emperor.

Having reached the territory of Madura he sent word to his father that the emperor had ordered him to behead him. But all the same he promised to get him excused if, at least then, he gave back the territory of the Pāṇḍya and surrendered himself to him. Nāgama Nāyaka sent back in reply that it should make no difference to the emperor whether the Pāṇḍya ruled in the province or himself, and that he was wrong in his order. Recounting the several acts of heroism of Viśvanātha, Nāgama Nāyaka sought to persuade him to join him saying that he had conquered the Pāṇḍya country only for Viśvanātha's sake. Viśvanātha then sent back saying that he did not want the conquered kingdom and that, if he submitted to him quietly, he would beg the emperor to pardon him. If, on the other hand, he chose to fight, God would have no mercy on him and he could not win. At this Nāgama Nāyaka was greatly distressed and marched with all his army against Viśvanātha.

There was then fought a big battle between the forces of the father and the son in which the father was defeated and taken prisoner by the son. Viśvanātha was very glad that he had been able to capture his father alive, and placing him on an elephant safely guarded, proceeded towards the capital. He sent intimation to the emperor about his victory and of his father Nāgama being with him as prisoner.

The emperor Krishna Dēva Rāya was much pleased with the news and praised the high qualities of Viśvanātha Nāyaka in public court. He also said that Viśvanātha had done him very great service previously. Once he destroyed a wild bison that was advancing upon Krishna Rāya with a single stroke of his sword. He had also marched against foreign kingdoms and brought them under subjection. The emperor expressed his view that it was very sinful to keep such an able general in a subordinate position and wanted to make him the ruler of a feudatory kingdom.

Ten days after this Viśvanātha Nāyaka led his father prisoner into the court of Krishna Rāya. When the emperor spoke to Nāgama Nāyaka on his treachery he began by recounting how he had been appointed viceroy of the Pāṇḍya country, and how he had spent vast sums of the imperial revenue and his own private money in bringing the kingdom to order.

When he offered the kingdom to the dispossessed Pāṇḍya after killing the Chōḷa usurper the Pāṇḍya said that he could not rule over so turbulent a province. Even then there was not perfect order throughout the country and several villages were not sending their revenues regularly to the treasury. The Pāṇḍya then said that he had no legitimate sons to succeed him as king, and that he would be content if Nāgama Nāyaka ruled the kingdom giving him adequate pension. But after Nāgama Nāyaka conquered the whole kingdom according to the agreement, the Pāṇḍya fled to the imperial court and made the complaint. When the Pāṇḍya heard this, he said that it was true that he had come to an agreement with Nāgama Nāyaka, and that he broke it only because the condition of his being allowed a decent position after the conquest was not properly fulfilled.

When the emperor expressed his anger at the Pāṇḍya for not stating the full facts earlier, Viśvanātha interceded on his behalf and begged the emperor not to be angry with the Pāṇḍya. Then the Pāṇḍya said that even then he had no objection to give over his kingdom to Viśvanātha Nāyaka according to the agreement. Then the emperor turned to Viśvanātha and expressed his profound satisfaction at his sense of duty in proceeding against his own father for the sake of the king, and bringing him to the court as a prisoner. He excused the faults of the father on the son's account, and gave them leave to return home for the day.

After they went home Viśvanātha begged pardon of his father for fighting against him for the sake of the king. He had his father anointed and made him wear new clothes, and after many charitable gifts fed a large number of Brahmans. Nāgama Nāyaka then showed his son the large amount of wealth that he had accumulated during his life-time, and asked him to take all. He said that the emperor would appoint him as viceroy over the Pāṇḍya country and directed him to spend the money in improving the temple of Mīnākshi and Sundarēśvara at the place, and in improving the productivity of the country by the construction of anicuts and irrigation canals.

Some days later the emperor summoned both the Pāṇḍya and Viśvanātha Nāyaka before him. He addressed the Pāṇḍya and asked him whether he still stuck to the agreement by which he gave the kingdom to Viśvanātha inasmuch as he had no legitimate heirs to succeed him. The Pāṇḍya replied that he had absolutely no objection to the procedure. He also said that even if he wanted to rule, he would not have a peaceful time of it in view of the hostility of the illegitimate successors of his predecessors who were at Tenkāśi, Śrīvilliputtūr and Rājāpāḷaiyam. Then the emperor turned to Viśvanātha and said that he would appoint him as the viceroy of the Pāṇḍya country, i.e. (the master of the southern throne).

Viśvanātha Nāyaka then proceeded with a large army to his new viceroyalty. When he reached Madura and saw the fort and palaces of the place, he formed a very poor impression of them having come from the imperial headquarters. He then summoned before him his subordinates Ariyanāyakam Mudaliyar and Bisapākam Kēśavappa Nāyuḍu, the general, and directed them to re-build the fort of Madura with eight gates, and with Bhairava's bastions all round. He also ordered them to construct afresh the temples of Mīnākshi and Sundarēśvara. When they said that the projects would cost a very large sum which the treasury could not afford just then, and counselled him to be content with the old and modest building, he said that he would advance the money amassed by his father (Nāgama Nāyaka) and directed them to complete the works soon.

Viśvanātha Nāyaka maintained the status of the old Pānḍya king with very great consideration. As he was very old he lived for only a few months and died. Then Viśvanātha became the sole ruler of the Pānḍya and Chōla kingdoms, and governed them as a subordinate of the emperor at Vidyānagar (Vijayanagar).

The emperor Krishnadēva Rāya died sometime after this and was succeeded by his younger brother Achyuta Rāya. His queen was Tirumalamma. Her younger sister Mūrtyamma was married to Chevvappa Nāyaka. Achyuta Rāya appointed this Chevva as sole viceroy over the Chōla country which had till then continued along with the Pānḍya country in the viceroyalty of Madura. Now it was detached from Madura and placed under a separate viceroy. Chevva after taking charge of his new viceroyalty built many towers, manṭapas and compounds (prākāras) to the temples of Aruṇāchalam (Tiruvaṇṇāmalai) and Vṛddhāchalam. At the capital, Tanjore, he constructed the new Śivaganga fort and the large fresh water tank Śivappa Nāyani Gunṭa after his own name. He made extensive grants to many temples and ruled peacefully for a considerable period.

He was succeeded by his son Achyutappa Nāyaka who had as his general and minister the famous Govinda Dīkshita. He ruled the kingdom in peace and prosperity for a considerable pericd. His son Raghunātha Nāyaka succeeded him. He was a scholar in all the Śāstras and maintained all the dharmas of the kingdom. He constructed the Ramaswami temple at Kumbhakōnam and founded many new Agrahāras. He patronised many literary works like Vijayavilāsa * and himself wrote works like the Rāmāyaṇa. Raghunātha ruled the kingdom in great glory.

His son Vijayarāghava Nāyaka succeeded him and made large additions to the forts of Tanjore and improved the palace. He began the construction of the four forts of Paṭṭukkoṭṭai, Atanḍāgy (Arantangi ?), Reḷātalli (?) and Tiruppattūr on a single day and made them very strong. He built the towers, manṭapas and prākāras of the large temple of Rājagōpala at Mannārguḍi. At Māyūra (Māyavaram) and Madhyārjuna (Tiruviḍaimaruḍūr) he constructed manṭapas that could hold ten thousand people at the same time near the bathing ghats on the Kaveri. He also made many munificent grants to other institutions. Every day before 1 yāma (9 o'clock) he used to feed 12,000 Brahmans in his kingdom and himself eat after that.

He used to go from his palace at Tanjore to the temple of Śrīrangam which was 3 āmaḍa (30 miles) distant daily. He had 50 changes of Boyees on the road and used to start early morning at sunrise and return after worshipping the God after 16 ghaḍis (12·24 o'clock).

Once Chokkanātha Nāyaka, the ruler of Madura, sent his relatives and agents (Sthānāpatis) to his court with presents of cloth and jewels to request from Vijayarāghava Nāyaka, the hand of one of his daughters. They told Vijayarāghava that the relationship between the two families was no new one and had continued from the time of Raja Pedda Vīrappa Nāyaka to that of Tirumala Śauri (Tirumala Nāyak). Vijayarāghava was very angry at the request since the grandfather of Chokkanātha (Tirumala Śauri) who had married Achyuta Raghunāthamma of the Tanjore house (probably sister of Raghunātha Nāyaka and daughter of Achyutappa) stabbed her for simply telling her husband that his new-built palace was not to be compared with her father's palace. The Tanjore royal family thereupon resolved that from that time there should be no more marriage relations between the two houses. Vijayarāghava wondered how the Madura sovereign could think of a marriage alliance with Tanjore in view of this previous action and dismissed the envoys with scant courtesy.

---

* Vijayavilāsa is an excellent Telugu poem written by the poet Chémakūra Venkaṭa Kavi and dedicated to Raghunātha who himself wrote the Rāmāyana in Telugu. This was translated into Sanskrit once more by the lady poet Madhuravāṇi who lived at his court. There was also a hall called Vijayavilāsam in the palace.

The extract given below carries the story so far. But the original continues it. Enraged at the insolent behaviour of Vijayarāghava, Chokkanātha Nāyaka ordered his commander of the troops (Daḷavāi) Venkatākrishnappa Nāyudu and the pēshkār (accountant) Chinnatambi Mudaliyar to proceed against Tanjore with an army. They concentrated all their troops at Trichinopoly and proceeded against the fort of Vallam which soon after fell into their hands. From Vallam they marched upon Tanjore and laid siege to the place. After sometime they were able to storm the fort and enter Tanjore. Then Vijayarāghava ordered his son Mannāru Dāsa whom he had for sometime imprisoned in golden chains to be released and brought before him. When he came before him both the father and son expressed regret for the past, and consulted as to what should be done. Mannār Dās said that in the actual circumstances of their position it was better to fight to the last without giving way. They prepared to fight to the death, and to prevent the enemy from triumphing and attaining his object after their deaths, ordered that on news of their deaths the harem should be blown up. The ladies of the harem approved of the step and awaited the signal.

Vijayarāghava and Mannār Dās with their few followers fought till all were killed. Just before the fall of Vijayarāghava one of his guards gave the signal and all the members of the harem were destroyed in the expiosion or by stabbing each other with swords and daggers. Just before this tragic event one of the queens of Vijayarāghava gave her young son who was four years old, to a nurse with all her jewellery which was worth a very large sum, and allowing her to escape, commissioned her to bring up the child. Chokkanātha Nāyaka assumed rule over the whole territory of Tanjore and appointed his foster brother Aḷagiri as governor of the country. The nurse who had escaped with the prince Chengamala Dās went to Negapatam where she and the boy were both secretly maintained by a wealthy merchant who gave the boy a good education and made him a good gymnast. Hearing about this one of the members of Vijayarāghava's court, a Niyogi, Rāyasam Venkanna by name, went to Negapatam and secretly collected some followers who still remained faithful to the house of Vijayarāghava. Collecting about 200 of these he escaped with Chengamala Dās and the nurse to Bijāpur. There they sought the assistance of the Sultan of Bijapur to reinstate Chengamala Dās once more as ruler of Tanjore. Just before leaving for Negapatam, Rāyasam Venkanna had commissioned some of the courtiers of Aḷagiri the ruler of Tanjore, to create hostilities between him and his master Chokkanātha of Madura.

Soon there arose some disputes between Chokkanātha and Aḷagiri and the former was waiting for an opportunity to proceed against his subordinate. Rāyasam Venkanna and Chengamala Dās after escaping to Bijapur concluded an agreement with the Sultan to make Chengamala Dās the ruler of Tanjore. The Sultan appointed Ekojee, the son of his Minister Shahji to lead the expedition against Tanjore. He marched with his army against the kingdom of Tanjore and first reduced the fort of Ayyampet. After its fall there was a severe battle between the forces of Aḷagiri and Ekojee in which Aḷagiri was completely defeated. He fled with the remnants of his troops to Tanjore. From there he wrote a supplicating letter to his former master the Nāyak of Trichinopoly for assistance and begged to be excused for his past wrongs. But Chokkanātha did not send any assistance. The troops of Ekojee approached the fort of Tanjore and were erecting batteries for its siege. Aḷagiri suspecting some treachery among his own followers within the fort, left the place with a few followers one night and escaped by way of Ariyalūr to the territory of Mysore.

On hearing of the flight of Aḷagiri, Venkanna arranged for the triumphal entry of Chengamala Dās and Ekojee into Tanjore, and made preparations for Chengamala Dās' coronation. The forces of Ekojee retired to Kumbhakōnam after the coronation, on receiving very substantial remuneration for their services and getting guarantees for the amounts that were due to the Sultan of Bijāpur to defray the expenses of the expedition. But soon there arose a dispute in the court of Chengamala Dās on his appointing the rich merchant of Negapatam who had protected him in his youth as his minister and commander-in-chief, a post to which Rāyasam Venkanna himself aspired. Being disappointed he escaped to Kumbhakōnam where Ekojee was with his troops and induced him to proceed against Chengamala Dās and become the ruler himself. Ekojee was unwilling at first.

But while these negotiations were going on news came that that Sultan of Bijāpur was killed in battle with Aurangázeb and his territories occupied. On hearing the news Ekojee made bold to proceed against Tanjore. But Rāyasam Venkanna had already written to Chengamala Dās that in spite of his remonstrances Ekojee was marching against Tanjore and advised him to escape from the fort, the best course that could be adopted in the circumstances. He wrote that they might regain Tanjore on a favourable opportunity. The young Raja of Tanjore and his minister were in great fear and escaped to Ariyalūr by night; and Ekojee was able to capture Tanjore at very little cost. Rāyasam Venkanna by his ability brought the whole kingdom firmly under Ekojee and restored order in the territory. But Ekojee and his friends thought that Venkanna was a dangerous servant considering how faithlessly he had acted to his former masters Aḷagiri and Chengamala Dās. They suspected that he might act in the same deceitful manner towards Ekojee and wished to keep him under restraint. But Venkanna came to hear of this in time and escaped secretly from Tanjore blaming his own genius. Thus Tanjore finally came under the Mahratta dynasty.

తంజావూరి యాంధ్రరాజులచరిత్ర.

ఆదిలో కృష్ణరాయలవారు కటకం మొదలుకొని కన్యాకుమారిదాకా దేశం లోపరుచుకొని సుఖసత్కథావినోదంతో విజయనగరములో రాజ్యం యేలుతూవుండగా, మధురలో చంద్రశేఖరపాండ్యుడున్నూ తంజావూరులో వీరశేఖరచోళుడున్నూ రాయలవారికి వశవర్తులై రాజ్యం చేస్తూవుండిరి. ఆలో తంజావూరు వీరశేఖరచోళరాజు బలాత్కారంగా మధుర చంద్రశేఖరపాండ్యున్ని జయించి ఆ రాజ్యం యావత్తు కట్టుకొని యేలసాగెను. అందువల్ల చంద్రశేఖరపాండ్యుడు యెత్తుపడి విజయనగరం రాయలసముఖానకు వచ్చి జరిగినవర్తమానం విన్నవించుకుంటూ "మాదగ్గిర కప్పం పుచ్చుకొని మమ్ము ఆజ్ఞలో నడిపించుకొని వస్తూవున్నారు. లోకంలో 'దుర్బలస్య బలంరాజా' అని న్యాయం వున్నది. మాకు గతియేమి ఆజ్ఞాపిస్తారో ఆలా నడుచుకొంటున్నాము. మాకు దిక్కు మీరుగాని మరియెవరూ లే"దంటే అప్పుడు రాయలవారు ఆ మాటలు విని ఆగ్రహపడి తమ తోశేఖానా అధికారి అయిన నాగమనాయని పిలిపించి దక్షిణరాజ్యం యావత్తూ మీ తోశేఖానాకు అడమానం వున్నదిగదా! యిట్లా వుండగా పాండ్యుడి రాజ్యం చోళుడు బలాత్కారంచేసి కట్టుకోవడ మేమిటి? మీరే సైన్యసమేతంగా పోయి ఆ దుష్టుడైన వీరశేఖరచోళరాజును తగినట్టు శిక్షచేయండి ఈ పాండ్యరాజుకు యథాప్రకారం రాజ్యం యిప్పించండి. చోళరాజ్యం జప్తీచేసి సరాకారు యిలాకాలో మనుష్యులను వుంచి మీ జమాబంది అర్థం

మాత్రం మీరు తీసుకొని తిరిగి రండి అని ఆజ్ఞాపించిరి. అప్పుడు పాండ్యరాజును తోడుకొని నాగమనాయనివారు దళసమేతంగావచ్చి వీరశేఖరచోళుణ్ణి శిక్షచేసి ఆ రాజ్యం తనవశం చేసుకొనిరి. తర్వాత మధురకు పోయి చోళుడు వుంచివున్న ఠాణాలను తరమగొట్టిరి. కాని రాయల వుత్తరువుప్రకారం పాండ్యుడికి యివ్వక ఆ రాజ్యమున్నూ తానే అపహరించుకొని అనేక దినములనుండి పాండ్యుడికి స్వాధీనంగాని గ్రామాలు యావత్తూ ఆజ్ఞలోనికి తెచ్చుకొని స్వతహాగా రెండు రాజ్యాలు యేలుకుంటూ వుండిరి. అప్పుడు పాండ్యరాజు తిరిగి విజయనగరం పోయి రాయలవారి దగ్గర "మీరయితే మాకు రాజ్యం యావత్తు కట్టియిస్మని నాగమనాయనివారిని అంపించినారుగాని ఆయన చోళరాజును కొట్టి ఆ రాజ్యం పాండ్యరాజ్యం రెండూ తానే కట్టుకొన్నాడు" అని ఫిర్యాదు చేసుకొన్నంతలో రాయలవారు నాగమనాయని పేరను ఆజ్ఞ వ్రాయించిరి. పాండ్యరాజ్యం పాండ్యుడికి పట్టం కట్టమంటే నీవు అపహరించుకొన్నావు. నిన్ను ఆ విధంగా రాజ్యమేలడానికి మేము అంపించలేదు. గనుక యీ ఆజ్ఞ చూస్తూనే చంద్రశేఖరపాండ్యుడికి పట్టం కట్టి అతి త్వరగా నీవు లేచి రమ్మని వ్రాయించినారు. అప్పుడు నాగమనాయనివారు జాబులువ్రాసినదేమనగా—ఈ గ్రామాలు యావత్తూ జాగ్రత్తచేసేటప్పటికి నేను అనేక ద్రవ్యం కర్చుచేసినాను. ఈ పాండ్యుడు ఇంతకులోనయినం మీదగ్గరికి రారాదా! ఇంత అరాచకంగా ఉన్న రాజ్యం మనకు స్వాధీనానకు గాదని ఇదివరదాకా ఊరికే ఉన్నాడు. ఇప్పుడు చోళరాజును కొట్టి రాజ్యం కట్టడంకాకుండా అరాచకంగా ఉన్న రాజ్యంకూడా స్వాధీనంలోనికి తేవడం చూచినాడు. ఇంతకు మునుపు రాజ్యం నాకు స్వాధీనానకు గాదు. మీరు యావత్తు కట్టుకొని నాకు అన్నవస్త్రాలకు మాత్రం జరిగిస్తే చాలును అని చెప్పుకొంటూ ఉండేవాడు ఇప్పుడు అతనికి ఆశపుట్టింది. అయితే నేమాయెను. అతనికి రాజ్యం ఇస్తే నగరికి శోఘారూకలుకూడా రావు.

మరిన్నీ ఇతను పాండ్యవంశం అని చెప్పుకోవడంమాత్రమే కాని జాతికి తక్కువ. దాసి కొమారుడు. రాజ్యం ఇతనికి అర్హంకాదు గనుకనే చోళరాజు కట్టుకొని యితణ్ణి వెళ్లగొట్టినాడు. దూరంగా ఉన్నాము గనుక ఈ జాతినీతులు మనకు తెలియలేదు. ఇంతకు నేను బహుదినములు తమ కొలువు కొలిచినాను. ఇక కొన్నిదినములు అయినా సుఖపడవద్దా! ఇదిగాక అనేక ద్రవ్యం యీ సంస్థానంమీద పెట్టి

యింతమాత్రం రాజ్యం స్వాధీనంలోనికి తెచ్చినాను. నా అర్థం యాపత్తు రాబట్టుకొని నేను వస్తానుకాని అంత స్వతంత్రం నేను వచ్చేది లేదు—అని సమాచారం వ్రాసి అంపించినంతలో రాయలువారికి బహు కోపం వచ్చింది. నాగమనాయడు మా ఆజ్ఞకు తప్పి నడచినాడు గనుక అతని తల మీరు ఎవరైనా తేగలరా అని అడిగెను. అప్పుడు నాగమనాయని కుమారుడు విశ్వనాథనాయనివారు లేచి రాయలవారి సముఖానకువచ్చి, నాకు ఉత్తరువిస్తే తెస్తానని అన్నారు. అప్పుడు రాయలవారు 'మీ తండ్రిగారి దగ్గరకు మీరుకూడాపోయి కలుసుకోవడానికి ఆజ్ఞ అడుగుతారా" అని ఆక్షేపిస్తే అప్పుడు విశ్వనాథనాయనివారు "ఎక్కడయినాకద్దా? ఏలినవారి సొమ్ము తింటూవున్నాము. స్వామికార్యం ప్రధానంకాని తండ్రి ఎక్కువకా'దని అన్నారు. అప్పుడు సర్కారు రాణువ అక్కర లేకుండా తన యెప్పటి బలం రెండు వేల గుఱ్ఱాలతో ఆరు వేల కాల్బలంతో మధురసీమకువచ్చి, తండ్రిగారి వద్దికి సమాచారం అంపించిన వయనం ఏమంటే—మీరు రాయలవారి ఆజ్ఞకు తప్పినడచినారు. మిమ్మును తలకొట్టి తెమ్మని ఉత్తరువు అయింది. అయితే నేమాయెను. ఇప్పుడయినా పాండ్య రాజ్యం పాండ్యులకి పట్టంకట్టి మీరు లేచివస్తే రాయలవారితో చెప్పి మాపు చేయిస్తాను రండని సమాచారం అంపిస్తే తిరుగా నాగమనాయనివారు తన కుమారుడివద్దికి కబురు అంపిన వైనం—రాయలవారిపట్టున నీవు సమస్తరాజ్యాలు సాధించినావుగదా ఇదిగాక నేనున్నూ చాలా రాజ్యం సాధించినాను. రెండు మూడు మార్లుపోయిన సంస్థానం నిలువబెట్టినాము. నీవు ఎంత మెహన్నతుచేసినా ఆ ఘనత నన్ను చెందవలెను గాని మరిఒకటికాదు. రాయలు విశ్వాసంకలిగినవాడే గనుక అయితే పాండ్య రాజ్యం ఉన్నప్పుడు దాసి కొమారుడు అనుభవిస్తే ఆయనకు వచ్చిందేమి? మనం అనుభవిస్తే రాకపోయిందేమి? నిన్ను బహు తపస్సుచేసి కన్నాము. ఏకపుత్ర విషయము; కాబట్టి నిష్కారణంగా నాతో ఎందుకు యుద్ధంచేస్తావు? ఇంతకూ ఈ వ్యాజ్యం కట్టడం నీకేమి త్తంగాని వేరే లేదు. తమతో కస్తురి సమాచారం అంపిస్తే తిరుగా విశ్వనాథనాయనివారు తండ్రిగారికి సమాచారం అంపించినవయినం ఏమంటే—స్వామికార్యానికి తప్పినడిచినారు గనుక మీరు తండ్రులు కారు నేను కొమారుణ్ణికాను. మీరు సంపాదనచేసిన రాజ్యమున్నూ నాకు అక్కరలేదు. తిన్నగా వస్తిరా ప్రభువారి సముఖానికితీసుకొని

పోయి ప్రాణానికి భయం లేకుండా చేయిస్తాను. అథవా ఒకవేళ యుద్ధం చేసినా గెలిచేపాటి బలము మీకు భగవంతుడు ఇవ్వడు. నా మనస్సులో ప్రతిజ్ఞ యేవిధంచేతనూ మిమ్ము తీసుకొనిపోయి రాయలవారియెదుట పెట్టడమే అదే సకలసామ్రాజ్యాలు ఏలడం గనుక తండ్రి అని విచారించను—అని సమాచారం అంపించినంతలో నాగమనాయనివారు బహు కష్టపడుతూ అన్నమాటలు—నేను ఈ కొమారుడు కలుగవలెనని బహు తపస్సుచేసి విశ్వనాథస్వామివారిని ప్రార్థించినందుకు నామీద కత్తియెత్తే కొమారుడు కలిగినాడు. ఈ కొమారుడు బ్రతికినా సరే చచ్చినా సరే అని తన తాలూకు రాణువ యావత్తు కూర్చుకొని యుద్ధానికి వచ్చెను. అప్పుడు ఘోరయుద్ధం అయింది నాగమనాయనివారు కొమారునికి చాలక వోడిపోయి దొరికినారు. దొరకగానే విశ్వనాథనాయనివారు ఇంతమాత్రం ప్రాణాలతోను దొరికినారు నకంచేసిన తపస్సు యొక్క బలం అని అంబారీమీద యెక్కించి చుట్టు తన పారా కడాయించి తీసుకవస్తూ ముందు అతిత్వరగా తమ తండ్రిగారికిన్ని తనకున్నూ అయినయుద్ధమున్నూ ఆయన దొరకినదిన్ని తాను ఖయిదు చేసి తీసికొనివస్తూ వున్నదిన్ని సమాచారం వ్రాయించి అంపించిరి. నాటికి రాయలవారు కచ్చేరికి గొప్ప సేనానాయకులను పిలిపించి సెలవిచ్చినమాటలు నాగమనాయని మీదికి దండు ఎత్తమంటే ఎవ్వడు మాచేత అయ్యేపనికాదు మీరుచూచి ఉత్తరువు ఇస్తే అన్యాయముగాపోయి చచ్చిపోతామని అంటిరిగదా! విశ్వనాథనాయడు స్వామికార్యంచోట తండ్రిని చేయించినపని చూచినారుగదా! అని ఆయన వ్రాయించి అంపించిన జాబులు చూపించినంతలో కూర్చున్న సభయావత్తు ఆశ్చర్యపడి స్వామి! అతను మనుష్యులలో పరిగణన అయిన వాడుకాడు. కేవలం విశ్వనాథస్వామే అని సభవారు అంతా స్తోత్రంచేసిరి. రాయలవారు యిరుభుజాలు పొంగి, యింతటి బంటును మనం ఏలినాముగదా అని సంతోషపడి అందరు ఉండగా అన్నమాటలు—విశ్వనాథనాయడు మనుష్యులలో పరిగణన అయిన వాడుకాడు అని మీరుచెప్పిన మాటలేని బుద్ధి ఆయనమన కొలువుకింద ఉంచుకోవడానికి యోగ్యుడయిన మనిషికాడు. ఇక ఆయనచేత కొలువు చేయించితే మనకు దోషంవస్తుంది మనతోను సమంగా సింహాసనాధిపత్యానికి యోగ్యుడు. ఇదిగాక అడవిదున్నపోతును నరికినవాడున్ను పరాయిదేశపు రాజుల దేశం కట్టుకొన్నవాడున్ను అయి రెండుమాన్లు ఫంస్థానం నిలిపినాడు. గనుక ఆయన వచ్చినతరువాత యెక్కడనయినా

రాజ్యంయిచ్చి మనతో సమంగా వుంచవలెను అన్నారు. అప్పుడు సభ
వారు అంతా విన్నపం చేసినమాటలు—స్వామీ విశ్వనాథనాయనివారికి
రాజ్యం అపేక్ష ఉంటే తండ్రిగారివద్దకి పోయినప్పుడు ఇద్దరు ఒకటిఅయి
ఆ రాజ్యముకట్టుకొని మనమీదికికూడా దండుఎత్తితే ఎదురు పోజాలకపో
దుము. ఆయన కేవలం స్వామివారియొక్క అంశముగనుక తమచోట
బహు విశ్వాసముగా అంత కార్యంచేసుకొని వస్తూవున్నారు. తమరు
సర్వజ్ఞమూర్తులుగనుక తమకు తెలియనిదేమి ఉన్నది? అని విన్నపంచేసి
నారు. మరి పదినిమలకు విశ్వనాథనాయనివారు తండ్రిని తీసుకువచ్చి
రాయలవారియెదుటను నిలపెట్టెను. రాయలవారు నాగమనాయణ్ణి
చూచి ఇంత విశ్వాసఘాతం చేసినావని అడిగితే అప్పుడు నాగమనాయని
వారు విన్నపం చేసినమాటలు—<u>పాండ్య రాజ్యం మీ తండ్రిగారు మా
యొక్క కోసేఖానామీనను తనఖాయిచ్చినారు.</u> నాటనుంచి అనేకద్ర
వ్యం నష్టపెట్టుకొన్నాము. ఇవిగాక ఇప్పుడు చోళరాజునుకొట్టి పాం
డ్యరాజుకు రాజ్యం యిప్పించి సెలవు ఇచ్చినారు. ఆ యుద్ధంలో ఇక్కడ
నుంచి తమరు ఇప్పించి అంపించిన అర్థంకాకుండా ఇంకా అనేక అర్థం
కర్చుఅయినది. ఇట్లా బహుశ్రమపడి చోళుణ్ణికొట్టి పాండ్యరాజ్యం యి
తనికి పట్టంకట్టించి పోతాము అంటే, ఈ పాండ్యుడు అన్నమాటలు—
చోళరాజును కొట్టడానకు తమ చేతగనుక సాధ్యపడినది. లేనట్టయితే ఎన్న
టికి స్వాధీనానికి రాకపోను ఇప్పటికిన్నీ రాజ్యం అరాచకంగా ఎవరి
గ్రామాలువారు అనుభవిస్తూ మనకు స్వాధీనానికిరాక ఉన్నారు. చోళ
రాజు నన్ను అన్యాయంచేసి రాజ్యంకట్టినాడన్న పేరుమాత్రమేగాని
ఆయనకూ ఈ గ్రామాలు యావత్తు స్వాధీనానికిరాలేదు. ఇంతకు మా
యొక్క శత్రువునుకొట్టినారు. ఇదేపదివేలు ఇదిగాక నాకున్న సం
తానములేదు. ఉన్నవారు అంతా ఉంపుడందాని కొడుకులు నాజీ
వం ఉన్నంతవరకూ మర్యాదగా జరుపుతూ నాకు అన్నవస్త్రాలకుమాత్రం
యిచ్చి నాపగవాడయిన చోళరాజుకు మాత్రంచెందనివ్వక నాపేరుగా
మీరే పలుకుతూ ఉంటేచాలునన్నాడు. అప్పుడు ఈ రాజ్యాలు యావ
త్తు బహు అరాజకముగా ఉన్నవి. బహుధనం వ్యయముచేసి రాజ్యం
బందోబస్తు చేసినాను. ఇప్పుడు మీదగ్గిరికి ఫిర్యాదుకువచ్చినాడు. అని
వారికి తమకు జరిగినకరార్లున్ను, తమకు వ్యయం చేసిన అర్థమున్ను రాయ
లవారికి తెలియబరచిరి. రాయలవారు చూచి అప్పుడు పాండ్యుణ్ణి
పిలిచి "నీవుచాలా పెద్దమనిషివని, నీమాటబహునిబద్ధి అని, మేము నమ్మి

కొని యింతమద్దస్తుచేసి అంపించినాము. ఈ సంగతులు నిజమగునా కాదా ? అని అడిగితే నిజమే నేను అన్నది కద్దుగాని నా శరీరం ఉన్నంతవరకు మర్యాదగా గడుపుమన్నాను. అందుకు అటార్ణవు అయిందిగనుక ఫిరియాదుకు వచ్చినానని అంటె మునుపు ఇట్లా చెప్పరాదా అని బహుకోపముచేసిరి. అప్పుడు విశ్వనాథనాయనివారు రాయలవారిని మనవి పూర్వకంగా పాండ్యుడిపై గర్హితం లేకుండా మాట్లాడవలెనని మనవిచేసుకొంటే విశ్వనాథనాయనివారి మాటలు చెల్లించిరి. అప్పుడు తిరుగ రాయలవారిని చూచి పాండ్యుడు అన్నమాటలు—నేను ఇతని కొమారుడు విశ్వనాథనాయనివారికి రాజ్యం వ్రాసియిచ్చినాను. నేను ఇప్పటికి ఆమాట తప్పలేదు. రాజ్యం విశ్వనాథనాయనివారికి పట్టంకట్టితే బహు సంతోషం అన్నంతట విశ్వనాథనాయనివారిని ప్రభువువారు చూచి మీ తండ్రిని ఖయిదులో తెచ్చి పెట్టి రవంతైనా తండ్రి అన్నమాట విచారించక, స్వామికార్యం ప్రధానం చేసుకొని తలకొట్టుతానని అన్నావుగనుక నిన్ను చూచి మీ తండ్రిచేసిన తప్పు క్షమించినాము. ఈక్షణం ఇంటికిపొమ్మని ఆజ్ఞాపించినారు. అప్పుడు నాగమనాయనివారికి కయిదు విడిపించి, ఇంటికితీసుకొని వచ్చి యికమీరు తండ్రులు నేను కొమారుణ్ణి ఇంత పర్యంతం నేను మీకు శత్రువును అని అనేక విధాలను తండ్రిగారిని వేడుకొని స్నానంచేయించి, నూతన వస్త్రములు కట్టబెట్టి, అనేక దానధర్మములుచేసి ఆమరునాడు అనేక బ్రాహ్మణ భోజనములుచేయించి తండ్రి కొమాళ్లు బహుయిష్టంగావుండిరి. నాయనివారు కొమారుణ్ణి చూచి నీవు రాజ్యాంగంచేస్తూ ఉండవలెనని యింతపనికి ఒప్పుకొన్నానే గాని వేరుకాదు. ఇక నేను పరలోక సాధనంచూచుకొంటాను. నాకు ఇక కావలసినది యేమి వున్నది కనుక ? నేను సంపాదనచేసిన అర్థం యీ వస్తువున్నది. అంతా తీసుకో ఇదిగాక నీకు రాయలవారు రాజ్యం ఇస్తారు. మర్యాదగా కాపాడుకొమ్మనగా, కొమారుడు మీరార్జించిన అర్థం నాకు అక్కరలేదు. మీరే దానధర్మములుచేసుకొని పరలోక సాధనంచూచుకొండని అన్నారు. అందుకు నాగమనాయనివారు ఎక్కడనైనా కద్దా ! బహుదినములు తపస్సుచేసి కన్నందుకు నీకు ఇంత మాత్రం అర్థమయినా పెట్టకపోతే బాగావుండదు అని తను పెద్దలు సంపాదనచేసిన అర్థమున్నూ ఇదిగాక తాము సంపాదనచేసిన అర్థమున్నూ కొమారునికి కనుపరచిన తర్వాత విశ్వనాథనాయనివారు కన్నులు తిరిగి యింత అర్థం ఎట్లా సంపాదనచేసినారో తెలియదు అని ఆశ్చర్యపోయిరి.

నాగమనాయనివారు కొమారుణ్ణిచూచి తిరిగా అన్నమాటలు — పాండ్య రాజ్యంలో మధురలో మీనాక్షిసుందరేశ్వరస్వామివారి దివ్యస్థలం ఉన్నది. ఆ మీనాక్షిదేవి ప్రత్యక్షదైవంగనుక నాకు ఒకనాటి రాత్రి స్వప్నంలో నీ కొమారుడు విశ్వనాథనాయడు నా సన్నిధానాన ఉండి రాజ్యమంతా ఏలడానికి బహు యోగ్యుడు అని చెప్ప ఉన్నది. ఈ అర్థమంతా తీసుకొనిపోయి పాండ్యదేశములో దేవస్థానాలిను, ఇంకా ఏర్లకు రాతికట్లున్నూ కట్టి అనేక ధర్మాలు చేస్తే నాకు పరలోకం కలుగుతుంది. అని అన్నారు. తర్వాత రాయలవారు విశ్వనాథనాయణ్ణి పాండ్యుణ్ణికూడా పిలిపించి ప్రత్యేకం పాండ్యునితోను అన్నమాటలు — నీకు ఉంపుడుదాని కొమారుడు ఒకడు మాత్రం ఉన్నాడుగాని తగిన సంతానం లేదు గదా! విశ్వనాథనాయనివారికి దేశం ఇవ్వడం బహుసమ్మతి అని ఆయన పేరంటికి వ్రాసియిచ్చి ఉన్నావు. అది సత్యమా అంటే అడిగినారు. అప్పుడు పాండ్యుడు అన్నమాటలు — నాకు సర్వథా దేశం అక్కర లేదు. ఒక వేళ నేను దేశం కావలెనని కోరినా చోళరాజు నన్ను ప్రాణంతో నిలవనివ్వడు. ఇదిగాక, మా తండ్రి తాతల ఉంపుడు సంబంధాలకు పుట్టిన వారు శ్రీవిల్లిపుత్తూరు, తెంగాశి, రాజపాళియం ఆ స్థలములలో ఉన్నారు. వారున్నూ తెలగా పరంగయ్యారు. నాగమనాయనివారు అన్ని స్థలములు సాధించినారుగాని ఆ అయిదు స్థలములు మాత్రం సాధించలేక పోయినారు. వారు పంచపాండవులని పేరు ఎత్తుకున్నారు. ఇంతకు నా పగవాళ్లు అయిన చోళరాజుకు ఈ పాండ్యులకు మాత్రం రాజ్యం ఇయ్యక విశ్వనాథనాయనివారు ఏలుతుంటే నాకు పరమసంతోషం. ఇప్పుడు రక్షించడానికి విశ్వనాథనాయుడు నాకు తండ్రివంటివాడు. అనగా అప్పుడు రాయలవారు విశ్వనాథనాయనివారిని పిలిచి పాండ్య రాజ్యానికి పట్టం కట్టుతాము. మాకు సమంగా దక్షిణసింహాసనాధిపతివి గా ఉండుమని ఆశీర్వచనం చేసి అడవి మహిషాన్ని ముక్కలుగా నరికి దుర్గకు బలి ఇచ్చినావు పరాయి దేశపు రాజులు సంస్థానంమీదికి వచ్చినపుడు హీనబలంతోను పోయి వారిని సంహారం చేసి సంస్థానం నిలువతీసినావు. ఇది గాక మీ తండ్రిగారు పోయి మమ్మును లక్ష్యం సేయక ఆజ్ఞ నిరాకరిస్తే స్వామికార్యమే ఎక్కువ అని పట్టితెచ్చి ఎదుటపెట్టి తల కొట్టుతానని అన్నావు. ఇంత మేలు నీవు చేసినప్పుడు, నిన్ను మరిస్తే మాకు దైవం సహాయము కాదు. లో వయసం నీవు రెండు మూడు పనులు చేసి మా దయ సంపాదన చేసుకొన్నప్పుడు నీకు రాజ్యం మాతో సమంగా కల్పిస్తామని అన్నాము. ఇది

గాక ఈ రాజ్యం నీ పరంగా ఉంటేనే కాని నగరికి తోఫా రూకలు కూడా రావు. యిక నీవు పాండ్య రాజ్యానికి పోయి దేశం బందోబస్తు చేస్తేనే గాని అనుకూలం కాదు. గనుక త్వరగా వెళ్లి దక్షిణ సింహాసనాధిపతి వికస్మని సమాధానం పరిచినారు. అంతట విశ్వనాథనాయనివారు దుర్గ మహాలక్ష్మిని తీసుకొని మధురకు వెళ్లేటప్పుడు తమ సేన అంతా ఇచ్చి బహు సంభ్రమంగా అంపించినారు. విశ్వనాథనాయనివారు అట్లా విచ్చేసి మధురసీమనున్ను పాండ్యశికోటనున్ను చూచేటప్పటికి రాయసంస్థానం చూచిన కన్నులకు ఏమీ రాణించక ఆరియనాయకం మొదలారిని బిసపాకం కేశవప్పనాయన్ని యిద్దరిని పిలిపించి యీ కోట మాకు ఉండడానికి అనుకూలం కాదు. మధురచుట్టు బైరవుడి బురుజులున్ను, ఎనిమిదిద్వారాలున్ను కలిగిన కోట, మీనాక్షిదేవికోవిల, సుందరేశ్వరస్వామివారి కోవిల కట్టించమని ఉత్తరవు చేసినారు. అప్పుడు అరియనాయకం మొదలారిన్ని కేశవప్పనాయడున్ను మనవి చేసిన వయినం—ఇంతపనికి మనదగ్గిర బొక్కసంలో అర్థం లేదు. ఇప్పుడు ఇంతలో ఇమిషీవుంటే మరికొన్ని దినములు జరిగిన తర్వాత మీచిత్తం వచ్చినట్టు పని చేస్తామని అన్నారు. అంతకు బహుకోపం చేసి మా తండ్రిగారు సంపాదన చేసిన అర్థం ఉన్నది. తెప్పిస్తాము ఇందువల్లను పని అవుతుంది. అని చెప్పి ఆధనంతో ఆ ఘనకార్యములు సాగించి నెరవేర్పించెను. వెనుకటి పాండ్యరాజును విశ్వనాథనాయనివారు ఎంతో గవురవంతో నడిపిరి. వృద్ధుడు గనుక ఆయన కొన్ని మాసములకు స్వర్గస్థుడాయెను. విశ్వనాథనాయనివారే చోళరాజ్యం పాండ్యరాజ్యం రెండు రాజ్యాలూ తమ మేలుబడికింద పెట్టుకొని విద్యానగరం రాయలవారికి లోనుగా పరిపాలనం జరుపుతూ వుండేవారు.

ఆ విధంగా కొన్ని సంవత్సరములు గడచిన తర్వాత శ్రీకృష్ణదేవరాయల తమ్ముడు అచ్యుతదేవరాయలవారు రాజ్యానికి వచ్చిరి. ఆయన భార్య తిరుమలమ్మ ఆమె చెల్లెలు మూర్తిమ్మను వివాహమాడిన చెవ్వప్పనాయనివారికి అచ్యుతదేవరాయలవారు స్త్రీధనంగా చోళరాజ్యం దయచేసి, పట్టాభిషిక్తుణ్ణి చేసి, కావలసిన వస్తువాహన సామగ్రినిన్ని యిచ్చి అక్కడకు పంపించిరి. చోళదేశానికి ప్రత్యేకంగా నాథుడు లేనందువల్ల విశ్వనాథనాయనివారినే గాక స్వజనంగా అక్కడ మరివొకరిని కూడా యేర్పరచవలెననే తలంపుతో అచ్యుతరాయలవారు ఈ విధముగా

చేసిరి. చెవ్వప్పనాయడు అకరూఢ విశ్వనాథనాయనివారికి పొంది వున్న రాజ్యం అధీనంలోనికి తెచ్చుకొనెను. ఆయన అరుణాచలం లోను వృద్ధాచలంస్థలంలోను అనేక గోపురప్రాకారమంటపాలు నిర్మించి తంజావూరులో శివగంగకోటకట్టించి తనపేర శివప్పనాయని కుంట అని తెటాకం త్రవ్వించి దేవాలయబ్రహ్మాలయాల కెంతో విశేషము గాస్థితులుకలుగచేసి బహుదినములు రాజ్యమేలెను. అటుతరువాత అతని కుమారుడు అచ్యుతప్పనాయడు గోవింద దీక్షితులకు దళకర్తప్రధానిక మిచ్చి బహుకీర్తిచంద్రుడుగా చోళదేశమందు అనేక అగ్రహారాలు దేవాలయబ్రహ్మాలయాదులైన అనేక ధర్మాలు కలుగజేసి చాలకాలం రాజ్యమేలెను.

తరువాత అతని కుమారుడు రఘునాథనాయడు సకల శాస్త్రములయందును మహాప్రవీణుడయి సకల ధర్మములు విచారించి కుంభకోణమందు రామస్వామిగుడికట్టించి ఎన్నో అగ్రహారములు తెటాకములు కలుగజేసి విజయవిలాసం మొదలయిన అనేక గ్రంథములు అందులోని రామాయణం మొదలయిన గ్రంథాలు రచించి మహాప్రసిద్ధుడుగా బహుదినాలు రాజ్యమేలెను. ఈయన కుమారుడు విజయరాఘవనాయడు పట్టాభిషిక్తుడై రాజ్యానకువచ్చి తంజావూరుకోట బలపరచి నగరు విస్తారముగా హెచ్చించెను. అతండాగె, పట్టుకోట, శేల్లాతల్లి, తిరుపత్తూరు. ఈ నాలుగు కోటలున్ను ఒక మహాత్మమందే ఆరంభించి రాతికోటలుగా కట్టించెను. మన్నారుగుడిలో రాజగోపాలస్వామికి గోపురమంటప ప్రాకారములు విస్తారముగ నిర్మించెను. మాయూరమందు మధ్యార్జునమందు కావేరిస్నానఘట్టములలో పున్యమంటపాలు పదివేల ప్రజవుండేటట్టు విశాలముగా కట్టించెను. అనేక దేవాలయబ్రహ్మాలయములకు నిరంతరస్థితి కలుగజేసెను. ఆయన ప్రతిదినము ఉదయమయిన జాములోగా పన్నెండువేల బ్రాహ్మణ్యానికి షడ్రసోపేతముగా జ్యేష్టాంశమిప్పించి తరువాత తాను భోజనముచేస్తూవుండేవాడు.

* * * * *

అప్పుమొదలు ఆ స్వామి అమ్మవార్లసన్నిధికి పోయేటందుకు తంజనగరానికిన్ని శ్రీరంగానికిన్ని ఉన్నదూరం మూడామడకున్ను యాభయి

జోళ్ల బోయీలను నిరంతరం తపాల ఉంచిరి. విజయరాఘవనాయనివారు ప్రతిదినం నాలుగు గడియలుముందే లేచి సూర్యోదయమయ్యేటందులో స్నాన జపపూజలన్నీ తీర్చుకొని ఆతపాలమీద శ్రీరంగానికిపోయి స్వామి దర్శనంచేసుకొని పదహారోగడియకు తిరిగివచ్చి భోజనముచేసేవారు ఈ విధముగా మహాభక్తితో నడుస్తూవుండగా కొన్నిదినాలకు పిమ్మట రాజాచొక్కనాథ నాయనింగారు తమ వివాహార్థముగా తంజావూరి రాజావిజయరాఘవనాయని వారివద్దికి తమ బంధువులను స్థానాపతులనుకూర్చి వారి భేటికి యోగ్యమయిన వస్త్రభూషణాదులున్ను ఇచ్చి అంపించిరి వారున్ను వచ్చి భేటిచేసికొన్నందున విజయరాఘవనాయనివారు వచ్చిన వర్తమానమేమి అని అడిగిరి. వారున్ను "మాయేలిన స్వామివారు తమ వివాహానికి కన్యకార్థము దేవర సముఖాన మనవి చేయవలసినదని అంపించగా వచ్చినాము. రాజా పెద్దవీరప్ప నాయనివారు మొదలుకొని రాజా తిరుమలశౌరిగారివరకున్ను నడచివచ్చిన సంబంధముగాని నూతన చుట్టరికముగాదు గదా! దేవరవారు దయచేసి శుభవార్త ఉత్తరువు చేయవలె" అని అడిగినందుకు రాజా విజయరాఘవ నాయనింగారు మహాకోపముతో "ఇంతైనా భయంలేక కన్యకను ఇమ్మని అడుగవచ్చినందుకు తగినశాస్తి చేయవలెను. గతమే వీరి పితామహుడైన తిరుమలశౌరికి మా అచ్యుతరఘునాథమ్మగారిని పట్టమహిషిగా వివాహం చేసినారు. ఆతడు క్రొత్తగా నగరుకట్టించి మా అచ్యుత రఘునాథమ్మగారికి కనుగొనపించినప్పుడు ఆమె హాస్యముగాను, తమతండ్రి నగరికి సమానంరాదని ఒకమాట అన్నందుకు సహించలేక బాకుతో పొడిచినాడు. ఆ సమాచారం యిన్నప్పటి మావారందరు ఇటువంటి దుష్కృత్యులకు తెలియక వివాహంచేస్తిమి ఇకమీద వారికి మనకు సంబంధములే అక్కర లేదని ప్రతిజ్ఞచేసినారు. ఇట్లా జరిగివుండగా తిరిగీ సంబంధంకావలెనని యే బుద్ధితో మా వారి మావద్దికి మిమ్మను పంపించినా'' డని వారు కొంచుకవచ్చిన భేటి వస్తువులు అంగీకారంచేయక వారికి బత్తెం భరణం విచారించక "మరేమయినా వేరు పనులు కలిగితే మా వద్దికి రావచ్చును. ఇటువంటి పనులు కోరి యికమీదవస్తే తగిన ఆజ్ఞ చేయింతు"మని ఉత్తరువిచ్చి కోటకు బయట కొంచుకొనిపోయి విడువమని సేవకులకు ఆజ్ఞాపించినారు. ఆమేరకు కోటకు బయట కొంచుపోయి విడిచినారు.

99

ŚIVATATTVARATNĀKARA.

[*By Keḷadi Basava.*]

Kallōla V, Taranga VIII.—After recounting the achievements of Bhadrabhūpāla of Keḷadi this work proceeds to narrate the story of his successors. Bhadra taught his nephew (elder brother's son), Doḍḍa Sankaṇṇa Nāyaka, the science of polity (Rājanīti) essential for kings, and installing him as his successor, died soon after. Doḍḍa Sankaṇṇa Nāyaka ruled his kingdom to the entire satisfaction of his subjects. Then the Governor of the Jambūradēśa, Virūpaṇṇa by name, withheld the tribute of his province from the Vijayanagar emperor and was evincing signs of hostility. Doḍḍa Sankaṇṇa Nāyaka defeated him and brought him as a prisoner before the emperor. Highly pleased with his conduct, the emperor invited him to go to the capital and live at court, leaving the kingdom in charge of his younger brother. He obeyed the command and was living at the capital. Soon after, he had two sons whom he named Rāma Rāja and Venkaṭappa Nāyaka respectively. The emperor was pleased when he found that Sankaṇṇa Nāyaka named his son after himself. He added the districts of Hoḷē Honnūr, Māsūr and Bēlmallūr to his governorship, and gave him permission to return to his province. He returned to his brother and lived there for a short period. When the Portuguese (Parangis) became hostile, the emperor summoned Sankaṇṇa Nāyaka once more for service. Placing him and his troops under the orders of his relative Viṭṭhalarāja he sent them against the Parangis (Portuguese) of Goa.* The two generals completely defeated the Portuguese, and, capturing the Governor of Goa, brought him a prisoner to the emperor. For this achievement the emperor presented him with the town of Mahādēvapura. He afterwards returned to his province and lived there. After a time he resolved on going

---

* This statement is perhaps in reference to the invasion under Rāmarāja-Timmarāja-Viṭṭala-dēvarāja to Travancore and the Pāṇḍya country. Having brought the south under his control in behalf of Sadāsivarāya of Vijayanagar, he marched along as far as Nandyal, as it seems, against Bijapūr. All these transactions must have taken place before the year A.D. 1544-45, the date of No. 140 of 1895 of the Epigraphist's collection. Whether the invasion against Goa also took place in this campaign is not clear although it is quite possible. The invasion of Goa in favour of Abdulla Adil as against his brother Ibrahim Adil Shah, the Meale Khan of the Portuguese, is about 7 years later. The Portuguese Governor who was taken prisoner is not identifiable as neither the Portuguese historians nor Ferishta mention any such in the lifetime of Rāmarāya (Danvers: The Portuguese in India I, Chapters XVII—XX, and Briggs' Ferishta III, 78—113).

on a pilgrimage to all the sacred shrines of India. On an auspicious day he went on his great pilgrimage first to the south.

Taranga IX.—After having visited all the sacred shrines in the south like Rāmēśvaram, and bathed in the sacred Tīrthas, he turned north. Seeing all the famous Śiva shrines (Lingas) on his way he ultimately reached Kāśi (Benares) on the sacred Ganges, and worshipped the far-famed Viśvēśa at the place. He then proceeded to Nīlakanṭha Nēpāḷa (Nepal), and after worshipping the God Kēdārēśa went to Kāsmir. From there he went to Kurukshētra and thence wanted to go to Delhi which was in ancient days called Indraprastha. While entering the city he saw (a sword hung) at one of the gates, and enquired what it signified. He was told by the gate-keeper that the sword was placed there by the chief Ankusa Khan to be taken down by anybody who would dare to fight with him. On hearing the story he wanted to imitate the acts of the Mahābhārata hero Bhima, at the gate of the Matsya king, and directed one of his followers to take down the sword. This was reported to Ankusa Khan by the gate-keeper who reported the matter to the emperor of Delhi. The emperor thereupon summoned Sankaṇṇa Nāyaka before him and, offering him a sword himself, directed him to fight a duel with Ankusa Khan. In the duel Śankaṇṇa Nāyaka managed to fell his opponent. Admiring his heroism the emperor of Delhi enquired about his history and, being pleased, presented him with valuable gifts and titles, as well a jaghir in his own territory. The jaghir that was made to him he gave to the God of Benares and constructed mutts, temples and gardens in the holy place.

He then returned to his own country and lived at a village called Vaṭavalli in the district of Māsūr. There he dreamt that a yogi directed him to construct various temples. At Keḷadi he constructed the temple of Vīrabhadra near the temple of Rāmēśvara.

Taranga X.—Sankaṇṇa Nāyaka constructed at Keḷadi and Ikkēri the temples of Rāmēśvara and Aghorēśvara respectively. He then installed his younger brother on the gadi and taught him the science of war.

Taranga XV.—After nominating Chikka Sankaṇṇa Nāyaka as his successor he retired from the administration and soon after died. Then his younger brother Chikka Sankaṇṇa Nāyaka governed the whole province without any opposition.

Taranga XVI.—After Chikka Sankaṇṇa Nāyaka ruled for a short time in peace, he had a son called Siddhappa Nāyaka whom he educated in all the vidyas. Once Sankaṇṇa Nāyaka's feudatory (Sāmanta) on the north-western side went over to the side of the Mlēccha (Muhammadan) ruler of Vijayāpura (Bijapūr), and Sankaṇṇa Nāyaka defeated him completely. When, after some more time, a Muhammadan (Mlēccha) chief Majjhula Khan came with his elephants and horses against him Sankaṇṇa Nāyaka defeated him and drove him away. He then defeated Bhairā Dēvi of Gerasappi (Gersoppa) and other chiefs, and got from them much wealth. He then annointed Venkaṭappa Nāyaka, his elder brother's son as his successor and nominated his younger brother Rāmarāja Nāyaka as yuvarāja (heir-apparent).

Kallōla VI, Taranga I.—Sankaṇṇa Nāyaka constructed a beautiful new town at Ikkēri and a magnificent palace in it. The new palace was provided with a beautiful theatre. He also had several literary works composed. At the village Sangaḷa he constructed a big tank and had a garden made there containing all kinds of trees and creepers.

Taranga VIII.

एवं भद्रमहीपालो ज्येष्ठभ्रातृतनूभवे ।
राज्ञामावश्यकीं तावद्राजनीतिमुपादिशत् ॥
ततस्स्वल्पैरहोभिः प्राग्दृष्टवान्काशिकापतिम् ।
शिवं कैलासधामानं दिदृक्षुरिव निर्ययौ ॥
ततो राज्यं समासाद्य दोड्डसंकण्णनायकः ।
आनन्दयत्कुवलयं राजा रम्यकलानिधिः ॥
जातु जम्बूरदेशेशो विरूपण्णाभिधानवान् ।
प्रख्यातस्सार्वभौमाय दातव्यां च करोपदाम् ॥
अदिशन्प्रातिकूलत्वमाचचारातिदर्पितः ।
तन्निगृह्य बलाद्धृत्वा हस्तेनैवानयत्प्रभोः ॥
सविधं सोऽपि सन्तुष्यन्नेवं वचनमब्रवीत् ।
एतादृक्शौर्यसंपन्नस्त्वमस्मत्सविधे वस ॥
निधेहि राज्यमनुजेष्व्यानायय कुटुम्बकम् ।
इत्याज्ञप्ते सविधगे याते कियद्दिनेऽहनि ॥
तस्योदभवतां श्रेष्ठौ महिष्यां क्रमशस्सुतौ ।
एकस्य रामराजाख्या रचितासीत्परस्य तु ॥

निर्मिता वेंकटप्पनायकाख्या तयोर्द्वयोः ।
सार्वभौमस्तदा स्वीयनामाङ्कनमवेक्ष्य सः ॥
होळेहोन्नूरुमासूरुबेलमल्लूरुदेशकान् ।
दत्वोपभोग्यानथ तं प्राहिणोत्स्वपुरं प्रति ॥
स च प्राप्यानुजाभ्याशं तेन साकमवर्तत ।
अनन्तरं परङ्गेषु सार्वभौमविरोधिषु ॥
पुनरेव समानाय्य मेळयित्वानुचेतनम् ।
नाम्ना विट्ठलराजेन यापयामास तान्प्रति ॥
ततस्तान्स्वैरिणो राजा गोवादेशनिवासिनः ।
पराभवत्सार्वभौमोऽनुजेन सह सङ्गतः ॥
ततो गोवापुराधीशं तस्मै जित्वार्पयत्यति ।
अस्मिन्प्रमुदितः प्रादान्महादेवपुरस्थलम् ॥
अनन्तरं प्राप्य राज्यं यातो निजपुरीं प्रति ।
अनुजेन समं कंचित्कालं सुखमवर्तत ॥
ततः कदाचित्पुण्यानां क्षेत्राणां तत्रवर्तिनाम् ।
लिङ्गानामपि तीर्थानामवलोकनकाङ्क्षया ॥
शकुनानि पुरस्कृत्य ततः शुभफलानि सः ।
प्रययौ प्रथमं तावत्ककुभं सेतुचिह्निताम् ॥

Taranga IX.

रामेश्वरादिलिङ्गानि नानाक्षेत्राणि तत्र च ।
दृष्ट्वा स्नात्वा च तीर्थेषु तत्रत्येषु च सादरम् ॥
दक्षिणां दिशमुन्मुच्य जगाहे दिशमुत्तराम् ।
दृष्ट्वा तत्रापि लिङ्गानि क्षेत्रतीर्थानि भूरिशः ॥
क्रमात्समासदत्काशीं भवाशीविषबर्हिणीम् ।
गङ्गां निजपयोबिन्दुसङ्गापहतदुष्कृताम् ॥
विश्वेशं चापि विश्वेशं यतः प्रापुस्सुरासुराः ।
प्राप्यावगाह्य बहुधा संपूज्यापि क्रमेण तान् ॥

निर्गत्य च ततो नीलकण्ठनेपाळमाश्रितः ।
केदारेशं ततो दृष्ट्वा प्राप्तः काश्मीरमण्डलम् ॥
कुरुक्षेत्रं ततोऽपश्यत् क्रमेणैव ततः परम् ।
ढिल्लीनामकमेतर्हि प्रागिन्द्रप्रस्थसंज्ञिकम् ॥
नगरं प्रेक्ष्य तस्यान्तःप्रवेशाय कृतस्पृहः ।
व्रजन्नसिं द्वारि बद्धमद्राक्षीदेकमग्रतः ॥
अपृच्छच्च प्रतीहारान् किमेतदिति कौतुकी ।
अयमङ्कुशखानेन शस्त्राशस्त्रिविधौ पटुः ॥
मया समं योद्धुकामो गृह्णात्विति निवेशितः ।
श्रुत्वेति वचनं तेषां स्मृत्वा पूर्वतनीं कथाम् ॥
कौरवप्रेरितो मात्स्यनगरे मल्लतल्लजः ।
बध्वा द्वारि गदां योद्धुं भीमेनासीन्निषूदितः ॥
मया निषूदनीयोऽयमिति निर्धारयन्हृदि ।
असिमानाययामास बद्धं तमनुयायिना ॥
श्रुत्वा सोऽङ्कुशखानोऽपि प्रतीहारमुखोक्तितः ।
तत्र प्रवृत्तं वृत्तान्तं सर्वमेवं न्यवेदयत् ॥
ढिल्लीश्वरेण सोऽप्येनमाकार्यनृपमादिशत् ॥
शस्त्राशस्त्रिरणं कर्तुं सह तेनासिमप्यदात् ।

* * * *

ततश्च नृपतिः खड्गं सर्वलक्षणसंयुतम् ।
हस्तेनादाय पुरतो विरोधिनमपातयत् ॥
शौर्यमस्येदृशं दृष्ट्वा हृष्टो ढिल्लिपुराधिपः ।
एतद्भृत्यान्पर्यपृच्छत्कुतुकी विस्मितान्तरः ॥
अयं कः कुत्र वसति स्वामी युष्माकमित्यपि ।
ततस्तं प्रति वृत्तान्तं स्वामिनस्तेप्यवादिषुः ॥
संकण्णनायको नाम पश्चिमस्यां नृपो दिशि ।
तीर्थयात्रापदेशेन स्वयमासीदुपागतः ॥

इत्याकर्ण्य वचस्तेषां तस्मै चात्यन्तविस्मितः ।
बिरुदं हरति(रित)च्छायपटाङ्कं केतनं ददौ ॥
बहुद्रविणदं देशं स्वदेशाभ्यन्तरेऽप्यदात् ।
वासांसि च विचित्राणि नूत्नान्याभरणानि च ॥
वितीर्णे तेन तं देशं काश्यामीश्वरतुष्टये ।
मठदेवालयारामधर्माविन्ययुञ्जत ॥
ततस्स्वदेशमागच्छन् देशात्तस्मात्क्रमेण सः ।
मासूरुदेशमासाद्य वटवल्लीति विश्रुते ॥
ग्रामे वसन्निशि स्वप्ने कंचिद्योगिनमैक्षत ।

* * * *

स्वं प्राप्य देशं केळदीरामेशागारसन्निधौ ।
निर्माय नगरं वीरभद्रमस्थापयत्ततः ॥

* * * *

Taranga X.

एवं शास्त्रानुसारेण श्रीमान्संकण्णनायकः ।
केळदीनाम्नि नगरे तथेक्केरीपुरान्तरे ॥
कारयित्वा शुभं गेहं तत्र स्थापितवान्क्रमात् ।
वीरभद्रेश्वरं तद्वदघोरेश्वरमेव च ॥
आगमोक्तविधानेन स्थानयोरनयोर्द्वयोः ।
पट्टाभिषेकमकरोत्पश्चान्निजकनीयसः ॥
अनुजाय विनीताय राज्ञामावश्यकीं नृपः ।
नीतिं चोपादिशत्तस्मै शत्रुनिग्रहसाधिकां ॥

Taranga XV.

ततः परं कतिपये दिने समतिवाहिने ।
संकण्णनायको ज्यायान् सनाम्नि स्वानुजन्मनि ॥
दत्तराज्यभरस्सोयमवर्तत शमोन्मुखः ।
भूयिष्ठानि शिवस्थानान्यालोक्य च समन्ततः ॥
उपरिष्ठानि सन्द्रष्टुमिव कैलासमासदत् ॥

ततस्तदनुजन्मापि चिक्कसंकण्णनायकः ।
अशात्रवां वसुमतीमशेषामन्वपालयत् ॥

Taranga XVI.

ततस्संप्राप्तराज्येऽस्मिन् चिक्कसंकण्णनायके ।
फलाभिवृद्ध्या नवया नवति क्षितिमण्डलम् ॥
ततः कतिपयेष्वेवं नीतेषु दिवसेष्वपि ।
सिद्धप्पनायकस्तस्माज्जातस्संकण्णनायकात् ॥
विद्याभिस्स बभौ चूतलताभिस्सुरभिर्यथा ।
एकदा स च संकण्णनायकस्समुपागतः ॥
विजयाख्यपुरस्थायिम्लेच्छसाहाय्यकोद्धतम् ।
वायव्यदिगवस्थायिसामन्तं पर्यभूत्ततः ॥
शत्रुपद्मवने दन्तीभूत्वा लक्ष्मीमुपाहरत् ।
पुनः कियद्दिनादूर्ध्वं महत्या सेनया सह ॥
योद्धुं मञ्जुलखानाख्ये म्लेच्छे च समुपागते ।
गजांस्तद्वाजिनश्चापि विजित्य तमपाहरत् ॥
अनन्तरं गेरसप्पिभैरादेवीमुखान्नृपान् ।
महीपतिः पराभूय तेभ्यो धनमुपाददौ ॥
ततः परं वेंकटप्पनायकं ज्यायसस्सुतम् ।
अभ्यषिञ्चन्निजे राज्ये यौवराज्येऽस्य चानुजम् ॥
संकण्णनायको रामराजनायकनामकम् ।

Kallōla VI, Taranga I.

इक्केरिनाम्नि देशे च रम्यं पुरमकल्पयत् ।
तत्र चाश्चर्यजनकं भवनं निरमापयत् ॥
तत्र नाटकशालां च विचित्रामुपपादयत् ।
प्रोद्यच्चमत्कृतीः किं च सत्कृतीरप्यकारयत् ॥
संगळाख्येऽपि च ग्रामे तटाकं च व्यधापयत् ।
तत्र नानाद्रुमलतारम्यमुद्यानमातनोत् ॥

100

ŚIVATATTVARATNĀKARA.

[*By Keḷadi Basava.*]

Kallōla VI, Taranga XIII.—After Venkaṭa* ruled his province for some years he had a son called Bhadrappa Nāyaka. This Bhadrappa had, while he was still young, by the grace of the god Vīrabhadra, a son named Vīrabhadra. Leaving the boy to be brought up by his grandfather, Bhadrappa Nāyaka, retired from the world having no taste for its vain pleasures, and became a recluse. After this Venkaṭappa Nāyaka was governing his province along with his grandson. Once while he was staying at the fortress of Hoḷe-Honnur, one† Hanuma attacked him with his forces greatly reinforced by those of the Mlēcchas (Muhammadans). Coming out of the place single, Venkaṭappa Nāyaka collected an army and defeated the besiegers of the fort completely.‡ He also defeated the troops of Majjula Khan who had come to the assistance of Hanuma and drove him back to his own territory. In token of this victory he erected a pillar of victory at Hānugallu (Hangal in Dharwar).

Then the elder brother of Hanuma wanted to come to terms with Venkaṭa and presented him with the places Lakkuhaḷḷi, Gājanūr and Shimoga. Venkaṭa accepted the treaty and sending back his erstwhile enemy stayed in camp on the Tungabhadra. Hanuma, on hearing that his brother concluded peace with Venkaṭa, opposed him with a big army. But Venkaṭa defeated him completely, and compelled him to take refuge in the town of Bāṇāvara. Venkaṭa then returned to his capital. He defeated his enemies in places like Dānivāsa and Kumbhase (Kumsi ?), and, having rooted them out, constructed fortresses like Hibbejāgara in their territory. After defeating some small chiefs and constructing the four kinds of fortresses in their territory, he attacked Bhairā Dēvi,§ the valiant lady who ruled the Tuḷu country. He captured her as a prisoner and annexed her territory to his own. After this he attacked Śankaranārāyaṇa Bhatta, the Brahman

* Venkaṭappa Nāyaka's inscriptions range from 1606 to 1629, Ep. Carn., Vol. VIII, p. 15.

† This may refer to one of the Hanumas mentioned in Hl. 34, Ep. Carn., Vol. VII. They were chiefs of Santē Beṇṇūr and belonged to the Pūvala family.

‡ A detailed account of this war is given in Ancient India, pages 292–94. Majjhula Khan seems to have been one of the officers under Ranadulla Khan.

§ This Bhairā Dēvi was the ruler of Gerasoppe. She was the sister of King Sāḷuva Malla, and, marrying the Pāndya king, gave birth to Dēva Rāya. An inscription of hers is noticed n the Mysore Archæological Report for 1916, page 69, paragraph 120.

governor of Vēṇupura (Bidrūr ?), and after capturing him in battle put him to disgrace, but spared his life since he was a Brahman. When the fort called Kauravadurga became the refuge of hostile people he defeated them completely and occupied it. He renewed and strengthened its fortifications, and renamed it Bhuvanadurga.

Within the citadel of the new fort he constructed the temples of the gods Śikharēśvara, Viśvēśvara, Lakshmīnārāyaṇa and Mailāra. Outside the citadel he constructed the temples of the gods Virūpāksha, Viṭṭhala, Narasimha, Vṛshēndra (Nandi), Vīrabhadra, Gurunātha and Kāḷikā, and erected dwelling-places throughout the place. At * Sringapura (Śrīngēri) he constructed a new Maṭha for the Svāmi, and founded an Agrahāra (Brahman settlement) there. He also had a big Maṭha constructed for the use of the Bhūrudras (the Śaiva priests of the Vīraśaiva or Basava persuasion). Venkaṭappa Nāyaka also constructed afresh the town of Anantaśivapura with its inward compound wall, and, constructing the temples of the gods Tāṇḍavēśvara and Ranganātha, endowed them with large estates for the permanent performance of worship therein. He also constructed there a Maṭha (called Champakasaras † for the use of Bhūrudras (Basava's followers). In the district of Ikkēri he constructed the new town Sadāśivasāgara provided with a grand palace for residence, and another for jalakrīḍa (playing in water).

Venkaṭappa Nāyaka also founded a new Agrahāra called Viśvanāthapura on the banks of the river Varadā and presented it to scholars. He also had many sacrifices like Vājapēya performed. He founded an Agrahāra called Vīrāmbāpura after his mother, and another called Abhinavavīrāmbāpura after his wife, and presented both of them to scholars. He also increased the worship of the deities Ādiśakti, Mahēśa (Śiva), Mūkāmbā, Subrahmanya and Śankaranārāyaṇa by means of large endowments. He also had by his patronage literary works written by scholars on Kāvya (poetry), Nātaka (drama), Dharma Śāstra (Law) and other subjects.‡

---

* The copper-plate recording the grant of this mutt has been noted in paragraph 111, page 65, of the Mysore Archæological Report for 1916.

† An inscription granting certain transit dues for the muṭt of the Champakasadasi-Mahattu at Anandapura (now Anantapura) is noted in Ep. Carn., Vol. VIII, page 15 and Sa. 123.

‡ The Triennial Catalogue of Manuscripts, Government Oriental Manuscripts Library, Madras, R. No. 1879, p. 2623, notes a commentary in Sanskrit of the Ṣiva Gitā portion of the Padmapurāna by this Venkaṭappa Nāyaka. The colophon of the work is herewith given.

इति श्रीमद्विशुद्धाद्वैतसिद्धान्तप्रतिष्ठापनैकधुरन्धरश्रीकेलदिवेङ्कटाद्रिनायक विरचितायां शिवगीताटीकायां षोडशोऽध्यायः ॥

Thus having got the seven sorts of Santāna (like the construction of a tank, etc.), possessing the eight sorts of wealth (Aiśvarya), ruling over a kingdom possessed of all the seven constituents (Saptānga), he became old not only by age but also by religious merit (Dharma), wealth (Artha), fame (Kīrti) and prosperity (Lakshmī).

He installed his grandson Vīrabhadra Nāyaka as his successor and taught him all the subjects that ought to be studied by kings. Vīrabhadra entrusted the whole management of the kingdom to Śivappa Nāyaka, his grand-uncle and the elder of the two sons, Śivappa and Venkṭappa, of Chikkasankaṇṇa Nāyaka.

Taranga XXVII.—After Venkaṭappa Nāyaka left the kingdom in the hands of Vīrabhadra, Vīrabhadra ruled it with the assistance of his able uncles Śivappa and Venkaṭappa, and was enjoying all the pleasures becoming a king. After Vīrabhadra had ruled the kingdom for a long time, he was opposed by his cousins or enemies (dāyādas) whom he defeated completely. Then the Governor of Basavāpaṭṭana, Hanuma Nāyaka of the Pūvala family, marched as far as Ikkēri with a Muhammadan (yavana) army, and returned after fighting with Vīrabhadra. But Vīrabhadra collected his own army and with it marched against the enemy's capital and captured it after defeating Hanuma completely.

Vīrabhadra was very sorry for not having a son, and, getting disgusted with the pleasures of the kingdom, called his two uncles before him, and, asking them to rule the kingdom in his stead, said that he would retire from the kingdom. When they remonstrated, he expostulated on the vanity of human happiness, and, giving the kingdom over to Śivappa,* had his coronation performed with due ceremony.

Kallōla VII, Taranga VI.—After Śivappa Nāyaka ruled the kingdom for some years delighted with the society of poets and scholars, he had a son whom he named Bhadra. He celebrated all the festivities associated with the birth of the son with due éclat.

Kallōla VII, Taranga XIV.—Śivappa Nāyaka ruled the whole kingdom assisted by his younger brother Venkaṭappa with great valour and liberality. Once Śivappa consulted with his younger brother about their duty to destroy the evil doers in the world. He

---

* The Chikkadēvarāyavamsāvaḷi says that Basava murdered the previous incumbent and usurped the gadi. If the statement of the Chikkadēvarājavijayam is correct, it should have been this Vīrabhadra Nāyaka that was murdered.

narrated how the capital of their emperor Vēlāpura (Vellore) had been occupied by his enemies, and how the emperor was wandering without a home. He proposed, therefore, that they should help the emperor get back his capital. When Venkaṭappa heard the proposal he entirely fell in with it and said that it was their imperative duty to help the emperor. Leaving his younger brother at the capital Śivappa marched with an army against Vellore. There he laid his camp outside the fort, and, constructing his own defences all round it as laid down in the Śāstras, began to blockade it. By this means he was able to take the fort of Vēlāpura (Vellore) and capture his enemy within it.

When the emperor Śrīranga Rāya heard of the news he came to Vellore to see Śivappa Nāyaka and felt very pleased when he met him. The emperor presented him with many titles like Rāmabāṇa, Paravāraṇavāraṇa. He also gave him a very costly ear ornament made of saphire, a very costly pearl, the emblems of the conch (Śankha) and the discus (Chakra), the umbrella called Jagajhampha, and also presented him with the head of his enemy. The emperor as well as Śivappa Nāyaka became very famous after this, the one for having got back his lost fortress and the other for having conquered it for the emperor. After this Śivappa defeated some feudatories of the emperor who were still recalcitrant and after handing over their territory to the emperor returned to his capital.

When he returned to his capital he founded an agrahāra called Śivarājapura and presented it to scholarly Brahmans. He also had several sacrifices like the Vājapeya performed in his name. He constructed many new forts in the province of Kēraḷa (Malabar), and there had many temples, wells and tanks restored. He made large endowments to many Śiva temples like those at Kēdāra, Benares (Kāśi), Śivagangā, Śrīśailam, Gōkarṇam and Rāmēśvaram. Śivappa presented a golden crown to the God Viśvēśa of Benares. He also made the various kinds of gifts (dānas) as laid down in the Śāstras. He then entrusted his two sons Bhadrappa Nāyaka and Somaśēkhara Nāyaka to be educated by his brother Venkaṭappa Nāyaka, to whom he taught the science of yoga.

Taranga XV.—After Śivappa Nāyaka died (became absorbed in Śivayōga), Venkaṭappa ruled the whole kingdom along with his two nephews.

Kallōla VIII, Taranga I.—Venkaṭappa ruled the kingdom for a long period ably and justly, and anointed his nephew Bhadrappa Nāyaka as his successor and taught him all that was essential to royalty. Bhadrappa Nāyaka ruled the kingdom with ability after Venkaṭa.

Taranga II.—When Bhadrappa Nāyaka had ruled for a considerable period, one of the subordinate chiefs (Sāmantas) on the east wanted to encroach upon his kingdom and attacked some fortresses on the frontier. He sent his army against them and defeating them in battle drove them away. Thinking that a king ought not to be contented like a Brahman, Bhadrappa wanted to capture the territories of his enemies. He marched against the ruler of Śīrya (Sīrā) and after driving him from his place, captured his fortress. When another chief to the north of his territory evinced a hostile attitude towards him he annexed his territory and restored it once more to him, when he sought refuge with the victor.

* One of Bhadra's enemies whose territory he annexed sought the assistance of the Muhammadan (Mlēccha) ruler of Vijayāpura (Bijapur). When the Sultan of Bijapur invaded his territory, Bhadra thought that he could not conquer him and so wisely concluded peace with him and returned to his capital.

Bhadra performed the gift called Hiraṇyagarbha at Tīrtharājapura (Tīrthahaḷḷi). At the town of Rāmachandrapura on the banks of the river Śarāvatī he had himself weighed against gold (tulāpurusha) and distributed the gold. He founded the three agrahāras Śivarājapura, Venkaṭāpura and Bhadrarājapura, so called after his uncle, his father and himself respectively. He also made extensive endowments to, and increased the worship of, Krishna worshipped at Uḍupa (Uḍipi), Guha or Subrahmaṇya at Subrahmaṇya, Śankaranārāyaṇa at Koṭīśvara and his own favourite goddess Mūkāmbā. Bhadrappa Nāyaka also constructed many monasteries for the use of the Bhūrudras (the followers of the Basava sect) and endowed them with lands. After ruling the kingdom thus meritoriously for a long time he nominated his younger brother Somaśēkhara Nāyaka to succeed him and taught him the science of archery.

Taranga V.—Sōmaśēkhara Nāyaka ruled the kingdom according to the Nītiśāstra and the people were very happy under him. When he was opposed by a number of enemies he killed some of them, destroyed the power of some and concluded peace with the others when they sought his refuge. At his capital he constructed a

* This may refer to one of the Hanumas of Santē Beṇṇūr or Channaya of Nāgamangaḷa who, according to the Chikkadēvarāyavamsāvaḷi, brought on the Bijapur invasion against Bhadra.

spacious monastery for the use of the Bhūrudras, and another for the viraktas (anchorites) among the Lingāyats. Before the latter he constructed a big tank filled with sweet water throughout the year. Around the tank he made a beautiful garden.

Sōmaśēkhara Nāyaka did not marry for a considerable period because he could not get a bride of high pedigree with the required accomplishments. Later he found that a lady Chennāmbā by name had all the necessary qualifications and married her. Chennāmbā is said to have been an incarnation of the goddess Mūkāmbā. Sōmaśēkhara told Chennamāmbā how in former times Mūkāmbā had taken several shapes and destroyed the demons (Rākshasas). He said that in the Kali age the Rākshasas had taken the shape of the Muhammadans and that they would be able to destroy them by worshipping the goddess. He told her how the people of all countries had flocked to their territory for safety and asked her to destroy the Muhammadans and protect all the refugees.

Taranga VII.—Sōmaśēkhara Nāyaka and Chennāmbā had a son who was named Basava. Directing his wife to rule the kingdom properly till Basava should come of age, Śōmaśēkhara died. Chennāmbā continued to rule the kingdom according to the advice of her husband.

Taranga VIII.—Chennāmbā ruled the kingdom possessed of the seven constituents (Angas) according to the Nītisāstra. She educated her son Basava, making him proficient in all the sciences (vidyas), and got his marriage performed with due ceremony. When some of her subordinate governors showed hostility she sent her generals against them and forced them to run away. After this she captured many elephants and horses belonging to their army, and resumed some of their important titles. When the Mlēccha (Muhammadan) ruler Avarangasāba (Aurangzeb) made war on Rāma Rāja who had the title Chatrādhipati, after conquering all the fifty-two countries, and wanted to capture his kingdom after defeating him, Rāma Rāja fled from his kingdom. Wandering hither and thither, he ultimately took refuge in the kingdom of Chennamāmbā.

On learning this Chennāmbā, reflecting that even great people are subject to adversity at times, received Rāma Rāja with kindness, and made him presents of valuable clothes and jewels. The Muhammadan general who was coming in pursuit of the fugitive prince was defeated by her army and driven back. The whole country from the Himalayas to the Śētu praised the heroism of

Chennāmbā on hearing of the defeat of Aurangazeb's army by her troops. She captured many elephants, horses and jewels from the enemies, and ruled the country without a rival. When after this some of her own feudatory chiefs (Sāmantas) evinced hostility she reduced them to subjection. She gave extensive lands to the goddess Mūkāmbā and founded an Agrahara called Chennāmbāpura after herself.

The work ends with a long colophon detailing the achievements of the author Basava. He says he was proficient in the science of Śivādvaita, and that he got his scholarship by the worship of the God Paramēśvara who is accompanied by Chidambara Śakti. The work itself is said to incorporate the essence of the various sciences and arts (vidyās) that are comprised in the Vēdas and the Āgamas (tantras).

After the colophon the author says that the prosperity of his kingdom was increased by the kindness of the god Vīrabhadra. He says that he ruled over the provinces of Gōrāshṭra (Goa), Tuḷu (Tauḷava), Malayāḷa (Kēraḷa), Mallarāshṭra and Traigarta. He had the titles of Parayaḍavamurāri and Kōṭikolāhala, had the distinction of the double sword (Asiyugaḷa), the title of the destroyer of the enemies' Saptānga and the banner of the yellow cloth. He was born in the family of Chauḍappa Nāyaka. He also uses the title of Rājādhirāja.

In the last verse of the work he says that the work was completed on Friday, the full moon day of the month Nabhasya (Āśvayuja) in the cyclic year Sarvadhārin, corresponding to the Śālivāhana Śaka year counted by the moon (1), fire (3), the seasons (6) and the earth (1) or Ś. 1631 or A.D. 1709–10.

Kallōla VI, Taranga XIII.

एवं वेङ्कटभूपालचरित्रं परमारभे ।
अथ वेङ्कटभूपालः कामशास्त्रोक्तवर्त्मना ॥
भार्यया सार्धमुद्यानसौख्यं समधिकं भजन् ।
राज्यं सुविलसन्नीतिप्राज्यं रक्षन्नवर्तत ॥
तस्मादजायत सुतो नाम्ना भद्रप्पनायकः ।
उदूढदीधितिः क्षीरवाराशेरिव कौस्तुभः ॥
तस्य बाल्ये वीरभद्रप्रसादप्राप्तसंभवः ।
तन्नामा तनुजो जज्ञे श्रिया तत्समतां गतः ॥

तं वीरभद्रनामानं पिता भद्रप्पनायकः ।
स्वतनूजं वेङ्कटप्पनायकस्य वशं व्यधात् ॥
ततो विषयवैराग्यवशाद्भद्रप्पनायकः ।
जानन्ननेहसाऽल्पेन परमाश्रममाश्रयत् ॥
अनन्तरं वेङ्कटप्पनायकः पुत्रसूनुना ।
वीरभद्राभिधानेन साकं सुखमवर्तत ॥
ततः कतिपयानेवमतिनीय स वासरान् ।
होळेहोन्नूरुनामाङ्के प्राकारेऽस्मिन्निषेदुषि ॥
सहायमधिकं लब्ध्वा म्लेच्छानां विपुलं बलम् ।
आगत्य चात्रणोद्दृप्तः सालं हनुमनामकः ॥
तदेकाकी वेङ्कटप्पनायको हयमुत्तमम् ।
आगत्य निर्गतः सालाद्बहिर्देशमवाप्य च ॥
सङ्गृह्य कियतीं सेनां पुनर्गत्वा च साहसी ।
तं हत्वा पूरयामास वप्रणाक्रमणं ततः ॥
तत्सहायागतं म्लेच्छं नाम्ना मञ्जुळखानकम् ।
योधयित्वा चिरं तस्यापसर्पणमकारयत् ॥
हानगल्लुस्थले कीर्त्यै जयस्थम्भं चखान च ।
हनुमस्य ततो ज्येष्ठः सन्धित्सुरमुना सह ।
लक्कुहळ्ळिगाजनूरुशीमोगेनामभिः श्रुतान् ॥
प्राकारानुपदं कृत्वा शरणं तं समाश्रयत् ।
शरणागतमत्यर्थं मानयित्वा सहामुना ॥
पारे तु तुङ्गभद्रायाः परस्मिन्शिबिरेऽवसत् ।
तस्यानुजोऽग्रजं दृष्ट्वा तं वैरिशरणागतम् ॥
अभ्याययौ योधयितुं बलेन महता सह ।
ततश्चायं नृपो जित्वा दूरमद्रावयच्च तम् ॥
विद्रुतः प्राविशत्पश्चात् बाणावरपुरान्तरम् ।
ततोऽयं स्वपुरं प्राप्य राजा सुखमवर्तत ॥

ततः परं दानिवासकुम्भसेप्रमुखस्थले ।
स्थितान्क्षुद्ररिपून्सर्वानुन्मूल्य तदनन्तरम् ॥
हिब्बेजागरमुख्येषु तेषां स्थानेषु सर्वतः ।
कारयामास दुर्गाणि दुष्प्रधर्षाणि विद्विषाम् ॥
सन्मण्डलीकसामन्तराजनामाङ्कितान् रिपून् ।
गळिताहंकृतीन्कृत्वा तेषां स्थानेषु भूयसा ॥
चतुर्विधानि मार्गाणि दुष्प्रधर्षाण्यकल्पयत् ।
ततस्तौळवराज्यस्य शासित्रीं बहुविक्रमाम् ॥
उपस्रुतप्रजां स्वैरं भैरादेवीं पराभवन् ।
बन्दीचकार तां तस्या राज्यमप्याक्रमीत्समम् ॥
ततःपरं कतिपयदिनेभ्यस्स महीपतिः ।
भट्टं वेणुपुरस्थं शङ्करनारायणाभिधम् ॥
सीमान्तस्थायिनां स्वैरमुपद्रवविधायिनम् ।
तं ब्राह्मणं तया निन्ये भङ्गं वधविनाकृतम् ॥
विप्राणामुचितो दण्डो यत्पुनर्मानखण्डनम् ।
इति नीतिमुपाश्रित्य गर्वनिर्वापणं व्यधात् ॥
यथाभिलाषैतैर्भोग्यभोज्यैस्तं प्रत्यपालयत् ।
जातु कौरवदुर्गाख्ये दुर्गदुष्टैरधिष्ठिते ॥
तां निगृह्याथ तद्दुर्गं बलिष्ठं विरचय्य च ।
ततोभुवनदुर्गाख्यां दुर्गस्यास्थप्रदाय च ॥
तस्योपरिष्ठाच्छिखरेश्वरविश्वेश्वराभिधौ ।
लक्ष्मीनारायणं चैव मैलारमपि संज्ञया ॥
दुर्गाद्बहिर्विरूपाक्षविट्ठलौ नरसिह्मकम् ।
वृषेन्द्रं वीरभद्रं च गुरुनाथं च काळिकाम् ॥
संस्थाप्य कारयामास भवनानि समन्ततः ।
तत्र शृङ्गपुराधीशस्वामिनां मठमातनोत् ॥
अग्रहारं च तत्रैव ब्राह्मणानामकल्पयत् ।
भूरुद्रास्पदमत्यर्थं महान्तं मठमातनोत् ॥

तेषामनितरापेक्षां भुवं भूयो वितीर्णवान् ।
अनन्तरं चाचसार्वभौमसंस्थानमागते ॥
अनन्तशिवपुर्याख्ये स्थले चानन्दनामके ।
पुरं निर्माप्य तस्यान्तःप्राकारं निरमापयत् ॥
तस्यान्तस्ताण्डवेशाख्यमालयेस्थापयच्छिवम् ।
तथैव रङ्गनाथाख्यदेवस्याप्यालयं नवम् ॥
निर्माप्य तस्य पूजार्थं क्षेत्रं भूरि विसृष्टवान् ।
तत्र निश्रेयसार्थं च भूरुद्राणां महात्मनाम् ॥
सन्मठं चम्पकसरोनामकं पर्यकल्पयत् ।
इक्केरिनाम्नि देशे च स सदाशिवसागरम् ॥
निर्माप्य नगरं तत्र राजगेहं विधाय च ।
मनोहरं जलक्रीडाप्रासादं चाप्यकारयत् ॥
वरदातटिनीतीरे विश्वनाथपुराह्वयम् ।
अग्रहारं च विद्वद्भ्यः कारयामास सादरम् ॥
वाजपेयादिकान्भूरि कारयन्नपि च क्रतून् ।
स्वमातृनाम्ना वीराम्बापुरमित्यतिविस्तृतम् ॥
वधूनाम्नाप्यभिनववीराम्बापुरनामकम् ।
अग्रहारद्वयं कृत्वा विद्वद्भ्यो व्यतरद्वरम् ॥
आदिशक्तेर्महेशस्य मूकाम्बाया विशेषतः ।
सुब्रह्मण्यस्य तद्वच्छङ्करनारायणेशितुः ॥
देवानामेतदादीनामुपचारक्रिया अपि ।
वर्धयामास तादर्थ्यात् क्षेत्राणि व्यतरत्तथा ॥
कृतीश्च कारयामास विद्वत्कृतचमत्कृतीः ।
काव्ये च नाटके धर्मशास्त्रादौ च महत्तराः ॥
एवं तटाकमुख्यं च प्राप्य सन्तानसप्तकम् ।
अष्टैश्वर्ययुतो रक्षन् सप्ताङ्गं राज्यमोजसा ॥
धर्मार्थकीर्तिलक्ष्मीभिरिवासौ वयसापि च ।
वृद्धत्वं प्राप्तवान् पौत्रं वीरभद्रप्पनायकम् ॥

अयोजद्राज्यलक्ष्म्या जरयाश्लिष्टविग्रहः ।
तस्मै राज्योपभोगांश्च सप्रपञ्चमुपादिशत् ॥
पितृव्यचिक्कसंकण्णनायकस्य तु पौत्रयोः ।
शिवप्पवेङ्कटप्पाख्यां जुषोनायकयोर्द्वयोः ॥
शिवप्पनायकायात्र सर्वनिर्वहणोद्यमम् ।
उपादिशद्वीरभद्रनायको राज्यशासनम् ।

Taranga XXVII.

बहुधासुभवेत्युक्त्वा वेङ्कटाक्षितिपालकः ।
पौत्रं राज्येऽभिषिच्यापि वीरभद्राख्यनायकम् ॥
ततः स्वयं च विरतः शिवयोगपरो भवेत् ।
अनन्तरं वीरभद्रनामधेयोऽथ भूपतिः ॥
विधानमनतिक्रम्य संसेवितरसायनः ।
दृढगात्रो महीपालयोग्यान्योगान् समाश्रयन् ॥
अवन्नवनिमार्याभ्यां पितृव्याभ्यां समं व्यधात् ।
शिववेङ्कटभूपाभ्यां वीरभद्रमहीपतिः ॥
बहुकालमवत्यस्मिन् साकं ताभ्यां वसुन्धराम् ।
दायादाः प्रबलैस्सार्धं आजग्मुर्योद्धुमुद्यताः ॥
तानुद्धतानयं युद्धे विद्विषस्समुपागतान् ।
धार्तराष्ट्रकशेषेण भीमसेन इवावधीत् ॥
जातु व्याधे तु बसवापट्टणाख्यपुराधिपे ।
नृपे पूवलवंशस्थे दृप्ते हनुमनामके ॥
आदाय यावनीं सेनामिक्केरिनगरावधि ।
आगत्य योधयित्वा तु प्रयाते स्वपुरीं प्रति ॥
तदा निजबलैस्सार्धं वीरभद्रमहीपतिः ।
ततःपर तुबसबापट्टणाख्यं निरुध्य च ॥
तत्प्राकारं समाक्रम्य सद्ध(?)एवं समं बलैः ।
हनुमन्नामकं तं च निर्जित्य निजतेजसा ॥

तद्राज्यलक्ष्मीं तत्काले परिणीय ततःपरम् ।
सप्ताङ्गं यौतकमिव ततोऽगृह्णन्महीपतिः ॥
ततोऽभीष्टितदायिन्याश्रितनन्दनसम्पदः ।
सन्तानवल्ल्यानापश्यदञ्चितं तनुजाङ्कुरम् ॥
एवं सञ्चिन्तयामास तदानीं मानसे नृपः ।
किं राज्येन विधातव्यं किं बलेन महीयसा ॥
किं भोगैरखिलैर्बाह्यैः फलं पुत्रं विना नृणाम् ।
नयनानन्दनो नैव नन्दनोऽस्माभिरीक्षितः ॥
अदर्शितात्मबाधं नो जन्म शास्त्रमिवाफलम् ।
यत्प्रसादेन लभ्यन्ते नृणामिष्टानि तं शिवम् ॥
उपास्य नश्वरं मुक्त्वा शाश्वतं फलमक्षुमः ।
इत्यालोच्य निजं राज्यं निधित्सुः स्वपितृव्ययोः ॥
आहूय तौ शिवक्ष्मापवेङ्कटक्षोणिपालकौ ।
युवां पितृव्यौ शृणुतं युवयोरुचितां महीम् ॥
युवां पालयतं नीत्येत्युदीरयति तावुभौ ।
अवोचतं भवानेव पालयत्ववनीमिमाम् ॥
इत्युदीरितमाकर्ण्य ताभ्यां प्रत्युत्तरं ददौ ।
आयुस्तरङ्गचपलं श्रीश्च सौदामिनी चला ॥
यौवनं त्रिदिनं नृणां कुतस्सौख्ये स्थिरत्वधीः ।
कुलाचला इव जनाः किं स्थिरत्वमुपागताः ॥

* * * *

इति निश्चित्य स परंपरया समुपागते ।
सिंहासने सभासद्भिरशेषैः परिवारिते ॥
आस्थानमण्डपे रम्ये सभालक्षणलक्षिते ।
धार्मिकैरपि नीतिज्ञैः क्रियानिर्वहणक्षमैः ॥
सुधर्माख्यामपि स्वस्मिन् समर्पयति योगतः ।
ध्रुवमारोपयामास प्रेम्णा स शिवभूपतिम् ॥

Kallōla VII, Taranga VI.

काव्यादीनां श्रुतिसुधावर्षकृद्भिर्वचोभरैः ।
आनन्दितान्तःकरणः सिंहासनवरे वसन् ॥
शशास धरणीं कृत्स्नां शिवनामा महीपतिः ।
एवं कतिपयेष्वस्य प्रयातेषु दिनेष्वभूत् ॥
शिवस्य जगतीभर्तुः कुमारो भद्रनामकः ।
तत्तत्कालोचितैस्तैस्तैरुत्सवैस्तनुजस्य सः ॥
आवर्तत महीपालो लब्धवानन्दपरम्पराम् ॥

Kallōla VII, Taranga XIV.

अनन्तरं तु चरितं शिवभूपस्य वर्ण्यते ।
वेङ्कटाख्येन सहितः शिवभूपः कनीयसा ॥
अभूदनन्यसामान्यविक्रमौदार्यसंयुतः ।
यथारुणेन घर्मांशुर्भुवनानि प्रकाशयेत् ॥
तथा कनीयसा साकमरक्षत् क्षितिमण्डलम् ।
अवन्नेवं महीं जातु भ्रात्रा साकमचिन्तयत् ॥
दुष्टानां निग्रहोऽवश्यं करणीयो महीभृता ।
इयं नीतिस्सर्वसिद्धा साम्प्रतं साप्युपस्थिता ॥
वेलापुरान्तःप्राकारमध्यवर्ती सुदुर्मदः ।
सार्वभौमप्रतीपत्वमुपेत्य विचरत्यसौ ॥
आक्रामदपि तत्स्थानं निगृह्याभ्यद्य तद्रिपुम् ।
सार्वभौमाय तत्स्थानं स्वीयं प्रत्यर्पयाम्यहम् ॥
इति वाचं जायसस्तु श्रुत्वा सोऽपीत्थमब्रवीत् ।
भ्रातः प्रभ्रष्टराज्याय स्थानप्रत्यर्पणं वरम् ॥
यशस्करं नृपाणां तु किमन्यत्तादृशं भवेत् ।
तस्मादवश्यकर्तव्यमिदमित्यमुनेरितः ॥
निधाय राज्यरक्षायै कनीयांसं विचक्षणः ।
तदाक्रमणमाकाङ्क्षन्ययौ वेलापुरीं प्रति ॥
ततो वेलापुरीं गत्वा चतुरङ्गबलान्वितः ।
प्राकाराच्च बहिस्तस्माच्छिबिरं प्रत्यकल्पयत् ॥

कोटाचक्रविधानज्ञैर्विज्ञाय च बलाबलम् ।
समन्ततश्च प्राकारं रुरोध सहसा बलैः ॥
दुर्गस्थो दुर्गमश्शत्रुरसाध्यो येन सिध्यति ॥

* * * *

शास्त्रलोकागतैरेवमुपायैश्शिवभूपतिः ।
वेलापुराख्यं प्राकारं सहसा स्वयमग्रहीत् ॥
ततोऽग्रहीत्करेणैव रिपुं तन्मध्यवर्तिनम् ।
श्रीरङ्गसार्वभौमस्तं श्रुत्वोदन्तं प्रहर्षितः ॥
वेलापुरं समायातः शिवभूपदिदृक्षया ।
ततस्समागतस्तेन प्राप्य तद्दर्शनोत्सवम् ॥
सन्तोषितः पराक्रान्तः स्थानप्रत्यर्पणाद्बहु ।
आदिशद्बिरुदान्यस्मै सार्वभौमा महीभृते ॥
रामबाणाभिधानं च वारणं परवारणम् ।
अमूल्यमिन्द्रनीलस्य कर्णाभरणमेव च ॥
मुक्ताफलमनर्घं च बिरुदे शंखचक्रके ।
जगझंपाभिधं छत्रं शात्रवं चापि मस्तकम् ॥
एवमादीनि बिरुदान्यर्पयित्वांशुकादिभिः ।
बहुधा मानयामास शिवभूपं महीपतिः ॥
कीर्त्या शिवमहीपालः स्थानप्रत्यर्पणोत्थया ।
सार्वभौमः पराक्रान्तनिजस्थानाप्तिकस्तथा ॥
तौ च स्वस्वेप्सितावाप्त्या तदाभूतां प्रहर्षितौ ।
तत्र स्थितांश्च सामन्तान् सार्वभौमविरोधिनः ॥
विजित्य कांश्चन नृपो दुष्प्रधर्षपराक्रमः ।
विजयी स्वपुरं गन्तुं प्रातिष्ठत महीपतिः ॥
ततस्स्वपुरमासाद्य चिरं सुखमवर्तत ।
तुङ्गभद्रानदीतीरे शिवराजपुराह्वयम् ॥
पर्याप्तक्षेत्रफलकमग्रहारमकल्पयत् ।
द्विजानतोषयद्वृत्तिमर्यादाभिश्च वृत्तिभिः ॥

यज्ञाद्भवति पर्जन्यः पर्ज्यन्यादन्नसम्भवः ।
इति शास्त्रादरचयद्वाजपेयादिकान्क्रतून् ॥
अनन्तरं केरळेषु भूरिदुर्गाण्यकल्पयत ।
जीर्णान् कूपतटाकांश्च नष्टान् देवालयानपि ॥
उद्दधारापरिमितान् स्वयशःकेतुना सह ।
केदारं भद्रपादं च काशीं चैव त्रियम्बकम् ॥
वैयाघ्रपादं साम्बाख्यं पुष्करं स्थाणुसंज्ञकम् ।
शिवगङ्गागुहारण्यरुद्रकोटिहरालयम् ॥
श्रीशैलं चैव गोकर्णपुण्यारण्याद्रिसंस्थितम् ।
रामेश्वरमिति ख्यातं सर्वपापप्रणाशनम् ॥
विश्वेश्वरस्य सौवर्णकिरीटादिसमर्पणम् ।
कारयामास देवस्य प्रत्यादाय महेशितुः ॥

* * * *

इति शास्त्रं समालोक्य शिवनामा महीपतिः ।
नानाविधानि दानानि महेशप्रीतयेऽदिशत् ॥
कनीयांसं ततः पुत्रं सोमशेखरनामकम् ।
विद्याभ्यासे वेंकटप्पनायकस्य वशं व्यधात् ॥
तस्मै सहैव पुत्राभ्यां प्रार्पयद्वसुधामपि ।
भद्रप्पनायकं चैव सोमशेखरनायकम् ॥
एतौ च बालकं प्रेम्णा नियतं परिपालयन् ।
नीत्या महीमिमां रक्षन् धर्मकीर्तिपराक्रमैः ॥
प्रवर्तयाखिलान् धर्मान् नृपाणामुचितान्बहिः ।
अन्तरङ्गे परं नित्यं शिवयोगपरो भव ॥
इत्युदीर्य नृपस्तस्मै योगविद्यामुपादिशत् ॥

Taranga XV.

एवं वेङ्कटभूपाय योगविद्यां प्रदर्शयन् ।

* * *

स्वयं शिवमहीपालः शिवयोगपरोऽभवत् ॥

ततो वेङ्कटभूपालः शशास धरणीमिमाम् ।
सुताभ्यामर्थकामाभ्यामिव धर्मस्समाहितः ॥

Kallōla VIII, Taranga I.

शिवभूपात्समासाद्य क्षमां स्वसहजक्षमः ।
स्वयं शिवमहीपालप्रोक्तधर्मेण संचरन् ॥
एकपत्नीव्रतपरः प्रकृतीरनुरञ्जयन् ।
सत्यव्रतैकनिरतश्शिवाधिक्यं विभावयन् ॥
श्रीवेङ्कटमहीपालो रक्षति स्म क्षमामिमाम् ॥
अवन्नेवं बहोः कालादवनीं स्वाग्रजन्मनः ।
कुमारमग्रजन्मानं नाम्ना भद्रप्पनायकम् ॥
अभिषिक्तं पदे स्वस्य कारयामास दाक्षिणम् ।
उपादिशदयं तस्मै व्यवहारक्रमानपि ॥
राज्यभारं बहोः कालाद्वहन् श्रान्त इवाधिकम् ।
मतिमान्निदधौ तस्मिन् सर्वधूर्वहणक्षमे ॥
ततः स्वयमभून्नित्यं शिवयोगैकतत्परः ।
ततो महीमहिपतिप्रतिमाने भुजे वहन् ।
भद्रप्पनायको नित्यं भूमण्डलमपालयत् ॥

Taranga II.

एवमस्मिन्बहोः कालादवति क्षितिमण्डलम् ।
पूर्वस्यां दिशि सामन्ते राज्याक्रमणकांक्षिणि ।
सीमोपान्तस्थितान्दुर्गप्राकारान्प्रतिरुन्धते ।
सेनाप्रधानमुखतस्ताञ्जित्वायं निवर्तयेत् ॥
द्विजवन्नैव सन्तुष्येत् स्वतः प्राप्तेन भूपतिः ।
इति नीत्या शात्रवीयराज्याक्रमणकाङ्क्षया ॥
निर्गत्य षड्विधैस्साकं बलैराक्रम्य चाभितः ।
भस्मशून्यमुखानेष प्राकारात्सहसाग्रहीत् ॥
ततश्शौर्यस्थितं चापि शौर्यतः परिकल्पयन् ।
ततश्चोत्तरसामन्ते कण्टकत्वमुपेयुषि ।
स्थानमाक्रम्य शरणं यातायास्मै यथापुरम् ॥

भ्रष्टराज्यायतत्स्थानमादिशत्कीर्तिवृद्धये ।
स्वस्थानाक्रमणक्लेशप्रतीकारचिकीर्षया ॥
विजयाख्यपुरस्थायी म्लेच्छानामधिनायकः ।
आनीतस्सहसा तेन साहाय्यकविधौ युधि ॥
भद्रभूपो न चास्माभिर्विजेतुं शक्यते बली ।
इत्यालोच्यामुना सन्धि विधाय स्वपुरं ययौ ॥
अनन्तरं भद्रभूपस्तीर्थराजपुरस्थले ॥
दानं हिरण्यगर्भाख्यमकरोदीशतुष्टये ।
ततश्शरावतीतीरे रामचन्द्रपुरस्थले ॥
तुलापुरुषदानं स सौवर्णं पर्यकल्पयत् ।
पितृनाम्नाग्रहारं च शिवराजपुराह्वयम् ॥
भुवं विसृज्य विपुलां विशेषेण व्यवर्धयत् ।
पितृव्यनाम्नाप्यकरोत् वेङ्कटापुरनामकम् ॥
स्वनाम्नाप्यकरोद्रम्यं भद्रराजपुराह्वयम् ।
उडुपक्षेत्रकृष्णस्य सुब्रह्मण्ये गुहस्य च ॥
कोटीश्वरेशितुः श्रीशंकरनारायणस्य च ।
इष्टदैवतमूकाम्बानाम्न्याश्शक्त्या महेशितुः ॥
देवानामेतदादीनामभिवर्ध्य च पूजनम् ।
भूरुद्राणां मठान् कृत्वा तेभ्यः क्षेत्राणि चादिशत् ॥
एवं धर्मेण वसुधां बहोः कालात्प्रपालयन् ।
स्वानुजं प्रौढवयसं राज्यधूर्वहनक्षमम् ॥
सोमशेखरनामानं मनसा संप्रधारयन् ।
सविशेषं धनुर्विद्यामुपदिश्य सविस्तरम् ॥
तस्मिन् राज्यं निचिक्षेप दक्षे भद्रमहीपतिः ॥

Taranga V.

अनीतिसंकुलं राज्यं सोमशेखरनायके ।
शासत्यनीतिरल्पापि न क्वचित्पर्यदृश्यत ॥

व्यञ्जयन्विषमेषुत्वं कामिनीष्वपि शत्रुषु ।
विग्रहेण स्वकीयेन प्रदिशत्यतिरिक्तताम् ॥
अस्मिन्कतिपयं कालं परिपालयति क्षितिम् ।
एनं प्रकोप्य सीमान्तप्राकारावरणान्नृपः ॥
सामन्तो हरिणास्सिंहमिव तस्याभजत्फलम् ।
पुनः क्षुद्रनृपान्कांश्चित् गळिताहंकृतीन्व्यधात् ॥
कांश्चिच्च शरणायातान् तत्तत्स्थानेष्ववर्तयत् ।
पुरोपान्ते मठं रम्यं भूरुद्राणां महात्मनाम् ॥
अनुग्रहं प्राप्तुकामो महान्तं निरमापयत् ।
पुरोपान्ते तथान्यत्र विरक्तानां मठं दृढम् ॥
लिङ्गाङ्गसङ्गिनां तुष्टयै कारयामास भक्तितः ।
तटाकं तस्य पुरतो महान्तं पर्यकल्पयत् ॥
मधुरेणाप्यशोष्येण जलेन परिपूरितम् ।
तटाकं परितश्चैव वृक्षोद्यानमकल्पयत् ॥
प्ररूढे यौवने स्वस्य विवाहकरणेच्छया ।
सदृशीं रूपरेखायां गुणेष्वपि कुले तथा ॥
स्त्रियमप्राप्य चोद्वाहे व्यलम्बत शिवो यथा ।
मूकाम्बिकांशसम्भूतां चन्नाम्बाख्यां मनोहराम् ॥
परिणीय विचिक्रीड तया रत्येव मन्मथः ॥
मधुराङ्गविलासाढ्या कुन्तळश्रीविराजिता ।
भूषिता सा द्वितीयेव राज्यश्रीर्हृद्यतामगात् ॥
एवं तया समं कालं कियन्तमतिवाहयन् ।
चन्नाम्बाख्यां कदाचित्स्वां वधूं प्रत्येवमुक्तवान् ॥
शृणु प्रिये पुरा देवान् परिभूय सुरारयः ।
तत्स्थलानि समाक्रम्य तेषां बाधां वितेनिरे ॥
तदा मूकाम्बिकादेवी निगृह्य दितिसम्भवान् ।
देवानामभयं प्रादात् सर्वेषामिति विश्रुतम् ॥
तदा कलियुगे दैत्यरूपैर्म्लेच्छैरुपद्रुतान् ।
पुण्यस्थलात्समस्ताच्च धर्मह्रासमवापितान् ॥

निर्गत्य सन्तस्सर्वेऽपि देशमस्माकमाश्रिताः ।
सुखेनैवोपजीवेयुः पुण्यदेशधियस्सदा ॥
अनन्तरं कियत्कालादेतद्देशमुपागतान् ।
म्लेच्छान्पराजितान्कृत्वा लोकानामभयं कुरु ॥
सर्वदेवशिरोरत्नेऽचिन्त्यरूपे महेश्वरे ।
भक्तिं सदापि कुर्वाणां भूतिं भूतिविवर्धिनीम् ॥

* * * *

Taranga VII.

इत्यनेन प्रकारेण सोमशेखरभूपतिः ।
अब्रवीच्चन्नमाम्बायै शिवपूजाविधिं ततः ॥
अस्माकं च विधानेन कृत्वा पट्टाभिषेचनम् ।
अयं कुमारो बसवप्पनायक इति श्रुतः ॥
प्रगल्भतां भजेद्यावद्राज्यभारविचारणे ।
तावन्महीमवन्त्येनां प्रजानां कुरु पालनम् ॥
इत्युदीर्य प्रियां राजा सोमशेखरनायकः ।
स्वनामधेययोग्यं स प्राप्तः परशिवास्पदम् ॥
अनन्तरं चन्नमाम्बाप्यष्टैश्वर्यसमन्विता ।
प्राणप्रियसमादिष्टसदाचारैकवर्तिनी ॥
अशिषत्सकलामुर्वीमुर्वीधरसुता यथा ॥

Taranga VIII.

सप्ताङ्गैस्सहिते राज्ये सर्वदैव च जाग्रति ।
शिवधर्मानाचरन्ती राज्यं नीत्या चकार सा ॥
अस्माकं सर्वविद्यासु कारयन्ती परिश्रमम् ।
विवाहमङ्गळमपि सर्वैर्भवमकारयत् ॥
कीर्त्या धर्मेण विक्रान्त्या रक्षन्त्या धरणीमिमां ।
सर्वसन्नाहेषु ततः सामन्तेषु कदाचन ॥
सीमोपान्तसमाक्रान्त्यै यतमानेषु द(र्प)नः ।
सेनामुख्यान्सह बलैः प्रेषयित्वा बलाधिकान् ॥

निगृह्य तद्बलं सर्वं विरचय्य पलायितम् ।
चलाद्रिसुभगान्नागानश्वान्विश्वातिशायिनः ॥
नानाविधानि बिरुदान्यतिमुख्यानि विद्विषाम् ।
आचकर्ष निजोत्कर्षं ख्यापयन्ती दिगन्तरे ॥
एवं क्षुद्रान्समुद्धृत्य सामन्तान्विनिगृह्णती ।
चकार शासनाधीनं सर्वं सामन्तमण्डलम् ॥
ततश्च सर्वयवनसार्वभौमस्थितिं गते ।
नृपश्रेष्ठान्द्विपञ्चाशत्संख्याकान्बलवत्तरान् ॥
उन्मूलवैरितां प्राप्तं छत्राधिपतिशब्दितं ।
रामराजनृपं जित्वा गृहीतुमभिवांछति ॥
म्लेच्छेऽवरङ्गसाबाख्ये समायाते बलीयसि ।
कालं प्रतीक्षमाणोऽथ निर्गत्य स सुधीस्ततः ॥
चरित्वा तत्रतत्रापि नृपो मार्गवशागतः ।
समागतोऽभवद्देशमिमं तु सपरिच्छदः ॥
स्वदेशं समुपायान्तं रामराजं विभाव्य सा ।
महतामपि शूराणां बलिनां नीतिवेदिनाम् ॥
पराभवस्तत्रतत्र पूर्वेषामपि दृश्यते ।

* * * *

तस्मादुपागतायास्मै सम्माननमिहोचितम् ।
इत्यालोच्य निजैस्सार्धं मन्त्रयित्वा च मन्त्रिभिः ॥
महार्घवस्त्रभूषाद्यैर्मानयामास मानितम् ।
अनुधाव्य तमायान्तमुद्धृतं म्लेच्छनायकम् ॥
वर्ण्यमानेनाब्धिनेव स्वबलेनानुधावितम् ।
स्वाम्याज्ञाचण्डवातेन प्रेर्यमाणे--वेणिना ॥
ज्वलन्तमधिकं भूयो महतामर्षवह्निना ।
सेनाप्रधानमुखतः पराजयमवापयत् ॥
तद्बलं चानयत्सर्वं यावनं शमनालयम् ।
अमेयबलपूर्णस्य समस्तधरणीशितुः ॥
यवनाधिपतेस्सैन्यं जेतुं कोऽप्यत्र न क्षमः ।
एषा विजितवत्यासीत्सैन्यं तस्यापि च स्वयम् ॥

असाधारणविक्रान्तिरियमित्यखिलैस्स्तुता ।
आसेतुहिमवत्पादं कीर्तीः प्राप सुनिर्मलाः ॥
एनां वार्तामुपश्रुत्य यवनाधिपतेस्ततः ।
सन्तुष्टान्नागतुरगवासोऽलङ्कारपूर्वकम् ॥
सम्मानं प्राप्य धरणीमपालयदशात्रवाम् ।
पुनः क्षुद्रांश्च सामन्तान् गळिताहंकृतीन्व्यधात् ॥
ततो विशेषसेवार्थं मूकाम्बायास्स्वभक्तितः ।
भूमिं वितीर्य पर्याप्तां स्वनामपरिचिह्निताम् ॥
अग्रहारं च चन्नाम्बापुरमित्यतिविश्रुतम् ।
निर्माप्य क्षितिदेवानां सद्वृत्तीः परिकल्प्य च ॥

Colophon.

इति श्रीमदनाद्यनन्तसकलतत्त्वोत्तीर्णषडध्वोपादानबिन्दुकारणचिदम्बरशक्तिसमन्वितपरमेश्वरप्रसादासादितशिवाद्वैतविद्याविशारदश्रीमत्केळदीबसवराजेन्द्रविरचितवेदागमान्तर्गतविविधविद्यातन्त्वसारभूतशिवतत्त्वरत्नाकरे — कल्लोले — तरङ्गः ॥

End.

श्रीवीरभद्रकरुणासमुपार्जितश्रीसाम्राज्यवैभवपराक्रमकीर्तिभाजा ।
गोराष्ट्रतौलवसकेरळमल्लराष्ट्रत्रैगर्तदेशपरिपालनदाक्षिणेन ॥
परयडवमुरारीकोटिकोलाहलेन प्रविशवितविशुद्धाद्वैतसिद्धान्तभूम्ना ।
असियुगळभृतांचद्वैरिसप्ताङ्गलक्ष्मीहरहरितपटोद्यत्केतनश्रीयुतेन ॥
चौडप्पनायकसमुन्मिषितान्ववायदुग्धाब्धिवृद्धिकरकैरवबान्धवेन ।
एकाङ्गवीररणरङ्गविहारधीरदोनेजपश्चिमसरस्वदधीश्वरेण ॥
स्वाभीष्टदायिकेळदीस्थिरवीरभद्रमुद्राबलेन परिपालयता धरित्रीं ।
राजाधिराजकेळदीबसवक्षितीन्द्ररत्नेन संविरचितेतिकृतिः प्रपूर्णा ॥
श्रीमत्युन्नतशालिवाहनशके चन्द्राग्न्यृतुक्ष्मामिते
वर्षे विश्रुतसर्वधारिणि तथा मासे नभस्याह्वये ।
वारे निर्जरवैरिणामपि गुरोः श्रीपौर्णमासीदिने
ग्रन्थोऽयं परिपूर्णतामवहत प्रख्यातसारार्थयुक् ॥

INDEX.

A

G

H

N

O

R

S

T